D1669944

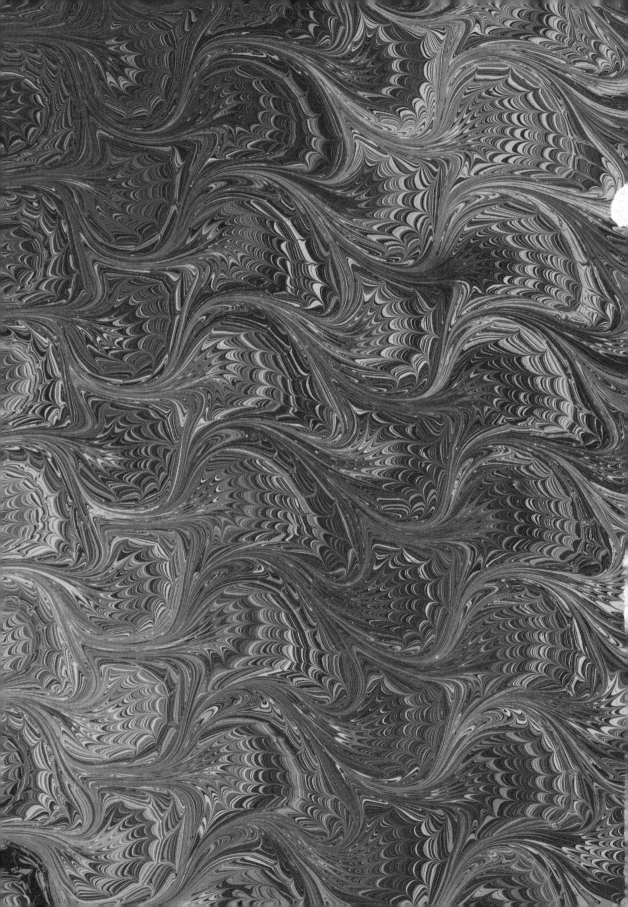

jovis

HER STORIES IN

Gerda Breuer

GRAPHIC DESIGN

Dialoge, Kontinuitäten, Selbstermächtigungen
Grafikdesignerinnen 1880 bis heute
Dialogue, Continuity, Self-Empowerment
Women Graphic Designers from 1880 until Today

Katja Lis (Design)

INHALT
CONTENTS

Inhaltsverzeichnis
Table of Contents

Vorwort

Als 2012 *Women in Graphic Design. Frauen und Grafik-Design 1890–2012* von Julia Meer und mir herausgegeben wurde, war dies die Zeit des lange nachwirkenden Postfeminismus.[1] Im Vorfeld begegnete uns viel Skepsis.

Heute wird von der „vierten Welle" des Feminismus gesprochen. Zu den alten Themen sind neue hinzugekommen. Es gründen sich Plattformen von Grafikdesignerinnen, neues Wissen über Design und dessen Geschichte fließt in die digitalen Enzyklopädien ein, geografische Ränder und ethnische Marginalisierung werden untersucht, ein verbindlicher Kanon und die Ausschließung von Frauen wird infrage gestellt. Dass die Designgeschichte der männlichen Heroen und der Ignoranz von Frauen nach wie vor ein großes Beharrungsvermögen aufweist, wird als Hinderungsgrund für eine „messy history"[2] (Martha Scotford) betrachtet, die Beiträge jenseits eines erklärten „guten Designs" und einer eindimensionalen Entwicklungsgeschichte zulässt. Gender bleibt dabei ein Fokus. An vielen Ecken und Enden wird heute über Grafikdesignerinnen gearbeitet.

Der vorliegende Band versucht, durch punktuelle historische Beispiele auf die durchgängige Präsenz von Frauen in der Designgeschichte hinzuweisen. Das Vorurteil, dass sie deshalb nicht erwähnt werden, weil es nur wenige Beispiele von Grafikdesignerinnen gab, hält sich bis heute hartnäckig – und das, obwohl schon viel Forschung stattgefunden hat.

Für die Disziplin Designgeschichte bedeutet dies, dass sie die Geschichte der Grafikdesignerinnen in ihre Erzählungen integriert: Das sind die vielen Initiativen von Frauen für Frauen, vor allem die Selbstermächtigungen. Viele von ihnen waren und sind getragen von weiblichen Vorbildern, von Dialogen und Kontinuitäten. „Design cannot change anything before it changes itself", war der Leitsatz des Swiss Design Network Summit „Beyond Change: Questioning the role of design in times of global transformation", 2018.[3]

Zur Revision einer Geschichtsschreibung über Frauen im Grafikdesign zählt deshalb auch, dass ihre reale Präsenz sichtbar wird und ihre nachträgliche Ausschließung nur verständlich wird, wenn die Kontextfaktoren beschrieben werden, die zu der Ignoranz führten.

1 Gerda Breuer & Julia Meer (Hg.): *Women in Graphic Design. Frauen und Grafik-Design 1880–2012*, Berlin: jovis Verlag, 2012.

2 Martha Scotford: Messy History vs. Neat History. Toward an Expanded View of Women in Graphic Design, *Visible Language* 28, Nr. 4 (Herbst 1994): 368–388.

3 Swiss Design Network Summit: Beyond Change: Questioning the Role of Design in Times of Global Transformation, 2018, https://swissdesignnetwork. ch/en/conferences/beyond-change (Abruf 14. Okt. 2022).

Preface

In 2012, when Julia Meer and I published *Women in Graphic Design: Frauen und Grafik-Design 1890–2012*, it was a period still under the lasting influence of postfeminism.[2] In the run-up to the book's publication, we encountered a great deal of skepticism.

Today, there is talk of the "fourth wave" of feminism. New topics have emerged next to the old ones. Women graphic designers are forming new platforms; new knowledge about design and its history is finding its way into digital encyclopedias; geographic peripheries and ethnic marginalization are being explored; and the idea that there is one authoritative canon is being questioned, along with the exclusion of women this has often entailed. That the design history of male heroes and women's ignorance continues to doggedly persist is viewed as an obstacle to a "messy history"[2] (Martha Scotford) that allows for contributions beyond what is deemed to be "good design" and a correspondingly one-dimensional history of its development. And yet gender remains a focus. No matter where you look, you will find discussions about women graphic designers.

In selecting pertinent historical examples, the present book aims to highlight the unbroken presence of women in design history. The misconception that no mention is made of women designers simply because there were so few of them persists to this day—and this despite all the research that has been done.

For the discipline of design history, this means integrating the history of women graphic designers into its historical narratives—the many initiatives by women for women, and above all those concerned with women's self-empowerment. Many of these women were and are underpinned by women role models, by dialogues and continuities. "Design cannot change anything before it changes itself": this was the guiding principle of the 2018 Swiss Design Network Summit "Beyond Change: Questioning the Role of Design in Times of Global Transformation."[3]

Revising a historiography of women in graphic design thus entails making their real presence visible, and that the only way to understand their exclusion from history is by describing the contextual factors that produced this ignorance.

1 Gerda Breuer & Julia Meer (eds.): *Women in Graphic Design: Frauen und Grafik-Design 1880–2012*, Berlin: jovis Verlag, 2012.

2 Martha Scotford: Messy History vs. Neat History: Toward an Expanded View of Women in Graphic Design, *Visible Language* 28, no. 4 (Autumn 1994): 368–388.

3 Swiss Design Network Summit: Beyond Change: Questioning the Role of Design in Times of Global Transformation, 2018, https://swissdesignnetwork. ch/en/conferences/beyond-change (accessed 14 Oct. 2022).

Dank

Die vorliegende Publikation ist nur mit der Unterstützung vieler zustande gekommen.

Ganz besonders bin ich Katja Lis zu Dank verpflichtet, die, zusammen mit Anna Voß, dem Band eine so schöne Form gegeben hat. Katja Lis hat von vornherein die Idee des Buches begeistert mitgetragen. Beide haben den Prozess der Kommunikation zusammen mit mir mit viel Geduld, Professionalität und Feingefühl glänzend gemeistert, sind auf meine Vorstellungen eingegangen und haben sie hervorragend umgesetzt.

Auch dem Team des jovis Verlags, der 2012 bereits die Publikation *Women in Graphic Design. Frauen und Grafik-Design 1890–2012* editiert hat, danke ich für die bewährte Arbeit, namentlich der Verlagsleiterin Doris Kleilein sowie den Mitarbeiterinnen Theresa Hartherz, Susanne Rösler und Charlotte Blumenthal, die den Band mit vielen guten Ideen bereichert haben.

Maike Kleihauer danke ich für das sorgfältige deutsche Lektorat und Michael Thomas Taylor für die professionelle Übersetzung und das Lektorat der englischen Texte.

Die Bereitschaft der Designer*innen, mir Abbildungen ihrer Werke bzw. Porträts zur Verfügung zu stellen, weiß ich sehr zu schätzen im Falle von Anja Kaiser, Leipzig, Luba Lukova, New York, Ellen Lupton, Maryland, sowie Golnar Kat Rahmani, David Morales, Rebecca Stephany, Berlin.

Bei der Bildbeschaffung haben mir viele geholfen. Hier habe ich mich besonders über die kollegiale Unterstützung von Bettina Richter, Museum für Gestaltung Zürich, und Dr. Birgit Nachtwey, Bahlsen-Archiv, Hannover, gefreut. Jenny Swadosh, New School Archives, danke ich für ihre Geduld bei der digitalen Übermittlung der Scans, Rebecca Odell vom Hackney Museum für ihre nicht nachlassenden Bemühungen, die Frauen des Lenthall Road Workshops ausfindig zu machen, Susan Mackie vom ehemaligen Red Women's Workshop für die Übermittlung zahlreicher Bilder.

Die oft komplizierte Bildbeschaffung – der Scans, tifs, jpgs, des Copyrights und des Personenrechts – hat viel Zeit in Anspruch genommen. Folgenden Frauen wie Männern bin ich für ihre Unterstützung sehr dankbar. Ihre Hilfe ging oft weit über die üblichen bürokratischen Auflagen hinaus: Joan Braderman, Heresies Film project; Nikki Braunton, Museum of London; Felix Brusberg, Galerie Brusberg, Berlin; Daniela Burger, *Missy Magazine*; Janine Dadier und Regina Wagner von der ETH-Bibliothek, Zürich; Melanie Glinicke, Olaf Guercke und Regine

Acknowledgments

This publication came about only with the support of many others.

I am especially indebted to Katja Lis, who, together with Anna Voß, has given the volume such a beautiful form. From the very beginning, Katja enthusiastically supported the idea for this book. Both of them brilliantly worked with me to manage our communication, displaying a great deal of patience, professionalism, and sensitivity; they listened to my ideas and were superb in making them happen.

I would additionally like to thank the team at jovis Verlag, who also published the earlier volume *Women in Graphic Design: Frauen und Grafik-Design 1890–2012*, especially its director Doris Kleilein and her colleagues Theresa Hartherz, Susanne Rösler, and Charlotte Blumenthal, all of whom contributed many good ideas that enriched the book.

I would like to thank Maike Kleihauer for the careful editing of the German and Michael Thomas Taylor for the professional translation and editing of the English texts.

Special thanks go to the designers who were willing to provide me with images of their works or portraits: Anja Kaiser (Leipzig), Luba Lukova (New York), and Ellen Lupton (Maryland), along with Golnar Kat Rahmani, David Morales, and Rebecca Stephany (Berlin).

Many people helped me acquire images, and here I am particularly grateful for the collegial support of Bettina Richter at the Museum für Gestaltung Zurich, and Dr. Birgit Nachtwey of Bahlsen Archive, Hannover. I thank Jenny Swadosh at the New School Archives for her patience in digitally providing the scans, Rebecca Odell of the Hackney Museum for her tireless efforts to locate the women of the Lenthall Road Workshop, and Susan Mackie of the former Red Women's Workshop for providing numerous images.

The process of image acquisition—of procuring scans, TIFS, and JPGs, along with copyright and personal rights—was complicated and took a great deal of time. I am very grateful to support from the following individuals, whose help often went far beyond the usual professional obligations: Joan Braderman, Heresies Film project; Nikki Braunton, Museum of London; Felix Brusberg, Galerie Brusberg, Berlin; Daniela Burger, *Missy Magazine*; Janine Dadier und Regina Wagner, ETH-Bibliothek, Zurich; Melanie Glinicke, Olaf Guercke, and Regine Schoch, Friedrich-Ebert-Stiftung, as well as

Schoch von der Friedrich-Ebert-Stiftung sowie Jonathan Menge, dem Direktor des Gender Justice Hub Asia (GEHA); Jessica Gysel von *Girls Like Us*; Autumn Haag, Department of Rare Books, Special Collection and Preservation, University of Rochester; Silke Haas, VG Bild-Kunst, Bonn; Martina Hoffmann, Schweizer Nationalbibliothek; Alice Herzog, Wallstein Verlag, Göttingen; Margitta Hösel, *Emma*, Köln; Babette Kaiserkern, Berlin; Roman Klarfeld, Das feministische Archiv, Berlin; Guerrilla Girl Käthe Kollwitz, New York; Dr. Magdalena Holzhey und Juliane Duft von den Krefelder Kunstmuseen; Chia Moan, ehemaliges Mitglied des Lenthall Road Workshop; Shaz Madani von *Riposte*; Thomas Matyk, Museum für angewandte Kunst Wien; Dr. Julia Meer, Museum für Kunst und Gewerbe Hamburg; David Morales von Philipp und Keuntje, Berlin; Johanna Merensky, fischerAppell Group; Dr. Gisela Notz, Historisches Forschungszentrum der Friedrich-Ebert-Stiftung; Stefanie Pöschl, Digitales Deutsches Frauenarchiv; Rachel Valinsky, *The New Woman's Survival Catalog*; Marion Beckers, Elisabeth Moortgat vom ehemaligen Verborgenen Museum, Berlin; Nastassja Wachsmuth, Terre des Femmes, Berlin; Sarah Zumkehr, Schweizerische Nationalbibliothek (NB), Bern. Besonderer Dank geht auch an Prof. Boris Gorin, Aachen, für die Übersetzung der russischen Texte.

Jonathan Menge, director of the Gender Justice Hub Asia (GEHA); Jessica Gysel, *Girls Like Us*; Autumn Haag, Department of Rare Books, Special Collection and Preservation, University of Rochester; Silke Haas, VG Bild-Kunst, Bonn; Martina Hoffmann, Swiss National Library; Alice Herzog, Wallstein Verlag, Göttingen; Margitta Hösel, *Emma*, Cologne; Babette Kaiserkern, Berlin; Roman Klarfeld, Das feministische Archiv, Berlin; Guerrilla Girl Käthe Kollwitz, New York; Dr. Magdalena Holzhey and Juliane Duft, Krefelder Kunstmuseen; Chia Moan, former member of the Lenthall Road Workshop; Shaz Madani, *Riposte*; Thomas Matyk, Museum für angewandte Kunst Wien; Dr. Julia Meer, Museum für Kunst und Gewerbe Hamburg; David Morales from Philipp und Keuntje, Berlin; Johanna Merensky, fischerAppell Group; Dr. Gisela Notz, Historisches Forschungszentrum der Friedrich-Ebert-Stiftung; Stefanie Pöschl, Digitales Deutsches Frauenarchiv; Rachel Valinsky, *The New Woman's Survival Catalog*; Marion Beckers and Elisabeth Moortgat, the former Verborgenes Museum, Berlin; Nastassja Wachsmuth, Terre des Femmes, Berlin; and Sarah Zumkehr, Swiss National Library (NL), Bern. Special thanks go to Boris Gorin, Aachen, who translated texts from Russian.

Mela Köhler, Postkarte der Wiener Werkstätte / Wiener Werkstätte postcard,
Nr./no. 532, 1911 © MAK Wien

Valentina Kulagina, Internationaler Frauentag – Tag der Kämpfe des Proletariats / International Day of Women Workers—
Militant Day of the Proletariat (We Will Be Ready to Repel the Military Attack on the USSR), Plakat/poster, 1931 © VG Bild-Kunst, Bonn,
Foto/photo: © Museum für Gestaltung Zürich, Plakatsammlung

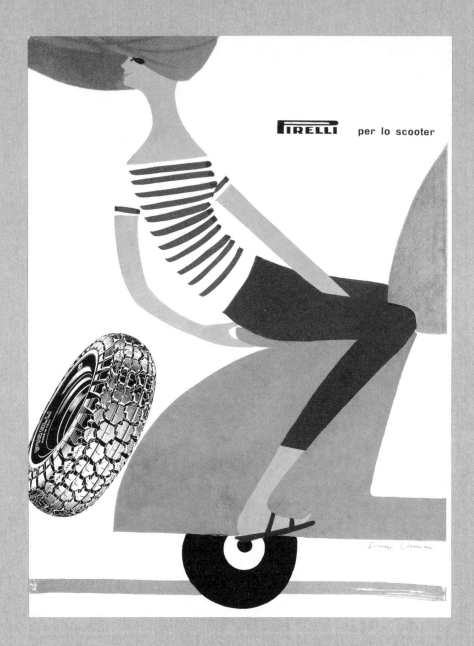

PIRELLI per lo scooter

50001
13

Lora Lamm, Kleinplakat/Werbeinserat für Reifen der Firma Pirelli / Small poster/advertisement for Pirelli tires, um/around 1959,
Foto/photo: © Museum für Gestaltung Zürich, Plakatsammlung

Ljubow Popowa, Cover der Zeitschrift / Cover of the magazine Muzykal'naia nov' (Musikalisches Neuland / Musical new land), Nr./no. 11, 1924

Bea Feitler, Plakat für die erste Ausgabe des Magazins / Poster for inaugural issue of the magazine Ms., Jul. 1972,

Margaret MacDonald Mackintosh, Menükarte für / Menu card design for Miss Cranston's Cafes auf der / at the Scottish Exhibition of National History, Art and Industry (1911), um/around 1911

Lora Lamm, Briefschaft für das Kaufhaus / Stationery for the department store La Rinascente, mode autunno inverno, 1960
© Museum für Gestaltung Zürich, Plakatsammlung

MARCH/1973 $1.00

WHO
VOTED FOR
RICHARD
NIXON?

Ms.

KATE
MILLETT: A
PERSONAL
STORY

DORIS LESSING'S
TERRIFIC NEW NOVEL ABOUT WOMEN, SEX, AND MIDDLE AGE

FLO: THE WITTY FEMINIST

TRAGEDIES IN
IRELAND

WHAT CONTRACEPTIVE TYPE ARE YOU?

SECRETS OF RAP GROUPS

THEY DIDN'T GET MARRIED AND THEY LIVED HAPPILY EVER AFTER ANYWAY

IND 35185

Bea Feitler, Titelblatt der / Cover for Ms. (Doris Lessing's Terrific New Novel about Women, Sex, and Middle Age), Mrz./Mar. 1973,
Foto/photo: © Bea Feitler papers, The New School Archives and Special Collection, The New School, New York, NY

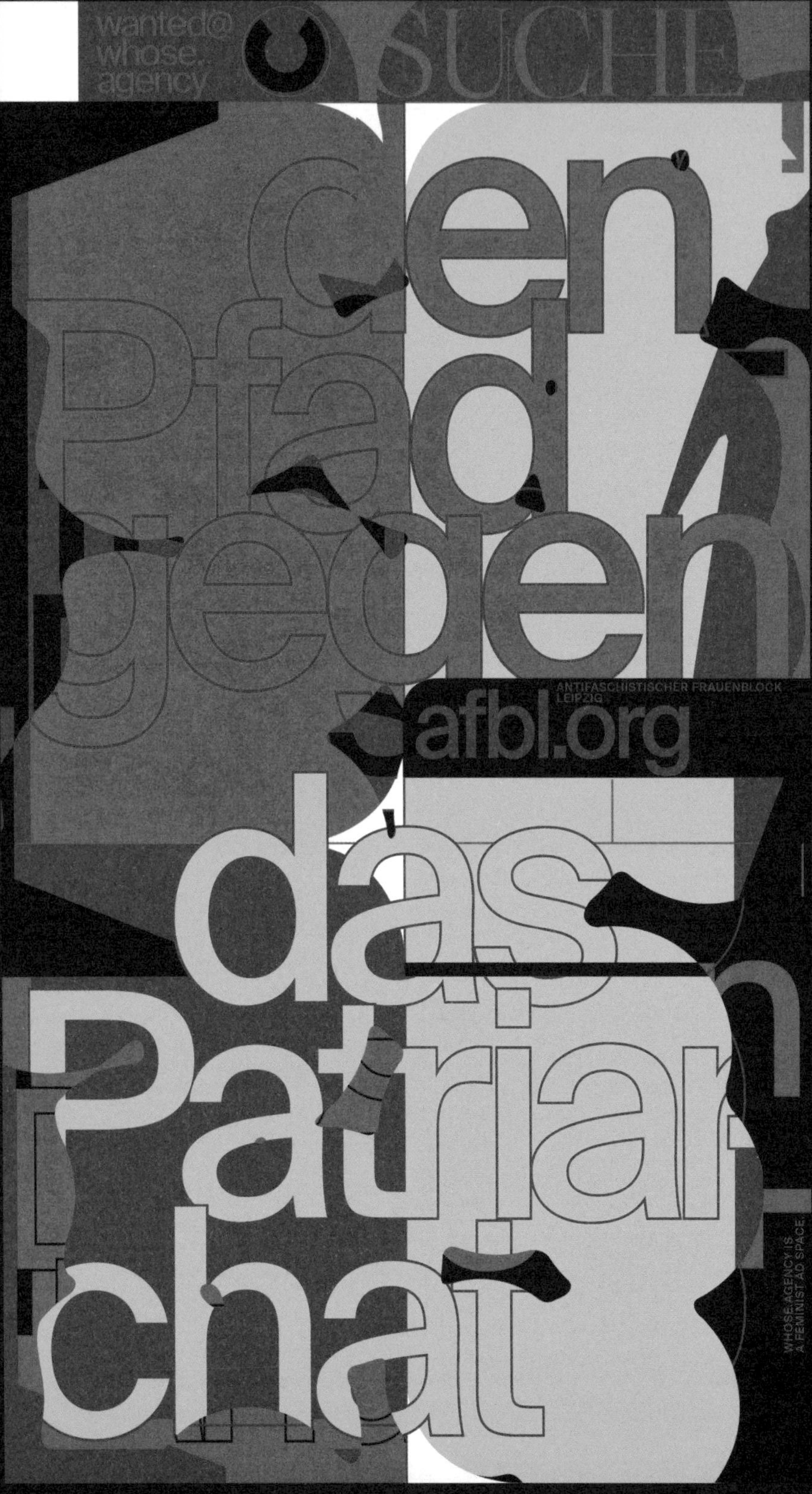

wanted@
whose.
agency

SUCHE

Gen
Pfad
gegen

ANTIFASCHISTISCHER FRAUENBLOCK
LEIPZIG

afbl.org

das
Patriar-
chat

WHOSE.AGENCY IS
A FEMINIST AD SPACE

Anja Kaiser, Whose.Agency, 2017 © Anja Kaiser

SCHLAG' DIR DIE ZÄHNE RAUS, MAN
HÖRT NUR NOCH DEIN FOTZENGESCHREI.
LOGGE MICH EIN BEI INSTAGRAM,
ES WIRD AUF STORY GETEILT.

AL GEAR – BONNIE & CLYDE
46.323 AUFRUFE

#UNHATEWOMEN

Gewalt gegen Frauen wird gefeiert. In Konzerthallen. Auf Schulhöfen. In Kinderzimmern.
Teile #UNHATEWOMEN und setze ein Zeichen gegen frauenverachtende Hate Speech.
Mehr auf unhate-women.com

Terre des Femmes, Kampagne gegen frauenverachtende Songtexte von deutschen Rappern unter dem Titel / Campaign against
misogynistic song lyrics by German rappers under the title #unhatewoman, Design: David Morales, 2020 © Philipp und Keuntje, Berlin

SO LONG AS WOMEN
ARE NOT FREE THE
PEOPLE ARE
NOT FREE

See Red Women's Workshop, So Long as Women Are Not Free, Plakat/poster, 1978 © See Red Women's Workshop (Mo Cooling)

Art + Feminism Wikipedia Edit-a-thon bei/at LACMA, organisiert von / coorganized by East of Borneo & Women's Center for Creative Work,
8. Mrz./Mar. 2015 © Saelwill

EINFÜHRUNG
INTRODUCTION

Die Designgeschichte wurde und wird zum guten Teil heute noch geschrieben als Erzählung mit einem Mangel an Designerinnen. Auch wenn aktuell der Trend zunimmt, Profile von berühmten Frauen im Design zu veröffentlichen, und eine neue feministische Welle ins Land schwappt, bleiben Frauen in Überblickswerken weit unterrepräsentiert. Wenn dennoch einige wenige aufgelistet sind, dann als Ausnahmen. Seit Beginn der Erzählungen wird konstant allenfalls eine Handvoll Designerinnen in der Geschichte erwähnt.

Wenngleich sich dieses Buch gegen das Verfahren sperrt, eine etablierte Erzählform lediglich um außergewöhnliche Frauen zu ergänzen, will es auch nicht einfach – in den Worten von Martha Scotford – eine „messy history" schreiben, eine dezentrale Präsentationsform, die der „neat history", der traditionellen männerdominierten Erzählform, entgegengesetzt wird.[1] All die verstreuten Mikroerzählungen von Grafikdesignerinnen, von denen es inzwischen eine Vielzahl gibt, laufen Gefahr, nicht in den breiten Strom der Designhistoriografie integriert zu werden.

Sie bleiben segregiert. Gerade aber die Unübersichtlichkeit vereitelt eine selbstverständliche Wahrnehmung.

Das Verfahren, eine „Hall of Fame"[2] lediglich durch eine „Hall of Femmes"[3] zu ergänzen, bestätigt eher den traditionellen Kanon einer Designhistoriografie, die sich aus herausragenden Einzelfiguren, den Pionier*innen und Hero*innen, den Innovator*innen und Erfinder*innen, die das „gute Design" vertreten, zusammensetzt. Deshalb soll die Designhistoriografie vor dem Horizont einer politischen, sozialen und kulturellen Entwicklung beschrieben werden, in der die „Hälfte der Menschheit" ihre Stimme erhebt. Bestimmte historische Zeitpunkte haben die Mobilisierung von Frauen befördert und in der Folge auch Grafikdesignerinnen oder grafisch arbeitenden Amateurinnen Gelegenheit gegeben, ihren Wünschen und Forderungen visuellen Ausdruck zu verleihen.

Die Anlässe hierfür sind vielfältig. In den Anfängen stand die Professionalisierung von Frauen im Vordergrund, ihr Wunsch nach Ausbildung und einer entsprechenden Berufstätigkeit. Darin verbarg sich oft eine Kritik an den Ungleichheitsverhältnissen der Geschlechter, was

Design history has largely been written, and continues to be written, as a narrative in which women are mostly missing. Even if we currently see a growing trend to publish profiles of famous women in design along with a new feminist wave in the West, women remain significantly underrepresented in surveys of the field. If they are listed at all, they are few in number and figure as exceptions. At most a handful of women designers are consistently mentioned in histories of design.

This book resists the approach of merely supplementing established narratives with the names of additional exceptional women. At the same time, it does not simply seek to write what Martha Scotford calls a "messy history"—a decentralized form of presentation that Scotford opposes to "neat history," the traditionally male-dominated narrative form.[1] There is a danger that the many, scattered micronarratives of women graphic designers we now find will fail to be integrated into the broad stream of design historiography, that they will remain segregated into individual accounts. And it is precisely this failure to achieve a more synthetic view that frustrates a perception of women designers as an essential part of design history.

The procedure of merely supplementing a "Hall of Fame"[2] with a "Hall of Femmes"[3] would just end up confirming the traditional canon of a design historiography composed of outstanding individual figures—of pioneers and heroes, innovators and inventors, be they men or women, who represent "good design." This book thus aims to write design history against the horizon of a political, social, and cultural development in which one half of humanity finds its voice. Certain historical moments have fostered the mobilization of women, thus also giving women graphic designers or amateurs working in the field opportunities to visually express their desires and demands.

The reasons for such a history are manifold. Its beginnings were focused on the professionalization of women—on their desire for education and a suitable professional livelihood. Yet this often obscured critiques of gender inequality, motivating many women to seek out alternatives less dependent on institutional structures. In

1 Martha Scotford: Messy History vs. Neat History. Toward an Expanded View of Women in Graphic Design, *Visible Language* 28, Nr. 4 (Herbst 1994): 367–387.
2 Seit 1920 ehrt die AIGA jährlich die besten Grafikdesigner*innen.
3 „Hall of Femmes" ist ein 2009 in Schweden gegründetes Projekt, das die Arbeit von Frauen in Art Direction und Design hervorheben will und entsprechende Publikationen über die Ausgelobten herausgibt.

1 Martha Scotford: Messy History vs. Neat History: Toward an Expanded View of Women in Graphic Design, *Visible Language* 28, no. 4 (Autumn 1994): 367–387.
2 Since 1920, the AIGA has honored the best graphic designers each year.
3 "Hall of Femmes" is a project founded in Sweden in 2009 that aims to highlight the work of women in art direction and design, with publications about those who receive the award.

zum Ergreifen von Alternativen in Eigeninitiative führte. Oder es waren politische Umbruchsituationen wie nach den russischen Revolutionen, die neue Vorstellungen vom Zusammenleben der Geschlechter förderten. Nicht durch Zufall hat das politische Ereignis außergewöhnliche Grafikdesignerinnen hervorgebracht. Der Markt spielte im Kontext der Kunstgewerbe-Reformbewegungen und ihrer Neubewertung der „Reklamekunst" für Frauen eine ausgleichende Rolle, die sie in den größtenteils männerbündischen Vereinigungen der modernen Designer nicht einnehmen konnten. Um 1910 und bis weit in die 1930er Jahre haben in Deutschland sehr viele Gebrauchsgrafikerinnen für Unternehmen gearbeitet. Nach Ende der 1960er Jahre setzten sich Frauenkollektive in Workshops durch, die für die Belange von Frauen eintraten und neue visuelle Formate durchspielten. Unter den Vorzeichen digitaler Vernetzung haben sich heute vermehrt internationale Plattformen gebildet. Rückblickend ist erkennbar, dass sich je nach historischem Kontext besondere Formen von Selbstermächtigung durch Frauen gebildet haben.

Die Frauenbewegungen

Begleitet wurden die historischen Konstellationen zu einem großen Teil von den „Wellen" der Frauenbewegungen. Für die Soziologin Ute Gerhard hat die Metapher der „Welle" Eingang in die Historiografie der Emanzipationsgeschichte gefunden, weil die vielen ungleichzeitigen Höhepunkte und Flauten den Gezeiten ähneln.[4] In der Tat sprechen Brit*innen und Anglo-Amerikaner*innen von „First Wave Feminism", wenn die Frauenbewegung des späten 19. Jahrhunderts und die der 1920er und 1930er Jahre gemeint sind, und von „Second Wave" für die Zeit nach 1970, während die Deutschen eher die Begriffe „alte" oder „historische" und „neue" Frauenbewegung bevorzugen. Heute greifen Grafikdesignerinnen wiederum auf das Bild der Welle zurück, wenn von der „dritten" und gegenwärtig der „vierten" Welle der Frauenbewegung gesprochen wird. Mit jeder Welle wurden neue Probleme behandelt. Grafikdesign kann dabei ein Seismograf dieser Bewegungen sein.

Zudem ist die Verschiedenheit der Erfahrungen von Frauen ein immer häufiger und viel diskutiertes Thema im internationalen Kontext. Ausgehend von den USA haben Schwarze Frauen in den 1950er Jahren gegen die Dominanz

other cases, it was moments of political upheaval, such as after the Russian revolutions, that promoted new ideas about the coexistence of the sexes. Not by chance did this political event produce exceptional women graphic designers. In the context of the decorative arts reform movements and its reassessment of commercial art or advertising, the market played a compensatory role by offering career opportunities when women were still largely excluded from mostly male associations of modern designers. Beginning around 1910 and well into the 1930s, a great many women commercial artists worked for companies in Germany. Post-1960, women's collectives took root in workshops that advocated for women's issues and explored new visual formats. And today, spurred on by digital networking, international platforms are increasingly taking shape. In retrospect, it can be seen that particular forms of self-empowerment have been shaped by women in ways that reflect the respective historical context.

The Women's Movements

One significant aspect of this history is that its constellations were accompanied by "waves" of women's movements. Sociologist Ute Gerhard argues that the metaphor of the "wave" has found its way into the historiography of emancipation movements because the many uneven peaks and lulls resemble tides.[4] Women in the English-speaking world do in fact speak of "first wave feminism" when referring to the women's movement of the late nineteenth century and that of the 1920s and 1930s, and of "second wave feminism" for the period after 1970, while Germans tend to prefer the terms "old" or "historical" and "new" for describing various phases of the women's movement. Today, graphic designers often take recourse to this same image when talking about a "third wave" and, now, a "fourth" wave of the women's movement. Each wave addressed new issues, and graphic design can serve as a seismograph of these movements.

In an international context, too, the diversity of women's experiences is an increasingly common and frequently discussed topic. Starting in the United States in the 1950s, Black women began to push back against the dominance of Western, "White" feminism. Criticizing feminists' universal claim to speak for all women, they have articulated how their own interests and experiences of injustice—often marked by

4 Ute Gerhard: *Atempause*, Frankfurt a. M.: Fischer, 1999.

4 Ute Gerhard: *Atempause*, Frankfurt a. M.: Fischer, 1999.

des westlichen, „weißen" Feminismus aufbegehrt. Sie kritisierten den universellen Anspruch von Feministinnen, für alle Frauen zu sprechen, denn sie fühlten sich in ihren Interessen und Unrechtserfahrungen, ihrer anderen – etwa der kolonialen – Geschichte der Ungleichheit nicht repräsentiert. Für diesen Denkansatz hat sich das Konzept der Intersektionalität durchgesetzt. Er ermöglicht neben den soziologischen Kategorien Geschlecht, Klasse und Ethnie die Beachtung weiterer struktureller Merkmale wie unterschiedliche soziale Milieus, geografische Randlagen, Alter, körperliche Behinderungen oder sexuelle Identitäten.

Die Bandbreite feministischer Positionen und Aktionsformen zeigt sich insbesondere im Bereich der visuellen Gegenkultur: in Workshops und selbstverlegten Zines sowie Graphic Novels oder Comics. Ihre Wirkung ist heute so breit akzeptiert, dass sie von renommierten staatlichen und städtischen Archiven gesammelt werden und auch NGOs zu dem Format der visuellen Kommunikation greifen, womit ein Blick auf die verschiedenen Anwendungsfelder, nicht nur von professionellen Grafikdesigner*innen, geworfen wird.

Es ist kein Zufall, dass in einem Land wie England, das die Jugendbewegungen wie kein anderes Land als Bestandteil seiner nationalen Identität betrachtet, den feministischen Workshops der 1970er Jahre und der lang anhaltende Riot-Grrrls-Bewegung, geleitet von jungen Frauen der alternativen Musikszene, besondere Beachtung geschenkt wird. Die Frauen kommunizierten mit Plakaten, eigenen Magazinen, Plattencovern und eigener Kleidung und verfolgten bewusst die Do-it-yourself-Methode, die visueller Ausdruck der Nonkonformität war. Alle waren der Frauenbewegung verpflichtet.

Erinnern

Insofern das vorliegende Buch von der Historiografie der Grafikdesignerinnen handelt, stellt sich auch die Frage: Wie wird erinnert?

In den meisten Fällen wird die Beachtung von Frauen in der Geschichte heute als Fortschrittsgeschichte erzählt. Wie Sabine Hark am Beispiel der feministischen Theoriebildung bemerkte, wird der Prozess des Erzählens von Geschichte oftmals in einer „simplen Taxonomie eines unterkomplexen ‚Früher' gegenüber einem komplexen ‚Heute'" dargestellt.[5] Die Geschichte

colonialism—have remained unrepresented in dominant histories. In this context, the notion of intersectionality has gained widespread currency. In addition to the sociological categories of gender, class, and ethnicity, it allows for consideration of other structural characteristics such as different social milieus, geographical peripheries, age, physical disabilities, or sexual identities.

The range of feminist positions and forms of action is particularly evident in the field of visual counterculture: in workshops and self-published zines, as well as graphic novels or comics. Their impact is now so widely accepted that they are collected by prestigious state and municipal archives, while NGOs are also turning to formats for visual communication. These developments provide a glimpse into the wide range of fields where design is employed, not just those in which professional graphic designers operate.

It is no coincidence that in a country like England, which regards youth movements as part of its national identity to an extent unlike any other, the feminist workshops of the 1970s and the long-running Riot Grrrls movement, led by young women in the alternative music scene, attract special attention. The women in these movements employed posters, their own magazines, record covers, and their own clothing as communication tools, while deliberately following do-it-yourself methods that serve to visually express nonconformity. All of these groups were committed to the women's movement.

Remembrance

To the extent that this book is about the historiography of women graphic designers, it also raises the question of how this remembrance takes shape.

In most cases today, attention to women in history is told as a story of progress. As Sabine Hark notes of feminist theorizing, the process of narrating history is often presented in a "simplistic taxonomy of a less sophisticated 'before' and a more complex 'today.'"[5] The history of the nineteenth century and of historical modernity seems to confirm that women had few opportunities for professional development. The date at which women were allowed to study at art academies— late in both symbolic and historical terms—is usually cited as one argument here, along with the

---

5 Sabine Hark: *Dissidente Partizipation. Eine Diskursgeschichte des Feminismus*, Frankfurt a. M.: Suhrkamp, 2005: 29.

5 Sabine Hark: *Dissidente Partizipation. Eine Diskursgeschichte des Feminismus*, Frankfurt a. M.: Suhrkamp, 2005: 29.

des 19. Jahrhunderts und der historischen Moderne scheint zu bestätigen, dass Frauen kaum berufliche Entfaltungsmöglichkeiten hatten. Ins Feld der Argumentation wird meist das späte symbolische und reale Datum der Zulassung von Frauen zum Studium an Kunstakademien angeführt, auch die vorherrschenden diskriminierenden bis misogynen Frauenbilder. Den Frauen fehlte angeblich die Ausbildung zur Künstlerin bzw. Gebrauchsgrafikerin, sie wurden von Eltern, Ehemann und der Gesellschaft generell daran gehindert, ihre Berufswünsche zu erfüllen, und auf die Rolle der Hausfrau, Mutter und Ehefrau festgelegt.

Im Folgenden soll an Beispielen darauf hingewiesen werden, dass dieses Narrativ nicht unbedingt einer historischen Realität entspricht. Frauen haben auch unter den Bedingungen größter Restriktionen Mittel und Wege gefunden, ihre Ambitionen als Grafikdesignerinnen in Eigenermächtigung umzusetzen. Zu den Eigeninitiativen zählten Privatschulen, die Frauen selbst gründeten, nationale Frauennetzwerke wie länderübergreifende Verbindungen. Das war insbesondere im 19. Jahrhundert und um die Jahrhundertwende der Fall. Von den 1960er bis in die 1990er Jahre waren Workshops und feministische Zines vorrangig.

Unter den Bedingungen besonderer designerischer Arbeitsformen, Anwendungsfelder, visueller Sprachen, neuer Formate über fast zwei Jahrhunderte kann von einer ausgeprägten Kontinuität des Grafikdesigns von Frauen gesprochen werden. Sie aus den Narrativen der Designhistoriografie angesichts der Dichte, der Kraft und Wirkmächtigkeit auszuschließen, ist kaum mehr nachvollziehbar.

Der Begriff Grafikdesign

Der Begriff Grafikdesign ist in der vorliegenden Publikation unterkomplex behandelt. Eine eigene Profession und entsprechende spezielle Ausbildung gab es über sehr lange Zeitstrecken noch nicht. Die meisten Frauen ließen sich anfangs als Künstlerinnen ausbilden und arbeiteten entweder in beiden Bereichen, den freien und den angewandten Künsten, oder sie deckten ein breites Feld an kunstgewerblichen Werken ab, zu denen auch die Gebrauchsgrafik zählte. Schon in der frühen Moderne hat die genaue Begriffsdefinition für Verwirrung gesorgt. „Gebrauchsgraphik, das ist ein Sammelbegriff, den es vor fünfzehn Jahren noch nicht gab, obgleich die Sache,

fact that prevailing images of women were often discriminatory and/or misogynistic. These histories have argued that women lacked training as artists or graphic designers; were prevented by parents, husbands, and society in general from fulfilling their career aspirations; and were confined to the role of housewife, mother, and wife.

The following will provide examples to show that this narrative does not necessarily correspond to historical reality. Even under the most restrictive conditions, women have found ways and means to transform their ambitions as graphic designers into self-empowerment. Initiatives launched outside traditional institutional structures included private schools founded by women themselves as well as national and transnational women's networks. This was especially the case in the nineteenth century and at the turn of the twentieth century. Beginning in the 1960s and through the 1990s, workshops and feminist zines were paramount.

Considering the changing conditions of particular forms of design work over two centuries—its fields of application, visual languages, and new formats—it is possible to speak of a pronounced continuity of graphic design by women. It is inexplicable to continue excluding women from the narratives of design historiography given how many women have played a part, with such significant power and influence.

The Term "Graphic Design"

This book employs the term "graphic design" in a broad, inclusive sense. A separate profession of graphic design, with correspondingly specific training, did not exist for a very long time. Most women initially trained as artists and either worked in both the fine and applied arts, or they were active in a broad field of decorative arts that included advertising and commercial art. Even in the early years of the modern period, the exact definition of the term caused confusion. "'Gebrauchsgraphik,'" typographer Fritz Helmut Ehmcke wrote in 1927, employing a word that means "applied art," "commercial art," or "advertising," "is a collective term that did not exist fifteen years ago, although the thing it denotes is ancient."[6] If used in strictly historical senses, terms such as "applied art," "commercial art," "commercial graphics," "design," "visual communication," and so on

6 F. H. Ehmcke in the article "Deutsche Gebrauchsgraphik" (1927), quoted from Jeremy Aynsley: Graphik-Design in Deutschland 1890–1945, Mainz: Hermann Schmidt, 2000: 11.

die damit bezeichnet wird, uralt ist", schrieb der Typograf Fritz Helmut Ehmcke 1927.[6] Die Anwendung der Begriffe „angewandte Kunst", „Nutzkünste", „Gebrauchsgrafik", „Design", „visuelle Kommunikation" etc. hätte jeweils einer eigenen Erklärung bedurft.

Insbesondere in den 1960er und 1970er Jahren spielten dann Aktivismus und Selbstermächtigung sowie die Methode des Do-it-yourself in den Workshops eine große Rolle und es kamen gleichermaßen Amateurinnen zum Zuge. Oder Frauen waren Art-Direktorinnen bei Zeitschriften, bei denen sie, zwar selbst einschlägig ausgebildet, Grafikdesign oftmals nur organisierten. Heute wiederum wollen sich Grafikdesignerinnen nicht mehr ausschließlich auf eine vordefinierte Form des Gestaltens beschränken, sondern öffnen sich mehreren künstlerischen Disziplinen und Formaten. Infolgedessen wird „Grafikdesign" pauschal als Arbeitsbegriff verwendet.

would have required a separate explanation in each case.

Especially in the 1960s and 1970s, activism and self-empowerment, in addition to the do-it-yourself method, played a major role in women's workshops, while amateur women designers begin to figure into the story in equal measure. Other women were art directors at magazines where they often only managed graphic design, rather than performing it themselves, despite having the requisite training. Today, however, women graphic designers no longer want to limit themselves exclusively to a predefined form of design; rather, they are often interested in exploring multiple artistic disciplines and formats. This book thus uses "graphic design" heuristically, as an umbrella term.

---

6 F. H. Ehmcke im Artikel „Deutsche Gebrauchsgraphik" (1927), zit. n.: Jeremy Aynsley: *Graphik-Design in Deutschland 1890–1945*, Mainz: Hermann Schmidt, 2000: 11.

EMANZI-PATION UND CHARITY

EMANCI-PATION AND CHARITY

Gebrauchsgrafikerinnen
in den USA um 1900
Women Commercial Artists
in the United States around 1900

Ethel Reed, Plakat zu / Poster for Albert Morris Bagby's New Novel
Miss Träumerei, Lamson, Wolffe & Co., 1895 © Library of Congress

Even before the significant change characterizing the second half of the nineteenth century, there were ways and means for women to acquire the knowledge they needed in art and design to work professionally as commercial artists. This was particularly the case in the United States.

For White upper-class women, offering instruction in design to younger women was initially a philanthropic field of activity. Soon, more and more women from the middle class took the opportunity to earn a living from commercial art. In many cases, they benefited from initiatives by other women that offered training and organized the sale of their work.

The fact that so many women working as commercial artists in the United States were able to advance professionally and gain public recognition before 1900 can be traced, most broadly speaking, to the US suffragette movement. One of the suffragettes' demands was that women should be able to lead autonomous lives. This stance resulted in numerous philanthropic institutions, such as private schools and workshops by women for women. However, the liberal and courageous spirit of these pioneering women can also be traced to other influencing factors, including an economically successful bourgeoisie that was still characterized by the pioneering spirit of a life in the New World. At first, most women commercial artists came from wealthy White families in New England who were able to finance an education for their daughters, even separately from academic institutions of learning, usually in the form of private lessons with artists. Many middle-class women found themselves in economically precarious situations. The enormous number of soldiers lost in the American Civil War (beginning in 1861) meant that many fathers and husbands who would been responsible for supporting their households were simply missing, leaving the women to support themselves. In this context, quite a number of women commercial artists were able to benefit from the educational institutions founded by the bourgeoisie.

In addition, art academies in the United States were more liberal than those in other countries, allowing women students to take drawing classes before this was possible elsewhere. The Pennsylvania Academy of the Arts, for example, admitted women students as early as 1844. A separate women's class was established in 1859 in which women students could work from clothed live models. Drawing from a female nude—

Bereits in der zweiten Hälfte des 19. Jahrhunderts gab es Mittel und Wege für Frauen, einschlägige Kenntnisse in Kunst und Design zu erwerben und Gebrauchsgrafik als Beruf auszuüben. Das war ganz besonders in den USA der Fall.

Jüngere Frauen in Design zu unterrichten, war zunächst ein philanthropisches Tätigkeitsfeld von Frauen der weißen Oberschicht. Bald nahmen mehr und mehr Vertreterinnen der Mittelschicht die Gelegenheit wahr, mit Gebrauchsgrafik ihren Lebensunterhalt zu verdienen. In vielen Fällen profitierten sie von Initiativen von Frauen, die ihnen eine Ausbildung ermöglichten und den Verkauf ihre Arbeiten organisierten.

Dass in den USA so viele Gebrauchsgrafikerinnen bereits vor 1900 beruflich avancieren konnten und öffentlich wahrgenommen wurden,

ist im weitesten Sinne der US-amerikanischen Suffragettenbewegung geschuldet. Eine ihrer Forderungen war, dass es Frauen möglich sein sollte, ein autonomes Leben zu führen. Aus dieser Haltung resultierten zahlreiche philanthropische Einrichtungen wie Privatschulen und Werkstätten von Frauen für Frauen. Der liberale und mutige Geist dieser Initiatorinnen ging aber auch auf weitere Einflussfaktoren zurück.

So gab es ein erfolgreiches Wirtschaftsbürgertum, das noch vom Pioniergeist eines Lebens in der Neuen Welt geprägt war. Anfangs stammten die meisten Gebrauchsgrafikerinnen aus wohlhabenden weißen Familien in Neuengland, die ihren Töchtern, auch unabhängig von der akademischen Lehre, eine Ausbildung finanzieren konnten, meist in Form von Privatunterricht bei Künstler*innen. Zahlreiche Frauen aus der Mittelschicht befanden sich in einer Notsituation. Aufgrund des hohen Verlusts an Soldaten im Sezessionskrieg (ab 1861) fielen Väter und Ehemänner aus, die ihre Existenz gesichert hätten. Nun mussten die Frauen ihren Lebensunterhalt selbst verdienen. Etliche Gebrauchsgrafikerinnen konnten in diesem Zusammenhang von den Bildungseinrichtungen, die Frauen aus dem Bürgertum gegründet hatten, profitieren.

Hinzu kam, dass die US-amerikanischen Kunstakademien im Vergleich mit anderen Ländern liberal waren. Sie erlaubten ihren Studentinnen früh den Zugang zu Zeichenklassen. Die Pennsylvania Academy of the Arts beispielsweise ließ Frauen bereits ab 1844 zum Studium zu. Eine separate Frauenklasse wurde 1859 eröffnet, wo Studentinnen nach bekleideten lebenden Modellen arbeiten konnten. Das Zeichnen nach einem weiblichen Akt – die Voraussetzung für das Studium der Malerei und Bildhauerei – war für sie ab 1868 möglich. Und dann war da selbstverständlich noch die US-amerikanische Arts-and-Crafts-Bewegung.

Die Arts-and-Crafts-Bewegung in den USA

Das Design von Büchern verdankt sich in weitem Maße der Arts-and-Crafts-Bewegung, die von England auf die Vereinigten Staaten übergegangen war.[1] William Morris und Emery Walker hatten in den 1890er Jahren in England die Kelmscott Press ins Leben gerufen und eine breite Reformbewegung der Buchgestaltung in Gang gesetzt, die in die Private-Press-Bewegung

1 Siehe insbes. Wendy Kaplan: *The Art That Is Life. The Arts and Crafts Movement in America, 1875–1920*, Boston: Bullfinch Press, 1987.

the prerequisite for studying painting and sculpture—was possible for these students beginning in 1868. And then, of course, there was also the American arts and crafts movement.

The Arts and Crafts Movement in the United States

The design of books can be traced in large part to the arts and crafts movement that spread from England to the United States.[1] When William Morris and Emery Walker launched the Kelmscott Press in England in the 1890s, they set in motion a broad reform movement in book design that resulted in the private press movement. The book was no longer regarded as a purely utilitarian object, but as a handcrafted aesthetic work.

Many women commercial artists from the American arts and crafts movement now found work in the art of making books. Like the British artists these women emulated, the American artists initially opposed industrial mass production, which they saw as failing to offer adequate quality. Instead, they developed a careful, well-crafted style of design for everyday objects of all kinds, characterized by an emphatically simple, functional aesthetic.[2]

The arts and crafts movement in the United States was centered in many places, with associations that formed all over the country. The city of Boston, influenced since its founding by English culture, offered particularly favorable terrain for the activities of artisans with its well-developed book trade. Boston-based printers and publishers were open to artistically sophisticated typography or calligraphy, and to new kinds of book decoration, illustration, and book covers. Boston was the first city to establish a society of arts and crafts. One of the first institutions dedicated to social reform in the United States was Hull House, Chicago. The house emerged from the settlement movement in 1889, at a time when 80 percent of Chicago's residents were European immigrants. For the most part, these newcomers

1 See especially Wendy Kaplan: *The Art That Is Life. The Arts and Crafts Movement in America, 1875–1920*, Boston: Bullfinch Press, 1987.
2 It was not so much the founding fathers of English arts and crafts, John Ruskin and William Morris, who were influential, but rather the second generation of architects and designers. These figures included Charles Robert Ashbee (1863–1942), who visited the United States in 1896, and Charles Francis Annesley Voysey (1857–1941), whose work became known in America primarily through magazines such as *The Studio*.

mündete. Das Buch galt von nun an nicht mehr als ein reines Gebrauchsobjekt, sondern als handwerklich hergestelltes ästhetisches Werk.

Aus der amerikanischen Arts-and-Crafts-Bewegung rekrutierten sich viele Gebrauchsgrafikerinnen, die im Bereich Buchkunst arbeiteten. Wie ihre britischen Vorbilder wandten sie sich zunächst gegen die industrielle Massenproduktion, die in ihren Augen keine angemessene Qualität auf den Markt brachte. Stattdessen entwickelten sie für Gebrauchsgegenstände jeglicher Art ein gediegenes Design, geprägt von einer betont schlichten, funktionalen Ästhetik.[2]

Das Arts and Crafts in den USA hatte viele Zentren, es bildeten sich Vereinigungen im ganzen Land. Die Stadt Boston, seit jeher durch die englische Kultur geprägt, bot mit ihrem ausgeprägten Buchgewerbe ein besonders günstiges Betätigungsfeld für die Kunsthandwerker*innen. Druckereien und Verlage vor Ort waren offen für künstlerisch anspruchsvolle Typografie, Kalligrafie, für Buchschmuck, Illustration und Bucheinbände. Boston war die erste Stadt, die eine Society of Arts and Crafts gründete. Eines der ersten Häuser für Sozialreformen in den USA war das Hull House in Chicago, das 1889 aus der Settlement-Bewegung hervorgegangen war. 80 Prozent der Einwohner Chicagos waren damals europäische Immigranten. Sie lebten überwiegend in desaströsen Lebensumständen in der von Korruption beherrschten Großstadt. Jane Adams, die Gründerin von Hull House, leitete die sozial- und bildungspolitische Einrichtung zusammen mit ihrer engsten Mitstreiterin Ellen Gates Starr und vielen anderen Frauen. Sie kümmerten sich um die prekären Lebensbedingungen der Migrant*innen in Chicagos naher West Side und bauten ein kulturelles Zentrum für Musik- und Theateraufführungen auf. Auch Ausstellungen wurden organisiert. Zu den aktiven Mitgliedern zählten viele Buchgestalterinnen wie Sarah Wyman Whitman (1842–1904), Julia DeWolf Addison (1866–1952), Mary Crease Sears (1880–1938) und Amy Maria Sacker (1872–1965).

Arts and Crafts folgte in den USA weniger einer strengen Philosophie als vielmehr einer individuellen philanthropischen Ausrichtung. Magazine wie *The Craftsman*, das von dem Möbeldesigner Gustav Stickley ab 1901 herausgegeben

2 Es waren weniger die Gründerväter des englischen Arts and Crafts, John Ruskin und William Morris, die Einfluss nahmen, als vielmehr die zweite Generation von Architekten und Designern, z. B. Charles Robert Ashbee (1863–1942), der die Vereinigten Staaten 1896 besuchte, und Charles Francis Annesley Voysey (1857–1941), dessen Werk vor allem durch Zeitschriften wie *The Studio* in Amerika bekannt wurde.

were housed under disastrous living conditions in a metropolis beset by corruption. Jane Adams, the founder of Hull House, ran the social and educational institution with her closest collaborator Ellen Gates Starr and many other women. These women endeavored to improve the precarious living conditions of immigrants in Chicago's Near West Side, where they built a cultural center for music and theater performances. They also organized exhibitions. Active members included many women book designers such as Sarah Wyman Whitman (1842–1904), Julia DeWolf Addison (1866–1952), Mary Crease Sears (1880–1938), and Amy Maria Sacker (1872–1965).

The arts and crafts movement in the United States was guided not so much by a rigid philosophy as by an inclination toward individual philanthropy. Magazines such as *The Craftsman*—published from 1901 by furniture designer Gustav Stickley, and edited in its early years by the seminal art historian and Syracuse University professor Irene Sargent (1852–1932)—spread the new ideas about design. Publishing numerous articles, Sargent became one of the leading women in the American arts and crafts movement. *House Beautiful* (from 1896) and *Ladies' Home Journal* (from 1883) were women's magazines that likewise increased the circulation of new ideas about object and graphic design.

Emancipation and Lifestyle

Quite a few of these women from the bourgeoisie led unconventional and independent lives, among them the book designer Margaret Neilson Armstrong (1867–1944), who was active, besides her focus on design, in many other fields from writing to botany. Together with other women, she traveled throughout the western United States and Canada in search of wild plants to draw. Several women were able to implement their ideas for the improvement of society with the help of a wealthy family or husband, sometimes even in collaboration with their partner. One such example was the extraordinary Candace Wheeler (1827–1923), whose initiatives, including in commercial graphics, are nothing short of legendary. Herself one of the first successful women in interior and textile design, she founded both the Society of Decorative Art (1877) in New York City and the New York Exchange for Women's Work (1878). These associations aimed to help women earn their own living by working with textiles and through other kinds of design. Financed

Candace Wheeler, Honeybees, Variation/variation, 1881, Foto/photo: © The Met Museum

wurde und dessen redaktionelle Schlüsselfigur in den ersten Jahren die Kunsthistorikerin und Professorin der Syrakus University Irene Sargent (1852–1932) war, verbreiteten die neuen Ideen. Durch die Publikation zahlreicher Artikel wurde Sargent zu einer der führenden Protagonistinnen der amerikanischen Arts-and-Crafts-Bewegung. *House Beautiful* (ab 1896) und *Ladies' Home Journal* (ab 1883) waren Frauenzeitschriften, die die Ideen des Objekt- und Grafikdesigns verbreiteten.

Emanzipation und Lebensstil

Nicht wenige der Frauen aus dem Bürgertum führten ein unkonventionelles und unabhängiges Leben wie die Buchdesignerin Margaret Neilson Armstrong (1867–1944), die neben ihrem gestalterischen Schwerpunkt in vielen anderen Fachgebieten tätig war, von der Schriftstellerei bis zur Botanik. Zusammen mit anderen Frauen reiste sie in die entfernt liegenden Regionen der Vereinigten Staaten und Kanadas, auf der Suche nach Wildpflanzen, die sie zeichnete. Etliche Frauen haben ihre sozialkritischen Ideen mithilfe einer reichen Familie oder eines wohlhabenden Ehemannes und teils in Zusammenarbeit mit ihrem Partner verwirklichen können, beispielsweise die außergewöhnliche Candace Wheeler (1827–1923). Ihre Initiativen, auch in der Gebrauchsgrafik, sind geradezu legendär. Selbst eine der ersten erfolgreichen Frauen im Interior- und Textildesign, gründete sie sowohl die Society of Decorative Art (1877) in New York City als auch die New York Exchange for Women's Work (1878). Diese Vereine sollten Frauen dabei unterstützen, ihren Unterhalt durch Textilarbeiten und andere Designarbeiten selbst zu erwirtschaften. Die Schule finanzierte sich durch Stiftungen wohlhabender Bürger*innen. Sie übernahm die Ausbildung und vertrieb die Produkte von Designerinnen. Auf diese Weise veränderte sie die allgemeine Wahrnehmung von künstlerischer Arbeit von Frauen. Was vormals als Freizeitbetätigung von Töchtern aus gutem Hause angesehen wurde, galt nun als Erwerbsarbeit. Beide Institutionen wurden ein Vorbild für vergleichbare Initiativen im ganzen Land.

Ethel Reed (1874–1912) wiederum, die erfolgreichste amerikanische Plakatkünstlerin des späten 19. Jahrhunderts, führte ein autonomes Privatleben jenseits aller Konventionen. Auch viele weitere Künstlerinnen pflegten einen neuen Habitus, kultivierten ein freies Leben und schlossen sich in Frauennetzwerken zusammen, wie das bei Elizabeth Coffin (1850–1930), Mary Cassatt

by donations from wealthy citizens, the school not only trained students but also distributed the products of women designers—thereby changing how women's artistic work was generally perceived. What had previously been considered a leisure activity for daughters from good homes came to be considered gainful employment. Both institutions became a model for similar initiatives across the country.

Another designer, Ethel Reed (1874–1912), who was the most successful American poster artist of the late nineteenth century, led an independent private life that cast aside all conventions. Many other women artists also developed a new social habitus, cultivated a free life, and joined women's networks. Prominent examples include Elizabeth Coffin (1850–1930), Mary Cassatt (1844–1926), Elizabeth Nourse (1859–1938), and Cecilia Beaux (1855–1942). These figures encouraged young women artists to develop work of their own. Women were already to be found in many influential positions in the United States before 1900 and took their own initiative in many ways.

Women Founders of Design Schools

Like the philanthropically oriented associations, the educational institutions founded by women had as their main objective the support of women for women. Most of the educational institutions founded by women became the cornerstone of today's national governmental or municipal educational institutions such as museums and design schools.

London's Female School of Design, founded in 1842, was the model for the Philadelphia School of Design for Women, now Moore College of Art and Design. Set up in Philadelphia in 1848 by Sarah W. Peter (1800–1877) in her own studio, it developed into the largest art academy in the country. Peter also established the Ladies' Gallery of Fine Arts, now the Cincinnati Academy of Fine Arts, becoming its first president. Like many other founders of such institutions, she was also responsible for raising the funds it required.

The New York School of Design for Women was founded by Susan Carter in 1852 and joined the Cooper Institute, now the Cooper Union for the Advancement of Science and Art, in 1859. The institution also rose to become one of the largest design schools in the country.

The Western Reserve School of Design for Women in Cleveland, founded in 1882, got its

Candace Wheeler, 1885

THIS IS AN ART SCHOOL AS WELL AS A BUSINESS HOUSE.

(1844–1926), Elizabeth Nourse (1859–1938) und Cecilia Beaux (1855–1942) der Fall war. Sie ermutigten junge Künstlerinnen zu eigenständiger Arbeit. Frauen waren in den USA bereits vor 1900 in vielen einflussreichen Positionen zu finden und ergriffen in vielfacher Hinsicht Eigeninitiative.

Gründerinnen von Designschulen

Wie die philanthropisch ausgerichteten Vereine hatten die von Frauen gegründeten Ausbildungsstätten hauptsächlich die Unterstützung von Frauen für Frauen zum Ziel. Die meisten der von Frauen gegründeten Ausbildungsstätten wurden zum Grundstein heutiger staatlicher oder kommunaler Bildungseinrichtungen wie Museen und Designschulen.

Die London's Female School of Design, die 1842 gegründet wurde, war das Vorbild für die Philadelphia School of Design for Women, heute Moore College of Art and Design. Sie wurde 1848 in Philadelphia von Sarah W. Peter (1800–1877) in ihrem eigenen Atelier eröffnet und entwickelte sich zur größten Kunstakademie im Lande. Peter etablierte außerdem die Ladies' Gallery of Fine Arts, heute Cincinnati Academy of Fine Arts, und wurde deren erste Präsidentin. Sie sorgte zudem, wie viele andere Initiatorinnen auch, für die Einwerbung der Finanzen.

The New York School of Design for Women wurde 1852 von Susan Carter gegründet und schloss sich 1859 dem Cooper Institute an, heute Cooper Union for the Advancement of Science and Art. Die Institution avancierte ebenfalls zu einer der größten Designschulen des Landes.

Die Western Reserve School of Design for Women in Cleveland, gegründet 1882, nahm ihren Anfang im Haus von Sarah M. Kimball (1818–1898), die als militante Suffragette galt. Sie ließ Frauen in Gebrauchsgrafik unterrichten, um sie auf das Berufsleben vorzubereiten. Später wurde die Schule umbenannt in Cleveland School of Art, ab 1949 in Cleveland Institute of Art.

Die New York School of Applied Design for Women entstand 1892 in New York City. Gründerin und treibende Kraft war Ellen Dunlap Hopkins (1854–1939). Außergewöhnlich in dieser Zeit war die Unterrichtung von Arbeiterinnen. Die Kurse der Schule umfassten ein breites Spektrum von Kunst und Design, unter anderem die Gestaltung von Bucheinbänden und Titelblättern, Interior Design, Tapeten- und Textildesign sowie Architektur. 1944 wurde die Institution umbenannt

start in the home of Sarah M. Kimball (1818–1898), who was considered a militant suffragette. She offered women training in commercial art to prepare them for professional life. The school was later renamed the Cleveland School of Art, and in 1949, the Cleveland Institute of Art.

The New York School of Applied Design for Women originated in New York City in 1892. Its founder and driving force was Ellen Dunlap Hopkins (1854–1939). Unusual for its time, the school taught working-class women. Its courses covered a wide range of art and design, including book cover and title page design, interior design, wallpaper and textile design, and architecture. In 1944, the institution was renamed the New York Phoenix School of Design when it merged with the Phoenix Art Institute, and in 1974 it was renamed the Pratt-New York Phoenix School of Design when it merged with the Pratt Institute.

The Women's Building

Among the most effective vehicles for achieving public impact at the time were the World's Fairs in the United States. In 1892, hundreds of women were busy preparing for the World's Columbian Exposition in Chicago. They were able to establish a Board of Women Managers, augmenting a previous board that had included only men, and eventually succeeded in building a structure of their own: The Women's Building,[3] which was also designed by a woman, Sophia Hayden (1868–1953). Harden was the first woman architect to graduate from the four-year program at the School of Architecture at the Massachusetts Institute of Technology (MIT) in Boston. Candace Wheeler was commissioned to design the building's interior. Women artists and graphic designers made further contributions.

Furnished exclusively by White, upper- and middle-class women, the edifice was nevertheless emblematic for the achievements of these segments of society. Women of color were systematically excluded. African American women in particular had pushed to be included, without success. Black journalist and activist Ida B. Wells then published the correspondence between Black activists and White organizers under the title *The Reason Why the Colored American Is Not in the World's Columbian Exposition*. The brochure was available not far from the Women's Building

3 The struggle for women's equal participation in the World Fair was described in detail by Jeanette Madeleine Weimann in *The Fair Women*, Chicago: Academy Books, ca. 1981.

in New York Phoenix School of Design, als sie sich mit dem Phoenix Art Institute vereinte, und 1974 in Pratt-New York Phoenix School of Design, als sie sich mit dem Pratt Institute verband.

The Women's Building

Eines der effektvollsten Medien, um öffentliche Wirkung zu erzielen, waren die Weltausstellungen in den USA. 1892 waren Hunderte von Frauen damit beschäftigt, die World's Columbian Exposition in Chicago vorzubereiten. Sie setzten durch, dass ein Board of Women Managers eingerichtet wurde, nachdem es ein solches bislang nur mit männlicher Besetzung gab. Schließlich konnten sie ein eigenes Gebäude für Frauen, The Women's Building,[3] errichten. Entworfen wurde es von einer Frau, Sophia Hayden (1868-1953), der ersten Architektin, die das Vier-Jahres-Programm der School of Architecture am Massachusetts Institute of Technology (MIT) in Boston abgeschlossen hatte. Candace Wheeler wurde beauftragt, das Innere des Gebäudes zu gestalten. Künstlerinnen und Grafikdesignerinnen steuerten weitere Beiträge bei.

Allerdings stand das Gebäude, das ausschließlich von weißen Frauen der Mittel- und Oberschicht ausgestattet wurde, symbolisch für die Errungenschaften ebenjener Schichten. Women of Color wurden systematisch ausgeschlossen. Insbesondere Afroamerikanerinnen hatten sich dafür eingesetzt, ebenfalls beteiligt zu sein, wurden aber abgelehnt. Die Schwarze Journalistin und Aktivistin Ida B. Wells veröffentlichte daraufhin den Briefwechsel zwischen den Schwarzen Aktivistinnen und den weißen Organisatorinnen unter dem Titel *The Reason Why the Colored American Is not in the World's Columbian Exposition*. Die Broschüre war unweit des Women's Building im Pavillon von Haiti erhältlich, jenes ersten unabhängigen Staates, der nach den Sklavenaufständen 1804 von Schwarzen Männern und Frauen gegründet worden war.[4]

The Women Graphic Designers Morse, Armstrong, and Whitman

Three equally esteemed women commercial artists dominated the art book design market in the United States at the end of the nineteenth century: Margaret Neilson Armstrong (1867-1944), Sarah Wyman Whitman, and Alice Cordelia Morse (1863-1961). While some women preferred working with handcrafted products, Sarah Wyman Whitman also supplied publishers who published mass-produced, machine-made goods.

One of the first woman graphic designers at the end of the nineteenth century was Alice C. Morse. Born in Ohio, she grew up middle class,

4 See Mary Pepchinski, Blinde Flecken: Auslassungen in frühen Darstellungen über Frauen in der Architekturgeschichte, *Arch+. Zeitschrift für Architektur und Urbanismus* (Zeitgenössische feministische Raumpraxis), no. 246 (2021): 52–60, on 54.

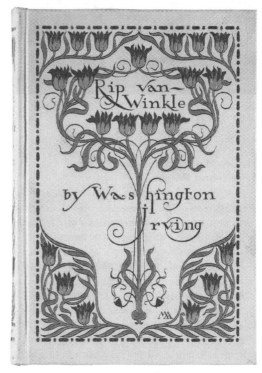

Margaret Neilson Armstrong, Bucheinband für / Book cover for Rip van Winkle von/by Washington Irving, Knickerbocker Press, 1899 © Gift of Friends of the Thomas J. Watson Library, The Metropolitan Museum

3 Der Kampf um die Beteiligung von Frauen wurde intensiv beschrieben in: Jeanette Madeleine Weimann: *The Fair Women*, Chicago: Academy Books, ca. 1981.

4 Siehe Mary Pepchinski: Blinde Flecken. Auslassungen in frühen Darstellungen über Frauen in der Architekturgeschichte, *Arch+. Zeitschrift für Architektur und Urbanismus* (Zeitgenössische feministische Raumpraxis), Nr. 246 (2021): 52–60, hier 54.

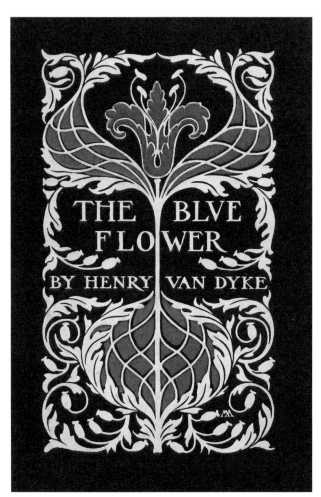

Margaret Neilson Armstrong, Bucheinband für / Book cover for The Blue Flower von/by Henry van Dyke, Charles Scribner's Son, 1902

Die Grafikdesignerinnen Morse, Armstrong, Whitman

Drei gleichermaßen geschätzte Gebrauchsgrafikerinnen dominierten Ende des 19. Jahrhunderts den US-amerikanischen Markt der künstlerischen Buchgestaltung: Margaret Neilson Armstrong (1867–1944), Sarah Wyman Whitman und Alice Cordelia Morse (1863–1961). Während einige Frauen handwerklich hergestellte Produkte bevorzugten, belieferte Sarah Wyman Whitman auch Verlage, die maschinenproduzierte Massenware herausgaben.

Eine der ersten Grafikdesignerinnen Ende des 19. Jahrhunderts war Alice C. Morse. In Ohio geboren, wuchs sie in der sozialen Mittelschicht auf. Sie profitierte von den sozialreformerischen Initiativen von Frauen. Morse studierte

later benefiting from women's social reform initiatives that allowed her to study drawing at the Woman's Art School of the Cooper Union for the Advancement of Science and Art (1879–1983) in Manhattan. After five years of design work at the Women's Glass Studio for leaded glass to be sold by Tiffany and Co., she decided to make a radical career change and returned to the Cooper Union, where from 1889 to 1891 she trained as an artist under the direction of Susan N. Carter. After that, she worked as a freelance book designer. Book covers designed by artists were not only popular at the time, but also commercially lucrative and an area where new design styles could develop.

In formal terms, Morse's aesthetic differed from that of Sarah Wyman Whitman and Margaret Neilson Armstrong. She cultivated an eclectic style and employed myriad forms of expression, often adapted to the public's taste. She borrowed from arts and crafts, art nouveau, neorococo, and classical periods such as the Renaissance, while also absorbing East Asian influences. In some cases, she combined styles, and this versatility was the foundation of her success. She continuously received commissions from the most prominent publishers such as Dodd, Mead & Company, Charles Scribner's Sons, and G. P. Putnam's Sons.

At the same time, she was committed to creating more professional visibility for women in their fields. In 1893, she chaired the subcommittee on book bindings, wood engravings, and illustrations of the Board of Women Managers in the Women's Building at the Chicago World's Fair. She also wrote a chapter in the handbook *Woman's Building* entitled "Women Illustrators," as well as designing the book cover of the *Distaff Series*, a compendium of six books written, designed, and typeset exclusively by women. The series was published by Harper & Brothers and sold in the Women's Building.

Sarah Wyman Whitman, also known as Sarah de St. Prix Wyman Whitman, is one of the most important women commercial artists during this early period of design history in the United States. Her association with the publisher Houghton, Mifflin & Co. led to advertisements announcing her work appearing from 1887 in *Publishers' Weekly*. In addition to her work as a painter and craftswoman for church windows, she became known primarily as a book designer. As a reaction to the often-ostentatious volumes in the years before 1880, she developed her own style with a pared-down design, foregoing splen-

Zeichnen an der Woman's Art School der Cooper Union for the Advancement of Science and Art (1879–1983) in Manhattan. Nach fünf Jahren Entwurfsarbeit im Women's Glass Studio für Bleiverglasungen der Firma Tiffany entschied sie sich für einen grundlegenden Berufswechsel und ging zurück zur Cooper Union, wo sie von 1889 bis 1891 eine Ausbildung als Künstlerin unter der Leitung von Susan N. Carter machte. Danach arbeitete sie als freie Buchdesignerin. Künstlerisch gestaltete Buchcover waren zu dieser Zeit beliebt, kommerziell lukrativ und ein Gebiet, in dem sich neue gestalterische Stile entwickeln konnten.

Morse unterschied sich formalästhetisch von Sarah Wyman Whitman und Margaret Neilson Armstrong. Sie kultivierte einen eklektischen Stil und bediente sich vieler Ausdrucksformen, die oft dem Publikumsgeschmack angepasst waren. Sie nahm Anleihen bei Arts and Crafts, Art nouveau, Neo-Rokoko und klassischen Perioden wie der Renaissance, auch ostasiatische Einflüsse nahm sie auf. In manchen Fällen kombinierte sie Stile. Ihre Vielseitigkeit war die Grundlage ihres Erfolges. Sie erhielt kontinuierlich Aufträge von den bekanntesten Verlagen wie Dodd, Mead & Company, Charles Scribner's Sons und G. P. Putnam's Sons.

Zugleich engagierte sie sich dafür, Frauen in ihrem Berufsfeld sichtbarer zu machen. 1893 war sie Vorsitzende des Unterausschusses für Bucheinbände, Holzstiche und Illustrationen des Board of Women Managers im Women's Building auf der Weltausstellung in Chicago. Zudem schrieb sie ein Kapitel im Handbuch *Woman's Building* mit dem Titel „Women Illustrators". Sie entwarf den Bucheinband der *Distaff Series*, ein Kompendium von sechs Büchern, die ausschließlich von Frauen geschrieben, gestaltet und gesetzt wurden. Die Serie wurde von Harper & Brothers herausgegeben und im Women's Building verkauft.

Sarah Wyman Whitman, auch Sarah de St. Prix Wyman Whitman genannt, zählt zu den bedeutendsten Gebrauchsgrafikerinnen der US-amerikanischen Frühzeit um 1890. Ihre Verbindung zu dem Verlag Houghton, Mifflin & Co. führte dazu, dass Werbung, die ihr Werk ankündigte, von 1887 an in *Publishers' Weekly* erschien. Neben ihrer Tätigkeit als Malerin und Kunsthandwerkerin für Kirchenfenster wurde sie vor allem als Buchgestalterin bekannt. Als Reaktion auf die häufig prunkvoll gestalteten Titel in den Jahren vor 1880 entwickelte sie einen eigenen Stil mit reduziertem Design, das heißt sie verzichtete auf prächtiges Ornament und auffällige Farben.

did ornamentation and flashy colors. The simplicity of the design meant that the book titles could be produced relatively inexpensively and were thus suitable for serial production. Whitman also nurtured young talent. She was a cofounder of the Boston Society of Arts and Crafts.

While Whitman was a pioneer, the 1890s saw the emergence of a host of young women artists who turned to commercial art, especially book art. Many were influenced by the private press movement in England. At the time, British magazines such as *The Yellow Book* and *The Studio* spread the ideas of art nouveau and the arts and crafts movement. In addition to Boston, publishers in other places, such as Stone & Kimball in Chicago and Thomas Mosher in Maine, published small, easy-to-read editions by avant garde writers with covers and title pages designed in the style of art nouveau. These volumes were modeled on traditional printing forms and methods of bookbinding, which revived the book as a work of art, and, through a focus on the material skills of craftspersons, bookmaking as an artisanal craft in its own right. Notable designers of the period include Bertha Stuart (1869–1953), Blanche McManus (1869–1935), Emma Reddington (Lee) Thayer (1874–1973), Amy Maria Sacker, and Marion Louise Peabody (1869–?).

Margaret Neilson Armstrong was highly acclaimed as one of the most prolific women commercial artists of the last decade of the nineteenth century. Her works are clearly recognizable not only because of her own style, but also because Armstrong furnished them with a signet consisting of her initials, the overlapping letters M and A. She and her sister Helen were influenced by one of the leading theorists and illustrators of the English arts and crafts movement, Walter Crane, and by the British children's book illustrator Kate Greenaway (1846–1901).

Armstrong first designed for the Chicago publishing house A. C. McClurg, and later for other publishers. She designed more than 270 book covers and dust jackets, about half of them for the New York publishing house Charles Scribner's Sons, whose catalog included works of highly renowned authors. Armstrong designed the cover for an edition of Washington Irving's *Rip van Winkel* in 1899, for example.

Around 1913, she turned to designing dust jackets, not least because they were less expensive. Her distinctive graphic style was so successful that publishers hired artists specifically to mimic her cover designs.

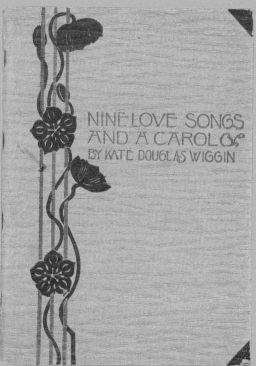

Sarah Wyman Whitman, Bucheinband für / Book cover for
The Great Remembrance and Other Poems von/by Richard Watson
Gilder, Houghton, Mifflin & Co., 1893 © Melinda Wallington;
Museum of Rochester, New York
Alice Cordelia Morse, Bucheinband für / Book cover for
Poems of Cabin and Field von/by Paul Laurence Dunbar,
Dodd Mead and Co., 1901
Margaret Neilson Armstrong, Bucheinband für / Book cover for
According to Season von/by Dana William Starr, 1902
Sarah Wyman Whitman, Bucheinband für / Book cover for
Nine Love Songs and a Carol von/by Kate Douglas Wiggin,
Houghton, Mifflin & Co., 1890 © Melinda Wallington;
Museum of Rochester, New York
Sarah Wyman Whitman, Bucheinband für / Book cover for
A Roman Singer von/by F. Marion Crawford, Houghton, Mifflin & Co.,
1884, Boston Public Library, Special Collection
Sarah Wyman Whitman, Bucheinband für / Book cover for
An Island Garden von/by Celia Thaxter, Houghton Mifflin & Co., 1894
© Melinda Wallington; Museum of Rochester, New York

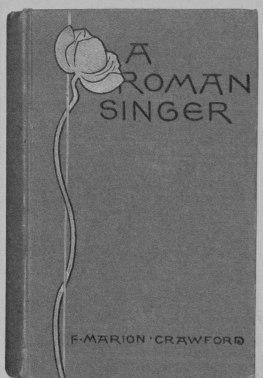

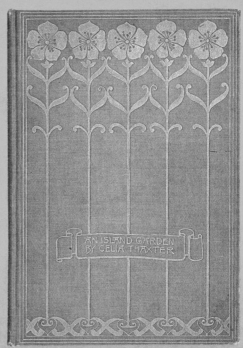

Sarah Wyman Whitman, Bucheinband für / Book cover for Being a Boy von/by Charles Dudley Warner, Houghton Mifflin & Co., 1897
© University of Rochester, New York, Rare Books, Special Collections & Preservation

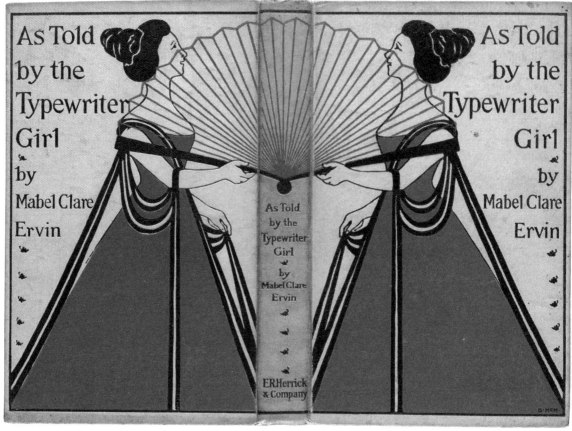

Blanche McManus, Bucheinband für / Book cover for As Told by the Typewriter Girl von/by Mabel Clare Ervin, E.R. Herrick & Co., 1898, The Metropolitan Museum of Art

Aufgrund der Schlichtheit der Gestaltung konnten die Buchtitel relativ kostengünstig produziert werden und eigneten sich somit für die serielle Produktion. Whitman förderte auch junge Talente. Sie war Mitbegründerin der Boston Society of Arts and Crafts.

War Whitman noch eine Pionierin, trat in den 1890er Jahren eine Vielzahl an jungen Künstlerinnen auf, die sich der Gebrauchsgrafik zuwandten, insbesondere der Buchkunst. Viele waren durch die Private-Press-Bewegung in England beeinflusst. Britische Zeitschriften wie *The Yellow Book* und *The Studio* verbreiteten in jenen Jahren die Ideen des Art nouveau und der Arts-and-Crafts-Bewegung. Neben Boston gaben auch Verlage in anderen Städten, etwa Stone & Kimball in Chicago and Thomas Mosher in Maine, kleine, gut lesbare Editionen von Avantgarde-Schriftsteller*innen heraus und ließen Einbände sowie Titelblätter im Stil des Art nouveau gestalten. Sie orientierten sich an traditionellen Druckformen und Methoden der Buch-

Blanche McManus, Illustration aus / Illustration from Alice's Adventures in Wonderland von/by Lewis Carroll, M.F. Mansfield and A. Wessels, 1899

binderei, welche das Buch als Kunstwerk und mit den manuellen Fähigkeiten der Handwerker*innen als Kunsthandwerk wiederaufleben ließen. Bedeutende Designerinnen dieser Zeit waren Bertha Stuart (1869–1953), Blanche McManus (1869–1935), Emma Reddington (Lee) Thayer (1874–1973), Amy Maria Sacker, Marion Louise Peabody (1869–?).

Margaret Neilson Armstrong wurde als eine der produktivsten Gebrauchsgrafikerinnen der letzten Dekade des 19. Jahrhunderts geschätzt. Identifizierbar sind ihre Arbeiten nicht nur aufgrund ihres eigenen Stils, sondern auch, weil Armstrong sie mit einem Signet aus ihren Initialen, die sich überlappenden Buchstaben M und A, versah. Sie und ihre Schwester Helen waren beeinflusst von einem der führenden Theoretiker und Illustratoren der englischen Arts-and-Crafts-Bewegung, von Walter Crane, und von der britischen Kinderbuchillustratorin Kate Greenaway (1846–1901).

Zunächst entwarf Armstrong für den Chicagoer Verlag A. C. McClurg und später auch für andere Verlage. Sie gestaltete mehr als 270 Bucheinbände und Buchumschläge, etwa die Hälfte davon für das New Yorker Verlagshaus Charles Scribner's Sons. Dort wurden auch Werke sehr renommierter Autoren herausgegeben. Armstrong entwarf 1899 beispielsweise das Titelblatt für eine Ausgabe von Washington Irvings *Rip van Winkel*.

Armstrong wandte sich um 1913 der Gestaltung von Schutzumschlägen zu, nicht zuletzt weil sie preisgünstiger waren. Ihr unverkennbarer grafischer Stil war so erfolgreich, dass die Verleger Künstler*innen speziell für die Nachahmung ihres Designs von Einbänden einstellten.

Ethel Reed

Die 1890er Jahre bildeten in den USA den Höhepunkt des künstlerischen Plakats jenseits der reinen Werbung. Schon 1896 richtete die Pennsylvania Academy of the Fine Arts eine Ausstellung über Plakate aus. Französische Beispiele des sogenannten Goldenen Zeitalters, von Toulouse-Lautrec, Steinlen, Chéret und anderen, waren nicht fremd in den USA. Designer*innen begannen in dieser Zeit, ihre Entwürfe zu signieren und schufen einen unverkennbaren eigenen Stil. Ende 1893 entwickelten Charles Scribner's Sons, J. B. Lippincott Company, The Century Company, Harper & Brothers, Stone & Kimball und andere Verleger den Plan, ihre eigenen Plakate zu drucken. Das Wettrennen unter den Verlagen

Ethel Reed

The 1890s marked the high point of art posters in the United States as a distinct genre separate from advertising. In 1896, for instance, the Pennsylvania Academy of the Fine Arts hosted a poster exhibition, while French examples of the so-called Golden Age by Toulouse-Lautrec, Steinlen, Chéret, and others were known in the United States. Women designers began to include their own signatures on their designs during this period and to create a distinctive style of their own. In late 1893, Charles Scribner's Sons, J. B. Lippincott Company, The Century Company, Harper & Brothers, Stone & Kimball, and other publishers each launched plans to print posters of their own. A race among the publishers commenced, and women commercial artists were right in the thick of it. Sarah Wyman Whitman, for example, created what became something of a house style for Houghton Mifflin and Company.

The Chap-Book, a small literary magazine and house journal of Stone and Kimbell, appeared twice monthly between 1894 and 1898. From the outset, the publishers engaged not only excellent authors, but also graphic designers from Europe such as Félix Vallotton and Henri de Toulouse-Lautrec. But the artist from this group who became the most famous was the American Will Bradley. Bradley designed the first six posters of *The Chap-Book*. Stone and Kimbell was also the American publisher of the English magazine *The Yellow Book*, which commissioned the contributions of many women graphic designers.

Although several American women poster artists emerged at the turn of the century, none of them achieved the fame of Ethel Reed, who garnered great attention with series of posters and illustrations for newspapers, magazines, and books. Reed was also active as a painter. During her brief period of success, she was hailed by US and European art critics as the greatest woman commercial artist in America. And her fame did not fade, as she is mentioned in all major histories of graphic design.

With their colorful and two-dimensional style, Ethel Reed's works can be considered as art nouveau. Like many other poster artists, she illustrated the upper-class world of beautiful women, leisure, and idleness.

Reed was born on 13 March 1874, in Newburyport, Massachusetts, as the daughter of an American photographer and an Irish immigrant. Her father died when she was eighteen years old, leaving the family in a dire financial situation. By and large she was self-taught, though she attended

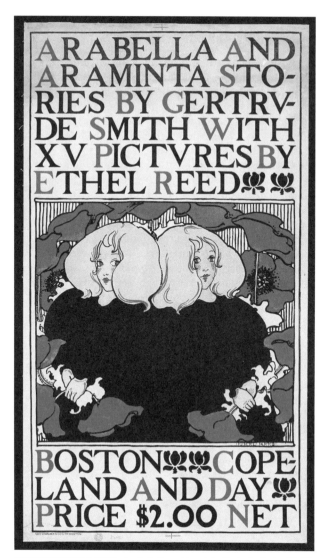

Ethel Reed, Plakat zu / Poster for Arabella and Araminta. Stories by Gertrud Smith, Copeland & Day, 1895 © Library of Congress

Ethel Reed, Ladies Want it Feb24, Plakat zu / Poster for The Boston Sunday Herald, 1874

begann. An ihm waren auch Gebrauchsgrafikerinnen beteiligt. Sarah Wyman Whitman schuf beispielsweise einen regelrechten Hausstil für Houghton Mifflin and Company.

The Chap-Book, ein kleines Literatur magazin und Hausblatt von Stone and Kimbell, erschien zwischen 1894 und 1898 zweimal monatlich. Von vornherein verpflichteten die Verleger nicht nur exzellente Autoren, sondern auch Grafikdesigner aus Europa wie Félix Vallotton und Henri de Toulouse-Lautrec. Am bekanntesten wurde aber der Amerikaner Will

Cowles Art School for a short time in 1893 after the family moved to Boston. American artist and illustrator Laura Coombs Hills (1859–1952) became her mentor. At the age of twenty, Reed had already achieved national fame as a poster artist. She received early attention in 1895 for a series of posters for the *Boston Sunday Herald* and worked above all for Copeland & Day and Lamson, Wolffe & Co. After moving to England, she contributed remarkable illustrations to *The Yellow Book*.

Widely lauded for her beauty, she posed for well-known photographers, among them Fred Holland Day and Frances Benjamin Johnston. She led a life marked by freedom. After breaking off an engagement, she never again entered into any conventional commitment and remained a single mother of two children. The private circle she built included many personalities from literature and art.

After ending her engagement, she traveled through Europe with her mother in 1896; a year later, the two settled in London, where Reed

Ethel Reed, Plakat zu / Poster for Is Polite Society Polite von/by Julia Ward Howe, Lamson, Wolffe & Co., 1895
© The Miriam and Ira D. Wallach Division of Art, Prints and Photographs: Art & Architecture Collection, The New York Library

Bradley. Die ersten sechs Plakate von *The Chap-Book* wurden von ihm gestaltet. Stone and Kimbell war auch der amerikanische Herausgeber des englischen *The Yellow Book*, zu dem viele Grafikdesigner*innen beitrugen.

Zwar traten einige amerikanische Plakatkünstlerinnen um die Jahrhundertwende hervor, allerdings erreichte keine von ihnen den Ruhm von Ethel Reed. Sie errang große Aufmerksamkeit mit Serien von Plakaten und Illustrationen für Zeitungen, Zeitschriften und für Bücher. Zugleich war Reed als Malerin tätig. In der kurzen Zeit ihres Erfolges wurde sie in den USA und Europa von der Kunstkritik als die größte amerikanische Gebrauchsgrafikerin gefeiert. Und auch im Nachhinein verblasste ihr Ruhm nicht. In allen Werken zur Geschichte des Grafikdesigns wird sie erwähnt.

Ethel Reeds Arbeiten werden in ihrem farbigen und flächigen Stil dem Art nouveau zugeordnet. Wie viele andere Plakatkünstler*innen auch illustrierte sie die Upper-Class-Welt der schönen Frauen, der Freizeit und des Müßiggangs.

continued to work as an illustrator. In England, however, she was unable to regain her former fame and disappeared from the public eye. Very little is known about her circumstances in her last years; she probably died in 1912 at the age of 38.

Geboren wurde Ethel Reed am 13. März 1874 in Newburyport in Massachusetts als Tochter eines amerikanischen Fotografen und einer irischen Einwanderin. Ihr Vater starb, als sie 18 Jahre alt war. In der Folge litt die Familie unter starken finanziellen Einschränkungen. Im Großen und Ganzen war sie Autodidaktin, besuchte aber 1893, nach dem Umzug der Familie nach Boston, für kurze Zeit die Cowles Art School. Die amerikanische Künstlerin und Illustratorin Laura Coombs Hills (1859-1952) wurde ihre Mentorin. Bereits im Alter von 20 Jahren erlangte Reed als Plakatkünstlerin nationalen Ruhm. Frühe Aufmerksamkeit erhielt sie 1895 für eine Serie von Plakaten für den *Boston Sunday Herald*. Sie arbeitete insbesondere für Copeland & Day und Lamson, Wolffe & Co. Nach ihrer Übersiedlung nach England trug sie mit bemerkenswerten Illustrationen zu *The Yellow Book* bei.

Wegen ihrer Schönheit stand sie bekannten Fotografen Modell, beispielsweise Fred Holland Day und Frances Benjamin Johnston. Sie führte einen freien Lebensstil. Nach der Auflösung einer Verlobung ging sie keinerlei konventionelle Bindung mehr ein und blieb alleinerziehende Mutter von zwei Kindern. In ihrem privaten Kreis versammelte sie viele Persönlichkeiten aus Literatur und Kunst um sich.

Nach dem Scheitern ihrer Verlobung reiste sie 1896 mit ihrer Mutter durch Europa, ein Jahr später ließen sich die beiden in London nieder, wo Reed weiterhin als Illustratorin arbeitete. In England konnte sie jedoch nicht mehr an ihren alten Ruhm anknüpfen und verschwand aus der öffentlichen Wahrnehmung. Über ihre Lebensumstände in späten Jahren ist sehr wenig bekannt, vermutlich verstarb sie 1912 mit 38 Jahren.

Literatur
Further Reading

Beauty for Commerce: Publishers' Bindings, 1830–1910, University of Rochester, Rare Books, Special Collections and Preservation, https:rbscp.lib.rochester.edu/3351 (Abruf/accessed 22. Jan. 2020).

Candace Wheeler. The Art and Enterprise of American Design, 1875–1900, Ausstellungskatalog / exhibition catalog, New Haven: Metropolitan Museum of Art, 2001.

Robert Judson Clark (Hg./ed.): *The Arts and Crafts Movement in America, 1876–1916*, Princeton: Princeton University Press, 1972.

Rebecca W. Davidson: *Unseen Hands. Women Printers, Binders, and Book Designers*, Ausstellungskatalog / exhibition catalog, Leonard L. Milberg Gallery for the Graphic Arts, Princeton: Princeton University Library, 2005.

Mindell Dubansky: *The Proper Decoration of Book Covers. The Life and Work of Alice C. Morse*, New York: Grolier Club, 2008.

Mindell Dubanksy: Alice Cordelia Morse (1863–1961), *Heilbrunn Timeline of Art History*, New York: The Metropolitan Museum of Art, 2000, http://www.metmuseum.org/toah/hd/mors/hd_mors.html (Abruf/accessed 1. Mai/May 2022).

Maud Howe Elliott: *Art and Handicraft in the Woman's Building of the World's Columbian Exposition*, Chicago, 1893.

Charles Gullans & John Espey: *Margaret Armstrong and American Trade Bindings* (Occasional Papers 6), Los Angeles: UCLA Library Department of Special Collections, 1991, https://archive.org/details/margaretarmstron00gull/ (Abruf/accessed 1. Mai/May 2022).

Leona M. Hudak & N. J. Metuchen: *Early American Women Printers and Publishers*, Lanham, Maryland: Scarecrow Press, 1978.

Wendy Kaplan: *„The Art That Is Life". The Arts and Crafts Movement in America, 1875–1920*, Boston: Bullfinch Press, 1987.

Margaret Armstrong Binding Collection. Decorative Bindings, Rare Book and Special Collections Reading Room, The Library of Congress, https://www.metmuseum.org/blogs/in-circulation/2020/armstrong-vitrine (Abruf/accessed 22. Jan. 2020).

Miriam Irwin Collection of Margaret Armstrong Book Design, University of Cincinnati, https://libapps.libraries.uc.edu/exhibits/margaretarmstrong/ (Abruf/accessed 22. Jan. 2020).

Ellen K. Morris & Edward S. Levin: *The Art of Publishers' Bookbindings 1815–1915*, Los Angeles: William Dailey Rare Books Ltd., 2000.

William S. Peterson: *The Beautiful Poster Lady. A Life of Ethel Reed*, New Castle, Delaware: Oak Knoll Press, 2013.

ARTS-AND-CRAFTS BEWEGUNG

ARTS AND CRAFTS MOVEMENT

Gilden und Netzwerke von Frauen
in England und Schottland
Guilds and Women's Networks
in England and Scotland

England war in der Ausbildung von Designer*innen ab Mitte des 19. Jahrhunderts besonders ambitioniert. Das Royal College of Art in London wurde 1837 in Somerset House als Government School of Design gegründet. 1853 zog die Schule um ins Marlborough House und wenig später in den Stadtteil South Kensington, an dieselbe Stelle wie das South Kensington Museum, das heutige Victoria and Albert Museum. Eine professionelle Ausbildung zum Grafikdesign wurde zwar erst ab Mitte des 20. Jahrhunderts angeboten, aber die Kunstschule wie auch das South Kensington Museum standen anfänglich unter dem Einfluss der Arts-and-Crafts-Bewegung und ihren Werkstätten. Sie waren daher sowohl der Gestaltung von Alltagsdingen als auch der angewandten Grafik gegenüber sehr offen.

Mit der Government School of Design waren etwa 130 freie Schulen im ganzen Land verbunden.[1] Die Curricula im Zeichnen wurden an Grundschulen gelehrt. Morgen- und Abendklassen waren den männlichen Studierenden vorbehalten, eine separate „Damenschule" ist ab 1848 in London erwähnt.[2] Es gab zudem zahlreiche weitere Schulen, die Frauen offenstanden.

May Morris (1862–1938) beispielsweise, die Tochter des legendären Arts-and-Crafts-Protagonisten William Morris, studierte textile Kunst an der South Kensington School of Design.[3] Die National Art Training School of South Kensington, von 1837 bis 1852 Vorläufer der School of Design, zählte zu den weltweit bedeutendsten Schulen, die sich dem Kunsthandwerk widmeten. Mehr als 1000 Studierende wurden jährlich in einem breiten Spektrum von Kunst und Design unterrichtet, wobei die Anzahl der Frauen überwog. Die Geschlechter wurden nach Klassen- und Arbeitsräumen eingeteilt, die Vorlesungen, die Bibliothek und andere gemeinschaftliche Einrichtungen standen allen offen. Die Abschlussprüfungen für weibliche und männliche Studierende unterschieden sich nicht, außer in den Fächern Architektur und Maschinenzeichnen.

In der Zeit zwischen 1880 und 1920 nahm die Zahl der Frauen, die als Buchkünstlerinnen arbeiteten, in England immens zu. Fast alle waren von den Ideen der Arts-and-Crafts-Bewegung geprägt, wonach die Gestaltung von Büchern eine

1 https://www.british-history.ac.uk/survey-london/vol38/pp74-96 (Abruf 23. Mrz. 2021).
2 https://sculpture.gla.ac.uk/view/organization.php?id=msib4_1267714397 (Abruf 24. Mrz. 2021).
3 Zoë Thomas: At Home with the Women's Guild of Arts. Gender and Professional Identity in London Studios, c. 1880–1925, *Women's History Review* 24, Nr. 6 (2015): 938–964, hier 964, DOI: 10.1080/09612025.2015.1039348.

Beginning in the mid-nineteenth century, England was particularly ambitious in training women designers. The Royal College of Art in London was founded in 1837 in Somerset House as the Government School of Design. In 1853, the school moved to Marlborough House and a short time later to the South Kensington neighborhood, on the same site as the South Kensington Museum, now the Victoria and Albert Museum. Although the art school did not offer professional training in graphic design until the mid-twentieth century, both it and the South Kensington Museum were initially influenced by the arts and crafts movement and its workshops. The institutions were thus quite open when it came to the design of everyday things and to applied graphics.

The Government School of Design also developed connections to some 130 independent schools across the country; its curriculum in drawing was taught in elementary schools.[1] Morning and evening classes were reserved for male students, and beginning in 1848 one finds mention of a separate "female school" in London.[2] Numerous other schools were also open to women.

1 See https://www.british-history.ac.uk/survey-london/vol38/pp74-96 (accessed 23. Mar. 2021).
2 See https://sculpture.gla.ac.uk/view/organization.php?id=msib4_1267714397 (accessed 24. Mar. 2021).

Esther & Lucien Pissarro, Holzschnitt für / Woodcut for
C'est d'Aucassin et de Nicolete von/by Francis William Bourdillon
Eragny Press, 1903

Helen Scholfield, Bucheinband in marokkanischem Leder mit Schmetterlings-Design zu / Book cover in Moroccan leather with butterfly design for More English Fairy Tales, Guild of Women-Binders, 1894, Foto/photo: Edward Nudelman, The Victorian Web

kunsthandwerkliche und künstlerische Aufgabe war. Vorbild war William Morris, der 1891 mithilfe seines Freundes Emery Walker die Privatdruckerei Kelmscott Press gründete, sich der Buchgestaltung aber schon vorher gewidmet hatte. Zu jener Zeit arbeiteten viele Künstlerinnen als Kalligrafinnen, Gestalterinnen von Bucheinbänden und Illustratorinnen. Unabhängig von ihrer akademischen Ausbildung, oder auch zusätzlich, schlossen sie sich in der 1898 gegründeten Guild of Women-Binders zusammen. Zu den bekanntesten Mitgliedern zählten Katharine Adams (1862–1952), Sybil Pye (1879–1958), Sarah Prideaux (1853–1933) und Alicia M. T. Amherst (1865–1941). Einige Frauen arbeiteten selbstständig mit renommierten Buchbindereien zusammen, beispielsweise Amherst mit J. Zaehnsdorf in London, Louise Powell (1865–1956) mit der Ashendene Press. Esther Pissarro (1870–1951) gründete mit ihrem Mann Lucien Pissarro 1894 die Eragny Press.

Guild of Women-Binders

Die Tatsache, dass die Nachfrage nach künstlerisch gestalteten Büchern wuchs, brachte den Privatmann Frank Karslake dazu, mit sei-

May Morris (1862–1938), for example, the daughter of legendary arts and crafts figure William Morris, studied textile arts at the South Kensington School of Design.[3] The National Art Training School of South Kensington, a forerunner of the School of Design from 1837 to 1852, was one of the world's most important schools devoted to arts and crafts. More than 1,000 students, most of them were women, were taught every year in a wide-ranging curriculum of art and design. The sexes had separate classrooms and workrooms, while the lectures, library, and other common facilities were open to all. The final exams for female and male students did not differ, except in the subjects of architecture and mechanical drawing.

In the period between 1880 and 1920, the number of women working as book artists vastly increased in England. Almost all of these designers were influenced by the ideas of the arts and crafts movement and its new understandings of book design. The movement's paragon was William Morris, who founded the private printing house Kelmscott Press in 1891 with the help of his friend Emery Walker, though he had already devoted himself to book design some time earlier. At this moment in history, many women artists worked as calligraphers, book cover designers, and illustrators. Separate from their academic training, or even to augment it, they joined together in 1898 to found the Guild of Women-Binders. Its best-known members include Katharine Adams (1862–1952), Sybil Pye (1879–1958), Sarah Prideaux (1853–1933), and Alicia M. T. Amherst (1865–1941). Some women worked independently with renowned bookbinders: Amherst, for instance, with J. Zaehnsdorf in London, or Louise Powell (1865–1956) with the Ashendene Press. Esther Pissarro (1870–1951) founded the Eragny Press with her husband Lucien Pissarro in 1894.

Guild of Women-Binders

Keen to profit from the growing demand for art books, the independently wealthy Frank Karslake initiated a commercial venture with his daughter Constance in 1898, the Guild of Women-Binders.

Karslake was a London bookseller and founder of the Hampstead Bindery. In 1897, he had discovered book bindings made by women at

3 Zoë Thomas: At Home with the Women's Guild of Arts: Gender and Professional Identity in London Studios, c. 1880–1925, Women's History Review 24, no. 6 (2015): 938–964, on 964, DOI:10.1080/09612025. 2015.1039348. S2CID 142796942.

ner Tochter Constance 1898 ein kommerzielles Unternehmen zu initiieren, die Guild of Women-Binders.

Karslake war ein Londoner Buchhändler und Gründer der Hampstead Bindery. 1897 hatte er auf einer Ausstellung Bucheinbände von Frauen entdeckt, unter anderem diejenigen der Schottin Annie S. Macdonald (1849–1924). Bald darauf, im Mai 1898, entwickelte er die Geschäftsidee, in seinem Londoner Buchladen ausschließlich von Frauen gestaltete kunsthandwerkliche Bucheinbände zu verkaufen. Er ermöglichte es Frauen, ihren Lebensunterhalt selbst zu verdienen. Zugleich ermutigte er sie, ihren eigenen künstlerischen Stil zu entwickeln.

Die „Ausstellung künstlerischer Buchbindearbeiten von Frauen" („Exhibition of Artistic Bookbinding by Women") von 1897/98 war ein großer Erfolg. Karslake erkannte, dass die Förderung von Frauen lukrativ sein konnte, und baute eine Art Agentur für einzelne Künstlerinnen auf.

Wie Arts and Crafts betrachtete sich die Guild of Women-Binders als Gegenbewegung zur zunehmenden fortschreitenden Mechanisierung der Buchherstellung und deren Massenproduktion Ende des 19. Jahrhunderts. Sie stellte der Entwicklung feine, kunstvolle Einbände von Hand entgegen, teils mit historischen Motiven und ebensolchem Dekor, aber zunehmend auch mit Elementen des Art nouveau.

Der Band *The Bindings of To-morrow: A Record of the Work of the Guild of Women-Binders and the Hampstead Bindery*, 1902 herausgegeben von der Guild of Women-Binders, führte katalogartig 50 Beispiele von Bucheinbänden in ganzseitigen Farbabbildungen auf.[4]

Letztendlich war das Unternehmen nicht erfolgreich und musste 1904 Insolvenz anmelden. Dennoch bewirkte die Guild of Women-Binders, dass zahlreiche Frauen hervortraten, die mit der Gestaltung von Bucheinbänden und künstlerischen Titelgestaltungen ihren Lebensunterhalt bestreiten konnten.

Women's Guild of Arts

Weil Frauen in der Art-Workers Guild, einer Gilde für Kunsthandwerker, nicht zugelassen waren (und das bis 1972), gründete May Morris 1907 die Women's Guild of Arts und blieb deren Präsidentin bis 1935. Sie war die treibende

4 *The Bindings of To-morrow. A Record of the Work of the Guild of Women-Binders and of the Hampstead Bindery*, London: Printed for the Guild of Women-Binders, 1902, https://archive.org/details/bindingsmorrow00Guil/page/n107/mode/2up (Abruf 10. Mai 2022).

an exhibition, including some from the Scottish woman Annie S. Macdonald (1849–1924). Soon after, in May 1898, he hit upon the business idea of exclusively selling book covers in his London bookstore that were designed as craft objects by women, making it possible for women to earn a living with their design work. At the same time, he encouraged these women to develop their own artistic style.

The *Exhibition of Artistic Bookbinding by Women* in 1897/98 was a smashing success. Realizing that promoting women could be lucrative, Karslake set up a kind of agency for individual women artists.

Like so many arts and crafts figures and institutions, the Guild of Women-Binders saw itself as a countermovement to the ever-increasing mechanization of book making and its mass production at the end of the nineteenth century. The guild sought to counter this development with elegant, luxurious artistic bindings made by hand, some with historical motifs and similar decorations, though increasingly also with elements of art nouveau.

Published in 1902 by the Guild of Women-Binders, *The Bindings of To-morrow: A Record of the Work of the Guild of Women-Binders and of the Hampstead Bindery* cataloged fifty examples of book bindings in full-page color illustrations.[4]

The company ultimately failed and had to file for bankruptcy in 1904. Nonetheless, the Guild of Women-Binders helped launch the careers of many women who were able to make a living designing book bindings and artfully designed covers.

4 *The Bindings of To-morrow: A Record of the Work of the Guild of Women-Binders and of the Hampstead Bindery*, London: Printed for the Guild of Women-Binders, 1902, https://archive.org/details/bindingsmorrow00Guil/page/n107/mode/2up (accessed 10. May 2022).

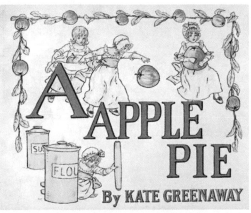

Kate Greenaway, Titelblatt zum Alphabet-Buch / Cover for the alphabet book A Apple Pie, Frederick Warne, 1886

THERE CAN SURELY BE NO DOUBT THAT THE WORK OF ARTISTS SHOULD BE JUDGED WITHOUT REGARD TO THE QUESTION OF SEX.

Feodora Gleichen, 1900

Kraft der Organisation. Ehrenvorsitzende war die Künstlerin Mary Annie Sloane (1867–1961). Die Gilde unterstützte alle Frauen, die in den Feldern von Arts and Crafts selbständig arbeiten wollten.

Aus dem generellen Interesse an Literatur und Buchgestaltung sind in England außergewöhnlich renommierte Kinderbuchautorinnen und -illustratorinnen hervorgegangen. Die bekanntesten sind Kate Greenaway und Beatrix Potter (1866–1943).

Die Situation in Schottland

Schottische Gebrauchsgrafikerinnen sind in der Designgeschichte vor allem mit der Glasgow School of Art verbunden. Zwar waren sie in erster Linie Malerinnen, haben aber auch, wie im Falle der Schwestern Margaret und Frances MacDonald, Bücher illustriert und Plakate gestaltet.

Im späten 19. und frühen 20. Jahrhundert war Glasgow eine boomende, wohlhabende Industriestadt. Ihre Bürger*innen legten Wert darauf, auch in Sachen Kultur anerkannt zu werden, und förderten dementsprechend die Ausbildung von Künstler*innen.

Schon 1845 wurde in der Stadt die Glasgow Government School of Design gegründet. Mit der Jahrhundertwende entwickelte sich die Glasgow School of Art unter der Leitung von Francis Newbery und seiner Frau Jessie zu einer modernen Schule, die Kunst und Design gleichstellte. Viele der Studierenden schlossen Freundschaft miteinander und mieteten Studios im Stadtzentrum an, zum Teil waren ihre Ateliers

Women's Guild of Arts

Because women were not allowed in the Art-Workers' Guild, which was established as a guild for men artisans (and remained so until 1972), May Morris founded the Women's Guild of Arts in 1907; she was the organization's driving force and remained its president until 1935. Its honorary chair was artist Mary Annie Sloane (1867–1961). The Guild supported all women who wanted to work independently in the fields of arts and crafts.

The general interest in literature and book design in England set the stage for exceptionally renowned women children's book authors and illustrators. Among them, the best known are Kate Greenaway and Beatrix Potter (1866–1943).

Margaret MacDonald Mackintosh, Titelblatt zu / Cover for Deutsche Kunst und Dekoration, 1902

Jessie M. King, Ex Libris auf japanischem Pergament für / Bookplate on Japanese vellum for **Charles D. Edwards**, 1907

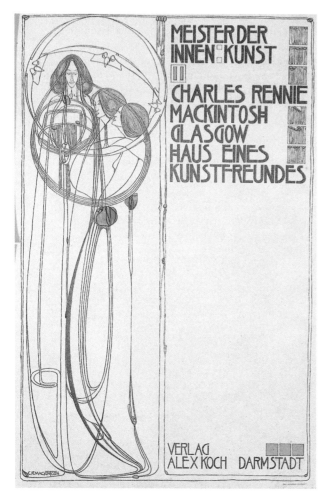

Margaret MacDonald Mackintosh, Titelblatt zur Mappe / Cover for the portfolio Haus eines Kunstfreundes (Meister der Innenkunst II) von/by Charles Rennie Mackintosh, Verlag Axel Koch, 1902

Frances MacDonald McNair,
Plakat für das / Poster for the
Glasgow Institute of the Fine Arts,
1896

The Situation in Scotland

The design history of women commercial artists from Scotland is mostly associated with the Glasgow School of Art. While these women were primarily painters, they also illustrated books and designed posters, as in the case of sisters Margaret and Frances MacDonald.

In the late nineteenth and early twentieth centuries, Glasgow was a booming, prosperous industrial metropolis. Its citizens placed a high value on cultural achievements, and accordingly supported artist training.

By 1845, the city saw the founding of the Glasgow Government School of Design. With the turn of the century, the Glasgow School of Art developed under the direction of Francis Newbery and his wife Jessie into a modern institution that treated art and design with equal importance. Many of the students became friends and rented studios downtown; in some cases, their studios were meeting places for artists, literary figures, and patrons, such as the studio of Jessie M. King (1875–1949) and Helen Paxton Brown (1876–1956). In 1882, a group of these women formed the Glasgow Society of Lady Artists to create a center for their artistic work.

Treffpunkte von Künstler*innen, Literat*innen und Mäzen*innen, wie das Studio von Jessie M. King (1875–1949) und Helen Paxton Brown (1876–1956). 1882 gründete eine Gruppe dieser Frauen die Glasgow Society of Lady Artists, um ein Zentrum für ihre künstlerischen Arbeiten zu schaffen.

Einige der Künstlerinnen wurden als „Glasgow Girls" bezeichnet. Der Begriff wurde erst spät geprägt, und zwar 1968 von William Buchanan. Im Essay über eine Ausstellung der sogenannten Glasgow Boys verwies er mit dieser Bezeichnung auf ein weibliches Pendant zu dieser Künstlergruppe von Männern. Tatsächlich waren die Glasgow Girls eher ein informeller Verbund, geprägt von individuellen, aber auch von Gruppenstilen. Der Begriff verfestigte sich jedoch. Jude Burkhauser organisierte 2001 den ersten

Überblick über das Werk der betreffenden Künstlerinnen mit dem Titel *Glasgow Girls. Women in Art and Design 1880–1920*. Der Beitrag von Frauen zur künstlerischen Entwicklung der schottischen Metropole ist seitdem untrennbar mit dem sogenannten Glasgow Style verbunden.

Der Glasgow Style integrierte Elemente der Arts-and-Crafts-Bewegung sowie nationale Rückbesinnungen auf die Kunst der Kelten und stand dem europäischen Jugendstil nahe. Künstlerinnen wie Jessie M. King, Annie French (1872–1965) und Jessie Newbery (1864–1948) übertrugen diesen unverwechselbaren Stil dann auf die angewandte Kunst, von Buchillustrationen, Plakaten, Tapeten und Stoffen bis hin zu Schmuck und Haushaltswaren. Zeitschriften wie *The Studio* verbreiteten ihre Drucke. Auch nahmen sie an internationalen Ausstellungen in München, Berlin, Wien und Turin teil. Ihr erfolgreiches Auftreten hatte Einzelausstellungen in Schottland und England zur Folge.

The Four

Die Schwestern Margaret (1864–1933) und Frances MacDonald (1873–1921) studierten beide an der Glasgow School of Art. Margaret heiratete 1900 den Architekten und Designer Charles Rennie Mackintosh, mit dem sie ein Jahr zuvor nach Liverpool gezogen war. Frances heiratete 1899 ihren langjährigen Freund James Herbert McNair. Zusammen bildeten die Genannten die Künstlergruppe The Four, die die schottische Schule des Jugendstils prägte. The Four verfolgte einen ganzheitlichen Ansatz in Kunst und Design, der alle materiellen Äußerungen einbezog, vom kleinsten Detail eines Alltagsobjekts bis hin zur Architektur.

Margaret MacDonald Mackintosh war die führende Künstlerin des schottischen Jugendstils und zählte mit ihren kunsthandwerklichen Arbeiten zu einer der einflussreichsten Gestalterinnen des Modern Style. 1900 stellten Margaret MacDonald Mackintosh und ihr Mann bei den Wiener Sezessionisten in der österreichischen Hauptstadt aus und beeinflussten dadurch die Arbeiten von Gustav Klimt und Josef Hoffmann. 1915 ließ sich das Paar in London nieder, wo es Teil der Künstlerszene von Chelsea wurde. Beide lebten von ihrer Erbschaft und dem Verkauf von Aquarellen und Textilentwürfen. Aufgrund ihres schlechten Gesundheitszustands musste Margaret ab 1921 ihre künstlerische Tätigkeit beenden. 1923 reiste sie wegen der niedrigeren Lebenshaltungskosten und des gesunden Klimas

Some of these women artists have come to be known as the Glasgow Girls. Yet the term was coined only long after they lived, by William Buchanan in 1968. Buchanan used it in an essay on an exhibition of works by the group of painters known as the Glasgow Boys to designate a corresponding group of women artists. The Glasgow Girls were nevertheless more of an informal group, characterized by individual styles as much as by any group style. The term, however, has become entrenched. Jude Burkhauser organized the first survey of the work of these women artists in 2001, under the title *Glasgow Girls: Women in Art and Design 1880–1920*. Since then, the contribution of women to the artistic development of the Scottish metropolis has been inseparable from what is now called Glasgow Style.

The Glasgow Style integrated elements of the arts and crafts movement along with a nationalistic return to Celtic art; it also shared an affinity with European art nouveau. Women artists such as Jessie M. King, Annie French (1872–1965), and Jessie Newbery (1864–1948) then transferred this distinctive style to the applied arts, in fields ranging from book illustrations, posters, wallpaper, and fabrics to jewelry and housewares. Magazines such as *The Studio* widely circulated their prints. These women also participated in international exhibitions in Munich, Berlin, Vienna, and Turin. Their success in these shows resulted in solo exhibitions in Scotland and England.

Schüler*innen der / Students from the Glasgow School of Art (Hintergrund/back: Francis MacDonald McNair; Mitte, v. r. n. l. / center, r. to l.: Margaret MacDonald Mackintosh, Katharine Cameron, Janet Aitken, Agnes Raeburn, Jessie Keppie, John Keppie; vorne, v. r. n. l. / front, r. to l.: Herbert McNair, Charles Rennie Mackintosh), 1890er Jahre / 1890s

Frances MacDonald McNair, Bucheinband und Grafik zu / Book cover and graphic for Das Eigenkleid der Frau von/by Anna Muthesius, Kramer & Baum, 1903, Courtesy of Kunstmuseen Krefeld

mit ihrem Ehemann nach Südfrankreich und verbrachte die folgenden Jahre im Hotel du Commerce in Port-Vendres. 1927 kehrten beide nach London zurück, lebten dort indes zurückgezogen.

Margaret MacDonald Mackintosh war überwiegend als Kunsthandwerkerin und Entwerferin von Flächenarbeiten tätig. Sie versuchte sich in verschiedensten Techniken und Materialien wie Metallarbeiten, Stickereien, Textilentwürfen und war besonders als Designerin von Innenräumen bedeutend. Sie erarbeitete Entwürfe für Teesalons und Privatwohnungen. Nachdem sie anfangs meist gemeinsam mit ihrer Schwester tätig war, verlagerte sich die Zusammenarbeit später auf ihren Ehemann. Im Fall des Willow Tearooms war sie an der Umgestaltung der Fassade beteiligt. 1901 entwarf das Ehepaar für den Wettbewerb „Haus eines Kunstfreundes" der deutschen Zeitschrift *Innendekoration* in Darmstadt, Deutschland, ein Wohnhaus mit Innenausstattung. Margaret MacDonald Mackintosh trug Illustrationen zu den Plänen bei. Die Planung für das Haus wurde nicht umgesetzt, aber in den 1990er Jahren in Glasgow nach den frühen Entwürfen realisiert.

The Four

The sisters Margaret (1864–1933) and Frances MacDonald (1873–1921) both studied at the Glasgow School of Art. Margaret married the architect and designer Charles Rennie Mackintosh in 1900, with whom she had moved to Liverpool a year earlier. In 1899, Frances married her longtime friend James Herbert McNair. Together, these two couples formed a group of artists known as The Four who shaped the Scottish school of art nouveau. The Four took a holistic approach to art and design that encompassed all forms of material expression, from the smallest detail of everyday objects to architecture.

Margaret MacDonald Mackintosh was the leading woman artist of Scottish art nouveau, and her work in the field of arts and crafts established her reputation as one of the most influential designers of British art nouveau modern style. In 1900 Margaret MacDonald Mackintosh and her husband exhibited their work with the Viennese secessionists in the Austrian capital, influencing Gustav Klimt and Josef Hoffmann. In 1915, the couple settled in London, where they became part of the Chelsea art scene. Both lived from their inheritance and from the sale of watercolors and textile designs. But poor health forced Margaret to stop her artistic activity beginning in 1921. In 1923, drawn by the lower cost of living and a healthy climate, she traveled with her husband to the south of France, where they spent the ensuing years at the Hotel du Commerce in Port-Vendres. In 1927 they both returned to a secluded life in London.

Margaret MacDonald Mackintosh was predominantly a craftswoman and designer of graphic works. She explored a wide variety of techniques and materials including metalwork, embroidery, and textile designs, and was especially significant as a designer of interior spaces, such as tea rooms and private apartments. At first mostly working together with her sister, she later shifted her collaboration to her husband. In the case of the Willow Tearoom, she was involved in redesigning the facade. In 1901 the couple designed a residence in Darmstadt, Germany, including its interior spaces, for the competition "An Art Lover's Home," staged by the German magazine *Innendekoration*. Margaret MacDonald Mackintosh contributed illustrations to the plans, which were not realized at the time, but only much later in the 1990s in Glasgow.

Nine years younger than her sister, Frances MacDonald McNair followed her older sibling's path in studying at the Glasgow School of Art. After her marriage to James Herbert McNair,

ERST WENN JEDE FRAU IHR EIGENER KÜNSTLER IST, WIRD DER GEDANKE DES EIGENKLEIDES IM GANZEN UMFANGE VERWIRKLICHT WERDEN KÖNNEN.

Anna Muthesius, 1903

Die neun Jahre jüngere Frances MacDonald studierte wie ihre Schwester an der Glasgow School of Art. Nach ihrer Hochzeit mit James Herbert McNair zog sie mit ihrem Mann nach Liverpool, wo beide an der School of Architecture and Applied Art unterrichteten.

1903 veröffentlichte Anna Muthesius, die Frau des einflussreichen Architekten und Kulturvermittlers Hermann Muthesius, der sich von 1896 bis 1903 als technischer Attaché für Architektur an der deutschen Botschaft in London aufhielt, das kleine, künstlerisch gestaltete Buch *Das Eigenkleid der Frau*. Es war für die Reformkleider-Bewegung in Europa von größter Bedeutung. Darin forderte Anna Muthesius zum eigenen Entwurf von Kleidern auf. Sie war der Artistic-Dress-Bewegung verbunden, in der viele Jugendstilkünstler, von Henry van de Velde bis Peter Behrens, tätig waren. Auch Frauen waren beteiligt, wie Anna Muthesius selbst, Maria Sèthe van de Velde und Else Oppler-Legband. Mit dem Begriff „Künstlerkleid" wurde Alltagskleidung beschrieben, die nach zeitgenössischen Kunstprinzipien entworfen wurde. Die Reformkleidung sollte es Frauen ermöglichen, sich freier zu bewegen, ohne dass einengende Korsetts und unhygienische Details, etwa eine Schleppe, den Bewegungsradius und ihre Gesundheit einschränkten. Auch viele Ärzte, die der Lebensreform nahestanden, waren der Reformkleider-Bewegung verbunden.

Der Einband des Büchleins wurde von Francis MacDonald MacNair mit einem Motiv im linearen Glasgow-Stil entworfen. Auffallend sind die grünen Bänder, die den Corpus und den Einband zusammenhalten.

Ab 1907 gab Frances regelmäßig Kunstunterricht an der Glasgow School of Art. In den folgenden Jahren schuf sie eine bewegende Reihe von Aquarellen, die sich mit den Themen Ehe und Mutterschaft beschäftigten, doch war sie mit ihren Arbeiten in der Öffentlichkeit nicht mehr erfolgreich.

she and her husband moved to Liverpool, where they both taught at the School of Architecture and Applied Art.

In 1903, Anna Muthesius, the wife of the influential architect and promoter of arts and crafts ideas, Hermann Muthesius, who served as technical attaché for architecture at the German embassy in London from 1896 to 1903, published a small, artfully designed book *Das Eigenkleid der Frau*—a title that might be anachronistically, though not inaccurately, translated as "Do-It-Yourself Women's Dress." The book was extremely influential for the dress reform movement in Europe, which promoted and designed clothing for women without corsets or other constricting elements, such as a train, that negatively impacted women's range of motion and health. In this book, Anna Muthesius encouraged people to design their own clothing, drawing from her association with the artistic dress movement, which included many art nouveau artists, from Henry van de Velde to Peter Behrens. Women, too, were involved: Maria Sèthe van de Velde and Else Oppler-Legban, in addition to Anna Muthesius herself. The term "Künstlerkleid" or "artist's dress" was used to describe everyday clothing designed following contemporary aesthetic principles, while reform clothing was intended to allow women to move more freely. Many doctors who were close to the life reform movement were also associated with the dress reform movement.

Francis MacDonald MacNair designed the cover of the small book with a linear Glasgow-style motif. The green bands holding together innerbook and cover are striking.

Beginning in 1907, Frances regularly taught art classes at the Glasgow School of Art. In the following years she created a moving series of watercolors dealing with the themes of marriage and motherhood, but her works no longer found public favor.

Literatur
Further Reading

G. Elliot Anstruther: *The Bindings of To-morrow. A Record of the Work of the Guild of Women-Binders and of the Hampstead Bindery*, London: Printed for the Guild of Women-Binders [Griggs & Son], 1902, https://archive.org/details/bindingsmorrow-00Guil/page/n107/mode/2up (Abruf/accessed 10. Mai/May 2022).

Gerda Breuer (Hg./ed.): *Arts and Crafts. Von Morris bis Mackintosh. Reformbewegung zwischen Kunstgewerbe und Sozialutopie*, Ausstellungskatalog / exhibition catalog, Darmstadt: Institut Mathildenhöhe Darmstadt, 1995.

Gerda Breuer: *Haus Eines Kunstfreundes. Mackay Hugh Baillie Scott, Charles Rennie Mackintosh, Leopold Bauer*, Stuttgart: Axel Menges Verlag, 2002.

Jude Burkhauser: *Glasgow Girls. Women in Art and Design, 1880–1920*, Edinburgh: Canongate Books, 2001.

Anthea Callen: *Angel in The Studio. Women in The Arts and Crafts Movement 1870–1914*, London: Astragal Books, 1979.

Janice Helland: *The Studios of Frances and Margaret MacDonald*, Manchester: Manchester University Press, 1995.

Lynn Hulse (Hg./ed.): *May Morris: Art & Life. New Perspectives*, Friends of the William Morris Gallery, 2017.

Peter Noever & MAK Wien: *Ein moderner Nachmittag. Margaret Macdonald Mackintosh und der Salon Waerndorfer in Wien*, Wien/Vienna: Böhlau Verlag, 2000.

Pamela Robertson: *Doves and Dreams. The Art of Frances MacDonald and James Herbert McNair*, Lund: Humphries Publishers, 2006.

M. H. Spielmann & G. S. Layard: *Kate Greenaway*, London: Adam and Charles Black, 1905.

Zoë Thomas: At Home with the Women's Guild of Arts: Gender and Professional Identity in London Studios, c. 1880–1925, *Women's History Review* 24, Nr./no. 6 (2015): 938–964, DOI: 10.1080/09612025.2015.1039348.

Zoë Thomas: *Women Art Workers and the Arts and Crafts Movement*, Manchester: Manchester University Press, 2022.

Marianne Tidcombe: *Women Bookbinders 1880–1920*, Newcastle & Delaware: Oak Knoll Press, 1996.

PROFESSIONALI-SIERUNG VON GEBRAUCHS-GRAFIK

PROFESSION-ALIZATION OF COMMERCIAL ART

Designerinnen
der Wiener Werkstätte
Women Graphic Designers
from the Wiener Werkstätte

Das Wien des Fin de Siècle wird häufig mit den misogynen Äußerungen berühmter Zeitgenossen in Verbindung gebracht. Auch über die Frauen der Wiener Werkstätte sind abwertende Äußerungen von Künstlern wie Adolf Loos, Julius Klinger und anderen bekannt. Loos sprach von den Designerinnen als „gelangweilte höhere Töchter", Klinger vom „Wiener Weiberkunstgewerbe" und der Architekt Oswald Haerdtl bezeichnete die Werkstätte als „unerhörte Pupperlwirtschaft".[1]

Zudem galt künstlerisches Arbeiten nur in bestimmten Bereichen als der Natur der Frau angemessen. Eine solche Haltung äußerte Rudolf Eitelberger von Edelberg. Er war der erste Direktor des 1863 nach dem Vorbild des South Kensington Museums in London (heute Victoria and Albert Museum) gegründeten k. k. Österreichischen Museums für Kunst und Industrie (heute Museum für angewandte Kunst, MAK) und der

Fin-de-siècle Vienna is often associated with the misogynistic statements made by famous contemporaries. And figures such as Adolf Loos and Julius Klinger are no exception, having left a legacy of disparaging remarks about the women of the Wiener Werkstätte. Loos described these women designers as "bored upper-class daughters"; Klinger spoke of the "applied arts of the Viennese broads"; and the architect Oswald Haerdtl called the Werkstätte a "scandalous bimbo business."[1]

Artistic work, moreover, was considered suitable for women's nature only in certain areas. Such an attitude was expressed, for instance, by Rudolf Eitelberger von Edelberg. Eitelberger was the first director of the k. k. Österreichisches Museum für Kunst und Industrie (the Imperial and Royal Austrian Museum of Art

---

1 Die Zitate sind dem Ausstellungskatalog Christoph Thun-Hohenstein, Anne-Katrin Rossberg & Elisabeth Schmuttermeier (Hg.): *Die Frauen der Wiener Werkstätte*, MAK – Museum für angewandte Kunst Wien, Basel: Birkhäuser, 2020 (S. 7) entnommen.

1 The quotes are taken from the exhibition catalog Christoph Thun-Hohenstein, Anne-Katrin Rossberg & Elisabeth Schmuttermeier (eds.): Women Artists of the Wiener Werkstätte, MAK—Museum für angewandte Kunst Wien, Basel: Birkhäuser, 2020 (p. 7): "gelangweilte höhere Töchter," "Wiener Weiberkunstgewerbe," and "unerhörte Pupperlwirtschaft."

Gruppenfoto in der Wiener Werkstätte / Group photo at the Wiener Werkstätte, **Charlotte Billwiller, Mathilde Flögl, Susi Singer, Marianne Leisching, Maria Likarz,** 1924 © MAK Wien

dem Museum angeschlossenen, 1867 gegründeten Kunstgewerbeschule. In den Statuten der Schule legte er fest, dass Frauen zwar als Studentinnen an seiner Schule willkommen seien, aber nur in bestimmten Studienfächern. In der katholisch geprägten Habsburgermonarchie galt es zudem als unschicklich, dass Frauen Aktzeichnen am lebenden Modell studierten, wiederum war genau dieser Unterricht eine unabdingbare Voraussetzung für das Studium der Fächer Malerei und Bildhauerei.

Dennoch lässt sich festhalten, dass es frauenfördernde Ausbildungsinstitutionen lange vor der Jahrhundertwende in Wien gab. Neben der Kunstgewerbeschule, die Frauen schon ab 1868 zuließ, existierte eine Kunstschule für Frauen und Mädchen, gegründet 1897 (später Wiener Frauenakademie), die halbstaatlichen Status hatte. Hinzu kamen Privatschulen von Künstler*innen, die Frauen in Zeichnen und Malen unterrichteten.

Vieles im Programm dieser Schulen für „Frauenkunst" entsprach den Lerninhalten von „Höheren Töchterschulen", die musische Fächer und Handarbeit förderten. Eine solche musische Erziehung sollte Frauen auf ihre spätere Rolle als Dame der Gesellschaft vorbereiten. Auch sollte die Kultivierung künstlerischer Talente Töchter aus Mittelklasse-Familien befähigen, aufzusteigen und in eine höhere soziale Schicht einzuheiraten. Der Wiener Frauen-Erwerb-Verein, der 1866 von frauenpolitisch interessierten Wienerinnen gegründet wurde – von 1873 bis 1897 war hier die Ehefrau von Eitelberger Präsidentin –, fokussierte sich dagegen auf eine Ausbildung, die die Erwerbsmöglichkeiten von Frauen verbesserte. Denn in der sogenannten Gründerzeit, die mit der ökonomischen Prosperität der österreichischen Industrie einherging, schätzte man den Wert der Frauenarbeit hoch ein.

Mit der Berufung der Professoren Josef Hoffmann, Koloman Moser und Alfred Roller an die Kunstgewerbeschule änderte sich die Ausbildung an dieser Institution wesentlich. Nach einer Schulreform des damaligen Direktors Felician von Myrbach stieg die Zahl der Studentinnen dramatisch. Ein liberaler Geist verbreitete sich und wurde noch gesteigert durch die Wiener Werkstätte, wo die Professoren mit ihren Studierenden, überwiegend Frauen, zusammenarbeiteten.[2]

Die „Wiener Werkstätte Produktiv Genossenschaft von Kunsthandwerkern in Wien" wurde am 19. Mai 1903 gegründet. Laut Statut wollte sie dem heimischen Kunsthandwerk neue

and Industry, today the Museum für angewandte Kunst, MAK) founded in 1863 on the model of the South Kensington Museum in London (today the Victoria and Albert Museum), and of the Kunstgewerbeschule (or School of Applied Arts), founded in 1867, that was attached to the museum. The bylaws he wrote for the school welcomed women as students, but only in certain fields of study. In the Catholic Habsburg monarchy, it was also considered unseemly for women to study nude drawing from a live model; yet precisely this instruction was seen as indispensable for studying painting and sculpture.

Nonetheless, we can say that educational institutions which nurtured women existed in Vienna long before the turn of the century. In addition to the Kunstgewerbeschule, which admitted women as early as 1868, there was a Kunstschule für Frauen und Mädchen (Art School for Women and Girls) founded in 1897 (later the Wiener Frauenakademie), which had semigovernmental status. Vienna also offered private schools run by artists who instructed women in drawing and painting.

Much of the program of these schools for "women's art" corresponded to the curriculum of the "höhere Töchterschulen" or finishing schools for upper-class girls, which promoted artistic subjects and manual labor. Such an education in the fine arts was intended to prepare women for their later role as ladies in elite society. Cultivating artistic talents was also seen as a means for daughters from middle-class families to ascend by marrying into a higher social class. The Wiener Frauen-Erwerb-Verein, or Vienna Women's Professional Association, founded in 1866 by Viennese women interested in the political goals of the women's movement (Eitelberger's wife was its president from 1873 to 1897), focused instead on fostering education that improved opportunities for women to make a living of their own. Indeed, during the decades of prosperous industrial growth in Austria that followed the revolutions in 1848, known in Austrian German as the *Gründerzeit,* women's work was given high value.

The appointment of three professors, Josef Hoffmann, Koloman Moser, and Alfred Roller to the Kunstgewerbeschule had a significant impact on education at this institution. Following a reform of the school by the director at the time, Felician von Myrbach, the number of women students increased dramatically. A liberal spirit grew more influential and was further enhanced by the Wiener Werkstätte, where professors

---

2 Elisabeth Johanna Michitsch: *Frauen – Kunst – Kunsthandwerk. Künstlerinnen in der Wiener-Werkstätte*, Diplomarbeit, Wien, 1993.

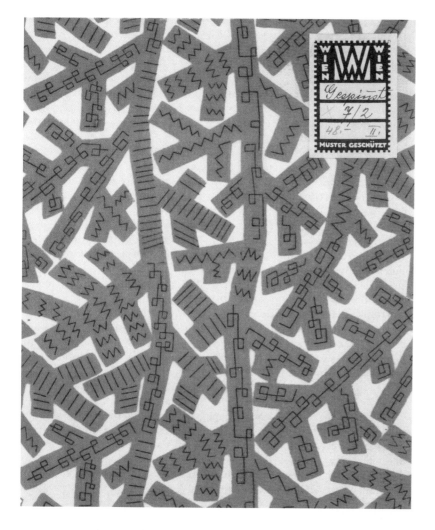

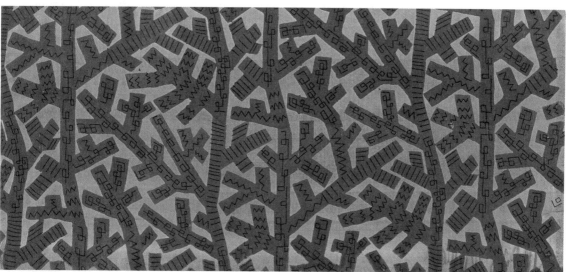

Felice Rex, WW-Stoffmuster / Wiener Werkstätte fabric design Gespinst, 1924 © MAK Wien

Impulse verleihen und von Menschen geschaffene Alltagsdinge künstlerisch „veredeln". Die künstlerischen Leiter waren Josef Hoffmann und Koloman Moser. Zur Geschäftsleitung gehörten auch Otto Primavesi und Moritz Gallia. Fritz Waerndorfer war ihr Financier (bis 1913). Ihr Vorbild war die Guild of Handicraft von Charles Robert Ashbee in England. Die Werkstätte war zeitweise so erfolgreich, dass sie Niederlassungen in New York, Berlin und Zürich hatte. Sie existierte bis 1932.

Die starke Präsenz von Frauen in der Werkstätte war bereits erkennbar in einer Vorläufereinrichtung, der 1900 gegründeten Wiener Kunst im Hause, die bis 1904 existierte.[3] Sie war das erste kommerzielle Unternehmen der Kunstgewerbeschule. Einige ihrer Mitglieder wie Jutta Sika (1877–1964) und Therese Trethan traten dann in die Wiener Werkstätte ein. Die Entwurfsbereiche von Kunst im Hause waren Holz, Metall, Glas, Ton, Leder, Papier und Leinen, und es wurden eigene Ausstellungen veranstaltet, die auch in Fachzeitschriften besprochen wurden. Die grafischen Arbeiten bezogen sich hauptsächlich auf Werbung für die Gruppe, beispielsweise in Form von Ausstellungseinladungen oder dem Verkaufskatalog.

Die Wiener Werkstätte als ein Meilenstein in der Modernisierung des Kunstgewerbes

Bis heute ist die Geschichte der berühmten Wiener Werkstätte vor allem mit den Namen der männlichen Gründer verbunden. Tatsächlich gab es viele Frauen in der Werkstätte, die in der Historiografie entweder übersehen oder nur im Kontext einzelner Werkgruppen erwähnt wurden. Eine Ausstellung des Wiener Museums für angewandte Kunst (MAK) machte 2021 unter dem Titel „Die Frauen der Wiener Werkstätte" auf den großen Anteil von Frauen an der Produktivität des Unternehmens aufmerksam. Rund 180 Künstlerinnen konnten bei den Recherchen namhaft gemacht werden.

Da die Gründungsmitglieder gleichzeitig Professoren an der Kunstgewerbeschule waren, konnten sie aus ihren Meisterklassen potenzielle Mitarbeiterinnen rekrutieren. Josef Hoffmann unterstützte zwar Frauen in der Architektur, dennoch nicht unbedingt in der Ausbildung als Architektinnen. Frauen wurden nicht zu Künstlerinnen oder Architektinnen ausgebildet, sondern zu Kunstgewerblerinnen. Folglich unterrichtete

worked together with their students—most of whom were women.[2]

The Wiener Werkstätte Produktiv Genossenschaft von Kunsthandwerkern in Wien, or Vienna Workshop Productive Cooperative of Craft Artists, was founded on May 19, 1903. As it declared in its founding documents, it aimed to invigorate arts and crafts in Vienna and to artistically "refine" everyday human-made objects. Its artistic directors were Josef Hoffmann and Koloman Moser, joined in other governing roles by Otto Primavesi and Moritz Gallia. Fritz Waerndorfer provided the financing (until 1913). Modeled on the Guild of Handicraft founded by Charles Robert Ashbee in England, it was so successful that it had branches for a time in New York, Berlin, and Zurich. The workshop existed until 1932.

The strong presence of women in the Werkstätte was already evident in one of its predecessors, Wiener Kunst im Hause, founded in 1900, which existed until 1904.[3] The first commercial enterprise set up by the Kunstgewerbeschule, it attracted students, including Jutta Sika (1877–1964) and Therese Trethan, who later joined the Wiener Werkstätte. The areas of design taught at Kunst im Hause were wood, metal, glass, clay, leather, paper, and linen, and the institution held its own exhibitions, which were also reviewed in professional journals. The graphic works produced by its student were mainly intended to advertise the group itself, such as exhibition invitations or the sales catalog.

The Wiener Werkstätte as a Milestone in the Modernization of Applied Arts

To this day, the history of the famous Wiener Werkstätte is associated primarily with the names of its male founders. In fact, there were many women in the workshop who have either been overlooked in historiography or mentioned only in the context of individual groups of works. In 2021, an exhibition at Vienna's Museum für angewandte Kunst, *Women Artists of the Wiener Werkstätte*, drew attention to the large contribution that women made to the workshop. Research for the exhibition was able to identify around 180 women artists.

2 Elisabeth Johanna Michitsch: Frauen—Kunst—Kunsthandwerk: Künstlerinnen in der Wiener-Werkstätte, diploma thesis, Vienna, 1993.

3 Elisabeth Schmuttermeier: Prelude to the Wiener Werkstätte: The Association "Wiener Kunst im Hause," in Thun-Hohenstein et al., *Women Artists of the Wiener Werkstätte*, 36–39.

3 Elisabeth Schmuttermeier: Auftakt zur Wiener Werkstätte: Die Vereinigung „Wiener Kunst im Hause", in Thun-Hohenstein et al., Die Frauen der Wiener Werkstätte (wie Anm. 1): 36–39.

Leopoldine Kolbe, Postkartenentwürfe für die / Postcard designs for the **Wiener Werkstätte**, Nr./no. 40, 43, 44 (oben/top), 36, 39, 32 (unten/bottom), 1907

Mela Köhler, Postkarte der Wiener Werkstätte / Wiener Werkstätte postcard, Nr./no. 518, 1911 © MAK Wien

Hofmann, am Ideal des Gesamtkunstwerkes orientiert, die vielseitig talentierten Frauen in Bereichen Dekor und Wohnen, damit sie die Architekturentwürfe der männlichen Studierenden ergänzten. Aus seiner Klasse gingen viele Frauen in die Wiener Werkstätte.

Zu Kriegszeiten nahm die Zahl der weiblichen Studierenden stetig zu, bis Frauen am Ende des Krieges in der Überzahl waren. Aus der Klasse von Koloman Moser gingen namhafte Kunstgewerblerinnen hervor wie Therese Trethan, Jutta Sika, Emilie Simandl, Mela Köhler (sie signierte bei der Wiener Werkstätte mit Koehler), Leopoldine Kolbe (1870–1912), Ella Max (1897–?), Gabi Magus Möschl (1887–1961), Dina Kuhn (1891–1963), Hedwig Schmidt, Marie Weißenberg (1900–?) und Agnes Speyer (1875–1942).

Grafische Arbeiten kamen in der Wiener Werkstätte beim Entwurf von Tapeten- und Textilmustern zum Zuge, vorzugsweise aber bei den Künstlerpostkarten. Die Geschäftsleitung legte großen Wert darauf, die eigenen Produkte zu bewerben. Sie bediente sich dabei des jungen, aber schon sehr erfolgreichen Mediums der Postkarte.

Insgesamt wurden zwischen 1908 und 1915 über 1000 verschiedene Künstlerpostkarten von 48 Künstler*innen entworfen. 40 Prozent der Entwürfe stammen von Frauen.[4] Bezeichnend ist, dass die Urheberschaft durch Namensnennung auf der Rück- oder Vorderseite nachgewiesen ist, was auf die Wertschätzung der Designer*innen hinweist. Die Auflagen betrugen schätzungsweise zwischen 200 und 1000 Stück pro Motiv. Die Zentralverkaufsstelle der Postkarten war das 1907 errichtete Stadtlokal der Wiener Werkstätte in der Innenstadt, es gab aber auch Filialen in Karlsbad und Marienbad sowie eine Verkaufsstelle der Niederlassung in Zürich.

Exemplarisch: drei Grafikdesignerinnen

Die Künstlerinnen, die die meisten Postkarten entwarfen, waren Mela Köhler, Maria Likarz, Fritzi Löw, Fritzi Berger und Hilde Jesser. Meist zeichneten sie Damen- und Kindermode.

Melanie Leopoldina (genannt Mela) Köhler (1885–1960) besuchte zunächst zwei Jahre lang die private Malschule von Franz Hohenberger und arbeitete anschließend als freischaffende Künstlerin. Von 1908 bis 1912 ließ sie sich an der Wiener Kunstgewerbeschule bei Moser und Bertold Löffler weiterbilden. Werke von ihr wur-

4 Elisabeth Schmuttermeier: Kleinkunstwerk Postkarte 1907–1919, in Thun-Hohenstein et al., Die Frauen der Wiener Werkstätte (wie Anm. 1): 79.

Mela Köhler, Postkarte der Wiener Werkstätte / Wiener Werkstätte postcard, Nr./no. 519, 1911 © MAK Wien

Since the founding members were also professors at the Kunstgewerbeschule, they were able to recruit potential women collaborators from their master classes. Josef Hoffmann supported women in architecture, though not necessarily their training as architects. Women were not trained as artists or architects, but as craft women. Guided by the ideal of the Gesamtkunstwerk, Hofmann accordingly taught his richly talented women student skills in the fields of decor and home design, which he believed would allow them to complement the architectural designs of the male students. Many women from his class later became part of the Wiener Werkstätte.

During the war, the number of women students steadily increased, until women outnumbered men by the end of the conflict. Koloman Moser's class produced renowned women in the applied arts, such as Therese Trethan, Jutta Sika, Emilie Simandl, Mela Köhler (who signed her name at the Wiener Werkstätte as Koehler), Leopoldine Kolbe (1870–1912), Ella Max (1897–?), Gabi Magus Möschl (1887–1961),

den bereits während der Schulzeit in *The Studio* veröffentlicht. Neben den Künstlerpostkarten für die Wiener Werkstätte arbeitete sie auch für andere Verlage wie den Postkartenverlag Brüder Kohn und für die Verlage Hugo Munk sowie Carl Konegen. Zudem war sie Mitarbeiterin der Zeitschrift *Wiener Mode* und entwarf Illustrationen für die Märchenbücher des Verlags. 1912 erhielt sie vom Museum für Kunst und Industrie in Wien ein Stipendium aus dem Rothschild-Fond, um in Paris studieren zu können. Nach ihrer Rückkehr gestaltete sie Verpackungen für die Keksfabrik Bahlsen in Hannover. Sie vernetzte sich mit einschlägigen Vereinigungen wie dem Deutschen als auch dem Österreichischen Werkbund. Als sie in den 1930er Jahren nach Schweden emigrierte, illustrierte sie weiterhin Postkarten, zeichnete Theater- und Ballettkostüme und illustrierte Bücher. Sie konnte ihren Unterhalt neben ihrer künstlerischen Arbeit durchaus mit angewandter Grafik verdienen.

Die zweite herausragende Grafikdesignerin der Wiener Werkstätte war Friederike „Fritzi" Löw (1892–1975). Sie besuchte von 1907 bis 1910 zunächst die Wiener Kunstschule für Frauen und Mädchen. Im Anschluss folgte von 1912 bis 1916 eine Ausbildung bei Josef Hoffmann, Alfred Roller und Oskar Strnad an der Wiener Kunstgewerbeschule. Anschließend war Löw von 1916 bis 1921 Mitarbeiterin der Wiener Werkstätte. 1938 emigrierte sie mit Zwischenstationen in Dänemark und England nach Brasilien. Dort war sie als Möbeldesignerin tätig. 1955 kehrte sie nach Wien zurück. In der Buchgestaltung arbeitete sie für die Verlage Strache, Gerlach & Wiedling und die Gesellschaft für graphische Industrie. In den Jahren 1915 bis 1922 illustrierte sie Märchen und Erzählungen bekannter Autoren mit Originallithografien, die als kleinformatige „Liebhaberausgaben" im Verlag Anton Schroll in Wien erschienen.

Von 1908 bis 1910 besuchte Maria Likarz (1893–1971) die Kunstschule für Frauen und Mädchen in Wien. Anschließend ließ sie sich bis 1914 an der Wiener Kunstgewerbeschule bei Josef Hoffmann und Anton Kenner ausbilden, auch in der Grafik. Von 1912 bis 1914 und von 1920 bis zur Auflösung 1931 war sie Mitarbeiterin bei der Wiener Werkstätte und dort vor allem in der Werbegrafik tätig. Sie entwarf Postkarten, Anzeigen, Plakate, Packpapiere, „Papeterien" und marmorierte Papiere. Später wandte sie sich der Keramik, Emaille und dann der Mode zu. Ihre Arbeiten waren häufig in Ausstellungen präsent. Von 1916 bis 1920 war sie als Lehrerin an der Kunstgewerbe-

Dina Kuhn (1891–1963), Hedwig Schmidt, Marie Weißenberg (1900–?), and Agnes Speyer (1875–1942).

Graphic work received attention at the Wiener Werkstätte in the design of wallpaper and textile patterns, but chiefly in artists' postcards. The school's administration made considerable effort to promote its own products, including via the new, yet already very successful, medium of the postcard.

In total, between 1908 and 1915, over 1,000 different artists' postcards were designed by forty-eight artists, with 40 percent of the designs coming from women.[4] What is telling is that authorship is indicated by a name placed on the front or back of the card—a sign of the recognition afforded to these women designers. The print runs are estimated to have been between 200 and 1,000 pieces for each motif. The central sales office for the postcards was the Wiener Werkstätte's urban location in the city center, built in 1907, but there were also branches in Karlovy Vary and Marienbad (today Mariánské Lázně), as well as a sales office of the branch in Zurich.

The Example of Three Women Designers

The women artists who designed the most postcards were Mela Köhler, Maria Likarz, Fritzi Löw, Fritzi Berger, and Hilde Jesser. Their work mainly consisted of drawing women's and children's fashion.

Melanie Leopoldina (called Mela) Köhler (1885–1960) first attended Franz Hohenberger's private painting school for two years and then worked as a freelance artist. From 1908 to 1912 she studied at the Vienna Kunstgewerbeschule under Moser and Bertold Löffler. Works of hers were already being published in *The Studio* while she was still in school. In addition to the artist postcards she created for the Wiener Werkstätte, she also worked for other publishers such as the postcard publisher Brüder Kohn and for the publishers Hugo Munk and Carl Konegen. She additionally contributed to the magazine *Wiener Mode* (Viennese fashion) and designed illustrations for the publisher's fairy tale books. In 1912 she received a scholarship to study in Paris, awarded by the Rothschild Fund from the Museum für Kunst und Industrie (Museum for Art and Industry) in Vienna. After returning, she designed packaging for the Bahlsen cookie factory in

4 Elisabeth Schmuttermeier: Postcards as Small Works of Art, 1907–1919, in Thun-Hohenstein et al., *Women Artists of the Wiener Werkstätte*, 79.

Maria Likarz, Postkartenentwurf für die / Postcard design for the Wiener Werkstätte, um/around 1911 © MAK Wien

schule Burg Giebichenstein in Halle an der Saale tätig und das erste weibliche Mitglied des Lehrkörpers. Mit ihrem Ehemann, dem jüdischen Arzt Richard Strauss, musste sie 1938 emigrieren, zunächst nach Kroatien und dann nach Italien, wo sie hauptsächlich als Keramikerin arbeitete.

Insgesamt spielten Frauen eine wichtige Rolle in der Wiener Werkstätte – auch im Führungsbereich. Es gab Werkstätten-Leiterinnen und eine Frau in Führungsposition: Helene Bernatzik (1888-1967) übernahm 1916 die Leitung der neu gegründeten Künstlerwerkstätte in der Neustiftgasse.

Maria Likarz, Postkartenentwurf für die / Postcard design for the Wiener Werkstätte, um/around 1911 © MAK Wien

Hannover. She cultivated networks with other design associations, including both the German and the Austrian Werkbund, and after she emigrated to Sweden in the 1930s, she continued to illustrate postcards, sketch designs for theater and ballet costumes, and illustrate books. She was certainly able to earn a living with applied graphic work alongside her artistic work.

The second outstanding woman graphic designer of the Wiener Werkstätte was Friederike "Fritzi" Löw (1892-1975). Löw first attended the Wiener Kunstschule für Frauen und Mädchen from 1907 to 1910. This was followed by training under Josef Hoffmann, Alfred Roller, and Oskar Strnad at the Vienna Kunstgewerbeschule from 1912 to 1916. Löw was subsequently an employee of the Wiener Werkstätte from 1916 to 1921. In 1938 she emigrated to Brazil, via Denmark and England, where she worked as a furniture designer. She returned to Vienna in 1955. As a book designer, she worked for the publishing houses Strache, Gerlach & Wiedling, and the Gesellschaft für graphische Industrie. Between 1915 and 1922, she illustrated fairy tales and stories by well-known authors with original lithographs, which were published as small-format bibliophile editions by the Anton Schroll publishing house in Vienna.

From 1908 to 1910, Maria Likarz (1893–1971) attended the Kunstschule für Frauen und Mädchen in Vienna. She then studied at the Kunstgewerbeschule with Josef Hoffmann and Anton Kenner until 1914, also in graphic design. At the Wiener Werkstätte, she was employed from 1912 to 1914, and again from 1920 until 1931 (when the workshop was disbanded), mainly producing advertising. She designed postcards, advertisements, posters, wrapping papers, papeterie, and marbled papers. Later, she turned to ceramics, works in enamel, and then fashion. Her works were frequently seen in exhibitions. From 1916 to 1920 she was a teacher at the Kunstgewerbeschule Burg Giebichenstein in Halle an der Saale and the first woman member of the teaching staff. She was forced to leave Vienna in 1938 with her husband Richard Strauss, a Jewish doctor, fleeing first to Croatia and then to Italy, where she worked mainly as a ceramic artist.

On the whole, women played an important role in the Wiener Werkstätte—as employees and as leaders. There were women workshop managers and one woman in a management position, Helene Bernatzik (1888-1967), who took over the newly founded artists' workshop in Neustiftgasse in 1916.

Literatur
Further Reading

Giovanni Fanelli & Ezio Godoli: *Art Nouveau Postcards*,
New York: Rizzoli, 1987.

Gottfried Fliedl: *Kunst und Lehre am Beginn der Moderne. Die
Wiener Kunstgewerbeschule 1867–1918*, Salzburg & Wien/Vienna:
Residenz Verlag, 1986.

Eva Kernbauer et al. (Hg./eds.): *Rudolf Eitelberger von Edelberg.
Netzwerker der Kunstwelt*, Wien/Vienna, Köln/Cologne & Weimar:
Böhlau Verlag, 2019.

Elisabeth Schmuttermeier: Die Wiener Werkstätte, in Robert
Waissenberger (Hg./eds.): *Wien 1870–1930. Traum und Wirklichkeit*,
Historisches Museum der Stadt Wien, Salzburg & Wien/Vienna,
1984: 145–150.

Christoph Thun-Hohenstein, Anne-Katrin Rossberg & Elisabeth
Schmuttermeier (Hg.): *Die Frauen der Wiener Werkstätte / Women
Artists of the Wiener Werkstätte*, MAK – Museum für angewandte
Kunst Wien, Basel: Birkhäuser, 2020.

„REKLAME-KUNST" AB 1900

"ADVER-TISING ART" FROM 1900

Deutsche Gebrauchsgrafikerinnen
und die Industrie
German Commercial Artists
and Industrial Clients

Ausbildung vor 1919

Die Wege der folgenden Gebrauchsgrafikerinnen veranschaulichen den mit viel Hoffnung verbundenen Beginn einer dynamischen gesellschaftlichen Entwicklung im Deutschen Reich und während der Weimarer Republik. Aufgewachsen in der Kaiserzeit unter den Bedingungen eines gesellschaftlichen Umbruchs, erlebten die Frauen, dass ihre Forderungen nach Gleichberechtigung teilweise Gehör fanden. Das betraf vor allem das Frauenwahlrecht, das ab 1918 den Weg zur Chancengleichheit für Frauen und Männer ebnen sollte.

Ab dem Frühjahr 1919 durften Frauen zudem an Kunstakademien in Deutschland studieren. Bis dahin mussten sie auf fachlich eingeschränkte „Damenklassen" in den Akademien, teure Privatschulen oder Privatateliers von Künstler*innen ausweichen. In Deutschland, wie in anderen Ländern auch, griffen Frauen zur Selbstermächtigung. Der bis heute existierende Verein der Künstlerinnen und Kunstfreundinnen zu Berlin, später Verein der Berliner Künstlerinnen genannt, unterhielt beispielsweise eine sogenannte Damenakademie, an der unter anderem berühmte Künstlerinnen wie Käthe Kollwitz (1867–1945) als Lehrerin tätig waren und an deren Zeichen- und Malschule Paula Modersohn-Becker (1876–1907) und Käte Lassen (1880–1956) ausgebildet wurden. Malerinnen der Neuen Sachlichkeit wie Lotte Laserstein und Jeanne Mammen sowie die Bildhauerinnen Emy Roeder, Renée Sintenis und Milly Steger profitierten vom Vereinsnetzwerk.

Im Gründungsjahr 1867 waren Frauen im Deutschen Reich allerdings noch nicht rechtsfähig, sodass ersatzweise Männer als Gründungsmitglieder fungierten; sie wurden später Ehrenmitglieder, ohne ordentliche Mitglieder zu sein. Der Verein der Berliner Künstlerinnen organisierte regelmäßig Ausstellungen, eine Zeichen- und Malschule auf akademischem Niveau (ab 1868), eine Darlehens- und Unterstützungskasse (ab 1868) und eine Pensions- und Rentenkasse (ab 1884).

Auch in München gab es einen Künstlerinnen-Verein. Er wurde 1882 gegründet, zwei Jahre später begann die Ausbildung in einer „Damenakademie" des Vereins. Die Schülerinnen konnten sich ihre Lehrer, meist Maler der Münchener Kunstakademie, selbst wählen. Andere Städte zogen nach.

Kunstgewerbeschulen, die in Deutschland ab etwa 1865 fast in jeder größeren Stadt entstanden, bildeten eine Brücke zur Ausbildung von künstlerisch tätigen Frauen. An diesen

Education before 1919

The paths of the commercial artists discussed here illustrate the beginning of a dynamic social change, associated with a great deal of hope, in the German Reich and during the Weimar Republic. Having grown up in Wilhelmine Germany during a period of great social upheaval, the women of this time finally saw their demands for equal rights partially being heard. This was particularly true of the movement for women's suffrage, which was to pave the way for equal opportunities for women and men beginning in 1918.

Clara Möller-Coburg/Ehmcke, Bastelbogen / Craft sheet „Syndetikon-Hampelmann", produziert von / produced by Otto Ring & Co., Berlin, um/around 1903, Courtesy of Kunstmuseen Krefeld

Clara Möller-Coburg/Ehmcke Reklamemarken für Fleckentferner der Firma Ring / Advertising stamps for spot remover produced by the Ring company, um/around 1908, Privatbesitz / privately owned

Einrichtungen gab es schon sehr bald kein Einschreibungsverbot mehr für Frauen, allerdings hatten diese Schulen nicht das Prestige der Kunstakademien. Eine große Rolle für die Berufstätigkeit von Frauen spielte das zu jener Zeit generell zunehmende Interesse an modernem Kunstgewerbe. Befördert durch den Vergleich auf Weltausstellungen, ging es darum, die Qualität des deutschen Kunstgewerbes durch eine moderne Gestaltung zu verbessern und international wettbewerbsfähig zu machen.

Vereine der angewandten Moderne

Es ist jedoch bezeichnend, dass in den Institutionen, die sich vom traditionellen Kunsthandwerk und dem historistischen Kunstgewerbe der Gründerzeit abwandten, gleichwohl der künstlerischen Behandlung moderner Alltagsgegenstände und der Architektur größte Aufmerksamkeit schenkten, keinesfalls frauenfreundliche Strukturen herrschten. Betrachtet man eine so mächtige Institution wie den Deutschen Werkbund, dann erkennt man darin eine Domäne mit tendenziell männerbündischen Zügen. 1907 fand sich unter den 16 Gründungsmitgliedern keine einzige Frau. 1908 wird der Vorstand samt Ausschüssen und Vertrauensleuten auf 49 Mitglieder erweitert, auch in diesen Kreis wird keine Frau aufgenommen. Von den 291 „Künstlern" dieses Jahrgangs (womit nicht nur bildende Künstler*innen bezeichnet wurden, sondern auch Architekt*innen, Designer*innen, Kunsthandwerker*innen, Fotograf*innen etc.) waren nur zwölf Künstlerinnen und darunter nur zwei Gebrauchsgrafikerinnen: die hoch geachtete Typografin Anna Simons (1871–1951) und Gertrud Kleinhempel (1875–1948), die zu jener Zeit als Fachlehrerin an die Handwerker- und Kunstgewerbeschule in Bielefeld berufen worden war. Dort leitete sie die Klasse für Flächen- und Textilkunst. Unter den 157 Unternehmer*innen sind nur fünf Frauen erwähnt. Und unter den 76 Sachverständigen für einzelne Branchen ist eine einzige Frau zu finden: die Wiener Schriftstellerin und Kunstkritikerin Berta Zuckerkandl (1864–1945). Der prozentuale Anteil der Frauen in der Vereinigung änderte sich im Laufe der Zeit nicht wesentlich. Auch 1919, zu Beginn der Weimarer Republik, nahm der Werkbund nach wie vor keine Frau in seinen Vorstand auf. Obwohl Frauen seinerzeit häufig als Symbolgestalten für Befreiung in der Kunst dienten und die Enthierarchisierung der Künste von den künstlerischen Avantgarden angestrebt wurde, führte diese Haltung in der Realität nicht zwangs-

From the spring of 1919, women were also allowed to study at art academies in Germany. Until then, they had been forced to resort to professionally restricted "ladies' classes" in the academies, or to expensive private schools or private artist studios. In Germany, as in other countries, women took actions to empower themselves. One example is the Verein der Künstlerinnen und Kunstfreundinnen zu Berlin (Berlin Association of Women Artists and Friends of Art), which still exists today and was later called the Verein der Berliner Künstlerinnen (Berlin Association of Women Artists). The association organized a *Damenakademie* (or women's academy), as it was called, with teachers that included such famous artists as Käthe Kollwitz (1867–1945) and students of drawing and painting who included Paula Modersohn-Becker (1876–1907) and Käte Lassen (1880–1956). New objectivity painters such as Lotte Laserstein and Jeanne Mammen, as well as the sculptors Emy Roeder, Renée Sintenis, and Milly Steger, benefited from the association's network.

When the academy was founded in 1867, however, women in the German Empire could not yet act in any legal capacity, which meant that men were required to function as founding members in the place of women. These men later became honorary members without full membership. The Verein der Berliner Künstlerinnen organized regular exhibitions, an academic-level drawing and painting school (from 1868), a loan and support fund (from 1868), and a pension and retirement fund (from 1884).

Munich, too, saw the founding of a women artists' association. Established in 1882, two years later it, too, began training women in its *Damenakademie*. The students could choose their own teachers, who were mostly painters from the Munich Kunstakademie. Similar associations in other cities soon followed.

Kunstgewerbeschulen (schools of applied arts), which sprang up in Germany from around 1865 in almost every major city, offered the first institutional educational opportunities for women working in the arts. These institutions very quickly ceased prohibiting women from enrolling, though they lacked the prestige of the art academies. The broadly growing interest at the time in applied arts played a major role in the careers open to women. Motivated in part by works shown at world exhibitions, figures in the field aimed to improve the quality of German applied arts through modern design and to make its products internationally competitive.

Änne Koken, Werbung für Appels Mayonnaise von der / Advertising for mayonnaise from the Delikatessen-Grosshandlung und Nahrungsmittel-Fabrik Heinrich Wilhelm Appel, 1909, Privatbesitz / privately owned

läufig zu einer egalitären Vergemeinschaftung der Geschlechter.

Der Zustand der Ablehnung von Frauen an den Kunstakademien widersprach der dynamischen Entwicklung des Marktes. Künstler*innen gründeten selbsttätig Werkstätten. Frauen hatten auf dem Markt größere Chancen als in den Akademien und den Vereinen der Reformkünstler. Sie mussten gleichwohl energisch den Weg der Möglichkeiten verfolgen, die sich ihnen mit vielen Umwegen und Hindernissen boten.

Die Hannoversche Cakes-Fabrik H. Bahlsen

Neben vielen anderen Unternehmen vergab auch die Firma Bahlsen ihre Werbeaufträge an Gebrauchsgrafikerinnen. Dazu zählten Mela Köhler, Änne Koken (1885–1919), Ella Margold (1886–1961), Clara Möller-Coburg (1869–1918) und Martel Schwichtenberg (1896–1945). Sie gestalteten die Fabrikarchitektur, Verkaufsläden, Schaufenster, Messestände, Verpackungen, Annoncen, Plakate, Reklame- bzw. Feldpostkarten und die zu dieser Zeit beliebten Reklamemarken.

Schon um die Jahrhundertwende hatte der Firmengründer Hermann Bahlsen (1859–1919) aus Hannover die Bedeutung eines Corporate Design für seine Firma erkannt und hierfür Künstler*innen der künstlerischen Reformbewegung, darunter erstaunlich viele Gebrauchsgrafikerinnen, hinzugezogen. Mit seinem außergewöhnlichen Verpackungsdesign hat sich das Hannoveraner Familienunternehmen einen Namen gemacht und ein Gesicht gegeben. Hermann Bahlsen gründete im Jahr 1889 die Hannoversche Cakes-Fabrik H. Bahlsen. Kekse waren zur Gründungszeit noch ein Luxusprodukt. Französische Biscuits

Associations of Applied Arts in the Modern Era

It is nevertheless telling that the institutions which turned away from traditional handicrafts and the historicist decorative arts of the *Gründerzeit*, and which were most concerned with an artistic approach to modern everyday objects and architecture, were hardly bastions of women-friendly structures. Such a powerful institution as the Deutscher Werkbund, for instance, clearly evinces characteristics of a domain dominated by men. In 1907, there was not a single woman among its sixteen founding members. In 1908, the board of directors, including committees and shop stewards, expanded to include forty-nine members; no women were admitted to this circle, either. Of the 291 "artists" in the year's class (which included not only visual artists, but also architects, designers, craftsmen and craftswomen, photographers, etc.), only twelve were women, and only two of them were commercial artists: the highly respected typographer Anna Simons (1871–1951) and Gertrud Kleinhempel (1875–1948), who had been appointed at the time as a specialist teacher at the Handwerker- und Kunstgewerbeschule in Bielefeld. In Bielefeld, Kleinhempel led the class for graphic art and textile art. Among the 157 entrepreneurs of companies, only five women are mentioned. And among the seventy-six experts for individual industries, we find but a single woman: the Viennese writer and art critic Berta Zuckerkandl (1864–1945). The percentage of women in the association did not change significantly over time. In 1919, at the beginning of the Weimar Republic, the Werkbund still failed to admit any women to its board. Women often served at the time as symbolic

Änne Koken, Reklamemarken für die Firma Bahlsen / Advertising stamps for the Bahlsen company, Serie C / C series, 1913,
Privatbesitz / privately owned

Mela Köhler, Reklamemarken für / Advertising stamps for H. Bahlsen Keksfabrik Hannover, Serie E / E series, ab/from 1914, Privatbesitz / privately owned

Martel Schwichtenberg, Entwurfszeichnung für eine Verpackung /
Design drawing for packaging, 1918–1924 © Bahlsen-Archiv, Hannover

Ella Margold, Entwurfszeichnung für eine Keksdose /
Design drawing for a cookie tin, 1915 © Bahlsen-Archiv, Hannover

figures for emancipation in art, and the artistic avant gardes strove to break down artistic hierarchies. Yet in reality this attitude did not necessarily lead to an egalitarian artistic community of all sexes.

The fact that women were still not being admitted to the art academies marked a contradiction to the dynamic development of the market. Artists themselves often founded their own workshops, and women had greater opportunities in the marketplace than in the academies and the associations of reform artists. They nevertheless had to pursue a path of possibilities that threw up many detours and obstacles in their way.

The Hannoversche Cakes-Fabrik H. Bahlsen

Like many other enterprises, the German company Bahlsen awarded its advertising contracts to some women commercial artists, among them Mela Köhler, Änne Koken (1885–1919), Ella Margold (1886–1961), Clara Möller-Coburg (1869–1918), and Martel Schwichtenberg (1896–1945). These women designed factories, stores, store windows, exhibitiostands, packaging, advertisements, posters, postcards for advertising, field postcards, and the advertising stamps that were so popular at the time.

und englische Cakes waren durch die Einfuhrzölle im Deutschen Reich teuer. Hermann Bahlsen war durch seine Englandaufenthalte mit dem Butterkeks-Markt vertraut. Keksdosen aus Blech und die Pappverpackungen sollten wie künstlerisch gestaltete Schmuckkästchen aussehen und den Konsument*innen das Gefühl geben, mit dem Kauf an einem gehobenen Lebensstil teilzuhaben. Die Entwerfer*innen der Dosen wurden namentlich erwähnt, zwar nicht immer auf den Dosen selbst, aber in der Werbung.

Bahlsen hatte längere Zeit in England gearbeitet und war dort mit der Arts-and-Crafts-Bewegung in Kontakt gekommen. Wie eine Reihe anderer Unternehmer in Deutschland verfolgte er das Ziel, seine unternehmerische Tätigkeit

mit der Idee der Ästhetisierung des Unternehmens und seiner Waren in Verbindung zu bringen. So war es von John Ruskin, William Morris und weiteren Protagonisten von Arts and Crafts formuliert worden. Gleichwohl waren die Ziele der englischen Protagonisten stärker als die der deutschen Unternehmen mit ethischen und politischen Zielen der Aufwertung von Arbeit verbunden.

Zum Corporate Design eines Unternehmens zählte, dass neben der ästhetisch ansprechenden Ausstattung der Verkaufsräume und Fabrikhallen auch die Außenwirkung der Firma von künstlerischen Maßstäben bestimmt sein sollte. Hierfür wählte Bahlsen kein einheitliches Design, auch beauftragte er nicht einen Künstler allein, wie die AEG den Architekten und Reformkünstler Peter Behrens, sondern er zog viele Künstler*innen und Gebrauchsgrafiker*innen hinzu. In den Anfängen ab etwa 1889 stammten sie alle aus den künstlerischen Reformbewegungen des Jugendstils, später entsprachen sie der Ausrichtung des Deutschen Werkbunds. Bahlsen selbst war Mitglied des Werkbunds.

Markendiskussionen, die später vor allem der Deutsche Werkbund aufgriff, wurden seit Ende des 19. Jahrhunderts geführt. Infolgedessen war es nicht ungewöhnlich, dass Künstler*innen für Werbung herangezogen wurden. Selbst solch renommierte Künstler wie Henri de Toulouse-Lautrec, Henry van de Velde, René Magritte, El Lissitzky, Kurt Schwitters setzten sich für künstlerische Produktreklame, typografisch anspruchsvolle Gestaltung von Geschäftsbriefen, Warenverpackungen und anderes mehr ein. Die Schokoladenfabrik Stollwerck, die Sektkellerei Henkell & Co., Daimler-Benz, Erdal, Kaffee Hag, Kulmbacher, Leitz, Lufthansa, Märklin, M.A.N., Pelikan, Henkel (Persil), Pfaff, Reemtsma, Zeiss (Jena) – sie und viele andere Unternehmen mehr arbeiteten mit Reformkünstler*innen zusammen.

Werbung von Gebrauchsgrafikerinnen

Clara Möller-Coburg, die den Namen ihrer Heimatstadt Coburg ihrem Eigennamen hinzufügte und nach ihrer Heirat mit dem Grafiker Fritz Helmuth Ehmcke auch den Namen ihres Mannes annahm, war von 1902 bis 1904 Mitarbeiterin in der zwei Jahre zuvor von ihrem Ehemann sowie Georg Belwe und Friedrich Wilhelm Kleukens gegründeten Steglitzer Werkstatt in Berlin. Die Werkstatt war eine der ersten und eine der renommiertesten Werbeagenturen in Deutsch-

Martel Schwichtenberg, Entwurf für eine Pappschachtel / Design for a cardboard box, 1929–1930 © Bahlsen-Archiv, Hannover

As early as the turn of the century, the company's founder Hermann Bahlsen (1859–1919) recognized the importance of corporate design and enlisted the help of artists from the artistic reform movement, including an astonishing number of commercial artists. The unusual packaging design of the Hannover-based family business allowed it to make a name for itself and become clearly recognizable on the market. Bahlsen founded the enterprise as the Hannoversche Cakes-Fabrik H. Bahlsen in 1889, when cakes and cookies were still a luxury product and import duties in the German Empire meant high prices for French biscuits and English cakes. He had become familiar with the butter cookie market from stays in England, where cookie tins and cardboard packaging were intended to resemble artistically designed jewelry boxes and give consumers the feeling that their purchase allowed them to participate in a high-class lifestyle. The designers of the tins were often mentioned by name—not always on the boxes themselves, but in the advertising for the products.

Bahlsen had worked in England for a long time, which brought him into contact with the arts and crafts movement. Like a number of other entrepreneurs in Germany, he sought to link his business activity with the idea of developing a striking aesthetic for the company and its goods. In this, he followed ideas expressed by John Ruskin, William Morris, and other arts and crafts figures. Nonetheless, these ideas from England were more closely linked to ethical and political goals of valorizing work than were those of German companies.

land. Ihr war auch eine kleine Steindruck-Handpresse für die lithografische Produktion angegliedert. Sie wurde vor allem durch den Industriellen Otto Ring, den Hersteller des erfolgreichen Klebstoffes Syndetikon, finanziert. Der Markenname „Syndetikon"[1] existierte ab 1880 und bezeichnete einen dickflüssigen Klebstoff, der nach 1900 der bekannteste Alleskleber in Deutschland wurde.

Ring ließ eine Reihe von Akzidenzdrucken in der Steglitzer Werkstatt fertigen, von denen Clara Möller-Coburg einige gestaltete, unter anderem Reklamemarken, Postkarten und Papierausschneidebögen, die als Werbematerial dienten. Auffallend ist, dass Möller-Coburg ihre Entwürfe mit einem eigenen Signet oder mit ihrem Namen versah. 1902 wurde der Werkstatt eine Schule für Buchgewerbe angegliedert, in welcher Buchkunst und andere kunstgewerbliche und künstlerische Fächer gelehrt wurden. Aus eigenen Mitteln baute Möller-Coburg in der Steglitzer Werkstatt die Abteilung für Kunst-Stickerei und Reformkleidung auf und unterrichtete auch an der Schule für Buchgewerbe. Zu den grafischen Entwürfen aus dieser Zeit gehören Vorsatzpapiere in verschiedenen farbigen Mustern, zum Teil auch auf Stoff gedruckt, und Gildezeichen für unterschiedliche Berufe. Unabhängig von der Werkstatt entwarf Möller-Coburg Textilarbeiten, Kinderkleidung, aber auch Spielzeug für die Deutschen Werkstätten und Werbung für die F. Baudler Rohrmöbelfabrik in Coburg sowie Verpackungen für die Parfümerie Hager in Stettin.

Neben Clara Möller-Coburg ist Änne Koken (1885–1919) unter den Frauen hervorzuheben, die als Werbegestalterinnen einen ähnlichen Weg gingen. Sie eröffnete 1910 in Hannover ein eigenes Atelier: Änne Koken, Werkstatt für angewandte Kunst. Von dort aus arbeitete sie für verschiedene namhafte Firmen, neben Bahlsen zum Beispiel für Appels Feinkost, die Lindener Samtfabrik, Günther Wagner (Pelikan) und die Hannoversche Waggonfabrik. Sie wurde zum „Künstlerischen Beirat" der Hannoverschen Cakes-Fabrik (Bahlsen) ernannt. Bei Bahlsen schuf Änne Koken zwei Serien von Reklamemarken: die Künstlermarken-Serie C ab Januar 1913 und F einen Monat später. In zwölf einzelnen Bildern illustriert sie den Entstehungsprozess der Bahlsen-Kekse von den Rohstoffzutaten über die Fertigung und den Vertrieb bis hin zum Konsum. Auf allen Marken ist ein kleiner Putto als Akteur abgebildet, der die jeweiligen Tätigkeiten verrichtet.

A company's corporate design was expected to apply artistic standards not only in fashioning aesthetically pleasing furnishings for the firm's salesrooms and factory halls, but also in shaping its public image. In realizing his own corporate design, Bahlsen did not choose any uniform vision or commission a single artist, in the way that AEG had commissioned the architect and reform artist Peter Behrens. Rather, he brought in many artists, including many who worked commercially. Initially, from about 1889, all of these artists came from the artistic reform movements of art nouveau; later they reflected the ideas of the Deutscher Werkbund, of which Bahlsen himself was a member.

Discussions about how to shape a brand, which would figure especially prominently for the Deutscher Werkbund, had been conducted since the end of the nineteenth century. One result was that it was not uncommon for artists to be employed in advertising. Even such renowned artists as Henri de Toulouse-Lautrec, Henry van de Velde, René Magritte, El Lissitzky, or Kurt Schwitters fought to apply artistic principles to objects such as product advertising, typographically sophisticated letterhead, and packaging for goods. Many large and well-known companies—among them, the chocolate factory Stollwerck, the sparkling wine producer Henkell & Co, Daimler-Benz, Erdal, Kaffee Hag, Kulmbacher, Leitz, Lufthansa, Märklin, M.A.N., Pelikan, Henkel (Persil), Pfaff, Reemtsma, and Zeiss (Jena)—worked together with reform artists.

Advertising Produced by Women Commercial Artists

Clara Möller-Coburg, who appended the name of her hometown Coburg to her own, and later took the name of her husband after she married the graphic artist Fritz Helmuth Ehmcke, worked from 1902 to 1904 in the Steglitzer Werkstatt in Berlin, which had been founded two years earlier by Fritz Helmuth Ehmcke, together with Georg Belwe and Friedrich Wilhelm Kleukens. The Werkstatt was one of the first, and the most renowned, advertising agencies in Germany. It included a small, hand-operated lithographic press for lithographic production, funded primarily by the industrialist Otto Ring, the manufacturer of the successful glue Syndetikon. The brand name "Syndetikon"[1] existed from 1880

1 Klaus Popitz: Syndetikon. Eine kleine Firma macht große Reklame, Begleittext zur Ausstellung der Kunstbibliothek der Staatlichen Museen Preußischer Kulturbesitz, Berlin, 1978.

1 Klaus Popitz: Syndetikon: Eine kleine Firma macht große Reklame, essay accompanying exhibition, Kunstbibliothek der Staatlichen Museen Preußischer Kulturbesitz, Berlin, 1978.

Clara Ehmcke (Möller-Coburg), Werbung für / Advertising for Syndetikon, 1911

Die Serie F wiederum führt fröhlich spielende, musizierende und Kekse konsumierende Kinder vor Augen. Dazu kommentiert ein Zweizeiler jeweils das Geschehen. Die Darstellungen sind bewusst naiv gehalten, vermutlich weil sie Kinder als Konsumenten ansprechen wollten.

Änne Koken begann ihre Tätigkeit als Künstlerin zunächst unter der Anleitung ihres Vaters, des Landschaftsmalers Gustav Koken. Anschließend studierte sie drei Jahre Malerei in München und kehrte dann nach Hannover zurück. Sie arbeitete erfolgreich als Werbegrafikerin. Zudem setzte sie sich für die Rechte von Frauen ein und war Mitglied im Verein für Deutsche Frauenkleidung und Kultur und im Deutschen Werkbund (Ortsverein Hannover). Im Jahr 1914 wurde sie als Beisitzerin in den Vorstand des Kestner-Museums gewählt. Im Haus der Frau auf der Werkbundausstellung in Köln 1914 findet man ihren Namen in der Sparte „Plakate, Reklamearbeiten, Buchgewerbe"; insgesamt waren 30 Teilnehmerinnen aus Deutschland und Österreich vertreten. Begleitet wird die Präsentation im Haus der Frau

and referred to a thick adhesive that after 1890 became the best-known all-purpose glue in Germany.

Ring had a series of commercial job prints produced in the Steglitz Werkstatt, some of which were designed by Clara Möller-Coburg, including advertising stamps, postcards, and paper cut-out sheets that served as promotional material. It is worth noting that Möller-Coburg included her own signet or name on her designs. In 1902, a school for book crafts was added on to the Werkstatt, where book arts and other crafts and artistic subjects were taught. Using her own funds, Möller-Coburg established a Department of Art Embroidery and Reform Clothing at the Steglitz Werkstatt; she also taught at the school for book crafts. Her graphic designs from this period include endpapers in various colored patterns, some of which were printed on fabric, and guild signs for various trades. Independent of the Werkstatt, Möller-Coburg designed textile works, children's clothing, and toys for the Deutsche Werkstätten and advertising for the F. Baudler

von einer Sonderausstellung Appel'scher Verpackungen von Änne Koken. Sie schuf 1909 einen Hummer zusammen mit einer Mayonnaise-Dose für die (damalige) Delikatessen-Grosshandlung und Nahrungsmittel-Fabrik Heinrich Wilhelm Appel. Als Markenzeichen der Firma hat es die Zeit bis heute überdauert.

Zwei weitere Künstlerinnen, die für Bahlsen „Reklamekunst" entwarfen, waren Ella Margold und Mela Köhler (1885–1960). Beim Ausbruch des Ersten Weltkriegs wurde Emmanuel Josef Margold zum Militärdienst eingezogen, die Entwurfstätigkeit für Bahlsen übernahm in dieser Zeit seine Frau Ella. Es ist zu vermuten, dass einige ihm zugeschriebene Entwürfe auf seine Frau oder auf ihre Unterstützung zurückgingen.

Mela Köhler ist die einzige Vertreterin der Wiener Werkstätte, die für Bahlsen tätig war. Die Grafikerin wurde vor allem durch eine große Zahl von Postkarten mit Modeentwürfen bekannt. Die Marken der zwölfteiligen Serie E, ab Januar 1914, greifen in bildlicher Darstellung das Motiv der Lebensstadien auf.

Als Schülerin von Koloman Moser war Mela Köhler von der Wiener Werkstätte beeinflusst, wo ihr Schwerpunkt auf Modeentwürfen lag. So erinnern die Postkarten von Bahlsen an Werbung für Mode, was wiederum auf den luxuriösen Charakter der Kekse anspielt. Zur neuen Mode zählten große Hüte, extravagante Kleidung und modische Accessoires und Pelze. Die Postkarten verweisen zugleich darauf, welch großen Gestaltungsspielraum die Firma den Künstler*innen gab.

Die Künstlerin, die in sehr umfassendem Maße für Bahlsen arbeitete, war die in Hannover

Änne Koken, Postkarte für die / Postcard for the Deutsche Werkbund-Ausstellung Cöln, 1914, Privatbesitz / privately owned

Rohrmöbelfabrik in Coburg, as well as packaging for the perfumery Hager in Stettin.

In addition to Clara Möller-Coburg, Änne Koken (1885–1919) stands out among the women who followed a similar path as designers of advertisements. She opened her own studio in Hannover in 1910—Änne Koken, Werkstatt für angewandte Kunst (Änne Koken, Workshop for Applied Arts)—where she worked for a number of well-known companies, such as Appels Feinkost, the Lindener Samtfabrik, Günther Wagner (Pelican), and the Hannoversche Waggonfabrik, in addition to Bahlsen. At Bahlsen's Hannoversche Cakes-Fabrik, she was even appointed to the "artistic supervisory board" and created two series of advertising stamps: the C series artist stamps from January 1913, and F series a month later. In twelve individual images, the C series illustrates the process of creating Bahlsen cookies, from the raw material ingredients through production, distribution, and consumption. All the stamps feature a small putto as the figure carrying out each task. The F series then presents children happily playing, making music, and enjoying cookies. A brief caption comments on what is happening in each case. The depictions are deliberately naive, presumably because they were meant to appeal to children as consumers.

Änne Koken first began her work as an artist under the guidance of her father, the landscape painter Gustav Koken. She then studied painting in Munich for three years before returning to Hannover, where she worked successfully as an advertising artist. She also campaigned for women's rights and was a member of the Verein für Deutsche Frauenkleidung und Kultur (Association for German Women's Clothing and Culture) and the German Werkbund (Hannover chapter). In 1914 she was elected to the board of the Kestner Museum as a nonvoting member. In the Haus der Frau (House of Women) at the Werkbund Exhibition in Cologne in 1914, her name was found in the section "Posters, Advertising Work, Book Crafts"; in total, thirty female participants from Germany and Austria were represented at the event. The presentation in the Haus der Frau was accompanied by a special exhibition of Appel's packaging by Änne Koken. In 1909 she designed a mayonnaise jar and a lobster graphic for Heinrich Wilhelm Appel, a wholesaler for delicatessens who also operated a food manufacturing plant. As the company's trademark, it has survived the test of time until today.

Two other women artists who designed "advertising art" for Bahlsen were Ella Margold

geborene Martel Schwichtenberg. Sie beschritt zunächst einen ähnlichen Ausbildungsweg wie die schon erwähnten Designerinnen. 1914 besuchte sie die private Kunstschule von Lothar von Kunowsky in Düsseldorf und nahm anschließend das Studium an der Düsseldorfer Kunstgewerbeschule auf.

Bereits 1914 ist sie, wie Änne Koken, mit ihren Arbeiten im Haus der Frau auf der Werkbund-Ausstellung in Köln zu sehen. 1917 begann sie, für die Firma Bahlsen Plakate und Verpackungen zu entwerfen. Ganz besonders trat sie zwischen 1916 und 1917, zusammen mit dem Bildhauer Bernhard Hoetger, mit dem visionären Projekt „TET-Stadt" hervor. Dieses städtebauliche Projekt sah eine Art Retortenstadt des Keksfabrikanten vor. Die Arbeiterstadt war für etwa 17.000 Menschen gedacht, die mit den Bahlsen-Werken verbunden waren. Der vorgesehene Name TET-Stadt bezog sich auf eine altägyptische Hieroglyphe. Sie bedeutet „ewig, dauernd" und sollte ein Hinweis sein auf die Haltbarkeit der Waren in den Keksdosen. Die Werbung mit dem Markenzeichen TET, mit denen Bahlsen-Produkte bis heute versehen sind, stammt weitgehend von Martel Schwichtenberg. Auch das Design der Stadt sollte sie übernehmen, während Bernhard Hoetger für die Konstruktion der Häuser und für die Plastiken zuständig war. 1919 gab man die Pläne für die TET-Stadt auf, doch die Werbung wurde in großem Maßstab realisiert.

Schwichtenbergs Entwürfe bezogen sich nicht nur auf Werbung, sondern sie gestaltete auch Bahlsen-Musterläden, die Innenausstattung der Fabrikgebäude, Firmen-Ausstellungen und anderes mehr. Am 23. November 1921 erhielt sie einen Anstellungsvertrag bei Bahlsen, der bis 1933 jährlich erneuert wurde. Mit Beginn des sogenannten Dritten Reichs emigrierte sie nach Südafrika. Für Bahlsen war sie indes weiterhin auf Honorarbasis tätig. Bis zu ihrem Tod 1945 soll sie 705 Reichsmark monatlich erhalten haben.

Gertrud Kraut nimmt eine Sonderrolle im Verbund der Designerinnen ein. Sie ließ sich von 1909 bis 1913 an der Debschitz-Schule in München ausbilden. Dorthin vergab Hermann Bahlsen Aufträge an die Keramische Werkstätte der Schule. Um 1912/13 gewann Gertrud Kraut, die die Keramikklasse der Debschitz-Schule leitete, einen von Bahlsen ausgelobten Wettbewerb und konnte einen unglasierten Steingut-Topf in den Farben Weiß, Hell- und Dunkelblau entwerfen Er wurde in München, offensichtlich in großer Stückzahl, produziert und auf einschlägigen Ausstellungen als vorbildliches Objekt präsentiert.

and Mela Köhler (1885–1960). At the outbreak of World War I, Emmanuel Josef Margold was called up for military service, and his wife Ella took over the design work for Bahlsen during his absence. We can assume that some of the designs attributed to him in fact stemmed from his wife or were realized with her assistance.

Mela Köhler was the only representative of the Wiener Werkstätte to work for Bahlsen, becoming known mainly for a large number of postcards with fashion designs. The stamps she designed for the twelve-part E series, from January 1914, portray the stages of life.

A student of Koloman Moser, Mela Köhler was influenced by the Wiener Werkstätte, where her focus was on fashion designs. Bahlsen's postcards, for example, are reminiscent of advertisements for fashion, which in turn was meant to evoke the luxurious character of the cookies. The new fashion included big hats, extravagant outfits, and highly styled accessories and furs. At the same time, the postcards are evidence of the great creative freedom the company gave the artists.

One woman artist who realized an unusually extensive body of work for Bahlsen was Martel Schwichtenberg, herself a native of Hannover. Her initial training followed the same path trod by the women designers noted above. In 1914, she attended Lothar von Kunowsky's private art school in Düsseldorf and then began studying at the Düsseldorf Kunstgewerbeschule.

As early as 1914, works by her were found —like those by Änne Koken—in the Haus der Frau at the Werkbund exhibition in Cologne. In 1917, she began designing posters and packaging for the Bahlsen company. She especially made her mark between 1916 and 1917 in the visionary project "TET City," together with the sculptor Bernhard Hoetger. This urban planning project envisioned a kind of planned city to be built by the cookie manufacturer—a workers' town intended for about 17,000 employees associated with the Bahlsen factories. The name created for the project, TET City, referred to an ancient Egyptian hieroglyph, which meant "eternal, permanent," and was intended to advertise the shelf life of the company's goods in its cookie tins. The advertising with the TET trademark, which is still found on Bahlsen products today, was largely created by Martel Schwichtenberg. Schwichtenberg was additionally to design the city, while Bernhard Hoetger was to be responsible for the construction of the houses and for sculptural works. In 1919, plans for TET City were abandoned, but the associated advertising was realized on a large scale.

Nach dem Zweiten Weltkrieg war Eva Grossberg (1924–2014) für die Gestaltung vieler Bahlsen-Blechdosen verantwortlich. Sie arbeitete als freie Designerin von 1949 bis 1989 für die Firma. Durch Diktatur und Krieg in ihrer Ausbildung und Berufstätigkeit behindert, studierte sie erst ab 1944 Bühnenbild und Malerei an der Kunsthochschule Weimar. Viele ihrer Dosen sind durch Pop Art und Op Art beeinflusst. Insgesamt entwarf sie mehr als 250 Dosen für die Firma.

Schwichtenberg's designs were not limited to advertising, however; she also designed Bahlsen sample stores, interior design for factory buildings, and company exhibitions, among many other projects. On 23 November 1921, she was given an employment contract with Bahlsen that was renewed annually until 1933. At the beginning of the Third Reich, she emigrated to South Africa, while continuing to work for Bahlsen through commissions. Until her death in 1945, she appears to have received 705 Reichsmark per month.

Gertrud Kraut plays a special role in this group of women designers for Bahlsen. She trained at the Debschitz School in Munich from 1909 to 1913, where Hermann Bahlsen awarded contracts to the school's ceramics workshop. Sometime around 1912/13, Gertrud Kraut, who taught the ceramics class at the Debschitz School, won a competition offered by Bahlsen that allowed her to design an unglazed earthenware pot in white, light blue, and dark blue. The pot was produced in Munich, apparently in large numbers, and presented at suitable exhibitions as a model object.

After World War II, Eva Grossberg (1924–2014) was responsible for the design of many Bahlsen tin cans. She worked as a freelance designer for the company from 1949 to 1989. Hindered in her education and career by dictatorship and war, she was only able to begin her studies in 1944 at the Kunsthochschule Weimar (Weimar Art Academy), where she studied stage design and painting. Many of her tins are influenced by pop art and op art. In total, she designed more than 250 containers for the company.

Literatur
Further Reading

F. H. Ehmcke, Clara Ehmcke, Düsseldorf (Flugschriften vom Deutschen Museum für Kunst in Handel und Gewerbe 1–2), Dortmund: Verlag Fr. Wilhelm Ruhfus, 1911.

Dieter Fuhrmann (Hg./ed.): Profession ohne Tradition. 125 Jahre Verein der Berliner Künstlerinnen, ein Forschungs- und Ausstellungsprojekt der Berlinischen Galerie in Zusammenarbeit mit dem Verein der Berliner Künstlerinnen, Berlin: Kupfergraben, 1992.

Tobias Hoffmann (Hg./ed.): Kunst und Keksdose. 125 Jahre Bahlsen, Köln/Cologne: Wienand, 2014.

Rüdiger Joppien: Die Hannoversche Keksfabrik Hermann Bahlsen auf der Werkbund- Ausstellung, in Der westdeutsche Impuls 1900–1914. Kunst und Umweltgestaltung im Industriegebiet. Die Deutsche Werkbundausstellung Cöln 1914, Ausstellungskatalog / exhibition catalog, Köln/Cologne: Kölnischer Kunstverein, 1984: 216–226.

Reiner Meyer: Die Reklamekunst der Keksfabrik Bahlsen in Hannover von 1889–1945, Niedersächsische Staats- und Universitätsbibliothek Göttingen, 1999, https://ediss.uni-goettingen.de/handle/11858/00-1735-0000-0006-B37F-3?show=full (Abruf/accessed 6. Feb. 2023).

POLITISCHES ENGAGEMENT POLITICAL ACTIVISM

Plakate von Künstlerinnen
und Grafikdesignerinnen
Posters by Women Artists
and Graphic Designers

„Women's March" und Suffragetten

Es sollen über 700.000 Menschen gewesen sein, die am 21. Januar 2017, einen Tag nach dem Amtsantritt von Donald Trump, in Washington auf die Straße gingen, um einen „Women's March" in Gang zu setzen. Sie griffen damit symbolisch die Traditionslinie der Suffragetten des späten 19. Jahrhunderts auf. Die Erinnerung an die Vorkämpferinnen des Frauenwahlrechts wurde dadurch wachgerufen, dass Trump öffentlich frauenfeindliche Äußerungen artikuliert hatte. Der neue Präsident der USA war der radikale Höhepunkt einer misogynen Rechten, von der man befürchtete, dass sie den Emanzipationsprozess von Frauen wieder rückläufig machen werde.[1]

Die USA sind stolz darauf, dass im Jahr 1870 im Staat Wyoming zum ersten Mal in der Weltgeschichte Frauen anlässlich einer bundesstaatlichen Wahl zur Urne gehen durften. Zwanzig Jahre später folgten drei weitere Bundesstaaten dem Beispiel. Am 3. März 1913, einen Tag vor der Amtseinführung des Präsidenten Woodrow Wilson, demonstrierten Tausende von Suffraget-

1 Die Bewegung in den USA ist allerdings geschwächt, weil gegen einige Organisatorinnen Antisemitismusvorwürfe laut wurden. Viele NGOs entzogen ihnen daraufhin die Unterstützung. Unter dem Motto „March On" organisierten sich indes Frauen weltweit neu.

The Women's March and the Suffragettes

According to reports, more than 700,000 people took to the streets of Washington, D.C. to kick off a Women's March on 21 January 2017, the day after Donald Trump's inauguration. Evoking the tradition set by the suffragettes from the late nineteenth century, the protest was spurred into action by a new president whose misogynistic remarks had been well documented in public. Trump was the radical culmination of a misogynist Right that the protesters feared would reverse the process of women's emancipation.[1]

Many in the US are proud that it was the state of Wyoming, in 1870, where women were allowed to vote in a statewide election for the first time in world history. Twenty years later, three other states followed suit. On 3 March 1913, one day before the inauguration of President Woodrow Wilson, thousands of suffragettes demonstrated on Washington's Pennsylvania Avenue. It was not until 18 August 1920 that the Nineteenth Amendment to the U.S. Constitution was ratified, granting women the right to vote.

1 The movement in the United States was weakened, however, when some of the organizers were accused of antisemitism, prompting many NGOs to withdraw their support. Meanwhile, women around the world reorganized under the slogan "March On."

Demonstration britischer Suffragetten vor einer Ausstellung von Frauen / In a procession to promote the Women's Exhibition, 1909
© Museum of London

Clémentine Hélène Dufau, La Fronde, Plakat/poster, 1898

Anna Sóos Korányi, Internationaler Frauenstimmrechts-Kongress, Budapest, 15.–20. Jun. 1913 / International Women's Suffrage Congress, Budapest, 15–20 Jun. 1913, **Plakat**/poster

ten auf der Washingtoner Pennsylvania Avenue. Erst am 18. August 1920 wurde das Nineteenth Amendment in der US-Verfassung ratifiziert, welches Frauen das Wahlrecht zugestand.

Bis ins 20. Jahrhundert durften Frauen in den meisten Ländern der Erde nicht wählen. Bei der schrittweisen Einführung des Frauenwahlrechts gab es nationale, teils große zeitliche Unterschiede: In der Schweiz wurde es erst 1971 (und auch nicht in allen Kantonen) eingeführt, während es in Neuseeland bereits seit 1893 bestand.

In allen Ländern gingen Frauen mit ihren Protestaktionen „auf die Straße" – ein öffentlicher Raum jenseits politischer Repräsentation, aber traditionell der Ort, an dem Demokratie eingefordert wurde. Auch die protestierenden Frauen in Washington griffen auf dieses erinnerungspolitische Symbol zurück: Die National Mall war der Ort ihrer Demonstrationen. Um ihre Identität als Aktivistinnen nach außen zu dokumentieren und nach innen zu sichern, griffen schon zu Zeiten der Suffragettenbewegung im 19. Jahrhundert militante wie gemäßigte Kämpferinnen auf visuelle Medien zurück, zum Beispiel Plakate, Flugblätter, Banner und Kleidermode. Heute noch beschwören die Protestierenden die traditionellen visuellen Formate, auch wenn ihnen ganz andere mediale Kommunikationsmittel zur Verfügung stehen. Zudem war soziales und politisches Engagement eines der Hauptaktionsfelder, in dem Grafikdesignerinnen ihre Fähigkeiten einsetzten. Immerhin stammen in Deutschland zwei der berühmtesten Plakate in der Frühzeit der Moderne von Frauen: Julie Wolfthorns SPD-Plakat *Vorwärts* von 1902 und *Nie wieder Krieg* von Käthe Kollwitz, 1924.

Into the twentieth century, women were not allowed to vote in most countries around the world. Yet the gradual introduction of women's suffrage took place at different times in different countries, with large gaps in between. In Switzerland, universal suffrage was not introduced until 1971 (and not in all cantons, either), while in New Zealand it has existed since 1893.

In all countries, women took their protests into the streets—a public space beyond formal political representation, yet traditionally where demands for democracy were expressed. The women protesting in Washington also took to the streets as a continuation of this tradition, staging their demonstrations on the National Mall. And in order to publicly mark their identity as activists and build internal solidarity, women campaigners since the suffragette movement in the nineteenth century, moderate and militant alike, have long resorted to visual media and signs—to posters, leaflets, banners, and fashions of dress. Today, protesters still turn to traditional visual formats, even though they have access to entirely different tools and media of communi-

Anna von Wahl, Plakat für die Kunstausstellung des Vereins der Künstlerinnen in der königlichen Akademie der Künste zu Berlin / Poster for the art exhibition of the Verein der Künstlerinnen in the Royal Academy of Arts in Berlin, um/around 1897

Bertha Margaret Boye, Votes for Women, Farblithografie / color lithography, 1911–1913

Verschränkung von sozialer und politischer Aktivität

Ab Mitte des 19. Jahrhunderts begannen Frauen, ihre Wahlberechtigung sowie das Recht auf eine Ausbildung und eigene Berufstätigkeit nach ihrem Wunsch einzufordern. Nicht wenige Künstlerinnen, die auch in angewandten Bereichen arbeiteten, gaben ihren Forderungen in Form von Wahl- und Protestplakaten Ausdruck.

Die wohl am häufigsten erwähnten politischen Plakate zu Anfang des 20. Jahrhunderts beziehen sich auf das Thema Wahlrecht für Frauen. *Woman's Suffrage* von Evelyn Rumsey Cary, 1905, und die Lithografie von Bertha M. Boye (1883–1930) *Votes for Women*, 1911, fehlen in keiner Auflistung. So bekannt diese Designerinnen sind, so wenig weiß man über sie.

Auch die Entwerferin eines der berühmtesten Bilder der Linken in Deutschland, die Künstlerin Julie Wolfthorn (1864–1944), war, wie ihr gesamtes Werk, lange nicht bekannt. Dabei war sie zu ihrer Zeit eine äußerst erfolgreiche

cation. And women graphic designers, too, have long found that social and political engagement is one of the main areas where they can deploy their skills. After all, two of the most famous posters in Germany in the early days of modernism were made by women: Julie Wolfthorn's SPD poster *Vorwärts* (Forward) from 1902 and *Nie wieder Krieg* (Never again war) by Käthe Kollwitz from 1924.

Intertwining of Social and Political Activity

Beginning in the mid-nineteenth century, women began demanding their right to vote, along with the right to receive an education and take up a profession of their choosing. More than a few women artists who also worked in applied fields expressed their demands in the form of election and protest posters.

Those political posters from the beginning of the twentieth century that are probably the most recognizable and discussed today all touch upon voting rights for women. Evelyn Rumsey

Plakat nach einem Motiv von / Poster based on a motif by Käthe Kollwitz, Nie wieder Krieg (Never again war), Auftraggeber*in unbekannt / client unknown, gedruckt von / printed by United Artists Ltd, Tel Aviv, 1924, IL, Foto/photo: © Museum für Gestaltung Zürich, Plakatsammlung

Käthe Kollwitz, Nie wieder Krieg, 1924

Cary's *Woman's Suffrage* from 1905 and Bertha M. Boye's (1883–1930) lithograph *Votes for Women* from 1911 would be included on any such list. Yet despite the fame of these women designers, often we know little about them or their work.

The designer of one of the most famous images made for the Left in Germany, the artist Julie Wolfthorn (1864–1944), long remained unknown, as did her entire body of work. She was nevertheless an extremely successful artist in her day, well-connected to important institutions such as the Deutscher Künstlerbund, the Verein Bildender Künstlerinnen zu Berlin, the Lyceum-Club, and the Berlin Secession. She had opportunities to present her works in many exhibitions in Germany and was one of the women who decisively shaped artistic life in Berlin. At the same time, she campaigned for women's rights and universal suffrage and worked to improve conditions for women artists. With the poster for the Social Democratic magazine *Vorwärts* in 1902, she created, for a militant political Left, an emblem that retained its potency for many years.

Yet if we look deeper, we find many other women artists working in applied graphic arts who have been largely ignored by histories of art and design. The reasons for this are legion, but they certainly include the fact that many obstacles were placed in the way of women's efforts to channel their talents into a career. Acquiring an education was itself difficult enough for women in the nineteenth century, and further hurdles awaited women in attempting to practice a profession or earn a living through work. For many years, they faced what Germaine Greer called the "obstacle race": a litany of restrictions imposed by public educational institutions and extending into their personal and professional life.[2]

This is especially true of the early period of the emancipation movement. Here, too, the exceptions confirm the rule. Many women artists were featured by name, for instance, in the magazine *Votes for Women*.

Founded in 1907 by Emmeline Pethick-Lawrence and her husband Frederick, until 1912 *Votes for Women* was the official weekly journal of the Women's Social and Political Union (WSPU), the leading organization of the English suffragette movement. The magazine was printed in the colors of the suffragettes—pink, white, and green—and copies were sold on the street for a penny. The WPSU organized major ad campaigns, including a bus that traveled around London, and set

Künstlerin, vernetzt mit einschlägigen Institutionen wie dem Deutschen Künstlerbund, dem Verein Bildender Künstlerinnen zu Berlin, dem Lyceum-Club und der Berliner Secession. Sie konnte ihre Werke in Deutschland in vielen Ausstellungen präsentieren und zählte zu den Frauen, die das künstlerische Leben in Berlin entscheidend mitprägten. Gleichzeitig setzte sie sich für Frauenrechte und das allgemeine Wahlrecht ein und engagierte sich für verbesserte Bedingungen für Künstlerinnen. Mit dem Plakat für die sozialdemokratische Zeitschrift *Vorwärts* schuf sie 1902 ein für lange Zeit wirkmächtiges Symbol einer kämpferischen politischen Linken.

Ein Blick unter die Oberfläche lässt viele weitere Künstlerinnen der angewandten Grafik hervortreten, die allerdings von der Design- und Kunstgeschichtsschreibung wenig erfasst sind. Das mag viele Gründe haben, aber mit Sicherheit den, dass dem Bestreben dieser Frauen, ihre Talente in eine Berufstätigkeit einfließen zu lassen, viele Hindernisse in den Weg gelegt wurden. War die Ausbildung für Frauen im 19. Jahrhundert schon schwierig genug, warteten in der Ausübung ihrer Arbeit weitere Hürden auf sie. Es gilt

2 Germaine Greer: *The Obstacle Race: Fortunes of Women Painters*, London: Secker & Warburg, 1980.

über viele Jahre, was Germaine Greer als „obstacle race"[2] bezeichnete: ein Hindernislauf durch die Restriktionen der kommunalen und staatlichen Ausbildungsstätten und darüber hinaus durch das Privat- und Berufsleben.

Das trifft insbesondere auf die frühe Zeit der Emanzipationsbewegung zu. Ausnahmen bestätigen auch hier die Regel. Viele Künstlerinnen sind zum Beispiel in der Zeitschrift *Votes for Women* namentlich erwähnt.

1907 von Emmeline Pethick-Lawrence und ihrem Mann Frederick gegründet, war *Votes for Women* bis 1912 das offizielle Wochenblatt der Women's Social and Political Union (WSPU), der führenden Organisation der englischen Suffragettenbewegung. Die Zeitschrift war in den Farben der Suffragetten, Rosa, Weiß und Grün, gedruckt und wurde zum Teil für einen Penny auf der Straße verkauft. Die WPSU organisierte große Anzeigenkampagnen, unter anderem mit einem Bus, der durch London fuhr, und stellte Dauerverkaufsstände im Zentrum von London auf. Die Mitglieder der Partei setzten sich in hohem Maße für die Distribution der Plakate und Handzettel ein, auch auf der Straße. Auf dem Höhepunkt der Kampagnen sollen bis zu 40.000 Exemplare im ganzen Land verkauft worden sein.

Gerade im Bereich des politischen Plakats sind viele Grafiker*innen anonym geblieben. Dass sie namentlich in der Regel nicht erwähnt

up permanent sales booths in central London. The members of the organization made exceptional efforts to distribute its posters and handbills, including on the streets. At the height of the campaigns, up to 40,000 copies were reportedly sold across the country.

Yet it is precisely in the area of political posters that many graphic designers have remained anonymous. The fact that these designers are usually not mentioned by name also stems from the fact that graphic design was not regarded with the same esteem as the so-called fine arts. Nevertheless, research in the last several years has been able to identify several examples of work by women.[3]

The following will describe two women artists from among the many women artists whose work was particularly engaged, socially and politically.

2 Germaine Greer: *The Obstacle Race: Fortunes of Women Painters*, London: Secker & Warburg, 1980; deutsche Ausgabe: *Das unterdrückte Talent. Die Rolle der Frauen in der bildenden Kunst*, Berlin: Ullstein, 1980.

3 See, among other studies, Briar Levit: *Baseline Shift: Untold Stories of Women in Graphic Design History*, New York: Princeton Architectural Press, 2021.

Briefmarke, Deutschland, 75 Cent, mit dem Motiv Nie wieder Krieg von Käthe Kollwitz, in Erinnerung an den Ausbruch des Ersten Weltkriegs 1914 / Stamp, Germany, 75 cents, with the motif Nie wieder Krieg by Käthe Kollwitz to commemorate the outbreak of World War I in 1914, 2014

Briefmarke, DDR, 25 Pfennig, mit einem Motiv von / Stamp, GDR, 25 pfennigs, with a motif by Käthe Kollwitz (Ausschnitt aus dem Plakat / detail from the poster Nie wieder Krieg)

Käthe Kollwitz, Auftragsarbeit für eine Kampagne des Frauen-sekretariats der Kommunistischen Partei Deutschlands (KPD) gegen den Paragrafen 218 / Commission for a campaign of the Women's Secretariat of the Communist Party of Germany (KPD) against Paragraph 218, **Plakat/poster, 1923**

Käthe Kollwitz (1867–1945)

In Germany, Käthe Kollwitz stands out as an artist whose protest posters have stood the test of time. In August 1924, on dates commemorating the tenth anniversary of the beginning of World War I, mass demonstrations took place all over Germany, organized—as in every year since 1920—by the action committee of the movement "Never Again War." With her eponymous poster for the Socialist Workers' Youth in Leipzig, Kollwitz created an antiwar image that became an icon. The German peace movement of the 1970s and 1980s chose this poster as its symbol, which it also gained attention far beyond Germany's borders. It shows a young man raising his hand to swear an oath, his left hand placed on his heart in affirmation and his mouth open as if to cry: "Never again war!"

In spite of the acclaim she received within artistic circles and her international reputation, Käthe Kollwitz had to struggle with all the adversities facing women artists and graphic designers of her time as they sought

DE OVERLEVENDEN   OORLOG AAN DEN OORLOG!

UITGEGEVEN DOOR HET INTERNATIONAAL VERBOND VAN VAKVEREENIGINGEN AMSTERDAM

Käthe Kollwitz, De Overlevenden. Oorlog aan den Oorlog! (Die Überlebenden. Krieg gegen Krieg / The survivors: war against war!), Auftragsarbeit für den / Commission for the Internationaal Verbond van Vakvereenigingen, Amsterdam, NL, Plakat/poster, 1923, Foto/photo: Museum für Gestaltung Zürich, Plakatsammlung

sind, ist auch darauf zurückzuführen, dass Grafik-design nicht dieselbe Wertschätzung besaß wie die sogenannte freie Kunst. Dennoch konnte die Forschung in den letzten Jahren etliche Beispiele weiblichen Engagements herausarbeiten.[3]

Im Folgenden sollen zwei Beispiele stellvertretend für die Künstlerinnen beschrieben werden, die mit ihrem Engagement besonders hervorgetreten sind.

Käthe Kollwitz (1867–1945)

In Deutschland ragt Käthe Kollwitz als die Künstlerin hervor, die mit ihren Protest-plakaten in die Geschichte eingegangen ist: Im August 1924, um den zehnten Jahrestag des Beginns des Ersten Weltkriegs herum, fanden in ganz Deutschland Massendemonstrationen statt, zu denen – wie in jedem Jahr seit 1920 – der Aktionsausschuss der „Nie wieder Krieg"-Bewegung aufgerufen hatte. Mit ihrem gleichnami-gen Plakat für die Sozialistische Arbeiterjugend in Leipzig schuf Kollwitz ein Anti-Kriegsplakat. Es wurde zu einer Ikone. Die Friedensbewegung der 1970er und 1980er Jahre wählte es zu ihrem Symbol, und auch weit über die Grenzen Deutsch-lands hinaus erlangte das Plakat Aufmerksamkeit. Darauf erhebt ein junger Mann die Hand zum Schwur, die Linke hat er zur Bekräftigung des Eids auf sein Herz gelegt, und sein Mund ist auf-gerissen wie zum Ruf: „Nie wieder Krieg!"

Trotz der Anerkennung in Künstlerkreisen und ihres internationalen Renommees hatte Käthe Kollwitz mit allen Widrigkeiten zu kämp-fen, denen Künstlerinnen und Grafikdesignerin-nen ihrer Zeit auf dem Weg zur Professionalisie-rung und während der Berufspraxis ausgesetzt waren. Mit großem Elan setzte sie sich für unte-re Volksschichten ein. Es waren einschneidende Erlebnisse im Laufe der deutschen Geschichte, die zu ihrem sozialen Engagement führten: die Empörung über die Grauen des Ersten Weltkrie-ges, dem ihr Sohn im Alter von nur 18 Jahren zum Opfer fiel, und zum Ende ihres Lebens die Dikta-tur des Nationalsozialismus, in der ihr Werk dis-kreditiert wurde. Nicht zuletzt hat sich Käthe Kollwitz mit mutigen Aktionen für die Gleichbe-rechtigung der Frau und deren prekäre Lebens- und Arbeitssituation eingesetzt.

Insgesamt schuf die Künstlerin 14 Plaka-te. Der größte Teil ihres Œuvres beinhaltet Gra-fiken, darunter zählen einige der Plakate zu den

3 Siehe u. a. Briar Levit: *Baseline Shift. Untold Stories of Women in Graphic Design History*, New York: Princeton Architectural Press, 2021.

to professionalize their labor and earn a living. She advocated with tireless vigor for the lower classes. What led to her social engagement was experiencing the drastic events of German his-tory: her outrage over the horrors of World War I, which claimed her son's life at the age of eighteen; and at the end of her life, the Nazi dictatorship, in which she found her work discredited. Last but not least, Käthe Kollwitz was courageous in fight-ing for equal rights for women and seeking to end their precarious living and working conditions.

She created fourteen posters in total. The largest part of her oeuvre consists of graphic works, and among these, it is several of her post-ers that are the most famous. Her first two works, the 1906 poster *Deutsche Heimarbeit-Ausstellung* (German home work exhibition) and the 1912 poster *Für Groß Berlin* (For greater berlin) set off scandals in the German Empire and were eventu-ally banned. She created further political posters mainly between 1919 and 1926, during the Weimar Republic.

Artistic Context

It was in Munich where the young artist Kollwitz experienced the breakthrough (led by Max Liebermann and Fritz von Uhde) of natural-istic open-air painting in her depiction of scenes from the everyday life of common people. She first turned to her subjects of working-class life in the same way as Liebermann, still free of any social criticism. According to Théophile-Alexandre Steinlen, the Internationale Gewerkschaftsbund (International Trade Union Confederation) com-missioned Kollwitz as the first woman to create a poster for Antiwar Day in September 1924, organized to commemorate the tenth anniver-sary of the outbreak of World War I. It was titled *Die Überlebenden: Krieg dem Kriege!* (The survi-vors: make war on war!) and appeared in several languages.

In 1891, Käthe Schmidt married the physi-cian Dr. Karl Kollwitz. However, she never played the role of woman at his side but led a completely independent life. The couple shared the same political convictions; Karl Kollwitz was a member of the Social Democratic Party, founded the Social Democratic Medical Association in 1913, and became a city councilor for the SPD in Berlin in 1919. He ran a practice for patients covered by public health insurance.

Käthe Kollwitz's commitment to the cause of poorly paid workers and their families carried risks. A lawsuit filed by a homeowners'

bekanntesten Werken. Ihre beiden ersten Arbeiten, das Plakat *Deutsche Heimarbeit-Ausstellung* von 1906 und das Plakat *Für Groß Berlin* von 1912, lösten im Deutschen Kaiserreich Skandale aus und wurden schließlich verboten. Weitere politische Plakate entstanden vorwiegend zwischen 1919 und 1926, in der Zeit der Weimarer Republik.

Künstlerischer Kontext

In München erlebte die junge Künstlerin den Durchbruch (angeführt von Max Liebermann und Fritz von Uhde) der naturalistischen Freilichtmalerei mit ihrer Darstellung von Szenen aus dem Alltagsleben des einfachen Volks. Zunächst wandte sie sich in ihren Sujets dem Arbeiterleben zu, anfangs wie Liebermann noch frei von jeglicher Sozialkritik. Nach Théophile-Alexandre Steinlen beauftragte der Internationale Gewerkschaftsbund Kollwitz als erste Frau mit einem Plakat für den Antikriegstag im September 1924, mit dem der zehnte Jahrestag des Ausbruchs des Ersten Weltkriegs begangen werden sollte. Es trägt den Titel *Die Überlebenden. Krieg dem Kriege!* und erschien in mehreren Sprachen.

1891 heiratete Käthe Schmidt den Arzt Dr. Karl Kollwitz. Sie war aber nie „die Frau an seiner Seite", sondern führte ein vollkommen eigenständiges Leben. Das Paar verband eine gleiche politische Orientierung, Karl Kollwitz war Mitglied der Sozialdemokratischen Partei, gründete 1913 den Sozialdemokratischen Ärzteverein und wurde 1919 Stadtverordneter der SPD in Berlin. Er führte eine kassenärztliche Praxis.

Das Engagement von Käthe Kollwitz für Volksschichten geringen Einkommens war riskant. Aufgrund der Klage eines Hausbesitzervereins wurde ihr Plakat *Für Groß Berlin*, das auf die Wohnungsnot der Stadt hinweist, verboten. Mit dem Plakat *Deutschlands Kinder hungern!* für die Internationale Arbeiterhilfe (IAH) wandte sich Käthe Kollwitz gegen die Not infolge der Inflation. Sie schuf 1920 *Drei Flugblätter gegen den Wucher*.

Für eine Frau ihrer Zeit übernahm Kollwitz ungewöhnlich viele verantwortungsvolle Ämter und erhielt die höchsten Ehrungen, und das, obwohl sie viele frauendiskriminierende Reaktionen erfuhr. Beispielsweise gehörte sie zu den Frauen, die 1904 eine Petition an den Akademiedirektor Anton von Werner in Berlin richteten, Frauen zum Studium zuzulassen. Frauen war seit 1882 das Studium ausdrücklich untersagt. Jahre später, 1919, wurde Kollwitz jedoch Professorin an der Preußischen Akademie der Künste in Berlin. Sie war die erste Frau, die je zur

Julie Wolfthorn, Werbung für das Magazin der Sozialdemokratischen Partei Deutschlands / Advertisement for the Social Democratic magazine **Vorwärts** (Foreward), Farblithografie / color lithography, vor/before 1902, gedruckt von / printed by Kunstanstalt Hollerbaum & Schmidt, Berlin

association led to her poster *Für Groß Berlin*, which called out the city's housing shortage, being banned. With the poster *Deutschlands Kinder hungern!* (Germany's children are starving!) for the Internationale Arbeiterhilfe (IAH) (International Workers' Aid), she similarly spoke out against the hardship caused by inflation. She created *Drei Flugblätter gegen den Wucher* (Three pamphlets against usury) in 1920.

For a woman of her time, Kollwitz took on an unusually large number of positions of responsibility and received the highest honors, and this despite the fact that she faced a great deal of discrimination. In 1904, for instance, she was one of the women who petitioned the academy director Anton von Werner in Berlin to admit female students. Women had been expressly forbidden to study at the institution since 1882. Years later,

Mitgliedschaft aufgefordert wurde. Von 1928 bis 1932 übernahm sie die Leitung des Meisterateliers für Grafik an der Akademie. Viele weitere Ämter folgten. So wurde sie Vorstandsmitglied der Berliner Secession. Nach der Spaltung der Vereinigung wechselte sie zur Freien Secession, deren Vorstand sie von 1914 bis 1916 angehörte.

Ende des Ersten Weltkriegs wurde sie Mitglied im Hauptausschuss des Bundes Neues Vaterland, der bedeutendsten deutschen pazifistischen Vereinigung zu jener Zeit. Bis 1924 war sie Mitglied des Zentral- bzw. Auslandskomitees der kommunistischen Internationalen Arbeiterhilfe (IAH). Für die Organisation entwarf sie das Plakat *Helft Russland*, um auf die Dürrekatastrophe im Wolgagebiet aufmerksam zu machen.

Mit Beginn des sogenannten Dritten Reichs wurde die Situation für Kollwitz ebenso wie für viele andere Künstler prekär. Mit der Drohung, die Preußische Akademie der Künste ansonsten zu schließen, wurden Heinrich Mann und Käthe Kollwitz 1933, mit der „Machtergreifung" der Nationalsozialisten, zum Austritt gezwungen.

Engagement für die Gleichberechtigung der Geschlechter

Käthe Kollwitz konnte, wie es zu ihrer Zeit üblich war, ihre Ausbildung nicht an Kunstakademien erhalten, sondern musste Privatunterricht bei Künstlern nehmen. Später besuchte sie die Berliner Künstlerinnenschule und danach eine vergleichbare Institution in München. Und wie viele andere Künstlerinnen dieser Zeit auch, zog sie nach Paris, wo sie sich 1904 in einem zweimonatigen Aufenthalt an der für Frauen zugänglichen Académie Julian ausbilden ließ.

Als Kollwitz auf der Großen Berliner Kunstausstellung mit ihrem Zyklus *Ein Weberaufstand* mit einer Medaille geehrt werden sollte – Max Liebermann als Mitglied der Preisjury wollte dies durchsetzen –, lehnte Kaiser Wilhelm II. die Verleihung entrüstet ab.

Fünf Jahre lang, von 1898 bis 1903, erhielt sie einen Lehrauftrag an der Berliner Künstlerinnenschule und unterrichtete Radieren sowie Zeichnen nach lebenden Modellen. Aktzeichnen nach einem lebenden Modell, eine wichtige Voraussetzung für Malerei und Bildhauerei, war Frauen zu jener Zeit verboten.

1906 entwarf Kollwitz ein Plakat für die „Deutsche Heimarbeit-Ausstellung" in Berlin, dessen Motiv eine erschöpfte Arbeiterfrau zeigt. Die Kaiserin lehnte den Besuch der Ausstellung ab, solange das Plakat öffentlich aushing. Aufgrund

however, in 1919, Kollwitz became a professor at the Preußische Akademie der Künste (Prussian Academy of Arts) in Berlin. She was the first woman ever asked to join. From 1928 to 1932, she was head of the master studio for graphic art at the academy. Many other such positions followed. She became a member, for instance, on the board of the Berlin Secession, and after the split of the association, she became engaged with the Free Secession, where she was also a member of the board from 1914 to 1916.

At the end of World War I, she became a member of the head committee of the Bund Neues Vaterland, the most important German pacifist association at the time. Until 1924, she was a member of the Central or Foreign Committee of the Communist International Workers' Aid (IAH). For the organization, she designed the poster *Helft Russland* (Help Russia) to draw attention to the drought disaster in the Volga region.

With the beginning of the Third Reich, the situation became precarious for Kollwitz, as it did for many other artists. Threatening, after they came to power in 1933, to otherwise close the Prussian Academy of Arts, the new Nazi rulers forced Heinrich Mann and Käthe Kollwitz to resign.

Fighting for Gender Equality

As was common in her day, Käthe Kollwitz was not allowed to receive an education at art academies but had to take private lessons from artists. Later she attended the Berliner Künstlerinnenschule (Berlin School for Women Artists) and then a similar institution in Munich. And like many other women artists of the time, she moved to Paris, where she trained for two months in 1904 at the Académie Julian, which was open to women.

When Kollwitz was to be honored with a medal at the Great Berlin Art Exhibition with her cycle *Ein Weberaufstand* (A weaver's revolt)—with prize-jury member Max Liebermann as the main advocate for her selection—Kaiser Wilhelm II indignantly refused his permission to confer the award.

For five years, from 1898 to 1903, Kollwitz held a teaching position at the Berlin Künstlerinnenschule and taught etching and drawing from live models. Nude drawing from live models, which was an important prerequisite for painting and sculpture, was forbidden to women at the time.

In 1906 Kollwitz designed a poster for the *Deutsche Heimarbeit-Ausstellung* in Berlin, with

Fun in the Sun

Luba Lukova, Fun in the Sun, Plakat/poster, 2008 © Luba Lukova

Luba Lukova, Plakat zu / Poster for The Taming of the Shrew von/by William Shakespeare, La MaMA E.T.C., 1998 © Luba Lukova

der vielen frauendiskriminierenden Erfahrungen gründete Kollwitz 1913 den Frauenkunstverband und blieb Erste Vorsitzende bis 1923.

In den Jahren 1924 und 1925 arbeitete Kollwitz für die Internationale Frauenliga für Frieden und Freiheit (IFFF), die unter anderem auf die moderne Kriegstechnologie, wie sie im Ersten Weltkrieg zum Einsatz gekommen war, und ihre schrecklichen Folgen aufmerksam machte.

Im Rahmen der Aktion „Entartete Kunst" wurden 1937 Arbeiten von ihr aus mindestens elf deutschen Museen beschlagnahmt.

Am 22. April 1945, wenige Tage vor Kriegsende, starb Käthe Kollwitz in Moritzburg. In Erinnerung an die überragende, engagierte Künstlerin wurden in Deutschland Schulen und Straßen nach ihr benannt. In mehreren Städten wurden Käthe-Kollwitz-Museen gegründet. Das Getty Research Institute in Los Angeles verfügt über die umfangreichste Kollwitz-Sammlung in den USA. Mit mehreren Briefmarkenmotiven ehrte die Deutsche Bundespost der Bundesrepublik Deutschland (BRD) die Künstlerin. Auch in der Deutschen Demokratischen Republik (DDR) erschienen zwei Briefmarken, die Plakate von ihr zeigten. Einer der ersten neuen Intercity-Express-Züge wurde nach ihr benannt. Sogar ein Asteroid erhielt ihren Namen. Die amerikanischen Protestkünstlerinnen Guerrilla Girls wählten sie unter anderem als eines ihrer Pseudonyme. Im Dezember 2017 wurde eine Büste von Käthe Kollwitz in die Ruhmeshalle Walhalla in Deutschland aufgenommen.

Luba Lukova

Auf das Werk von Käthe Kollwitz bezieht sich die junge amerikanisch-bulgarische Grafikdesignerin Luba Lukova, die in den letzten Jahren auf sich aufmersam machte. Soziale Gerechtigkeit, Diversität und Teilhabe sind ihre Kernthemen, von Immobilienspekulation über Kriegsschauplätze, ungleicher Lohn, Zensur und Korruption bis hin zu Umweltbedingungen. Zwar betrachtet sich Lukova nicht als Feministin,[4] doch verbindet sie Themen von Gerechtigkeit immer wieder mit der Situation der Frau in der Gesellschaft. Dazu hat sie 1999 die Serie *Women of the Bible* ediert und 2001 eine Ausstellung unter dem Titel „The Printed Woman" organisiert. Des Weiteren existieren eine Reihe von Arbeiten, in denen die Situation von Frauen im Mittelpunkt stehen wie *I Scream, Fun in the Sun, See Cheese.*

4 Vortrag „Penny Stamps", University of Michigan, von Luba Lukova, in Luba Lukova: Graphic Guts, YouTube (29. Jan. 2022).

a motif showing an exhausted working woman. The empress refused to visit the exhibition as long as the poster was publicly displayed. Spurred to action by the discrimination she experienced as a woman, Kollwitz founded the Frauenkunstverband (Women's Art Association) in 1913, where she remained first chairwoman until 1923.

In 1924 and 1925 Kollwitz worked for the Internationale Frauenliga für Frieden und Freiheit (The International Women's League for Peace and Freedom, IFFF), which strove, among other aims, to draw attention to the use of modern war technology in World War I and its terrible consequences.

As part of the "Degenerate Art" campaign in Nazi Germany, works by Kollwitz were confiscated from at least eleven German museums in 1937.

On 22 April 1945, a few days before the end of the war, Käthe Kollwitz died in Moritzburg. Many schools and streets named in her honor maintain the memory of Kollwitz as an outstanding, engaged artist, in addition to Käthe Kollwitz museums founded in several cities. The Getty Research Institute in Los Angeles has the most extensive Kollwitz collection in the United States. The Deutsche Bundespost of the Federal Republic of Germany (FRG) has also honored Kollwitz with several stamp motifs, as did the postal service in the German Democratic Republic (GDR) with two stamps featuring posters by Kollwitz. One of the first new Intercity Express trains carried her name, which has even been bestowed upon an asteroid. The American protest artists Guerrilla Girls used it, as well, as one of their pseudonyms. In December 2017, a bust of Käthe Kollwitz was added to the Valhalla Hall of Fame in Germany.

Luba Lukova

Garnering attention in recent years, the young American-Bulgarian graphic designer Luba Lukova is one artist who refers back to the work of Käthe Kollwitz. Social justice, diversity, and equal participation are her core issues, with a specific focus on a range of problems that includes real estate speculation, war zones, unequal pay, censorship, corruption, and environmental conditions. Although Lukova does not consider herself a feminist,[4] she repeatedly links themes of justice with the situation of women in society. Examples include her 1999 series *Women of the Bible*

4 Lecture, "Penny Stamps," delivered by Luba Lukova at the University of Michigan, in Luba Lukova: Graphic Guts, YouTube (accessed 29. Jan. 2022).

Lukova ist in Plovdiv, Bulgarien, geboren und studierte an der National Academy of Fine Arts in Sofia. Sie wanderte 1991 in die USA aus. Kurz darauf wurde sie von *New York Times Book Review* angestellt und gründete ein eigenes Studio in New York City.

Lukova hat einen sehr einfachen, expressiven Autorenstil. Er zeichnet sich durch starke Kontraste, harte Konturen, eindeutige Symbole und Metaphern aus, die schnell zu erfassen sind. Die Farben sind plakativ, die Sujets reduziert und vereinfacht, die Typografie teils in Handschrift. Trotz ihrer eigenständigen Stilistik wird sie mit historischen Vorbildern aus dem niederländischen Expressionismus wie Holzstichen von M. C. Escher und anonymen Protestplakaten in Verbindung gebracht. 2008 gab sie die Plakatserie *Soziale Gerechtigkeit* heraus. In den folgenden Jahren entwarf sie Arbeiten für humanitäre Organisationen, Universitäten, Broadway-Produktionen, Choreografien und für die War Resisters League. Lukovas Werk ist in höchstem Maße anerkannt, geehrt und weltweit mit Preisen dotiert. Werke von ihr sind unter anderem aufgenommen in den Sammlungen des Museum of Modern Art, New York City, dem Denver Art Museum, der Library of Congress in Washington, D. C., der Bibliothèque Nationale de France in Paris und dem Zürcher Museum für Gestaltung. „Designing Justice"[5] ist der Titel einer Wanderausstellung, die von September 2017 bis März 2022 in vielen US-amerikanischen Städten zu sehen war und die Vielfalt ihrer Sujets aufzeigte.

and the exhibition she organized in 2001 entitled *The Printed Woman*. A number of other works by her highlight the situation of women, such as *I Scream, Fun in the Sun, or See Cheese*.

Born in Plovdiv, Bulgaria, Lukova studied at the National Academy of Fine Arts in Sofia. She emigrated to the United States in 1991. Shortly thereafter, she was hired by the *New York Times Book Review*, and she was able to establish her own studio in New York City.

Lukova has a very simple, expressive authorial style, characterized by strong contrasts, hard contours, and unambiguous symbols and metaphors that can be quickly grasped. Her colors are striking, her subjects reduced and simplified, and her typography partly rendered in handwriting. Despite her distinct style, she is associated with historical models from Dutch expressionism such as wood engravings by M. C. Escher and anonymous protest posters. In 2008, she produced a series of posters under the title of *Social Justice*. In the ensuing years, she designed work for humanitarian organizations, universities, Broadway productions, and choreographic performances, and for the War Resisters League. Lukova's work has attracted worldwide praise, recognition, and honors. Works by her are held in the collections of the Museum of Modern Art, New York City, the Denver Art Museum, the Library of Congress in Washington, D.C., the Bibliothèque nationale de France in Paris, and the Zurich Museum of Design, among others. *Designing Justice*[5] is the title of a traveling exhibition that was on display in many US cities from September 2017 to March 2022, showcasing the diversity of her subjects.

5 https://www.lukova.net/lukova-traveling-exhibitions (Abruf 28. Jul. 2022); siehe Ausstellungskatalog: *Luba Lukova. Designing Justice*, Clay & Gold, 2022.

5 https://www.lukova.net/lukova-traveling-exhibitions (accessed 28. Jul. 2022); see exhibition catalog, *Luba Lukova: Designing Justice*, Clay & Gold, 2022.

Literatur
Further Reading

Heike Carstensen: *Leben und Werk der Malerin und Graphikerin Julie Wolfthorn (1864–1944). Rekonstruktion eines Künstlerinnenlebens*, Marburg: Tectum Verlag, 2011.

Steven Heller: Separated at Birth: Lifting Luba Lukova, *Print* 58, Nr./no. 2 (2004): 16.

Meredith James: By Women, for Women. Suffragist Graphic Design, in Briar Levit (Hg./ed.): *Baseline Shift. Untold Stories of Women in Graphic Design History*, New York: Princeton Architectural Press, 2021: 62–74.

Dorothee Linnemann (Hg./ed.): *Damenwahl. 100 Jahre Frauenwahlrecht*, Frankfurt a. M.: Societäts-Verlag, 2018.

Liz McQuiston, Guido Costa, Nan Goldin & Enrique Juncosa: *Suffragettes to She-Devils. The Developing Role of Graphics in the Struggle for Women's Liberation and Beyond*, London: Phaeton, 1997.

SUFFRA-GETTEN SUFFRAG-ETTES

Frühes Corporate Design
und Kommunikationsdesign
in England
Early Corporate and
Communication Design
in England

Eines der bekanntesten englischen Netzwerke von Künstler*innen, Intellektuellen und Wissenschaftler*innen zu Anfang des 20. Jahrhunderts war die Bloomsbury Group. Sie wurde vor allem durch eines ihrer Mitglieder, die Schriftstellerin und Galionsfigur der Frauenemanzipation, Virginia Woolf, weit über die Grenzen des Landes bekannt. Diese Gruppe setzte sich, wie so viele andere in dieser Zeit, die zur kulturellen Modernisierung Englands beitragen wollten, mit bildender Kunst, Literatur, Wissenschaft und politischer Theorie und Aktion auseinander.

Beeinflusst von der Arts-and-Crafts-Bewegung und ihren Ausläufern in der Private-Press-Bewegung haben auch Virginia Woolf und ihr Ehemann Leonard mit einer Privatpresse gearbeitet. Nachdem sie zunächst in ihrem Privathaus Bücher von Hand gesetzt und dann auf einer gebraucht erstandenen Minerva-Tiegeldruckpresse eigenhändig gedruckt hatten, gründeten sie bald darauf, im Juli 1917, einen Verlag, dessen Bücher von kommerziellen Druckern hergestellt wurde: die Hogarth Press.

Die Gemengelage aus einem künstlerischen Leben, das alle Lebensbereiche neu gestalten wollte und den Lebensstil der Einzelnen durchdrang, baute auf einem breiten Spektrum an künstlerischen Tätigkeiten auf – sie flossen auch in die neuen Medien, Newspapers und neue Magazine, ein, in denen Illustrationen und Karikaturen eine große Rolle spielten, wie *The Yellow Book, Punch* etc., in Literatur und Poesie, Grafikdesign und Karikatur, politische Diskurse und tagesaktuelle Berichterstattung.

Die Suffragetten

Weniger bekannt ist, dass in England auch Suffragetten mit künstlerischen Mitteln arbeiteten und eine regelrechte Werbestrategie im Sinne eines Corporate Design aufbauten. Im Gedächtnis geblieben sind eher die Fotografien von ihren spektakulären radikalen Demonstrationen mit den dilettantischen Schriftplakaten, die häufig genug von der wenig wohlgesonnenen Presse karikiert wurden. Doch Frauenrechtlerinnen agierten gleichermaßen mit Formaten durchaus moderner visueller Kommunikation. Eines der Zentren dieser künstlerischen Ausgestaltung war das Suffrage Atelier.

Der Kampf der Frauen für das Wahlstimmrecht – *women's suffrage* – wurde schon Mitte des 19. Jahrhunderts, im Viktorianismus, zu einem zentralen sozialen und politischen Anliegen. Die Kampagnen zielten weit über das

One of the most famous English networks of artists, intellectuals, and scientists at the beginning of the twentieth century was the Bloomsbury Group, internationally known today primarily through one of its members, the writer and champion of women's emancipation, Virginia Woolf. Like so many other groups at the time who worked to achieve a more culturally modern England, it too engaged with visual art, literature, and science, along with politics in both theory and practice.

Influenced by the arts and crafts movement and its offshoots in the private press movement, Virginia Woolf and her husband Leonard also turned to the new presses producing handcrafted books. After first typesetting books by hand in their own home and then printing them by hand on a second-hand Minerva platen press they had purchased, they soon established a publishing

Suffrage Atelier, Postkarte/postcard, um/around 1909–1914

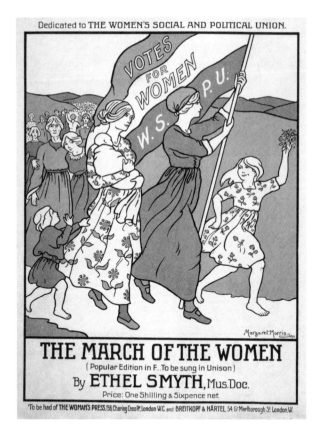

Dedicated to THE WOMEN'S SOCIAL AND POLITICAL UNION.

THE MARCH OF THE WOMEN
(Popular Edition in F...To be sung in Unison)
By **ETHEL SMYTH**, Mus.Doc.
Price: One Shilling & Sixpence net.
To be had of THE WOMAN'S PRESS,156 Charing Cross R? London W.C. and BREITKOPF & HÄRTEL, 54 G? Marlborough S? London W.

Margaret Morris, The March of the Women, Plakat/poster, 1911
© Museum of London

company in July 1917 whose books were produced by commercial printers: the Hogarth Press.

The vibrant tension of an artistic creativity that sought to reshape all areas of life, while also permeating individual lifestyles, drew from a broad spectrum of artistic activities. These also left their mark on new media, newspapers, and magazines in which illustrations and caricatures played a major role (such as *The Yellow Book*, *Punch*, etc.), in addition to literature and poetry, graphic design and caricature, political discourse, and daily news reporting.

The Suffragettes

What is less well known is that in England suffragettes also employed art to achieve their aims and developed nothing less than a full advertising strategy resembling what we would today call a corporate design. The historical memory that has persisted is rather the photographs of their spectacular, radically political demonstrations with dilettantish, handmade posters, frequently caricatured at the time by a press that was hardly sympathetic to their aims. Yet women's rights activists also mobilized forms of visual communication that were entirely modern. One center of such artistic expression was the Suffrage Atelier.

Women's suffrage became a central social and political concern during the mid-nineteenth century, in the Victorian Age. Yet the goals of the suffragette campaigns went far beyond the issue of voting rights in seeking to redefine traditional gender norms, end discrimination, and achieve equal civic rights for women.

Sarah Grand's 1894 essay "The New Aspect of the Woman Question" both sparked and popularized the phenomenon of the "new woman." In contrast to the traditional Victorian woman, the "new woman" was to be independent, strong-willed, and free to make decisions that went beyond her traditional field of activity, the home. The public therefore played a major role in the development of this new image of womanhood.

It was also hoped that powerful social and political associations would contribute to shaping this new type of woman. In 1897, the National Central Society for Women's Suffrage and the Central Committee of the National Society for Women's Suffrage merged to form the National Union of the Women's Suffrage Societies (NUWSS). These groups coordinated and guided the actions of women involved in the movement. The Women's Social and Political Union (WSPU) was founded

Thema Wahlrecht hinaus und wollten traditionelle Geschlechternormen neu definieren, Diskriminierung beenden und eine gleichberechtigte Staatsbürgerschaft für Frauen erreichen.

Sarah Grand's Essay „The New Aspect of the Woman Question" von 1894 war ein Auslöser für das Phänomen „Neue Frau" und popularisierte es zugleich. Im Gegensatz zur traditionellen viktorianischen Frau sollte die „Neue Frau" selbstständig, willensstark und frei in ihren Entscheidungen sein, die über ihr traditionelles Aktionsfeld, das Haus, hinausgingen. Die Öffentlichkeit spielte daher eine große Rolle bei der Entfaltung der neuen Weiblichkeit.

Zur Bildung eines neuen Frauentyps sollten auch mächtige Verbände beitragen. Die National Central Society for Women's Suffrage und das Central Committee of the National Society for Women's Suffrage schlossen sich 1897 zur National Union of the Women's Suffrage Societies (NUWSS) zusammen. Sie steuerten die Aktionen der Frauen und verbanden sie untereinander. Die Women's Social and Political Union (WSPU) wurde im Oktober 1903 von Emmeline Pankhurst gegründet und war eine reine Frauenpartei. Sie

Plakatdemonstration der Suffragetten / Poster demonstration of the suffragettes, 1908 © Museum of London

war mit den Gewerkschaften der Arbeiter*innen verbunden. Obwohl sie ursprünglich nicht militant war, wurde sie zunehmend radikaler in ihren Aktionen.

Nach 1900 avancierten die militanten Suffragetten zu Protagonistinnen moderner und aufsehenerregender politischer Inszenierungen. Dabei spielten Visualisierungen eine große Rolle, wie sie sich in zahlreichen Fotografien, Plakaten, Flyern und Symbolen niederschlugen. Spektakuläre Auftritte waren nun eine Strategie, öffentliche Aufmerksamkeit zu erreichen. Tatsächlich berichteten alle Zeitschriften des Landes über die WSPU. Die Frauen erprobten bewusst den zivilen Ungehorsam mit demonstrativen Protestformen und entwarfen neue ikonografische Stilmittel, um ihre Anliegen medienwirksam zu positionieren. Sie setzten auf Skandale, Störaktionen, Zwischenrufe im Parlament, Unterbrechungen bei Theateraufführungen und Kirchenpredigten. Ihre Banner „Votes for Women" kamen häufig zum Einsatz. Erste Verhaftungen von Aktivistinnen hatten ein enormes Medienecho zur Folge. Der Ideenreichtum der Suffragetten, ihre Forderungen visuell zu kommunizieren, kannte kaum Grenzen.

Eine Frau, die die Votes for Women verkauft /
British suffragette with a poster, selling the Votes for
Women magazine, zwischen/between 1900 & 1919

Unterstützung holten sich die Frauen bei Künstler*innen. Eines der bekanntesten Ateliers war das Suffrage Atelier. Militante Suffragetten wie gemäßigte Suffragistinnen-Organisationen beauftragten es, Illustrationen für ihre Zeitschriften, Embleme, Flaggen, Banner, Abzeichen, Plakate, Flyer bis hin zur Kleidermode zu entwerfen. Die von dem Atelier konzipierten Symbole wurden wieder und wieder bei den Protesten gezeigt und dienten der Stärkung der inneren wie äußeren Identität der Gruppe. Die Aktivistinnen trugen bei ihren Demonstrationen und Prozessionen Kleider in verschiedenen Farben und sogar Uniformen ihrer Organisation, wodurch sie in den Medien leicht erkennbar waren. Ikonografische Sujets des Martyriums und der Heroisierung waren wesentlich für ihre bildhaften Inszenierungen. So stießen beispielsweise der Beginn der Hungerstreiks der verhafteten militanten Suffragetten

in October 1903 by Emmeline Pankhurst as an all-women's party with strong ties to labor unions. Though not originally militant, its actions became increasingly radical.

After 1900, the militant suffragettes became more and more successful in garnering public attention through bold acts of political theater. Visual representations played a major role here, as reflected in numerous photographs, posters, flyers, and symbols. Spectacular public events and campaigns became an intentional strategy to increase the visibility of the movement. And indeed, print media in Great Britain widely reported on the WSPU. Its activists deliberately tested strategies of civil disobedience through public forms of protest, and they designed new styles and iconographies to ensure their demands would resonate in public. They relied on actions that provoked public outrage—on disruptions, heckling during sessions of parliament, and interruptions of theater performances or sermons, frequently carrying "Votes for Women" banners. The first arrests of women activists produced enormous media coverage, matched in impact by the suffragettes' inventiveness in themselves using visual media to communicate their demands.

This included turning to artists for support, and one of the most famous studios engaged in this effort was the Suffrage Atelier. Both militant suffragettes and moderate suffragist organizations commissioned the studio to design illustrations for their magazines, emblems, flags, banners, badges, posters, flyers—and even to design their clothing. The symbols created by

A Patriot (Alfred Pearse), The Modern Inquisition Treatment of Political Prisoners under a Liberal Government, Plakat/poster, 1910. Gezeigt wird eine Sufragette, die zwangsernährt wird. / Poster showing a suffragette prisoner being force-fed.

The Cat and Mouse Act, The Liberal Cat, Plakat/poster, herausgegeben von der / published by the Women's Social and Political Union (WSPU). Das Plakat bezieht sich auf den Hungerstreik der verhafteten Suffragetten. / The poster refers to the hunger strike of suffragettes who had been arrested.

und die darauf folgenden Zwangsernährungen auf eine breite öffentliche Resonanz. Szenen der Zwangsernährung wurden auf Plakaten und in Grafiken für die Presse dargestellt. Das bekannte Plakat *Modern Inquisition* von 1910 nutzte die WSPU erfolgreich, um ihre Gegner öffentlich zu diskreditieren. Die Organisation erfuhr in dieser Zeit einen enorm hohen Mitgliederzulauf und eine Welle öffentlicher Zustimmung. Das Plakat *The Liberal Cat*, 1914, anlässlich des Prisoners Temporary Discharge for Ill Health Act erfreut sich auch heute noch großer Beliebtheit.

Die Suffragetten sahen sich als Opfer der Politik des Staates, organisierten sich in den 1910er Jahren in einem „Guerrilla Warefare" und agierten mit paramilitärischen, irregulären kleinen Überraschungsattacken.

The Venture:
An Annual of Art and Literature

1903 wurde das kleine Magazin *The Venture: An Annual of Art and Literature* von W. Somerset Maugham und Laurence Housman herausgegeben und bei John Baillie in London und ab 1905 bei The Arden Press in Leamington produziert. Das Magazin, das einmal im Jahr erschien, markiert den Beginn einer regelrechten Welle der Beschäftigung mit sozialpolitischen Ideen von neuer Weiblichkeit. Erstaunlicherweise waren beide Herausgeber der Zeitschrift Männer, doch sie unterstützten die Suffragettenbewegung und nahmen an deren Aktionen teil. Laurence Housman (1865–1959) war eine zentrale Figur in der Men's League for Women's Suffrage, die sich 1907 etablierte.

In den Ausgaben von *The Venture* wird die enge Verbindung von Kunst, Grafikdesign, Literatur und den neuen Ideen der Feminist*innen offenbar. Die Schriften verknüpften die Ideen von Emanzipation mit denen von Menschenrechten und sozialer Gerechtigkeit und halfen den Frauen, ihre eigene Situation zu reflektieren.

Das Suffrage Atelier

Das Suffrage Atelier war ein Künstler*innenkollektiv, das die Demonstrationen der Suffragetten in England visuell begleitete. Es wurde im Februar 1909 von Laurence Housman, seiner Schwester Clemence (1861–1955) und Alfred Pearse (1855–1933) gegründet und betrachtete sich als Arts-and-Crafts-Vereinigung, die Frauen unterstützte. Sie produzierte Werbung für die Suffragettenbewegung, Banner, Postkarten, Plakate und Dekorationen für Festumzüge.

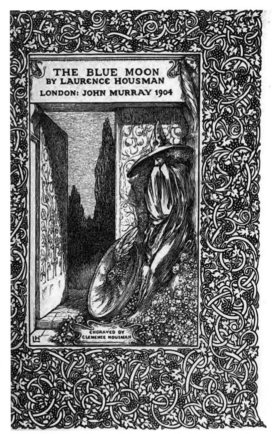

Clemence Housman, Grafik zu / Graphic for The Blue Moon von/by Laurence Housman, John Murray, 1904

the studio were repeatedly displayed at protests, where they served to give the group a coherent public identity and strengthen its internal cohesion. At their demonstrations and public parades, the activists wore clothing in different colors, or sometimes even uniforms from their respective organizations, which made them easily recognizable for the press. Iconographic motifs of martyrs and heroes were essential to these visual stagings. The start of hunger strikes by militant suffragettes who had been arrested, for instance, along with the forced feedings that followed, provoked a widespread public response. Force-feeding scenes were depicted on posters and in graphic works for the press. The well-known poster *Modern Inquisition* from 1910 was successfully used by the WSPU to publicly discredit its opponents—in a period when the organization experienced a tremendous influx of members and a wave of public approval. The poster *The Liberal Cat*, 1914, to protest the Prisoners Temporary Discharge for Ill Health Act, is still widely admired today.

Hilda Dallas, Werbeplakate für das Wochenblatt / Advertising posters for the weekly paper Votes for Women, 1903 & 1909

Hilda Dallas, Plakat für die Zeitschrift /
Poster for the magazine The Suffragette, 1903

The suffragettes saw themselves as victims of the state's policies, and organized their activities in the 1910s as a kind of guerrilla warfare operating with paramilitary, irregular small-scale surprise attacks.

The Venture:
An Annual of Art and Literature

In 1903, the small magazine *The Venture: An Annual of Art and Literature* first appeared, edited by W. Somerset Maugham and Laurence Housman and printed by John Baillie in London, and from 1905 by The Arden Press in Leamington. Appearing once a year, the magazine marked the beginning of a remarkable wave of engagement with sociopolitical ideas of new womanhood. Though both editors of the magazine were surprisingly men, they supported the suffragette movement and participated in the actions it staged. Laurence Housman (1865–1959) was a central figure in the Men's League for Women's Suffrage, founded in 1907.

Laurence Housman war Illustrator und Schriftsteller, der in einflussreichen englischen Magazinen wie *The Yellow Book, The Pageant* und *The Dial* veröffentlichte. Er studierte mit seiner Schwester Clemence Kunst an der Lambeth School of Art und dem Royal College of Art in London. Auch Clemence war zugleich Schriftstellerin. Sie gab unter anderem den Roman *The Were-Wolf* (1896) heraus, eine allegorische Fantasie über die sich ändernde Rolle der Neuen Frau. Illustrationen zeichnete sie für die Bücher ihres Bruders, *The Blue Moon* (1904) und *Moonshine & Clover* (1922), sowie für das Magazin *The Venture*. Der Schwerpunkt der Zeitschriftenbeiträge lag darauf, die Errungenschaften von Frauen zu betonen, die Bedeutung von Künstlerinnen zu unterstreichen und Feminismus in Verbindung mit einer künstlerisch anspruchsvollen Visualisierung zu bringen.

Politisch waren die Geschwister seelenverwandt, Clemence wurde eine der zentralen Figuren der Suffragettenbewegung, Laurence engagierte sich in einem Feministen-Club für Männer.

Alfred Pearse war Illustrator. Seine Zeichnungen und Karikaturen wurden unter anderem in *The Illustrated London News*, *The Boy's Own Paper*, *The Strand Magazine* und im *Punch* abgedruckt. Er illustrierte eine große Anzahl Bücher. Ab 1909 zeichnete er unter dem Pseudonym A Patriot wöchentlich einen Cartoon für das 1907 gegründete Suffragetten-Magazin *Votes for Women*.[1]

Das Atelier wurde ein Zentrum für politische Aktivitäten. Zu seinen Mitgliedern zählten auch weitere Personen, vor allem professionelle Illustrator*innen, aber auch Amateur*innen. Die meisten Illustrationen und Plakate waren in Blockdrucken wie Holzschnitten angefertigt und meist gedruckt in schwarzer oder weißer Tusche. Das Atelier führte Workshops für Druckgrafik, Bannerherstellung, Zeichnen und Schablonieren durch und veranstaltete Wettbewerbe. Seine Politik bestand darin, nur das zu lehren, was schnell reproduziert und verbreitet werden konnte. Techniken wie Holz- und Linolschnitt zählten dazu.

Das Suffrage Atelier war auch darin einzigartig, dass es den Künstlerinnen Lohn zahlte für ihre Arbeiten. So konnten Frauen Teile ihres Lebensunterhaltes verdienen. Darüber hinaus organisierte das Atelier ein Bildungsprogramm, das sich auf frauenemanzipatorische Themen spezia-

The issues of The Venture reflect the close connection in the suffragette movement between art, graphic design, literature, and new feminist ideas. The texts it published linked ideas of emancipation with others about human rights and social justice and helped women reflect on their own situation.

The Suffrage Atelier

The Suffrage Atelier was a collective of artists who contributed visual representations to support the suffragette demonstrations in England. It was founded in February 1909 by Laurence Housman, his sister Clemence (1861–1955), and Alfred Pearse (1855–1933) and considered itself to be an arts and crafts association that supported women. Its productions for the suffragette movement included advertising, banners, postcards, posters, and decorations for parades.

Laurence Housman was an illustrator and writer whose work appeared in influential English magazines such as *The Yellow Book*, *The Pageant*, and *The Dial.* He studied art with his sister Clemence at the Lambeth School of Art and the Royal College of Art in London. Clemence, too, was a writer, whose published works included the novel *The Were-Wolf* (1896), an allegorical fantasy about the changing role of the new woman. She drew illustrations for her brother's books, *The Blue Moon* (1904) and *Moonshine & Clover* (1922), and for *The Venture* magazine. The texts she wrote focused on highlighting women's achievements, emphasizing the importance of women artists, and making connections between feminism and artistically sophisticated forms of visual representation.

Politically, the siblings were kindred spirits; Clemence became one of the central figures of the suffragette movement, and Laurence became involved in a feminist club for men.

Alfred Pearse was an illustrator. His drawings and caricatures appeared in *The Illustrated London News*, *The Boy's Own Paper*, *The Strand Magazine*, and *Punch*, among others, and he illustrated a large number of books. From 1909, he drew a weekly cartoon under the pseudonym A Patriot for *Votes for Women*, the suffragette magazine founded in 1907.[1]

The atelier, whose members mainly consisted of professional illustrators, with some

1 Siehe https://spartacus-educational.com/wvotesm.htm (Abruf 22. Aug. 2022).

1 See https://spartacus-educational.com/wvotesm.htm (accessed 22. Aug. 2022).

Laurence Housman, Titelblatt für / Cover for The Were-Wolf von/ by Clemence Housman, John Lane at the Bodley Head / Way and Williams, 1896

lisierte, lud zu Vorträgen ein und organisierte Schreibkurse. Es hatte einen großen Zulauf von beiden Geschlechtern. Sie wurden ermutigt, ihr Design einzureichen für entsprechende Printmedien und an Gemeinschaftsarbeiten teilzunehmen.

Parteipolitisch war das Atelier verbunden mit einem Zweig der militanten Women's Social and Political Union (WSPU). Laurence Housman entwarf die Flagge der Partei. Clemence Housman wie ihr Bruder waren angesehene Mitglieder der WSPU. Für die Partei wurde ein Großteil der Plakate und Illustrationen im Suffrage Atelier hergestellt und in ihren Ladenketten sowie über überregionale Zeitungen vertrieben.

Laurence Housman bekannte sich offen zu seiner Homosexualität und engagierte sich dafür, dass Homosexuelle nicht diskriminiert wurden. Er schloss sich deshalb einer Geheimgesellschaft namens Order of Chaeronea an, die Fragen der Geschlechteridentitäten diskutierte und sich für eine Liberalisierung in diesem Bereich einsetzte. Weiterhin war er Mitbegründer der British Society for the Study of Sex Psychology. Housman war davon überzeugt, dass auch Männer die Frauenemanzipation unterstützen sollten, und gründete daher mit Israel Zangwill, Henry Brailsford und vielen anderen Schriftstellern, Journalisten und politischen Aktivisten die Men's League for Women's Suffrage. Er war

amateurs, became a center for political activities. Most of the illustrations and posters were made in block prints, such as woodcuts, and mostly printed in black or white ink. The atelier conducted workshops in printmaking, banner making, drawing, and stenciling, in addition to holding competitions. Its guiding principle was to teach only what could be quickly reproduced and disseminated; these included techniques such as woodcut and linocut.

The Suffrage Atelier was also unique in that it paid women artists wages for their work, enabling these women artists to partially support themselves. The atelier further organized an educational program specializing in topics related to women's emancipation, invited guests to give lectures, and organized writing courses. The program attracted many participants of all sexes, who were encouraged to submit designs of their own for the print media in which they were working and to participate in community outreach.

Politically, the atelier was allied with a branch of the militant Women's Social and Political Union (WSPU), whose flag had been designed by Laurence Housman. Both Clemence Housman and her brother were respected WSPU members. Most of the posters and illustrations used by the party were produced in the Suffrage Atelier and distributed in the atelier's chain stores and through national newspapers.

Laurence Housman openly acknowledged his homosexuality and fought to prevent discrimination against homosexuals. Among other things, he took up membership in a secret society called the Order of Chaeronea—a group that discussed questions of gender and sexual identity and advocated for more liberal positions. He was moreover a cofounder of the British Society for the Study of Sex Psychology. Firm in his belief that men should also support women's emancipation, Housman founded the Men's League for Women's Suffrage with Israel Zangwill and Henry Brailsford, along with many other writers, journalists, and political activists. He was concurrently active in another group of male feminists, the Men's Social and Political Union.

Other members of the Suffrage Atelier included Edith "Edy" Alisa Geraldine Craig (1869-1947). Craig was an acclaimed theater director, costume designer, and actor who also became involved in the suffragette movement. Her own origins were connected to the arts and crafts movement: her father was the famous architect and designer Edward William Godwin; and her brother, Edward Gordon Craig, was a set designer

Suffrage Atelier, What a Woman May Be, and Yet Not Have the Vote, Plakat/poster, 1913, Schlesinger Library, RIAS, Harvard University

gleichzeitig in einer anderen Gruppe von männlichen Feministen aktiv, der Men's Social and Political Union.

Zu den weiteren Mitgliedern des Suffrage Ateliers zählte Edith „Edy" Alisa Geraldine Craig (1869–1947). Sie war eine anerkannte Theaterdirektorin, Kostümdesignerin und Schauspielerin und engagierte sich in der Suffragettenbewegung. Craig stammte aus einem der Arts-and-Crafts-Bewegung verbundenen Elternhaus, ihr Vater war der berühmte Architekt und Designer Edward William Godwin, ihr Bruder war einer der angesehensten Vertreter eines modernen Theaters sowie Bühnenbildner: Edward Gordon Craig.

Obwohl die Mitglieder des Ateliers verschiedenen sozialen Schichten entstammten, zeigt sich an diesem Beispiel einmal mehr, dass die Suffragettenbewegung in eine kulturell aufgeschlossene moderne Mittel- und Oberschicht eingebettet war. Auch Edith Craig führte einen liberalen Lebensstil und lebte in einer lesbischen Ménage-à-trois mit der Dramaturgin Christabel Marshall und der Künstlerin Clare „Tony" Atwood.

Ein weiteres Mitglied war die in Japan geborene Hilda Dallas (1878–1958), von der einige bekannte Titelblätter des Magazins *Votes for Women* stammen. 1901 wurde sie Studentin an der Slade

and one of the most respected advocates of a modern theater.

Although the members of the atelier came from different social classes, this example shows once again that the suffragette movement was embedded in a modern, open-minded, progressive middle and upper class. Edith Craig also led a liberal lifestyle, as part of a lesbian ménage-à-trois with playwright Christabel Marshall and artist Clare "Tony" Atwood.

Another member of the atelier was Japanese-born Hilda Dallas (1878–1958), designer of several well-known covers of the magazine *Votes for Women*. In 1901 Dallas became a student at the Slade School of Fine Art in London and was later responsible for the graphic design of many of the suffragettes' campaigns. At the same time, she was herself a committed pacifist suffragette and held a leadership position at the WSPU. She raised funds for the party and designed sets and costumes for antiwar theater productions. At WSPU, she served as head of a subdivision of the party. She was a member of the Suffrage Atelier from its founding.

The suffragette sales shops often featured seasonal window displays with gift items, postcards, and literature about the movement.

School of Fine Art in London und zeichnete verantwortlich für das Grafikdesign vieler Aktionen der Suffragetten. Gleichzeitig war sie selbst engagierte pazifistische Suffragette und in Führungsposition bei der WSPU. Sie akquirierte finanzielle Mittel für die Partei und entwarf Bühnenbilder und Kostüme für das Antikriegstheater. Bei der WSPU vertrat sie eine Unterabteilung. Gleich zu Anfang war sie Mitglied des Suffrage Ateliers.

Die Verkaufsläden der Suffragetten hatten saisonale Schaufensterdekorationen mit Geschenkartikeln, Postkarten und entsprechender Literatur. Im Laden der Kilburn High Road soll eine Schaufensterpuppe gestanden haben, die nach einem Plakat von Hilda Dallas gekleidet war und ein Plakat von ihr in der Hand hielt. Die Frauenfiguren sollten junge Frauen auffordern, sich für das Frauenstimmrecht einzusetzen.

Das Anti-Suffrage Alphabet

Das *Anti-Suffrage Alphabet* wurde von Laurence Housman gestaltet und von Leonora Tyson, einer Organisatorin der WSPU, herausgegeben. Die illustrierten Verse beschrieben, dem Alphabet folgend, die unwürdige Unterordnung der Frau und ermutigten zur Opposition. Jede Edition wurde von Hand gefertigt. Das Heft spielte bei der Akquise von Geldmitteln für die Suffragetten-Kampagnen eine Rolle. Es wurde in *Votes for Women* kurz vor Weihnachten 1911 abgebildet.

Eine der Grafikdesignerinnen war die Amerikanerin Pamela Colman Smith (1878–1951), die in New York am Pratt Institute of Art and Design studiert hatte. Sie war eine Freundin von Edith Craig und ihrer Partnerin Christabel Marshall. Während ihres Aufenthalts in England illustrierte sie auch für *The Venture*, war Mitglied des Suffrage Ateliers und schuf mehrere Plakate für das Atelier wie *A Bird in the Hand*. Sie illustrierte zahlreiche Bücher, und ihre Arbeiten wurden in ganz Europa und den USA ausgestellt.

Künstlerinnen und Grafikdesignerinnen hatten einen erheblichen Anteil an der Frauenbewegung. Es gab noch andere Vereinigungen wie die Artists' Suffrage League (1907–ca. 1918). Aufgrund gemeinsamer Überzeugungen vernetzten sie sich untereinander und agierten teilweise weltweit. Sie erweiterten ihre Arbeit im Sinne einer modernen Public Relation, in vielen Fällen ausgehend von der Arts-and-Crafts-Bewegung und deren Verständnis für die politische Wirkmacht von Kunst und Handwerk sowie dem Bemühen, dass beides sich mit dem aktuellen Leben durchdringen möge.

It is said that a mannequin stood in the Kilburn High Road store, dressed to resemble the figure in a poster from Hilda Dallas that it was also holding in its hands. Such figures were meant to urge young women to stand up for women's suffrage.

The Anti-Suffrage Alphabet

The *Anti-Suffrage Alphabet* was designed by Laurence Housman and edited by Leonora Tyson, a WSPU organizer. Written as illustrated verses for each letter of the alphabet, the book described the disgraceful oppression of women and made a plea for readers to oppose it. Each copy was made by hand, and the book played a role in raising funds for the suffragette campaigns. It was advertised in *Votes for Women* just before Christmas 1911.

One of the graphic designers was the American Pamela Colman Smith (1878–1951), who had studied in New York at the Pratt Institute of Art and Design. Smith was a friend of Edith Craig and her partner Christabel Marshall. During her stay in England she also drew illustrations for *The Venture*, was a member of the Suffrage Atelier, and created several posters for the Atelier, such as *A Bird in the Hand*. She illustrated numerous books, and her work was exhibited throughout Europe and the United States.

Women artists and graphic designers played a significant role in the women's movement. Other associations important to this history include the Artists' Suffrage League (1907–ca. 1918). Spurred on by common convictions, these groups developed close connections with each other and in some case acquired a global reach. They expanded their work into what we might call a form of public relations, often building on the arts and crafts movement and its understanding of how the ideals and products could have a political impact in becoming part of everyday life.

Literatur
Further Reading

Myriam Boussahba-Bravard: Vision et visibilité. La Rhétorique visuelle des Suffragistes et des Suffragettes Britanniques 1907–1914, *Lisa e-journal* 1, Nr./no. 1 (2003): 42–54.

Maria DiCenzo: *Feminist Media History. Suffrage, Periodicals, and the Public Sphere*, Basingstoke & Hampshire: Palgrave Macmillan, 2011.

Jana Günther: Suffragetten. Mediale Inszenierung und symbolische Politik, in Paul Gerhard (Hg./ed.): *Das Jahrhundert der Bilder. 1900 bis 1949*, Göttingen: Vandenhoeck & Ruprecht, 2009: 108–115.

Jana Günther: Die politischen Bilder und radikalen Ausdrucksformen der Suffragetten. Bilder der Heroisierung, des Martyriums und der Radikalität in der britischen Suffragettenbewegung, *kunsttexte.de*, 1/2009, https://edoc.hu-berlin.de/bitstream/handle/18452/8237/guenther.pdf (Abruf/accessed 7. Feb. 2023).

Meredith James: By Women, for Women. Suffragist Graphic Design, in Briar Levit (Hg./ed.): *Baseline Shift. Untold Stories of Women in Graphic Design History*, New York: Princeton Architectural Press, 2021: 62–74.

Dorothee Linnemann (Hg./ed.): *Damenwahl. 100 Jahre Frauenwahlrecht*, Frankfurt a. M.: Societäts-Verlag, 2018.

Liz McQuiston, Guido Costa, Nan Goldin & Enrique Juncosa: *Suffragettes to She-Devils. The Developing Role of Graphics in the Struggle for Women's Liberation and Beyond*, London: Phaeton, 1997.

Tara Morton: Changing Spaces: Art, Politics, and Identity in the Home Studios of the Suffrage Atelier, *Women's History Review* 21, Nr./no. 4 (2012): 623–637, DOI: 10.1080/09612025.2012.658177.

Harold L. Smith: *The British Women's Suffrage Campaign, 1866–1928*, Boston: Addison Wesley Longman Ltd, 1998.

Lisa Tickner: *The Spectacle of Women. Imagery of the Suffrage Campaign, 1907–1914*, Chicago: University of Chicago Press, 1988.

RUSSLAND UND DIE MODERNE

RUSSIAN MODERNISM

Vision einer
geschlechtergerechten
Gesellschaft
A Vision of a Society
with Gender Equality

Künstlerinnen haben die russische Avantgarde im besonderen Maße geprägt. Infolge des Auftrags der sozialistischen Revolutionen zu Anfang des 20. Jahrhunderts, sich von der hohen Kunst abzuwenden und Kunst und Leben miteinander zu verbinden, haben sich viele der angewandten Kunst zugewandt: dem Grafikdesign, der Bühnengestaltung, der Mode und der Architektur. Eine erhebliche Anzahl an Künstlerinnen, die gleichberechtigt am Aufbau der neuen Gesellschaft mitwirken wollten, konnte sich zwischen 1907 und den 1920er Jahren profilieren.

Im Programm der Staatlichen Freien Kunstwerkstätten WCHUTEMAS (ab 1927 WCHUTEIN in Moskau, der berühmtesten Ausbildungsstätte zwischen 1920 und 1930, arbeiteten die neuen Künstler*innen mit einem viele Sparten umfassenden Kunstbegriff, der insbesondere den privilegierten Status der „reinen" Kunst auflösen und sich Bereichen der angewandten Kunst zuwenden sollte. Visuelle Kommunikationsmedien wie Plakate, Flugblätter und Bücher waren besonders begehrte Tätigkeitsfelder. Die Künstler*innen konnten dennoch einerseits ihre kühnen Entwürfe realisieren, die dem Suprematismus und Kubismus, das heißt der reinen Kunst, verbunden waren, auf der anderen Seite wollten sie soziale Utopien ausmalen. Denn ihre eigentliche Entwicklungsdynamik bezogen revolutionäre Plakate und Bücher aus ihrer diskursiven Einbettung: dem Aufruf, eine neue Gesellschaft zu entwerfen.

Außergewöhnlich viele Frauen waren an diesem Prozess beteiligt. Ljubow Popowa (1889–1924) beispielsweise leitete zusammen mit Alexander Wesnin an den WCHUTEMAS die Anfangskurse der Malerei-Fakultät. 1920 schufen beide das Modell einer Theatertruppenparade in Moskau für die III. Internationale, für die der Regisseur und emphatische Anhänger des sowjetischen Theaters, Wsewolod Emiljewitsch Meyerhold, die Regie übernehmen sollte. Dort war eine aus geometrischen Formen gebildete „Zukunftsstadt" mit Pyramiden und an Maschinenteile erinnernden Rädern zu sehen. Wesnin, Popowa, Alexandra Exter (1882–1949), Alexander Rodtschenko und Warwara Stepanowa (1894–1958) zeigten 1921 auf der Ausstellung „5 × 5 = 25" in Moskau ihre abstrakten geometrischen Arbeiten und stellten sich damit bewusst gegen den Expressionismus, der für sie Subjektivismus, Individualismus und folglich eine privilegierte Kunst verkörperte. Insbesondere die neue Stilrichtung des Konstruktivismus wollte den praktischen Nutzen von Kunst betonen. In Zusammenhang

Alexandra Exter, Illustration für den Essay / Illustration for the essay Picasso I Okrestnosti (Picasso und Umgebung / Picasso and his milieu), Tsentrifuga, 1917 (Titelblatt / title page)

The impact of women artists on the Russian avant-garde has been especially pronounced. Following the call issued by the socialist revolutions from the early twentieth century to turn away from high art and combine art and life, many devoted their efforts to applied art: graphic design, stage design, fashion, and architecture. Between 1907 and the 1920s, a significant number of women artists who were keen to participate on equal footing with men in building a new society were able to make their mark.

The program of the state art and technical schools VKHUTEMAS (from 1927, VKHUTEIN) in Moscow, the most well-known center for artistic training in the Soviet Union between 1920 and 1930, advanced a concept of art encompassing many disciplines, with the special aim of dissolving the privileged status of "pure" art and turning toward fields of applied art. Visual communication media such as posters, flyers, and books were especially popular with the students. The artists were nevertheless also able to realize bold new designs associated with artistic currents of

Valentina Kulagina, Heldinnen der Arbeit, verstärken Sie die heroischen Brigaden, beherrschen Sie die Technik, mehren Sie die Kader mit proletarischen Spezialisten / Heroines of Labor!—Strengthen the Heroic Brigades, Master the Technique, Increase the Cadres with Proletarian Specialists, Plakat/poster, 1931 © VG Bild-Kunst, Bonn, Foto/photo: © Museum für Gestaltung Zürich, Plakatsammlung

pure art, such as suprematism and cubism, while envisioning social utopias, as the revolutionary posters and books they produced were animated above all by the discourse in which they were embedded—demands for the design of a new society.

An unusually large number of women were involved in this process. Lyubov Popova (1889 – 1924), for example, together with Aleksander Vesnin, taught the beginners' courses in painting at VKHUTEMAS. In 1920, the two of them worked together to create the model of a parade of theater troupes in Moscow for the Third International, to be directed by Vsevolod Emilyevich Meyerhold, the towering figure of Soviet theater. It featured a "city of the future" formed from geometric shapes with pyramids and wheels resembling the parts of a machine. In Moscow in 1921, Vesnin, Popova, Aleksandra Ekster (1882-1949), Aleksander Rodchenko, and Varvara Stepanova (1894-1958) exhibited their abstract geometric works at the show "5 × 5 = 25" as a deliberate rejection of expressionism, which for them embodied subjectivism and individualism, and thus privileged art. The new style of constructivism especially aimed to emphasize the practical use of art, including utopian visions for a "gender politics of equality."[1]

Women were equal partners in these art movements, often living in personal and work communities together with their husbands and friends, who were equally committed to mobilizing art in the service of a new society. Yet the names of these women—Olga Rozanova (1886-1918), Aleksandra Ekster, Natalia Goncharova (1881-1962), Lyubov Popova, Varvara Stepanova, Nadezhda Udaltsova (1885-1961), Valentina Kulagina (1902-1987), and Valentina Khodasevich (1894-1970)—are less wellknown today than men from the Russian avant-garde such as Kazimir Malevich, Vladimir Tatlin, El Lissitzky, Aleksander Rodchenko, or Vladimir and Georgii Stenberg. The contribution of women to the Russian avant-garde has nevertheless garnered increasing attention in recent years.

The conditions for women to participate in artistic activity were particularly favorable in Russia. Though one of the most backward countries in Europe, and a state dominated by agriculture, it was marked by several peculiarities regarding the role of women that distinguished it from Western Europe. Following the "great

mit dieser Kunstrichtung steht auch die Utopie einer „Geschlechterpolitik der Gleichheit".[1]

Frauen waren in diesen Kunstrichtungen gleichberechtigte Partnerinnen, oft lebten sie in einer Lebens- und künstlerischen Arbeitsgemeinschaft mit ihren Ehemännern und Freunden, die ebenfalls Protagonisten der Kunst im Dienste einer neuen Gesellschaft waren. Die Namen Olga Rosanowa (1886-1918), Alexandra Exter, Natalja Gontscharowa (1881-1962), Ljubow Popowa, Warwara Stepanowa, Nadeschda Udalzowa (1885-1961), Valentina Kulagina (1902-1987) und Valentina Chodassewitsch (1894-1970) sind der Nachwelt weniger bekannt, wird doch die russische Avantgarde mit Künstlernamen wie Kasimir

1 Viktoria Schmidt-Linsenhoff: Die Ikonographie der Gleichheit und die Künstlerinnen der russischen Avantgarde, *Kritische Berichte* 20, Nr. 4 (1992): 5–25, hier 24. Die Autorin weist auf die Risiken hin, die die Idee der Geschlechterneutralität barg.

1 Viktoria Schmidt-Linsenhoff: Die Ikonographie der Gleichheit und die Künstlerinnen der russischen Avantgarde, *Kritische Berichte* 20, no. 4 (1992): 5–25, on 24. Schmidt-Linsenhoff points especially to the risks inherent to the idea of gender neutrality.

Malewitsch, Wladimir Tatlin, El Lissitzky, Alexander Rodtschenko, Wladimir und Georgi Stenberg verbunden. Dennoch hat die Aufmerksamkeit für den Beitrag der Frauen an der russischen Avantgarde in den letzten Jahrzehnten merklich zugenommen.

Die Voraussetzungen für die Beteiligung von Frauen am künstlerischen Geschehen waren in Russland besonders günstig. Obwohl eines der rückständigsten Länder Europas und überwiegend ein Agrarstaat, gab es in Hinblick auf die Rolle der Frau einige Besonderheiten, die das Land von Westeuropa unterschied. Frauen war es schon seit Beginn des 19. Jahrhunderts infolge der „Großen Reformen" Alexanders II. erlaubt, ein Hochschulstudium zu absolvieren und die Kaiserliche Akademie der Künste in St. Petersburg sowie andere staatliche Kunstschulen zu besuchen. Künstlerinnen, die aus bürgerlichen oder adligen Häusern stammten, reisten in andere Länder Europas und tauschten sich mit der Avantgarde in Frankreich, Italien und Deutschland aus. Wie in Westeuropa diente auch der Privatunterricht von Künstler*innen der Vorbereitung auf ein späteres Studium.

Von der Orientierung an den Ismen westeuropäischer Kunst abrückend, entstand in der Sowjetunion eine eigenständige und neuartige Ausrichtung von (angewandter) Kunst, die der Visualisierung eines „neuen Lebens" dienen sollte bis hin zu Sujets im Dienste der Propaganda im Stalinismus. Die Künstlerinnen profitierten dabei von der neuen Rolle der Frau nach der Revolution und setzten sich für den Aufbau einer sozialistischen Gesellschaft ein.

Aber auch unabhängig vom politischen Wandel gab es Initiativen, die didaktische Neuerungen in die Ausbildung von angewandter Kunst einführten. Die bekannteste war die Stroganow-Zeichenschule, die der äußerst wohlhabende russische Offizier, Archäologe, Kunstsammler und Mäzen Graf Sergei Grigorjewitsch Stroganow gründete und finanzierte. 1825 startete er die erste Zeichenschule für Kunst und Handwerk in Moskau. Begabte Kinder konnten dort unabhängig von ihrer sozialen Herkunft kostenlosen Unterricht erhalten. Er leitete die Schule, die heute Moskauer Stroganow-Akademie für Kunst und Industrie genannt wird, zwölf Jahre lang. Olga Rosanowa zählte neben Alexander Rodtschenko zu den bekanntesten Schüler*innen. Die Schule umfasste auch eine Frauenabteilung und Sonntags-Zeichenkurse, in denen Menschen jeden Alters und sozialer Herkunft die Kunst des Malens erlernen konnten. Die Bildungseinrichtung war

reforms" of Alexander II at the beginning of the nineteenth century, women had been allowed to study at universities and to attend the Imperial Academy of Arts in St. Petersburg, as well as other state art schools. Women artists who came from bourgeois or aristocratic homes traveled to other countries in Europe and exchanged ideas with the avant-garde in France, Italy, and Germany. As in Western Europe, private lessons helped women artists prepare for later studies.

Turning away from the various isms of Western European art, an independent and new kind of (applied) art emerged in the Soviet Union that was expected to help visualize a "new life" in the Soviet state, even producing material for propaganda under Stalinism. Women artists benefited from the new opportunities afforded to women after the Russian Revolution and worked to build a socialist society.

But even independent of any political changes, Russia saw initiatives that introduced innovations into applied arts education. The most famous was the Stroganov School of Drawing, financed by the extremely wealthy Russian officer, archaeologist, art collector, and patron Count Sergei Grigoryevich Stroganov; it opened in 1825 as the first school for applied arts in Moscow. Gifted children could receive instruction free of charge, regardless of their social circumstances or background. Stroganov directed the school, now called the Moscow State Stroganov Academy of Industrial and Applied Arts, for twelve years. Its most famous alumni have included Olga Rozanova, as well as Aleksander Rodchenko. The school also included a women's department and Sunday drawing classes where people of all ages and social backgrounds could learn the art of painting. Administratively subordinate to the Ministry of Finance, the academy was reorganized and incorporated into VKHUTEMAS, where it split into several independent institutions in 1930.

Natalia Goncharova, Lyubov Popova, Olga Rozanova, Nadezhda Udaltsova, Aleksandra Ekster, and Varvara Stepanova are among the important pioneers of the avant-garde before and during the Russian Revolution. They taught in Moscow at the free state studios SVOMAS or VKHUTEMAS, designed product art, agitated in books and essays, and worked to articulate theoretical justifications for their positions.

Vera Adamovna Gicevič, Für die sozialistische Gesundheitsschmiede – Für den proletarischen Park der Kultur und der Erholung /
For the Socialist Health Forge—For the Proletarian Park of Culture and Recreation, Plakat/poster, 1932 © VG Bild-Kunst Bonn,
Foto/photo: © Museum für Gestaltung Zürich, Plakatsammlung

Valentina Kulagina, Kunstausstellung der Sowjetunion, Plakat/poster, 1931, in Auftrag gegeben vom / commissioned by Kunstsalon Wolfsberg, Zürich © VG Bild-Kunst, Bonn, Foto/photo: © Museum für Gestaltung Zürich, Plakatsammlung

dem Finanzministerium unterstellt. Die Schule wurde reorganisiert und in die WCHUTEMAS aufgenommen. 1930 spaltete sie sich in mehrere unabhängige Institutionen auf.

Natalja Gontscharowa, Ljubow Popowa, Olga Rosanowa, Nadeschda Udalzowa, Alexandra Exter und Warwara Stepanowa zählen zu den bedeutenden Pionierinnen der Avantgarde vor und während der Russischen Revolution. Sie lehrten in Moskau an den freien staatlichen Ateliers SWOMAS oder WCHUTEMAS, entwarfen Produktkunst, agitierten in Büchern und Aufsätzen und arbeiteten an theoretischen Begründungen ihrer Positionen.

Bedeutung der Frauen in den Revolutionen

Der revolutionäre Umbruchprozess zu Anfang des 20. Jahrhunderts betraf Frauen in Russland besonders.

Die totale Autorität des Zaren war in der Kirche verankert gewesen. Die Institutionen, Familie und Ehe sowie Scheidungen standen unter religiöser Kontrolle und damit auch die Rolle der Frau, die dem Ehemann rechtlich gesehen untergeordnet war. Bauern- und Arbeiterfrauen mussten neben ihrer Arbeit auf dem Feld und in der Fabrik zusätzlich den Haushalt führen und die Kinder aufziehen.

Einige Wochen nach der Oktoberrevolution wurde die Ehe durch die zivile Partnerschaft ersetzt. Die Scheidung war ohne jegliche Begründung auf Antrag einer der beiden Partner möglich, denn die neue kommunistische Regierung war auf die Zerstörung der Institution Familie aus. Die Frau sollte aus ihrer von Religion und Zarismus vorgeschriebenen Rolle der Mutter, Ehefrau und Hausfrau befreit und ihre Arbeitskraft für die neue Gesellschaft eingesetzt werden. Die Frauen wurden mit dem geschlechtsneutralen Wort „Kamerad" angesprochen, ebenso wie alle männlichen Sowjetbürger.

Auch viele weitere Änderungen wurden zugunsten von Frauen eingeführt. Russland war das erste Land der Welt, in dem die Gleichstellung von Mann und Frau rechtlich verankert wurde. Das Wahlrecht für die Frauen wurde in Sowjetrussland noch vor Großbritannien und Deutschland eingeführt. Die Frauen durften über ihr eigenes Geld verfügen. 1920 wurde Russland das erste Land, in dem die Abtreibung auf Wunsch der jeweiligen Frau legalisiert wurde. Dennoch wurden viele Ziele nicht erreicht. Auch wenn Frauen in der Arbeitswelt zunehmend eine Art Gleichberechtigung erlangten, war ihr Lohn meist

The Importance of Women in the Revolutions

The revolutionary changes at the beginning of the twentieth century particularly affected women in Russia.

The tsar's total authority had been anchored in the church. Institutions such as the family and marriage, as well as divorce, were under religious control, as was the social and legal status of women, who were legally subordinate to their husbands. Peasant and worker women were expected to manage the household and raise the children, in addition to their work in the fields and in the factory.

Several weeks after the October Revolution, religious marriage was replaced by the institution of civil partnership. Divorce became possible at the request of either partner, with no justification needing to be given, as the new Communist government aimed to destroy the existing institution of the family. Women were to be freed from the roles of mother, wife, and housewife prescribed by religion and tsarism, their labor to be employed in the service of the new society being built. And as with all male Soviet citizens, women too came to be addressed by the gender-neutral term "comrade."

Many other changes were also introduced that benefited women. Russia was the first country in the world in which equality between men and women was enshrined in law, and women's suffrage was introduced in Soviet Russia before Great Britain and Germany. Women were allowed to dispose of their own money, and in 1920, Russia became the first country to legalize abortion if women sought it. Nevertheless, many goals of this social reorganization were not achieved. Even though women increasingly gained a measure of equality in the workforce, their wages usually remained lower than men's because they mainly lacked formal skills or training. They were, moreover, unable to penetrate the center of power, which continued to be reserved for men.

Artist Couples

The artistic avant-garde in Russia saw an unprecedented number of artist couples in which women did not play a subordinate role or take the role of muse, as had so often been the case. Such intimate partnerships aimed at a creative symbiosis and lived the utopia of communally organized art production.

Art historian Ada Raev has pointed out that the prominent position of women artists in

geringer als der der Männer, weil sie überwiegend ungelernt waren. Auch in das Zentrum der Macht konnten sie nicht vorstoßen. Das blieb weiterhin dem männlichen Teil der Bevölkerung vorbehalten.

Künstlerpaare

In Zusammenhang mit der künstlerischen Avantgarde in Russland ist eine beispiellose Häufung an Künstlerpaaren zu verzeichnen, bei denen die Frauen meist keinen untergeordneten Part spielten oder die Rolle der Muse einnahmen. Das Künstlerpaar zielte auf eine kreative Symbiose und lebte die Utopie einer vergemeinschafteten Kunstproduktion.

Die Kunsthistorikerin Ada Raev hat darauf hingewiesen, dass die herausragende Position von Künstlerinnen in der nachrevolutionären Zeit nicht allein auf die neuen politischen Umstände zurückzuführen ist. Raev führt weitere Faktoren an wie die liberale russische Adelskultur, das Ideal einer partnerschaftlichen Ehe, den Kult um die Dichterin Georg San, die die Gleichheit der Geschlechter und sexuelle Freiheit proklamierte, sowie die Tatsache, dass Frauen relativ früh Zugang zur Hochschulbildung hatten.[2] Dennoch haben sich die Revolutionen zu Anfang des neuen Jahrhunderts ganz offensichtlich als Beschleuniger der Frauenemanzipation ausgewirkt.

Zu den vielen Künstlerpaaren zählen Natalja Gontscharowa und Michail Larionow. Beide lebten seit ihrer Studienzeit in Russland und später in Frankreich fast sechzig Jahre zusammen. In der Rezeption treten sie entweder mit Einzelmonografien hervor oder als Initiatoren bekannter Künstler*innen- und Ausstellungsvereinigungen wie „Karo-Bube", „Eselsschwanz" oder „Zielscheibe", als Vertreter*innen von bestimmten Kunstgattungen wie der Szenografie oder der Buchkunst. Vor allem waren sie die wichtigsten Vertreter*innen des Neoprimitivismus, einer an der russischen Volkskunst angelehnten, radikal anti-akademischen Kunst. Sowohl als Paar als auch als Einzelpersonen nehmen sie in der Geschichte der russischen Avantgarde einen festen Platz ein.[3]

Ein weiteres bekanntes Paar waren Warwara Stepanowa und Alexander Rodtschenko.

Ljubow Popowa, Cover der Zeitschrift / Cover of the magazine Muzykal'naia nov' (Musikalisches Neuland / New musical territory), Nr./no. 1, 1923

the postrevolutionary period did not solely stem from the new political circumstances. She cites other factors such as the liberal Russian aristocratic culture, the ideal of marriage based on partnership, the cult of the poet Georg San, who advocated for gender equality and sexual freedom, and the fact that women had relatively early access to higher education.[2] Nevertheless, the revolutions at the beginning of the new century clearly accelerated women's emancipation.

Among the many such couples are Natalia Goncharova and Mikhail Larionov, who lived together from their time as students for almost sixty years in Russia and later in France. Scholars have largely examined them either in monographs devoted to their individual bodies of work; as initiators of well-known artist and exhibition associations, such as Karo Bube, Eselsschwanz, or Zielscheibe; or as representatives of certain art genres such as scenography or book art. Above all, they were the most important representatives of neoprimitivism, a radically antiacademic art based on Russian folk art. Both

2 Ada Raev: *Russische Künstlerinnen der Moderne 1870–1930. Historische Studien. Kunstkonzepte, Weiblichkeitsentwürfe*, München: Wilhelm Fink Verlag, 2002.

3 Ada Raev: Eine „zweistellige Formel" des russischen Neoprimitivismus. Natalija Gončarova und Michail Larionov, DOI: 10.7788/9783412319526-007.

2 Ada Raev: *Russische Künstlerinnen der Moderne 1870–1930: Historische Studien. Kunstkonzepte, Weiblichkeitsentwürfe*, Munich: Wilhelm Fink Verlag, 2002.

Sie verknüpften Öffentliches und Privates ebenso wie ihre Kunst mit Theorie.

Ihre Entwürfe verbanden Ljubow Popowa und Alexander Wesnin mit Massenspektakeln, Theaterbühnen, der neuen Architektur und visionärer Städteplanung. Olga Rosanowas visuelle Poesie entwickelte sich im Austausch mit dem Dichter Alexej Krutschonych. Es entstanden Schlüsselwerke transnationaler futuristischer Buchkunst. Valentina Kulagina und Gustav Klucis setzten Fotomontagen für ihre Propaganda- und Werbeplakate ein. Weitere Paare waren Jelena Guro (1877–1913) und Michail Matjuschin, Xenia Boguslawskaja (1892–1973) und Iwan Puni, Sarra Lebedewa (1892–1967) und Wladimir Lebedew, Nina Simonovič-Efimova (1877–1948) und Iwan Efimow, Vera Nikolskaya (1890–1864) und Alexander Nikolsky, Lilja Brik (1891–1978) und Ossip Brik bzw. Wladimir Majakowski. Ob temporär liiert oder verheiratet, in einer Liebes-, Lebens- und Arbeitsgemeinschaft verbunden, waren sie Verbündete in der gemeinsamen Utopie. Einige Frauen praktizierten die freie Liebe. Die Paare formulierten infolgedessen nicht nur in der Kunst avantgardistische Ziele, sondern praktizierten auch in ihrem Lebensstil die neuen politischen Ideale.

Von der Staffelei auf die Straße und in die Schulen

Da die Revolution mit großen utopischen Ideen und der Vorstellung von einer gleichberechtigten Gesellschaft – insgesamt vom „neuen Menschen" – verbunden war, war sie gekoppelt an eine Atmosphäre größter Experimentierfreude in Kunst, Architektur, Theater, Literatur und Mode.

Ljubow Popowa, Bühnenbild für Der großmütige Hahnrei / Stage plan for The Magnanimous Cuckold von/by Wsewolod Emiljewitsch Meyerhold, Bild aus dem Essay „Ingenieure der Massen" / picture for the "Engineers of the Masses" essay, 1922

as a couple and as individuals, they occupy a firm place in the history of the Russian avant-garde.[3]

Another famous couple from this period was Varvara Stepanova and Aleksander Rodchenko, who combined public and private aspects of their lives as well as their own art with theory.

In their designs, Lyubov Popova and Aleksander Vesnin were influenced by mass spectacles, theater stages, new forms of architecture, and visionary urban planning. Olga Rosanova's visual poetry developed in dialogue with the poet Aleksei Kruchyonykh, producing key works of transnational futurist book art. Valentina Kulagina and Gustav Klutsis employed photomontage to produce their propaganda and advertising posters. Other artist couples included Jelena Guro (1877–1913) and Mikhail Matyushin; Kseniya Boguslavskaya (1892–1973) and Ivan Puni; Sarra Lebedeva (1892–1967) and Vladimir Lebedev; Nina Simonovič-Efimova (1877–1948) and Ivan Efimov; Vera Nikolskaya (1890–1864) and Aleksander Nikolsky, Lilya Brik (1891–1978) and Ossip Brik, later with Vladimir Mayakovsky. Whether they were together only for some time or married, these couples lived partnerships of love, life, and work, allied in realizing a shared utopia. Some women also practiced free love, in partnerships that not only articulated avant-garde aims in art but also practiced new political ideals in their lifestyles.

From the Easel onto the Street and into the Schools

Bound up with grand utopian ideas and the notion of an equal society, and generally with the ideal of a "new human being," the Russian Revolution fomented an atmosphere of extreme experimentation in art, architecture, theater, literature, and fashion.

After the October Revolution of 1917 and the abolition of academies and schools of arts and crafts, artistic education was reformed by the introduction of the Free State Art Workshops, out of which the VKHUTEMAS developed in Moscow in 1920. These were art universities for fine and applied arts. The schools were divided into eight faculties: painting, sculpture, architecture, graphic arts, textiles, ceramics, metalwork, and woodwork. The goal was to develop skills in product design and train "artist-engineers" who would deliver industrial mass production to build Soviet industry.

3 Ada Raev: Eine „zweistellige Formel" des russischen Neoprimitivismus: Natalija Gončarova und Michail Larionov, DOI: 10.7788/9783412319526-007.

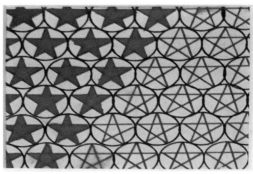

Ljubow Popowa, Design für industriell hergestelltes Textil „Sterne in Kreisen" / Fabric design „Stars in Circles", Rouge Grand Palais, um/ around 1923

Ljubow Popowa, Design für industriell hergestelltes Textil „Streifen in Schwarz-Weiß-Rosa" / Fabric design „Black-White-Pink", um/around 1923

Ljubow Popowa, Design für industriell hergestelltes Textil / Fabric design, um/around 1924

Nach der Oktoberrevolution 1917 und der Abschaffung der Akademien und Kunstgewerbeschulen wurde das künstlerische Ausbildungswesen durch die Einführung der Freien Staatlichen Kunstwerkstätten reformiert, aus denen sich 1920 in Moskau die WCHUTEMAS entwickelten. Dabei handelte es sich um Kunsthochschulen für freie und angewandte Künste. Sie gliederten sich in acht Fakultäten: Malerei, Skulptur, Architektur, Grafik, Textil, Keramik, Metall- und Holzbearbeitung. Ziel war die Entwicklung eines Produktdesigns und die Ausbildung von „Künstler-Ingenieuren", die industrielle Massenproduktion für den Aufbau der Industrie liefern sollten.

Die Bedeutung von Büchern

„Bücher. Zu allen Wissensbereichen", lässt Alexander Rodtschenko eine junge Frau rufen. Ursprünglich, 1925, als Werbung für den Leningrader Staatsverlag gedacht, hat das Plakat inzwischen geradezu ikonischen Status und veran-

The Significance of Books

"Books! In all branches of knowledge!," is what Aleksander Rodchenko has a young woman shout in his 1925 poster. Originally intended as an advertisement for the Leningrad State Publishing House, the poster has now acquired an almost iconic status, illustrating the new visual language of postrevolutionary Russia with its photomontage technique, geometric lines, and striking colors. As a motif, it has been adapted and reused many times.

Among the most important tasks facing the young Soviet Union was teaching the masses to read and, in particular, emancipating women. At the same time, books and magazines were expected to employ new forms of visual design in heralding the establishment of a society marked by equality. In their new social role as workers and political subjects, women thus increasingly became the subject of illustrations, just as women graphic designers became deeply involved in their design.

Plakat, nach dem Werbeplakat „Bücher. Zu allen Wissenschaftsbereichen" von Alexander Rodtschenko für den russischen Staatsverlag GOSZIAT / Poster after the advertising poster „Books" by Aleksander Rodchenko for the Russian state publishing house GOSZIAT, 1925. Erstausgabe / First edition 2000, Die Messe der Ideen, Leipzig, Foto/photo: © Museum für Gestaltung Zürich, Plakatsammlung/Anonymous

schaulicht mit seiner Fotomontage, der geometrischen Linienführung und den plakativen Farben die neue visuelle Sprache des nachrevolutionären Russlands. Als Motiv wurde und wird es bis heute vielfach variiert.

Zu den wichtigsten Aufgaben der jungen Sowjetunion zählten die Alphabetisierung der Massen und insbesondere die Emanzipation der Frauen. Zugleich sollten Bücher und Zeitschriften mit einem neuen visuellen Erscheinungsbild vom Aufbau einer gleichberechtigten Gesellschaft künden. So waren Frauen in ihrer neuen gesellschaftlichen Rolle der berufstätigen und politisch aktiven Frau vermehrt Sujet der Abbildungen, und Grafikdesignerinnen beteiligten sich in hohem Maße an der Gestaltung.

Besondere Bedeutung hatten Kinderbücher. Mit veränderten Inhalten und experimenteller Gestaltung wollten Russinnen helfen, eine neue Generation auf den grundlegenden Wandel der Gesellschaft vorzubereiten. Eine Reihe von Grafikdesignerinnen, etwa Maria Sinjakowa und Wera Jermolajewa (1893–1937), entwickelten neue Typen von Kinderbüchern.

Die Schwestern Olga und Galina Chichagova (1886–1958 und 1891–1966) nahmen

Children's books were particularly important here. By providing new content and experimental design, Russian women sought to help prepare a new generation for the fundamental transformation of society. A number of women graphic designers, such as Maria Sinyakova and Vera Yermolayeva (1893–1937), developed new types of children's books.

Together with lyricist Nikolai Smirnov, the sisters Olga and Galina Chichagova (1886–1958 and 1891–1966) began work on what they called the "production book for children" in 1922. The aim was to teach children about the new age of technology. Characteristic for political agitation in the Soviet system was propaganda for new ideals of labor, for workers who would be energized and active. Any sentimental and romantic aspects of the world of children were to be cast aside. The Chichagova sisters had studied at the Stroganov Academy of Applied Arts in Moscow before the revolution, and then took courses in the Fundamentals Department at VKHUTEMAS before transferring to the Polygraphic Department at the same institution. From 1922, they favored working in photomontage and photography for Soviet graphic design.

1922 zusammen mit dem Texter Nikolai Smirnov die Arbeit an dem von ihnen so genannten „Produktions-Kinderbuch" auf. Kindern sollte die neue Zeit der Technik vermittelt werden. Typisch für die Agitation des Sowjetsystems war die Propaganda für neue Berufsideale, für Tatkraft und Aktivität. Alles Sentimentale und Romantische der Kinderwelt sollte keine Beachtung finden. Die Schwestern hatten vor der Revolution an der Moskauer Stroganow-Schule für angewandte Kunst studiert und anschließend Kurse an der Grundlagenabteilung der WCHUTEMAS belegt, ehe sie an die dortige Polygrafische Abteilung wechselten. Ab 1922 bevorzugten sie die Fotomontage und die Fotografie für sowjetisches Grafikdesign.

Valentina Chodassewitsch, Valentina Kulagina, Warwara Stepanowa, Natalia Pinus (1901–1986) und Jelisaweta Ignatowitsch fanden attraktive Betätigungsfelder im Bereich der zunehmend massenhaft verbreiteten Bildmedien wie Plakaten und Zeitschriften. Auch Propagandaausstellungen boten sich an, in denen Fotografie und die Fotomontage an Bedeutung gewannen.

Insbesondere Warwara Stepanowa konzentrierte sich mit Beginn der 1920er Jahre für drei Jahrzehnte auf Grafikdesign, vor allem die Gestaltung von Büchern. Gut vertraut mit den neuesten Tendenzen im In- und Ausland, verhalf sie ab 1923/24 allein und in Zusammenarbeit mit Rodtschenko Zeitschriften und Verlagen mit einer ganzheitlichen Gestaltung zu einer Art eigenem Corporate Design.

Politische Agitation

Viele Plakate hatten mit den politischen Entwicklungen zunehmend agitatorischen Charakter. Kollektivierung und Industrialisierung waren in der Sowjetunion in vollem Gange und Frauen wurden als Arbeitskräfte benötigt. Sie wurden ermutigt, eine ganze Reihe von Berufen zu ergreifen, darunter „männliche" wie Traktorfahrer oder Lokführer. Was die Agitationsplakate der Stalin-Zeit betrifft, sind weniger Entwerfer*innen bekannt, wenngleich sie zu dieser Zeit besonders gefragt waren. Viele stellten sich in den Dienst des Terrorsystems, das seine Propaganda für den neuen Staat und seine technischen und ökonomischen Errungenschaften durch die visuellen Medien lauthals verkündete. Ebenso wie beim Sozialistischen Realismus der späteren Zeit ist auch hier davon auszugehen, dass viele Frauen am Design beteiligt waren. Propaganda-Poster proklamierten, wie eine sowjetische Frau sein sollte. Frauen wurden aufgerufen, aktive

Valentina Khodasevich, Valentina Kulagina, Varvara Stepanova, Natalia Pinus (1901–1986), and Yelizaveta Ignatovich found attractive areas of work in the new visual media, with their growing mass circulation, such as posters and magazines. Propaganda exhibitions, in which photomontage and photography were becoming increasingly important, also offered artists an opportunity to showcase their work.

Varvara Stepanova in particular focused on graphic design, and above all on book design, for three decades beginning in the 1920s. Well versed in the latest trends at home and abroad, from 1923/24 onwards she employed holistic principles to help magazines and publishing houses create what we might call their own corporate design schemes, both on her own and in collaboration with Rodchenko.

Political Agitation

Political events meant that many posters took on an increasingly agitational character. Collectivization and industrialization were in full swing in the Soviet Union, and women were needed as labor. Women were encouraged to take up a whole range of occupations, including previously "male" activities such as tractor driver or train driver. Still, comparatively fewer design-

Olga & Galina Chichagova, Titelbild des Kinderbuchs /
Cover of the children's book **Puteshestvie Charli** (Die Reise von Charlie / The journey of Charlie), Gosizdat, 1924

Mitglieder der sowjetischen Gesellschaft zu sein. Mithilfe von Plakaten wurden ihnen die Vorteile dieses Lebens erklärt und in einer didaktischen Attitüde die Mängel des Lebens in der Vergangenheit.

Das Künstlerpaar Gustav Klucis und Valentina Kulagina repräsentiert die letzte Generation der russischen Avantgarde. Beide hatten sich 1920 in Moskau während des Studiums an den WCHUTEMAS kennengelernt und kurz danach geheiratet. Als überzeugte Kommunist*-innen traten sie für „Produktionskunst" ein, das heißt sie dienten mit Plakaten, Buch- und Zeitschriftenillustrationen der Propaganda für das neue System. Fotomontagen waren häufig das geeignete Medium, um das Massenpublikum mit einer Art Wirklichkeitssimulation zu erreichen. Für ihre Montagen schöpften sie aus einem ab 1924 gemeinsam angelegten „semiprivaten" Fotoarchiv. Beide blieben bis zum Tode Klucis – er fiel dem stalinistischen Terror zum Opfer und wurde 1938 hingerichtet – zusammen. Allerdings zeugen Kulaginas Tagebuchnotizen von einer durchaus ambivalenten Beziehung, in der sich die jüngere Künstlerin zur bloßen Mitarbeiterin ihres Partners degradiert fühlte.

Auch wenn infolge der Revolutionen die vollständige Gleichberechtigung der Frauen per Gesetz verankert wurde, sah die Praxis oftmals anders aus. Trotz vieler Experimente mit dem „neuen Leben" brachen patriarchale Strukturen durch. Der wirtschaftliche Niedergang und die Not während des Bürgerkriegs und der Diktatur des Stalinismus hatten Existenznöte zur Folge, denen auch Künstler*innen unterlagen. Viele von ihnen kamen zu Tode, wurden inhaftiert und ermordet.

Dennoch: Die vor- und nachrevolutionäre Zeit in Russland erlaubte den Frauen einen weder in Westeuropa noch in außereuropäischen Ländern erreichten Grad an Autonomie.

ers of agitation posters from the Stalinist era are known today, despite the fact that they were particularly in demand at the time. Many put themselves at the service of Stalin's system of terror, which employed visual media to trumpet propaganda for the new state and its technical and economic achievements. As with Socialist realism of the later Stalinist period, it can be assumed that many women were involved in design work. Propaganda posters proclaimed new ideals of a Soviet woman, calling on women to be active members of Soviet society. Posters were used to explain to women the advantages of this new way of life, along with didactic explanations of the privations of life before the revolution.

The artist couple Gustav Klutsis and Valentina Kulagina represent the last generation of the Russian avant-garde. The two met in Moscow in 1920 while studying at the VKHUTEMAS and married shortly thereafter. As convinced communists, they advocated for "production art," that is to say, they produced propaganda for the new system in the form of posters along with book and magazine illustrations. Photomontages were often the medium they chose to reach a mass audience through a kind of simulated reality. For their montages, they drew on a "semiprivate" photographic archive they had created together starting in 1924. The two remained together until Klutsis's death—he became a victim of the Stalinist terror and was executed in 1938. However, notes in Kulagina's diary testify to a quite ambivalent relationship in which the younger artist felt degraded to the status of a mere employee of her partner.

Even though the revolutions had enshrined full equality for women into law, in practice things often looked different. Despite many experiments with the "new life," patriarchal structures persisted. The economic decline and hardship during the Russian civil war and Stalin's dictatorship produced existential difficulties that also affected artists. Many of them perished as they were imprisoned and then murdered.

Nonetheless, the pre- and postrevolutionary period in Russia allowed women a degree of autonomy not achieved at the time in Western Europe or non-European countries.

Literatur
Further Reading

John E. Bowlt & Matthew Drutt (Hg./eds.): *Amazonen der Avantgarde. Alexandra Exter, Natalja Gontscharowa, Ljubow Popowa, Olga Rosanowa, Warwara Stepanowa und Nadeschda Udalzowa*, Berlin: Deutsche Guggenheim, 1999.

Ingried Brugger, Heike Eipeldauer & Florian Steininger (Hg./eds.): *Liebe in Zeiten der Revolution. Künstlerpaare der russischen Avantgarde*, Heidelberg: Kehrer, 2015.

Magdalena Dabrowski (Hg./ed.): *Ljubow Popowa*, München/Munich: Prestel Verlag, 1991.

Hubertus Gaßner & Eckhart Gillen: *Zwischen Revolutionskunst und sozialistischem Realismus. Dokumente und Kommentare. Kunstdebatten in der Sowjetunion von 1917 bis 1934*, Köln/Cologne: DuMont, 1979.

Selim Khan-Magomedov: *Vhutemas. Moscou 1920–1930*, 2 Bde./vols., Paris: Editions du Regard, 1990.

Aleksandra Michajlovna Kollontaj: *Autobiographie einer sexuell emanzipierten Kommunistin*, Berlin: Guhl, 1980.

Ada Raev: Varvara Stepanova. Konstruktivistin aus Überzeugung, in Katharina Sykora, Annette Dorgerloh, Doris Noell-Rumpeltes & Ada Raev (Hg./eds.): *Die Neue Frau. Herausforderung für die Bildmedien der Zwanziger Jahre*, Marburg: Jonas-Verl. für Kunst und Literatur, 1993: 67–82.

Ada Raev: *Russische Künstlerinnen der Moderne (1870–1930). Historische Studien. Kunstkonzepte. Weiblichkeitsentwürfe*, Habilitationsschrift / habilitation thesis, Humboldt-Universität zu Berlin 1999, München/Munich: Wilhelm Fink Verlag, 2002.

Richard Stites: *The Women's Liberation Movement in Russia. Feminism, Nihilism and Bolshevism 1860–1930*, Princeton: Princeton University Press, 1978.

Margarita Tupitsyn: *Natalia Pinus. Female Delegate, Worker, Shock-worker (1931), Soviet History*, https://sovietpropagandawordpressco.wordpress.com/women/natalia-pinus-female-delegate-worker-shock-worker/ (Abruf/accessed 10. Aug. 2022).

EXPERIMENTE IN POLITISCHER TEILHABE

EXPERIMENTS IN POLITICAL PARTICIPATION

Die Druckwerkstätten
See Red Women's Workshop,
Lenthall Road Workshop
und Notting Hill Press
The See Red Women's Workshop,
Lenthall Road Workshop,
and Notting Hill Press

Während der Unruhen im Mai 1968 besetzten Aktivist*innen das Lithografie-Studio der Kunstakademie L'École des Beaux-Arts in Paris und gründeten das Kollektiv Atelier Populaire. Dieses wollte die Streikenden der Protestbewegung gegen die Regierung Charles de Gaulles unterstützen. Ihre Plakate klebten sie an die Wände der Häuser in ganz Frankreich. Sie wurden zu den bekanntesten Dokumenten der Revolte von Studierenden im symbolischen Jahr 1968. Die Autorschaft der Aktivist*innen trat in den Hintergrund. Zudem galt das wilde Plakatieren als illegal. Heute werden die ephemeren Dokumente im Original wie Kunstwerke in einschlägigen Marketingplattformen gehandelt oder in Neuauflagen reproduziert.

Weniger bekannt ist, dass es auch Frauenkollektive gab, die sich mit ihren Plakatwerkstätten der Neuen Frauenbewegung in den 1970er Jahren verschrieben. Durch neue Drucktechniken wurde vor mehreren Dekaden, genauso wie heute, die Teilhabe an alternativen und kritischen Diskursen erleichtert, insbesondere wenn die Ressourcen preiswert und leicht zugänglich waren beziehungsweise sind. Was heute digitale Technologien sind, war in den späten 1960er und in den 1970er Jahren der Siebdruck. Vor dem Hintergrund der Neuen Frauenbewegung ermöglichten es die benutzerfreundlichen Techniken, autonome Projekte in Hinblick auf eine demokratische Partizipation, das heißt die Gleichberechtigung der Frauen, zu verwirklichen.

Sowohl in den USA als auch in Europa bildeten sich im Zuge einer Politisierung der Jugend zahlreiche kollektiv geführte Druckwerkstätten, die die mediale Autonomie der Gruppen garantieren sollten. In ihnen wurden vor allem radikale Zines, Plakate und Flyer gedruckt, teils mithilfe von professionell ausgebildeten Designer*innen oder Künstler*innen, oft aber von Amateur*innen.

Das Drucken war bis weit ins 20. Jahrhundert eines der gebräuchlichsten Werkzeuge, radikal-alternative und demokratische Ziele durchzusetzen. Kritik an der gängigen Medienpraxis von Werbung und Glanzmagazinen war ein Fokus der neuen politischen Zirkel; sie kam insbesondere von den zahlreichen linken Gruppierungen der Jugendbewegung. Auch die in diese Szene eingebettete Frauenbewegung nahm die Gelegenheit wahr, ihre Ziele über Werkstätten, die nur von Frauenkollektiven geführt wurden, zu verfolgen.

In fast allen Städten in Großbritannien gab es in dieser Zeit Frauen-Druckwerkstätten, in

See Red Women's Workshop, A Call to all Tenants, Plakat/poster, 1974
© See Red Women's Workshop

During the May 1968 riots in Paris, activists occupied the lithography studio of the L'École des Beaux-Arts and founded the collective Atelier Populaire, seeking to support strikers in the protest movement against the government of Charles de Gaulle. They affixed their posters to the walls of buildings all over France, which became the most widely known documents of the student revolts in the symbolic year of 1968. The authorship of the activists receded into the background, especially since putting up posters without permission was considered illegal. Today, the original ephemera are traded like works of art on various marketing platforms or reproduced in new editions.

What is less well known is that there were also women's collectives whose poster workshops dedicated themselves to the second-wave feminist movement in the 1970s. Then as now, new printing technologies facilitate participation in alternative and critical discourse, especially when resources are inexpensive and easily accessible. What digital technologies are today,

See Red Women's Workshop, Anfertigen eines Plakatlayouts /
Working on poster layout © See Red Women's Workshop

silk-screen printing was in the late 1960s and in the 1970s. And for second-wave feminists, user-friendly techniques made it possible to independently realize projects that expressed democratic ideals in giving women the rights and means of equal political participation.

Both in the United States and in Europe, numerous workshops run by collectives were formed as the younger generation was politicized; their aim was to guarantee the independence of the groups from larger, commercial media structures. The workshops mainly printed radical zines, posters, and flyers, sometimes with the help of professionally trained designers or artists, but often with work by amateurs.

Until well into the twentieth century, printing was one of the most common tools for realizing radically alternative, democratic goals. The new political circles, and especially the many left-wing groups of the youth movement, focused on criticizing the widespread print-media practices of advertising and producing glossy magazines. The women's movement within this scene also seized the opportunity to pursue its goals through workshops run entirely by women's collectives.

There were women's printing workshops in almost every city in Britain during this period, with some thirty in London alone. Their printing tools were often donated or purchased as used, and they used spaces that were commonly rent-free or low-rent, sometimes located in squats. Silk-screen printing and small offset lithography techniques offered the best conditions for printing inexpensively, and it was comparatively easy to learn how to use them. The women's collectives consciously pursued the goal of the *Do It Yourself* (DIY) movement, among other ideals, emphasizing, for example, a new work ethic based in non-hierarchical organization, as well as collaborative exchange of technical know-how. In most cases, their work addressed issues related to discrimination against women. They also intentionally engaged with male-identified technology in order to combat conventional gender roles and expectations. Many women's collectives were embedded in local political and social networks of others who shared their aims and were active in areas including social welfare, child care, sexual education, and health. The groups were an expression of a cultural countermovement and thus of alternative forms of self-empowerment.

Feminist women's printing collectives included Women in Print in London, Moss Side Community Press in Manchester, and the

London sollen allein 30 existiert haben. Die Druckwerkzeuge waren oft gebraucht gekauft oder gespendet, die Räume mietfrei oder hatten niedrige Mieten, manchmal befanden sie sich in besetzten Häusern. Siebdruck- und Kleinoffsetlitho-Technologien waren die besten Voraussetzungen, preiswert zu drucken, und ihre Handhabung war vergleichsweise leicht erlernbar. Die Frauenkollektive verfolgten bewusst das Ziel des Do-it-yourself (DIY) und vieles mehr: Beispielsweise legten sie Wert auf ein neues Arbeitsethos, das heißt auf eine nichthierarchische Organisation, sowie auf den partnerschaftlichen Wissensaustausch von Fähigkeiten. In den meisten Fällen behandelten sie Themen die Frauendiskriminierung betreffend. Auch setzten sie sich bewusst mit männlich identifizierter Technik auseinander, um so gegen geschlechtsspezifische Rollenzuschreibungen anzugehen. Viele Frauenkollektive waren ein-

See Red Women's Workshop, Fight the Cuts, Plakat/poster, 1975 © See Red Women's Workshop

gebettet in lokale politische und soziale Netze von Gleichgesinnten und bewegten sich unter anderem in den Bereichen soziale Fürsorge, Kinderbetreuung, sexuelle Aufklärung und Gesundheit. Sie waren Ausdruck einer kulturellen Gegenbewegung und somit einer alternativen Selbstermächtigung.

Zu den feministischen Frauendruckerei-Kollektiven zählten beispielsweise Women in Print in London, Moss Side Community Press in Manchester und die Sheffield Women's Printing Co-operative. Die bekanntesten waren das Plakat-Kollektiv See Red Women's Workshop, Lenthall Road Workshop und Notting Hill Press, alle drei in London.

See Red Women's Workshop

Gegründet wurde See Red Women's Workshop 1974 von den Kunststudentinnen Prudence Stevenson, Julia Franco and Susan Mackie. In den 16 Jahren seiner Existenz schlossen sich der Werkstatt mehr als 40 Frauen an. Ziel der Druckerei war es, der Women's-Liberation-Bewegung visuellen Ausdruck zu verleihen. Die Frauen produzierten Drucksachen aller Art, unter anderem Plakate, Postkarten, Kalender und bedruckte T-Shirts. Aber es ging nicht nur darum, *was* sie produzierten und *wie*, sondern vor allem darum: *wer* produzierte und für *wen*. Zentral war, dass sich Frauen in Solidarität untereinander übten, weshalb auch solche gruppenpsychologischen Formate wie *consciousness raising* ihre Arbeit begleiteten. Sie solidarisierten sich mit anderen Gruppierungen, die für die Befreiung von Frauen kämpften. Die Themen, die die Werkstatt bespielte, behandelten viele verwandte Anliegen der Protestbewegung wie Veröffentlichungsrechte, Flüchtlingspolitik und Rassismus, Gewalt gegen Frauen, Frauen in Gefängnissen und lesbische Rechte.

Zum Beispiel produzierte See Red Women's Workshop eine Serie von Plakaten zur Gesundheit von Frauen. Im Rahmen der Plakatserie *Our Body* visualisierte er den weiblichen Körper, klärte über Verhütung auf und vieles mehr. Über den eigenen Körper selbst zu bestimmen, war eines seiner selbsterklärten Ziele. Die Berliner Frauengruppe Brot und Rosen veröffentlichte 1972 in diesem Zusammenhang ein Frauenhandbuch mit dem Titel *Abtreibung und Verhütungsmittel*. Die Schrift wurde in der deutschen Frauenbewegung zu einem Standardwerk. Ein Jahr zuvor hatte The Boston Women's Health Collective eine Aufklärungsbroschüre mit dem Titel *Our Bodies, Ourselves* veröffentlicht, die

See Red Women's Workshop, Black Women Will Not Be Intimidated, Plakat/poster, 1980/81 © See Red Women's Workshop

Sheffield Women's Printing Co-operative. The best known were the poster collective See Red Women's Workshop, Lenthall Road Workshop, and Notting Hill Press, all three of which were located in London.

See Red Women's Workshop

See Red Women's Workshop was founded in 1974 by art students Prudence Stevenson, Julia Franco, and Susan Mackie. Over the sixteen years of its existence, more than forty women joined the workshop, which aimed to visually express ideas from the women's liberation movement. The women produced printed materials of all kinds, including posters, postcards, calendars, and printed T-shirts. Yet what mattered in their work was not only *what* they produced and *how*, but above all about *who* was producing and for *whom*. In this regard, it was crucial that the women practiced solidarity with one another, giving rise to forms of group psychology such as consciousness raising. The women showed solidarity with other groups fighting for the liberation of women. The topics the workshop covered addressed many related concerns raised by the protest movement such

See Red Women's Workshop, Girls Are Powerful, Plakat/poster, 1979 © See Red Women's Workshop

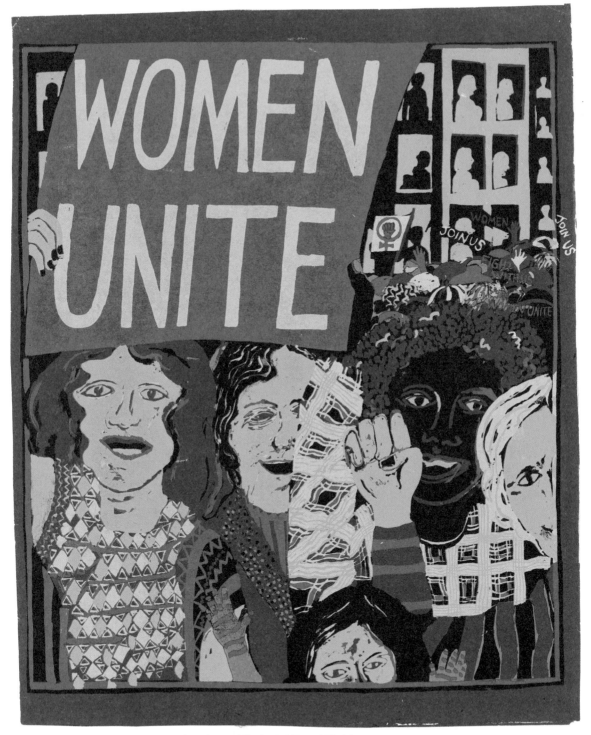

See Red Women's Workshop, Women Unite, Plakat/poster, 1973 © See Red Women's Workshop

See Red Women's Workshop, Right on Jane, Plakat/poster, 1977/78 © See Red Women's Workshop

sowohl in den USA als auch in England stark wahrgenommen wurde. Vermutlich ist der Titel der Plakatserie *Our Body* von See Red Women's Workshop diesem Vorbild entlehnt. Mit der Initiative schlossen sich die Frauen der Women's-Health-Bewegung an, das sich gegen männlich geprägte Gesundheitspolitik wandte. Indem See Red Women's Workshop das Medium Plakat nutzte, um Frauenrechte zu stärken, kritisierte er zugleich die visuelle Konsumkultur seiner Zeit, die negative Stereotypen von Frauen verbreitete.

Die Technik des Siebdrucks war zu dieser Zeit noch preiswert. Außerdem wurde sie außerordentlich attraktiv durch die Drucke von berühmten Künstlern wie Andy Warhol, der das Druckverfahren schon 1962 für seine *Marilyn*-Porträts nutzte. Auch andere Pop-Art-Künstler haben diese Technik bevorzugt wie Arthur Okamura, Robert Rauschenberg, Roy Lichtenstein und Harry Gottlieb.

Die technische Methode des Siebdrucks erforderte nur ein Minimum an Ausrüstung und konnte an jedem noch so kleinen Ort aufgebaut werden. Um 1978 hatte See Red Women's Work-

as publication rights, refugee policy and racism, violence against women, women in prisons, and lesbian rights.

See Red Women's Workshop, for example, produced a series of posters on women's health under the title of *Our Body* that visualized the female body, provided information about contraception, and much more. Having control over one's own body was one of the workshop's selfdeclared goals. And it was in the same context that the Berlin women's group Brot und Rosen published a women's handbook in 1972 entitled *Abtreibung und Verhütungsmittel* (Abortion and contraceptives). The text became a touchstone for the German women's movement. A year earlier, The Boston Women's Health Collective had published an educational brochure titled *Our Bodies, Ourselves*, which was well received in both the United States and England. The title of the poster series *Our Body* by See Red Women's Workshop was likely inspired by this brochure. This women's initiative was intended as part of the women's health movement and sought to support its aims of opposing the male domination of

Lenthall Road Workshop (Chia (Pat) Moan und Kathy Andrew), A Woman's Cycle, Plakat/poster, 1979 © Lenthall Road Workshop (Chia (Pat) Moan und Kathy Andrew)

Lenthall Road Workshop (Mo Cooling), Rolling Sisters, Plakat/poster, um/around 1983 © Lenthall Road Workshop (Mo Cooling)

shop zusätzlich eine Dunkelkammer, in der die Frauen Fotografien entwickeln konnten. Die Werkstatt zog mehrmals innerhalb Londons um. Zuletzt war sie gegenüber der Offset-Lithografie-Werkstatt Women in Print lokalisiert, und beide Gruppen benutzten gemeinsam die Dunkelkammer. Sie finanzierten sich durch Verkäufe ihrer Drucksachen und durch städtische Unterstützung.

Lenthall Road Workshop

Lenthall Road Workshop (LRW) wurde 1975 von drei Frauen, Chia Moan, Viv Mullett and Jenny Smith, als kommunale Siebdruck- und Fotografie-Werkstatt in Hackney, im Nordosten Londons, gegründet. Sie übernahmen eine schon existierende Siebdruck-Werkstatt und wandelten sie in einen *community printing workshop* um. Er diente etwa 15 Jahre lang als kommunales Zentrum.

Wie viele andere Werkstätten erhielt die Initiative finanzielle Unterstützung von kommunalen Einrichtungen wie Community Art Panel (ACGB) und von Centerprise, einer Organisation, die 1971 einen der ersten *community bookshops* eröffnete. Dort wurde unter anderem die Federation of Workers Writers and Community Publishing (FWWCP) gegründet.

Insgesamt setzten sich die Gruppen, mit denen LRW zusammenarbeitete, aus dem üblichen Spektrum der kommunalen, linken, sozialen und kulturellen Initiativen der politischen Jugendbewegung zusammen. Dazu zählten Hausbesetzer*innen, antifaschistische Gruppen, „Kinderläden" und Frauen, die in sozialen Berufen arbeiteten.

health care policy. By using the medium of the poster to strengthen women's rights, See Red Women's Workshop simultaneously criticized the ways in which the visual consumer culture of its time propagated negative stereotypes of women.

The technique of silk-screen printing was still inexpensive when the workshop was founded. It also gained extraordinary attention through the prints of famous artists such as Andy Warhol, who used the printing process as early as 1962 for his *Marilyn* portraits. Other pop artists, such as Arthur Okamura, Robert Rauschenberg, Roy Lichtenstein, and Harry Gottlieb, also favored this technique.

The advantage of the technique was that it required only a minimum of equipment and could be set up in almost any space, no matter how small. Around 1978, See Red Women's Workshop also offered a darkroom where women could develop photographs. The workshop moved several times within London, finally ending up across the street from the offset lithography workshop Women in Print, with whom it shared a darkroom. The women of workshop supported themselves by selling the items they printed, with additional financial backing from the city of London.

Lenthall Road Workshop

Lenthall Road Workshop (LRW) was founded in 1975 by three women, Chia Moan, Viv Mullett, and Jenny Smith, as a community silk-screen printing and photography workshop in Hackney, in northeast London. They took over an existing silk-screen printing workshop and transformed it into a community printing workshop, which served as a community center for some fifteen years.

Mit seiner Druckerei wollte LRW zum sozialen Wandel beitragen. Das Frauenkollektiv engagierte sich in verschiedenen lokalen Gruppen der politischen Bewegungen und sozialen Organisationen. Beispielsweise öffnete es seine Werkstatt für Schulkinder und Frauen aus der Nachbarschaft und bot Kurse im Drucken an. Ziel war es, die Sichtbarkeit von Frauen zu erhöhen, Frauen mit besonderen Bedürfnissen eine Öffentlichkeit zu verschaffen, Minderheiten in der westlichen Welt eine Stimme zu geben und generell die Vorherrschaft des „weißen Mannes" und der heteronormativen Geschlechterbeziehungen im öffentlichen Leben zu hinterfragen.

In der Ära vor der digitalen Kommunikation war ein solch kreativer Ort für den Austausch der Frauen untereinander von besonderer Bedeutung. Sie entwarfen gemeinsam Plakate und lernten Drucken in einer reinen Frauenumgebung. Von 1975 bis in die 1980er Jahre hinein arbeitete LRW zusammen mit Gruppen wie Women's Aid, der Black Lesbian and Gay Support Group und dem Hackney Urban Studies Centre. 1977 gründeten sie Hackney Girls Project, einen alternativen Jugendclub für Mädchen, lehrten Selbtverteidigungstechniken, unterstützten Sportaktivitäten und neue Netzwerke und versuchten insgesamt, Mädchen mehr Sicherheit in der städtischen Umgebung zu verschaffen.

In den 1980er Jahren gehörten zur Kerngruppe Schwarze Arbeiterfrauen. Lenthall Road Workshop war folglich vor allem daran interessiert, Frauen aus dem unmittelbaren Arbeiterviertel zu ermutigen, ihre Teilhabe an der Gesellschaft zu artikulieren, aber auch im Alltagsleben Solidarität zu erproben.[1]

Notting Hill Press

Notting Hill Press wurde 1968 von Beryl Foster und Linda Gane gegründet. Beide waren Krankenschwestern in der Ausbildung und involviert in den neu entstehenden kommunalen Aktivismus von Notting Hill, einem Stadtteil von London. Die Community rekrutierte sich aus der Häuserkampfszene und den antirassistischen Protesten, den Radikalen der Gegenkultur und einem breiten Spektrum an linksorientierten Friedensgruppen und Angehörigen der Anti-

Like many other workshops, the initiative received financial support from sources such as the Community Art Panel (of the Arts Council of Great Britain) and Centerprise, an organization that opened one of the first community bookshops in 1971. The Federation of Workers Writers and Community Publishing (FWWCP), among other organizations, was founded here.

Overall, the groups with which LRW worked were composed of the usual spectrum of community, leftist, social, and cultural initiatives from the political youth movement. These included squatters, antifascist groups, alternative cooperatively organized preschools, and women working in professions dedicated to helping others and building community.

LRW wanted its print shop to contribute to social change. The women's collective was involved in various local groups from related political movements and social organizations. It opened its workshop to school children and women from the neighborhood, for instance, offering courses in printing. Its goal was to increase the visibility of women, to provide a public sphere for women with particular needs, to give a voice to minorities in the Western world, and to generally challenge the dominance of "White men" and of heteronormative gender relations in public life.

In the era before digital communications, a creative site of this kind played a particularly important role in enabling sharing between women. Women collaborated in designing posters and learned print-making in an all-women environment. From 1975 into the 1980s, LRW worked with groups such as Women's Aid, the Black Lesbian and Gay Support Group, and the Hackney Urban Studies Centre. In 1977, they founded Hackney Girls Project, an alternative youth club for girls, taught self-defense techniques, supported sports activities and new networks, and in general tried to make girls feel safer in the urban environment.

In the 1980s, the core group included Black working-class women. Lenthall Road Workshop was accordingly primarily interested in encouraging women from the surrounding working-class neighborhood to claim equal rights and an equal place in the community, while also advancing strategies of solidarity in everyday life.[1]

1 Siehe Rebecca Odell: *Women on Screens. Printmaking, Photography and Community Activism at Lenthall Road Workshop 1970s–1990s*, 30. Jun. 2022, https://hackneyhistories.hackney.gov.uk/2022/06/30/lenthall-road-workshop-1970s-1990s-beginnings/ (Abruf 15. Aug. 2022). Unter demselben Titel wurde 2019 eine Ausstellung im Hackney Museum gezeigt.

1 See Rebecca Odell: *Women on Screens: Printmaking, Photography and Community Activism at Lenthall Road Workshop 1970s–1990s*, 30. Jun. 2022, https://hackneyhistories.hackney.gov.uk/2022/06/30/lenthall-road-workshop-1970s-1990s-beginning/ (accessed 15. Aug. 2022). An exhibition was shown at the Hackney Museum in 2019 under the same title.

Vietnam-Krieg-Bewegung. Mit der Notting Hill People's Association bildete sich eine informelle Plattform der verschiedenen Initiativen. Vor diesem Hintergrund erwarben Foster und Gaines eine *offset litho printing press*, absolvierten einen zweiwöchigen Ausbildungskurs und gründeten Notting Hill Press (NHP).

Die besondere Attraktivität von Druckereiwerkstätten wie NHP beschreibt Foster im Rückblick folgendermaßen: „In the 1960's printing was a powerful medium. Organisations, groups and movements all sought to get their message across to others and to put their information in print. [...] Controlling the means of production had a particular appeal to anyone wanting to make a revolution and the offset lithographic process could make these means more affordable and flexible. It could deliver long runs, colour printing, flexible graphics and even photographs."[2]

NHP war von entscheidender Bedeutung für die wöchentlich erscheinende Zeitschrift *People's News*. Das Magazin trug dazu bei, die heterogenen Gruppierungen der alternativen Szene von Notting Hill und ihre übergreifenden gemeinsamen Interessen zu verbinden. Es druckte die gesamte Bandbreite der Themen des Stadtteils ab: vom Wohnungswesen über Streiks, von radikalen Zeitungen der Schwarzen Bürger des Stadtteils über alternative neue Unternehmen bis hin zu den Anliegen der offenen Jugendarbeit und der lokalen Skinheads. Mit diesem breiten Spektrum von Aktivitäten und Orientierungen fungierte das Blatt als eine Art Nachbarschaftshilfe in der alternativen Szene.

Die Druckerei durchlief verschiedene Stadien und kursierte unter mehreren Namen wie Cress Press, Printshop West 11 und Words Illustrated, blieb aber in ihrer sozialen und politischen Ausrichtung konstant.

Notting Hill Press

Notting Hill Press was founded in 1968 by Beryl Foster and Linda Gane. Both women were nurses in training who were engaged in the emerging community activism of Notting Hill, a borough of London. The community recruited members from the scene of militant urban squatters and antiracist protesters, counterculture radicals, and a broad spectrum of left-leaning groups fighting for peace, as well as members of the anti-Vietnam War movement. The Notting Hill People's Association took shape as an informal platform for these various initiatives. It was in this context that Foster and Gaines purchased an offset litho printing press, completed a two-week training course, and founded Notting Hill Press (NHP).

Looking back, Foster describes the special appeal of print shops such as NHP as follows: "In the 1960's, printing was a powerful medium. Organisations, groups and movements all sought to get their message across to others and to put their information in print. ... Controlling the means of production had a particular appeal to anyone wanting to make a revolution and the offset lithographic process could make these means more affordable and flexible. It could deliver long runs, colour printing, flexible graphics and even photographs."[2]

NHP was crucial for the weekly magazine *People's News*. The magazine helped to connect the widely different groups from Notting Hill's alternative scene and their overarching common interests. It printed work reflecting the entire spectrum of pressing issues and topics in the borough: housing availability, strikes, radical newspapers run by members of the Black community, alternative new businesses, the concerns of independent youth work, and local skinheads. With its broad range of activities and orientations, the paper functioned as a kind of neighborhood community center for the alternative scene.

The print store went through various stages and several names, including the Cress Press, Printshop West 11, and Words Illustrated, but its social and political aims remained unchanged.

2 Foster, 2017, zit. nach https://blogs.bl.uk/english-anddrama/2020/03/community-printing-in-north-kensington-the-beryl-foster-archive.html (Abruf 15. Aug. 2022).

2 Foster, 2017, quoted from https://blogs.bl.uk/english-and-drama/2020/03/community-printing-in-north-kensington-the-beryl-foster-archive.html (accessed 15. Aug. 2022).

Literatur
Further Reading

Jess Baines: Experiments in Democratic Participation:
Feminist Printshop Collectives, *Cultural Policy, Criticism and
Management Research*, Nr./no. 6 (Herbst/Autum 2012): 29–51.

Eileen Cadman, Gail Chester & Agnes Pivot:
Rolling Our Own. Women As Printers, Publishers and Distributors,
London: Minority Press Group, 1981.

David Crowley: Design Magazines and Design Culture,
in Rick Poynor (Hg./ed.): *Communicate! British Independent
Graphic Design*, London: Lawrence King, 2004: 182–199.

Carol Kenna, Lynn Medcalf & Rick Walker:
Printing is Easy ...? Community Printshops 1970–1986,
London: Greenwich Mural Workshop, 1986.

Rebecca Odell: Women on Screens. Printmaking, Photography and
Community Activism at Lenthall Road Workshop 1970s–1990s,
30. Jun. 2022, https://hackneyhistories.hackney.gov.uk/2022/06/30/
lenthall-road-workshop-1970s-1990s-beginnings/
(Abruf/accessed 15. Aug. 2022).

Prudence Stevenson, Susan Mackie, Anne Robinson & Jess Baines:
See Red Women's Workshop. Feminist Posters 1974–1990,
London: Four Corners Books, 2016.

FRAUEN IM BUCH-GEWERBE

WOMEN IN THE BOOK TRADE

Kontinuität feministischer
Selbstermächtigung
Continuities of Feminist
Self-Empowerment

1893 – Distaff Series des Woman's Building, Chicago

Unter der Leitung von Candace Wheeler, einer herausragenden US-amerikanischen Designerin und Mäzenin, wurden sechs kleine Bücher über künstlerische Arbeiten von Frauen 1893 im Woman's Building auf der Weltausstellung in Chicago ediert. Ihr Titel lautete *Distaff Series*.[1] Die Booklets waren mit der Schreibmaschine geschrieben. Sie kosteten nur je einen Dollar und konnten in der Bibliothek des Woman's Building erworben werden.

Mehr als 39 Artikel wurden für die *Distaff Series* gesammelt, die Veröffentlichung übernahm der Verlag Harper & Brothers. Sie hatten Titel wie „Woman and the Higher Education", verfasst von Anna C. Brackett. Auch einige literarische Texte von Autor*innen waren dabei. Candace Wheeler steuerte neben „Household Art" zwei weitere Essays bei: „The Philosophy of Beauty Applied to House Interiors" und „Decorative and Applied Art". Die Grafikdesignerin Alice C. Morse entwarf die Einbände der *Distaff Series*.

Vermutlich bildete diese Initiative den Auftakt für die Herausgabe vergleichbarer Veröffentlichungen von Frauen im Buchgewerbe zu späteren Zeiten.

1902 – Guild of Women-Binders: über die Zukunft des Buchbindens

Ein weiteres Beispiel für den Hinweis auf weitgehend unentdeckte Frauen im Buchgewerbe war der 1902 von der Guild of Women-Binders herausgegebene Band *The Bindings of To-morrow. A Record of the Work of the Guild of Women-Binders and of the Hampstead Bindery*.[2] Die Guild of Women-Binders war ein Kollektiv von Künstlerinnen, das eine Vielzahl von sorgfältig gestalteten Bucheinbänden in der Zeit zwischen 1898 und 1904 herstellte und vertrieb. Es wurde von Frank (Francis) Karslake (1864–1917), Buchantiquar und

Dun Emer Press bei der Arbeit, mit Elizabeth Corbet Yeats vor der Handpresse, Beatrice Cassidy mit der Tintenrolle, Esther Ryan beim Korrigieren der Andrucke / The Dun Emer Press at work: Elizabeth Corbet Yeats standing at the hand press, Beatrice Cassidy standing to roll ink, Esther Ryan at a table correcting proofs, um/around 1903

1893—The Distaff Series of the Woman's Building, Chicago

Under the direction of Candace Wheeler, a prominent American designer and patron of the arts, six small books of women's artistic works were produced in 1893 in the Woman's Building at the Chicago World's Fair. Their title was *Distaff Series*. The booklets were typewritten, cost only a dollar each, and could be purchased at the Woman's Building Library.

More than thirty-nine articles were collected for the *Distaff Series* and published by Harper & Brothers, with titles like "Woman and the Higher Education," written by Anna C. Brackett. The series also included some literary texts. Candace Wheeler contributed two essays in addition to "Household Art": "The Philosophy of Beauty Applied to House Interiors" and "Decorative and

[1] Die Bibliothek der Harvard University gibt Einblick in zwei der Bücher unter der Rubrik „CURIOSity Digital Collections", siehe: https://curiosity.lib.harvard.edu/women-working-1800-1930/catalog?f%5Bplace-of-origin_ssim%5D%5B%5D=New+York&f%5Bseries_ssim%5D%5B%5D=Distaff+series&f%5Bseries_ssim%5D%5B%5D=The+distaff+series&view=list (Abruf 24. Aug. 2022). Siehe auch das Kapitel Wayne A. Wiegand, Sarah Wadsworth: „By Invitation Only". The American Library Association and the Women's Building Library of the World's Columbian Exposition, in Mary Hawkesworth (Hg.): *Feminist Practises. Signs on the Syllabus*, unpaginiert, digitale Version abrufbar als *digital reader* der University of Chicago Press.

[2] *The Bindings of To-morrow. A Record of the Work of the Guild of Women-Binders and of the Hampstead Bindery*, mit einer kritischen Einleitung von G. Elliot Anstruther, London: Printed for the Guild of Women-Binders, 1902.

Buchhändler mit einem Buchladen in Charing Cross, London, ins Leben gerufen.

Die Initiative betonte die Tradition eines weiblichen Handwerks, das mit dem Herstellen und Gestalten von Manuskripten in westeuropäischen Ordenshäusern eine lange Tradition hatte. Ein urkundliches Dokument im Kloster San Jacopo di Ripoli in Florenz von 1476 verweist beispielsweise auf Frauen, die als Druckerinnen gearbeitet haben. Junge Frauen wurden oft von ihren Vätern oder Ehemännern ausgebildet, um die Arbeit in den Druckereien zu unterstützen, nicht selten übernahmen sie nach dem Tod ihrer männlichen Verwandten die Leitung der Unternehmen.

Im 19. Jahrhundert war das Druckergewerbe sowohl in Europa als auch in den Vereinigten Staaten von Männerzünften beherrscht. Frauen durften nur schlecht bezahlte Hilfsarbeiten ausüben. Doch es gab Ausnahmen. Die Frauenrechtlerin und Verlegerin Emily Faithfull (1835–1895) zum Beispiel gründete 1860 die Victoria Press in London, um Frauen das Handwerk zu lehren. Frauen waren hier als Buchdruckerinnen beschäftigt, Männer übernahmen nur einen Teil der Pressearbeit, vor allem schwere körperliche Arbeit. Trotz Feindseligkeiten in der Druckergewerkschaft und Sabotageakten erwarb sich die Victoria Press großes Renommee. Königin Victoria ernannte sie sogar zum „Printer and Publisher in Ordinary to Her Majesty".

Die Irin Elizabeth Corbet Yeats (1868–1940) gründete die Dun Emer Press, um junge Frauen in der Berufsausbildung als Druckerinnen praktisch zu trainieren. Die Dun Emer Guild (1902–1964) war ein irischer Textilworkshop, der 1902 von Evelyn Gleeson zusammen mit Elizabeth und Lily Yeats unter dem Namen Dun Emer Industries and Press entstand. Yeats zählte zum Kreis um William Morris in London, war von dessen sozialen und politischen Ideen beeinflusst und der Arts-and-Crafts-Bewegung sowie der Celtic Renaissance verbunden.

Eine der ersten Druckereien in den USA, deren Besitzerinnen Frauen waren, war die Women's Co-operative Printing Union, 1868 in San Francisco gegründet. Augusta Lewis Troup (1848–1920), Journalistin und Setzerin für Susan B. Anthonys Zeitung *The Revolution*, wurde 1870 zur korrespondierenden Sekretärin der International Typographical Union gewählt, eine der ersten Frauen in einem nationalen Gewerkschaftsbüro. Ab der Mitte des 19. Jahrhunderts fanden die Frauen vor allem Unterstützung durch die Arts-and-Crafts-Bewegung.

Applied Art." The covers for the series were designed by graphic designer Alice C. Morse.[1]

This initiative likely set the stage for comparable publications by women in the book trade in later years.

1902—Guild of Women-Binders: On the Future of Bookbinding

Another example pointing to largely undiscovered women in the book trade was the 1902 volume published by the Guild of Women-Binders, *The Bindings of To-morrow: A Record of the Work of the Guild of Women-Binders and of the Hampstead Bindery*.[2] The Guild of Women-Binders was a collective of women artists who produced and distributed a variety of carefully designed book bindings between 1898 and 1904. The guild was started by Frank (Francis) Karslake (1864–1917), a seller of new and antique books with a shop in Charing Cross, London.

The initiative emphasized the tradition of a female craft that had a long history in Western European ecclesiastical orders in the production and design of manuscripts. An official document in the monastery of San Jacopo di Ripoli in Florence from 1476, for example, refers to women who worked as printers. Young women were often trained by their fathers or husbands to assist with the work in the print shops, and not infrequently they took over the management of the ventures after the death of their male relatives.

In the nineteenth century, the printing trade in both Europe and the United States was dominated by male guilds. Women were only allowed to do poorly paid, unskilled work. But there were exceptions. Women's rights activist and publisher Emily Faithfull (1835–1895), for example, founded the Victoria Press in London in 1860 to teach women the craft. Women were employed at this press as book printers, while men took on only part of the production

---

1 Harvard University library gives a glimpse of two of the books under the rubric of "CURIOSity Digital Collections"; see https://curiosity.lib. harvard.edu/women-working-1800-1930/catalog?f[place-of-origin_ ssim][]=New+York&f[series_ssim][]=Distaff+series&f[series_ssim] []=The+distaff+series&view=list (accessed 24. Aug. 2022). See also the chapter Wayne A. Wiegand, Sarah Wadsworth: By Invitation Only: The American Library Association and the Women's Building Library of the World's Columbian Exposition, Chicago, 1893, in Mary Hawkesworth (ed.): *Feminist Practices: Signs on the Syllabus*, unpaginated, digital version available as a digital reader from the University of Chicago Press.

2 *The Bindings of To-morrow: A Record of the Work of the Guild of Women-Binders and of the Hampstead Bindery*, with a critical introduction by G. Elliot Anstruther, London: Printed for the Guild of Women-Binders, 1902.

WE WERE CONVINCED THAT IF WE WERE TO BE HEARD, IF OUR WORDS WERE TO BE PUBLISHED, WE WOULD HAVE TO CONTROL THE PROCESS OF PUBLISHING. AND THAT, FOR US AT THAT TIME, MEANT LEARNING TO PRINT.

Lilian Mohin, 1993

A Typografic Discourse →
for The Distaff Side of Printing, a book by ladies

From Jane Grabhorn's typographic laboratory
Jumbo Press San Francisco 1937

Bookmaking on the Distaff Side (A Typografic Discourse for The Distaff Side of Printing: A Book by Ladies. From Jane Grabhorn's Typographic Laboratory, von/by Jane Grabhorn), New York: Distaff Side, 1937, Graphic Arts Division, Princeton University Library

Bekannt ist auch die private Druckerei Hogarth Press des Ehemanns der Schriftstellerin Virginia Woolf (1882–1941), in der beide limitierte und künstlerisch wertvoll gestaltete Belletristik produzierten. Bertha Matilda Sprinks Goudy (1869–1935), eine amerikanische Typografin und Mitinhaberin der Village Press, hat sich ebenso einen Namen gemacht wie Jane Bissell Grabhorn (1911–1973), eine amerikanische Künstlerin, Typografin, Buchbinderin und Druckerin, die in der Grabhorn Press ihres Ehemanns und dessen Bruders arbeitete. 1937 eröffnete sie eine eigene Druckerei, die Jumbo Press, die für ihre experimentelle und künstlerische Ausrichtung bekannt wurde.

Doch viele Frauen blieben unbekannt. *The Bindings of To-morrow* wollte sie wieder ins Gedächtnis rufen.

work—mainly heavy physical labor on the presses. Despite hostilities in the printers' union and acts of sabotage, the Victoria Press earned a vaunted reputation, even being appointed by Queen Victoria as "Printer and Publisher in Ordinary to Her Majesty."

Irishwoman Elizabeth Corbet Yeats (1868–1940) founded the Dun Emer Press to provide young women vocational training as printers. The Dun Emer Guild (1902–1964) was an Irish textile workshop established in 1902 by Evelyn Gleeson with Elizabeth and Lily Yeats under the name Dun Emer Industries and *Press*. Yeats belonged to the circle surrounding William Morris in London, was influenced by his social and political ideas, and was associated with the arts and crafts movement and the Celtic renaissance.

One of the first printing companies in the United States to be owned by women was the Women's Co-Operative Printing Union, founded in San Francisco in 1868. Augusta Lewis Troup (1848–1920), journalist and typesetter for Susan B. Anthony's newspaper *The Revolution*, was elected corresponding secretary of the International Typographical Union in 1870, as one of the first women in a national union office. Beginning in the mid-nineteenth century, women found support primarily through the arts and crafts movement.

Another well-known press was the private printing house Hogarth Press owned by the husband of the writer Virginia Woolf (1882–1941), which published limited editions and belles lettres featuring sophisticated artistic design. Bertha Matilda Sprinks Goudy (1869–1935), an American typographer and coowner of the Village Press, made her mark, as did Jane Bissell Grabhorn (1911–1973), an American artist, typographer, bookbinder, and printer who worked at the Grabhorn Press, owned by her husband and his brother. In 1937, she opened her own print shop, the Jumbo Press, which became known for its experimental and artistic approach.

Many women in the book trade nevertheless remained unknown. *The Bindings of To-morrow* sought to rekindle their memory.

1937 – Kritik am herkömmlichen Buchgewerbe: Bookmaking on the Distaff Side

Geradezu ikonischen Charakter unter denjenigen Frauen, die mit dem Buchgewerbe zu tun haben, hat das Buch *Bookmaking on the Distaff Side*. Es wurde 1937 von einer kollaborati-

1937—Criticism of the Conventional Book Trade: Bookmaking on the Distaff Side

One book that enjoyed nearly iconic status among women involved with the book trade was *Bookmaking on the Distaff Side*, named after a collaborative association of American women

ven Vereinigung amerikanischer Verlegerinnen mit dem Namen Distaff Side herausgegeben. Angeführt wurde die Gruppe von Edna Beilenson (1909–1981). Das Buch ist nur in einer Auflage von 100 Exemplaren erschienen und deshalb heute sehr selten in Sammlungen oder auf dem antiquarischen Markt zu finden.

Bookmaking on the Distaff Side wurde ausschließlich von Frauen gestaltet und gedruckt. Das Buch vereint Beiträge von Schriftstellerinnen, Grafikdesignerinnen, Buchbinderinnen, Typografinnen, Illustratorinnen und Verlegerinnen aus verschiedenen kleinen Druckereien. Enthalten sind Essays, Satiren, persönliche Erfahrungen, Gedichte, programmatische Texte und typografische Experimente. Die Gestaltung zeichnet sich aus durch unterschiedliche Papier- und Schriftarten sowie ein individuelles Layout für die Beiträge. Da die einzelnen kleinen Verlage, die einen Beitrag lieferten, in der Tradition der Private-Press-Bewegung standen, sind die Essays äußerst sorgsam, manchmal per Hand, gefertigt. Der Name der Grafikdesignerinnen und anderer Mitarbeiter*innen ist jeweils erwähnt. Wie Edna Beilenson bemerkte, war das Buch aus der Empörung heraus geschrieben worden, dass Frauen im Buchgewerbe zu wenig Aufmerksamkeit erfuhren. Das Buch sollte einen überzeugenden Beitrag zur Geschichte des weiblichen Buchgewerbes leisten. Es wurde zusammengestellt, gebunden und veröffentlicht von Jumbo Press.

Edna Beilenson war eine amerikanische Typografin, Druckerin, Schriftsetzerin und Grafikdesignerin. Von 1931 bis zum Tod ihres Ehemannes Peter Beilenson 1962 war sie Mitinhaberin der bibliophilen Peter Pauper Press und danach alleinige Inhaberin bis zu ihrem Tod 1981.

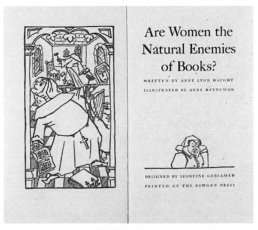

Bookmaking on the Distaff Side (Are Women the Natural Enemies of Books? von/by Anne Lyon Haight), New York: Distaff Side, 1937, Graphic Arts Division, Princeton University Library

publishers, Distaff Side, who published it in 1937. The group was led by Edna Beilenson (1909–1981). Published in an edition of just one hundred copies, the work is now extremely rare in collections or on the antiquarian market.

Bookmaking on the Distaff Side was designed and printed exclusively by women. It brings together contributions from women working as writers, graphic designers, bookbinders, typographers, illustrators, and publishers at various small presses. The contributions comprise essays, satires, personal experiences, poems, programmatic texts, and typographic experiments. The design is distinguished by various types of paper and typographies, as well as a customized layout for the articles. Because the individual small publishers who contributed hailed from the tradition of the private press movement, the essays are extremely carefully crafted, sometimes by hand. The names of the women who worked as graphic designers and other collaborators are mentioned in each case. As Edna Beilenson noted, the book was motivated by outrage that women were not receiving enough attention in the book trade. It was intended to make a compelling contribution to the history of women in the field. It was edited, bound, and published by Jumbo Press.

Edna Beilenson was an American typographer, printer, typesetter, and graphic designer. From 1931 until the death of her husband, Peter Beilenson, in 1962, she was coowner of the bibliophile Peter Pauper Press and then sole owner until her death in 1981. Under her leadership, members of the collective endeavor later founded the Distaff Press, which published several issues on women and the book trade. Over the course of her life, she acquired a considerable reputation, being elected the first president of the American Institute of Graphic Arts (AIGA), a position she held from 1958 to 1960.

In *Bookmaking on the Distaff Side*, Biruta Sesnan wrote a piece titled "CPW," meaning Club of Printing Women. The contribution was designed by the members of the club and printed by Kalkhoff Press, New York. Jane Grabhorn composed "A Typographic Discourse for The Distaff Side of Printing. A Book by Ladies: From Jane Grabhorn's Typographic Laboratory," while Edna K. Rushmore wrote about two women printers from the American colonial period. The article was hand typeset by hand and printed by The Golden Hind Press in Madison, New Jersey.

Jessica Thompson published "A Short History of Ladies-in-Printing in Connecticut: Based on Some Very Thorough, Careful, &

Fred & Bertha Goudy, Werbemarke von / Advertising stamp from The Village Press, 1904

Unter ihrer Führung gründeten Mitglieder des kollektiven Werks später die Distaff Press, die mehrere Ausgaben zum Thema Frauen und Buchgewerbe veröffentlichte. Im Laufe ihres Lebens hat sie sich ein beachtliches Renommee erworben: Sie wurde zur ersten Präsidentin des American Institute of Graphic Arts (AIGA) gewählt, eine Position, die sie von 1958 bis 1960 innehatte.

Biruta Sesnan schrieb in *Bookmaking on the Distaff Side* einen Beitrag mit dem Titel „CPW". Die Initialen standen für Club of Printing Women. Gestaltet wurde der Artikel von den Mitgliedern ebenjenes Clubs, gedruckt wurde er bei der Kalkhoff Press, New York. Jane Grabhorn verfasste „A Typografic Discourse for The Distaff Side of Printing: A Book by Ladies: From Jane Grabhorn's Typographic Laboratory". Edna K. Rushmore schrieb über zwei Druckerinnen aus der amerikanischen Kolonialzeit. Der Artikel war von Hand gesetzt und wurde von The Golden Hind Press, Madison, New Jersey, gedruckt.

Jessica Thompson veröffentlichte „A Short History of Ladies-in-Printing in Connecticut: Based on Some Very Thorough, Careful, & Exhausting Guesswork." Edna Beilenson gab „Men in Printing" heraus, gestaltete ihren Text selbst und druckte ihn bei der Peter Pauper Press. Mary D. Alexander wiederum veröffentlichte „A Few Disadvantages of Being a Woman", gestaltet und gedruckt ebenfalls von ihr selbst bei der University of Chicago Press.

Exhausting Guesswork." Edna Beilenson published "Men in Printing," designing her own text in an edition produced by the Peter Pauper Press. Mary D. Alexander, in turn, published "A Few Disadvantages of Being a Woman," also designed and printed by herself at the University of Chicago Press.

Anne Lyon Haight (1891–1977), an American author and rare book collector, became well known with the essay "Are Women the Natural Enemies of Books?" The title refers to William Blake's *The Enemies of Books* from 1880, which enumerated fire, ignorance, bookworms, bookbinders, collectors, and even children among the book's foes. Blake's list does not mention women, but as Haight points out, history offered enough examples of women described as enemies of books.

One of many other contributions was a letter that Gertrud Stein offered for publication.

One of two texts that stood out in being written by a man was a remembrance of his wife by the renowned typographer Frederic W. Goudy. She, too, was a typographer, who had worked with him at the jointly owned Village Press and passed away two years before the book was published. Frederic W. Goudy named his one hundredth typeface Bertham in her memory. Two years later, he also published a tribute to her under the title *Bertha M. Goudy: Recollections by One Who Knew Her Best* (Marlboro, NY:

Bekannt wurde Anne Lyon Haight mit „Are Women the Natural Enemies of Books?". Haight (1891-1977) war eine amerikanische Autorin und Sammlerin von seltenen Büchern. Mit dem Titel bezieht sie sich auf William Blakes *The Enemies of Books* von 1880, der alle Feinde von Büchern auflistet – Feuer, Ignoranz, Bücherwürmer, Buchbinder, Sammler bis hin zu Kindern. Frauen sind zwar in der Aufzählung nicht erwähnt, aber, wie die Autorin meinte, gab es genug Beispiele in der Geschichte, die Frauen als Feinde von Büchern beschrieben.

Einer von vielen weiteren Beiträgen war ein Brief von Gertrud Stein, den sie für die Veröffentlichung zur Verfügung stellte.

Eine von zwei männlichen Ausnahmen unter den Texten von Frauen war der renommierte Typograf Frederic W. Goudy, der die Erinnerungen an seine Frau Bertha M. Goudy herausgab. Sie war ebenfalls eine Typografin gewesen, die mit ihm in der gemeinsamen Village Press zusammenarbeitete. Zwei Jahre zuvor war sie gestorben. Frederic W. Goudy bezeichnete seine hundertste Schrifttype Bertham, in Erinnerung an seine Frau. Zwei Jahre später wiederum veröffentlichte er eine Hommage an seine Frau unter dem Titel: *Bertha M. Goudy: Recollections by One Who Knew Her Best* (Marlboro, NY: The Village Press, 1939), und die Frauen der Distaff Press publizierten 1958 *Bertha S. Goudy: First Lady of Printing.*

1980er und 1990er Jahre – Frauenbuchläden und die Women-in-Print-Bewegung

In den 1970er und 1980er Jahren entstanden auf breiter Ebene und in vielen Ländern Frauenbuchläden. Sie konzentrierten sich auf Literatur von Frauen, feministische Theorie, Kinderliteratur, Gesundheitsbücher für Frauen und sämtliche Formen gedruckter Arbeiten, die von Frauen gestaltet waren: Bücher, Plakate, Magazine, Pamphlete, Broschüren, Handzettel. Die Öffentlichkeit, die durch Druck-Erzeugnisse hervorgerufen wurde, war für die Frauenbewegung außerordentlich wichtig. Sprache wurde zudem als ein Werkzeug betrachtet, das Ausschluss und Unterdrückung bewirken konnte. Genauso aber konnten Worte in Form von Reden, Pamphleten, Poesie oder Polemik Instrumente der Befreiung sein.

Der erste Frauenbuchladen in den 1970er Jahren war Amazon in Minneapolis und ICI: A Woman's Place in Oakland, USA. Im Laufe der nächsten beiden Dekaden entstanden viele ver-

The Village Press, 1939), and in 1958 the women of the Distaff Press published *Bertha S. Goudy: First Lady of Printing.*

The 1980s and 1990s: Women's Bookstores and the Women in Print Movement

In the 1970s and 1980s, women's bookstores emerged on a broad scale in many countries. They focused on literature by women, feminist theory, children's literature, women's health books, and all kinds of printed works designed by women, whether books, posters, magazines, pamphlets, brochures, or handbills. The public sphere generated and sustained by this printed matter was extremely important for the women's movement. Language was regarded as a tool with the power to exclude or oppress—and yet it could also serve, in speeches, pamphlets, poetry, or debates, as an instrument of liberation.

The first women's bookstore in the 1970s was Amazon in Minneapolis and ICI: A Woman's Place in Oakland, California. Over the next two decades, many similar shops sprang up, especially in North America. These establishments were an integral part of the women in print movement, which was driven by the initiative of women themselves and dovetailed with the work of women activists aiming to create a female public sphere. Its authors included feminists of color, such as Audre Lorde, June Jordan, bell hooks, and Gloria Anzaldúa. And among feminist publishers, or those associated with feminism, one name stands out: Kitchen Table: Women of Color Press, which was closely allied with the National Black Feminist Organization (NBFC). The publishing house also served as an international platform for women of color, distributing titles, for instance, from other independent small presses. It influenced women activists in liberation movements across the globe, including in Latin American countries. The publisher also sought with its work to challenge heterosexual norms and to give voice to LGBTQT+ individuals.

Another venture was Onlywomen Press, an early radical feminist publisher and printer founded in London in 1974 by lesbians Lilian Mohin, Sheila Shulman, and Deborah Hart. Lesbian feminism was defined not merely by sexual orientation; rather, like feminism in general, as well as lesbian and gay studies and queer theory, it articulated a fundamental critique that bound together the various concerns of these allied movements, challenging heteronormative under-

gleichbare Läden, vor allem in Nordamerika. Sie waren ein integraler Bestandteil der Women-in-Print-Bewegung, das auf Eigeninitiative beruhte und mit aktivistischen Frauen korrespondierte, die eine weibliche Öffentlichkeit herstellen wollten. Zu den Autorinnen gehörten Feminists of Color, darunter Audre Lorde, June Jordan, bell hooks und Gloria Anzaldúa. Zu diesen feministischen Verlagen, wie auch denjenigen, die dem Feminismus verbunden waren, zählte Kitchen Table: Women of Color Press, der der National Black Feminist Organisation (NBFC) nahestand. Der Verlag diente auch als internationale Plattform für Women of Color, zum Beispiel vertrieb er Titel anderer unabhängiger kleiner Druckereien. Er beeinflusste Aktivistinnen der Befreiungsbewegungen, unter anderem in lateinamerikanischen Ländern. Durch ihre Arbeit versuchte der Verlag zugleich, heterosexuelle Normen in Frage zu stellen und LGBTQ (Abkürzung für Lesbian, Gay, Bisexual, Transgender, Queer) eine Stimme zu geben.

Ein weiteres Unternehmen war Onlywomen Press, ein früher radikaler feministischer Verlag mit Druckerei, der 1974 in London von den Lesben Lilian Mohin, Sheila Shulman und Deborah Hart gegründet wurde. Lesbischer Feminismus ist nicht allein durch eine sexuelle Orientierung charakterisiert, sondern verbindet, ähnlich wie der Feminismus generell sowie die Lesben- und Schwulenforschung und die Queer-Theorie, die verschiedenen Initiativen durch seine grundsätzliche Kritik: Er stellt die heterosexuellen Geschlechtervorstellungen als Norm infrage und arbeitet systematische Zusammenhänge heraus. Grundsätzlich ist dieser Feminismus deshalb intersektional orientiert.

2020 – Natural Enemies of Books.
A Messy History of Women in Printing
and Typography

Seit der Mitte des 20. Jahrhunderts hat sich die Situation für Frauen im Buchgewerbe grundlegend verändert: Frauen übernahmen Druckarbeiten und Grafikdesign jeder Art, von der Leitung einer Zeitung und Zeitschrift wie die legendäre US-amerikanische Verlegerin und Herausgeberin Katharine („Kay") Graham bis hin zur technischen Leitung von Druckereien. Ein sehr hoher Prozentsatz von Positionen im amerikanischen Buchgewerbe ist von Frauen besetzt, wenngleich der Tatbestand des Gender-Pay-Gap und der Mangel an Frauen in leitenden Positionen nicht aufgehoben ist.

standings of gender and elaborating the systematic underpinnings of discrimination or oppression. Such an approach is what makes this kind of feminism fundamentally intersectional.

2020—Natural Enemies of Books:
A Messy History of Women in Printing
and Typography

Since the middle of the twentieth century, the situation for women in the book trade has changed radically: women have taken over print work and graphic design of every kind, from running newspapers and magazines (as the legendary American publisher and editor Katharine "Kay" Graham did) to directing the technical work of print shops. A very high percentage of positions in the American book industry are held by women, although the reality of the gender pay gap and the lack of women in senior positions persists.

In 2020, the collective of graphic designers MMS (Maryam Fanni, Matilda Flodmark, and Sara Kaaman) from Sweden published a book titled *Natural Enemies of Books: A Messy History of Women in Printing and Typography* with Occasional Papers press. The title refers to Anne Lyon Haight's essay "Are Women the Natural Enemies of Books?," which appeared in 1937 in *Bookmaking on the Distaff Side*, with the publication of this essay figuring prominently in MMS's account. Among other things, the collective examines how working and living conditions have changed for women graphic designers since 1937.

Focusing on the labor movement in Sweden in addition to feminism, MMS aims to follow the example of its predecessors in making voices heard who would otherwise remain silent. The women they foreground include Jess Baines of See Red Women's Workshop, the second-wave feminist, left-wing group run as a women's collective that produced silk-screen protest posters in London in the 1970s and 1980s as a way of strengthening their local community. Figures emphasized by MMS also include women historians, graphic designers, writers, journalists, and economists, as well as members of trade and labor unions, who have played a significant part in the often-precarious situation of women in today's book trade.

All of the examples discussed in this chapter moved away from stereotypes of graphic design and design historiography that focus primarily on individual designers, the book object, and "good" design, to emphasize instead the diversity of voices comprised by their contributions.

2020 gab das Kollektiv der Grafikdesignerinnen MMS (Maryam Fanni, Matilda Flodmark und Sara Kaaman) aus Schweden ein Buch heraus mit dem Titel *Natural Enemies of Books. A Messy History of Women in Printing and Typography*, erschienen im Verlag Occasional Papers. Der Titel bezieht sich auf Anne Lyon Haights Beitrag „Are Women the Natural Enemies of Books?" in *Bookmaking on the Distaff Side* von 1937. Die Veröffentlichung selbst ist dann auch die Referenz, auf die sich MMS bezieht. Unter anderem untersucht das Kollektiv, was sich für Grafikdesignerinnen in Hinblick auf ihre Arbeits- und Lebensbedingungen seit 1937 geändert hat.

MMS, deren Schwerpunkt neben dem Feminismus die Arbeiterbewegung in Schweden ist, will, wie ihr Vorbild, Stimmen zu Gehör bringen, die ansonsten nicht zu Wort kommen. Da ist Jess Baines von See Red Women's Workshop, der als Frauenkollektiv geführten linken Gruppe, die in den 1970er und 1980er Jahren in London im Rahmen der Stadtteilarbeit und der zweiten Frauenbewegung Protestplakate im Siebdruckverfahren druckte. Da sind Historikerinnen, Grafikdesignerinnen, Schriftstellerinnen, Journalistinnen, Ökonom*innen, auch Vertreterinnen der Gewerkschaft, die einen Beitrag zur besonderen, oft vom Prekariat gezeichneten Situation von Frauen im Buchgewerbe heute beisteuern.

Alle erwähnten Beispiele rücken zugleich von Stereotypen des Grafikdesigns und der Designhistoriografie ab, die sich vorwiegend auf einzelne Entwerfer*innen, das Buchobjekt und auf das „gute" Design konzentrierten, und betonen die Vielstimmigkeit ihrer Beiträge.

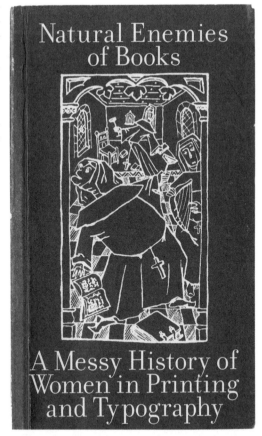

MMS [Maryam Fanni, Matilda Flodmark & Sara Kaaman] (Hg./eds.), The Natural Enemies of Books: A Messy History of Women in Printing and Typography, London: Occasional Papers, 2020
© Occasional Papers, 2020

Literatur
Further Reading

Eileen Cadman, Gail Chester & Agnes Pivot:
Rolling Our Own. Women in Printing, Publishing and Distribution,
London: Minority Press-Group, 1980.

James P. Danky & Wayne A. Wiegand (Hg./eds.): *Women in Print.*
Essays on the Print Culture of American Women from the Nineteenth
and Twentieth Centuries, Madison: University of Wisconsin Press,
2006.

Jane Grabhorn: *The Compleat Jane Grabhorn: A Hodgepodge*
of Typographic Ephemera. Three Complete Books Broadsides
Invitations: Greetings Placecards &c.,&c. San Francisco:
The Jumbo Press / Grabhorn-Hoyem, 1968.

Kristen Hagen: *Women in Print. The Feminist Bookstore*
Movement: Lesbian Antiracism and Feminist Accountability,
Durham, NC: Duke University Press, 2016.

Mallory Haselberger: The Feminist Possibilities of Print:
Jane Grabhorn's Jumbo Press, *Alphabetes*, 1.2020,
http://www.alphabettes.org/the-feminist-possibilities-of-print-
jane-grabhorns-jumbo-press/ (Abruf/accessed 9. Aug. 2022).

Dean Irvine: *Editing Modernity. Women and Little-Magazine*
Cultures in Canada 1916–1956, Toronto: University of Toronto Press,
2008.

MMS [Maryam Fanni, Matilda Flodmark & Sara Kaaman] (Hg./eds.):
The Natural Enemies of Books. A Messy History of Women
in Printing and Typography, London: Occasional Papers, 2020.

Gillian Murphy: „Balancing on a Razor's Edge": Running the Radical
Feminist Lesbian Onlywomen Press, *Women. A Cultural Review* 32,
Nr./no. 3–4 (2021): 442–456.

Lois Rather: *Women as Printers*, Oakland, CA: The Rather Press,
1970.

AMERIKA-NISCHE ALTERNATIV-KULTUR

AMERICAN COUNTER-CULTURE

The New Woman's
Survival Catalog

The New Woman's
Survival Catalog

The New Woman's Survival Catalog wurde 1973 in Anlehnung an den einflussreichen Whole Earth Catalog herausgegeben, den der Fotograf, Aktivist und Verleger Stewart Brand zwischen 1968 und 1972 publizierte. Brands Buch war ein Produktkatalog der amerikanischen Alternativkultur: In mehreren Ausgaben stellte der Autor ein Kompendium von Produktlisten, grafischen Schaubildern und pädagogischen Tipps für Kommunard*innen, die das Landleben bevorzugten, und andere Vertreter*innen der Hippie-Bewegung zusammen. Auf dem Cover des ersten Whole Earth Catalog war eine Fotografie der Erde abgebildet, die die NASA ein Jahr zuvor von einem ihrer Satelliten aufgenommen hatte. Sie sollte das Bewusstsein für die Fragilität des Planeten fördern helfen.

Der Whole Earth Catalog verfolgte ein neues, heute, in Zeiten von digitalen Plattformen selbstverständliches, aber zur damaligen Zeit kaum verbreitetes Konzept: Nutzer*innen sammelten für andere Nutzer*innen ihr Wissen und Können und stellten es kostenlos zur Verfügung.

Zugleich war das Unternehmen in Buchform gegossener Zeitgeist, wegweisend für die nutzerorientierte Gegenwart avant la lettre, eine Art „Google in Papierform",[1] wie Steve Jobs den Katalog nannte. Obwohl das Buch eine breite Palette von Angeboten wie Kleidung, Bücher, Werkzeuge, Saatgut und vieles mehr aufführte und testete, verkaufte der Herausgeber die Produkte nicht selbst, sondern gab lediglich Empfehlungen und Kontaktadressen weiter. Zugleich vermittelte der Katalog schon in den 1960er und 1970er Jahren ein neues Umweltbewusstsein, Werkzeuge für ein Überleben auf dem Planeten, kurz: eine Hilfe zur Selbsthilfe.

Auch The New Woman's Survival Catalog strebte Survival-Strategien an, diesmal für eine patriarchalisch geprägte Welt, und vermittelte ein neues Bewusstsein von Frauen. Zusammengestellt war er von der Literaturwissenschaftlerin Kirsten Grimstad und der Sozialwissenschaftlerin Susan Rennie, drei weitere Frauen kamen hinzu. Er sollte eine feministische Alternative für die kulturellen Aktivitäten der 1970er Jahre sein.

Grimstad und Rennie waren im Sommer 1973 zwei Monate lang durch die USA gereist und hatten verschiedene Organisationen und Einzelpersonen befragt, um Informationen zu sammeln.

The New Woman's Survival Catalog was published in 1973 in the style of the influential Whole Earth Catalog published between 1968 and 1972 by photographer, activist, and publisher Stewart Brand. Brand's book was a product catalog of American counterculture: across multiple issues, the author put together a compendium of product lists, graphic charts, and educational tips for commune members living a rural lifestyle and other adherents of the hippie movement. The cover of the first Whole Earth Catalog featured a photograph of the Earth that NASA had taken a year earlier from one of its satellites. It was meant to promote an awareness for the fragility of the planet.

The Whole Earth Catalog pursued a new concept that is taken for granted today in the age of digital platforms but was not at all common at the time: users worked together to gather their knowledge and skills for others, making them available free of charge.

At the same time, the project was pure zeitgeist printed in book form, pioneering today's user-oriented present avant la lettre—a kind of "Google in paperback form," as Steve Jobs called it.[1] Although the book listed and tested a wide

[1] Quoted from NZZ, https://www.nzz.ch/feuilleton/das-internet-vor-dem-internet-ld.1393491 (accessed 28. Feb. 2022). See also Anna Wiener: The Complicated Legacy of Stewart Brand's "Whole Earth Catalog," The New Yorker, 16. Nov. 2018.

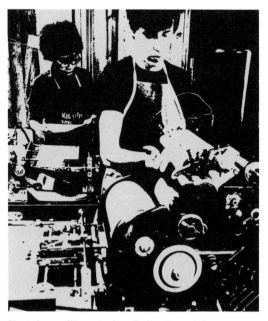

Illustration aus / Illustration from The New Woman's Survival Catalog, hg. von / ed. by Kirsten Grimstad & Susan Rennie, 1973/2019. Courtesy of Kirsten Grimstad, Susan Rennie & Primary Information

[1] Zit. n. NZZ, https://www.nzz.ch/feuilleton/das-internet-vor-dem-internet-ld.1393491 (Abruf 28. Feb. 2022). Siehe auch Anna Wiener: The Complicated Legacy of Stewart Brand's „Whole Earth Catalog", The New Yorker, 16. Nov. 2018.

Illustration aus / Illustration from The New Woman's Survival Catalog, hg. von / ed. by Kirsten Grimstad & Susan Rennie, 1973/2019. Courtesy of Kirsten Grimstad, Susan Rennie & Primary Information

range of offerings that included clothing, books, tools, seeds, and more, the publisher did not sell the products himself but merely provided recommendations and contact addresses. Still, at a remarkably early moment in the history of the environmental movement, the catalog conveyed a new environmental consciousness in the 1960s and 1970s, along with tools for survival on the planet. In short, it offered help for self-help.

The New Woman's Survival Catalog likewise aimed at survival strategies, albeit in this case for a patriarchal world, while conveying a new feminist consciousness. It was compiled by literary scholar Kirsten Grimstad and social scientist Susan Rennie, joined later by three other women. It was meant to be a feminist alternative to the cultural happenings of 1970s.

To gather information, Grimstad and Rennie had traveled throughout the United States for two months in the summer of 1973, interviewing various organizations and individuals. They visited bookstores and independent publishers, women's health centers, and crisis centers for women who had been the victims of rape. Richly illustrated, the book served as a directory of feminist initiatives and activities in the second wave of the women's movement, listing, for instance, addresses for crisis centers or other sources of help for those who had suffered sexual violence, along with educational and medical advice. It published references to artistic groups that aligned with the counterculture scene and were led by women; it made suggestions on how to acquire funding for DIY projects; and it gathered together a wealth of tips on how women could shape their own lives and find support. While the scope was intended to be worldwide, the focus largely remained on the United States.

The book itself was designed in the spirit of the do-it-yourself movement, with elements that included self-drawn lists, numerous hand-drawn illustrations, and instructions on how to make books or posters. No value was placed on technical perfection. The catalog was printed in black and white throughout, with only the cover in bright red. In the days of glamorous fashion magazines, it was far from a glossy product. *The New Woman's Survival Catalog* challenged women to take charge of their own, feminist interests. On its final pages, the editors boldly present the catalog's production process with photographs and descriptions under the title "Making the Book," first printed by Berkeley Publishing Company.

Dazu zählten Buchläden und unabhängige Verlage, Gesundheitszentren für Frauen und Krisenzentren für vergewaltigte Frauen. Das bilderreiche Buch ist ein Verzeichnis feministischer Initiativen und Aktivitäten in der „zweiten Welle" der Frauenbewegung: aufgelistet werden Beratungsadressen, beispielsweise bei Vergewaltigung, und es werden pädagogische und medizinische Tipps gegeben. Es gibt Hinweise auf künstlerische Gruppen, die zur Alternativszene passen und von Frauen geleitet werden. Für Do-it-yourself-Projekte werden Vorschläge gemacht, wie man eine Finanzierung akquiriert. Das Buch versammelt eine Fülle an Tipps, wie Frauen ihr Leben selbst gestalten und sich Unterstützung besorgen können. Zwar waren weltweite Informationen intendiert, doch konzentrierte sich der Katalog weitgehend auf die USA.

Gestaltet war das Buch, ganz im Geist der Do-it-yourself-Bewegung, mit selbstgezeichneten Listen, sehr vielen von Hand gezeichneten Illustrationen sowie Anleitungen, wie beispielsweise Bücher oder Plakate selbst hergestellt werden können. Auf technische Perfektion wurde kein Wert gelegt. Der Katalog ist durchgehend in Schwarz-Weiß gehalten, nur der Einband ist leuchtend rot. In Zeiten der glamourösen Modezeitschriften war er alles andere als eine

The New Woman's
Survival
Catalog

A Woman-made Book

The New Woman's Survival Catalog, hg. von / ed. by Kirsten Grimstad & Susan Rennie, 1973/2019 (Titelblatt / cover). Courtesy of Kirsten Grimstad, Susan Rennie & Primary Information

The New Woman's Survival Catalog, hg. von / ed. by Kirsten Grimstad & Susan Rennie, 1973/2019 (Innenseiten / inside pages). Courtesy of Kirsten Grimstad, Susan Rennie & Primary Information

Glanzbroschüre. *The New Woman's Survival Catalog* forderte auf, feministische Interessen in die eigene Hand zu nehmen. Auf den letzten Seiten stellen die Herausgeberinnen unter dem Titel „Making the Book" den Herstellungsprozess des Kataloges anhand von Fotografien und Beschreibungen dezidiert dar. Das Buch wurde zuerst in der Berkeley Publishing Company gedruckt.

Zwei Jahre später folgte *The New Woman's Survival Sourcebook*, herausgegeben bei Knopf.

2019 erschien eine faksimilierte Neuauflage des *New Woman's Survival Catalog* bei der Non-profit-Organisation Primary Information in einer Auflage von 4000 Exemplaren.

Heute ist *The New Woman's Survival Catalog* eine unverzichtbare Quelle für die Erforschung feministischer Bewegungen der 1970er Jahre in den USA.

The catalog was followed two years later by *The New Woman's Survival Sourcebook*, published by Knopf. More recently, in 2019, a facsimile reprint of *The New Woman's Survival Catalog* was published by the nonprofit organization Primary Information in a print run of 4,000 copies.

Today, *The New Woman's Survival Catalog* is an indispensable resource for studying the feminist movements of the 1970s in the United States.

Illustration aus / Illustration from The New Woman's Survival Catalog, hg. von / ed. by Kirsten Grimstad & Susan Rennie, 1973/2019.
Courtesy of Kirsten Grimstad, Susan Rennie & Primary Information

Literatur
Further Reading

The New Woman's Survival Catalog. A Woman-Made Book
(1973), New York: Primary Information, 2019.

ZINES
ZINES

Feministische Gegenkultur
der 1970er bis 1990er Jahre
Feminist Counterculture
from the 1970s to the 1990s

Chrysalis

No. 2

Chrysalis: A Magazine of Women's Culture, Nr./no. 2 (1977), Titelblatt mit einem Ausschnitt des Gemäldes / cover with a detail of the painting Die Dichtung umarmt die Malerei (Poetry embraces painting) von/by Angelika Kauffmann, 1782

Frauenkollektive und DIY

Zines, aus dem englischen *magazine* abgeleitet, sind Publikationen mit geringem Umfang und kleiner Auflage. Sie werden häufig von Amateur*innen entworfen und geschrieben, zum großen Teil in eigener Werkstatt hergestellt, im Selbstverlag publiziert und vertrieben durch alternative oder Underground-Netzwerke. Solche Zeitschriften entstanden weltweit im Zuge der politischen Gegenbewegungen der späten 1960er und vor allem der 1970er Jahre und erlebten in den 1990er Jahren durch die Bewegung der Riot Grrrls noch einmal einen Höhepunkt.

Für die frühen Zines gilt, dass sich ihre Akteur*innen meist in lokalen Räumen bewegten, den Stadtteilen von Großstädten, und sich auf ein Netz miteinander verbundener Mitglieder mit unterschiedlichen Ausrichtungen vor Ort stützten. Alle bewegten sich in einer, meist linken, Gegenkultur, waren folglich weniger Fans, wie im Fall der Fanzines (im strengen Sinne ein Magazin,

Women Collectives and DIY

Produced in small formats with a small circulation, zines (a shortened form of magazines) are frequently designed and written by amateurs, largely in workshops of their own, and are often self-published and distributed through alternative or underground networks. This kind of publication emerged around the world in the wake of the political countermovements of the late 1960s and especially the 1970s, epitomized again in the 1990s with the Riot Grrrls movement.

The producers of early zines were mostly active in local spaces, in the neighborhoods of big cities, while relying on a network of local members with differing concerns and agendas. All of these publications participated in a mostly left-wing counterculture, meaning zine producers were not so much mere consumers or fans who made fanzines for themselves, but collaborators with shared political worldviews. Women-only groups also formed during this time, addressing issues of their own. Almost every nation in Europe saw feminist zines emerge.

All of them pushed back against the glossy magazines with a global reach, such as *Vogue*, *Harper's Bazaar*, or *Elle*, which mostly originated in the United States and propagated a fashionable yet traditional image of women. These magazines nevertheless offered women graphic designers, art directors, and photographers a field where they had extraordinary opportunities for development. Many of these professionals were simultaneously involved in alternative or underground magazines.

For much of the twentieth century, an aesthetics built upon disruption and the dissolution of boundaries served as the tool of women avant-gardists and especially social reformers, characterized by low-tech, do-it-yourself (DIY), cut-and-paste approaches. These women pioneered tactics of culture jamming, creative activism, and the antiadvertising movement of brandalism; by setting out on their own path, they sought to resist the political mainstream, the advertising industry, and capitalism in general. Posters were anonymously pasted on street walls, handbills were distributed on the street, and information was spread in the alternative press.

Allied with the DIY movement of the time, the feminist zines valued being proactive without conforming to the standards of good design and sophisticated printing techniques. Their dilettantish and amateurish qualities were thus not rooted in unprofessionalism, but in a conscious decision against established forms of design.

das von Fans für Fans gemacht wird) oder Konsumenten, sondern Gleichgesinnte in ihrer politischen Ausrichtung. Es haben sich in dieser Zeit auch reine Frauengruppen gebildet und ihre eigenen Themen behandelt. Fast jede Nation in Europa hat feministische Zines hervorgebracht.

Alle opponierten gegen die weltweit agierenden Hochglanzmagazine wie *Vogue*, *Harper's Bazaar*, *Elle* und viele mehr, die meist von den USA ausgingen und in denen ein modisches, gleichwohl traditionelles Frauenbild propagiert wurde. Diese Magazine boten Grafikdesignerinnen, Art-Direktorinnen und Fotografinnen allerdings ein Terrain, in dem sie sich außerordentlich entfalten konnten. Viele dieser Professionellen waren gleichzeitig in alternativen oder Underground-Magazinen engagiert.

Über weite Strecken des 20. Jahrhunderts war eine Ästhetik der Störung und Entgrenzung das Werkzeug der Avantgardist*innen und insbesondere der Sozialreformer*innen. Es war durch Low-tech-, Do-it-yourself- und Cut-and-paste-Ansätze gekennzeichnet. Dies waren die Taktiken des Culture Jamming, des kreativen Aktivismus und des Brandalismus, die sich durch selbst gesetzte Ziele dem politischen Mainstream, der Werbung und generell dem Kapitalismus widersetzen wollten. Ihre Plakate wurden anonym an die Straßenwände geklebt, Handzettel auf der Straße verteilt und ihre Informationen in der alternativen Presse verbreitet.

Der DIY-Bewegung dieser Zeit verbunden, ging es den feministischen Zines um Eigeninitiative ohne Anpassung an die Standards guter Gestaltung und ausgefeilter Drucktechniken. Das Dilettantische und Amateurhafte beruhte also nicht auf Unprofessionalität, sondern es wurde gegen das anerkannte Design ausgespielt. Diesem unterstellten die Frauen Komplizenschaft mit dem Kommerz und eine Ästhetisierung des frauenunterdrückenden Lebensstils.

Solche Zines waren im Kontext der Neuen Frauenbewegung angesiedelt. Herausgeberinnen und Produzentinnen waren Frauenkollektive. Teils waren Amateurinnen unter den Produzentinnen, teils junge einschlägig ausgebildete Grafikdesignerinnen, Künstlerinnen, die sich das Handwerk der grafischen Gestaltung aneigneten, und Journalistinnen. In ihrer Non- und Anti-Ästhetik opponierten sie gegen die Themen der Frauen- und Modejournale, die sich mit Haushalt, Kochrezepten und Kosmetik beschäftigten. Sie wollten nicht zur Dominanz der festgelegten Gender-Rollen beitragen, das heißt nicht zur Reduktion von Frauen auf die Rolle der aufopfernden Mutter,

The women who made them accused traditional design of being complicit with commercial interests and of aestheticizing a lifestyle that oppressed women.

Zines of this kind, edited and produced by women's collectives, often emerged in the context of the new women's movement. Some of the producers were amateurs, while others were young women graphic designers with professional training, women artists who learned the craft of graphic design, or women journalists. With their nonaesthetics and antiaesthetic stance, they opposed the themes of women's and fashion journals, which focused on house and home, cooking recipes, and cosmetics. They wanted to avoid contributing to the dominance of fixed gender roles, that is to say, to the reduction of women to the role of the self-sacrificing mother, the perfect housewife, and the domestically subservient but fashionably dressed spouse. Empowering themselves, they sought out autonomous spaces of democratic participation. Most were convinced that they could change society with their efforts.

Their activity went far beyond the boundaries of graphic design to affect how they organized their work or communicated with different social and ethnic groups; it was concerned with many issues crucial to women such as childcare, sexuality, and health education. Many of these women were also associated with lesbian feminism. Pointing out intersectional entanglements was one of their main objectives. And although many members of the women's collectives were White, Western, and from the middle class, they also worked together with communities of color where they lived—and in England and the United States, especially with the Black community. The following examples of the zines that they produced are indicative of their diversity.

Spare Rib

Spare Rib emerged from the British counterculture of the late 1960s and existed between 1972 and 1993. The title alludes to the biblical legend in which Eve was created from Adam's rib. Yet it also plays on an ambiguity: spare ribs as grilled meat, an American barbecue classic.

The magazine was founded in 1972 by Marsha Rowe and Rosie Boycott, but was run as a women's collective with several other women. In the early issues, important feminists such as Betty Friedan, Germaine Greer, Margaret Drabble, and Alice Walker authored pieces supporting the movement, though unknown women had a voice,

der perfekten Hausfrau und der dienenden, aber modisch gekleideten Ehefrau. Mit ihrer Selbstermächtigung suchten sie nach autonomen Freiräumen demokratischer Teilhabe. Die meisten waren davon überzeugt, mit ihrem Beitrag die Gesellschaft verändern zu können.

Ihre Aktivität ging weit über die Grenzen grafischer Gestaltung hinaus und betraf beispielsweise die Organisation ihrer Arbeit, die Kommunikation mit verschiedenen sozialen und ethnischen Gruppen, Kinderbetreuung, Aufklärung über Sexualität und Gesundheit und vieles mehr. Viele Akteurinnen waren dem lesbischen Feminismus verbunden. Auf intersektionale Verflechtungen hinzuweisen, war eines ihrer Hauptanliegen. Wenngleich viele Mitglieder der Frauenkollektive der weißen westlichen Mittelschicht angehörten, integrierten sie doch auch andere Ethnien, je nach Stadtteil: in England und den USA insbesondere die *Black community*. Einige wenige Beispiele sollen auf das vielfältige Spektrum der Zeitschriften hinweisen.

Spare Rib

Spare Rib entstand aus der britischen Gegenkultur der späten 1960er Jahre und existierte zwischen 1972 und 1993. Der Titel spielt auf die biblische Legende an, wonach Eva aus der Rippe Adams geschaffen wurde. Gleichzeitig zielt er auch auf eine Doppeldeutigkeit: Spare Ribs sind Grillfleisch, ein BBQ-Klassiker aus den USA.

Gegründet wurde das Magazin 1972 von Marsha Rowe und Rosie Boycott, wurde aber als Frauenkollektiv mit mehreren weiteren Frauen geführt. In den frühen Ausgaben schrieben bedeutende Feministinnen wie Betty Friedan, Germaine Greer, Margaret Drabble und Alice Walker entsprechende Artikel, aber auch unbekannte Frauen kamen zu Wort. Die Themen bewegten sich im großen Spektrum von *class*, *race* und *gender*.

Der provokante und humorvolle, gleichzeitig aber auch ernsthafte und engagierte Inhalt der Zeitschrift war eine Herausforderung für dessen visuelle Sprache. Die Cover waren oft provozierend und bissig gestaltet. Wechselnde unbekannte junge Designer*innen und Fotograf*innen waren zwar damit befasst, die Herausforderung aufzugreifen, doch das visuelle Konzept stammte von Kate Hepburn und Sally Doust. Kate Hepburn hatte an der Central School of Art and Design in London (heute University of the Arts) studiert, anschlie-

too. Topics ranged across the broad spectrum of class, race, and gender.

Polemical and humorous, while also serious and engaging, the magazine's content posed a challenge for its visual language. The covers were often designed to be provocative and biting. A number of unknown young women designers and photographers took up the challenge of these designs, but the visual concept came from Kate Hepburn and Sally Doust. Kate Hepburn had studied at the Central School of Art and Design in London (today the University of the Arts), then at the Royal College of Art. Sally Doust attended Brighton College and graduated from Goldsmiths' College in London. Both had met in the late 1960s at *Vogue Australia*.

Spare Rib pursued progressive journalism and wrote about taboo subjects such as women's sexuality, as well as domestic violence. Its editors were inspired by journalism's alternative, underground scene. Rosie Boycott worked for a year at the radical magazine *Frendz*, while Marsha Rowe worked simultaneously for the Australian underground magazine Oz. Both were inspired by the New York underground magazine *RAT*, by the feminist groups Redstockings and Weatherwomen, and by the guerrilla theater group Women's International Terrorist Conspiracy from Hell (W.I.T.C.H.)

Editorial decisions were made collaboratively. *Spare Rib* did not pursue any ideological position, but saw itself as a platform for various left-wing camps such as socialist feminism, lesbian groups, Black feminism, and others. What united these groups was an anticapitalist stance, the view that women were being exploited as consumers, and the belief that standard forms of graphic design were supporting these systems.

Instead of the glossy paper used in the glamorous women's magazines, matte sheets were chosen, and working tools were scissors, glue, and paper scraps. The women designers stuck their layouts together with adhesive to produce templates for the London lithographic printer J. H. Pauli. *Spare Rib* was bound together with staples, its news pages and other articles printed on colored paper with colored ink, with a different color combination for every monthly issue. The cover was printed in two tones. Photographs and illustrations came from friends, many of whom had studied together. The issues were financed by advertising, though the editors found it extremely difficult to find advertisers whose ads were not sexist.

Spare Rib: A Women's Liberation Magazine, Nr./no. 122
(Sept. 1982), Titelblatt/cover

Spare Rib: A Women's Liberation Magazine,
Nr./no. 66 (Jan. 1978), Titelblatt/cover

Heresies:
A Feminist Publication on Art and Politics

As part of the feminist art movement, the journal *Heresies: A Feminist Publication on Art and Politics* was founded in New York and produced by the Heresies Collective between 1977 and 1992. Its twenty-seven issues were overseen by a group of volunteers assembled separately for each issue under the name "mother collective." Each issue had its own style of design and theme— a kind of noncorporate design. The production was always DIY. Some of the pages were handwritten, some typeset. Because so many people were involved in the production of the booklets, and because the group was organized in a way that rejected any hierarchy, each individual issue was uniquely different in its style, format, and layout. The editors found it important to reflect about their own work, as they wanted to show that women are able to work together in a patriarchal society as a collective to fight discrimination.

"Each of us worked on every page of this magazine, a slow and frustrating process, but one from which we learned a great deal: about each other, about editorial and mechanical skills, about the collective process itself, about our subject—feminism, art and politics—and about what it means to be political in a real active, living situation," was the declaration printed and signed in the first issue by Joan Braderman, Harmony Hammond, Elizabeth Hess, Arlene Ladden, Lucy Lippard, and May Stevens.[1] Early members included some women who became famous in the scene or later, such as Lucy Lippard and Miriam Schapiro. In one of the last issues, the editors left the first pages blank to invite readers to formulate a contribution of their own.[2]

Topics included feminist theory, art, film, design and design history, queer life, violence against women, working-class women, outsiders, and geographical peripheries. *Heresies* nevertheless drew criticism from people of color who felt excluded because most of the women in the collective were from the White middle class. The zine discussed this critique, though without ever really resolving the issue.

ßend am Royal College of Art. Sally Doust besuchte das Brighton College und machte ihren Abschluss am Goldmiths's College in London. Beide hatten sich in den späten 1960er Jahren kennengelernt bei der *Vogue Australia*.

1 *Heresies* 1, no. 1 (Jan. 1977): 3, quoted from facsimiles of the original *Heresies* published by No More Nice Girls Productions, 2022, http://heresiesfilmproject.org/archive/ (accessed 3.8.2022).
2 *Heresies* has now also published their entire archive online: http://heresiesfilmproject.org/archive/ (accessed 10.2.2023).

Spare Rib vertrat einen progressiven Journalismus und schrieb über Tabuthemen wie weibliche Sexualität ebenso wie über häusliche Gewalt. Die Herausgeberinnen waren angeregt worden durch die journalistische Alternativ- und Undergroundszene. Rosie Boycott arbeitete ein Jahr bei dem radikalen Magazin *Frendz*, Marsha Rowe gleichzeitig für das australische Underground-Magazin *Oz*. Inspirationen erhielten sie von der New Yorker Underground-Zeitschrift *RAT*, durch die feministischen Gruppen Redstockings und Weatherwomen wie auch von der Guerilla-Theatergruppe Women's International Terrorist Conspiracy from Hell (W.I.T.C.H.)

Die Entscheidungen der Redaktion wurden gemeinschaftlich getroffen. *Spare Rib* verfolgte keine ideologische Position, sondern verstand sich als Plattform für verschiedene linke Positionen wie sozialistischer Feminismus, lesbische Gruppen, *Black feminism* und andere. Was sie verband, war eine antikapitalistische Haltung, die Auffassung, dass Frauen als Konsumentinnen ausgebeutet werden und dass das übliche Grafikdesign in diesem Zusammenhang eine dienende Rolle spielte.

Statt glänzenden Papiers der glamourösen Frauenmagazine wurden matte Blätter gewählt. Gearbeitet wurde mit Schere, Kleber und Papierschnipseln. Die Designerinnen verwendeten ein Klebelayout, um Vorlagen für den Londoner Lithodrucker J. H. Pauli herzustellen. *Spare Rib* wurde mit Heftklammern gebunden. Die Nachrichtenseiten und andere Artikel wurden auf farbigem Papier mit bunter Tinte gedruckt: Jede Monatsausgabe wählte eine andere Farbkombination. Der Titel war zweifarbig. Fotografien und Illustrationen lieferten Freund*innen, viele davon Kommiliton*innen aus der Zeit des Studiums. Die Ausgaben finanzierten sich durch Werbung, allerdings war es sehr schwer für die Herausgeberinnen, Anzeigenkunden zu finden, deren Werbung nicht sexistisch war.

Heresies.
A Feminist Publication on Art and Politics

Das feministische Journal *Heresies. A Feminist Publication on Art and Politics* ging von New York aus und wurde zwischen 1977 bis 1992 vom Heresies Collective produziert. Es war Teil der Feminist-Art-Bewegung. Die 27 Ausgaben wurden von einer Gruppe von Ehrenamtlichen betreut, die sich jedes Mal individuell zusammensetzte und unter dem Namen „mother collective" firmierte. Jede Ausgabe hatte einen eigenen

OZ, Nr./no. 33 (Feb. 1971), Titelblatt/cover: Norman Lindsay

Chrysalis: A Magazine of Women's Culture

Chrysalis: A Magazine of Women's Culture, published in Los Angeles from 1977 to 1981, has now become well known. The term "chrysalis" is taken from zoology and refers to one stage in an insect's process of metamorphosis, usually a butterfly, as it changes from an ugly larva to an immobile pupa and then a fully grown insect.

The magazine has received a great deal of attention in part because of its association with the legendary institution of the Woman's Building, the feminist arts center in downtown Los Angeles, whose members Kirsten Grimstad and Susan Rennie founded the publication as a noncommercial project. Both had been involved in the production of self-help books such as *The Woman's Survival Catalog* and *The New Woman's Survival Sourcebook*. Beyond women's issues, the magazine also took up political, literary, and artistic themes. It was particularly close to the movement of consciousness raising groups as a kind of knowing that would allow individuals to break free from predetermined norms and discover their own identity. Highly prevalent in feminist circles, this method was developed in the late 1960s by the New York Radical Women, an early feminist group.

Chrysalis featured contributions by well-known authors such as Black lesbian activist Audre Lorde, artist Judy Chicago, and art critic Lucy Lippard. The magazine covered a wide range of topics including ecology, pornography, feminist theories, religion, lesbian and feminist art, and literature.

A Feminist Publication on Art & Politics

HERESIES

Women's Traditional Arts
The Politics of Aesthetics

$3.00

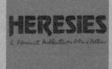

Heresies, Titelblätter einiger Ausgaben / Cover of several issues, 1977–1992 © Heresies Collective, New York City

gestalterischen Stil und ein eigenes Thema – eine Art Non-Corporate-Design. Die DIY-Methode war für die Gruppe verbindlich. Zum Teil waren die Seiten handschriftlich gestaltet, zum Teil gesetzt. Wegen der Beteiligung von vielen an der Herstellung der Hefte und wegen des egalitären Anspruchs, der jede Hierarchie ablehnte, waren die einzelnen Ausgaben der Hefte sehr unterschiedlich in Stil, Format und Layout. Die Reflexion der Arbeit war für die Herausgeberinnen wichtig, weil sie zeigen wollten, dass Frauen in der Lage sind, in einer patriarchalen Gesellschaft kollektiv zusammenzuarbeiten und gemeinsam gegen die Diskriminierungen vorzugehen.

„Each of us worked on every page of this magazine, a slow and frustrating process, but one from which we learned a great deal: about each other, about editorial and mechanical skills, about the collective process itself, about our subject – feminism, art and politics – and about what it means to be political in a real active, living situation", heißt es in der ersten Ausgabe von den Unterzeichnerinnen Joan Braderman, Harmony Hammond, Elizabeth Hess, Arlene Ladden, Lucy Lippard, May Stevens.[1] Zu den frühen Mitgliedern zählten Personen, die in der Szene oder später berühmt wurden wie Lucy Lippard und Miriam Schapiro. In einer der letzten Ausgaben ließen die Herausgeberinnen die ersten Seiten leer, um Leserinnen aufzufordern, ihren Beitrag zu formulieren.[2]

Die Themen bezogen sich beispielsweise auf feministische Theorie, Kunst, Film, Design und Designgeschichte, queeres Leben, Gewalt gegen Frauen, Arbeiterfrauen, Außenseiterinnen, geografische Randlagen. Kritik erntete *Heresies* dennoch von People of Color, die sich ausgeschlossen fühlten, weil die meisten Frauen des Kollektivs aus der weißen Mittelschicht stammten. Dieser Einwand wurde zwar diskutiert, aber bis zum Schluss nicht wirklich ausgeräumt.

Chrysalis. A Magazine of Women's Culture

Chrysalis. A Magazine of Women's Culture hat inzwischen Berühmtheit erlangt. Das Blatt erschien von 1977 bis 1981 in Los Angeles.

Der Begriff „Chrysalis" ist der Zoologie entnommen und beschreibt den Prozess der Metamorphose eines Insekts, meist eines Schmetter-

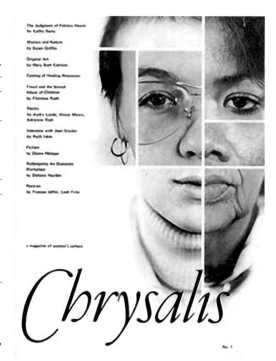

Chrysalis. A Magazine of Women's Culture, Nr./no. 1 (1977), Titelblatt/cover, Entwurf/design: Sheila Levrant de Bretteville

The first issue was designed by Sheila Levrant de Bretteville, who also developed the logo. She was part of the core group from the Woman's Building and served on the editorial board.

Despite its popularity, the paper managed to publish only ten issues over the three years of its existence because of financial difficulties, printing its final issue in 1981.

Emanzipation

Many of the magazines discussed here are from England and the United States, with only a few from other countries. Among these, the Swiss feminist magazine *Emanzipation* is a prominent example.[3] The magazine was published from 1975 to 1996 in Basel and later in Bern by the Zurich-based Organisation für die Sache der Frauen (OFRA, Organization for the Cause of Women), becoming a crucial outlet for the new women's movement of the time. OFRA wanted to combine feminism with socialism. The organization had taken over the magazine from the POCH group, a left-wing activist party that existed until 1990. OFRA had numerous chapters

---

1 *Heresies* 1, Nr. 1 (Jan. 1977): 3, zitiert n. den Faksimiles der originalen *Heresies*-Ausgaben von No More Nice Girls Productions, 2022, http://heresiesfilmproject.org/archive/ (Abruf 3. Aug. 2022).

2 Auch bei *Heresies* ist das Archiv inzwischen vollständig online: http://heresiesfilmproject.org/archive/ (Abruf 10. Aug. 2022).

3 The journal can be viewed as an e-periodical at https://www.e-periodica.ch/digbib/volumes?UID=ezp-001 (accessed 7. Jan. 2022).

lings, von einer hässlichen Larve über die bewegungslose Puppe bis hin zum erwachsenen Vollinsekt.

Das Magazin hat nicht zuletzt dadurch viel Aufmerksamkeit erfahren, weil es mit der legendären Institution des Woman's Building, dem feministischen Kunstzentrum in Downtown Los Angeles, in Verbindung gebracht wird. Gründerinnen des nichtkommerziellen Magazins waren Kirsten Grimstad und Susan Rennie vom Woman's Building. Beide waren involviert gewesen in der Produktion von Selbsthilfebüchern wie *The Woman's Survival Catalog* und *The New Woman's Survival Sourcebook*. Über Frauenbelange hinaus integrierte das Blatt auch weitere politische, literarische und künstlerische Themen. Besonders nahe stand es der Bewegung der Selbsterfahrungsgruppen, einer auf subjektiver Wahrnehmung basierenden Erkenntnisform, die dazu verhelfen sollte, sich von vorgegebenen Normen zu lösen und eine eigene Identität zu entdecken. Diese in feministischen Kreisen höchst verbreitete Methode wurde Ende der 1960er Jahre von den New York Radical Women, einer frühen feministischen Gruppe, entwickelt.

Charakteristisch für *Chrysalis* ist die Beteiligung bekannter Autorinnen wie die Schwarze lesbische Aktivistin Audre Lorde, die Künstlerin Judy Chicago und die Kunstkritikerin Lucy Lippard. Das Magazin behandelte ein breites Spektrum an Themen wie Ökologie, Pornografie, feministische Theorien, Religion, lesbische und feministische Kunst und Literatur.

Die erste Ausgabe gestaltete Sheila Levrant de Bretteville, die auch das Logo entwickelte. Sie zählte zur Kerngruppe des Woman's Building und war Mitglied des Editorial Board.

Trotz seiner Beliebtheit erreichte das Blatt wegen finanzieller Schwierigkeiten über die drei Jahre seiner Existenz nur zehn Ausgaben und war 1981 gezwungen, die Edition einzustellen.

Emanzipation

Viele der untersuchten Magazine stammen aus England und den USA, wenige aus anderen Ländern. Zu letzteren zählt die Schweizer feministische Zeitschrift *Emanzipation*.[3] Das Magazin erschien von 1975 bis 1996 in Basel und später in Bern. Es wurde von der Organisation für die Sache der Frauen (OFRA) in Zürich herausgegeben und war ein Medium der Neuen Frauenbewegung dieser Zeit. OFRA wollte Feminismus mit

across the country, employing both existing political instments and noninstitutional protests to advocate for women's political issues. The magazine reported on women's discrimination in Switzerland and abroad.

Since women's suffrage and voting rights were not introduced in Switzerland until 1971 (authorized by a federal referendum in which only men could take part, and at first not even in all cantons), making Switzerland one of the last countries in Europe to grant women full civil rights, this journal was especially significant.

In its first issues, the magazine was set in several columns on simple newsprint and illustrated with amateurishly reproduced photographs and drawings. From the mid-1980s onward, the issues were more elaborate with equally well-produced design concepts in multiple colors, though they never reached the level of professional design brochures, as they remained true to a low-cost DIY ethos.

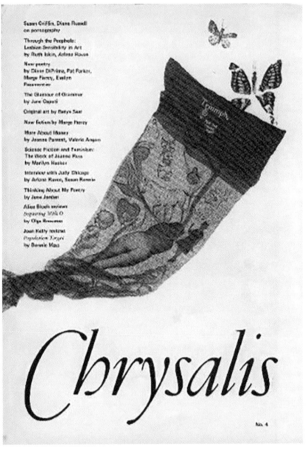

3 Die Zeitschrift ist als E-Periodica einsehbar, https://www.e-periodica.ch/digbib/volumes?UID=ezp-001 (Abruf 7. Jan. 2022).

Chrysalis. A Magazine of Women's Culture, Nr./no. 4 (1980), Titelblatt/cover

Emanzipation: Die feministische Zeitschrift für kritische Frauen 8, Nr./no. 1 (Feb. 1982), Titelblatt/cover

Emanzipation: Die feministische Zeitschrift für kritische Frauen 10, Nr./no. 1 (Jan./Feb. 1984), Titelblatt/cover

Emanzipation: Die feministische Zeitschrift für kritische Frauen 12, Nr./no. 1 (Jan./Feb. 1986), Titelblatt/cover

La revue Sorcières

A French example of a feminist publication is *La revue Sorcières: Les femmes vivent.*[4] Founded in 1975 by writer, journalist, and college professor Xavière Gauthier (pseudonym of Mireille Boulaire), the feminist magazine appeared in twenty-four issues until 1982. Visually, it stood out more from more DIY feminist publications, as it frequently featured photographic work by professional women artists. Although it considered itself allied with the Mouvement de libération des femmes (MLF), it devoted itself more intensively to the cultural scene of literature, theater, and art, where many of its women artists also worked. Its illustrations were accordingly often large-format and full-page. The magazine emphasized subjective dimensions of women's experience through interviews with its contributors. Discussions in the editorial meetings pro-

4 Ana Bordenave: La revue Sorcières (1975–1982), un espace de représentation féministe entre arts visuels et littérature, *Archives of Women Artists, Research and Exhibitions Magazine,* https://aware-womenartists.com/magazine/la-revue-sorcieres-1975-1982-un-espace-de-representation-feministe-entre-arts-visuels-et-litterature/ (accessed 10. Jan. 2023).

Sozialismus verbinden. Die Organisation hatte die Zeitschrift von der POCH-Gruppe übernommen, einer linken aktivistischen Partei, die bis 1990 existierte. Die OFRA hatte landesweit zahlreiche Sektionen. Mit existierenden politischen Instrumenten sowie nichtinstitutionellen Protestaktionen setzte sie sich für frauenpolitische Fragen ein. Die Zeitschrift berichtete über Frauendiskriminierung im eigenen Land und über dessen Grenzen hinaus.

Da das Frauenstimmrecht und Wahlrecht in der Schweiz erst 1971 eingeführt wurde (durch eine eidgenössische Volksabstimmung des männlichen Teils der Bevölkerung und auch nicht in allen Kantonen), kommt dieser Zeitschrift eine besondere Bedeutung zu. Denn die Schweiz war in Europa eines der letzten Länder, das Frauen volle Bürgerrechte zusprach.

In den ersten Ausgaben war das Magazin auf einfachem Zeitungspapier mehrspaltig gesetzt, bebildert mit dilettantisch reproduzierten Fotografien und Zeichnungen. Ab Mitte der 1980er Jahre waren die Titel aufwendiger mit entsprechenden Designentwürfen und mehreren Farben gestaltet, wenngleich sie nie den Status von professionellen Designbroschüren erhielten, sondern sich am kostengünstigen DIY orientierten.

La revue Sorcières

Ein französisches Beispiel ist *La revue Sorcières*,[4] mit dem Untertitel *Les femmes vivent*. Gegründet 1975 von der Schriftstellerin, Journalistin und Hochschulprofessorin Xavière Gauthier (Pseudonym von Mireille Boulaire), erschien das feministische Blatt mit 24 Ausgaben bis 1982. Visuell hebt sich das Magazin stärker von den DIY-orientierten feministischen Zeitschriften ab, da es häufiger Werke von professionellen Künstlerinnen ablichtete. Zwar betrachtete es sich als verbunden mit dem Mouvement de libération des femmes (MLF), dennoch widmete es sich intensiver der kulturellen Szene von Literatur, Theater und Kunst, aus der auch viele der Künstlerinnen stammten. Die Abbildungen sind deshalb häufig großformatig und ganzseitig. Der subjektive Aspekt wurde durch Interviews mit den Teilnehmerinnen betont. Die Diskussionen in den

moted exchange between the women artists and confidence in their own abilities, and it could almost be described as a form of consciousness raising. Many women were politically radical in their views.

Courage, Die Schwarze Botin, Emma

As in other countries, the literature produced in West Germany by second wave feminism—or the new women's movement, the Neue Frauenbewegung, as it is called in German—was characterized by a variety of contributions capturing individual experience and expressing opinions in techniques of self-awareness as political practice that have been called a "politics of subjectivity."[5] In addition, the movement produced a plethora of what is known as gray literature, including theories of feminism, along with translations of related texts from other countries. Women's magazines were only one form of exchange.

In 1976/77, three magazines with national circulation were founded in West Germany by women involved in the independent women's movement; the publications were intended as tools for readers to explore and fashion their own identity as women and to foster communication between women: *Courage*, *Emma*, and *Die Schwarze Botin* (The black messenger). They were united by the impression that the women of the "movement" had neither a language, nor concepts, nor a theory of their own that reflected women's experiences. They felt constrained by the male leftist groups who saw women's issues as only a secondary contradiction of revolutionary practice.

In West Berlin, the feminist monthly Courage, founded by women including Sibylle Plogstedt, Sabine Zurmühl, Barbara Duden, Christa Müller, and Monika Schmid, appeared from 1976 to 1984. The title Courage was a reference to the main character of the picaresque novel published in 1670 by Hans Jakob Christoffel von Grimmelshausen: *Trutz Simplex, or Descriptions of the Life of Courage, a Woman Swindler and Vagabond*. The same figure had been the inspiration for Bertolt Brecht's famous play from 1938/39, *Mother Courage and Her Children*. Grimmelshausen describes his "Gypsy" figure as an independent, fierce woman caught amid the moral devastation of the Thirty Years' War.

---

4 Ana Bordenave: La revue Sorcières (1975–1982), un espace de représentation féministe entre arts visuels et littérature, *Archives of Women Artists, Research and Exhibitions Magazine*, https://awarewomenartists.com/magazine/la-revue-sorcieres-1975-1982-un-espace-de-representation-feministe-entre-arts-visuels-et-litterature/ (Abruf 10. Jan. 2023).

5 Michaela Wunderle: *Politik der Subjektivität: Texte der italienischen Frauenbewegung*, Suhrkamp: Frankfurt a. M., 1977.

Redaktionssitzungen förderten den Austausch und das Selbstbewusstsein der Künstlerinnen und kamen einem *consciousness raising* nahe. Viele Künstlerinnen nahmen eine politisch radikale Position ein.

Courage, Die Schwarze Botin, Emma

Wie in anderen Ländern auch war die Literatur zur Neuen Frauenbewegung in Westdeutschland charakterisiert durch eine Vielfalt von Erfahrungsberichten und Meinungsäußerungen, die der „Politik der Subjektivität"[5] und der Übung in Selbsterfahrung als politischer Praxis entsprachen. Daneben gab es eine Fülle an sogenannter grauer Literatur bis hin zu Theorien zumFeminismus, samt den Übersetzungen einschlägiger Literatur aus anderen Ländern. Frauenzeitschriften waren dabei nur ein Format des Austauschs.

Als Organe der Selbstfindung weiblicher Identität und der Kommunikation gründeten sich 1976/77 in der BRD drei überregionale Zeitschriften der autonomen Frauenbewegung: *Courage*, *Emma* und *Die Schwarze Botin*. Es verband

5 Michaela Wunderle: *Politik der Subjektivität. Texte der italienischen Frauenbewegung*, Suhrkamp: Frankfurt a. M., 1977.

Die Mitarbeiterinnen Christa Müller (hinten Mitte), Barbara Weber, Adelheid Zöfelt und Heidi Stein in einem Büroraum mit unbekannten Personen, an der Wand hängen die Titelseiten der Courage-Ausgaben 1 bis 4 / The women employees Christa Müller (back center), Barbara Weber, Adelheid Zöfelt, and Heidi Stein in an office room with unknown persons, in the background, cover pages of Courage issues 1 to 4 hang on the wall, Foto/photo: © Das feministische Archiv

The magazine was regarded as a platform for the independent left-wing feminist scene, and it also saw itself as an alternative to the feminist magazine *Emma*, which still exists today. In addition to covering current political issues, the magazine tackled sensitive taboo topics such as domestic violence, prostitution, clitoral circumcision in Africa, rape, postmenopausal sex, abortion and its effect on women's mental health, child abuse and, of course, the general exclusion of women from politics and business. At the same time, it was more engaged with theoretical discourses than the other two of these German magazines.

Its circulation grew to 70,000 copies, with magazines sold deliberately at kiosks in order to reach broad sections of the population. Today, the Friedrich-Ebert-Stiftung has made a full digital copy of the journal available online.[6]

The magazine *Die Schwarze Botin: Frauenhefte* (The black messenger: journals for women) played a special role beginning in the fall of 1976. It saw itself as a voice within the new women's movement in West Germany and West Berlin, while also expressing criticism of the movement from a feminist perspective.

Even if *Die Schwarze Botin* was ultimately overshadowed (like *Courage*) by *Emma*, the magazine offered a platform for women authors who later became known far beyond feminist circles for their writings on literature, visual art, and (feminist) cultural theory: Rita Bischof, Silvia Bovenschen, Gisela Elsner, Elfriede Jelinek, Ursula Krechel, Julia Kristeva, Elisabeth Lenk, Eva Meyer, Heidi Pataki, Heidi von Plato, Christa Reinig, Sarah Schumann, Ginka Steinwachs, Gisela von Wysocki, and many others. Working together, the journalist and writer Gabriele Goettle and the historian Brigitte Classen (from 1980) bore editorial responsibility. After a two-year break starting in 1983, Branka Wehowski, a lawyer, took over the editorship alongside Brigitte Classen. The writer Elfriede Jelinek took charge of the editions in Vienna, as did the Germanist and translator Marie-Simone Rollin in Paris. The publisher and financial backer was the architect Marina Auder. After thirty-one issues, the last edition appeared in 1987.

The journal brought together a wide range of disciplines and forms of artistic expression including scientific papers, essays, literary texts and poems, collages, short commentaries, satires, and illustrations. It saw itself as a platform for

6 See http://library.fes.de/courage/ (accessed 24. May 2022).

aktuelle frauenzeitung
COURAGE 4

April 1979, 4. Jahrgang, 3 DM, A 1700 EX

Atomkraft

Frankreich ffr. 7,00 Dänemark dkr. 10,00 Italien L 1200 Luxemburg ffr. 52,00 Niederlande nfl. 4,00 Österreich öS 25,00 Portugal Esc. 45,00 Schweden skr. 6,50 Schweiz sfr. 3,30 USA/Canada/Übersee $ 1,75

Klage gegen Siemens • Hugenottinnen • Dicke duck dich
Go-In für's 2. Frauenhaus • Kritik an der DFI • Technikerinnen-Treffen

R. Groven, Plakat für die norwegische Aktion / Poster of the Norwegian initiative Aksjon mot Atomkraft (Aktion gegen Atomkraft / Action against nuclear power), 1977, auf dem Titelblatt von / on the cover of Courage. Aktuelle Frauenzeitung 4, Nr./no. 4 (1979)

Den gleichen Dreck für weniger Geld

Wilma, Käte, Hedwig, Lilo und Dorothea.

Fotos: Barbara Metzlaff

Wer es in den Zeitungen liest, begreift nur schwer, daß es dabei um Menschen geht. »Die Privatisierung der öffentlichen Reinigung, heißt es da, »steigt rapide an.« Was bedeutet das? In Hamburg zum Beispiel sind davon 8300 Putzfrauen betroffen, die täglich insgesamt 4900 Gebäude reinigen.

Die Stadt zahlt dafür jährlich 193 Millionen Mark. Nun sollen 20 Millionen eingespart werden – dreimal darf man (und vor allem auch frau) raten, auf wessen Rücken!

Viele Städte haben schon gehandelt. Und so wird verfahren: Manche Stadt entläßt die Putzfrauen, die dann von privaten Firmen wieder eingestellt und an denselben Arbeitsplatz zurückgeschickt werden. Nun putzen dieselben Frauen denselben Dreck, nur für weniger Geld. Sie verdienen ein Drittel, das heißt im Durchschnitt 2 Mark 50 weniger. Anderswo läßt man die öffentlichen Putzfrauen »aussterben«, das heißt, es werden keine neuen mehr eingestellt.

In der Männerpresse wird über diesen Skandal auf die üblich flapsige Art und Weise berichtet. So zum Beispiel in der »Süddeutschen Zeitung«, die über die Reaktion der Hamburger FDP berichtet, sie habe »mit staatlich gelenkten Putzfrauen wenig im Sinn« und mehr mit »privater Sauberkeit im öffentlichen Schrubbdienst«.

Hört sich nett an, »private Sauberkeit«, oder? Ist sogar zutreffend. Denn all diese öffentlichen Putzfrauen dürfen abends privat weiter machen! Nur – so hat es die FDP nicht gemeint.

Argument der öffentlichen Haushalte für dieses Manöver: So sparen wir Geld ein. Ein sehr kurzsichtiges Argument. Denn auf lange Sicht wird das teurer für die öffentliche Hand als die frühere Lösung. Frauen und Steuerzahler zahlen drauf – nur einer profitiert: der private Unternehmer. Wie, das zeigt der nachstehende Bericht von Barbara Schleich.

Emma (Mrz./Mar. 1977), Doppelseite / double page 32–33 © EMMA Frauenverlag

sie der Eindruck, dass die Frauen der „Bewegung" weder über eine Sprache, über Begriffe noch über eine eigene Theorie verfügten, die die Erfahrungen von Frauen reflektierten. Von den männlichen linken Gruppen fühlten sie sich insofern eingeengt, als die Frauenthematik als Nebenwiderspruch revolutionärer Praxis galt.

In West-Berlin erschien von 1976 bis 1984 die feministische Monatszeitschrift *Courage*. Zu den Gründerinnen zählten Sibylle Plogstedt, Sabine Zurmühl, Barbara Duden, Christa Müller und Monika Schmid. Der Titel *Courage* (französisch für „Mut") bezieht sich auf die Hauptfigur von Hans Jakob Christoffel von Grimmelshausens Roman *Trutz Simplex oder Lebensbeschreibungen der Ertzbetrügerin und Landstörzerin Courasche* von 1670. Er wurde von Bertolt Brechts berühmtem Theaterstück *Mutter Courage und ihre Kinder*, 1938/39, aufgenommen. Grimmelshausen beschreibt eine „Zigeunerin" als autonome kämpferische Frau inmitten der sittlichen Verwahrlosung des Dreißigjährigen Krieges.

Die Zeitschrift galt als Plattform der autonomen linksfeministischen Szene und ver-

Emma (Mrz./Mar. 1977), Titelblatt/cover
© EMMA Frauenverlag

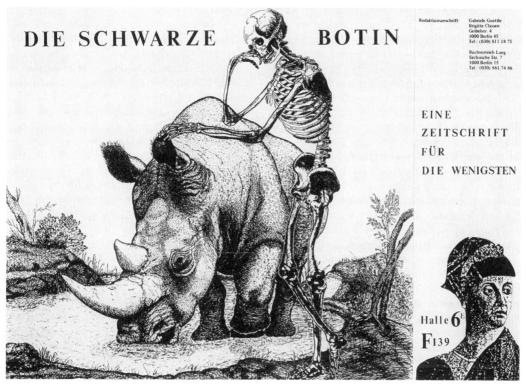

DIE SCHWARZE BOTIN

EINE
ZEITSCHRIFT
FÜR
DIE WENIGSTEN

Redaktionsanschrift: Gabriele Goettle
Brigitte Classen
Geibelstr. 4
1000 Berlin 45
Tel.: (030) 811 18 75

Buchvertrieb Lang
Sächsische Str. 7
1000 Berlin 15
Tel.: (030) 881 74 86

Halle 6
F139

Illustration aus der Zeitschrift / Illustration from the magazine Die Schwarze Botin

stand sich gleichzeitig als Alternative zur feministischen Zeitschrift *Emma*, die bis heute existiert. Neben aktuellen politischen Themen nahm sie auch heikle Tabuthemen auf wie häusliche Gewalt, Prostitution, Klitorisbeschneidung in Afrika, Vergewaltigung, Sex nach der Menopause, Abtreibung und Abtreibungstrauer, Kindesmissbrauch und selbstverständlich die generelle Ausgrenzung von Frauen aus Politik und Wirtschaft. Gleichzeitig setzte sie sich stärker als die beiden anderen Zeitschriften mit theoretischen Diskursen auseinander.

Ihre Auflage erreichte bis zu 70.000 Exemplare. Sie wurden bewusst auch an Kiosken verkauft, um breite Bevölkerungsschichten zu erreichen. Die Friedrich-Ebert-Stiftung in Deutschland stellt heute ein Volldigitalisat der Zeitschrift zur Verfügung.[6]

Eine besondere Bedeutung hat das Periodikum *Die Schwarze Botin. Frauenhefte* ab Herbst 1976, das sich ebenfalls als Akteurin der Neuen Frauenbewegung in der BRD und West-Berlin verstand, diese aus feministischer Sicht aber auch einer Kritik unterzog.

6 Siehe http://library.fes.de/courage/ (24. May 2022).

feminist theory and the possibilities of its aesthetic expression, offering a public space to various disciplines and theoretical formats, and to different feminist positions. Feminist cultural criticism and social critique were engaged via aesthetic means. In the wake of feminism's "fourth wave," this journal, once nearly forgotten, is now again receiving greater attention.

The magazine *Emma* was founded in 1977 by a collective and later continued under the sole editorship of the journalist Alice Schwarzer. Aimed to appeal to women and men alike, it dealt more broadly with women's issues, equal opportunities for men and women, and current feminist happenings. The publication developed no distinct corporate design of its own, but rather modeled itself on traditional illustrated magazines.

In contrast to the other two magazines from West Germany discussed here, which are more closely associated with the period of the new women's movement, *Emma* remains the prototypical outlet for a feminist public sphere in Germany. And especially through its editor, it has achieved an ongoing level of public visibility that has often been accompanied by controversy.

Wenngleich sie, wie *Courage*, im Rückblick im Schatten der *Emma* steht, ist *Die Schwarze Botin* mit Autorinnen verbunden, die später weit über feministische Kreise hinaus mit ihren literarischen, bildkünstlerischen und theoretischen Schriften bekannt wurden: Rita Bischof, Silvia Bovenschen, Gisela Elsner, Elfriede Jelinek, Ursula Krechel, Julia Kristeva, Elisabeth Lenk, Eva Meyer, Heidi Pataki, Heidi von Plato, Christa Reinig, Sarah Schumann, Ginka Steinwachs, Gisela von Wysocki und viele andere. Die Redaktionsleitung hatten die beiden Herausgeberinnen, die Journalistin und Schriftstellerin Gabriele Goettle und die Historikerin Brigitte Classen (ab 1980), inne. Nach einer zweijährigen Pause ab 1983 übernahm die Juristin Branka Wehowski neben Brigitte Classen die Redaktion. Die Schriftstellerin Elfriede Jelinek besorgte die Ausgaben in Wien und die Germanistin und Übersetzerin Marie-Simone Rollin in Paris. Verlegerin und Sponsorin wurde die Architektin Marina Auder. Nach 31 Ausgaben erschien das letzte Magazin im Jahr 1987.

Die Zeitschrift versammelte ein breites Spektrum an Disziplinen und künstlerischen Ausdrucksformen, wie wissenschaftliche Aufsätze, Essays, literarische Texte und Gedichte, Collagen, Glossen, Satiren und Illustrationen. Sie verstand sich als Plattform feministischer Theorie und ihrer ästhetischen Ausdrucksmöglichkeiten. Sie gab verschiedenen Disziplinen und theoretischen Formaten ebenso Raum wie unterschiedlichen Positionen im Feminismus. Feministische Kulturkritik und Kritik der Gesellschaft wurden mit ästhetischen Mitteln behandelt. Im Zuge der „vierten Welle" des Feminismus hat die fast vergessene Zeitschrift wieder größere Beachtung erfahren.

Die Zeitschrift *Emma* wurde 1977 von einem Kollektiv gegründet und später von der Journalistin Alice Schwarzer allein fortgeführt. Sie beschäftigte sich allgemeiner mit Frauenthemen, der Chancengleichheit von Männern und Frauen und mit aktuellen feministischen Ereignissen und wollte Frauen und Männer gleichermaßen ansprechen. Die Zeitschrift hat kein ausgeprägtes eigenes Corporate Design entwickelt, sondern entspricht eher einer gängigen Illustrierten.

Entgegen den beiden anderen Zeitschriften, die sich stärker mit der Zeit der Neuen Frauenbewegung verbinden, steht *Emma* in Deutschland prototypisch für feministische Medienöffentlichkeit und erreichte insbesondere durch Alice Schwarzer eine bis heute andauernde, oft umstrittene Medienöffentlichkeit.

Al-Raida, The Pioneer

Other feminist magazines from this period, however, come from countries that differ from those of the West. *Al-Raida, The Pioneer* for example, engages the situation of women in the Arab world. Founded in 1976 and still in existence today, the journal is a bilingual, interdisciplinary project published by the Arab Institute for Women (AiW) at the Lebanese American University in Beirut. *Al-Raida* serves as a platform for young women and activists in Arab countries. It advocates for women's rights and gender issues, promotes creative processes in fields such as literature, visual arts, and photography, and provides information on interdisciplinary academic research.

Radicalization in the 1990s: Riot Grrrls

While the majority of feminist zines from the 1970s demanded in their programmatic texts that men and women work in tandem to change the ways they lived together, in the 1990s other women writers, most of them young, wrote radicalized manifestos calling for women themselves to work to change the popular image of womanhood.

The ground for this radicalized approach had been prepared with activist Jo Freeman's "Bitch Manifesto" from 1968, which strategically and affirmatively appropriated and resignified this slur for women. Freeman's move was a common tactic among feminists, but what she brought to this creative appropriation was the claim that women can also be aggressive, stubborn, independent, dominant, big, loud, not pretty, or clumsy. The trait shared by all "bitches," in short, was of refusing to identify with given gender stereotypes of women. Like the Riot Grrrl manifesto decades later, the "Bitch Manifesto" offered a new model of subjectivity, paired with another possibility of realizing solidarity and collective action.

Riot Grrrl was not just the name for a single group, but an amalgamation of several bands of young women in the feminist wave of the 1990s that all belonged to the feminist underground hardcore punk movement. The three r's in the naming also refer to the angry growling that the girls used as provocation.

The movement protested against sexism in general, against abuse, domestic violence, and the silence with which it they are so often met, and more broadly against patriarchy and capitalism. Still, the aim was not only to express

Al-Raida, bilinguale Zeitschrift der / bilingual journal of the Lebanese American University, ab/beginning Mai/May 1976

Al-Raida, The Pioneer

Andere Zeitschriften wiederum stammen aus Nationen, die den westlichen nicht vergleichbar sind. *Al-Raida, The Pioneer* beispielsweise handelt von der Situation der Frauen in „arabischen Welten". 1976 gegründet und bis heute bestehend, ist sie ein zweisprachiges interdisziplinäres Journal, herausgegeben vom Arab Institute for Women (AiW) an der Lebanese American University in Beirut. *Al-Raida* dient als Plattform für junge Frauen und Aktivistinnen in arabischen Ländern, setzt sich für Frauenrechte und Gender-Themen ein, fördert kreative Prozesse, auch im Bereich Literatur, bildende Kunst, Fotografie, und informiert über akademische interdisziplinäre Forschung.

Radikalisierung in den 1990er Jahren: Riot Grrrls

Während die Mehrzahl der feministischen Zines der 1970er Jahre in ihren programmatischen Texten unter anderem eine konsensuale Veränderung des Zusammenlebens von Mann und Frau forderten, radikalisierten einige Autorinnen, vor allem junge Frauen, mit den 1990er Jahren in ihren Manifesten die Vorstellungen davon, wie sich vor allem das Bild der Frau selbst zu ändern hatte.

Bereits das „Bitch-Manifest" der Aktivistin Jo Freeman aus dem Jahr 1968 hatte diese Attitüde vorbereitet. Der abwertende und ausgrenzende Begriff „Bitch" bedeutete eigentlich Hündin oder Hure, wurde aber strategisch erwendet und affirmativ umgedeutet. Insoweit entsprach Freeman einer verbreiteten Taktik der Feministinnen. Doch verband sie mit dieser Um-

women's anger, but also to empower women, and especially young girls, by giving them a voice. In addition to bands known for spectacularly provocative performances, the movement sought to express its perspective on feminism, punk, and punk activism by producing small magazines.Bands on the music scene included Bikini Kill, Bratmobile, Calamity Jane, Sleater-Kinney, and Heavens to Betsy.

The all-women bands of American punk and grunge, exemplified in the band Bikini Kill and one of its earliest lead singers, Kathleen Hanna, emerged in the early 1990s, in New York City and especially in Olympia, the capital of Washington state. With their criticism of the male-dominated punk scene, these young women wanted to make themselves heard, and they quickly became known beyond the United States through the musical groups that emerged from within the movement and through self-produced and self-published fanzines. These magazines were used by fans to grow a community.

This was also the period in which grunge emerged, a music style that mixed rock, punk, and metal. The music had a loud and hard edge, with guitar sounds that were "dirty" and strange. Less physically imposing than their male counterparts, girls from these bands were often not taken as seriously as they would have wanted, and the topics they sang about were marginalized as women's issues, hardly appearing at all in songs by the male grunge bands. In response, the women's bands wrote protest lyrics and performed on stage in ways that often broke taboos. Claiming their rebellious identity as girls, they deliberately worked to smash any notions that women must be ladies, or even the idea that they should be perceived as women. Aggressive punk music was a

widmung den Anspruch, dass Frauen auch aggressiv, stur, unabhängig, dominant, groß, laut, nicht hübsch, tollpatschig sein können. Allen „Bitches" sollte gemeinsam sein, dass sie sich nicht mit den vorgegebenen Geschlechterstereotypen der Frau identifizieren. Wie das Riot-Grrrl-Manifest Jahrzehnte später stellte das Bitch-Manifest ein neues Angebot an Subjektivität bereit und zugleich eine andere Möglichkeit der Solidarisierung und Kollektivierung.

Riot Grrrl war nicht nur die Bezeichnung für eine einzelne Gruppe, sondern ein Zusammenschluss mehrerer Bands junger Frauen in der Feminismus-Welle der 1990er Jahre. Sie zählte zur feministischen Underground-Hardcore-Punkbewegung. Die drei „r" in der Namensgebung verweisen auch auf das wütende Grollen, das die Girls provozierend äußerten.

Die Bewegung protestierte gegen Sexismus allgemein, Missbrauch, Schweigen, häusliche Gewalt und generell gegen das Patriarchat und den Kapitalismus. Sie äußerte nicht nur ihre Wut, sondern suchte Frauen, insbesondere Mädchen, zu stärken und ihnen eine Stimme zu geben. Neben den Musikbands und entsprechend spektakulär-provozierenden Auftritten versuchte sie, ihre Perspektive auf die Bewegung, den Punk und seinen Aktivismus über kleine Zeitschriften zum Ausdruck zu bringen. Zu den Bands der Musikszene zählten Bikini Kill, Bratmobile, Calamity Jane, Sleater-Kinney und Heavens to Betsy.

Die reinen Frauen-Bands des amerikanischen Punk und Grunge entstanden zu Beginn der 1990er Jahre insbesondere in Olympia, der Hauptstadt des US-Staates Washington, durch die Band Bikini Kill und eine ihrer frühesten Frontsängerinnen, Kathleen Hanna, sowie in New York City. Mit ihrer Kritik an der männerdominierten Punkszene wollten sich die jungen Frauen Gehör verschaffen und wurden schnell über die Landesgrenzen hinaus bekannt durch eigene Musikgruppen und durch selbstverfertigte und -aufgelegte Fanzines. In den Magazinen wollten die Fans andere Fans ansprechen.

In dieser Zeit entwickelte sich der Grunge, eine Musikrichtung aus Rock, Punk und Metal. Der Sound war laut und hart, Gitarrentöne „dreckig" und schräg. Da Mädchen den männlichen Bandmitgliedern oft körperlich unterlegen waren, wurden sie nicht so ernst genommen, wie sie es erwarteten. Zudem kamen „ihre" Themen in den männlichen Grunge-Bands nicht vor. Dagegen setzten die Frauenbands Protesttexte und Bühnenperformances, die oft Tabus verletzten. Sie wollten bewusst undamenhaft sein und bean-

perfect way for these girls to denounce constricting gender norms.

The groups expressed a DIY ethic that not only allowed women to express themselves through their music, but also to articulate their opinions and reflect on their personal experiences in the zines they produced or on handouts they distributed. Their unique style, which emphasized rough editing, applied not only to the music but also to these zines, with a severe layout produced by cutting-and-pasting texts and images on paper that had been torn from their original source or cut out with scissors.

Topics addressed by the Riot Grrrl movement included gender equality and artistic self-realization, as well as the need for women musicians to manage their own careers. To make this happen, they created alternative production and distribution structures, founded their own record labels, and designed their albums themselves. The resistance strategies employed by many of the riot grrrls are characterized by communicative guerrilla tactics and by exaggeration. The aim was to expose and attack norms defining what was considered "feminine" and "normal."

The number of all-girl bands exploded, along with a wealth of fanzines that were often used to print band manifestos.

Titelblatt des deutschen Metal-Magazins / Cover of the German magazine Ablaze, Nr./no. 10

spruchten auch nicht, als Frauen wahrgenommen zu werden, sondern bekannten sich zu ihrem Mädchenleben. Die aggressive Punkmusik war für sie ein perfektes Mittel, die einengenden Geschlechternormen anzuprangern.

Diese Gruppen äußerten eine Do-it-yourself-Ethik, die es Frauen ermöglichte, sich nicht nur mit ihrer Musik auszudrücken, sondern auch ihre Meinungen zu artikulieren und persönliche Erfahrungen in ihrer Zine oder auf Handzetteln, die sie verteilten, wiederzugeben. Ihr einzigartiger Stil, der den groben Schnitt betonte, bezog sich nicht nur auf die Musik, sondern zeigte sich in den Zines durch ein hartes Klebelayout von gerissenen oder mit der Schere geschnittenen Papierschnipseln.

Thematisiert wurden im Rahmen der Riot-Grrrl-Bewegung neben der Gleichberechtigung der Geschlechter und künstlerischer Selbstverwirklichung die Selbstverwaltung der Musikerinnen. Um ihre Autonomie zu festigen, schufen sie alternative Produktions- und Vertriebsstrukturen, gründeten eigene Plattenlabels und gestalteten ihre Albencover selbst. Die Widerstandsstrategien vieler Riot Grrrls zeichnen sich durch kommunikative Guerillataktiken und durch Überzeichnung aus. Damit sollten die Bedeutungen dessen, was als „weiblich" und „normal" galt, aufgedeckt und angegriffen werden.

All-Girl-Bands schossen wie Pilze aus dem Boden und schrieben eine Fülle von Fanzines. Sehr oft druckten sie darin ihre Manifeste ab.

Die Riot Grrrls machten sich schnell in der Öffentlichkeit bekannt und wurden von der Presse als Thema aufgegriffen. Dennoch blieb die Bewegung ein relativ kurzes Phänomen in der Presse, unter anderem weil die Bands die Medien boykottierten. Dagegen wurde ihre Form der Performance von populären Bands und Sängerinnen wie den Spice Girls, Madonna und Lady Gaga vereinnahmt, wobei allerdings die Ursprungsidee des Protestes verblasste. Es entstand zudem das konsumkulturelle Medienphänomen der Girlies, die von den anfänglichen radikalisierten Ideen abwichen und einen popkulturell geprägten Feminismus vertraten. Eine politische Dimension erhielten sie allerdings wieder durch die russische Band Pussy Riot, die explizit gegen die einengenden Frauenrollen rebellierte und entsprechend harte staatliche Sanktionen erfuhr. Pussy Riot beruft sich explizit auf die Band Bikini Kill als Vorbild.

The Riot Grrrls quickly gained public visibility, spurring media attention to their activities. Nevertheless, in the press the movement remained a relatively short-lived phenomenon, in part because the bands boycotted the media. Their form of performance was, however, co-opted by popular bands and singers such as the Spice Girls, Madonna, and Lady Gaga, even as their original idea of staging protest faded. They were also an inspiration for the consumer-culture-based media phenomenon of the girlies, which abandoned the initially radicalized positions of the Riot Grrrls to tout a feminism influenced by pop culture. Yet this strand of performance again took a political turn with the Russian band Pussy Riot, whose open rebellion against constricting gender roles prompted harsh state sanctions. Pussy Riot explicitly invoke the band Bikini Kills as one of their role models.

Pussy Riot, 2012 © Foto/photo: Denis Bochkarev

Literatur
Further Reading

Agatha Beins: *Liberation in Print. Feminist Periodicals and Social Movement Identity* (Since 1970: Histories of Contemporary America), Athen/Athens, GA: University of Georgia Press, 2017.

Fi Churchman, Kate Hepburn & Sally Doust: Radical Platform, *Eye Magazine* 25, Nr./no. 97 (2018).

Fabienne Dumont: *Des sorcières comme les autres. Artistes et féministes dans la France des années 1970*, Presses universitaires de Rennes, 2014.

Laurel Forster & Joanne Hollows (Hg./eds.): *Women's Periodicals and Print Culture in Britain, 1940s–2000s. The Postwar and Contemporary Period*, Edinburgh: Edinburgh University Press, 2020.

Danièle Lenzin & Edith Mägli: *Die Sache der Frauen. OFRA und die Frauenbewegung in der Schweiz*, Zürich/Zurich: Rotpunkt, 2000.

The Liberation in Print Collective: *Feminist Findings.* Begleitheft der Ausstellung in Le Signe / publication to accompany the exhibition in Le Signe, Chaumont, Frankreich/France, Aug. 2020.

Katharina Lux: *Kritik und Konflikt. Die Zeitschrift „Die Schwarze Botin" in der autonomen Frauenbewegung*, Wien/Vienna: Mandelbaum Verlag, 2022.

Heresies Magazine (1977–1993), Ausstellung/exhibition, University of Victoria Libraries, Herbst/Autum 2017, https://omeka.library. uvic.ca/exhibits/show/movable-type/paper/heresies (Abruf/accessed 30. Mai/May 2022).

Gisela Notz: *Die Frauenzeitschrift Courage*, Friedrich-Ebert-Stiftung, o. J. / n.d. [2008].

Katja Peglow & Jonas Engelmann (Hg./eds.): *Riot Grrrl Revisted. Geschichte und Gegenwart einer feministischen Bewegung*, Mainz: Ventil Verlag, 2011, 2. Aufl./ed. 2013.

Marsha Rowe: *Spare Rib Reader*, Harmondsworth, Middlesex: Penguin Books, 1982.

Teal Triggs: *Fanzines: The DIY Revolution*, San Francisco, CA: Chronicles Books, 2010.

Vojin Saša Vukadinović: *Die Schwarze Botin. Ästhetik, Polemik, Satire 1976–1980*, Göttingen: Wallstein Verlag, 2020.

US-AMERI-KANISCHE VORBILDER

AMERICAN ROLE MODELS

Sheila Levrant de Bretteville,
Martha Scotford, Ellen Lupton
und andere

Sheila Levrant de Bretteville,
Martha Scotford, Ellen Lupton,
and Others

Briefmarke des U.S. Postal Service vom 26. Aug. 1970, herausgegeben zum Gedenken an den 19. Zusatzartikel der Verfassung der Vereinigten Staaten, der 1919 das gleichberechtigte Stimmrecht der Frauen bestätigte, Design: Ward Brackett / U.S. Postal Service stamp dated 26 Aug. 1970, issued to commemorate the 19th Amendment to the United States Constitution, which affirmed women's equal voting rights in 1919, design: Ward Brackett

Es sind vor allem Amerikanerinnen, die als *role models* für den heutigen Wandel in der Haltung junger Grafikdesignerinnen im Westen geschätzt werden. Ihre Aktivitäten waren eingebettet in die „zweite Welle" des Feminismus der 1960er und 1970er Jahre. Diese hat in den USA früher begonnen als auf dem europäischen Kontinent. Zusätzlich zu den programmatischen Werken der Grafikdesignerinnen spielt es eine bedeutende Rolle, dass sie fast alle als Lehrerinnen an einschlägigen Schulen ihren Einfluss auf die neue Generation geltend machen konnten.

Seit den 1950er Jahren hatte sich in den USA ein allgemeiner gesellschaftlicher Wertewandel angekündigt, in dessen Zusammenhang auch die neue Frauenbewegung stand. Er war eng verbunden mit der Civil-Rights-Bewegung, insbesondere mit den Kampagnen gegen Rassendiskriminierung. Neben der afroamerikanischen Bür-

It is primarily American women who stand out as role models for today's change in attitudes among young women graphic designers in the West. These women were active as part of the second wave of feminism during the 1960s and 1970s, which started earlier in the United States than on the European continent. In addition to their programmatic work as graphic designers, one factor that plays a significant role in this history is that almost all of them were able to have an impact on the new generation as teachers at design schools.

Beginning the 1950s, the United States witnessed a general shift in social values, which also provided the context for second wave feminism. This new wave of feminism was closely associated with the civil rights movement, and especially with its campaigns to fight racial discrimination. In addition to the African-American

gerrechtsbewegung spielten auch Proteste von Homosexuellen sowie Arbeiter*innen eine Rolle. Es war die Zeit der Studierendenproteste, der Friedensbewegungen gegen den Vietnamkrieg und der Erprobung alternativer Lebensformen, etwa bei den Hippies. Der radikalen Frauenbewegung ging es vor allem um die psychologische Befreiung der Frauen, wobei der Kampf gegen sexuelle Unterdrückung eine zentrale Rolle spielte.

Eine der bekanntesten Protagonistinnen der zweiten Frauenbewegung war Betty Friedan. Sie schrieb 1963 ihr erstes Buch mit dem Titel *The Feminine Mystique* (dt. *Der Weiblichkeitswahn*), in dem sie die Rollenzuschreibung der Frau als Hausfrau, Ehefrau und Mutter kritisierte. Zugleich wirkte sie damit auf die in der amerikanischen Frauenbewegung ausgeprägte Hinwendung zum *consciousness raising* ein. Übung in Selbsterfahrung und Bewusstwerdung war für sie politische Praxis. Zusammen mit anderen Feministinnen gründete sie 1966 die National Organization of Women (NOW), eine der bedeutendsten Interessenvertretungen von Frauen.

Einflussreiche Grafikdesignerinnen waren Sheila Levrant de Bretteville, Lorraine Wild und Katherine McCoy, Muriel Cooper, Martha Scotford und April Greiman. Sie waren keine Repräsentantinnen *der* Frauenbewegung, aber sie waren mobilisierende Akteurinnen, die sich in zeitlichen Verflechtungszusammenhängen bewegten, gemeinsame Interessen verfolgten, Machtbalancen infrage stellten und alternative Organisationsformen erprobten. So unterschiedlich sie in Ausdrucksformen und Tätigkeitsfeldern auch waren, haben sie doch zu einem neuen Designkonzept beigetragen, in dem sich feministische Kreativität entfalten konnte. Sie stellten den normativen Kanon infrage, bevorzugten individuelle und subjektive Lösungen und entwickelten neue Formate.

Insbesondere die programmatischen Äußerungen von Sheila Levrant de Bretteville und Martha Scotford werden von jüngeren Designhistorikerinnen und Grafikdesignerinnen durchgängig als Referenz zitiert.

Sheila Levrant de Bretteville

Die Grafikdesignerinnen Sheila Levrant de Bretteville (geb. 1940 in Brooklyn, New York City) ist eine der bekanntesten Protagonistinnen, die eine Neueinschätzung weiblicher Werte im Design forderten.

Eines der topografischen Zentren des Wandels war Los Angeles. 1973 gründeten dort

civil rights movement, protests by homosexuals and workers also made their mark. This was the time of student protests, the peace movements against the Vietnam War, and a desire to explore alternative lifestyles, as seen for instance among the hippie movement. The main aim of the radical women's movement was to liberate women psychologically, with the struggle against sexual oppression playing a central role.

One of the most famous figures of second wave feminism was Betty Friedan, whose first book, *The Feminine Mystique* (1963), criticized how the roles of housewives, wives, and mothers were traditionally ascribed to women. At the same time, Friedan influenced the turn toward consciousness raising that was pronounced in the American women's movement; for her, training in consciousness raising was a form of political practice. Together with other feminists, in 1966 Friedan founded the National Organization of Women (NOW), one of the most important advocacy groups for women.

Influential women graphic designers included Sheila Levrant de Bretteville, Lorraine Wild, and Katherine McCoy, Muriel Cooper, Martha Scotford, and April Greiman. These women did not represent any *one single* women's movement; operating in historically entangled contexts, they rather served as mobilizing forces as they pursued common interests, questioned balances of power, and tested alternative forms of organization. However widely their modes of expression and fields of activity differed, they helped formulate a new concept of design that allowed feminist creativity to flourish. They questioned the design canon and the norms on which it was based, favored solutions that were individual and subjective, and developed new design formats.

Younger women design historians and graphic designers consistently reference, in particular, the programmatic statements of Sheila Levrant de Bretteville and Martha Scotford.

Sheila Levrant de Bretteville

The graphic designer Sheila Levrant de Bretteville (born in 1940 in Brooklyn, New York) is one of the best-known figures to have called for a reassessment of female values in design.

One center of the changes this spurred was Los Angeles, where artist Judy Chicago, Sheila Levrant de Bretteville, and art historian Arlene Raven founded the Woman's Building in 1973. The women founded this institution to further

DIVERSITY AND INCLUSIVENESS ARE OUR ONLY HOPE. IT IS NOT POSSIBLE TO PLASTER EVERYTHING OVER WITH CLEAN ELEGANCE. DIRTY ARCHITECTURE, FUZZY THEORY AND DIRTY DESIGN MUST ALSO BE OUT THERE.

Sheila Levrant de Bretteville, 1993

die Künstlerin Judy Chicago, Sheila Levrant de Bretteville und die Kunsthistorikerin Arlene Raven das Woman's Building. Es sollte feministischen Programmen, Aktivitäten und Künstlerinnen dienen, weil die Gründerinnen der Meinung waren, dass etablierte Museen und Galerien Kunst von Frauen nicht ausstellten – ein häufig reklamierter Zusammenhang, auf den noch in den 1980er Jahren die anonym agierenden feministischen Aktivistinnen Guerrilla Girls mit spektakulären Aktionen in New York City hinwiesen. Sie wollten auf die Übermacht „weißer Männer", die den Kanon bestimmten, aufmerksam machen. In den 1970er Jahren kam es zu einem Zusammenschluss einiger Künstlerinnen, die eigene Galerien eröffneten und sich darin vorrangig mit Kunst und Grafikdesign von Frauen beschäftigten. Die Frauen spielten auch in der Ausbildung eine große Rolle: 1970 hatte Judy Chicago am Fresno State College ein Feminist Art Program (FAP)

feminist concerns, activities, and artists in response to their perception that established museums and galleries were not exhibiting art by women. This was a complaint that would continue to be made for years, its importance still being underscored into the 1980s through the spectacular, anonymous actions staged by the feminist Guerrilla Girls in New York City. The founders of the Woman's Building wanted to draw attention to the preponderance of the "White men" defining the art and design canon. In the 1970s, a number of women artists joined forces to open their own galleries, where they focused primarily on women's art and graphic design. Women also played a major role in education: in 1970 Judy Chicago had founded a Feminist Art Program (FAP) at Fresno State College, which was then reestablished under the same name a year later with artist Miriam Schapiro at the California Institute of the Arts in Los Angeles.

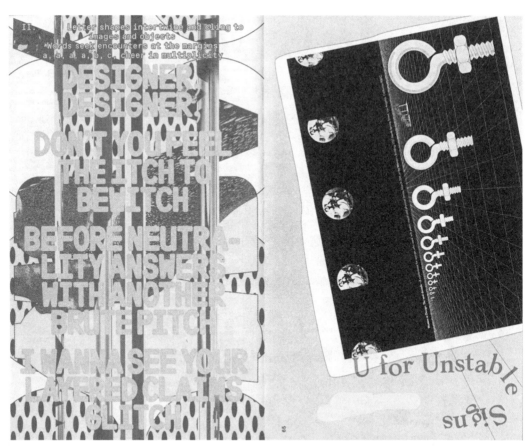

Innenseiten des Buchs / Inside pages of the book Glossary of Undisciplined Design von/by Anja Kaiser & Rebecca Stephany, Spector Books, 2021, mit einem Ausschnitt aus Sheila Levrant de Brettevilles Plakat / with an excerpt from Sheila Levrant de Bretteville's poster Women in Design: The Next Decade …, 1975 © Anja Kaiser, Rebecca Stephany

gegründet und zusammen mit der Künstlerin Miriam Schapiro am California Institute of the Arts in Los Angeles ein gleichnamiges Programm verfolgt.

1973 taten sich dann Chicago, Levrant de Bretteville und Raven, alle drei Lehrerinnen des California Institute of the Arts, zusammen und gründeten den Feminist Studio Workshop (FSW), ein zweijähriges Studienprogramm zur künstlerischen Ausbildung von Frauen. Das Gebäude, in dem es stattfand, nannten die Frauen Woman's Building, in Anlehnung an das gleichnamige Ausstellungsgebäude auf der World's Columbian Exposition in Chicago von 1893. Im Gebäude befanden sich auch noch weitere feministische Einrichtungen wie die National Organization for Women und ein Sisterhood Bookstore. Zu den Programmen zählten Kurse für Kunst, Grafikdesign und Literatur sowie Consciousness-raising-Gruppen zu Themen wie Gewalt und Sexualität, Lohn und Arbeit, Rassismus und Missbrauchserfahrungen. Das Haus diente zugleich als Forum für Künstlerinnen, deren Werke in der etablierten Kunstszene nicht gezeigt wurden.

Eingebettet waren Neuansätze im Grafikdesign in ein großes Spektrum von weiteren künstlerischen Initiativen. Es bildeten sich am Woman's Building der Schreibkurs von Deena Metzger mit teils bekannten feministischen Schriftstellerinnen wie Audre Lorde. Dann war dort das Women's Improvisational Theatre sowie die Feminist Art Workers, die interaktive Performancearbeiten aufführten. Ein weiteres Projekt war Ariadne: A Social Art Network, das Performances durchführte, die auf Gewalt gegen Frauen aufmerksam machten, das Lesbian Art Project (LAP) und die Great American Lesbian Art Show (GALAS).

Nach der Schließung des Hauses bildete sich das Women's Graphic Center, das Levrant de Bretteville mitgründete. Sie gab dort Kurse nur für Frauen. In ihrer Lehre ermunterte sie die Studentinnen, Projekte zu gestalten, denen ihre eigenen Erfahrungen als Frau zugrunde lagen.

Kurz nachdem Craig Hodgetts zum stellvertretenden Dekan der School of Design am California Institute of the Arts ernannt worden war, bat man sie, das Branding der neuen School of Design zu entwerfen. 1970 gestaltete sie das programmatische Plakat und den Flyer *Taste and Style Just Aren't Enough*. Sie wies darauf hin, dass die formalästhetische Sprache des normativen Kanons im Design nicht ausreichte für zeitgemäßes Design, sondern dass weitere Kontextfaktoren eine Rolle spielen sollten.

Sheila Levrant de Bretteville, Ausschnitt aus einem Plakat, zusammengesetzt aus Quadraten zur Farbe Pink / Detail from a poster composed of squares on the color pink, 1973 © Sheila Levrant de Bretteville

In 1973, Chicago, Levrant de Bretteville, and Raven—at the time all three of them teachers at the California Institute of the Arts—then teamed up to create the Feminist Studio Workshop (FSW), a two-year program of study for women's arts education. The women called its physical home the Women's Building, in reference to the building of the same name at the 1893 World's Columbian Exposition in Chicago. The building also housed other feminist institutions such as the National Organization for Women and a Sisterhood Bookstore. Its programs included courses in art, graphic design, and literature, as well as consciousness raising groups on topics such as violence and sexuality, wages and work, racism and experiences of abuse. The building also served as a forum for women artists whose works were not being shown in the established art scene.

New approaches to graphic design were embedded in a wide range of other artistic initiatives. Deena Metzger's writing class took shape at the Woman's Building with participants including well-known feminist writers such as Audre Lorde.

Die Schule suchte in der damaligen Zeit nach einem neuen Selbstverständnis und wollte mehr als eine übliche Designschule sein. Für den Entwurf sprach de Bretteville drei Hauptthemen an: Ökologie, menschliches Verhalten und Technik. Bei dem Plakat arbeitete sie zusammen mit der afroamerikanischen Künstlerin Betye Irene Saar, die in den 1970er Jahren zu den Vertreterinnen der Black-Arts-Bewegung zählte.

De Bretteville forderte die Studierenden auf, sich von den Stilen der Designtrends zu distanzieren. Vielmehr sollten sie ihre subjektiven Perspektiven einbringen und auf relevante soziale und politische Themen der Zeit Bezug nehmen. Sie selbst engagierte sich in der Anti-Kriegs- und Bürgerrechtsbewegung. Texte über die Befreiungspädagogik des brasilianischen Autors Paulo Freire zählten zur Grundlagenlektüre ihrer Kurse wie auch die der radikalen Feministinnen Shulamith Firestone und Eva Figes. So entstand der erste Studiengang für Frauendesign am CalArts.

Pluralität, Zusammenarbeit und Partizipation waren neue Werte. Letzteres betonte sie insbesondere an der Yale-Universität in den 1990ern: Designer*innen sollten mit dem Publikum in eine Interaktion treten und die sozialen Folgen ihrer eigenen Praxis stärker reflektieren. Auch Amateur*innen wurden in den Entwurfsprozess einbezogen. Auf diese Weise sollten Gemeinschaften entstehen. In einer von ihr gestalteten Sonderausgabe der Zeitschrift *Everywoman* aus dem Jahr 1970 erhielten beispielsweise alle Autorinnen gleichberechtigt eine eigene Doppelseite.

Ein Beispiel für ein partizipatorisches Werk ist *Pink*. 1973 wurde de Bretteville vom American Institute of Graphic Arts gebeten, für eine Ausstellung ein Kunstwerk mit den Maßen 30 × 30 Zoll über eine Farbe ihrer Wahl zu gestalten. Sie entschied sich für die Farbe Pink, unterteilte den Bereich in Quadrate, von denen sie manche leer ließ und manche an Freunde und Studentinnen der Schule verteilte. Sie forderte sie auf, ihre eigene Version der Bedeutung der Farbe Pink zu beschreiben. Wie ein Quilt wurden die Quadrate zusammengefügt und ergaben auf diese Weise ein pluralistisches Ganzes.

1974 wurde sie mit ihrem Poster für die „Women in Design: The Next Decade"-Konferenz bekannt, für welches sie eine Blueprint-Methode aus der Architektur verwendete. Die Wahl des Materials wurde von ihr getroffen, weil es preiswert war, außerdem ist es Planmaterial, das auf einen Entwurf hinweist. Die gerasterte Landschaft war beeinflusst von den utopischen Zeich-

The center also included the Women's Improvisational Theatre and the Feminist Art Workers, who performed interactive performance works. Other projects in the building included Ariadne: A Social Art Network, which staged performances calling attention to violence against women, as well as the Lesbian Art Project (LAP) and the Great American Lesbian Art Show (GALAS).

After the Women's Building closed, Levrant de Bretteville cofounded the Women's Graphic Center, which offered courses only for women. In her teaching, de Bretteville encouraged her students to create projects based on their own experiences as women.

Shortly after Craig Hodgetts was named associate dean of the School of Design at the California Institute of the Arts, she was asked to design the branding for the new academic unit. In 1970 she designed the programmatic poster and flyer *Taste and Style Just Aren't Enough*; she argued that the formal aesthetic language of the normative canon in design was not suitable for contemporary design, and that other contextual factors must also play a role.

At the time, the school was seeking to position itself in a new, atypical way. In her design, de Bretteville addressed three main issues: ecology, human behavior, and technology. For the poster, she collaborated with the African-American artist Betye Irene Saar, who was one of the representatives of the Black arts movement in the 1970s.

De Bretteville urged students to distance themselves from the styles of design trends and instead contribute their subjective perspectives and engage with relevant social and political issues of the time. She herself was involved in the antiwar and civil rights movements. Central texts for the course included works on liberation pedagogy by Brazilian author Paulo Freire, along with those by radical feminists Shulamith Firestone and Eva Figes. This led to the first degree program in women's design, at CalArts, defined by the new values of plurality, collaboration, and participation. Later teaching at Yale University in the 1990s, De Bretteville particularly emphasized participation: designers, she argued, should interact with the public and reflect more on the social consequences of their own practice. The design process, she continued, should also include amateur designers, fostering the creation of communities. In a special edition of the magazine *Everywoman* that she designed in 1970, for example, all of the women authors were given equal space with their own double-page spread.

nungen der italienischen Gruppe des Radical Design Superstudio, die sie während ihrer Zeit in Mailand kennengelernt hatte. Innerhalb einer Raster-Landschaft waren besondere Ringschrauben aufgestellt. Diese Schrauben hatte sie als feministische Symbole kreiert, sie wurden zu Ikonen der Bewegung. Sie entwarf eine Kette, welche eine Ringschraube als Anhänger hat, die „Strength without a fist" (deutsch: „Stärke ohne eine Faust") sowie das biologische Symbol der Frau darstellen sollte. Die Bilder im Mond sind Ausschnitte aus dem Werk von Angelika Kaufmann, einer schweizerisch-österreichischen Malerin aus dem 18. Jahrhundert, die sich emanzipatorischen Themen von Frauen zuwandte, europaweit agierte und eine äußerst erfolgreiche Managerin ihres eigenen Werkes war.

1981 gründete de Bretteville den Fachbereich Kommunikationsdesign am Otis Art Institute der Parsons School of Design in Los Angeles, dessen Vorsitzende sie bis 1990 war. Danach wurde sie zur Direktorin des Studiengangs für Grafikdesign ernannt und wurde die erste Grafikdesignerin, die eine Anstellung auf Lebenszeit an der Yale School of Art erhielt. Mit ihren neuen Lehrmethoden hatte sie großen Einfluss darauf, dass sich das Design an der Schule langfristig veränderte.

Sheila Levrant de Bretteville erhielt zahlreiche Ehrungen und wurde unter anderem mit mehreren Ehrendoktorwürden ausgezeichnet. Gleichwohl erfuhr sie auch herbe Kritik von ihren Kollegen. Ihre Designhaltung wurde als „postmodern" diskreditiert. Die Konfrontation ging sogar so weit, dass der äußerst renommierte Grafikdesigner Paul Rand 1992 seine Position an der Yale-Schule aus Protest aufgab. In dem Artikel „Confusion and Chaos: The Seduction of Contemporary Graphic Design" formulierte Rand eine Erklärung und bezeichnete das postmoderne Design als „faddish and frivolous" (dt. modisch und frivol) und „harbor[ing] its own built-in boredom" (dt. seine selbstgemachte Langeweile verbergend).[1]

De Bretteville, die auch in den 1980er Jahren als erfolgreiche kommerzielle Designerin und Künstlerin sowie als Lehrerin an Designschulen arbeitete, hat ihre feministische Haltung nie aufgegeben. Für die Vermittlung ihrer Ideen spielt Ellen Lupton eine nicht unbedeutende Rolle, sie hat sich in Interviews mit Sheila Levrant de Bret-

[1] Paul Rand: Confusion and Chaos: The Seduction of Contemporary Graphic Design, *AIGA Journal of Graphic Design* 10, Nr. 1 (1992), https://www.paulrand.design/writing/articles/1992-confusion-and-chaos-the-seduction-of-contemporary-graphic-design.html (Abruf 2. Jul. 2022).

Another example of a participatory work is *Pink*. In 1973, de Bretteville was asked by the American Institute of Graphic Arts to create a 30×30-inch artwork for an exhibition about a color of her choice. She decided on the color pink and divided the area into squares—some of which she left blank and some of which she distributed to friends and women students at the school. She asked the recipients to describe what the color pink meant to them. The squares were joined together in the form of a quilt, creating a pluralistic whole.

In 1974, she gained notice for the conference poster "Women in Design: The Next Decade," which she created using the architectural medium of a blueprint. She chose this format not only because it was inexpensive, but because it inherently signals the process of design. With a nearly empty landscape consisting of a white grid on a blue background, the poster was influenced by the utopian drawings of the Italian radical design group, Superstudio, which she had encountered during her time in Milan. A row of eyebolts with a unique shape receded diagonally across the grid into the distance: clearly recognizable as feminist appropriations of the symbol for the Roman goddess Venus, they became icons of the movement. The idea stemmed from necklaces she had designed with an eyebolt as a pendant, taking the biological symbol for the female sex to symbolize "strength without a fist." The painting visible in the moon that appears in phases across the top are taken from the work of Angelika Kaufmann, an eighteenth-century Swiss-Austrian painter who engaged with themes of women's emancipation, worked all across Europe, and was extremely successful in managing her own career.

In 1981, de Bretteville founded the Department of Communication Design at the Otis Art Institute of the Parsons School of Design in Los Angeles, serving as its chair until 1990 and subsequently being appointed director of the Graphic Design Program; she later also became the first woman graphic designer to receive tenure at the Yale School of Art. With her new methods as a teacher, she had a lasting influence in changing how design was taught at the school.

Sheila Levrant de Bretteville has received numerous honors, including several honorary doctorates. Yet she also drew harsh criticism from some of her colleagues, who discounted her design stance as "postmodern." This conflict became so bitter that in 1992 the highly renowned graphic designer Paul Rand resigned from his position at Yale in protest. He articulated his rea-

teville intensiv mit ihrem Konzept auseinandergesetzt. Zudem gab sie in jüngster Zeit ihr Buch *EXTRA BOLD. A Feminist Inclusive Anti-racist Nonbinary Field Guide for Graphic Designers* heraus, das ganz in der Tradition der von de Bretteville angestoßenen Ausrichtung steht. Auch in der jüngeren Geschichte des etablierten Grafikdesigns sind solche Positionen bekannt: beispielsweise bei Katherine McCoy, die in den siebziger Jahren zusammen mit ihrem Mann an der Cranbrook Academy Grafikdesign lehrte. Sie ermöglichte Studierenden, ihre eigenen Meinungen und Visionen zu artikulieren.

Martha Scotford

Quasi zu „Urtexten" moderner feministischer Theorie im Grafikdesign wurden die Schriften von Martha Scotford, insbesondere „Messy History vs. Neat History: Toward an Expanded View of Women in Graphic Design" von 1994.[2] Sie analysiert in diesem Essay die prekäre Situation von Grafikdesignerinnen in ihrem Berufsfeld und geht insbesondere auf die Designgeschichtsschreibung ein, die den Eindruck erweckt, als hätten Frauen keinen signifikanten Beitrag geleistet. Die Perspektive der Frauen hatte sie bereits drei Jahre früher skizziert, nämlich in ihrem Artikel „Is There a Canon of Graphic Design?",[3] der für mehr Diversität wirbt.[4]

Selbst Buchdesignerin, war Scotford durch designtheoretische und -historische Abhandlungen, durch ihre kuratorische Tätigkeit und die Designlehre an einschlägigen Schulen bekannt. Der Fokus lag dabei häufig auf Frauen im Grafikdesign und feministischer Theorie. Unter anderem gab sie eine Monografie über die Designerin Cipe Pineles heraus und betonte auch hier deren Beitrag zu einem solidarischen Handeln unter Frauen in ihrem Beruf.[5] Dem Kanon in der Designgeschichtsschreibung, der „neat history", stellt Scotford die Pluralität verschiedener Ansätze entgegen.

sons in an article entitled "Confusion and Chaos: The Seduction of Contemporary Graphic Design," calling postmodern design "faddish and frivolous" and "harbor[ing] its own built-in boredom."[1]

De Bretteville, who also worked in the 1980s as a successful commercial designer and artist and as a teacher at design schools, never abandoned her feminist stance. Ellen Lupton has played a not insignificant role in spreading Sheila Levrant de Bretteville's ideas, above all in interviews in which the two women discussed them at length. She has also recently published a book, *EXTRA BOLD: A Feminist Inclusive Anti-racist Nonbinary Field Guide for Graphic Designers,* that builds on the tradition initiated by de Bretteville. Similar positions can also be found in the more recent history of graphic design: one thinks here, for instance, of Katherine McCoy, who (together with her husband) taught graphic design at Cranbrook Academy of Art in Bloomfield Hills, Michigan. Her work, too, allowed students to articulate their own opinions and visions.

Martha Scotford

The writings of Martha Scotford, and in particular "Messy History vs. Neat History: Toward an Expanded View of Women in Graphic Design" from 1994, became the closest things to foundational texts possessed by modern feminist theory in graphic design.[2] This essay analyzes the precarious situation of women graphic designers in their professional field and specifically addresses the historiography of design, which gives the impression that women have not made any significant contributions. Aiming to promote more diversity,[3] Scotford had outlined the perspective of women three years earlier in her article "Is There a Canon of Graphic Design?"[4]

2 Martha Scotford: Messy History vs. Neat History: Toward an Expanded View of Women in Graphic Design, *Visible Language* 28, Nr. 4 (Herbst 1994): 367–387.

3 Martha Scotford: Is There a Canon of Graphic Design?, *AIGA Journal of Graphic Design* 9, Nr. 2 (1991).

4 Siehe auch Martha Scotford: Is There a Canon of Graphic Design History?, Nachdruck in Steven Heller & Marie Finamore (Hg.): *Design Culture. An Anthology of Writing from the AIGA Journal*, New York: Allworth Press, 1997, und: Martha Scotford: Googling the Design Canon, *Eye Magazine* 17, Nr. 68 (Mai 2008).

5 Martha Scotford: *Cipe Pineles. A Life of Design*, New York: W. W. Norton & Co, 1999; siehe auch ihren Artikel The Tenth Pioneer, *Eye Magazine* 5, Nr. 18 (Herbst 1995), https://www.eyemagazine.com/feature/article/the-tenth-pioneer (Abruf 2. Jul. 2022).

1 Paul Rand: Confusion and Chaos: The Seduction of Contemporary Graphic Design, *AIGA Journal of Graphic Design* 10, no.1 (1992), https://www.paulrand.design/writing/articles/1992-confusion-and-chaos-the-seduction-of-contemporary-graphic-design.html (accessed 2. Jul. 2022).

2 Martha Scotford: Messy History vs. Neat History: Toward an Expanded View of Women in Graphic Design, *Visible Language* 28, no. 4 (Autumn 1994): 367–387.

3 See also Martha Scotford: Is There a Canon of Graphic Design History?, reprinted in Steven Heller & Marie Finamore (eds.): *Design Culture: An Anthology of Writing from the AIGA Journal*, New York: Allworth Press, 1997, and Martha Scotford: Googling the Canon, *Eye Magazine* 17, no. 68 (May 2008).

4 Martha Scotford: Is There a Canon of Graphic Design?, *AIGA Journal of Graphic Design*, 9, no. 2 (1991).

evolution of humanity and technology, creation and creativity. For that, she created a giant, human-sized, double-sided poster, 33×76.5 inch (84×194 cm) that could be folded down to the standard, 32-page-format of Design Quarterly.

It took Greiman more than six months to develop, design and output the poster on her laser printer. She began working on a Macintosh 128K, the original Apple Macintosh personal computer, released in early 1984, and then, upon its release later that year, continued on a 512K. With an initial selling price of \$3,195 (around \$7,600 or 6,300 euros in 2020, taking inflation into account), the 512K was a very expensive, slow, bulky and, by today's standards, prehistoric device.

With limited possibilities for design that such a basic device would offer, the work is a technical masterpiece in many respects. The defining image is a digitized, life-size, two-headed portrait of Greiman's naked body. It was captured as live video stills from her Sony Beta camera using MacVision, a device that could digitize stills from composite video. Once all the images were captured, Greiman managed to import the stills from MacVision to MacDraw, where she composed the collage, as well as importing bitmapped typography and images that she had drawn in MacPaint. As MacDraw only offered one visual layer to work with, the process was as much trial and error as it was time-consuming as each visual or textual element was automatically merged into one big, bitmapped surface. During the process, entering command-Z, making copies of all major changes in the layout, as well as practicing one's impromptu composition skills, were a designer's best friend. Once the collage was finished, Greiman had to print it out on her LaserWriter as 21 US-letter-sized parts; the print office she worked with then

tiled the pages together to capture it on film in order to create a single source for offset printing. Greiman titled the issue Does It Make Sense?

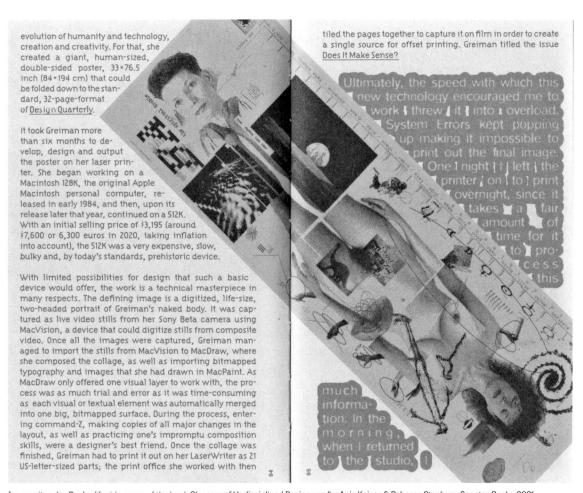

Innenseiten des Buchs / Inside pages of the book Glossary of Undisciplined Design von/by Anja Kaiser & Rebecca Stephany, Spector Books, 2021, mit einem Ausschnitt aus April Greimans Plakat / with an excerpt from April Greiman's poster Does it make sense?, 1986 © Anja Kaiser, Rebecca Stephany

„Underground matriarchy"

Im selben Jahr, in dem Martha Scotford ihren berühmten Aufsatz über „messy history" schrieb, tauschten sich Ellen Lupton, Grafikdesignerin und Design-Kuratorin am Cooper-Hewitt Museum, New York, und Laurie Haycock Makela, Designdirektorin des Walker Art Center, Minneapolis, per Fax über Frauen im Grafikdesign aus. Ihr Gespräch wurde im selben Jahr in der Designzeitschrift *Eye* veröffentlicht. Sie nannten den Beitrag „Underground matriarchy. Women who have shaped the profession by their own work and by enabling those around them".[6]

Demzufolge sind Männer zwar immer noch an vorderster Front im aktuellen Design, dennoch wird der Einfluss der Frauen im Hintergrund, oder besser: im Untergrund, als bedeutend beschrieben. Sie sprechen Frauen eine Wirkung im Sinne eines Matriarchats zu, die Studentinnen stark beeinflusst. Denn viele Grafikdesignerinnen waren zugleich Lehrerinnen an Designhochschulen: April Greiman, Sheila Levrant de Bretteville, Lorraine Wild und Katherine McCoy, Muriel Cooper, Carol Devine Carson und Mildred Friedman, die sich alle radikal von modernistischen Positionen abwandten und eine stärkere Subjektivität forderten.

Das „underground matriarchy" sollte aber nicht das „old boys' network", das über lange Zeit Frauen ausschloss, durch ein „exclusive new girl's network" ersetzen, sondern den sozialen Kontext von Design betonen und den Wert von Pluralität, subjektiver Interpretation und Partizipation herausstreichen.

A book designer herself, Scotford was known for her treatises on design theory and history, her curatorial work, and her design teaching at leading schools. Her work often focused on women in graphic design and feminist theory, including a book on the designer Cipe Pineles—further proof of her contributions to fostering professional solidarity among women.[5] Scotford juxtaposes the canon in design historiography, which she calls "neat history," to the plurality of approaches that maintain differing perspectives.

"Underground Matriarchy"

The same year that Martha Scotford wrote her famous essay on messy history, Ellen Lupton, graphic designer and design curator at the Cooper-Hewitt Museum, New York, and Laurie Haycock Makela, design director of the Walker Art Center, Minneapolis, exchanged ideas about women in graphic design via fax. Their conversation was published the same year in the design magazine *Eye*. They called the article "Underground Matriarchy: Women Who Have Shaped the Profession by Their Own Work and by Enabling Those around Them."[6]

They argued that while men were still at the forefront of design in their day, the influence of women in the background, or rather the underground, was significant. The impact they attribute to women can be understood in terms of a matriarchal influence that strongly influences women students, because many women graphic designers were also teachers at design colleges: April Greiman, Sheila Levrant de Bretteville, Lorraine Wild and Katherine McCoy, Muriel Cooper, Carol Devine Carson, and Mildred Friedman were all designers and educators who radically turned away from modernist positions in calling for stronger forms of subjectivity.

This "underground matriarchy," however, was not meant to replace the "old boys' network" that had so long excluded women with an "exclusive new girl's network." Rather, they called for it to emphasize the social context of design and to highlight the value of plurality, subjective interpretation, and participation.

6 Ellen Lupton & Laurie Haycock Makela: Underground Matriarchy. Women Who Have Shaped the Profession by Their Own Work and by Enabling Those around Them, *Eye Magazine* 4, Nr. 14 (Herbst 1994), https://www.eyemagazine.com/feature/article/underground-matriarchy (Abruf 2. Jul. 2022).

5 Martha Scotford: *Cipe Pineles: A Life of Design*, New York: W. W. Norton & Co, 1999; see also her article The Tenth Pioneer, *Eye Magazine* 5, no. 18 (Autumn 1995), https://www.eyemagazine.com/feature/article/the-tenth-pioneer (accessed 2. Jul. 2022).
6 Ellen Lupton & Laurie Haycock Makela, Underground Matriarchy, *Eye Magazine* 4, no. 14 (Autumn 1994), http://www.eyemagazine.com/feature/article/underground-matriarchy (accessed 2. Jul. 2022).

Literatur
Further Reading

Julian Beinart, Giancarlo de Carlo & Julian Beinart (Hg./eds.):
Sheila Levrant de Brettevile: Feminist Design, in Space and Society /
Spazio e Societa, Boston: MIT Press, 1986.

Sheila Levrant de Bretteville: Some Aspects of Design
from the Perspective of a Woman Designer,
Icographic. A Quarterly Review of International Visual
Communication Design, Nr./no. 6 (1973).

Ellen Lupton: Sheila Levrant de Bretteville: Dirty Design
and Fuzzy Theory, *Eye Magazine*, Nr./no. 13 (1992).

Ellen Lupton: Reputations: Sheila Levrant de Bretteville,
Eye Magazine 2, Nr./no. 8 (Herbst/Autum 1993),
https://www.eyemagazine.com/feature/article/reputations-
sheila-levrant-de-bretteville (Abruf/accessed 2. Jul. 2022).

Ellen Lupton & Laurie Haycock Makela: Underground Matriarchy.
Women Who Have Shaped the Profession by Their Own Work and
by Enabling Those around Them, *Eye Magazine* 4, Nr./no. 14
(Herbst/Autumn 1994), https://www.eyemagazine.com/feature/
article/underground-matriarchy (Abruf/accessed 4. Nov. 2022).

Jan van Toorn (Hg./ed.): *Design beyond Design*,
Maastricht: Jan van Eyck Academie Editions, 1998.

Terry Wolverton: *Insurgent Muse. Life and Art at the*
Woman's Building, San Francisco: City Light Books, 2002.

EINE FRAUENDOMÄNE

A WOMAN'S DOMAIN

Art-Direktorinnen von Vogue,
Harper's Bazaar und
anderen Lifestyle-Zeitschriften
Women as Art Directors of Vogue,
Harper's Bazaar, and
Other Lifestyle Magazines

Die Jahre der großen Mode- und Life-style-Zeitschriften in den USA und ihrer Dependancen in Europa waren auch die großen Zeiten amerikanischer Grafikdesignerinnen. Früh, in den 1910er und 1920er Jahren, prägte Helen Dryden (1887–1981) das Erscheinungsbild der Zeitschrift *Vogue*. Sie kreierte das Bild der modernen amerikanischen Frau der weißen Mittelschicht und der Upper Class, das sie im Laufe ihrer Karriere dann auch einem neuen Zeitgeist anpasste.

Dryden trat mit einem eigenen Stil in der *Vogue* auf. Sie wurde durch ihre von Art nouveau und später Art déco beeinflussten Titelgestaltungen und Anzeigen bekannt. Zunächst fand ihr für damalige Verhältnisse reduzierter Dryden-Stil wenig Anerkennung, sogar bei der *Vogue* selbst. Erst das Verlagshaus Condé Nast erkannte die Qualität ihrer Zeichnungen. Ihre Titelblätter prägten dann von 1909 bis 1922 die *Vogue*. Als sie die Modezeitschrift nach dreizehn Jahren verließ, gestaltete sie als Freelancerin unter anderem regelmäßig die Cover des *Delineator*-Magazins.

Eine frühe Art-Direktorin war Cipe Pineles (1908–1991), eine Immigrantin aus Österreich, die in Brooklyn aufwuchs. 1932 begann sie als Assistentin von M. F. Agha, der Art-Direktor von *Vogue* und *Vanity Fair* war und seinen Zeitschriften ein neues, an europäischen modernen Strömungen orientiertes Image verleihen wollte. Er ließ Pineles große Freiheit, was Layout und die Einbeziehung von Fotografie anbetraf. 1942 wurde sie dann Art-Direktorin von *Glamour*, später, von 1947 bis 1950, von *Seventeen*, von 1950 bis 1959 von *Charm* und von 1959 bis 1961 von *Mademoiselle*. Alle Magazine wandten sich bewusst an jüngere Leserinnen.

Die Grafikdesignerin und Designwissenschaftlerin Martha Scotford hat auf die moderne aufklärerische Haltung gegenüber Frauen in diesen Zeitschriften hingewiesen – und das unmittelbar nachdem sie ihre Kritik am Designkanon und der männlich dominierten Designhistoriografie formuliert hatte. Unter der Überschrift „Taking women seriously"[1] geht sie darauf ein, wie die Zeitschrift *Seventeen* in den 1940er Jahren junge Frauen, „Teenager" genannt, als eigene Altersgruppe „erfand". Frauen waren bis dato, vor allem in der Kleidung und ihrem Lebensstil, entweder Kinder oder Erwachsene. Zudem macht sie darauf aufmerksam, dass die Zeitschrift *Charm* sich in den 1950er Jahren Berufsfrauen zuwandte, ihr Untertitel lautete: „Die Zeitschrift für Frauen,

1 Martha Scotford & Cipe Pineles: The Tenth Pioneer, *Eye Magazine* 5, Nr. 18 (Herbst 1995), https://www.eyemagazine.com/feature/article/the-tenth-pioneer (Abruf 3. Aug. 2022).

Helen Dryden, Titelblatt für die / Cover for Vogue, 1. Jul. 1919

The era of the big fashion and lifestyle magazines in the United States, and of their related publications in Europe, coincided with the capital years of American women graphic designers. Quite early in this history, in the 1910s and 1920s, Helen Dryden (1887–1981) deeply influenced the look of the magazine *Vogue*. She created the image of the modern American woman from the White middle and upper class, later adapting it to the new zeitgeist over the course of her career.

Dryden entered onto the scene with a style of her own in *Vogue*. She became known for her cover designs and advertisements influenced by art nouveau and later art déco. Initially, her signature Dryden style, which was quite reduced for her day, received little recognition, even at *Vogue*, until the publishing house Condé Nast recognized the quality of her drawings. Her covers then became emblematic for *Vogue* from 1909 to 1922. When she left the fashion magazine after thirteen years, her freelance work included regularly designing the covers of the magazine *Delineator*.

One early woman art director was Cipe Pineles (1908–1991), an immigrant from Austria

BEING A MAGAZINE DESIGNER IS A LITTLE BIT LIKE BEING AN ORCHESTRA CONDUCTOR.

Ruth Ansel, 2010

Helen Dryden, Werbung für LUX, veröffentlicht 1928 in der deutschen Fachzeitschrift Gebrauchsgraphik /
Advertisement for LUX, published in 1928 in the German trade journal Gebrauchsgraphik

die arbeiten".[2] Scotford folgert: „Both were ground-breaking women's magazines."

Zugleich beschreibt sie, dass die Zeitschriften, unabhängig von den Leserinnen, eine Frauendomäne waren. Helen Valentine war Herausgeberin, Cipe Pineles die Grafikdesignerin, Promotion Director war Estelle Ellis. Alle anfangs um die 30 Jahre alt, waren sie während mehr als zwölf Jahren täglich in Kontakt. Es verband sie eine enge persönliche und professionelle Beziehung. Alle drei Frauen waren verheiratet und wurden von ihren Männern als Berufsfrauen anerkannt und unterstützt. Es war die Zeit, in der Simone de Beauvoir ihr Buch *The Second Sex* (1949) herausgab und 13 Jahre, bevor Betty Friedan mit *The Feminine Mystique* maßgeblich auf die amerikanische Frauenbewegung einwirkte. Auch wenn die Frauen sich nicht als Feministinnen verstanden, sogar ihre Bedenken öffentlich äußerten und den Standard zeitgenössischer Konstruktionen des Weiblichen nicht grundsätzlich durchkreuzten, haben sie doch Frauenleben in ihren Zeitschriften unterstützt. Scotford kommt zu dem Schluss: „I would call these women proto-feminists."[3]

Auch in weiteren Lifestyle-Zeitschriften spielten Frauen eine große Rolle. Die Grafikdesignerinnen Bea Feitler (1938–1982) und Ruth Ansel (geb. 1938) waren herausragende Art-Direktorinnen bei *Harper's Bazaar*. In den 1960er und 1970er Jahren arbeiteten sie darüber hinaus für andere Zeitschriften. Ansel war in den 1970er Jahren Art-Direktorin vom *New York Times Magazine* und in den 1980ern für *House & Garden, Vanity Fair* und *Vogue*. Bea Feitler entwarf Titelblätter für *Ms.*, *Rolling Stone* und *Vanity Fair*.

Miki Denhof (1912–2000) arbeitete ab 1945 für Condé Nast und war Promotion Art Director für *Vogue*. Die Fotografin und Grafikdesignerin Lillian Bassman (1917–2012) war in den 1940ern bis in die 1960er Jahre Art-Direktorin bei *Junior Bazaar* und später bei *Harper's Bazaar*.

Eine besondere Vertreterin ihrer Profession war in den 1980er Jahren Gail Anderson bei *Rolling Stone*. Während alle anderen erwähnten Art-Direktorinnen zwar den Stil der jeweiligen Zeitschrift prägten, oft durch die Konzeption und die Wahl von Fotograf*innen, aber keinen eigenen Autorenstil im Grafikdesign selbst kreierten, brachte neben Helen Dryden insbesondere Gail Anderson ihren eigenen Stil am stärksten ein. Sie war in dem legendären Musik-Magazin 15 Jahre lang in leitender Position.

who grew up in Brooklyn. In 1932, Pineles began working as an assistant to M. F. Agha, the art director of *Vogue* and *Vanity Fair* who wanted to give his magazines a new look oriented toward modern European trends. He gave Pineles broad freedom to design the layout and include photography. In 1942 she became art director of *Glamour*, and later, of *Seventeen* (1947–50), *Charm* (1950–59), and *Mademoiselle* (1959–61). All of these magazines were deliberately aimed at younger women readers.

Graphic designer and design scholar Martha Scotford has emphasized the modern progressive attitude toward women in these journals—a point she made immediately after formulating her critique of the design canon and male-dominated design historiography. Under the heading "Taking Women Seriously,"[1] she addresses how the magazine *Seventeen* "invented" young women, or "teenagers," as their own age group in the 1940s. Until then, especially in their dress and lifestyle, women had been regarded as either children or adults. She further points to the fact that the magazine *Charm* addressed professional women in the 1950s, announced by the publication's subtitle: "The magazine for women who work." Scotford concludes: "Both were groundbreaking women's magazines."[2]

At the same time, she describes how these magazines were a woman's domain even apart from their readers. Helen Valentine served as an editor, Cipe Pineles as a graphic designer, and Estelle Ellis as a promotion director. All in their early thirties when they started out, they remained in daily contact for more than twelve years, developing a close personal and professional relationship. All three women were married and were recognized and supported by their husbands as professional women. This was the time when Simone de Beauvoir published her book *The Second Sex* (1949), and thirteen years before Betty Friedan had a major impact on the American's women movement with *The Feminine Mystique*. Even if these three women designers did not see themselves as feminists and publicly voiced their misgivings about feminism, shying away from fundamentally challenging or disrupting constructions of femininity from their day, they did support women's lives in their journals. Scotford concludes: "I would call these women proto-feminists."[3]

2 Ebenda.
3 Ebenda.

1 Martha Scotford & Cipe Pineles: The Tenth Pioneer, *Eye Magazine* 5, no. 18 (Autumn 1995), https://www.eyemagazine.com/feature/article/the-tenth-pioneer (accessed 3. Aug. 2022).
2 Scotford, Pineles, The Tenth Pioneer.

Bea Feitler, Plakat für eine Ausgabe des Magazins / Poster for an issue of the magazine Ms., Jul. 1972,
Foto/photo: © Bea Feitler papers, The New School Archives and Special Collections, The New School, New York, NY

Bea Feitler, Titelblatt der / Cover for Ms., Jan. 1975
© The New School Archives and Special Collection, The New School, New York, NY

Nicht selten arbeiteten einige der erwähnten Frauen zusammen und förderten einander. Beispielsweise gestaltete Bea Feitler 1978 den Umschlag zum Jubiläumsbuch des seit 1901 herausgegebenen US-Magazins *House & Garden*, das von Condé Nast Publications ediert wurde und sich auf Innenarchitektur, Unterhaltung und Gartengestaltung spezialisierte. Die Herausgeberin war Mary Jane Pool, die seit 1970 zugleich Herausgeberin von *House & Garden* war. Die Journalistin Caroline Seebohm betreute den redaktionellen Teil und Miki Denhof, die zu diesem Zeitpunkt Creative Director von Condé Nast Books war, gestaltete den gesamten Innenteil des Buches. Das ganze Projekt war folglich in Frauenhand.

Wie Martha Scotford kritisch anmerkt, waren die Zeitschriften zugleich alles andere als Produkte einer Gegenkultur: „[...] they were, after all, successful commercial products within a booming post-war capitalist economy."[4]

Es waren vor allem die Magazine *Harper's Bazaar* (ab 1867) und *Vogue* (ab 1892) in New York, die nicht nur die neueste Mode präsentierten, sondern auch den Lebensstil der High Society vorführten. Sie beschrieben, was „in" und was „out" war, und beeinflussten mit ihren vie-

Women also played a major role in other lifestyle magazines, as well. Graphic designers Bea Feitler (1938–1982) and Ruth Ansel (b. 1938), for instance, were prominent art directors at *Harper's Bazaar*; and later, in the 1960s and 1970s, they also worked for other magazines. In the 1970s, Ansel was an art director at the *New York Times Magazine* and in the 1980s for *House & Garden*, *Vanity Fair*, and *Vogue*. Bea Feitler designed covers for *Ms.*, *Rolling Stone*, and *Vanity Fair*.

Miki Denhof (1912–2000) worked for Condé Nast beginning in 1945 and was a promotion art director for *Vogue*. Photographer and graphic designer Lillian Bassman (1917–2012) was an art director from the 1940s to the 1960s at *Junior Bazaar* and later at *Harper's Bazaar*.

One exceptional woman designer in the 1980s was Gail Anderson at *Rolling Stone*. Apart from Helen Dryden, the women art directors mentioned in this chapter did not create their own authorial style of graphic design, even though they did shape the style of their respective maga-zines, often through the design approach and choice of photographers. Following the path blazed by Dryden, however, Gail Anderson emerged as the woman director from this period who most strongly developed and implemented her own style. She held a senior position at the legendary music magazine for fifteen years.

Not infrequently, some of the women mentioned here worked together and supported each other. In 1978, for example, Bea Feitler designed the cover for the book celebrating the anniversary of *House & Garden*, a Condé Nast Publications title in print since 1901 that specialized in interior design, entertainment, and garden design. The editor was Mary Jane Pool, who since 1970 had also been the editor of *House & Garden*. The journalist Caroline Seebohm was in charge of the editorial section and Miki Denhof, at that time a creative director at Condé Nast Books, was the sole designer for the interior of the book. The entire project was thus in the hands of women.

At the same time, as Martha Scotford critically notes, the magazines were anything but products of a counterculture: "they were, after all, successful commercial products within a booming post-war capitalist economy."[4]

It was mainly the magazines *Harper's Bazaar* (from 1867) and *Vogue* (from 1892) in New York that not only presented the latest fashions, but also showcased the lifestyle of high society. These publications described what was in and what was out and, with their many sister publi-

4 Ebenda.

3 Scotford, Pineles, The Tenth Pioneer.
4 Scotford, Pineles, The Tenth Pioneer.

len Dependancen in Europa Lifestyle und Design weltweit. Die amerikanische *Vogue* hatte allein 18 „Geschwister". In Deutschland erschien eine eigene Ausgabe seit 1928. Die verschiedenen Eigner der Zeitschriften wie Condé Nast (*Vogue*) und der „Medienbaron" William Randolph Hearst (*Harper's Bazaar*) bauten regelrechte Medienimperien auf.

Charakteristisch für fast alle Hochglanzmagazine war ihre Nähe zu Kunst und Fotografie. Die Herausgeber*innen wählten begabte Grafikdesigner*innen aus, die das Talent hatten, das besondere Etwas dieser Mischung zu erkennen und der Zeitschrift einen eigenen unverwechselbaren Stil zu geben. Die Berufsgruppe war nicht nur für das visuelle Erscheinungsbild zuständig – dies vor allem –, sondern sie verfügte zugleich über Kreativität, Führungs- und Teamqualitäten und über Kenntnisse der Produktionsabläufe. Die Frauen verkörperten Erfolg, gut bezahlte Stellen, das Talent zum Netzwerken mit Personen in den verschiedensten kreativen Berufen und das Gespür für den Geschmack der *happy few*.

Neben den Art-Direktorinnen arbeiteten auch auffallend viele Frauen als Chefredakteurinnen in den Modezeitschriften. Die erste bei *Vogue* war Josephine Redding, seit 1988 Anna Wintour. Das Renommee dieser Frauen war groß, nicht nur in ihren eigenen, sondern auch in Kunstkreisen. Modebewusste Frauen wie Jackie Kennedy, Intellektuelle wie Susan Sontag zählten zu ihrem gesellschaftlichen Milieu. Hervorragende Fotograf*innen, die sie auswählten, sind mit ihren Werken für die *Vogue* und *Harper's Bazaar* in die Fotografiegeschichte eingegangen.

Anfangs waren Baron Adolphe de Meyer, Edward Steichen, Man Ray, Cecil Beaton, Jacques-Henri Lartigue und George Hoyningen-Huene – die gesamte Garde der berühmten Fotografen der Zeit – vertreten. Später dann beauftragte *Vogue* aufwendige Fotostrecken und engagierte Fotografen wie Helmut Newton und Peter Lindbergh. Auch Künstler erschienen mit ihren Werken in der Zeitschrift wie Pablo Picasso und Salvador Dalí sowie Literaten wie Truman Capote und Aldous Huxley und Schauspieler wie Richard Burton und Marcello Mastroianni. Mit der Wahl dieser Größen wollte sich die *Vogue* ein kultiviertes Image verleihen. In manchen Bereichen war sie avantgardistisch, zum Beispiel führte sie eine innovative Typografie und Fotografie ein. Bereits 1932 zeigte sie eine Farbfotografie auf dem Cover. Im August 1974 wurde zum ersten Mal ein afroamerikanisches Model auf dem Titel abgebildet.

Mit dem Art Director Alexey Brodovitch wurde *Harper's Bazaar* ein dominierendes Stilmagazin seiner Epoche. Auch diese Zeitschrift

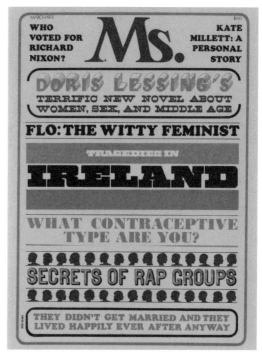

Bea Feitler, Plakat für eine Ausgabe des Magazins / Poster for an issue of the magazine Ms., Jul. 1972, Foto/photo: © Bea Feitler papers, The New School Archives and Special Collections, The New School, New York, NY

cations in Europe, influenced lifestyle and design worldwide. The American *Vogue* alone had eighteen "siblings." In Germany, a separate edition has appeared since 1928. The various owners of magazines such as Condé Nast (*Vogue*) and of the media baron William Randolph Hearst (*Harper's Bazaar*) built up veritable media empires.

A distinguishing feature of almost all glossy magazines was a proximity to the fields of art and photography. The editors selected talented graphic designers who had a unique ability to recognize this mix's special something and to give each magazine its own distinctive style. Graphic designers were not only responsible for a publication's visual appearance, their main task; they were also expected to employ creativity, leadership and team skills, and knowledge of production processes. The women embodied success, well-paying jobs, a knack for networking with people in a variety of creative professions, and a sense for the tastes of the happy few.

In addition to art directors, a striking number of women also worked as editors-in-chief of fashion magazines. The first at *Vogue* was Josephine Redding, and since 1988, Anna Wintour. These women enjoyed a commanding reputation, not only among their peers but also in art circles. Fashion-conscious women such as Jackie Kennedy

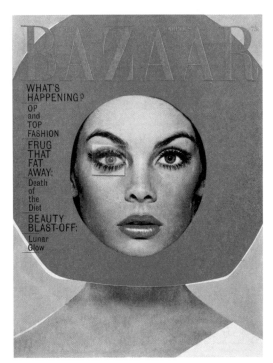

Bea Feitler, Model Jean Shrimpton, Harper's Bazaar (Apr. 1965), Art-Direktion / art direction: Bea Feitler & Ruth Ansel, Foto/photo: Richard Avedon © 2022 The Richard Avedon Foundation, The New School Archives and Special Collection, The New School, New York, NY

hatte legendäre Chefredakteurinnen. 1936 kam die US-amerikanische Modedesignerin und Mode-Kolumnistin Diana Vreeland als Redakteurin für Mode und Design zu *Harper's Bazaar* und wurde deren Chefredakteurin.[5] Von 1963 bis 1971 übernahm sie diese Position beim amerikanischen *Vogue Magazine*. Vreeland selbst entstammte einer wohlhabenden New Yorker Familie und war eine Szene-Größe der Stadt. In den Sixties spielte sie die Rolle eines Stars im US-Modejournalismus und hatte ein gutes Gespür für hervorragende künstlerische Beiträge. Fotografinnen wie Louise Dahl-Wolfe lieferten allein 86 Titelfotos. Renommierte Fotograf*innen wie Man Ray, Diane Arbus und Richard Avedon arbeiteten für das Magazin. Avedons Bild des Models Jean Shrimpton mit pinkfarbenem Helm im Courrèges-Look avancierte zu einer Ikone. Die Zeitschriften reflektierten auch die wechselnde Rolle der Frau in der Gesellschaft. Dennoch blieben sie „in erster Linie ein Coffeetable-Heft, also ein Blatt zum Blättern".[6]

or intellectuals such as Susan Sontag belonged to their social milieu. With their works for *Vogue* and *Harper's Bazaar*, outstanding photographers they selected have gone down in photographic history.

Initially these photographers included Baron Adolphe de Meyer, Edward Steichen, Man Ray, Cecil Beaton, Jacques-Henri Lartigue, and George Hoyningen-Huene—the entire vanguard of famous photographers of the day. *Vogue* then later commissioned lavish photo spreads, hiring photographers such as Helmut Newton and Peter Lindbergh. Artists also appeared in the magazine, with works by visual artists such as Pablo Picasso or Salvador Dalí or by literary figures such as Truman Capote or Aldous Huxley alongside features on actors such as Richard Burton or Marcello Mastroianni. In choosing these celebrated figures, *Vogue* aimed to project a sophisticated image. In some areas the magazine was even avant-garde, such as in its introduction of innovative typography and photography. Quite early, in 1932, it began featuring a color photograph on the cover. In August 1974, it chose an African-American model for the cover for the first time.

With the art director Alexey Brodovitch, *Harper's Bazaar* became one of the dominant style magazines of its era. And it, too, had legendary women in the position of editor-in-chief.[5] In 1936, US fashion designer and fashion columnist Diana Vreeland joined *Harper's Bazaar* as fashion and design editor, later becoming its editor-in-chief. From 1963 to 1971, she held this position at the American *Vogue Magazine*. Vreeland came from a wealthy New York family and was already a prominent socialite in her own right. In the 1960s she became a star of US fashion journalism, with a good sense for illustrious artistic contributions. Women photographers such as Louise Dahl-Wolfe provided eighty-six cover photos alone. Renowned photographers such as Man Ray, Diane Arbus, and Richard Avedon worked for the magazine. Avedon's image of model Jean Shrimpton wearing a pink helmet in a look by Courrèges became iconic. These magazines also reflected the changing role of women in society. They nevertheless remained "primarily coffee-table publications, that is to say, magazines meant to be browsed and not seriously read."[6]

5 Eleanor Dwight: *Diana Vreeland*, New York: Morrow, 2002.
6 Sebastian Hammelehle über *Harper's Bazaar*: Deutsche Ausgabe „Harper's Bazaar". Das Bling-Ding, https://www.spiegel.de/kultur/gesellschaft/harper's-bazaar-a-919434.html (Abruf 21. Nov. 2021).

5 Eleanor Dwight: *Diana Vreeland*, New York: Morrow, 2002.
6 Sebastian Hammelehle on *Harper's Bazaar*, Deutsche Ausgabe "Harper's Bazaar": Das Bling-Ding, https://www.spiegel.de/kultur/gesellschaft/harper's-bazaar-a-919434.html (accessed 21. Nov. 2021).

Literatur
Further Reading

Cipe Pineles Golden & Martha Scotford: *Cipe Pineles. A Life of Design*, New York: Norton Book for Architects and Designers, 1998.

Julia Ryff: *Lillian Bassman (1917–2012)*, Köln/Cologne: Böhlau Verlag, 2016.

Martha Scotford & Cipe Pineles: The Tenth Pioneer, *Eye Magazine* 5, Nr./no. 18 (Herbst/Autumn 1995), https://www.eyemagazine.com/feature/article/the-tenth-pioneer (Abruf/accessed 3. Aug. 2022).

André Stolarski & Bruno Feitler (Hg./eds.): *O design de Bea Feitler*, São Paulo: Cosac Naify, 2012.

POST-FEMINISTISCHE UND QUEER-FEMINISTISCHE MAGAZINE

POSTFEMINIST AND QUEER-FEMINIST MAGAZINES

Kontinuität und Diskontinuität
Continuity and Discontinuity

Die Skepsis, der die sogenannte dritte Welle der Frauenbewegung in den 1990er Jahren der Neuen Frauenbewegung der 1970er Jahre begegnete, hat zu viel diskutierten Ausdrucksformen geführt. Es erschienen Zeitschriften von Frauenkollektiven, die zwar feministische Themen behandelten, die aber eine andere Ausrichtung hatten als ihre Vorläuferinnen. Diese neuen Magazine, die von jungen Frauen fast in jeder westlichen Nation herausgegeben wurden oder nationenübergreifend operierten, reflektier(t)en häufig, wie sich „ihr" Feminismus von der früheren Emanzipationsbewegung unterscheidet. Nur: Um welchen Feminismus handelt es sich? Wie können Genderthemen mit Unterhaltung, Pop und Politik verbunden werden? Und: Erfasst der Begriff Gender ihre Ausrichtung überhaupt noch? Es scheint, dass Feminismus sich immer weiter ausdifferenziert und zu einem Diskurs zwischen verschiedenen Positionen wird.

Zu dem neuen Typ von unabhängigen Zeitschriften, die bis heute erscheinen, zählen *Missy Magazine* in Deutschland, *Girls Like Us*, ausgehend von Amsterdam und Belgien sowie Grafikdesignerinnen aus Stockholm mit einem sehr weiten Vertriebsnetz, *an.schläge* in Österreich, *Riposte*, ein britisches Magazin und eine Online-Plattform, *Causette* in Frankreich, *Bitch: Feminist Response to Pop Culture* in den USA und viele mehr. Sie alle integrieren Grafikdesign als wesentliches Format ihrer Aussagen, wobei ihre Ästhetik vor allem an der Popkultur orientiert war und ist. Die Grafik ist, bis auf Ausnahmen wie *Girls like Us* und *Riposte*, plakativ, oft auch schrill und provozierend, ohne allerdings die Widerständigkeit des DIY der 1960er und 1970er Jahre und deren bewusste Ablehnung gängiger Ästhetik nachzuahmen.

Durch ihre scheinbar widersprüchlichen Aussagen befördern die Magazine den Verdacht, feministische Anliegen zu kommerzialisieren und zu trivialisieren. Vor allem die englische Kulturwissenschaftlerin Angela McRobbie hat den Typus der jungen Frau kritisiert, der diese Magazine betreibt.[1] Sie stimmt mit Rosalind Gill in ihrer kritischen Position überein: Der Postfeminismus „[...] eignet sich feministische wie auch antifeministische Ideen sowohl an, als er sie auch ablehnt, und ist eng mit dem Neoliberalismus verbunden", heißt es bei ihr.[2] Trotz Mikroformen von Frauen-

The skepticism with which the third wave of the women's movement in the 1990s met second wave feminism from two decades earlier provoked widely discussed forms of expression. Women's collectives produced journals that continued to engage with feminist issues, but with an entirely different take than their predecessors. These new magazines, published by young women in almost every Western nation or operating internationally, often reflect (on) how "their" feminism differed from the earlier movement for women's emancipation. Yet their perspectives raise further questions: What kind of feminism are we talking about? How can gender issues be connected to entertainment, pop culture, and politics? And does the concept of gender even still capture their concerns? It seems that feminism is becoming more and more differentiated as it develops into a discourse between various positions.

This new type of independent magazine, still being published today, includes *Missy Magazine* in Germany; *Girls Like Us*, produced by women graphic designers in Amsterdam, Belgium, and Stockholm and boasting a very wide distribution network; *an.schläge* in Austria; the British magazine *Riposte*; the online platform *Causette* in France; *Bitch: Feminist Response to Pop Culture* in the United States; and many more. All of them integrate graphic design as an essential format for the statements they make, although their aesthetics were and are primarily geared toward pop culture. The visuals, with exceptions like *Girls Like Us* and *Riposte*, are bold, often garish, and provocative, without however emulating the rebellious DIY stance of the 1960s and 1970s and its conscious rejection of the prevailing aesthetic.

Such seemingly contradictory positions can arouse suspicion that these publications commercialize and trivialize feminist concerns. The English cultural scholar Angela McRobbie, in particular, has criticized the type of young woman that she identifies as running these magazines.[1] In her critical stance, she agrees with Rosalind Gill: "Postfeminism," she writes, "both appropriates and rejects feminist and antifeminist ideas, and it is closely linked to neoliberalism."[2] Despite the existence of women's collectives on a microscale and the international phenomenon

1 Angela McRobbie: Post-feminism and Popular Culture, *Feminist Media Studies* 4, Nr./no. 3 (2004), DOI: 10.1080/1468077042000 309937.
2 Rosalind Gill: Die Widersprüche verstehen. (Anti-)Feminismus, Postfeminismus, Neoliberalismus, *Bundeszentrale für politische Bildung*, 20. Apr. 2018, https://www.bpb.de/shop/zeitschriften/apuz/267938/die-widersprueche-verstehen/ (Abruf 20. Jul. 2021).

1 Angela McRobbie: Post-feminism and Popular Culture, *Feminist Media Studies* 4, Nr./no. 3 (2004), DOI: 10.1080/1468077042000 309937.
2 Rosalind Gill: Die Widersprüche verstehen: (Anti-)Feminismus, Postfeminismus, Neoliberalismus, *Bundeszentrale für politische Bildung*, 20. Apr. 2018, https://www.bpb.de/shop/zeitschriften/apuz/267938/die-widersprueche-verstehen/ (accessed 20. Jul. 2021).

kollektiven und trotz des nationenübergreifenden Phänomens vergleichbarer Magazine schwören die jungen Frauen einerseits einer feministischen Ideologie ab, obwohl sie sich gleichzeitig als einer „vierten Welle" des Feminismus zugehörig betrachten. Die Herausgeberin Jessica Gysel von *Girls like Us* beschrieb dies wie folgt: „Fourth wave feminism is a nebulous beast. Shape-shifting, label-changing, name-calling, it's an inclusive, exclusive, girls club which spends more time gazing into the camera at its own Face Tuned reflection than practising the love it preaches in vowelless Instagram hashtags."[3]

Und Sara Kaaman, die Grafikdesignerin des Magazins, schrieb dazu: „*Girls like Us* is more or less female [...] it begins, acknowledging the slippery, non-binary nature of gender. [...] *Girls like Us* is an investigation in the form of a magazine."[4]

Der Begriff Postfeminismus

Wenn diese Zeitschriften als postfeministisch firmieren, dann muss darauf hingewiesen werden, dass der Begriff Postfeminismus in Deutschland unterschiedlich verwendet wird. Während er zum einen eine wertneutrale Bezeichnung für die historische Kontinuität ist, das heißt lediglich auf die Zeit nach der Zweiten Frauenbewegung verweist, ohne den Feminismus für obsolet zu erklären, und auf Transformationen des Feminismus eingeht, ist er zum anderen, vor allem seit den 1990er Jahren, mit einer Ablehnung des Feminismus verbunden. Das Präfix „Post-" steht dann für die Überwindung emanzipatorischer Forderungen. Viele Vertreter*innen dieser Form von Postfeminismus plädieren für Selbstverantwortung und reklamieren eine individuelle Entscheidungsfreiheit, die keinen politisch-ideologischen Gesamtinteressen untergeordnet ist. Allein wegen ihrer Forderung nach Partikularität ist unter diesen Frauen eine Vielzahl von Positionen zu erkennen. Oft verbinden sie sich mit lauten, provozierenden Gesten, sind eine Art von Popfeminismus und werden als unpolitisch kritisiert. Zumindest ist es irritierend, dass sie häufig mit Geschlechterklischees jonglieren und sie überzeichnen.

Subversive Affirmation ist aber ein Mittel für die Frauen, Distanz zu den konventionellen Aussagen zu schaffen, indem sie diese übertreiben und durch die vordergründige Bestätigung in ihr Gegenteil verwandeln. Überidentifizierung bedeu-

of comparable magazines, these young women renounced a feminist ideology even as they consider themselves to belong to a "fourth wave" of feminism. Editor Jessica Gysel of *Girls Like Us* described this as follows: "Fourth wave feminism is a nebulous beast. Shape-shifting, label-changing, name-calling, it's an inclusive, exclusive, girls club which spends more time gazing into the camera at its own Face Tuned reflection than practising the love it preaches in vowelless Instagram hashtags."[3]

Sara Kaaman, the magazine's graphic designer, further noted: "*Girls Like Us* is more or less female ... it begins, acknowledging the slippery, non-binary nature of gender. ... *Girls Like Us* is an investigation in the form of a magazine."[4]

The Concept of Postfeminism

If these journals operate under the banner of postfeminism, then it must be noted that this term is used in a particular way in Germany. On the one hand, the term designates a historical continuity without any value judgment, meaning it merely refers to the period after the second wave of the women's movement without declaring feminism obsolete, thus addressing transformations of feminism. On the other hand, especially since the 1990s, it has been associated with a rejection of feminism. In this view, the prefix "post" stands for the overcoming of demands for emancipation. Many proponents of this form of postfeminism call for personal responsibility in rejecting any kind of individual freedom that is not subordinated to overall political-ideological interests. On this account alone, the insistence of these postfeminists on particularity entails that they recognize a multiplicity of positions. They often join together with loud, provocative gestures, articulating a kind of pop feminism that some criticize as apolitical. At the very least, it is disconcerting that they often play with gender stereotypes and their exaggeration.

Subversive affirmation, however, offers women a means to create distance from conventional positions: exaggerating them merely appears to confirm them, while in fact it transforms them into their opposite. Overidentification means taking a position precisely within the logic of the prevailing order in order to attack it from inside. Alienation disrupts the

---

3 Siehe https://www.itsnicethat.com/articles/jessica-gysel-on-girls-like-us-070617 (Abruf 11. Jan. 2022).
4 Ebenda.

3 See https://www.itsnicethat.com/articles/jessica-gysel-on-girls-like-us-070617 (accessed 11. Jan. 2022).
4 See https://www.itsnicethat.com/articles/jessica-gysel-on-girls-like-us-070617 (accessed 11. Jan. 2022).

Postfeminist and Queer-Feminist Magazines

Sara Kaaman, Jessica Gysel &
Katja Mater, 2021

RETHINKING THE FUTURE WHILE DIGGING INTO THE PAST.

Plakat zur Ausstellung / Poster for the exhibition The F* word. Guerrilla Girls und feministisches Grafikdesign, Kuratorin/curator: Dr. Julia Meer, Museum für Kunst und Gewerbe Hamburg, 2023 © Museum für Kunst und Gewerbe Hamburg, Grafik: Rimini Berlin, Motiv/motif: Guerrilla Girls, 2023

seemingly normal process of communication, which in turn again creates distance from positions that seem normal and familiar. This reveals that the pejorative interpretative of postfeminism described above does not accord with how the movement sees itself.

Club Culture as Reference

Unlike their predecessors from the 1960s and 1970s, the new crop of magazines draws inspiration from club culture, among other sources. Yet it is also symptomatic that many of their proponents are active within established institutions, often teaching at universities or in workshops in museums. This means they can no longer be called expressions of an alternative scene or subculture.

Like most postfeminist positions today, they are broadening their focus to include an *intersectional* perspective. Rather than reducing oppression to the "classical" forms of belonging structured by class, race, and gender, they consider the multiple identities of individuals and the power dynamics produced when different forms of discrimination interact. Deliberately employing a patchwork of theories and of design forms and formats, they playfully move between positions with the freedom of creative experimentation.

Looking back at the history of the club culture movement, one can see (anti)aesthetic elements even within the youth culture of punk rock in the 1970s as it developed in New York City and London. While the movement's protagonists intentionally stood out in these early years with their provocative appearance, rebellious attitude, and nonconformist behavior, in the 1990s

Guerrilla Girls, Do Women Have to Be Naked to Get into the Met. Museum?, Plakat/poster, 1989 © Guerrilla Girls, courtesy guerrillagirls.com

tet, sich zwar innerhalb der Logik der herrschenden Ordnung aufzustellen, sie dabei aber gerade dort anzugreifen. Verfremdung stört den scheinbar normalen Kommunikationsprozess. Dadurch wird erneut Distanz zur Normalität und Vertrautem geschaffen. Es lässt sich zeigen, dass das abwertende Deutungsmuster von „Postfeminismus" kein Bestandteil der Selbstbeschreibung ist.

Club culture als Referenz

Anders als ihre Vorläuferinnen aus den 1960er und 1970er Jahren schöpfen die neuen Magazine ihre Anregungen unter anderem aus der *club culture*. Symptomatisch aber ist auch, dass viele ihrer Vertreterinnen sich zugleich im Rahmen etablierter Institutionen bewegen, der Lehre an Hochschulen und in Workshops von Museen beispielsweise. Sie sind deshalb keine Alternativ- oder Subkultur mehr.

Wie die meisten heutigen postfeministischen Positionen erweitern sie ihre Ausrichtung auf eine intersektionale Perspektive. Sie reduzieren sie nicht auf die „klassischen" Unterdrückungsformen in den Bereichen *class*, *race* und *gender*, bei denen klassenspezifische, ethnische und geschlechtliche Zugehörigkeit in den Fokus rücken. Vielmehr beziehen sie individuelle Mehrfachidentitäten und Machtdynamiken mit ein, die sich durch das Zusammenwirken verschiedener Diskriminierungsformen ergeben. Mit einem bewusst eingesetzten Patchwork an Theorien, gestalterischen Formen und Formaten jonglieren sie im Freiraum kreativer Erprobungen.

Blickt man zurück auf die Geschichte der Club-Culture-Bewegung, kann man (anti-)ästhetische Elemente bereits in der Jugendkultur des Punk-Rock in den 1970er Jahren erkennen, der sich in den Großstädten New York City und London abspielte. Während ihre Akteur*innen zu dieser Zeit durch ein provozierendes Aussehen, eine rebellische Haltung und nonkonformistisches Verhalten auftraten, politisierte sich die Bewegung in den 1990er Jahren stärker. Sehr bald wurde sie ein großer kommerzieller Erfolg und innerhalb einer Jugendszene Mainstream. Nach wie vor spielte sie mit Ausdrucksformen einer Gegenkultur und behielt ihre hedonistischen, subversiven und permissiven Qualitäten bei. Sie bezog sich nicht nur auf Musik, sondern entwarf auch eigene Ausdrucksformen im Mode- und Grafikdesign wie beispielsweise bei Plakaten, Zines und Plattencovern.

Anfang der 1990er Jahre entstand innerhalb der amerikanischen Punkmusikszene it became even more political. It soon found huge commercial success, however, and became mainstream for some young people, though nevertheless continuing to play with ways of expressing a counterculture and retaining its hedonistic, subversive, and permissive qualities. Ultimately it was not only in music, but also in creating its own forms of expression in fashion and graphic design, in formats such as posters, zines, and record covers, that its influence was felt.

In the early 1990s, a feminist movement also emerged within the American punk music scene, initially in response to the dominance of male musicians in the alternative scene and their misogynistic lyrics and stage performances. Feminists protested against the perception of young girls as cute and naive.[5] Many of the magazines discussed here, such as *Missy Magazine*, directly engaged with this perception in order to counteract it. For decades, visual languages and forms of action have referred to subcultures or demonstrated against the models propagated by official cultures. Recognized American artists, too, such as Barbara Kruger and Jenny Holzer, followed the Guerrilla Girls in adopting the visual language and practices of advertising in order to convey their messages in a swift and striking form.

The magazines described below are thus able to draw from a wealth of discussions that articulated, expanded, and gave visual form to early forms of postfeminist theories in the fields of artistic and graphic design.

Missy Magazine

Missy Magazine has been published since the end of 2008—at first quarterly with a circulation of 15,000 copies, and now today in a print run that has doubled. It carries a subtitle: "Pop Culture for Women." The founders, publishers, and editors were and still are Sonja Eismann, Stefanie Lohaus, and Chris Köver. The magazine is self-published.

In its editorials and editorial contributions, *Missy Magazine* presents itself as a counterproject to conventional women's magazines, criticizing in particular the norms about women's bodies and about beauty that these publications often propagate and reinforce. *Missy Magazine*, for instance, features close-ups portraits of women that have not been touched up. The magazines often pick up on tendencies that are not necessarily linked to feminist positions

5 Alison Piepmeier: *Girl Zines: Making Media, Doing Feminism*, New York: New York University Press, 2009.

auch eine feministische Bewegung, die zunächst auf die Dominanz männlicher Musiker
in der alternativen Szene und auf deren frauenfeindliche Texte bzw. Bühnenauftritte reagierte.
Ihr Protest wandte sich gegen die Wahrnehmung
von jungen Mädchen als niedlich und naiv.[5] Viele
der Magazine wie *Missy Magazine* greifen diese Wahrnehmung auf, um sie zu konterkarieren.
Seit Jahrzehnten beziehen sich visuelle Sprachen
und Aktionsformen auf die Subkultur oder sie
demonstrieren gegen diejenigen der offiziellen
Kulturen. Auch anerkannte amerikanische Künstlerinnen wie Barbara Kruger und Jenny Holzer
übernahmen von den Guerrilla Girls die Visualität
und die Praxis der Werbung, um ihre Botschaften
in einer schnellen und plakativen Form zu über-
mitteln.

Die im Folgenden beschriebenen Magazine können sich deshalb auf eine Fülle an Diskussionen beziehen, die postfeministische Theorien
im künstlerischen und grafikdesignerischen Bereichen bereits vorformulierten, erweiterten und
visuelle Angebote bereitstellten.

Missy Magazine

Missy Magazine erschien ab Ende 2008,
zunächst vierteljährlich mit einer Auflage von
15.000 Exemplaren, heute hat sich die Druckaufla-
ge verdoppelt. Das englische Wort „missy" bedeutet „kleines Fräulein". Der Untertitel lautet „Popkultur für Frauen". Gründerinnen, Herausgeberinnen und Redaktion waren und sind bis heute
Sonja Eismann, Stefanie Lohaus und Chris Köver.
Die Zeitschrift erscheint im Eigenverlag.

In den Editorials und redaktionellen Beiträgen präsentiert sich *Missy Magazine* als Ge-
genentwurf zu konventionellen Frauenzeitschriften, insbesondere werden die dort vermittelten
Körper- und Schönheitsnormen kritisiert. So sind
beispielsweise unretuschierte Nahaufnahmen
von Frauenporträts zu sehen. Die Zeitschriften
greifen häufig Tendenzen auf, die nicht unbedingt
allein an feministische Positionen gekoppelt sind,
wie die Body-Positivity-Bewegung, die sich gegen
den Selbstoptimierungszwang richtet, dem Mädchen schon in jungen Jahren unterliegen. Wie bei
der Neuen Frauenbewegung animieren sie Frauen
dazu, Tätigkeiten zu übernehmen, die üblicher-
weise Männern zugeschrieben werden, verwei-
gern sich aber auch nicht traditionellen Frauen-
arbeiten wie Stricken, Nähen, Kochen. Sie geben
sich liberal und unverkrampft. Dies gilt auch für

alone, such as the body positivity movement,
which is directed against the pressure that girls
face from a young age to optimize themselves. As
with second wave feminism, these publications
encourage women to take on activities usually
attributed to men, while also not refusing traditional women's work such as knitting, sewing, and
cooking. They present themselves as liberal and
open-minded, including in their attitude toward
symbols of femininity such as red lipstick or
fashionable clothing. The editorial staff of *Missy
Magazine* self-deprecatingly describes itself as
megalomaniacal, presumptuous, rebellious, and
resistant to advice, thus providing a playful, provocative, and experimental contrast to discourses
of theory and science.

Missy's graphics team—a visual communications collective called "Zoff," German for a
quarrel—describes their thinking about design
thus: "We are committed to a society of the
many, to the democratization of democracy, to
emancipatory politics. We work at the intersection of design, art, and politics. We believe
in visual communication that breaks stereotypes, that continues to deconstruct images.
We believe in communication that offers a new
perspective and aims to shift power relations—

Missy Magazine, Nr./no. 2 (2009), Titelblatt/cover © Missy Magazine;
Art-Direktion / art direction: Nicole Ibele & Julia Steinbrecher,
Foto/photo: Nina Lüth, Fotoassistenz / photo assistant: Dariusz
Brunzel, Haare/Make-up / hair/make-up: Nadja Lakluk

5 Alison Piepmeier: *Girl Zines. Making Media, Doing Feminism*, New
York: New York University Press, 2009.

MISSY
MAGAZINE

Pop, Politik
& Feminismus

03/2021
Juni–Juli
Deutschland €5,50 – L €6,50
AT €6,20 – CH Sfr 10,30

Klitoris:
Lange nicht
gesehen

Resilienz:
Was kann
der Hype?

Neue
Typen!
16 Seiten
femi-
nistisches
Design

DAWN
RICHARD

Independent Woman

Missy Magazine, Nr./no. 3 (2021), Titelblatt/cover © Missy Magazine; Art-Direktion / art direction: Daniela Burger; Grafik/graphic: Lisa Klinkenberg,
Stefanie Rau, Lena Rossbach; Foto/photo: Jasmine Durhal

Weiblichkeitssymbole wie den roten Lippenstift oder modische Kleidung. Die Redaktion von *Missy Magazine* bezeichnet sich selbstironisch als größenwahnsinnig, anmaßend, aufmüpfig und beratungsresistent, womit sie das Spielerische, Provozierende, Experimentelle der Theorie und der Wissenschaft gegenüberstellt.

Das Missy-Grafikteam „Zoff", ein Kollektiv für visuelle Kommunikation, beschreibt die Überlegungen bei den Gestaltungsfragen wie folgt: „Wir setzen uns ein für eine Gesellschaft der Vielen, für die Demokratisierung der Demokratie, für eine emanzipatorische Politik. Wir arbeiten an der Schnittstelle von Design, Kunst und Politik. Wir glauben an eine visuelle Kommunikation, die mit Stereotypen bricht, die die Dekonstruktion von Bildern vorantreibt. An eine Kommunikation, die einen Perspektivwechsel bietet und auf eine Verschiebung der Machtverhältnisse zielt. Eine Kommunikation, die eher zum Nachdenken anregt als überzeugen zu wollen. Eine Kommunikation, die Empowerment und konkrete politische Wirksamkeit ermöglicht. Wir plädieren für eine Kommunikation, die danach fragt, wer spricht. Eine Kommunikation, die sich sozialer Determinismen und visueller Kodierung bewusst ist. Eine Kommunikation, die eher inklusive Räume der sozialen Interaktion gestaltet als eine exklusive Ästhetisierung des Diskurses anstrebt."[6]

an.schläge. Das feministische Magazin

an.schläge. Das feministische Magazin wurde bereits 1983 in Wien gegründet und existiert bis heute. Eine Kontinuität zur Geschichte der Frauenzines in den Dekaden davor ist durchaus erkennbar, wenn das Heft sich als „indispensable democratic tool for exercising criticism and control"[7] betrachtet, das trotz der #MeToo-Öffentlichkeit nach wie vor notwendig sei. Ihr Programm formuliert die Zeitschrift wie folgt: „Die an.schläge beleuchten […] das aktuelle politische, gesellschaftliche und kulturelle Geschehen aus einer konsequent feministischen Perspektive. Das Magazin greift außerdem Themen auf, die sonst kaum vorkommen: Wir berichten über sozialen Protest und ‚Politik von unten', schreiben über Körper, Sex und Selbstbestimmung, analysieren die Entwicklungen in der neuen Arbeitswelt, nehmen wissenschaftliche Diskurse kritisch unter die Lupe und porträtieren upcoming [sic] female Artists aus Kunst & Pop."[8]

communication that provokes thought more than it aims to persuade, that fosters empowerment and real political efficacy. We advocate for communication that asks who is speaking, for communication that is aware of how social determination and visual coding operate, for communication that designs inclusive spaces to support social interaction rather than striving for an exclusive aestheticization of discourse."[6]

an.schläge: Das feministische Magazin

an.schläge: Das feministische Magazin—its title a play on words meaning both "(key) strokes" and "attacks"—was founded in Vienna in 1983 and still exists today. One certainly finds a continuity with the history of women's zines from the 1960s and 1970s in the magazine's description of itself as an "indispensable democratic tool for exercising criticism and control" that continues to be necessary despite the public presence of #MeToo.[7] The magazine formulates its program as follows: "The an.schläge … illuminate current political, social, and cultural events from a resolutely feminist perspective. The magazine also takes up topics that are rarely covered elsewhere: we report on social protest and grassroots politics; we write about bodies, sex, and self-determination, analyze developments in the new world of work, take a critical look at scientific discourses, and profile up-and-coming women artists from art & pop."[8]

Girls Like Us

One women's magazine with professional-level graphic design is *Girls Like Us*, with two graphic designers on staff in addition to guest designers. The magazine strives for a "european design sensibility—modern, fresh and cutting edge" (Kathrin Hero), as it says in its inaugural issue.[9]

The magazine started in Amsterdam in 2005 as a collaboration between two women, Belgian art critic Jessica Gysel and graphic designer Kathrin Hero. It developed into a larger women's collective, with three members living in Brussels, plus Kathrin Hero in Amsterdam, Sara Kaaman and Stina Löfgren in Stockholm, and Vela Arbutina in Switzerland. Today, Katja Mater and

6 Siehe https://gleichungleich.designverein.net/
zoff-kollektiv/ (Abruf 28. Jul. 2022).
7 Siehe https://anschlaege.at/ueber-uns/ (Abruf 28. Jul. 2022).
8 Ebenda.

6 See https://gleichungleich.designverein.net/
zoff-kollektiv/ (accessed 28. Jul. 2022).
7 See https://anschlaege.at/ueber-uns/ (accessed 28. Jul. 2022).
8 See https://anschlaege.at/ueber-uns/ (accessed 28. Jul. 2022).
9 See http://kathrinhero.nl/projects/world-of-glu-magazine/
(accessed 4. Sep. 2022).

Girls Like Us

Ein Frauenmagazin, das mit der Professionalität von Grafikdesign arbeitet, ist *Girls Like Us*. Es beschäftigt zwei Grafikdesignerinnen sowie Gastdesignerinnen. Das Heft strebe eine „[...] european design sensibility – modern, fresh and cutting edge" (Kathrin Hero) an, heißt es im ersten Heft.[9]

Die Zeitschrift startete 2005 in Amsterdam als Kooperation von zwei Frauen, der belgischen Kunstkritikerin Jessica Gysel und der Grafikdesignerin Kathrin Hero. Es entwickelte sich zu einem größeren Frauenkollektiv, von denen drei Mitglieder in Brüssel leben, außerdem Kathrin Hero in Amsterdam, Sara Kaaman und Stina Löfgren in Stockholm sowie Vela Arbutina in der Schweiz. Heute gehören Katja Mater und Sara Kaaman zum *editorial team*. Hinzu kommen einige Mitarbeiter*innen und ein größeres unterstützendes Netzwerk in verschiedenen Städten in aller Welt. Die Arbeitsform eines Kollektivs ist von besonderer Bedeutung für das Magazin: „As you know, we have a soft spot for collectives, collaborations, friendships and support structures. People doing things with other people: loving, working, organising, living. These strategies for surviving together form an underlying thread throughout all our issues."[10]

Zunehmend öffnete sich das Magazin einem weiteren Spektrum von Kollektivität jenseits der Gender-Binarität: „We write. She, they, them, he writes. All bodies write."[11] Mit dem Begriff „Bodies" wird vermutlich auf die Wunschproduktion der Körper jenseits kanonisierter Festlegungen angespielt, wie sie in den 1970er Jahren von Psychoanalytikern wie Gilles Deleuze und Félix Guattari in *Anti-Ödipus* (1972) beschrieben wurde. Sie waren es, die Kritik an der Psychoanalyse und vor allem an der Unterwerfung des Subjekts unter die männlich geprägte Struktur der Kultur äußerten. Die weiblichen Gegenstücke waren die Schriften von Hélène Cixous, Luce Irigaray, Julia Kristeva und anderen. *Depatriarchizing* ist, wie bei den Vorbildern, auch heute bei *Girls Like Us* das Zauberwort einer Auflehnung gegen den normativen Kanon von Kulturtechniken. Sowohl das Schreiben wie auch die thematische Gestaltung der Hefte sperren sich gegen tradierte Aneignungsformen. So müssen die Hefte nicht unbedingt linear

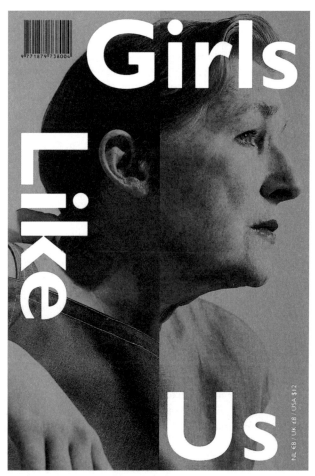

Girls Like Us 2, Nr./no. 3 (2012), Grafikdesign / graphic design: Vela Arbutina; auf dem Titelblatt / on the cover: Alice Carey, eine AIDS-Akivistin aus New York / a New York-based AIDS activist

Sara Kaaman are part of the editorial team, supported by several additional employees and a larger network of individuals in various cities around the world. The working form of a collective is particularly important for the magazine: "As you know, we have a soft spot for collectives, collaborations, friendships and support structures. People doing things with other people: loving, working, organising, living. These strategies for surviving together form an underlying thread throughout all our issues."[10]

Increasingly, the magazine has opened up to a wider spectrum of collective communities and endeavors beyond the gender binary: "We write. She, they, them, he writes. All bodies write."[11] The term "bodies" presumably alludes to

9 Siehe http://kathrinhero.nl/projects/world-of-glu-magazine/ (Abruf 4. Sep. 2022).

10 Editorial, *Girls Like Us* 8, „Family", 2016.

11 Sara Kaaman, Jessica Gysel & Katja Mater [Redaktion, *Girls Like Us*]: Anyone with a Link Can Edit, in Brad Haylock & Megan Patty (Hg.): *Art Writing in Crisis*, London: Sternberg Press, 2021: 179–191, hier 179.

10 Editorial, *Girls Like Us* 8, "Family," 2016

11 Sara Kaaman, Jessica Gysel & Katja Mater, editors of *Girls Like Us*: Anyone with a Link Can Edit, in Brad Haylock & Megan Patty (eds.): *Art Writing in Crisis*, London: Sternberg Press, 2021: 179–191, on 179..

gelesen werden, sondern präsentieren sich als ein Netz miteinander verbundener „Plateaus".[12] Auch verschiedene Textsorten werden unkonventionell beachtet: „Quotes, fiction, Autofiction, Speculative writing, Sci-fi, Dystopias and imaginary worlds. It's about images. Dream-state projects. Freeflowing, undefined experiments."[13] Die Art des Schreibens legt Wert auf die weibliche Differenz in Sprache und Text, wie sie Hélène Cixous in ihrem Konzept einer *écriture feminine* beschreibt.[14]

Girls Like Us arbeitet in einem breiten Spektrum von Kulturinitiativen und kreativen Projekten, der Lehre am Sandberg Instituut in Amsterdam, dem International Amsterdam Film Festival, dem Mauritshuis, der Utrecht Graduate School of Visual Art and Design und vielen anderen mehr. Gysel gründete bereits 2002 das Magazin *KUTT*, eine lesbische Version des Magazins von Homosexuellen *BUTT*. *Girls Like Us* sollte eine Gegenposition zu den stereotypen Klischees der lesbischen Kultur sein, indem es Spaß, Mode, Subversion, Kunst, Musik und Literatur zusammenfügte, um alternative Lebenswege aufzuzeigen. Das Heft wurde zunächst zweimal im Jahr herausgegeben, folgt aber zunehmend selbstgesetzten Zeitpunkten: „We appear in print when the feeling is right ... We are makers of our own time. Our shared documents live in a constant state of flux."[15]

Vorbild von *Girls Like Us* ist das amerikanische Magazin *Heresies. A Feminist Publication on Art and Politics*, das von 1977 bis 1993 vom *Heresies Collective* herausgegeben wurde. Jede Ausgabe wurde als Collage beschrieben, jeweils von einem anderen Kollektiv gestaltet. Anders als bei diesem Vorbild ist heute indes die nationenübergreifende Arbeit, die durch die digitalen tools ermöglicht wird. Bewusst ist sich die Redaktion von *Girls Like Us* allerdings auch der Bedingungen, unter denen digitale Plattformen in kapitalistischen Überwachungssystemen arbeiten.

Eine besondere Rolle in den Heften der neuen Zeitschrift spielt die Auseinandersetzung

the "desiring-production" of bodies beyond canonized determinations that was described in the 1970s by psychoanalysts Gilles Deleuze and Félix Guattari in *Anti-Oedipus* (1972). It was they who articulated critiques of psychoanalysis and, above all, of the subject's subordination to cultural structures shaped by men and masculinity. Female counterparts to these positions took shape in the writings of Hélène Cixous, Luce Irigaray, Julia Kristeva, and others. For these earlier critiques as for *Girls Like Us* today, dismantling patriarchy is the key motto for resisting the normative canon of cultural techniques. Both the writing and the thematic design of the magazines defy traditional forms of appropriation, allowing them to be read not in linear fashion, but as a network of interconnected "plateaus."[12] Space is also given to various types of unconventional text: "Quotes, fiction, autofiction, speculative writing, sci-fi, dystopias and imaginary worlds. It's about images. Dream-state projects. Free-flowing, undefined experiments."[13] As Hélène Cixous describes with her concept of an *écriture feminine*, this kind of writing values female difference in language and text.[14]

Girls Like Us works in a wide range of cultural initiatives and creative projects—teaching at institutions that include the Sandberg Instituut in Amsterdam, the International Amsterdam Film Festival, the Mauritshuis, and the Utrecht Graduate School of Visual Art and Design. In 2002, Gysel founded the magazine *KUTT*, a lesbian version of the *BUTT*, a magazine for "international homosexuals." *Girls Like Us* was meant to occupy a counterposition to the stereotypical clichés of lesbian culture, bringing together fun, fashion, subversion, art, music, and literature to highlight alternative ways of living. The magazine was initially published twice a year, but has increasingly appeared according to its own schedule: "We appear in print when the feeling is right ... We are makers of our own time. Our shared documents live in a constant state of flux."[15]

12 Vgl. Gilles Deleuze & Félix Guattari: *A Thousand Plateaus* (1987), in ihrem Text „Rhizomes" von 1976, der in der englischen Übersetzung von *A Thousand Plateaus* als „Introduction: Rhizome" abgedruckt wurde, rufen die beiden Autoren zu einem untergründigen Netz von Verbindungen auf. In Westdeutschland wird *Rhizom* getrennt 1977 im Merve Verlag, Berlin, herausgegeben und *Tausend Plateaus. Kapitalismus und Schizophrenie* 1992 ebenfalls im Merve Verlag, Berlin.
13 Sara Kaaman et al.: Anyone with a Link Can Edit (wie Anm. 11): 181.
14 Siehe Hélène Cixous: *Le rire de la meduse et autre ironies*, Paris: Galilée, 1975; deutsche Ausgabe: Das Lachen der Medusa, in Esther Hutfless, Gertrude Postl, & Elisabeth Schäfer (Hg.), Wien: Passagen Verlag, 2013.
15 Sara Kaaman et al.: Anyone with a Link Can Edit (wie Anm. 11): 180.

12 See Gilles Deleuze & Félix Guattari: *A Thousand Plateaus* (1987); in their 1976 text "Rhizomes," included in the English translation of *A Thousand Plateaus* as "Introduction: Rhizome," the two call for an underground network of connections. In West Germany, *Rhizom* was published separately in 1977 by Merve Verlag (Berlin), followed by Tausend Plateaus: Kapitalismus und Schizophrenie in 1992, also with Merve Verlag (Berlin).
13 Sara Kaaman et al., Anyone with a Link Can Edit, 181.
14 See Hélène Cixous, *Le rire de la meduse et autres ironies*, Paris: Galilée, 1975; English edition: The Laugh of the Medusa, in Julie Rivkin & Michael Ryan (eds.): *Literary Theory: An Anthology*, Oxford: Blackwell Publishing, 1996: 940–955.
15 Sara Kaaman et al, Anyone with a Link Can Edit, 180.

mit der Geschichte, ein Re-reading und eine Revision von Erzählungen: „Hidden life, underground life, life under the radar. Herstories forgotten never told, never surfaced.“[16] Der Ertrag einer eigenen Geschichte von Frauen ergibt für sie eine neue Form von Kollektivität.

Riposte. A Magazine for Women

Die Zeitschrift ist ein Beispiel jener privatwirtschaftlich arbeitenden Magazine der *creative industry*, die Ästhetik und Inhalte von feministischen Journalen aufgreifen. Sie wendet sich an eine junge liberale Frauenszene und formuliert die Vielfalt neuer politischer und sozialer Haltungen in Wort und Bild. Durch eine ausgefeilte professionelle Ästhetik unterscheidet sie sich von vielen der besprochenen Zeitschriften.

Den Launch des Magazins kündigte Rachel Steven 2013 in einem Interview mit der Herausgeberin Danielle Pender wie folgt an: „Riposte is a new women's magazine promising intelligent editorial and beautiful design.“[17] Da das Erscheinungsbild der zweimal im Jahr edierten Zeitschrift eine so große Bedeutung hat, engagierte die Leitung eine Creative-Direktorin: Shaz Madani, London, und einen Photo Director: Gem Flechter.

Der Begriff Riposte geht auf eine Technik des Fechtens zurück, wobei eine erfolgreiche Attacke der jeweiligen Gegner*innen mit einem Gegenangriff gekontert wird. Aus dem Französischen stammend, bedeutet er hier auch „schlagfertige Antwort“.

16 Ebenda.
17 Nelly Ben Hayoun features in *Riposte Magazine*, Words by Rachael Steven, 19 November 2013, Interview with Danielle Pender, https://nellyben.com/riposte-magazine-2 (Abruf 29. Mai 2022).

Riposte: A Magazine for Women, Nr./no. 13 (2021), The Care Issue, Titelblatt/cover © Riposte

The model for *Girls Like Us* is the American magazine *Heresies: A Feminist Publication on Art and Politics*, which was published from 1977 to 1993 by the *Heresies Collective*. Each issue was envisioned to be a collage, each designed by a different collective. What is different today, however, is the international cooperation made possible by digital tools. The editors of *Girls Like Us* are nonetheless also aware of the conditions under which digital platforms operate in capitalist systems of surveillance.

The new journal places special emphasis on engaging with history, on rereading and revisioning narratives: "Hidden life, underground life, life under the radar. Herstories forgotten never told, never surfaced."[16] For them, the boon of a women's history told by and for women is a new form of collectivity.

Riposte: A Magazine for Women

Riposte is an example of those private-sector magazines in the creative industry that adopt the aesthetics and content of feminist journals. It addresses an audience of young, liberal women by expressing a diversity of new political and social attitudes in its texts and images. What sets it apart from many of the other magazines discussed here is its polished, professional aesthetics.

Rachel Steven announced the magazine's launch in 2013 in an interview with editor Danielle Pender: "Riposte is a new women's magazine promising intelligent editorial and beautiful design."[17] Since the biannual magazine places such a premium on its look, its executives hired a creative director, Shaz Madani (based in London), and a photo director, Gem Weaver.

Originating from French, the term "riposte" refers to a fencing technique in which a successful attack by the opponent is met with a counterattack. Here it also means a "quick-witted response."

The magazine's text selection and design embodies a particular stance; its mantra is "openness and honesty."[18] One of its values is furthermore "diversity" in the creative industry.

The editor is a journalist and creative consultant in London. Although *Riposte* is an independent platform, it is in a certain sense also

16 Sara Kaaman et al, Anyone with a Link Can Edit, 180.
17 Nelly Ben Hayoun features in *Riposte Magazine*, Words by Rachael Steven, 19 November 2013, Interview with Danielle Pender https://nellyben.com/riposte-magazine-2 (accessed 29. May 2022).
18 Nelly Ben Hayoun features in *Riposte Magazine*.

Die Zeitschrift verkörpert in ihrer Textauswahl und ihrer Gestaltung eine Haltung. Ihr Mantra ist „openness and honesty", eine Art Political Correctness.[18] Eine ihrer Ausrichtungen ist auch Diversität in der Kreativindustrie.

Die Herausgeberin ist Journalistin und Creative Consultant in London. In gewisser Weise ist *Riposte*, wenngleich eine unabhängige Plattform, auch ein Sprachrohr für ihre Agentur Riposte Studio, von der aus sie mit Brands wie Adidas, Ace & Tate, Toast, Nike and COS zusammenarbeitet und mit gemeinnützigen Organisationen Ausstellungen und Events kreiert oder ihre PR begleitet. Zu solchen gemeinnützigen Organisationen zählen Slow Factory oder Plan International, eine Organisation für die Rechte von jungen Mädchen, und Amnesty International UK sowie die Plattform *Squarespace* für Start-ups von Kreativen.

Der Bogen der Essays und Features spannt sich von Kunst, Design, Ökonomie, Politik bis zum Reisen. Da kann eine Heroin der Bewegung, Sheila Levrant de Bretteville, ebenso zu Wort kommen wie weniger bekannte Frauen aus der islamischen Welt. Die erste Ausgabe befasste sich beispielsweise mit Françoise Mouly, der Redakteurin und Mitbegründerin des *Raw*-Magazins. *Raw* war eine Anthologie von Comics, die von Françoise Mouly und ihrem Ehemann, dem Karikaturisten Art Spiegelman, zwischen 1980 und 1991 herausgegeben wurde. Ein anderes Heft geht auf die Body-Positivity-Bewegung ein, die sich für die Abschaffung diskriminierender Schönheitsideale einsetzt. Die Queer-Szene ist ebenso vertreten, desgleichen Vertreterinnen vieler ethnischer Gruppen weltweit. Am Beispiel der CICLO-Textile-Technologie wird zudem über nachhaltige Wirtschaft berichtet, die sich gegen Kunststoffmaterialien wie Polyester und Nylon wendet. Dabei kommen Interviewpartnerinnen aus der Wissenschaft zu Wort.

Ein tiefer gehender Blick auf diese Zeitschriften mit ihrer lustvollen Kreativität offenbart, welche Fülle an aktuell kritischen Themen sie abdecken, und vor allem, wie entschieden ihre Haltung gegenüber gegenwärtigen sozialen Problemen ist. Vor diesem Hintergrund erscheint die Kritik an diesem Zeitschriftentypus eindimensional. Dass diese Zeitschriften immer auch in den Netzen des Neoliberalismus agieren, ist den meisten Herausgeberinnen sehr wohl bewusst.

a mouthpiece for its agency Riposte Studio—a base from which it collaborates with brands such as Adidas, Ace & Tate, Toast, Nike, and COS and creates exhibitions and events with nonprofit organizations, or supports their PR. Nonprofits with which it has worked include Slow Factory, Plan International (an organization that fights for the rights of young girls), and Amnesty International UK, as well as the *Squarespace* platform for start-ups by creatives.

The essays and features range from art, design, economics, and politics to travel. It offers space to heroines of the movement, such as Sheila Levrant de Bretteville, and to lesser-known women from the Islamic world. The first issue, for example, focused on Françoise Mouly, the editor and cofounder of the magazine *Raw*. *Raw* was an anthology of comics edited by Mouly and her husband, cartoonist Art Spiegelman, between 1980 and 1991. Another issue was dedicated to the body positivity movement and its fight against oppressive ideals of beauty. The queer scene is also present in the magazine, along with representatives of many ethnic groups worldwide. One feature on CICLO textile technology reports on a sustainable economy that endeavors to eliminate plastic materials such as polyester and nylon. Women from the scientific community are also given a voice in interviews.

A deeper look at these magazines, with their joyful creativity, reveals the plethora of current critical issues they cover and, above all, just how resolutely they take a position vis-à-vis contemporary problems. Seen thus, criticisms leveled at this type of magazine appear one-dimensional. The fact that these journals always operate within neoliberal networks is something most of their editors are well aware of.

18 Ebenda.

Literatur
Further Reading

Agatha Beins: *Liberation in Print. Feminist Periodicals and Social Movement Identity* (Since 1970: Histories of Contemporary America), Athen/Athens, GA: University of Georgia Press, 2017.

Gesche Gerdes: Der Postfeminismus-Vorwurf. Beobachtungen zum feministischen Selbstkonzept junger Theaterkünstlerinnen und Journalistinnen am Beispiel des Missy Magazin, *Gender. Zeitschrift für Geschlecht, Kultur, Gesellschaft* 4, Nr./no. 1 (2012): 9–23.

Rosalind Gill: Die Widersprüche verstehen. (Anti-)Feminismus, Postfeminismus, Neoliberalismus, *Bundeszentrale für politische Bildung*, 20. Apr. 2018, https://www.bpb.de/shop/zeitschriften/apuz/267938/die-widersprueche-verstehen/ (Abruf/accessed 20. Jul. 2021).

Sara Kaaman, Jessica Gysel & Katja Mater: Anyone with a Link Can Edit, in Brad Haylock & Megan Patty (Hg./eds.): *Art Writing in Crisis*, London: Sternberg Press, 2021.

Angela McRobbie: Post-feminism and Popular Culture, *Feminist Media Studies* 4, Nr./no. 3 (2004), DOI: 10.1080/1468077042000309937.

DIVERSITY UND GESCHICHTE

DIVERSITY AND HISTORY

Women of Color
in den USA
Women of Color
in the United States

Dass Women of Color im US-amerikanischen Grafikdesign erfolgreich arbeiten können, entsprechend wahrgenommen werden und durch Preise Anerkennung erhalten, ist noch nicht lange der Fall. Frühe Beispiele vor den 1960er Jahren sind äußerst selten, über weite Strecken schien Design von BIPOCs (Abkürzung von Black, Indigenous, People of Color) unsichtbar. Für die hier erwähnten Designerinnen war der Zugang zu einer US-amerikanischen Ausbildung kein grundsätzliches Problem mehr. Doch wenn es um Ehrungen in den einschlägigen Institutionen geht, findet man sie nur vereinzelt.

Eine herausragende Person ist indes Gail Anderson (geb. 1962). Ihre Familie stammt aus Jamaica, sie selbst wurde in New York geboren. Nach einem Studium an der School of Visual Arts in New York City, beispielsweise bei der legendären Grafikdesignerin Paula Scher, arbeitete sie in verschiedenen bedeutenden Firmen und war unter anderem langjährige Art-Direktorin bei der designorientierten Musikzeitschrift *Rolling Stone*. Hier konnte sie ihren unangepassten, expressiv-eklektischen Stil erproben, der mit verschiedenen Schrifttypen traditioneller als auch neuer Quellen spielt. Sie kombinierte sie unkonventionell. Dennoch hat sie bewusst keinen eigenen Autoren-Stil entwickelt, sondern blieb offen für immer neue Kombinationen. Sie entwickelte eine Art Zettelkasten mit allen möglichen Fetzen von Typografie, skurrilen Buchstabenformen aus traditionellen und kitschigen Materialien, aus Metall oder Holz. Häufig speiste sich ihr typografisches Material aus der Geschichte, das heißt, dass sie traditionelle Schriften keineswegs ablehnte, sondern sie als Bereicherung und Anregung für ein neues Schriftbild betrachtete. Auch Handschriften zählten dazu. Zusammen mit dem Grafikdesigner und -kritiker Steven Heller stellte sie historische Schriften vor, und Autor*innen setzten sich zugleich mit neuesten Fonts auseinander, unter anderem in dem von ihr gestalteten Buch *New Vintage Type*. Besonders eingängig ist auch ihr Hang zu starker Farbigkeit und vorgefundenem anonymen Alltagsdesign. Aus so unterschiedlichen Quellen entstand ein Schriftbild, das oft als exzentrisch gewertet wurde, aber dennoch viele Nachahmer*innen fand. Es war ihre Auffassung von Diversität im Design: demonstrativ und symbolisch.

Für eine Woman of Color ungewöhnlich, hat sie viele Ehrungen erhalten. Schon 2008 empfing sie eine Medaille des American Institute of Graphic Arts (AIGA), der größten Vereinigung von professionellen Designer*innen in

In the United States, it is only recently that women of color have been able to work successfully in graphic design—to be recognized for their work and garner awards. Early examples before the 1960s are extremely rare; for long stretches, design by BIPOCs (short for Black, Indigenous, people of color) seemed invisible. For the women designers discussed here, access to an education in the United States was no longer a fundamental problem, but the number of those who have been honored by design institutions is limited.

One outstanding example, however, is Gail Anderson, born in 1962 in New York to a family from Jamaica. After studying at the School of Visual Arts in New York City with teachers that included the legendary graphic designer Paula Scher,

Gail Anderson, Briefmarke zur Erinnerung an den 150. Geburtstag der Emanzipationsproklamation / Stamp commemorating the 150th anniversary of the Emancipation Proclamation © 2014 Gail Anderson

Titel von / Cover of New Vintage Type: Classic Fonts for the Digital Age, von/by Steven Heller & Gail Anderson, designt mit / designed with Jessica Disbrow, Thames & Hudson, 2009 © Thames & Hudson

den USA und die wohl höchste Auszeichnung für Grafikdesigner*innen. 2009 gewann sie den Richard Gangel Art Director Award. Die Ehrungen für ihr Werk folgten von solch renommierten Institutionen wie der Society of Publication Designers, des Type Directors Club, des Art-Directors Club, Graphis, Communication Arts and Print. Sie erhielt 2018 als erste Women of Color den Cooper Hewitt National Design Award für ihr Lebenswerk. Zugleich war sie die dritte Frau, die diesen Preis überhaupt empfing. Heute sind ihre Arbeiten Bestandteil der Sammlungen des Cooper Hewitt, Smithsonian Design Museum und der Library of Congress. In der

Anderson worked for various major companies, holding positions such as art director for many years at the design-conscious magazine *Rolling Stone*. At *Rolling Stone*, she was able to test out her nonconformist, expressive-eclectic style, which plays with various typefaces from both traditional and new sources. Her approach was to combine them in unconventional ways. Yet she intentionally refrained from developing her own authorial style, instead remaining continually open to new combinations. She developed a kind of card catalog with all kinds of scraps of typography, with quirky letterforms made of traditional and kitschy materials, of metal or wood. Her typographic material

STEVEN HELLER & GAIL ANDERSON

TELLSTELLDtellstellsels
tellstellstellstells
TELLSTELLSTELLStells!!!
!!!!!!!!!!!!
tellstellstells
Tellstells
telldtelltells tellstells

TELLS

Thames & Hudson

Titel von / Cover of Type Tells Tales von/by Steven Heller & Gail Anderson, Thames & Hudson, 2017 © Thames & Hudson

Illustration der Grafikdesignerin / Illustration of Graphic Designer
Sylvia Harris © Creative Repute, LLC

Kunstkritik wird sie als „Designlegende" bezeichnet.

Doch immer noch sind People of Color, insbesondere Frauen, in der Welt des Grafikdesigns Pionier*innen. Sylvia Harris (1953–2011) beispielsweise, die noch in den 1960er Jahren die Tumulte um die Segregation Schwarzer Bürger*innen in ihrer Heimatstadt Richmond, Virginia, hautnah miterlebte, hat sich in ihrer Karriere als Designerin für soziale Projekte eingesetzt. Am 25. April 2014 erhielt sie posthum die AIGA-Medaille. Im Gedenken an ihre Arbeit schuf dieselbe Institution den Sylvia Harris Citizen Design Award, der professionelle Designer*innen ehrt, die ein konstruktives Projekt verwirklichten, das sich auf das öffentliche Leben fokussiert. Das Bemühen, ein defizitäres Geschichtsverständnis zu korrigieren und sich von der Haltung der *white supremacy* zu verabschieden, ist in den USA heute in den einschlägigen Designinstitutionen deutlich spürbar.

Black history

Mit ihrem Bestreben, im US-amerikanischen Design sichtbarer zu werden und gleichberechtigte Entfaltungsmöglichkeiten zu erhalten, often drew inspiration from history, meaning she did not reject traditional typefaces at all but regarded them as a means of enriching and spurring the development of new forms. Hand-drawn fonts were among them. In *New Vintage Type*, for instance, a book which she designed and published together with graphic designer and critic Steven Heller, she presented historical typefaces, while other authors engaged with the latest fonts. Her penchant for strong color and anonymous, everyday found design is also particularly striking. From such diverse sources, a typeface emerged that was often considered eccentric, but nevertheless found many imitators. This reflected her take on diversity in design: demonstrative and symbolic.

Unusual for a woman of color, Anderson has received many honors, including a 2008 medal from the American Institute of Graphic Arts (AIGA), the largest association of professional designers in the United States—arguably the highest award for graphic designers—as well as the Richard Gangel Art Director Award in 2009. Honors for her work then followed from such prestigious institutions as the Society of Publication Designers, the Type Directors Club, the Art Directors Club, Graphis, and Communication Arts and Print. In 2018, she became the first women of color to receive the Cooper Hewitt National Design Award for her life's work. She was also the third woman ever to receive this award. Today, her work is held by collections of the Cooper Hewitt, Smithsonian Design Museum and the Library of Congress. Art critics have called her a design legend.

People of color, especially women, nevertheless remain pioneers in the world of graphic design. Sylvia Harris (1953–2011), for instance, who as late as the 1960s experienced first-hand the turmoil provoked by the segregation of Black citizens in her hometown of Richmond, Virginia, remained committed to social projects throughout her career as a designer. She was posthumously awarded the AIGA Medal on 25 April 2014. In memory of her work, the same institution created the Sylvia Harris Citizen Design Award, which honors professional designers who have realized a constructive project focused on public life. Efforts to correct a deficient understanding of history and move beyond attitudes influenced by White supremacy are clearly noticeable today in leading design institutions in the United States.

können Women of Color auf diesem Kontinent auf eine lange Tradition des Protests zurückgreifen.

Viele der heutigen Initiativen der People of Color können sich auf die Geschichte der Civil-Rights-Bewegung berufen. Sie war vielleicht die größte und relevanteste Bewegung in den Vereinigten Staaten in den 1960er und 1970er Jahren, durch die auch Künstler*innen und Designer*innen ermutigt wurden, eigene Gruppen zu bilden. Dazu zählte die Black-Arts-Bewegung (BAM) zwischen 1960 und 1970. Die Spiral Group, ein New Yorker Kollektiv afroamerikanischer Künstler*innen von 1963 bis 1965, war eine weitere von vielen Gruppen. Ein experimenteller und eklektischer Stil war typisch für die Gruppe, insbesondere aber diskutierte sie über Theorie, kreative Integrität und künstlerische Freiheit Schwarzer Künstler*innen und die Rolle, die People of Color im sozialen Wandel einnehmen sollten. Eine weitere wichtige Vereinigung war AfriCobra (African Commune of Bad Relevant Artists), eine Gruppe aus Chicago, die sich 1968 zusammenfand. Schwarze Ästhetik stand im Zentrum ihrer Projekte. Where We At (WWA) bildete sich im Frühjahr 1971 anlässlich einer gleichnamigen Ausstellung in der Acts of Art Gallery in Greenwich Village, organisiert von 14 Schwarzen Künstlerinnen. WWA wurde eine Plattform,

Black History

In striving to become more visible in US design and to be given equal opportunities to develop their skills, American women of color can draw on a long tradition of protest.

Many initiatives launched by people of color today can be traced to the history of the civil rights movement. Perhaps the largest and most consequential development in the United States during the 1960s and 1970s, the movement also encouraged artists and designers to form groups of their own. These included the Black arts movement (BAM) between 1960 and 1970 and the Spiral Group, a New York collective of African American artists from 1963 to 1965, among many others. The Spiral Group was characterized by an experimental and eclectic style, but in particular it pursued discussions about topics including art theory, the creative integrity and artistic freedom of Black artists, and the role to be played by people of color in effecting social change. Another important association was AfriCobra (African Commune of Bad Relevant Artists), a Chicago-based group

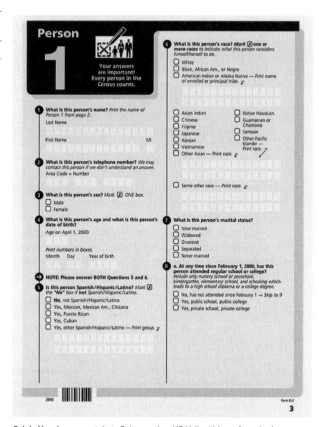

Seite aus dem US-Volkszählungsformular 1990 / Page from the 1990 United States Census Form, abgerufen von / retrieved from census.gov

Sylvia Harris, neu gestaltete Seite aus dem US-Volkszählungsformular/ Redesign of the United States Census Form, 2000, abgerufen von / retrieved from census.gov

in der afroamerikanische Frauen aufgerufen wurden, sich und ihre eigene Ästhetik zu artikulieren. Ähnlich wie AfriCobra organisierten sie zahlreiche Workshops in Kulturzentren, Schulen und Gefängnissen und boten Kurse für Schwarze Jugendliche an.[1]

Auch Schwarze US-amerikanische Grafikdesignerinnen schlossen sich zusammen, um als Netzwerk größere Beachtung zu finden. Dazu gehört die Plattform *Black Art Story*, in der die Mitglieder ihr Profil vorstellen. Zu den African American Stamp Artists in der ESPER Stamp Society[2] zählen neben männlichen Vertretern auch drei Women of Color: die Grafikdesignerinnen Higgins Bond, Synthia St. James und Andrea Pippins. Sie können sich beispielsweise auf Ausstellungen im Metropolitan Museum in New York berufen. Überall sind die Grenzen zwischen Kunst und Grafikdesign fließend.

Eine weitere Gruppe ist die Non-Profit-Organisation Scope of Work (SOW), die sich seit 2016 unter der Leitung von Eda Levenson und Geneva White für junge People of Color einsetzt. Sie wollen Designer*innen, Fotograf*innen, Filmemacher*innen und weitere Berufsgruppen im Feld der Kreativwirtschaft unterstützen und gegen die Disproportion der Einstellungen von BIPoC ankämpfen. Laut *Design Census 2019* von *Eye on Design*, AIGA, sind nur 16,2 Prozent der Designer*innen aus den Reihen der BIPoC bei Stellenbesetzungen zu finden.

Weitere Organisationen sind Where are the Black Designers? (seit 2020), die eine digitale Plattform etablierten, Konferenzen abhalten, einen Newsletter herausgeben und eine webbasierte *slack community* bilden. Sie wurde gegründet von der Designerin Mitzi Okou. Hinzu kommt auch @Black Girls Code (seit 2011),[3] die sich auf die Durchsetzung von *diversity* im Webdesign konzentrieren und jungen Women of Color zwischen 7 und 17 Jahren Ausbildungsprogramme anbieten. Inzwischen gibt es 13 Abteilungen der Gruppe in den USA und eine in Johannesburg.

that came together in 1968. Black aesthetics was the main focus of their projects. Where We At (WWA) was organized by fourteen Black women artists in the spring of 1971 at the Acts of Art Gallery in Greenwich Village on the occasion of an exhibition of the same name. WWA became a platform that called upon African American women to express themselves and articulate their own distinct aesthetic. Similar to AfriCobra, the group organized a large number of workshops in cultural centers, schools, and prisons and offered courses for Black youth.[1]

Women graphic designers of color from the United States also joined together to gain greater attention and respect as a network. One such effort was the platform *Black Art Story*, which allowed members to present a profile of themselves. African American stamp artists in the ESPER Stamp Society include men as well as three women of color: graphic designers Higgins Bond, Synthia St. James, and Andrea Pippins.[2] Their work has been recognized, for instance, through exhibitions at the Metropolitan Museum in New York, reflecting the generally fluid boundaries between art and graphic design.

Another such group is the nonprofit Scope of Work (SOW), which has been advocating for young people of color since 2016 under the leadership of Eda Levenson and Geneva White. SOW seeks to support designers, photographers, filmmakers, and other professionals in creative industries and to fight against disproportionately low levels of hiring BIPOC in the field. According to *Design Census 2019* by *Eye on Design*, AIGA, BIPOC designers constitute only 16.2 percent of new hires.

Other such organizations include Where Are the Black Designers? (since 2020), who have established a digital platform and created a web-based community, in addition to organizing conferences and publishing a newsletter. The organization was founded by the designer Mitzi Okou. These efforts are complemented by the work of @BlackGirls Code (since 2011),[3] which focuses on fostering diversity in web design by offering educational programs to young women of color ages

---

1 Siehe die Wanderausstellung „We Wanted a Revolution: Black Radical Women, 1965–85. A Sourcebook", Californian African American Museum, Brooklyn Museum, New York, 2017. WWA veröffentlichte eine Broschüre mit dem Titel „Where We At. Black Women Artists: A Tapestry of Many Fine Threads the history and Mission of the Abun-dant Evidence. Black Women Artists of the 1960s and 70s".
2 https://www.esperstamps.org/african-american-stamp-artists (Abruf 10. Jul. 2022).
3 www.blackgirlscode.com (Abruf 7. Jul. 2022).

1 See the catalog to the traveling exhibition *We Wanted a Revolution: Black Radical Women, 1965–85: A Sourcebook*, Californian African American Museum, Brooklyn Museum, New York, 2017. WWA published a brochure entitled "Where We At. Black Women Artists: A Tapestry of Many Fine Threads the History and Mission of the Abundant Evidence. Black Women Artists of the 1960s and 70s."
2 See https://www.esperstamps.org/african-american-stamp-artists (accessed 10. Jul. 2022).
3 See www.blackgirlscode.com (accessed 7. Jul. 2022).

Decolonization

Decolonization beschränkt sich als Terminus längst nicht mehr auf Diskussionen um People of Color oder auf die Angelegenheiten von marginalisierten sozialen Gruppen und deren Teilhabe am Mainstream. Er weitet sich aus zur Infragestellung des etablierten Designkanons der westlichen Welt und dessen Hierarchisierung von „gutem" Design und Design von Randgruppen.

Folglich begleitet die Diskussion viele transnationale Initiativen und ist nicht mehr nur auf den US-amerikanischen Kontext konzentriert. Ursprünglich diente der Begriff dazu, die Loslösung der Kolonien von ihren fremden Kolonialherren zu beschreiben. Heute umfasst der Begriff ein ganzes Bündel an Ideen. Meist richtet sich die Argumentation gegen die Vorherrschaft des Westens und seine weißen privilegierten Bürger*innen. Zunehmend beschäftigen sich Kongresse und Universitätsprogramme, Buchpublikationen und digitale Plattformen mit dem Thema, um Designforschung und Designpraxis hinsichtlich ihrer Narrative zu transformieren. „Wer spricht?" ist nun eine grundlegende Frage. Für viele People of Color ist dies nicht mehr eine Frage der Partizipation und Anpassung, sondern der Artikulation ihrer eigenen, von Geschichte und Kultur geprägten Perspektive. Die europäische und US-amerikanische Welt betrachtet diese Bewegung als Paradigmenwechsel.

Während sich die Diskussionen bislang weitgehend auf die akademische Lehre bezogen, weiten sie sich inzwischen auf viele Netzwerke aus. Neben solchen Design-Organisationen, die sich für *Black history* einsetzen, orientieren sich die meisten neueren Initiativen an Fragen von Diversität. Einige wenige vertreten auch neue Prinzipien von Arbeitsorganisation, beispielsweise Creative Repute®, eine Agentur für Grafikdesign und Webdesign, die in Philadelphia, Pennsylvania, ansässig ist. Sie arbeitet laut Programm nur mit sozial orientierten Organisationen zusammen. Auf ihrer Homepage heißt es: „We are black-owned and women-led." Von der Agentur stammt der Webauftritt „Women of Color in the Graphic Design Industry" der AIGA.[4]

Intersektionalismus

Viele der Frauen sind Repräsentantinnen einer Programmatik, die intersektional arbeitet, das heißt, sie betrachten Geschlecht in einem

seven to seventeen. The group now has thirteen chapters in the United States and one in Johannesburg.

Decolonization

As a term, decolonization has long since ceased to be limited to discussions about people of color or the affairs of marginalized social groups and their participation in mainstream society. It has expanded to contest the established, Western design canon and its hierarchy of "good" design and design by marginalized groups.

Discussions about decolonization thus play a part in many transnational initiatives and are no longer focused solely on the US context. Originally, the term was used to describe the emancipation of colonies from their foreign colonial masters. Today, the term encompasses a whole host of ideas. Mostly, its claims are directed against Western domination and its privileged White citizens. Increasingly, conferences and university programs, as well as book publications and digital platforms, are taking up the issue in ways that are transforming the structuring narratives of design research and practice. "Who is speaking?" has become a fundamental question. For many people of color, this is no longer a matter of social and political participation or of learning to fit in to dominant social structures, but of articulating their own perspective as it is shaped by history and culture. In Europe and the United States, this movement is often seen as part of a paradigm shift.

While discussions initially took place mainly in university courses, they have expanded to play a part in many other contexts. In addition to design organizations that advocate for Black history, most of the newer initiatives are committed to issues of diversity. Several also represent new principles for organizing work, such as Creative Repute®, a graphic design and web design agency based in Philadelphia. It describes its own program as working only with organizations that have a social focus and notes on its homepage: "We are black-owned and women-led." This agency was responsible for designing AIGA's webpages on "Women of Color in the Graphic Design Industry."[4]

---

4 https://www.creativerepute.com/women-color-graphic-design-industry/ (Abruf 24. Nov. 2021).

4 See https://www.creativerepute.com/women-color-graphic-design-industry/ (accessed 24. Nov. 2021).

Geflecht von verschiedenen Diskriminierungen. Die Ursprünge des Konzepts der Intersektionalität liegen im Schwarzen Feminismus, der afroamerikanischen Arbeiter*innen-Bewegung und der Critical Race Theory der 1980er Jahre. Die Protagonistinnen beklagten, dass die besondere Situation Schwarzer Frauen generell wie auch in der Neuen Frauenbewegung kaum beachtet wurde. Die Frauenbewegung werde von weißen bürgerlichen Frauen dominiert, die Black-Consciousness-Bewegung in den USA wiederum einseitig von Schwarzen Männern.

Einer der bedeutendsten Beiträge zur Intersektionalität war der Aufsatz „Demarginalizing the Intersection of Race and Sex" (1989) der afroamerikanischen Juraprofessorin Kimberlé Crenshaw, die darin Kritik an der US-amerikanischen Rechtsprechung übte. Sie wies darauf hin, dass spezifische Diskriminierungen von Schwarzen Frauen gerichtlich nicht anerkannt wurden. Seit Ende der 1980er Jahre ist Intersektionalität eine der zentralen analytischen Kategorien der Critical Race Theory und der Gender Studies.

Popularisierung

Die Forderung, People of Color gleichberechtigte Aufmerksamkeit zu schenken, hat viele designorientierte Ausdrucksformen gefunden. Eine beliebte sind T-Shirts oder Sticker, die der Haltung ihrer Besitzer*innen Ausdruck verleihen sollen. Die Firma Redbubble, die 2006 in San Francisco gegründet wurde, bringt solche Print-on-Demand-Shirts heraus, die auf Design von unabhängigen Designer*innen und Amateur*innen basieren. Viele der Aufdrucke greifen Zitate und Porträts von People of Color auf.

Intersectionality

Many of these women are representatives of a programmatic approach that works through an intersectional lens, that is to say, they view gender as part of a wider structure of forms of discrimination. The concept of intersectionality originates in Black feminism, the African American labor movement, and critical race theory as first articulated during the 1980s. Those who developed the concept decried the fact that the particular situation of Black women in general, and specifically in second wave feminism, had received little attention. The women's movement, it argued, was dominated by White middle-class women, while the Black consciousness movement in the United States was exclusively dominated by Black men.

One of the most significant contributions to intersectionality was the essay "Demarginalizing the Intersection of Race and Sex" (1989) by African American law professor Kimberlé Crenshaw, written as a critique of the American legal system. Crenshaw showed that specific discrimination against Black women has not been recognized by the courts. Since the end of the 1980s, intersectionality has been a central analytical category in both critical race studies and gender studies.

Popularization

The demand to give equal attention to people of color has found many forms of expression that employ design. T-shirts and stickers, for example, are particularly popular as ways to express their owner's attitude. Redbubble, founded in San Francisco in 2006, produces such print-on-demand shirts from designs by independent and amateur designers, many engaging with quotes from and portraits of people of color.

T-Shirt mit einem Bild von / T-shirt with a picture of **Audre Lorde**, vertrieben von / distributed by **Redbubble**

Literatur
Further Reading

Ahmed Ansari: What a Decolonisation of Design Involves: Two Programmes for Emancipation, *Beyond Change. Questioning the Role of Design in Times of Global Transformations*, 3.2008, http://www.decolonisingdesign.com/actions-and-interventions/publications/2018/what-a-decolonisation-of-design-involves-by-ahmed-ansari/ (Abruf/accessed 7. Aug. 2021).

Ece Canlı: Designing with/against Cherophobia, 7.2022, https://futuress.org/stories/designing-with-against-cherophobia (Abruf/accessed 1. Jul. 2021).

Angela Davis: Reflections on the Black Woman's Role in the Community of Slaves, *The Black Scholar* 3, Nr./no. 4 (Dez./Dec. 1971): 2–15.

bell hooks: *Ain't I a Woman. Black Women and Feminism*, Boston: South End Press, 1981.

Audre Lorde: *Selected Works of Audre Lord*, hg. v. / ed. by Roxane Gay, New York: W. W. Norton & Company, 2020.

Claudia Mareis & Nina Palm (Hg./eds.): *Design Struggles. Intersecting Histories, Pedagogies, and Perspectives*, Amsterdam: Valiz, 2021.

Katherine Morris, Rujeko Hockley & Stephanie Weissberg: *We Wanted a Revolution: Black Radical Women. A Sourcebook, 1965–85*, New York: Brooklyn Museum, 2017.

Michelle Wallace: „Black Macho – Damals und Heute" und andere Aufsätze, in Diederich Diederichsen (Hg./ed.): *Yo! Hermeneutics. Schwarze Kulturkritik. Pop, Medien, Feminismus*, Berlin: Edition ID-Archiv, 1993.

DECOLO-NIZING ALS DESIGN-PRINZIP

DECOLO-NIZING AS A DESIGN PRINCIPLE

„Arabische Welten"
"Arab Worlds"

Von „arabischen Welten" zu reden, ist nicht unproblematisch, weil der Nahe Osten und seine Kulturen geprägt sind von territorialen Komplexitäten, weit verstreuten Diaspora-Gemeinschaften und von transnationalen und hybriden Identitäten, die sich, vor allem in Zusammenhang mit der Migration, zwei oder mehreren kulturellen Räumen gleichermaßen zugehörig fühlen.[1] Es ist folglich nicht möglich, von einer geschlossenen arabischen Kultur zu sprechen.[2]

Hinzu kommt, dass der sogenannte Orient überlagert ist mit Imaginationen und Projektionen. Seit dem 18. Jahrhundert und auch heute noch sind seine Staaten „Randgeografien" und „das Andere". Der eurozentrische westliche Blick ist geprägt von einer binären Logik des Eigenen und Fremden, des Okzidents und Orients.[3]

Es war das Buch *Orientalism* (dt. *Orientalismus*) des palästinensischen, in Jerusalem geborenen und in den USA lehrenden Literaturwissenschaftlers Edward W. Said (1935–2003), das 1978 zuerst erschien und den westlichen Blick auf die arabische Welt ins Zentrum seiner Abhandlung rückte. Für ihn war der „Orientalismus" ein Konstrukt der westlichen Welt. Er wurde zugleich ein Schlüsselbegriff imperialismus- und kolonialismuskritischer Debatten, ist in die *postcolonial studies* eingeflossen und wurde zum Standardinstrumentarium literaturwissenschaftlicher Untersuchungen und anderer Disziplinen.

Es sind laut Said mehrere Faktoren, die westliche Vorstellungen von „arabischen Welten" beeinflussen, etwa Identität, Imagination und Hegemonie. Durch die imaginierte Unterlegenheit des „Ostens" stabilisiert die Projektion der Europäer zugleich ihre eigene Identität.

Saids Kernthese, wonach orientalistische Diskurse den Orient überhaupt erst produziert haben, ist heute aktueller und diskussionswürdiger denn je. Befeuert werden die Debatten durch zahlreiche Ereignisse wie 9/11, die Kriege im Nahen Osten, die Migration, auch unter genderspezifischen Perspektiven, beispielsweise bei der Kopftuch-Debatte, dem Hidschāb für arabische Frauen, dem Verbot von Bildung für Frauen sowie den vie-

Speaking of "Arab worlds" is not unproblematic, as the Middle East and its cultures are characterized by complex disagreements about borders, widely dispersed diaspora communities, and transnational and hybrid identities that feel, especially in the context of migration, as though they belong equally to two or more cultural spaces.[1] It is thus not possible to speak of any single, cohesive Arab culture.[2]

The so-called Orient is overlaid with fantasies and projections. Since the eighteenth century and still today, its states have figured as marginal geographies emblematic of the Other. The Eurocentric Western view is characterized by a binary logic of the self and the Other, the familiar and the foreign, the Occident and the Orient.[3]

It was the 1978 book *Orientalism* by the Palestinian literary scholar Edward W. Said (1935–2003), born in Jerusalem and educated in the United States (where he also taught), that sharpened an awareness of how the Western world has long looked at the Arab world. The title of his book was the name he gave to this perspective. The term has since become a key concept in critical debates about imperialism and colonialism—having been integrated into postcolonial studies and become a fundamental tool for research in literary studies and other fields.

1 On hybrid identities in Europe, see Johny Pitts: Afropean: *Notes from Black Europe*, London: Allan Lane, 2019.
2 See https://www.bpb.de/shop/zeitschriften/apuz/32223/hybride-identitaeten-muslimische-migrantinnen-und-migranten-in-deutschland-und-europa/ (accessed 3. Aug. 2022).
3 *Geographies and Art Histories: Diaspora, Decolonizing, and Praxis*, panel organized by Andrew Gayed and Chanda Carey at the annual con-ference of the College Art Association, New York, 13. Feb. 2019.

1 Vgl. zu den Hybridexistenzen in Europa Johny Pitts: *Afropean. Notes from Black Europe*, London: Allan Lane, 2019; deutsche Ausgabe: *Afropäisch. Eine Reise durch das schwarze Europa*, Berlin: Suhrkamp, 2020.
2 https://www.bpb.de/shop/zeitschriften/apuz/32223/hybride-identitaeten-muslimische-migrantinnen-und-migranten-in-deutschland-und-europa/ (Abruf 3. Aug. 2022).
3 *Geographies and Art Histories. Diaspora, Decolonizing, and Praxis*, Beitragscluster in Andrew Gayed und Chanda Carey, College Art Association, The Annual Conference, New York, 13. Feb. 2019.

Typografie-Workshop mit Golnar Kat Rahmani an der Universität der Künste (UdK) in Berlin / Typography workshop with Golnar Kat Rahmani at the University of the Arts (UdK) in Berlin, 2018

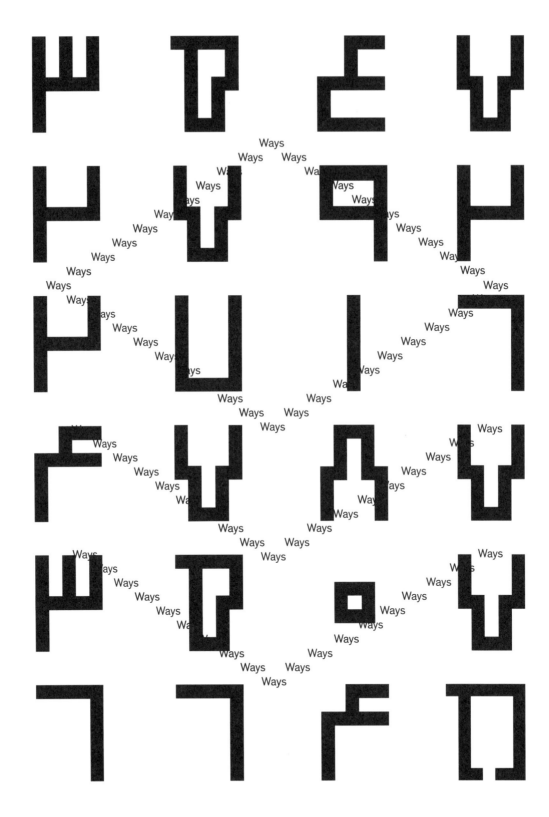

Golnar Kat Rahmani, Typografie-Plakat / typography poster © Golnar Kat Rahmani

len Restriktionen von im Westen selbstverständlichen Rechten und Freiheiten in Saudi-Arabien.

Der Neo-Orientalismus ist dabei deutlich politischer und ideologischer gefärbt. Antimuslimischer Rassismus und islamophobe Ablehnung gehen verschärft darin ein. Die pauschale Gleichsetzung von Islam und Terrorismus, Frauenfeindlichkeit und Konservativismus hat zugenommen.[4]

Eng damit verbunden ist die Vorstellung von der Rückständigkeit und einer verzögerten Aufklärung der arabischen Welt, insbesondere des fehlenden Anschlusses an die Moderne. Im Falle von Design und des hegemonialen Anspruchs von westlichen Designnormen führte dieses Urteil dazu, arabisches Design weitgehend zu ignorieren oder nur dann zu akzeptieren, wenn es der westlichen Moderne entsprach.

Kaum mehr zu überschauen sind die im Anschluss an Saids Veröffentlichung entstandenen Studien zum Themenkomplex Gender und Orientalismus. In diesem Zusammenhang steht auch die Vorstellung von einer Frauenfeindlichkeit des Islam. Selten sind die gängigen Denkmuster und die pauschalen Urteile über den Orient so differenziert analysiert worden wie bei Christina von Braun und Bettina Mathes in ihrem Buch über die Verschleierung der muslimischen Frau.[5] Sie vergleichen die kulturellen Hintergründe der Verhüllung des Frauenkörpers mit denen der hiesigen Freizügigkeit – also die angeblich unemanzipierte Kopftuchträgerin mit der emanzipierten westlichen Frau –, und gehen auf den Symbolgehalt der Polarisierung und die Hintergründe vermeintlicher Wahrheiten ein, auch mit Blick auf die Geschichte.

Wer sich folglich in Auseinandersetzungen mit „dem Orient" befindet, bewegt sich in einer langen Tradition von Diskursen. Die Designpraxis in der europäischen Geschichte hat viel dazu beigetragen, den Exotismus in die westliche Alltagswelt einzulagern. Designer*innen haben die Fantasie über den sogenannten Orient beeinflusst und gefestigt. Allein die Verpackungsindustrie des 19. und frühen 20. Jahrhunderts für Luxuslebensmittel wie Zigaretten hat die Bilderwelt des „Orients" mit luxurierender Vielfalt überschwemmt. Sich dieser affirmativen Vergangenheit aus designtheoretischer Perspektive zu stellen, ist ein bislang noch nicht eingelöstes Desiderat der Disziplin.

4 Vgl. Claudia Brunner et al.: Okzidentalismus konkretisieren, kritisieren, theoretisieren, in dies. et al. (Hg.): *Kritik des Okzidentalismus. Transdisziplinäre Beiträge zu (Neo-)Orientalismus und Geschlecht*, Bielefeld: transcript, 2010: 11–21, hier 11–12.

5 Christina von Braun & Bettina Mathes: *Verschleierte Wirklichkeit. Die Frau, der Islam und der Westen*, Berlin: Aufbau, 2007.

Said argues that several factors influence Western conceptions of Arab worlds, among them identity, imagination, and hegemony. He shows how projections about the inferiority of the "Orient" allow Europeans to stabilize their own identity.

His core thesis—that it was Orientalist discourses which produced the Orient in the first place—is more pertinent and worth discussing today than ever before. These debates have been fueled by a number of events including 9/11, the wars in the Middle East, and migration, as well as gender-specific perspectives, such as controversies over headscarves or the hijab, education bans for women, and many other gender-based restrictions on rights and freedoms in Saudi Arabia that are taken for granted in the West.

Neo-Orientalism is even more overtly political and ideological—shaped more intensely by anti-Muslim racism and Islamophobic disapproval and accompanied by a growing, sweeping equation of Islam and terrorism, of misogyny and conservatism.[4]

4 See Claudia Brunner et al.: Okzidentalismus konkretisieren, kritisieren, theoretisieren, in Claudia Brunner et al. (eds.): *Kritik des Okzidentalismus: Transdisziplinäre Beiträge zu (Neo-)Orientalismus und Geschlecht*, Bielefeld: transcript, 2010: 11–21, on 11–12.

Ganzeer, Mask of Freedom, 2011. Aufkleber aus der Ausstellung / Sticker from the exhibition Be with the Revolution: Street Art und Grafikdesign in den arabischen Protesten seit 2011, Museum für Kunst und Gewerbe Hamburg, 2022 © Ganzeer

Fanons „weiße Maske"

Mit der politischen Dekolonisierung trat im Westen allerdings die Auseinandersetzung mit der eigenen Kultur arabischer Länder wenig in Erscheinung, vereinzelt haben arabische Autor*innen sie hingegen mit wenigen, in Europa aber stark rezipierten Texten beschrieben. Sie wurden mit dem bewaffneten Konflikt um die Unabhängigkeit Algeriens von Frankreich von der französischen und später auch der deutschen Intelligentsia besonders wahrgenommen. Erneut tauchen in heutigen Designdiskursen über Dekolonisierung die Schriften des in Martinique geborenen französischen Autors und Freiheitskämpfers Frantz Fanon (1925–1961) auf.[6] Er war ein Vordenker der Dekolonisierung.

Insbesondere sein Werk *Peau noire, masques blancs* (*Schwarze Haut, weiße Masken*), das 1952 in Paris erschien, geht auf die psychischen Folgen der Kolonialzeit ein. In ihr beschreibt Fanon, der 1953 zum Leiter der psychiatrischen Abteilung der Klinik von Blida-Joinville in der französischen Kolonie Algerien berufen wurde, wie der Schwarze Mensch in eine neurotische Situation geworfen wird, wenn er in einer weißen Gesellschaft aufwächst. Er erscheine den Weißen als minderwertig, gleichzeitig seien Weiße für ihn mit ihrer Kultur nachahmenswert. People of Color, wie Fanon selbst, hatten in Algerien nach einem langen und blutigen Unabhängigkeitskrieg seit 1947 zwar die französische Staatsangehörigkeit erhalten und waren formal Franzosen, wurden jedoch von den weißen Kolonialherren als Bürger zweiter Klasse behandelt. Der Bürgerkrieg endete 1962 mit der Unabhängigkeit Algeriens. Er war einer der weltweit größten Kriege der Dekolonisierung. Dennoch bleibt, so Homi K. Bhabha im Vorwort, ein „Schwarzer Mann" immer ein „weiß maskierter schwarzer Mann", um in einer (post) kolonialen Welt ernst genommen zu werden.[7] Fanon beschrieb zugleich die Mittel, wie sich die „kolonisierten Subjekte" von ihrer tiefsitzenden Entfremdung befreien können. Die aufgeklärte französische Intelligentsia – die Fanon auch selbst rezipierte wie beispielsweise den Begriff der „Subjektkonstruktion" bei Maurice Merleau-Ponty –, wurde von seinen Thesen sehr beeinflusst.

A closely related projection concerns the supposed backwardness and delayed enlightenment of the Arab world, and especially its lack of connection to modernity. In the case of design and the hegemonic claims of Western design norms, this judgment has led many to largely ignore Arab design or to accept it only when it conforms to Western modernity.

The number of studies on gender and Orientalism that have emerged in the wake of Said's theses has been vast. Yet one focus that has clearly emerged in this research has been an interrogation of the belief that Islam is hostile to women. And there are few works to have analyzed widespread patterns of thought or sweeping generalizations about the "Orient" in such a differentiated fashion as Christina von Braun and Bettina Mathes's book on the veiling of Muslim women.[5] Von Braun and Mathes compare the veiling of women's bodies in Arab countries and its various cultural contexts to supposedly more liberal attitudes in the Western world, that is to say, they juxtapose the supposedly unemancipated Muslim women who wear headscarves with supposedly emancipated Western women. Their analysis explores the symbolic significance of the polarization surrounding this issue, as well as the putative truths behind it, taking into account historical context.

Those who confront notions about the "Orient" thus find themselves faced with long-standing discursive traditions. Design practice in European history has moreover done much to embed exoticism into the everyday Western world. Designers have influenced and consolidated such Orientalist fantasies and their imagery, not least on the richly designed packaging used in the nineteenth and early twentieth centuries for luxury goods such as cigarettes. Employing design theory to confront this history of embracing such Orientalist discourse is a task remaining for the discipline.

Fanon's "White Mask"

After political decolonization, however, there was little engagement in the West with the culture in these Arab countries, though individual Arabic authors did describe it in a limited number of texts that were widely read in Europe. As the armed conflict erupted over Algerian independence from France, these texts were especially noticed by French and later also German intellectuals. Today, the writings of Martinique-

---

6 Zunächst in französischer Sprache veröffentlicht: Frantz Fanon: *Peau noire, masques blancs*, Paris: Seuil, 1952; deutsche Ausgabe.: *Schwarze Haut, weiße Masken*, Frankfurt a. M.: Syndikat, 1980.
7 Fanon, Schwarze Haut, weiße Masken 1980 (wie Anm. 6), 11.

5 Christina von Braun & Bettina Mathes, *Verschleierte Wirklichkeit: Die Frau, der Islam und der Westen*, Berlin: Aufbau, 2007.

Dekolonisierung und Diversität

Statt eines Alteritätsdiskurses wird heute zunehmend eine interkulturelle Kommunikation gefordert, auch in Designdiskursen und in der Designpraxis. Kritische (Selbst-)Befragungen des westliche Wissenschaftssystems generell und Reflexionen der akademischen Produktion, etwa die Critical Whiteness Studies, schließen an die alte Orientalismus-Debatte an.[8] Solche Auseinandersetzungen stehen im Design erst am Anfang. Sie befinden sich aber nicht durch Zufall verstärkt im Zentrum epistemischer Fragen, vor allem der Infragestellung des Designkanons und der Anerkennung von mehr Diversität sowie der Methode der Intersektionalität.

Eine Lösung, um der komplexen Verwendungs- und Gebrauchsgeschichte europäischer Repräsentationen des „Orients" aus dem Weg zu gehen, scheint zu sein, arabischstämmige Menschen selbst zu Wort kommen zu lassen.

Der Gender-Aspekt steht dabei in einem Kreuzungspunkt verschiedener sozialer, kultureller oder politischer Einflussfaktoren. Zu den Akteurinnen der neuen epistemischen Zugänge zu Design gehören viele Designerinnen, die sich als Lehrerinnen, Mitglieder eines Netzwerks und/oder Leiterinnen von Design-Agenturen für Frauenbelange einsetzen. Zugleich bemühen sie sich, die Eigenständigkeit arabischer Kulturen zu bewahren.

Einige dieser Grafikdesigner*innen haben eine Ausbildung in Europa oder den USA genossen und leben dort. Teils haben sie, neben ihrer Designpraxis, Lehrämter an Akademien inne. Sie untersuchen die aus den Unterdrückungsmechanismen der kolonialen Zeit resultierenden Überschneidungen von Gender, Sprache, Kultur, Politik und Ethnizität in ihren eigenen Ursprungsländern oder den Zusammenhängen ihrer neuen Wohnorte. Unter der Grundbedingung der Verwerfung der Binarität von „gutem" und „schlechtem" Design betonen sie die Vielsprachigkeit von Design. Zugleich wird der Zustand derjenigen Länder aufgearbeitet, die aufgrund der Kolonisierung an den Rand der anerkannten Designwelt gedrängt wurden und deren Design und Kunsthandwerk als subaltern gewertet werden.

Für die Kanonbildung ist in ihren Augen vor allem die westliche Moderne verantwortlich, die zu einer Grundlage globaler kolonialistischer

born French author and freedom fighter Frantz Fanon (1925–1961) are once again appearing in contemporary design discourses on decolonization.[6] Fanon was a pioneering figure in the decolonization movement.

His book *Peau noire, masques blancs* (*Black Skin, White Masks*), published in Paris in 1952, addresses in particular the psychological consequences of the colonial period. In it, Fanon, who was appointed head of the psychiatric department of the Blida-Joinville hospital in the French colony of Algeria in 1953, describes how the Black man is thrown into a neurotic situation growing up in a White society. White people see Black people as inferior, he argues, and yet at the same time Black people see Whites and their culture as worthy of imitation. After the long and bloody war of independence that began in 1947, people of color in Algeria, such as Fanon himself, possessed French citizenship and were formally French, but they were treated as second-class citizens by the White colonial rulers. The civil war ended in 1962 with Algeria's independence. It was one of the world's largest wars of decolonization. Nevertheless, according to Fanon, the "black man" is trapped in a dilemma, even in the post-colonial world, that he "wants to be white" and is "sealed in his whiteness."[7] At the same time, Fanon described the means by which "colonized subjects" can free themselves from this deep-seated alienation. Progressive French intellectuals whom Fanon also read, such as Maurice Merleau-Ponty (known for his concept of "subject construction"), were also deeply influenced by Fanon's ideas.

Decolonization and Diversity

Today we find a growing plea for intercultural communication in place of a discourse of alterity, and this is a demand that extends into discourses and practices of design. Critical (self-)interrogation of the Western academic system in general, as well as specific reflections on academic production (such as are found in critical Whiteness studies), are building on the old Orientalism debate.[8] Yet this engagement is only just beginning in design. However, it is no coincidence that it is increasingly playing a crucial part in epistemo-

8 Vgl. stellvertretend Katharina Walgenbach: „Die weiße Frau als Trägerin deutscher Kultur". Koloniale Diskurse über Geschlecht, „Rasse" und Klasse im Kaiserreich, Frankfurt a. M.: Campus Forschung, 2006.

6 Published originally in French as Peau noire, masques blancs, Paris: Seuil, 1952; English edition: Black Skin, White Masks, New York: Grove Press, 1967.

7 Frantz Fanon: Black Skin White Masks, 11.

8 For a representative discussion, see Katharina Walgenbach: "Die weiße Frau als Trägerin deutscher Kultur": Koloniale Diskurse über Geschlecht, "Rasse" und Klasse im Kaiserreich, Frankfurt a. M.: Campus Forschung, 2006.

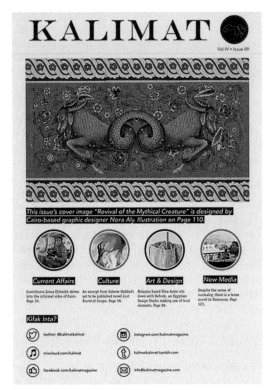

Kalimat Magazine 4, Nr./no. 9 (2014), Titelblatt/cover

Matrix von Macht und Hierarchien wurde. Beispielsweise versammelte das Modernity/Coloniality Project in Lateinamerika von Ende 1990 bis Ende 2020 eine Reihe von Konferenzen und Symposien. Zu den Teilnehmer*innen zählten Theoretiker*innen aus verschiedenen lateinamerikanischen und karibischen Ländern und unterschiedlichen Disziplinen wie Philosophie, Pädagogik, Literaturkritik, Anthropologie, Soziologie und Gender Studies. Unter intersektionaler Perspektive wurden die Diskriminierungsmechanismen oder auch die Selbstwahrnehmung von arabischen Frauen und generell Women of Color deshalb in der Kreuzung von Rassismus und Sexismus betrachtet. Sie forderten, dass neue Narrative entworfen werden und neue diskursive Rahmenbedingungen für Empowerment geschaffen werden. Design wird betrachtet als eine offene Praxis.

Eine Vertreterin dieser Designhaltung ist die in Kuwait geborene Danah Abdulla. In ihrer Doktorarbeit mit dem Titel *Design Otherwise. Towards a Locally-Centric Design Education Curricula in Jordan*, die sie 2018 am Department of Design des Goldsmiths, University of London einreichte, beschreibt sie pädagogische Maßnahmen einer Designlehre, die den Tatbestand der „kolonisierten Subjekte" (Fanon) miteinbezieht.

logical issues in design, in particular the questioning of the design canon and in a growing recognition of greater diversity and the method of intersectionality.

One way to avoid the complex history of how European representations of the "Orient" have been employed seems to have been to let people of Arab descent speak for themselves.

The gendered aspect of this endeavor stands at the intersection of various social, cultural, and political influences. Proponents of these new epistemic approaches to design include many women designers who advocate for women's issues as teachers, members of networks, and artists or directors of design agencies. At the same time, these women are striving to preserve the independence of Arab cultures.

Some of these graphic designers live and work in Europe or the United States, where they received their training. In some cases, they have accepted teaching positions at design schools in addition to their design practice. They examine the intersections of gender, language, culture, politics, and ethnicity that result from the oppressive mechanisms of the colonial period in the countries from which they originally hail or the countries where they now live. Fundamentally rejecting the binary of "good" and "bad" design, they emphasize the diversity of ways in which the craft makes meaning. At the same time, they are working to shed light on the conditions of countries that colonization pushed to the margins of the recognized design world, and whose design and craftwork are regarded as subaltern.

In their view, it is Western modernity, as the foundation of global colonialist matrixes of hierarchical power structures, that is primarily responsible for the formation of *the* design canon as a single body of exemplary works. This view is evident, for instance, in the work of the Modernity/Coloniality Project, which organized a series of conferences and symposia in Latin America from the end of 1990 to the end of 2020. Participants included theorists from various Latin American and Caribbean countries and diverse disciplines such as philosophy, pedagogy, literary criticism, anthropology, sociology, and gender studies. These conferences explored an intersectional perspective on the mechanisms of discrimination against, and the self-perception of, Arab women and other woman of color, focusing on the interplay of racism and sexism. They called for the fashioning of new narratives and the creation of new discursive frameworks to enable empowerment. This perspective sees design as an open practice.

Gleichzeitig ist Danah Abdulla Gründungsmitglied der digitalen Plattform *Decolonising Design*. Diese Plattform unterstützt ähnlich interessierte Designwissenschaftler*innen und organisiert internationale Kongresse, bei denen Themen wie Politik der Migration, indigenes Wissen, Geschlechterproblematik, sexuelle Vielfalt, Abbau von strukturellem Rassismus und die Praxis von respektvollem Umgang mit anderen menschlichen und nichtmenschlichen Wesen besprochen werden. Ihre Mitglieder experimentieren mit vielfältigen und komplexen Denkweisen, die mit dem Konzept des *decolonizing design* verbunden sind. Sie plädieren für performatives Mapping und Storytelling, die die unterschiedlichen westlichen und arabischen Kontexte respektieren. Als Entwurfshaltung empfiehlt Abdulla *disciplinary disobedience*, das heißt, die Normen traditioneller Ideen von „gutem" Design werden verworfen zugunsten eines kontextorientierten Zugangs zu Design. Ein selbstverständlicher Bestandteil dieser Denkweise ist auch eine gendersensible Orientierung, weshalb bei Kongressen, Symposien, Publikationen immer auch Beiträge zu den geschlechterspezifischen Machtstrukturen zählen.

Danah Abdulla gründete 2010 zudem das *Kalimat Magazine*, ein unabhängiges, Non-Profit-Magazin über arabische Kultur. Es existierte bis 2016. Als Plattform zielte es darauf ab, die diversen Stimmen der arabischen Kultur an Designdiskussionen zahlreicher werden und ihre speziellen Erfahrungen und Ausrichtungen einfließen zu lassen.[9]

Ihre Sichtweisen vermittelt sie im Rahmen verschiedener Lehrpositionen: als Programmdirektorin für Grafikdesign in Camberwell, Chelsea, und den Wimbledon Colleges of Art, University of the Arts London (UAL). Vorher lehrte sie an der Brunel University und der Design School am London College of Communication (UAL).

Die „nicht lateinischen" Schriften

Ein bedeutendes Sujet in Debatten über Dekolonisierung ist die Schrift, die als „nicht lateinisch" bezeichnet wird und die arabische Alphabete mit indigenen, Thai- und anderen Typografien verbindet. Allein durch ihre Schrift ist der Wirkungsradius arabischer Designer*innen in westlichen Welten begrenzt.

Die iranische, in Berlin lebende Designerin Golnar Kat Rahmani widmet sich insbeson-

Books are written in Cairo, published in Beirut and Read in Baghdad, Werbeplakat für / advertising poster for the Kalimat Magazine

One representative of this approach to design is Kuwaiti-born Danah Abdulla. In her doctoral dissertation entitled *Design Otherwise: Towards a Locally-Centric Design Education Curricula in Jordan*, submitted in 2018 to the Department of Design at Goldsmiths, University of London, she describes pedagogical strategies of a design education that would incorporate the fact of "colonized subjects" (Fanon). Danah Abdulla is also a founding member of the digital platform *Decolonising Design*. This platform supports design scholars with similar interests and organizes international congresses to discuss topics such as the politics of migration, Indigenous knowledge, gender issues, sexual diversity, dismantling structural racism, and the practice of respectful treatment of other human and nonhuman beings. Its members experiment with diverse and complex ways of thinking associated with the notion of "decolonizing design." They argue for performative mapping and storytelling that respect differing Western and Arab contexts. Abdulla recommends "disciplinary disobedience" as an approach to design, that is to say, discarding the norms of traditional ideas of "good" design in favor of a method that is sensitive to context. It goes without saying that one aspect of this way of thinking is a sensitivity to gender, which is why congresses, symposia, and publications concerned with this approach always include contributions on gender-specific power structures.

Golnar Kat Rahmani, Modekollektion / fashion collection
Namak-e Safar (Der Geschmack einer Reise / The taste of a Journey),
Berlin, 2020 © Golnar Kat Rahmani

In 2010, Danah Abdulla also founded the *Kalimat Magazine*, an independent, nonprofit magazine about Arab culture. The magazine continued until 2016. As a platform, it aimed to empower the diverse voices of Arab culture by increasing their presence in discussions about design and incorporating the specific experiences and perspectives they bring.[9]

She also shares her perspectives through various teaching positions: as program director of graphic design at the Camberwell, Chelsea, and Wimbledon Colleges of Art, University of the Arts London (UAL). She previously taught at Brunel University and the Design School at the London College of Communication (UAL).

"Non-Latin" Scripts

A significant topic in debates about decolonization is the notion of "non-Latin" scripts, which serves as a rubric including not only Arabic alphabets but also Indigenous, Thai, and other typographies. The very script of Arabic limits the scope of influence that Arab designers enjoy in Western contexts.

9 See, among other scholars, Danah Abdulla: Nuclear. Nuqta: A Conversation with Muiz, 10.2012, https://kalimatmagazine.com/ Nuclear-Nuqta-A-conversation-with-Muiz (accessed 6. Aug. 2022).

dere der arabischen Typografie. Sie studierte Grafikdesign an der Universität von Teheran und anschließend Visuelle Kommunikation an der Weißensee Kunsthochschule Berlin. 2016 gründete sie das Studio Kat Rahmani, das sich auf Kommunikationsdesign in den Bereichen der Typografie spezialisiert hat.

Ein charakteristisches Projekt von ihr ist *Type & Politics*, eine Plattform, die sie 2018 gründete. Damit will sie auf die ideologischen und politischen Konnotationen von arabischer Schrift und deren Verwendung in unterschiedlichen Kontexten aufmerksam machen, vor allem auf die negativen Konnotationen im Zusammenhang mit heutigen islamophoben Tendenzen.

Ein weiteres Projekt ist ein Modelabel, bei dem sie sich mit persischer Kalligrafie, insbesondere dem quadratischen Kufi-Stil, ein klassischer Stil in ihrer Heimat, auseinandersetzt. Bei der Modekollektion „Namak-e-Safar" geht es um Distanzen, in diesem Fall zwischen Berlin und ihren Heimatstädten wie Teheran, Damaskus, Kairo, Sari, Doha, Bagdad, Kabul. Nummern geben die Kilometer zwischen Berlin und den Städten an. Die Agentur organisiert parallel Workshops und Vorträge, um den interkulturellen Austausch und Wissenstransfer zu unterstützen.

Streetart und Grafikdesign in den arabischen Protesten seit 2011

Ein weiteres Beispiel, arabische Stimmen selbst zu Wort kommen zu lassen und auf die Situation von gestalterischen Aktionen in arabischen Ländern aufmerksam zu machen, ist die kleine Ausstellung „Be with the Revolution" im Museum für Kunst und Gewerbe in Hamburg, die vom 31. März 2022 bis zum 2. April 2023 gezeigt wurde. Sie verweist auf die Rolle von Streetart und Grafikdesign in den Protesten der arabischen Welt seit 2011.

In besonderem Maße verbunden ist sie mit der als Arabischer Frühling bekannten Serie von Protesten und Aufständen in der arabischen Welt. Sie begannen mit der Revolution in Tunesien und gingen über auf verschiedene Staaten des Nahen Ostens und Nordafrikas (Maghreb und Ägypten), und waren gerichtet gegen die autoritären Systeme der jeweiligen Länder. Hinzu kamen die Grüne Bewegung im Iran (2009) und die Gezi-Proteste in der Türkei (2013). Der zunächst erfolgreiche Protest, der unter anderem auf eine konsequente Verwirklichung der Menschenrechte abzielte, ist inzwischen mit vielen Enttäuschungen verbunden und durch andere Tagesereignisse überschattet.

In her work, Iranian, Berlin-based designer Golnar Kat Rahmani is particularly concerned with Arabic typography. In 2016, after studying graphic design at the University of Tehran and then visual communication at the Weißensee Kunsthochschule Berlin, she founded Studio Kat Rahmani, which specializes in communication design in the various fields of typography.

One of her signature projects is *Type & Politics*, a platform she founded in 2018. The project aims to draw attention to the ideological and political connotations of Arabic script and its use in various contexts, and especially to the negative connotations bound up with contemporary currents of Islamophobia.

Another project of hers is a fashion label in which she explores Persian calligraphy, and in particular the rectilinear kufic style that is classic in her homeland of Iran. Her fashion collection Namak-e-Safar, by contrast, takes up the topic of distances, in this case between Berlin and the many cities that she has come to call home, including Tehran, Damascus, Cairo, Sari, Doha, Baghdad, and Kabul. The use of numbers in the collection indicates the distance in kilometers between Berlin and these cities. The agency also organizes workshops and lectures to support intercultural exchange and knowledge transfer.

Street Art and Graphic Design in the Arab Protests since 2011

Another example of letting Arab voices speak for themselves and drawing attention to creative initiatives in Arab countries is the small exhibition *Be with the Revolution* shown at the Museum für Kunst und Gewerbe in Hamburg from 31 March 2022 to 2 April 2023. The exhibition highlights the role of street art and graphic design in the protests in the Arab world since 2011.

It focuses especially on the series of protests and uprisings in the Arab world that are known as the Arab Spring. These uprisings began with the revolution in Tunisia and spread to various states in the Middle East and North Africa (Maghreb and Egypt); they were directed against the authoritarian systems of the countries in which they took place. They were followed by the Green Movement in Iran (2009) and the Gezi protests in Turkey (2013). After experiencing initial success, these protests and their demands, including the consequential recognition of human rights, have met with significant disappointment and been overshadowed by other current events.

By expressing both hopes and their criticisms, street artists and graphic designers have

Bei den Hoffnungen und der Kritik haben Streetart-Künstler*innen und Grafikdesigner*innen eine eigene Rolle gespielt. Sie verbreiteten ihre Arbeiten „auf der Straße" und in digitalen Räumen, thematisierten Feminismus und sexualisierte Gewalt, legten Wert auf die Wiederentdeckung der arabischen Schrift als politische Sprache und erinnerten an die Opfer der Proteste. So kritisiert Bahia Shehab mit ihrem Graffito eines blauen BHs die sexualisierte Gewalt, die durch die Gegenreaktion auf die Proteste ausgelöst wurde. Sie erinnerte beispielsweise an die Entkleidung einer jungen ägyptischen Frau durch die Polizei auf dem Tahir-Platz in Kairo.

Besonders bemerkenswert an dieser Ausstellung ist die enge Kooperation mit den beteiligten Künstler*innen und Designer*innen aus ihren eigenen Ländern oder dem Exil, wie Ammar Abo Bakr, Bahia Shehab, Ganzeer, Hanadi Chawaf, Mark Nickolas, Marwan Shahin, Mohamed Gaber, Nadia Khiari, Sajad Mustafa Zuabil, Siwar Kraytem, Sulafa Hijazy, Taqi Spateen, Zoo Project.

Nach wie vor ist die Sensibilität für Information und für Beispiele von Designpraxis und -diskursen, die aus „arabischen Welten" stammen und sich mit der Wechselwirkung westlicher und östlicher Kulturen auseinandersetzen, in europäischen Designdiskursen, in der Designpraxis und bei vermittelnden öffentlichen Institutionen nur wenig ausgeprägt.

played their own part in these movements. They have disseminated their work on the street and in digital spaces; they have addressed feminism and sexualized violence, emphasized the importance of rediscovering Arabic script as a political language, and fostered remembrance of the victims the uprisings have claimed. Bahia Shehab's graffito of a blue bra, for instance, criticizes the sexualized violence unleashed by the backlash against the protests. Her work is a call to remember how police stripped a young Egyptian woman in Tahir Square in Cairo.

What is particularly remarkable about this exhibition is its close cooperation with the participating artists and designers, whether they be living in their own countries or in exile—a list that includes Ammar Abo Bakr, Bahia Shehab, Ganzeer, Hanadi Chawaf, Mark Nickolas, Marwan Shahin, Mohamed Gaber, Nadia Khiari, Sajad Mustafa Zuabil, Siwar Kraytem, Sulafa Hijazy, Taqi Spateen, and the Zoo Project.

There is still little awareness in European discourses and practices of design, and in the public institutions that exhibit and communicate their ideas, about information and examples of design practice and discourse that originate in "Arab worlds," and that explore how Western and Eastern cultures interact.

Typografie-Workshop mit Golnar Kat Rahmani an der Universität der Künste (UdK) in Berlin / Typography workshop with Golnar Kat Rahmani at the University of the Arts (UdK) in Berlin, 2018

Literatur
Further Reading

Danah Abdulla: Melancholy and a Palestinian Sadness,
Journal of Visual Culture 20, Nr./no. 2 (2021): 160–161.

Bernd Adam: *Saids Orientalismus und die Historiographie
der Moderne. Der „ewige Orient" als Konstrukt westlicher
Geschichtsschreibung*, Hamburg: Diplomica, 2013.

Iman Attia (Hg./ed.): *Orient- und IslamBilder. Interdisziplinäre
Beiträge zu Orientalismus und antimuslimischem Rassismus*,
Münster: Unrast, 2007.

Ian Buruma & Avishai Margalit: *Okzidentalismus. Der Westen
in den Augen seiner Feinde*, München/Munich: Hanser, 2005.

Ece Canlı: Lachen bringt Tränen, *Missy Magazine*, Nr./no. 3
(Jun.–Jul. 2021): 56–59.

Frantz Fanon: *Peau noire, masques blancs*, Paris: Seuil, 1952;
deutsche Ausgabe / German edition: *Schwarze Haut, weiße Masken*,
Frankfurt a. M.: Syndikat, 1980; englische Ausgabe / English edition:
Black Skin, White Masks, New York: Grove Press, 1967.

Claudia Mareis & Nina Paim (Hg./eds.): *Design Struggles.
Intersecting Histories, Pedagogies, and Perspectives*,
Amsterdam: Valiz, 2021.

Walter Mignolo: The Collective Project Modernity/Coloniality/
Decoloniality, 11. Nov. 2017, http://waltermignolo.com/
the-collective-project-modernitycolonialitydecoloniality/
(Abruf/accessed 6. Jul. 2020).

Edward Said: *Orientalism*, New York: Pantheon Books, 1978;
deutsche Ausgabe / German edition: *Orientalismus*, Frankfurt a. M.:
S. Fischer, 1981.

Markus Schmitz: *Kulturkritik ohne Zentrum.
Edward W. Said und die Kontrapunkte kritischer Dekolonisation*,
Bielefeld: transcript, 2008.

Burkhard Schnepel, Gunnar Brands & Hanne Schönig (Hg./eds.):
*Orient – Orientalistik – Orientalismus. Geschichte und Aktualität
einer Debatte*, Bielefeld: transcript, 2011.

Christina von Braun & Bettina Mathes: *Verschleierte Wirklichkeit.
Die Frau, der Islam und der Westen*, Berlin: Aufbau, 2007.

POSITIONEN HEUTE

CONTEMPORARY POSITIONS

Die „vierte Welle"?
The "Fourth Wave"?

Von einer „vierten Welle" der Frauenbewegung kann auch im Grafikdesign gesprochen werden. Um die Jahrtausendwende und noch bis in die 2010er Jahre hinein galt vielen „der" Feminismus der 1970er Jahre als überholt, ideologisch und verkrampft. Emanzipation erschien insbesondere jungen Frauen als obsolet, insofern sie in der Zwischenzeit eingelöst sei.

Unterschiedliche Lebenserfahrungen, Haltungen und Kontexte haben eine einheitliche Frauenpolitik aufgeweicht. Ein besonderes Kennzeichen ist ihre Diffusität und verschiedene parallel verlaufende individuelle feministische Aktionsformen der neuen Zeit. Eine organisierte feministische Bewegung besteht nicht mehr, in deren Namen politisch gehandelt wird. Gründe sind unter anderem die Aufweichung des Konzepts der Zweigeschlechtlichkeit und die zunehmende Kritik an der Idee einer kollektiven Identität der Frau, intersektionale Aspekte, eine zunehmende Beachtung der Lebensbedingungen von sozialen Randgruppen und Randgeografien. Diversität ist inzwischen zu einem beachtenswerten kulturellen Kriterium auch der großen Grafikdesignverbände geworden, allen voran der amerikanischen AIGA, die in ihrer Sonderrubrik *Eye on Design* viele neue Beispiele aus der Praxis von diversem Design behandelt.

Doch gleichzeitig hat auch eine Reihe von Ereignissen, von denen viele glaubten, dass sie längst zu den Errungenschaften modernen Lebens zählen, zu Irritationen geführt und die Debatten über Feminismus neu entflammt. Rechte von Frauen, die als gesichert und unverhandelbar galten, wurden erneut infrage gestellt.

Dazu gehört die unter dem Hashtag #MeToo kursierende Empörung über sexualisierte Gewalt. Auslöser war die Beschuldigung des mächtigen Filmproduzenten Harvey Weinstein in der *New York Times* vom 5. Oktober 2017 durch die Schauspielerinnen Ashley Judd und Rose McGowan, die ihm sexuelle Belästigung vorwarfen. Aufgefordert, mit dem Bekenntnis „Me too" vergleichbare Erlebnisse öffentlich zu machen, entstand eine Welle an Reaktionen über die sozialen Medien. Die Opfer waren zumeist junge Frauen in abhängigen und prekären Verhältnissen, deren Täter Männer in einflussreichen Machtpositionen waren, besonders in der Film- und Fernsehbranche, dem Theater und generell der Kreativwirtschaft.

Um einen ähnlichen Fall ging es bei dem französischen Politiker der sozialistischen Partei Frankreichs, Dominique Strauss-Kahn, dem sexuelle Belästigung eines Zimmermädchens in den

In graphic design, too, we can speak of a "fourth wave" of the women's movement. Around the turn of the millennium and even into the 2010s, many considered "the" feminism of the 1970s to be outdated, ideological, and overly rigid. Emancipation seemed obsolete, especially to young women, since its aims seemed to have been achieved.

A variety of different life experiences, attitudes, and contexts have moreover diluted any unified feminist politics. A particular feature of today's feminism lies in its diffuse quality, in various individual forms of feminist action running parallel to one another. There no longer exists any organized feminist movement under which political actors claim to operate. Reasons for this shift include the blurring of binary notions of sex and the growing critique of the idea that women share a collective identity; intersectional factors; and a growing consideration of the living conditions of marginalized social groups and geographies. Diversity has now become a noteworthy value even among the major graphic design associations, led by the American AIGA, whose special design section *Eye on Design* overs many examples from the practice of diverse design.

At the same time, however, a series of events pointing to problems that are widely thought to have been overcome have also caused irritation and reignited debates about feminism. Women's rights, which many had regarded as secure and beyond all debate, were once again called into question.

Among these events was the outrage over sexualized violence that spread worldwide under the hashtag #MeToo. The movement was triggered by the accusations of sexual harassment made in the *New York Times* on 5 October 2017 against Harvey Weinstein, a powerful film producer, by actors Ashley Judd and Rose McGowan. Spurred on to bring similar experiences to public attention with the confession "me too," a wave of reactions emerged via social media. The victims were mostly young women in subordinate positions and precarious circumstances, while the perpetrators were men in influential positions of power, especially in the film and television industries, theater, and the creative sector overall.

Another case involved Dominique Strauss-Kahn, a French politician from the Socialist Party, who was accused of sexual assault by a maid in the United States. As with other cases from the #MeToo movement, this assault prompted an intense debate about women's autonomy that varied from country to country, even as it erupted simultaneously.

ES GIBT ALSO NICHT EINEN FEMINISMUS, SONDERN VIELE.

Ilse Lenz, 2018

TERRE DES FEMMES

DIE BITCH MUSS BÜGELN, MUSS SEIN. WENN NICHT, GIBT'S PRÜGEL, MUSS SEIN.

KURDO & MAJOE – CHARLIE SHEEN
24.539 AUFRUFE

#UNHATEWOMEN

Gewalt gegen Frauen wird gefeiert. In Konzerthallen. Auf Schulhöfen. In Kinderzimmern.
Teile #UNHATEWOMEN und setze ein Zeichen gegen frauenverachtende Hate Speech.
Mehr auf unhate-women.com

Terre des Femmes, Kampagne gegen frauenverachtende Songtexte von deutschen Rappern unter dem Titel / Campaign against misogynistic song lyrics by German rappers under the title #unhatewoman, Design: David Morales, 2020 © Philipp und Keuntje, Berlin

USA vorgeworfen wurde. Wie bei #MeToo wurde nun, zu einem bestimmten historischen Zeitpunkt, die individuelle Tat zu einer intensiven, von Nation zu Nation unterschiedlich geführten Debatte über die Autonomie von Frauen.

Mit der Bewerbung um das Amt des amerikanischen Präsidenten durch Donald Trump und dessen sexistische und rassistische Äußerungen setzte ebenfalls eine Welle der öffentlichen Empörung ein.

In der ganzen westlichen Welt lösten diese spektakulären Fälle eine Massenmobilisierung aus. Dazu zählte der „Women's March on Washington" einen Tag nach der Amtseinführung des Präsidenten Trump, der bewusst an die Demonstrationen der Suffragetten im 19. Jahrhundert anknüpfte. Nicht nur in der amerikanischen Hauptstadt, sondern rund um den Globus schlossen sich Frauen den Solidaritätskundgebungen Sisters Marches an. Gerüstet mit Plakaten, Stickern, Buttons, Handzetteln benutzten sie dabei durchaus traditionelle visuelle Formate, wie auch der Ort des Geschehens nicht nur das digitale Netz, sondern vor allem die Straße war. Abtreibungsdebatten in den USA, die krasse Frauenunterdrückung in Saudi-Arabien und Afghanistan, die nicht enden wollende Diskussion um den Gender-Pay-Gap oder die zunehmenden sprachlichen Verunglimpfungen von Frauen in den populären Medien – sehr viele der alten Diskriminierungen bestehen bis heute, und einige emanzipatorische Errungenschaften sind in heftigem Maße rückläufig.

Wenngleich heute eine Vielfalt von neuen Ansätzen im Grafikdesign besteht, die Position gegen die Diskriminierungen von Frauen und die binäre Logik heterosexueller Geschlechteridentitäten einnehmen, sollen einige wenige exemplarisch die verschiedenen Positionen vor Augen führen. Nicht wenige beziehen sich auf eine eigene Tradition feministischer Proteste.

Beispiel: Stiftungen und NGOs

Viele Stiftungen und NGOs wie Terre des Femmes und die Friedrich-Ebert-Stiftung in Deutschland widmen sich vermehrt hartnäckigen Formen der Geschlechterdiskriminierung und setzen Grafikdesign ein, um auf alte und aktuelle Probleme aufmerksam zu machen.

In der Kampagne #unhatewomen haben Grafikdesigner*innen beispielsweise in besonders wirkungsvoller Weise auf die gewaltverherrlichende und frauenverachtende Sprache in deutschen Rap-Songs hingewiesen. „Gewalt gegen

Donald Trump's campaign to become US president and his sexist and racist remarks set off a similar wave of public outrage.

Throughout the Western world, these spectacular cases triggered mass mobilization at the highest political levels. This included the Women's March on Washington the day after President Trump's inauguration—a protest that deliberately echoed the demonstrations of the suffragettes in the nineteenth century. Not only in the American capital, but around the globe, women joined the solidarity rallies known as the Sisters Marches. Equipped with posters, stickers, buttons, and flyers, they employed thoroughly traditional visual formats, as their actions unfolded not just online but above all on the street. Whether one points to debates about abortion in the United States, the blatant oppression of women in Saudi Arabia and Afghanistan, the neverending discussion about the gender pay gap, or the increasing linguistic denigration of women in the popular media: quite a number of long-standing forms of discrimination still persist to this day, and some gains made by movements for women's emancipation are being dramatically eroded.

Although one finds a variety of new approaches in graphic design today that take a stand against the discrimination of women and the binary logic of heterosexual gender identities, highlighting just a few can exemplify the various positions. Many of them draw from a unique tradition of feminist protests.

Example: Foundations and NGOs

Many foundations and NGOs, such as Terre des Femmes and the German Friedrich-Ebert-Stiftung, are increasingly addressing persistent forms of gender discrimination and using graphic design to draw attention to both old and current problems.

In a campaign called #unhatewomen, for example, graphic designers employed a particularly effective means of drawing attention to language in German rap songs expressing misogyny and glorifying violence. "Violence against women is not always just physical," it says. "Language, too, can be violence. Verbal violence against women is listened to, liked, and celebrated by millions—making it part of our everyday lives and language."[1]

1 See https://www.unhate-women.com/de/ (accessed 10. Jul. 2022).

Philipp und Keuntje, 2022
#unhatewomen. Terre des Femmes

WIR SCHLUGEN DIE RAPPER MIT IHREN EIGENEN WAFFEN: IHREN TEXTEN.

Graphic Novel aus der Serie / Graphic Novel from the series
Asian Icons for Gender Justice, Friedrich-Ebert-Stiftung, Bangladesh
Office: The High-Altitude Sit-in Protester von/by Kang Ju-ryong,
Illustratorin/illustrator: Cha Fun-Hye © Friedrich-Ebert-Stiftung

Graphic Novel aus der Serie / Graphic novel from the series
Asian Icons for Gender Justice, Friedrich-Ebert-Stiftung, Bangladesh Office, Ever living Rokeya: Pioneer of Women's Rights and
Gender Justice in Bangladesh von/by Tania Hoque, Illustratorin/
illustrator: Nahida Nisha © Friedrich-Ebert-Stiftung

Frauen ist nicht immer nur physisch", heißt es dort. „Auch Sprache kann Gewalt sein. Verbale Gewalt gegen Frauen wird millionenfach gehört, geliked und gefeiert – und so zum Teil unseres Alltags und unserer Sprache."[1]

Mit Plakaten und Videos im Netz fordert Terre des Femmes zur Bekämpfung und Strafverfolgung von Hasskriminalität gegen Frauen und Mädchen auf. Grafikdesigner*innen, in diesem Fall David Morales, Executive Creative Director, zusammen mit Grafikdesignerinnen der Berliner Kreativagentur Philipp und Keuntje, haben für ihre Entwürfe zahlreiche Preise gewonnen. Die Gestaltung der Plakate ist unspektakulär, große Porträtaufnahmen von Frauen werden mit Zitaten aus den Rap-Songs konfrontiert, dazu die Zahl der Aufrufe in den sozialen Medien aufgelistet. In dieser dokumentarischen Form wirkt die simple Konfrontation besonders beeindruckend.

Ein weiteres Beispiel sind asiatische Graphic Novels von Heroinnen der Geschichte. 2021 gaben Jonathan Menge und Isabelle Mischke

With posters and online videos, Terre des Femmes calls for combating and prosecuting hate crimes against women and girls. Designers for the campaign—in this case, executive creative director David Morales working together with graphic designers from the Berlin-based creative agency Philipp und Keuntje—have won numerous awards for their work. The design of the posters is unspectacular: large portraits of women are juxtaposed with quotes from rap songs, along with a list of the number of views on social media. In this documentary format, the sparse juxtaposition is especially impressive.

Another example is Asian graphic novels of heroines in history. In 2021, Jonathan Menge and Isabelle Mischke published an anthology of twelve graphic novels from Asian countries for the Friedrich-Ebert-Stiftung. Under the title *Icons of Gender Justice: Paving the Way for Women's Rights in Asia*,[2] twelve individual stories

1 Siehe https://www.unhate-women.com/de/
(Abruf 10. Jul. 2022).

2 See https://www.fes.de/themenportal-die-welt-gerecht-gestalten/
weltwirtschaft-und-unternehmensverantwortung/artikel-in-
weltwirtschaft-und-unternehmensverantwortung/icons-of-gender-
justice (accessed 7. Jul. 2022).

im Auftrag der Friedrich-Ebert-Stiftung eine Anthologie von zwölf Graphic Novels aus asiatischen Ländern heraus. Unter dem Titel *Icons of Gender Justice. Paving the Way for Women's Rights in Asia*[2] wurde jeweils eine eigene Geschichte von zwölf außergewöhnlichen Frauen und ihrem Kampf für mehr Geschlechtergerechtigkeit in Form von Bildgeschichten gestaltet. Die Illustrator*innen waren jeweils unterschiedliche Grafikdesigner*innen. Die Initiator*innen wollten darauf aufmerksam machen, dass in Asien, wie überall auf der Welt, die Ikonen politischer und sozialer Befreiungskämpfe nicht nur Männer waren. Aus diesem Grund wurden mutige Frauen vorgestellt, um Asiat*innen neue Vorbilder anzubieten. Es sind vorwiegend historische Personen aus jeweils einem anderen asiatischen Land und der Pazifik-Region.

Internationalisierung

Die sogenannte vierte Welle der Frauenbewegung zeichnet sich durch zunehmende Internationalisierung aus. Grafikdesignerinnen von allen Kontinenten sind durch das Internet miteinander vernetzt. Es verbindet sie fast immer ein intersektionaler Zugang zur Designgeschichte und ihren Diskursen, wobei der Rahmen mit den Begriffen *gender*, *culture*, *ethnicity* und *class* abgesteckt ist. Diskriminierung hat viele Formen, die sich zum Teil in einer Person überschneiden und dadurch zu einer jeweils besonderen Erfahrung führen. Labels wie *depatriarchizing* und *decolonizing*, eine Infragestellung westlicher Dominanz, eine antirassistische Haltung, die Neigung zum Aktivismus, kollektive und kooperative Organisationsformen und das Zurückdrängen einer rein akademischen Auseinandersetzung verbinden die Grafikdesignerinnen mit Vertreterinnen anderer Professionen. Bemerkenswert ist dabei auch die Beschäftigung mit der Geschichte von Design und mit feministischen Traditionen. Hier, wie in der Geschichte auch, spielen Frauenkollektive und Selbstermächtigung eine große Rolle, allerdings nun mit neuen Kommunikations- und Distributionsformen sowie mit neuen Formaten.

Beispiel: Frauenkollektive

Ein solches feministisches Frauenkollektiv ist das schwedische MMS. Sein Name ist aus

2 Siehe https://www.fes.de/themenportal-die-welt-gerecht-gestalten/weltwirtschaft - und - unternehmensverantwortung / artikel - in - weltwirtschaft-und-unternehmensverantwortung/icons-of-gender-justice (Abruf 7. Jul. 2022).

of extraordinary women and their strugle for more gender justice were combined in a graphic novel anthology. Each story was illustrated by a different graphic designer. The book's creators wanted to draw attention to the fact that in Asia, as everywhere else in the world, the icons of struggles for political and social liberation were not just men. To do so, they presented courageous women as new Asian role models. The women are mainly historical figures, each from a different Asian country and the Pacific region.

Internationalization

The fourth wave of the women's movement is characterized by increasing internationalization. Graphic designers from all continents are connected online. They are almost always united by an intersectional approach to design history and its discourses, framing it in terms of gender, culture, ethnicity, and class. Discrimination takes many forms, some of which overlap in their effects on a single person, producing experiences that are individually unique. Labels such as "depatriarchizing" and "decolonizing," along with a questioning of Western dominance, an antiracist stance, an inclination towards activism, collective and cooperative forms of organization, and moving beyond a purely academic debate, create commonalities between women graphic designers and women working in other positions. Noteworthy among these fourth wave feminists is a preoccupation with the history of design and with feminist traditions. Women's collectives and self-empowerment play a major role here, as they have historically, but now with new forms of communication and distribution as well as new formats.

Example: A Women's Collective

One such feminist women's collective is the Swedish MMS, whose name is constructed from the initials of its members: Maryam Fanni, Matilda Flodmark, and Sara Kaaman. It explores the present and history of women graphic designers.

Originally from Stockholm, where some of them teach part-time at the art academy, the three graphic designers have been conducting research since 2012. "Graphic design, socialism and feminism" is the telling title under which they have been collaborating with the Worker's Educational Association (ABF) in Stockholm since 2015.

den Initialen der Mitglieder konstruiert: Maryam Fanni, Matilda Flodmark und Sara Kaaman. Es setzt sich mit der Gegenwart und Geschichte von Grafikdesignerinnen auseinander.

Aus Stockholm stammend und teilweise dort an der Kunsthochschule lehrend, organisieren die drei Grafikdesignerinnen seit 2012 Forschung. „Graphic design, socialism and feminism", unter diesem bezeichnenden Titel führen sie seit 2015 eine Zusammenarbeit mit The Worker's Educational Association (ABF) in Stockholm durch.

Eine besondere Initiative war 2018 ihre Buchveröffentlichung *Natural Enemies of Books. A Messy History of Women in Printing and Typography*.[3] Unter dem gleichen Titel veranstalteten sie dazu eine Ausstellung. Der Titel erinnert bewusst an das Buch *Bookmaking on the Distaff Side*, das 1937 von einer Gruppe von Frauen aus dem Druckereigewerbe herausgegeben wurde. Es war von vielen Frauen aus dem Buchgewerbe – Grafikdesignerinnen, Verlegerinnen, Setzerinnen, Autorinnen – mit eigenen Beiträgen zur persönlichen Berufserfahrung und jeweils eigener Gestaltung, bis hin zu individuell ausgewähltem Papier, zusammengesetzt worden und wollte die prekäre Situation von Frauen im Buchgewerbe beleuchten. Gleichzeitig ist die Veröffentlichung ein Symbol für partizipative Arbeit unter Frauen. Das Buch von MMS ist nun Anlass, auf die vielen Personen hinzuweisen, die an der Buchproduktion heute beteiligt sind, auf ihre Probleme aufmerksam zu machen und sie zu Wort kommen zu lassen.

Mit dem Softwareprogramm The Name of the Game erstellte MMS Statistiken zu Designwettbewerben und Designpreisen in Schweden und zwar nach geografischen Gesichtspunkten und Gender-Aspekten. Interviews mit Designerinnen versuchen zugleich zu ergründen, welche Effekte Designpreise haben bzw. welche Designprodukte ausgelobt werden und welche ausscheiden. Die Ergebnisse decken sich mit Untersuchungen nach Gender-Aspekten in anderen Ländern. Da solche Statistiken selten, wenn überhaupt, von den verantwortlichen Staaten, Kommunen oder Verbänden durchgeführt werden, sind sie ein wesentlicher Baustein in der Argumentation bezüglich der Schieflage, in der sich der Proporz von Frauen und Männern im Grafikdesign nach wie vor befindet.

A unique project in 2018 was their book publication *Natural Enemies of Books: A Messy History of Women in Printing and Typography*,[3] accompanied by an eponymous exhibition. The title deliberately plays off of the book *Bookmaking on the Distaff Side*, published in 1937 by a group of women in the printing trade. This book, which aimed to shed light on the precarious situation of women in the trade, was assembled by many women working in the business, including graphic designers, publishers, typesetters, and authors. It consisted of pieces written by the women themselves reflecting on their personal experience in the trade, with each contribution boasting a unique design, even down to the individually selected paper. At the same time, the publication is a symbol of participatory work among women. In the present context, MMS's book serves as an occasion to draw attention to the many people involved in book production today—to acknowledge their problems and give them a voice.

Using the software program The Name of the Game, MMS compiled statistics on design competitions and design awards in Sweden according to criteria of location and gender. At the same time, interviews with women designers sought to discover the effects of design prizes or which design products receive awards and which are eliminated. The results are consistent with studies in other countries that focus on gender. Since such statistics are rarely, if ever, produced by the relevant states, municipalities, or associations, they are an essential component of arguments highlighting the unequal proportion of men and women that still persists in graphic design today.

Example: Design Platforms

A number of initiatives for a new perspective on design are currently originating from Switzerland. depatriarchise design is a Basel-based nonprofit organization. Initially a blog responding to a call-for-action criticizing the design scene for being apolitical, the group formally established itself in 2017. It aimed to support the voices of "womxn, BIPoC [sic], LGBTQIA+, people with disabilities, migrants and refugees, and others from marginalized backgrounds" in publicly articulating their concerns. Designers Maya Ober and Nina Paim from Basel are its codirectors.[4]

3 *Natural Enemies of Books. A Messy History of Women in Printing and Typography* ist eine Anthologie, herausgegeben von MMS und im Frühjahr 2020 von Occasional Papers, London, editiert.

3 *Natural Enemies of Books: A Messy History of Women in Printing and Typography* is an anthology edited by MMS and published in early 2020 by Occasional Papers (London).
4 See https://depatriarchisedesign.com (accessed 30. Jun. 2022).

Screen printing im Workshop von Clara Philips während ihrer Ausstellung / Screen printing in Clara Philips's workshop during her exhibition Warm Friends, Cold Cash in der / at the Kunsthalle Stockholm, 2015, v. l. n. r. / from left to right: Sara Kaaman, Matilda Flodmark (mit ihrem Kind / with her child Elis) & Maryam Fanni, 2015 © MMS

Beispiel: Design-Plattformen

Von der Schweiz gehen einige Initiativen zu einer neuen Perspektive auf Design aus. depatriarchise design ist eine in Basel ansässige Non-Profit-Organisation. Die Gruppe bildete sich 2017 zunächst infolge eines *call for action* als Blog und kritisierte die Designszene, die ihr apolitisch erschien. Sie versuchte deshalb, Stimmen von „womxn, BIPoC, LGBTQIA+, people with disabilities, migrants and refugees, and others from marginalized backgrounds"[4] zu unterstützen mit dem Anliegen, ihnen eine Öffentlichkeit zu verschaffen. Die Designerinnen Maya Ober und Nina Paim aus Basel sind Co-Direktorinnen.

depatriarchise design übt grundsätzliche Kritik am Design-Kanon von „gutem" Design und plädiert für größere Diversität. Vor allem möchten die Protagonistinnen soziale und politische

depatriarchise design is fundamentally critical of the design canon of "good" design and argues for greater diversity. Above all, its protagonists want to expose social and political practices that are discriminatory and to highlight alternatives. Maya Ober developed the teaching program Imagining Otherwise at the University of Art and Design (FHNW) in Basel, in which she explores how intersectionality shapes design practice. She also directs the Educating Otherwise program.

In 2021, depatriarchise design (Anja Neidhardt and Maya Ober) merged with the nonprofit organization common-interest, which was founded in 2018. In 2019, common-interest created the website *Futuress*, which developed a year later into an online magazine and platform. Its members hail from five continents. *Futuress* announces itself with the subtitle "Where feminism, design and politics meet."[5] The group is

4 https://depatriarchisedesign.com (Abruf 30. Jun. 2022).

5 See https://futuress.org (accessed 10. Feb. 2023).

Futuress #1, v. l. n. r. / from left to right: Abigail Scheider, Noemi Parisi, Mio Kojima, Nina Paim, Otto Paim, Maya Ober, Nour Sea Ober, Ann Kern, Sabrina Vinzen, Cherry-Ann Davies & Alice Fada, 2022 © Futuress

Gepflogenheiten aufdecken, die diskriminierend sind, und Alternativen aufzeigen. Maya Ober entwickelte an der Hochschule für Gestaltung und Kunst (FHNW) in Basel das Lehrprogramm „Imagining Otherwise", in dem sie untersucht, wie Intersektionalität die Designpraxis bestimmt. Sie leitet gleichzeitig das Programm „Educating Otherwise".

2021 schloss sich depatriarchise design (Anja Neidhardt und Maya Ober) mit der Non-Profit-Organisation common-interest zusammen, die sich 2018 gegründet hatte. 2019 schuf common-interest die website *Futuress*, die sich ein Jahr später als Online-Magazin und Plattform entwickelte. Mitglieder sind Personen von fünf Kontinenten. *Futuress* wirbt mit dem Untertitel „Where feminism, design and politics meet".[5] Die Gruppe setzt sich zusammen aus Vertreter*innen von Design, Literatur, Journalistik, Verlags-

composed of representatives from design, literature, journalism, publishing, science, education, visual arts, and activism. The group has general goals that are very similar to those of depatriarchise design: "to radically democratize design education and amplify marginalized voices."[6]

Another significant platform is *Decolonising Design*.[7] As the editors write, here too participants formulate a fundamental critique of the narratives of design history and design theory. In particular, the editors lament the exclusion of once-colonized countries, as well as the dominance of Eurocentric perspectives on design and the transmission of corresponding knowledge that shapes current design production.

5 https://futuress.org (Abruf 10. Feb. 2023).

6 See https://futuress.org (accessed 10. Feb. 2023).
7 See https://www.decolonisingdesign.com (accessed 30. Jun. 2022).

wesen, Wissenschaft, Pädagogik, bildender Kunst und Aktivismus. *Futuress* verfolgt sehr ähnliche allgemeine Ziele wie depatriarchise design: „to radically democratize design education and amplify marginalized voices".[6]

Eine weitere bedeutende Plattform ist *Decolonising Design*.[7] In den Worten der Redaktion üben die Vertreter*innen auch hier grundsätzliche Kritik an den Narrativen von Designgeschichte und Designtheorie. Besonders beklagt wird der Ausschluss von einstmals kolonisierten Ländern, außerdem die Dominanz eurozentrischer Perspektiven auf Design und die Vermittlung von entsprechendem Wissen, das die aktuelle Designproduktion prägt.

Grafikdesignerinnen als Lehrerinnen

Eine vergleichsweise junge Tradition ist die Verbindung vieler Grafikdesignerinnen mit Hochschulen. Als Lehrerinnen hatten und haben sie wesentlichen Einfluss auf Diskurse und Praxis von Design der nachfolgenden Generation.

Bereits in der zweiten Hälfte des 20. Jahrhunderts spielten Frauen eine signifikante Rolle in der Lehre von Grafikdesign. Sie stellten den Design-Kanon infrage, initiierten fachspezifische Diskussionen und agierten als Kunstkritikerinnen, Verlegerinnen und Kuratorinnen. Sie sind das *underground matriarchy*, von dem Ellen Lupton sprach.[8] Fast alle Grafikdesignerinnen, die in den 1970er Jahren zu Berühmtheit gelangten, bekleideten Positionen an einschlägigen Designakademien. Ihre Präsenz darf allerdings nicht darüber hinwegtäuschen, dass der gesamte Bereich der Lehre immer noch eine Männerdomäne war und ist. Und das, obwohl in Design-Studiengängen Frauen überwiegen, desgleichen in den entsprechenden Berufszweigen. Auffallend wenige Frauen sind allerdings in oberen Führungspositionen vertreten. Laut GWA-Diversity-Studie (Gesamtverband Kommunikationsagenturen GWA e. V.) sind 2021 etwa 60 Prozent aller Angestellten im Agenturbereich weiblich. Auf Geschäftsführungsebene sind es nur noch 18 Prozent, 12 Prozent davon sind Kreativ-Direktorinnen. Der Gender-Pay-Gap in Agenturen beträgt über alle Mitarbeiter*innen 6,5 Prozent. Im Management ist

Women Graphic Designers as Teachers

A comparatively recent tradition is the affiliation of many women graphic designers with universities. As teachers, these women have significantly influenced and continue to impact the following generation's discourses and practice of design.

As early as the second half of the twentieth century, women played a significant role in the teaching of graphic design. They challenged the design canon, initiated specialized discussions, and were active as art critics, publishers, and curators. They comprise the underground matriarchy discussed by Ellen Lupton.[8] Almost all of the women graphic designers who rose to prominence in the 1970s held positions at various design schools. However, their presence should not obscure the fact that the entire field of teaching mainly was and remains a domain dominated by men, and this despite the fact that women predominate in design courses and in the corresponding professions. Conspicuously few women are nevertheless represented in upper management positions. According to a study on diversity authored by the Gesamtverband Kommunikationsagenturen (General Association of Communication Agencies, GWA e. V.), around 60 percent of all agency employees were women in 2021. At the executive level, the figure drops to 18 percent, with only 12 percent of those being women creative directors. The gender pay gap in agencies across all employees is 6.5 percent, and it is most pronounced among management. About half of women aged thirty-five and older work part-time. This proportion hardly decreases as age increases. Currently, the proportion of women at the German Art Directors Club (ADC) is 16.7 percent; when it comes to juries, only eight out of twenty-nine are chaired by women, and only 20 percent of jurors are women.[9]

Example:
Anja Kaiser and Rebecca Stephany

One especially significant example of the particular intersection between graphic design, activism, and established institutions such as universities, museums, and urban art galleries is the

6 Ebenda.
7 https://www.decolonisingdesign.com (Abruf 30. Jun. 2022).
8 Ellen Lupton & Laurie Haycock Makela: Underground Matriarchy. Women Who Have Shaped the Profession by Their Own Work and by Enabling Those around Them, *Eye Magazine* 4, Nr. 14 (Herbst 1994), https://www.eyemagazine.com/feature/article/underground-matriarchy und https://ellenlupton.com/Underground-Matriarchy (Abruf 11. Apr. 2022).

8 Ellen Lupton & Laurie Haycock Makela: Underground Matriarchy: Women Who Have Shaped the Profession by Their Own Work and by Enabling Those around Them, *Eye Magazine* 4, no. 14 (Autumn 1994), https://www.eyemagazine.com/feature/article/underground-matriarchy and https://ellenlupton.com/Underground-Matriarchy (accessed 11. Apr. 2022).
9 See Eva-Maria Schmidt: Die Zukunft ist weiblich, *HORIZONTmagazine*, ADC festival newspaper, 29. Apr. 2021: 2.

er am stärksten ausgeprägt. Etwa die Hälfte der Frauen ab 35 Jahren arbeitet in Teilzeit. Dieser Anteil geht später kaum wieder zurück. Aktuell liegt der Anteil von Frauen beim deutschen Art Directors Club (ADC) bei 16,7 Prozent, bei Jurys haben 8 von 29 Frauen den Vorsitz, 20 Prozent der Juror*innen sind weiblich.[9]

Beispiel:
Anja Kaiser und Rebecca Stephany

Ein besonderes und signifikantes Beispiel für die spezifische Vernetzung von Grafikdesign, Aktivismus und etablierten Institutionen wie Hochschulen, Museen bzw. städtischen Kunstgalerien ist die Aktion „Whose.Agency" von Anja Kaiser 2018 in Leipzig, Deutschland.

Die ausgebildete Grafikdesignerin studierte unter anderem an der Burg Giebichenstein Kunsthochschule Halle. Ihr Fokus lag dort auf Typografie und Editorial Design. Ab 2012 setzte sie das Studium am Sandberg Instituut in Amsterdam fort bis zum Masterabschluss mit der Arbeit „Sexed Realities. To Whom Do I Owe My Body?". Darin setzte sie sich mit dem weiblichen Körper als Projektionsfläche verschiedenster Wünsche und Zuschreibungen auseinander. Dabei erschloss sie sich das ihr bislang wenig bekannte Territorium der digitalen Medien.

Anja Kaiser war künstlerische Mitarbeiterin im Lehrgebiet für Schrift und Typografie an der Burg Giebichenstein und hat heute eine Vertretungsprofessur an der Hochschule für Grafik und Buchkunst Leipzig inne. 2017 gewann sie den Preis INFORM der Galerie für zeitgenössische Kunst (GfZK), Leipzig, der mit einem Preisgeld verbunden war. Sie entschloss sich, eine digitale Werbekampagne im Leipziger Stadtraum mit bewegten Bildern zu organisieren. Mit der Frage „Whose.Agency?" betitelt, wollte sie die Wirkmacht von Aktivist*innen jenseits von Werbefirmen erproben, die sich im öffentlichen Raum artikulieren. Sie benutzte bereits vorhandene digitale City-Light-Werbeflächen, die ansonsten für die ökonomische Verwertung von Firmen vermietet wurden.

Anja Kaiser bewegt sich in einem feministisch-aktivistischen Umfeld. Auf der Einladung zur Aktion waren explizit aktivistische Gruppen angesprochen, sich mit eigenen Textbausteinen zu beteiligen: „queer, punks, homo core babes, not grrrrrlz, DIY witches & anarchist punk players". Die Aktivist*innen hatten bislang meist

Whose.Agency initiative started by Anja Kaiser 2018 in Leipzig, Germany.

Trained as a graphic designer, Kaiser studied at the Burg Giebichenstein Kunsthochschule Halle, among other institutions. Her focus in Halle was on typography and editorial design. Starting in 2012, she continued her studies at the Sandberg Instituut in Amsterdam, where she received a master's degree with the thesis "Sexed Realities: To Whom Do I Owe My Body?". In her thesis, she dealt with the female body as a screen for projections of a wide variety of desires and attributions. In the process, she explored the territory of digital media with which she had previously had little experience.

Kaiser held a position as artistic assistant in the Department of Typeface and Typography at Burg Giebichenstein and currently holds a visiting professorship at the Leipzig Academy of Visual Arts. In 2017 she won the INFORM prize of the Galerie für zeitgenössische Kunst (GfZK), Leipzig, which comes with a monetary award. Using the money, she then organized a digital advertising campaign based on video images in Leipzig's urban space. Called Whose.Agency?, the campaign sought to test the effectiveness of independent activists in conveying their message publicly, without the involvement of advertising firms. It used existing digital ad space known as City Lights that was otherwise rented out by companies for commercial purposes.

Anja Kaiser operates in a feminist-activist environment, explicitly inviting activist groups to participate with their own short texts: "queer, punks, homo core babes, not grrrrrlz, DIY witches & anarchist punk players." Previously, activists had mostly been able to draw attention to themselves by illegally using public spaces for advertising. Kaiser demanded that they instead "provide spaces for feminist resistance classified ads." She wanted to give individuals and groups a voice in urban space and to oppose the purely economic use of the city, as a space that is emblematic of democracy. She accordingly considers her work to be a form of political action: "I seek to form alliances, with the aim of both making visible and fueling the political demands of a feminist community within the ubiquitous world of commodity exchange."[10]

Numerous contributors produced classified ads as part of this project, including Abt

9 Vgl. Eva-Maria Schmidt: Die Zukunft ist weiblich, *HORIZONTmagazin*, ADC-Festivalzeitung, 29. Apr. 2021: 2.

10 Interview with Anja Kaiser conducted by Julia Meer, Museum für Kunst und Gewerbe Hamburg, https://www.museumsfernsehen. de/julia-meer-im-gespraech-mit-grafikdesignerin-und-kuenstlerin-anja-kaiser-designblicke/ (accessed 10. Feb. 2023).

Anja Kaiser, Whose.Agency, 2017 © Anja Kaiser

auf illegalen Flächen auf sich aufmerksam machen können. Kaisers Aufforderung lautete: „[...]
biete Flächen für widerständige feministische
Anzeigen". Sie wollte Einzelnen und Gruppen
eine Stimme im städtischen Raum geben, sich der
rein ökonomischen Verwertung des städtischen
Raums, der als Symbol der Demokratie gilt, ent-
gegensetzen. Folglich betrachtet sie ihre Arbeit
als politische Aktion: „[...] es (ist) mir ein Anliegen,
Allianzen zu bilden, um politische Forderungen
einer feministischen Gemeinschaft im allgegen-
wärtigen Warentausch sichtbar zu machen und zu
befeuern."[10]

Kleinanzeigen im Rahmen dieses Projekts
verfassten unter anderem Abt. Handlungspotential,

10 Interview Anja Kaiser mit Julia Meer, Museum für Kunst und
Gewerbe Hamburg, https://www.museumsfernsehen.de/julia-meer-
im-gespraech-mit-grafikdesignerin-und-kuenstlerin-anja-kaiser-
designblicke/ (Abruf 10. Feb. 2023).

Handlungspotential, AFBL (Antifaschistischer
Frauenblock Leipzig, AK Unbehagen), Feministischer Lesekreis, Blaue Distanz, Bliss Vienna,
böse& gemein Kollektiv, depatriarchise design,
e*vibes—für eine emanzipatorische Praxis, Hazy
Borders, MONAliesA Leipzig—Feministische
Bibliothek, outside the box—Zeitschrift für feministische Gesellschaftskritik, Pro Choice Sachsen,
Young Girl Reading Group, and others. Further
ads came from individuals.

In 2021, Anja Kaiser additionally published the book *Glossary of Undisciplined Design*
together with Rebecca Stephany. In the book, both
women extend their critique of the established
criteria for "good design." Feminist social critique
is an essential element of their intentionally
undisciplined research tools and forms of visual
communication. These range from print media to
installations, video works, performances, curatorial practice, and art critical writing. They are
marked, on the one hand, by a return to the history of graphic design, and on the other, by posi-

Rebecca Stephany, Projektvorstellung mit performativer Verkaufsshow der / Project presentation with performative sales show of 200 Sisters Souvenirs, Badischer Kunstverein, Karlsruhe. SuperSale Talkshow am/on 20. Jun. 2018, Fotograf/photographer: Felix Grünschloss

AFBL (Antifaschistischer Frauenblock Leipzig, AK Unbehagen), Feministischer Lesekreis, Blaue Distanz, Bliss Vienna, böse & gemein Kollektiv, depatriarchise design, e*vibes – für eine emanzipatorische Praxis, Hazy Borders, MONAliesA Leipzig – Feministische Bibliothek, outside the box – Zeitschrift für feministische Gesellschaftskritik, Pro Choice Sachsen und Young Girl Reading Group. Hinzu kamen Einzelpersonen.

Darüber hinaus gab Anja Kaiser 2021, zusammen mit Rebecca Stephany, das Buch *Glossary of Undisciplined Design* heraus. Beide führen darin ihre Kritik am etablierten „guten Design" fort. Feministische Gesellschaftskritik ist ein wesentliches Element ihrer bewusst undisziplinierten Forschungsinstrumente und visuellen Artikulationen. Sie reichen von Printmedien über Installationen, Videoarbeiten, Performances bis hin zu kuratorischer Praxis und kunstkritischem Schreiben. Dabei spielt zum einen die Rückbesinnung auf die Geschichte von Grafik-

tions in design theory, especially Martha Scotford's idea of a "messy history" from the 1990s and the design pedagogical curriculum for women formulated by Sheila Levrant de Bretteville at CalArts in the 1970s. Such new articulations can thus build on an existing genealogy of women's work in design, even if it is rather limited.

The feminist perspective is also the focus of Rebecca Stephany's artistic work. Stephany studied at the Gerrit Rietveld Academie and the Sandberg Instituut in Amsterdam. Until 2022, she was professor of communication design at the Staatliche Hochschule für Gestaltung Karlsruhe; today she is professor of editorial design at the Kunsthochschule Kassel.

In 2018, she realized *200 Sisters Souvenirs* at the Badischer Kunstverein Karlsruhe, subtitled *200 Jahre Ausstellungskataloge, Randnotizen und launische Bilder, a feminist exhibition (mis)reading*—in English: 200 years of exhibition catalogs, marginal notes, and moody images, a feminist

design eine Rolle. Zum anderen werden designtheoretische Positionen reflektiert, insbesondere Martha Scotfords Idee von einer „messy history" in den 1990er Jahren oder das designpädagogische Curriculum für Frauen von Sheila Levrant de Bretteville an der CalArts in den 1970er Jahren. Die neuen Artikulationen bauen bereits auf einer, wenn auch bislang sehr eingeschränkten, Genealogie weiblicher Artikulationen im Design auf.

Die feministische Perspektive steht auch im Fokus der künstlerischen Arbeit von Rebecca Stephany. Sie studierte an der Gerrit Rietveld Academie und am Sandberg Instituut in Amsterdam. Bis 2022 war sie Professorin für Kommunikationsdesign an der Staatlichen Hochschule für Gestaltung Karlsruhe, heute ist sie Professorin für Redaktionelles Gestalten an der Kunsthochschule Kassel.

2018 führte sie am Badischen Kunstverein Karlsruhe die Aktion „200 Sisters Souvenirs" durch, die den Untertitel trug: „200 Jahre Ausstellungskataloge, Randnotizen und launische Bilder, a feminist exhibition (mis)reading". Sie ging zurück auf eine Recherche von 300 Publikationen des Archivs im Kunstverein aus feministischer Perspektive. Daraus entstanden ein Katalog und eine begleitende Produktlinie.

„200 Sisters Souvenirs" macht aufmerksam auf die vielen unbekannten, in Gemälden und Skulpturen dargestellten Frauen sowie die wenigen Künstlerinnen, deren Werke in der zweihundertjährigen Geschichte des Badischen Kunstvereins gesammelt wurden. Auch die Ausstellungskataloge im Archiv sollten „anders" gelesen werden, insbesondere nach intersektionalen Kriterien. Die Archivrecherche sollte „übersetzt" werden in brauch- und tragbare Objekte, unter anderem Schrumpffolienanhänger mit Bildfragmenten aus dem Katalogarchiv und grafische Elemente aus dem Magazin *LAVA*, einem Karlsruher Frauenmagazin, das zwischen 1989 und 1994 mit 13 Ausgaben erschien.

Neues Wissen und Aktivismus

Die noch vor einigen Jahren in der Wissenschaft als nicht zitierfähige Online-Enzyklopädie Wikipedia hat sich dem neuen Wissen über Designerinnen gewidmet und macht sie mit großer Akribie auch außerhalb eines akademischen Kontextes bekannt. Geschichte spielt dabei eine große Rolle. Seit 2015 hat die internationale Kampagne „WikiD" (Women, Wikipedia, Design) ein internationales Netzwerk, finanziert

Flyer für den / Flyer for the Wikipedia Edit-a-thon-Event Art+Feminism, an der Universität von / at University of Nevada, Las Vegas, 2016

exhibition (mis)reading. The exhibition grew out of a study that applied a feminist lens to 300 publications from the Kunstverein's archive. The result was a catalog and an accompanying product line.

200 Sisters Souvenirs calls attention to the many unknown women depicted in paintings and sculptures, and to the few women artists whose works have been collected during the two hundred year history of the Badischer Kunstverein. The exhibition catalogs in the archive are also meant to be read "differently," in particular through an intersectional lens. The intention was to "translate" the archival research into usable and wearable objects, including shrink-wrap tags with image fragments from the catalog archive and graphic elements from the magazine *LAVA*, a women's magazine that appeared in thirteen issues in Karlsruhe between 1989 and 1994.

durch die gemeinnützige Wikimedia Foundation, zu enormer Wissensvermittlung und -erweiterung im Netz beigetragen. Als eines der meistgenutzten Onlinemedien, insbesondere von jungen Nutzer*innen, hat die Enzyklopädie einen großen Einfluss auf Grafikdesign und dessen Geschichte.

Zu den digitalen Tools zählen sogenannte Edit-a-thons. Diese Wortschöpfung resultiert aus der Kombination von *to edit* (bearbeiten) mit dem Wort „Marathon". Autor*innen können hierbei Artikel erstellen oder verbessern. Die Mitglieder geben neuen Nutzer*innen häufig Hilfestellung beim Verfassen ihrer Beiträge. Ursprungsorte der Wikipedia-Edit-a-thons waren häufig Büros spezifischer Wikimedia-Chapter, die an Hochschulen in den USA, Kanada, Österreich oder der Schweiz stattfanden oder an Kulturinstitutionen wie Museen und Archiven.

Art+Feminism ist ein Edit-a-thon, das mit dem Ziel gegründet wurde, Wikipedia um das Thema „Frauen in der Kunst" zu ergänzen sowie Frauen zur Mitarbeit an der Wikipedia-Plattform zu befähigen. Das Edit-a-thon nahm seinen Ausgang 2014 in New York und findet seitdem weltweit jedes Jahr im März, um den Internationalen Frauentag herum, statt.

Die Notwendigkeit zur Bildung der Medi-a-thons sahen Frauen im *gender trouble* gegeben, konkret in der Unterrepräsentanz ihrer Themen in der Enzyklopädie. Denn laut einer Studie, die 2011 von der Wikimedia Foundation durchgeführt wurde, sind trotz des angeblich egalitär zugänglichen Formats der Website *Wikipedia* mehr als neunzig Prozent ihrer Beitragenden männlich. Es sind inzwischen solch renommierte Institutionen wie das Museum of Modern Art in New York City, das die Medi-a-thons unterstützt, in Kooperation mit Universitäten wie Stanford, Berkeley und Cornell. Seit 2014 wurden Veranstaltungen unter anderem in Australien, Kanada, Kambodscha, Indien, Neuseeland sowie in vielen europäischen Ländern durchgeführt. Weitere an den Sitzungen beteiligte Institutionen zählen zu den weltweit renommiertesten Häusern und auch Universitäten, etwa in Ghana und Mexiko-City.

Die Inhalte, die Teilnehmer*innen der Medi-at-thons aufbereiten, werden in einem Koordinationsforum auf Wikipedia erfasst, überprüft und kontrolliert, bevor sie veröffentlicht werden.

Im Bereich Design ist die bereits erwähnte Veranstaltung „wikiD" angesiedelt, ein internationales Gemeinschaftsprojekt der Agenturen Parlour, Melbourne, Architexx, New York, und n-ails, Berlin. Allerdings bestehen die beteiligten Gruppen aus Architektinnen, wenngleich auch

New Knowledge and Activism

Even a few years ago, many in academia considered the online encyclopedia Wikipedia to be an unreliable source. It has nevertheless dedicated itself to new knowledge about women designers and is assiduously making them known outside of an academic context. History figures prominently in this knowledge. Since 2015, the international campaign WikiD (Women, Wikipedia, Design)—an international network funded by the nonprofit Wikimedia Foundation—has made enormous contributions to knowledge transfer and expansion on the internet. As one of the most used online sources, especially by young people, the encyclopedia has a great influence on graphic design and its history.

Digital tools include "edit-a-thons" in which authors create or edit entries. Participants often provide assistance to new users in writing their posts. The Wikipedia edit-a-thons often originated in specific Wikimedia chapters at universities in the United States, Canada, Austria, or Switzerland, or at cultural institutions such as museums and archives.

Art+Feminism is an edit-a-thon founded with the goal of adding the topic of "women in the arts" to *Wikipedia*, and of empowering women to contribute to the *Wikipedia* platform. The edit-a-thon started in New York in 2014 and has been held worldwide every March since then, around International Women's Day.

Women saw in today's gender trouble the need to found such mediathons, motivated specifically by the underrepresentation of women's subjects in the encyclopedia. One study conducted by the Wikimedia Foundation in 2011, for instance, showed that more than 90 percent of Wikipedia's contributors are male, despite the website's ostensibly egalitarian model of access. Such prestigious institutions as the Museum of Modern Art in New York City are now supporting these mediathons, in cooperation with universities such as Stanford, UC Berkeley, and Cornell. Since 2014, events have been held in Australia, Canada, Cambodia, India, New Zealand, and many European countries. Other institutions involved in the sessions include some of the world's most prestigious publishing houses and universities, in places as diverse as Ghana and Mexico City.

The content produced by participants in the mediathons is recorded, reviewed, and checked in a coordination forum on Wikipedia before it is published.

The event wikiD mentioned above is likewise situated in the field of design, as a joint

Designerinnen berücksichtigt werden.[11] Auch „wikiD" führt Schreibwerkstätten durch, um die Unterrepräsentanz von Frauen in der digitalen Plattform zu beheben.

Bei heutigen Positionen im Design sind plurale Perspektiven auf die Gegenwart und Vergangenheit von Bedeutung. Sie überschreiten die festgelegten Grenzen der Disziplin Design, genauso wie die Initiativen in der Designpraxis nicht nur von einem „Herrschaftswissen" der Profession ausgehen. Der Genderaspekt steht dabei im Zentrum eines internationalen Verständigungsraums für die Vielfalt der Ansätze.

international project of the agencies Parlour in Melbourne, Architexx in New York, and n-ails in Berlin. Although the participants from the agencies are women architects, women designers do play a part.[11] wikiD also conducts writing workshops to address the underrepresentation of women in the digital platform.

For contemporary positions in design, multiple perspectives on the present and past are important. They transcend the established boundaries of the discipline, just as initiatives in design practice do not necessarily assume that the profession possesses any "authoritative" knowledge about design. Gender features instead as a crucial factor within an international space of communication and understanding constituted by a diversity of approaches.

---

11 Unter den vielen Beispielen sei erwähnt: Wiki Women Design: Unlocking the Contributions of Belgian Female Designers on Wikipedia, https://www.archdaily.com/955712/wiki-women-design-unlocking-the-contributions-of-belgian-female-designers-on-wikipedia/60377c86f91c812230000403-wiki-women-design-unlocking-the-contributions-of-belgian-female-designers-on-wikipedia-image (Abruf 22. Aug. 2022).

11 Among the many examples, it is worth mentioning Wiki Women Design: Unlocking the Contributions of Belgian Female Designers on Wikipedia, https://www.archdaily.com/955712/wiki-women-design-unlocking-the-contributions-of-belgian-female-designers-on-wikipedia/60377c86f91c812230000403-wiki-women-design-unlocking-the-contributions-of-belgian-female-designers-on-wikipedia-image (accessed 22. Aug. 2022).

WikiD (Women Wikipedia Design), Edit-a-thon auf der / at the Melbourne Art Book Fair, 2017

Literatur
Further Reading

Sara Boboltz: Editors Are Trying to Fix Wikipedia's Gender and
Racial Bias Problem, *The Huffington Post*, 15. Apr. 2015,
https://www.huffpost.com/entry/wikipedia-gender-racial-
bias_n_7054550 (Abruf/accessed 1. Jul. 2022).

Siân Evans, Jacqueline Mabey & Michael Mandiberg:
Editing for Equality. The Outcomes of the Art+Feminism Wikipedia
Edit-a-thons, *Art Documentation. Journal of the Art Libraries
Society of North America* 34, Nr./no. 2 (Herbst/Autumn 2015):
194–203, DOI: 10.1086/683380.

Anja Kaiser & Rebecca Stephany (Hg./eds.): *Glossary of
Undisciplined Design*, Leipzig: Spector Books, 2021.

Michelle R. Smith: Giving Female Scientists Their Due,
The Philadelphia Inquirer, 17. Okt./Oct. 2013, https://www.inquirer.com/
philly/news/nation_world/20131017_Giving_female_scientists_their_
due.html (Abruf/accessed 1. Jul. 2022).

AUSKLANG
CONCLUDING THOUGHTS

Die Aufsätze der vorliegenden Publikation führen punktuell Beispiele im Grafikdesign von Frauen aus über eineinhalb Jahrhunderten vor Augen. Es sind konzentrierte Ereignisse und kollektive Phänomene, in denen Frauen sich neue Arbeitsfelder eroberten und in den meisten Fällen für Frauen eintraten. Der Fokus der Buchpublikation liegt auf einem Überblick, die Beispiele ließen sich noch um viele mehr erweitern.

Das, was so häufig mit Design verbunden wird, nämlich dass es sich in den Dienst seiner Auftraggeber*innen stellt und deren Wünsche bestmöglich erfüllt, tritt in den vorliegenden Beispielen zurück. Vielmehr verweisen sie auf den Spielraum von Autonomie, den Grafikdesign hat.

Es war meine Absicht zu zeigen, wie dicht und kontinuierlich die Auseinandersetzung der Grafikdesignerinnen mit dem eigenen Geschlecht und den Wirkungsmöglichkeiten ihrer Arbeit ist und dass sie nicht erst mit dem fortgeschrittenen 20. Jahrhundert begann. Am häufigsten begleiteten die Aktivitäten den allgemeinen emanzipatorischen Prozess der Frauen zur jeweiligen Zeit, nicht selten waren sie den Frauenbewegungen in Form besonderer symbolischer Handlungen und Formate direkt verbunden.

Während die (Sozial-)Geschichte von Künstlerinnen in den letzten Jahrzehnten vermehrt Beachtung gefunden hat, ist dies bei Designerinnen in Deutschland nicht der Fall. Eine Ausnahme stellt das Bauhaus dar, bei dem die besondere Geschichte der Studentinnen und Lehrerinnen früh aufgearbeitet wurde und mit dem 100. Gründungsjubiläum der Schule 2019 noch einmal besonders in den Fokus rückte. Allerdings spielen Grafikdesignerinnen an dieser Schule fast keine Rolle.

Die Aufarbeitung der Designgeschichte in diesem Land profitiert jedoch von den Untersuchungen in der benachbarten Disziplin Kunstgeschichte, vor allem deshalb, weil es Ähnlichkeiten zwischen der Ausbildung von Künstlerinnen und Grafikdesignerinnen gab. In der frühen Moderne genossen die meisten Frauen, die später im Grafikdesign arbeiteten und überhaupt bekannt wurden, eine künstlerische Ausbildung. Sie bevorzugten deshalb bildhafte Medien wie Plakate und Akzidenzdrucke und die sogenannte Flächenkunst bei Textilien, Tapeten, Vorsatzpapieren etc., bei denen sie ihre bildkünstlerischen Fähigkeiten anwenden konnten.

In Deutschland liegen insbesondere aus den 1970er und 1980er Jahren, der Zeit der grundlegenden Neuorientierung des Fachs Kunstgeschichte und der Erweiterung ihrer Grenzen zur

The essays in this publication present select examples of graphic design by women over a century and a half. They focus in on individual events while panning out to wider collective phenomena in which women conquered new fields of work and, in most cases, advocated for women. The book primarily aims to provide an overview, though its examples could be expanded to include many more.

The basic condition so often associated with design—that it is practiced to serve clients and to fulfill their wishes in the best possible way—is given less priority in the book's examples. The book points instead to the autonomy often exercised by graphic design.

My intention has been to reveal the richness and continuity in the history of how women graphic designers have engaged with their own gender and the potential impact of their work, and to show that this history did not begin only in the latter half of the twentieth century. Most often, their activities went hand in hand with the general process of women's emancipation at the time; not infrequently, they were directly linked to women's movements in the form of acts and formats of visual expression that had exceptional symbolic value.

While the (social) history of women artists has received increased attention in recent decades, this is not the case for women designers in Germany. One exception is the Bauhaus, where the special history of women students and teachers was addressed early on and foregrounded once again with the one-hundredth anniversary of the school's founding in 2019. However, women graphic designers played almost no role at this school.

The reappraisal of design history in Germany nevertheless does benefit from research in the neighboring discipline of art history, primarily because there were similarities between the training of women artists and graphic designers. In the early years of the modern era, most of the women who later worked in graphic design and became known at all enjoyed an artistic education. This meant they tended to prefer pictorial media such as posters and commercial prints and other two-dimensional formats such as art for textiles, wallpaper, endpapers, etc. to which they could apply their skills in pictorial art.

There are many studies of women artists in Germany, especially from the 1970s and 1980s—a period marked by a fundamental reorientation of the discipline of art history and an expansion of its boundaries toward social history.

Sozialgeschichte hin, viele Analysen über Künstlerinnen vor. Nicht wenige dieser Forschungen überschreiten die auch für das Fach Designgeschichte so charakteristische Konzentration auf herausragende Einzelfiguren und deren Monografien sowie auf Vertreterinnen ihres Fachs, die die Augenhöhe mit dem männlich dominierten Kanon der Disziplin unter Beweis stellen wollten. Einige Untersuchungen stellten mit dieser Aufarbeitung zugleich die theoretischen Prämissen der Disziplin Kunstgeschichte infrage.[1]

Doch kann diese kunstgeschichtliche Forschung wiederum nicht ohne Weiteres auf die Designgeschichte übertragen werden. Bleiben wir noch einmal bei der Zeit um 1900. Hier ist zwar die Ausbildungssituation von Künstlerinnen und Designerinnen in vielen Fällen vergleichbar: Sie waren – trotz bisweilen heftiger Proteste – bis 1919 weitgehend ausgeschlossen vom Studium an staatlichen Kunstakademien in Deutschland, und auch danach verlief die Umsetzung der gesetzlichen Liberalisierung nicht problemlos. Doch gleichzeitig rückte die Gebrauchsgrafik im Zusammenhang mit der Kunstgewerbe-Reformbewegung zu jener Zeit in den Vordergrund. Nun wurden Tätigkeitsfelder ideologisch aufgewertet, die bislang als minderwertig gegenüber den sogenannten freien Künsten galten. Gerade deswegen wurden sie nun auch für Männer attraktiv. Viele Interessengruppen im modernen Design waren zu einem sehr hohen Prozentsatz von Männern besetzt. Sie waren meist sogar männerbündisch. Das gilt in Mitteleuropa für die Werkbünde (in Deutschland ab 1907), das gilt auch beispielsweise für den hochkarätig besetzten deutschen Ring Neuer Werbegestalter (1928–1933), in dem auch Grafikdesigner aus benachbarten Ländern versammelt waren. Keine einzige Frau wurde in diesen Kreis aufgenommen. In der privaten Vorbildersammlung, die einer der berühmtesten Grafikdesigner der Moderne, Jan Tschichold, hinterließ, findet sich unter den 45 renommierten Vertretern des Fachs ebenfalls keine einzige Frau.[2] Die Beispiele ließen sich bis heute vielfach fortsetzen.

Quite a few of these studies go beyond a focus on outstanding individual figures and their own writings or books about them, which is as characteristic of design history as it is of art history; they moreover widen their view beyond women who wished to prove that they were on a par with the male-dominated canon of the discipline. And as part of this reappraisal, some studies also questioned the theoretical premises of the discipline of art history itself.[1]

Nevertheless, as noted above, this art historical research cannot so easily be applied to design history. Allow us to return once again to the period around 1900. Here, the situation characterizing the training of women artist and women designers is comparable in many ways: despite sometimes vehement protests, women in both groups were largely excluded from studying at state art academies in Germany until 1919, and even after that the implementation of legal liberalization did not proceed without friction. At the same time, however, commercial art gained significance in the wake of the arts and crafts reform movement of the day. Fields of activity that had previously been considered inferior to the so-called fine arts soon enjoyed an ideological revalorization. And precisely for this reason, they now became attractive to men. A large percentage of stakeholders in modern design were men. Most groups or associations of designers even reflected the masculinist ethos of the quasi-military men's associations that sprung up in the nineteenth and early twentieth centuries. In Central Europe, this was true of the Werkbünde (in Germany from 1907), as it was, for example, of the highly elite German group Ring Neuer Werbegestalter, or Ring of New Advertising/Publicity Designers (1928–1933), which also included graphic designers from neighboring countries. Not a single woman was admitted to this circle. In the private collection of model designs left by one of the most famous graphic designers of the modern era, Jan Tschichold, there is also not a single woman among the forty-five renowned representatives of the profession.[2] Examples of this kind could be continued into the present day.

[1] Exemplarisch hierfür sei Renate Berger genannt: *Malerinnen auf dem Weg ins 20. Jahrhundert. Kunstgeschichte als Sozialgeschichte*, Köln: DuMont, 1982.

[2] Patrick Rössler ist einer der sehr wenigen Vertreter seines Fachs, die dieses Defizit überhaupt problematisieren. Siehe Patrick Rössler: Mitteilungen in der eindringlichsten Form. Jan Tschichold, der Ring Neue Werbegestalter und die Neue Typographie, in: ders. & Mirjam Brodbeck (Hg.): *Revolutionäre der Typographie*, Göttingen: Wallstein Verlag, 2022: 18–33, hier 27.

[1] Renate Berger is a good example here: *Malerinnen auf dem Weg ins 20. Jahrhundert: Kunstgeschichte als Sozialgeschichte*, Cologne: DuMont, 1982.

[2] Patrick Rössler is one of the very few scholars in his field to have even problematized this lack of women. See Patrick Rössler: Mitteilungen in der eindringlichsten Form: Jan Tschichold, der Ring Neue Werbegestalter und die Neue Typographie, in Patrick Rössler & Mirjam Brodbeck (eds.): *Revolutionäre der Typographie*, Göttingen: Wallstein Verlag, 2022: 18–33, on 27.

Doch wo sind all die Designerinnen geblieben, die eine Ausbildung an Kunstgewerbeschulen erhielten? Die Unterrichtsanstalt des Kunstgewerbemuseums Berlin entstand 1868, vergleichbare Schulen gründeten sich daraufhin in jeder größeren Stadt in Deutschland. Zwar waren kunstgewerbliche Schulen weniger angesehen als Kunstakademien, doch ihre Zulassungsregeln waren lockerer, weshalb sich viele Frauen dort ausbilden ließen. Studiert man die Archive der Kunstgewerbeschulen, die in Deutschland erst allmählich aufgearbeitet werden, dann finden sich dort die Namen zahlreicher Studentinnen. Ihr Lebensweg wird indes nur äußerst selten weiterverfolgt, da die Frauen nach ihrer Ausbildung offensichtlich in weniger bekannten Tätigkeitsfeldern und Berufen arbeiteten.

Das Gebot der Sachlichkeit in den 1910er Jahren und die daraus resultierenden Definitionen des Funktionalismus hatten zur Folge, dass Design zunehmend mit bildender Kunst konkurrierte. Hinzu kam die Industrie, die die Werbung als ein Mittel zur Absatzsteigerung entdeckte und folglich reichlich Arbeitsmöglichkeiten für Designer*innen bot. Die zahlreichen Männer, die sich nun der Produktgestaltung und der Gebrauchsgrafik zuwandten, etwa Peter Behrens, Henry van de Velde, Adolf Loos, Josef Frank, Richard Riemerschmid und viele andere mehr, betrachteten dieses Arbeitsgebiet als Gewinn für ihren ganzheitlichen Gestaltungsansatz.

Das Narrativ insbesondere der deutschen Designgeschichte wertet die Kunstgewerbe-Reformbewegung als entscheidenden Motor für die Entstehung der eigenen Disziplin, doch es beschreibt eine männlich dominierte Entwicklung. In den meisten Fällen besteht in der begleitenden Kommentierung des Designgeschehens und in der Rezeption kein Problembewusstsein für die Unterrepräsentanz von Frauen. Dass Grafikdesignerinnen in der Geschichte selten vorkommen, hat die Auffassung von der Minderwertigkeit weiblichen Designs gefördert. Die ausgeprägte Tendenz in jener Zeit zur Selbstermächtigung und zum Aktivismus, zur Lektüre einer großen Bandbreite von Publikationen über Frauen und Kunstgewerbe, darunter auch viele Ratgeber für junge Frauen, wird geradezu ignoriert. Dieser Ausschließung unterlagen bis vor Kurzem auch die Kunstgewerbeschulen, deren Geschichte nur sehr zögerlich aufgearbeitet und nur sehr selten in Hinblick auf ihre Studentinnen und Lehrerinnen analysiert wird.

In anderen Ländern wie England und den USA herrscht eine wesentlich größere

But what became of all the women designers who received training at schools of applied arts or arts and crafts? The Unterrichtsanstalt des Kunstgewerbemuseums Berlin (Teaching Institute of the Berlin Museum of Applied Arts) was founded in 1868, followed by similar schools in every major city in Germany. Although schools of applied arts were less prestigious than art academies, rules for admission were less strict, which allowed many women to gain training. Careful research in the archives of schools of applied arts in Germany, which are only now being explored, is revealing the names of many students who were women. Only rarely, however, is follow-up research done to trace their lives, as these women worked after their training in fields and professions that were evidently less well known.

The influence of objectivity as an aesthetic movement in the 1910s and the resulting definitions of functionalism meant that design increasingly competed with fine art. Industry, too, soon entered the mix, in discovering advertising as a way to increase sales that soon offered ample job opportunities for designers. The numerous men who now turned to product design and commercial art, such as Peter Behrens, Henry van de Velde, Adolf Loos, Josef Frank, Richard Riemerschmid, and many others, saw this field of work as a boon for their holistic approach to design.

The narrative of German design history in particular holds up the arts and crafts reform movement as a crucial driver for its own emergence as a discipline, yet the narrative it tells is largely dominated by men. In most cases, there is no awareness of the problem of women's underrepresentation in the analysis of crucial events in design history or their reception. The fact that women graphic designers rarely appear in historiography has fostered the notion that design by women is inferior. The marked tendency in the late nineteenth and early twentieth centuries toward women's self-empowerment and activism—along with the wide readership for a range of publications about women and the applied arts, including many guidebooks for young women—is virtually ignored. Until recently, this historical blindness included the schools of applied art, whose history has been examined only slowly, and very rarely with an eye toward their women students and teachers.

In other countries, such as England and the United States, there is a much greater willingness—producing a great deal more scholarship—to write the history of the nameless women who worked in the background of industrial compa-

Bereitschaft und wissenschaftliche Aktivität, namenlosen Frauen, die im Hintergrund von Industrieunternehmen gearbeitet haben, eine Geschichte zu geben. Dazu zählt die Forschung von Cheryl Buckley, bezogen auf die Keramikindustrie,[3] und Fiona Ross und Alice Savoie, die Monotype-Industrie betreffend.[4] Auch Genealogien werden aufgedeckt, wie dies die schwedische Gruppe MMS in ihrer Auseinandersetzung mit dem 1937 von Frauen herausgegebenen Buch *Bookmaking on the Distaff Side* leistet. In allen Fällen ist die Forschung über die Designgeschichte von Frauen eng mit der Kritik an den Narrativen der Designgeschichte verbunden.

In der heutigen Zeit fördern vor allem internationale digitale Kommunikationsmedien den Austausch untereinander. Es bilden sich eigene Zirkel und Netzwerke. Trotz einer „vierten Welle" des Feminismus, wie sie von ihren Vertreterinnen selbstredend genannt wird, kann man hier nicht unbedingt von einer Bewegung sprechen. Gefeiert wird aber die nationenübergreifende Kommunikation, die Liberalität in den Lebensformen, die Pluralität der ästhetischen Vorlieben, wie sie von dem großen theoretischen Vorbild Martha Scotford beschrieben wird, die Infragestellung des ästhetischen Kanons, der geografischen und ethnischen Hierarchien. In dieser Vielzahl der Orientierungen ist sich die jüngere Generation einig.

Auch wenn nicht mehr von einer Emanzipationsbewegung im klassischen Sinne gesprochen werden kann, besteht doch ein großes Unbehagen, dass der lange Arm patriarchalischer Strukturen immer noch wirkmächtig ist. Dieser Zustand wird auch heute noch mit dem Instrument der Statistik beschrieben, wenn in den Überblickswerken auf die Asymmetrie der Geschlechter aufmerksam gemacht wird. Das Narrativ der Ausschließung von Grafikdesignerinnen hält sich trotz gleichzeitiger Präsenz und Vielfalt von Fraueninitiativen hartnäckig: Männer geben den Ton an, sie sind es, die Geschichte schreiben.[5] Immer noch erscheint das neue Wissen über Grafikdesignerinnen mehrheitlich in einer feministischen Parallelwelt angesiedelt zu sein. Es hat die Machtbalance zwischen den Geschlechtern noch

nies. We can name here Cheryl Buckley's work on the ceramics industry,[3] or that of Fiona Ross and Alice Savoie on the monotype industry.[4] Genealogies are also being uncovered, as the Swedish group MMS does in their examination of the 1937 book *Bookmaking on the Distaff Side*, published by women. In all cases, research on the history of women's design is closely tied to critiques of the narratives that have structured design history in general.

In today's world, digital communication media that effortless cross national borders are particularly powerful in promoting mutual exchange. Women are forming their own circles and networks. Despite a fourth wave of feminism, as its protagonists call it, one cannot necessarily speak of a movement here. What is being celebrated, however, is cross-national communication, liberal ways of life, a plurality of aesthetic preferences in the sense described by the trenchant theoretical model of Martha Scotford, and a questioning of the aesthetic canon and of geographical and ethnic hierarchies. The younger generation is united in this multiplicity of positions.

Even if one can no longer speak of an emancipation movement in the classical sense, there is still a great deal of unease that the long arm of patriarchal structures retains its pull. Today, these circumstances are reflected in survey statistics that draw attention to inequalities between men and women. And historical narratives excluding women from graphic design persists despite the fact that one also finds a diversity of women's initiatives: men here set the agenda; they are the ones who have mostly written history.[5] Meanwhile, the new knowledge about women graphic designers that does come to light appears to remain confined to a parallel, feminist world. It has not yet been able to equalize the balance of power between men and women, or to enter mainstream awareness.

In a 2018 empirical analysis, for instance, Farah Kafei and Valentina Vergara (two students at Pratt Institute in New York) found that in design faculties in the United States, the majority—about 75 percent—of graphic design students are women. The majority of professors, in turn,

3 Cheryl Buckley: *Potters and Paintresses. Women Designers in the Pottery Industry, 1870–1955*, Women's Press, 1990.
4 *Women in Type. A Social History of Women's Role in Type Drawing*, https://research.reading.ac.uk/women-in-type/ (Abruf 22. Okt. 2022).
5 Siehe u. a. das eklatante Missverhältnis der Geschlechter bei Jens Müller & Julius Wiedermann (Hg.): *The History of Graphic Design*, Bd. 1: *1890–1950*, Bd. 2: *1960–Today*, Köln: Taschen, 2018 & 2020.

3 Cheryl Buckley: *Potters and Paintresses: Women Designers in the Pottery Industry, 1870–1955*, London: Women's Press, 1990.
4 *Women in Type: A Social History of Women's Role in Type Drawing*, https://research.reading.ac.uk/women-in-type/ (accessed 22. Oct. 2022).
5 For an example, see the glaring gender imbalance in Jens Müller & Julius Wiedermann (eds.): *The History of Graphic Design*, vol. 1, *1890–1950*, vol. 2, *1960–Today*, Cologne: Taschen, 2018 & 2020.

Guerrilla Girls, Dieses Franzbrötchen repräsentiert die 400.000 grafischen Arbeiten im MK&G. Dieser Krümel steht für die Arbeiten von Frauen: 1,5 % (This pastry represents the 400,000 graphic works in the MK&G. The crumb represents the works of women: 1.5%), Plakat/poster, 2022 © Courtesy of Guerrilla Girls, Foto/photo: Museum für Kunst und Gewerbe Hamburg

nicht ausgeglichen und ist nicht in den Mainstream eingeflossen.

Farah Kafei and Valentina Vergara beispielsweise, Studentinnen des Pratt Institute in New York, haben 2018 in ihrer empirischen Analyse festgestellt, dass in den Designfakultäten der Vereinigten Staaten die Mehrheit der Grafikdesign-Studierenden Frauen sind, rund 75 Prozent. Die Mehrheit der Professor*innen wiederum ist männlich, rund 75 Prozent. Teil der empirischen Studie war die Bitte an Designstudierende, innerhalb von wenigen Minuten so viele Designer*innen in der Geschichte zu nennen wie möglich. Im Ergebnis waren mehr als 70 Prozent der genannten Personen Männer.

Diese Recherche deckt sich mit Untersuchungen nach Gender-Aspekten in anderen Ländern. Das schwedische Frauenkollektiv MMS beispielsweise veröffentlichte drei statistische Auswertungen der wichtigsten Design-Preise in Schweden zwischen 2005 und 2014. Danach wurden zwei Drittel an Männer verliehen und nur ein Drittel an Frauen. Bei Art-Direktor*innen steigerte sich die Differenz auf drei Viertel der Preise für Männer und ein Viertel für Frauen.

are male—also around 75 percent. One part of the empirical study asked design students to name as many designers from history as they could within several minutes. In the results, more than 70 percent of those named were men.

This study is consistent with research in other countries that focuses on gender. The Swedish women's collective MMS, for example, published three statistical assessments of the most important design awards in Sweden between 2005 and 2014. It showed that two-thirds were awarded to men and only one-third to women. For art directors, the difference increased to three-quarters of the prizes given to men and one-quarter to women.

Still, sources and information are fragmented. Some public archives are gradually opening up and granting open-source access to their treasures of works by women graphic designers, such as the British Library or the Museum of London (some of these works have entered the libraries and museum archives through private collections, that is to say, they were not directly acquired by the museums themselves). In the holdings of other archives, by contrast, there are dis-

Doch der Zustand ist durchaus disparat. Einige öffentliche Archive öffnen sich allmählich und gewähren den Open-Source-Zugang zu ihren Schätzen an Werken von Grafikdesignerinnen, wie die British Library oder das Museum of London (einige der Werke sind über Privatsammlungen in die Bibliotheken und Museumsarchive gelangt, das heißt nicht von den Museen selbst gesammelt worden). In den Beständen anderer Archive wiederum spiegelt das Geschlechterverhältnis einen extremen Disproporz. So resultierte eine Bestandsaufnahme von 2021/22 der Kunstbibliothek in Berlin unter dem Titel „Frühe Plakate 1840-1914" in einer konkreten Statistik: Unter den 997 Namen von Entwerfer*innen waren nur 40 weiblich.

Eine Überprüfung des Archivbestands der Plakatsammlung im Museum für Kunst und Gewerbe Hamburg, ergab 2023, dass von 400.000 Arbeiten nur 1,5 Prozent von Frauen sind. Diese Schieflage kommentierten die amerikanischen Guerrilla Girls in ihrer Ausstellung „The F* Word. Guerrilla Girls und feministisches Grafikdesign" im selben Jahr mit einem spektakulären Plakat, auf dem neben einem Franzbrötchen ein Krümel liegt. Der verschwindend geringe Anteil von Frauen an der gesamten Sammlung ist folglich nur als solcher zu bezeichnen.

Selbstermächtigung und Aktivismus

Für die meisten Initiativen im Grafikdesign, die eine Veränderung der Situation von Frauen anstrebten, ist die Strategie der Selbstermächtigung zentral. Selbstermächtigung will das Bestehende verändern, protestiert gegen Missverhältnisse und zeigt Alternativen auf. Der Aktivismus ist geprägt von zivilem Ungehorsam: Regeln werden bewusst gebrochen mit dem Ziel, Freiräume zu erobern. Um diesen Protest kommunizieren zu können, bedarf es nicht nur einer dezidierten Haltung und neuer utopischer Entwürfe, sondern auch einer neuen visuellen Sprache. Alternative Medien- und Kulturproduktion dienen dazu, neues Wissen und neue Bedeutung zu produzieren und gesellschaftliche Prozesse zu verändern. Insbesondere in der Gegenkultur haben sich Magazine, Grrrl- und Queer-Zines, Ladyfeste, Plattenlabels, Radical Crafting und diverse andere Projekte entfaltet.

Angesichts der Fülle der unterschiedlichen Fraueninitiativen im Grafikdesign, wie sie die vorliegende Publikation vor Augen führt, ist die Frage obsolet, ob eine „His-Story" allein Designgeschichte repräsentiert und ob es reicht,

proportionately more sources and materials about men than women. A 2021/22 inventory of the Kunstbibliothek in Berlin, for instance, titled "Frühe Plakate 1840-1914" (Early posters 1840-1914) produced a concrete statistic: among the 997 names of designers, only 40 were female.

In 2023, a review of the archival holdings of the poster collection at the Museum für Kunst und Gewerbe in Hamburg revealed that of 400,000 works, only 1.5 percent were by women. In the same year, the American Guerrilla Girls commented on this imbalance in their exhibition *The F* Word: Guerrilla Girls and Feminist Graphic Design* with a spectacular poster featuring a crumb next to a *Franzbrötchen*, a sweet cinnamon pastry for which Hamburg is known. A mere crumb, the poster says, is the only way to describe the vanishingly small proportion of women in the collection as a whole.

Self-Empowerment and Activism

In most initiatives in graphic design that sought to change the circumstances of women, the strategy of self-empowerment played a crucial part. Strategies of self-empowerment aim to change the status quo, protest against inequalities, and point to alternatives. Activism is characterized by civil disobedience: rules are deliberately broken with the aim of claiming spaces of freedom. Yet communicating such protest requires not only a determined attitude and new utopian designs, but also a new visual language. Alternative media and forms of cultural production serve to produce new knowledge and meaning and to change social processes. Within counterculture, especially, these have developed as magazines, grrrl and queer zines, ladyfests, record labels, radical crafting, and various other projects.

Given the wealth of diverse women's initiatives in graphic design presented in this publication, the question of whether a His-Story alone represents design history, and whether it is sufficient to cite individual women graphic designers rather than a broad sweep of collective manifestations, can be dismissed as obsolete. Looking behind the surface of this history reveals a specific genealogy of women in design—one in which women's initiatives neither exist in isolation from each other nor figure as exceptions within a larger story.

einzelne Grafikdesignerinnen zu zitieren, statt einen weiten Bogen kollektiver Erscheinungsformen zu spannen. Der Blick hinter die Oberfläche der Erzählung offenbart eine eigene Genealogie der Geschichte von Frauen im Design, Fraueninitiativen bestehen nicht mehr disparat nebeneinander und sind keine Ausnahmen.

AUSGEWÄHLTE LITERATUR
SELECTED BIBLIOGRAPHY

Isabelle Anscombe: *A Woman's Touch. Women in Design from 1860 to the Present Day*, London: Viking Adult, 1984.

Ruth Artmonsky: *Designing Women. Women Working in Advertising and Publicity from 1920s to the 1960*, London: Artmonsky Arts, 2012.

Anja Baumhoff: *The Gendered World of the Bauhaus. The Politics of Power at the Weimar Republic's Premier Art Institute, 1919–1932*, Bern: Peter Lang, 2001.

Ruth Becker & Beate Kortendiek (Hg./eds.): *Handbuch Frauen und Geschlechterforschung. Theorie, Methoden, Empirie*, Wiesbaden: VS Verlag für Sozialwissenschaften, 2004.

Agatha Beins: *Liberation in Print. Feminist Periodicals and Social Movement Identity* (Since 1970: Histories of Contemporary America), Athen/Athens, GA: University of Georgia Press, 2017.

Izzy Berenson & Sarah Honeth: *Clearing the Haze. Prologue to Postmodern Graphic Design Education through Sheila de Bretteville*, Design. Insight Design Lecture Series, 26. Apr. 2016, https://walkerart.org/magazine/clearing-the-haze-prologue-to-postmodern-graphic-design-education-through-sheila-de-bretteville-2 (Abruf/accessed 22. Okt./Oct. 2022).

Tulga Beyerle & Klara Nemeckova (Hg./eds.): *Gegen die Unsichtbarkeit. Designerinnen der Deutschen Werkstätten Hellerau, 1898 bis 1938*, Ausstellungskatalog / exhibition catalog, Staatliche Kunstsammlungen Dresden, München/Munich: Hirmer Verlag, 2018.

Silvia Bovenschen: *Die imaginierte Weiblichkeit. Exemplarische Untersuchungen zu kulturgeschichtlichen und literarischen Präsentationsformen des Weiblichen*, Frankfurt a. M.: Suhrkamp, 1979.

Uta Brandes: *Gender Design. Streifzüge zwischen Theorie und Empirie*, Basel: Birkhäuser, 2017.

Gerda Breuer & Elina Knorpp (Hg./eds.): *Gespiegeltes Ich. Fotografische Selbstbildnisse von Frauen in den 1920er Jahren*, Berlin: Nicolai, 2013.

Gerda Breuer & Julia Meer (Hg./eds.): *Frauen und Grafik-Design / Women in Graphic Design 1890–2012*, Berlin: Jovis Verlag, 2012.

Cheryl Buckley: Made in Patriarchy. Toward a Feminist Analysis of Women and Design, *Design Issues* 3, Nr./no. 2 (Herbst/Autumn 1986): 3–14.

Cheryl Buckley (1986): Made in Patriarchy II: Researching (or Re-Searching) Women and Design, *Design Issues* 36, Nr./no. 1 (Winter 2020): 19–29, DOI: 10.1162/desi_a_00572.

Anne Burdick: Design without Designers, Vortrag am / lecture given on 29.4.2009, School of Design Strategies at Parsons The New School for Design, New York.

Judith Butler: *Gender Trouble. Feminism and the Subversion of Identity*, New York: Routledge, 1990; deutsche Ausgabe / German edition: *Das Unbehagen der Geschlechter*, Frankfurt a. M.: Suhrkamp, 2003.

Rebecca W. Davidson: *Unseen Hands. Women Printers, Binders, and Book Designers*, Ausstellungskatalog / exhibition catalog, Leonard L. Milberg Gallery for the Graphic Arts, Princeton: Princeton University Library, 2005.

Magdalena Droste: Beruf Kunstgewerblerin, in Landesgewerbeamt Baden-Württemberg & Design Center Stuttgart (Hg./eds.): *Frauen im Design. Berufsbilder und Lebenswege seit 1900*, Katalog/catalog, Stuttgart: Design Center Stuttgart, 1989: 174–201.

Kirsten Grimstad & Susan Rennie (Hg./eds.): *The New Woman's Survival Catalog*, 1973, Faksimile/facsimile, Brooklyn: Primary Information, 1973.

Marjan Groot et al. (Hg./eds.): *MoMoWo. Women Designers, Craftswomen, Architects and Engineers between 1918 and 1945*, Ljubljana: Založba ZRC, 2017.

Jerome Harris: Black Graphics: Celebrating Designers of Color, *Afropunk*, 25. Nov. 2018, https://afropunk.com/2018/09/black-graphics-celebrating-designers-of-color/ (Abruf/accessed 14. Feb. 2023).

Anne-Kathrin Herber: *Frauen an deutschen Kunstakademien im 20. Jahrhundert. Ausbildungsmöglichkeiten für Künstlerinnen ab 1919 unter besonderer Berücksichtigung der süddeutschen Kunstakademien*, Dissertation/dissertation, Heidelberg, 2009.

bell hooks: *Ain't I a Woman. Black Women and Feminism*, Boston: South End Press, 1981.

bell hooks: *Black Looks. Race and Representation*, Boston: South End Press, 1992; deutsche Ausgabe / German edition: *Black Looks. Popkultur – Medien – Rassismus*, Berlin: Orlanda, 1994, Neuaufl. 2019.

bell hooks: *Feminism is for Everybody*, Cambridge, MA: South End Press, 2000; deutsche Ausgabe / German edition: *Feminismus für alle*, Münster: Unrast, 2021.

International Union of Women Architects (Hg./eds.): *Architektinnenhistorie. Zur Geschichte der Architektinnen und Designerinnen im 20. Jahrhundert. Erste Zusammenstellung*, Berlin: Selbstverlag, 1984.

Anja Kaiser & Rebecca Stephany (Hg./eds.): *Glossary of Undisciplined Design*, Leipzig: Spector Books, 2021.

Michaela Karl: *Die Geschichte der Frauenbewegung*, Ditzingen: Reclam, 2011; 6. Aufl./ed. 2020.

Jennifer Kaufmann-Buhler, Victoria Rose Pass & Christopher S. Wilson (Hg./eds.): *Design History beyond the Canon*, London, New York, Oxford, New Delhi & Sydney: Bloomsbury Visual Arts, 2019.

Pat Kirkham (Hg./ed.): *Women Designers in the USA, 1900–2000. Diversity and Difference*, Ausstellungskatalog / exhibition catalog, The Bard Graduate Center for Studies in the Decorative Arts, Design and Culture, New Haven: Yale University Press, CT, 2000.

Katharina Kurz & Pia Berger (Hg./eds.): Nicht mein Ding – Gender im Design, Ausstellung im / exhibition in HfG-Archiv, Ulm, 2019.

Alexandra Lange: The Hidden Women of Architecture and Design, https://www.newyorker.com/culture/cultural-comment/the-hidden-women-of-architecture-and-design (Abruf/accessed 22. Aug. 2022).

Ilse Lenz: Von der Sorgearbeit bis #MeToo. Aktuelle feministische Themen und Debatten in Deutschland, in Bundeszentrale für politische Bildung, aus Politik und Zeitgeschichte, https://www.bpb.de/shop/zeitschriften/apuz/267940/von-der-sorgearbeit-bis-metoo/ (Abruf/accessed 10. Okt./Oct. 2021).

Briar Levit: *Baseline Shift. Untold Stories of Women in Graphic Design History*, New York, NY: Princeton Architectural Press, 2021.

Sheila Levrant de Bretteville: Some Aspects of Design from the Perspective of a Woman Designer, *Icographic. A Quarterly Review of International Visual Communication Design*, Nr./no. 6 (1973).

Audre Lorde: *Sister Outsider. Essays and Speeches*, Berkeley: Crossing Press, 1984; deutsche Ausgabe / German edition: *Sister Outsider. Essays*, Berlin: Hanser, 2021.

Ellen Lupton: Colophon: Women Graphic Designers, in Pat Kirkham (Hg./ed.): *Women Designers in the USA, 1900–2000*, New Haven: Yale University Press, 2000: 363–381.

Ellen Lupton & Laurie Haycock Makela: Underground Matriarchy. Women Who Have Shaped the Profession by Their Own Work and by Enabling Those around Them, *Eye Magazine* 4, Nr./no. 14 (Herbst/Autumn 1994), https://www.eyemagazine.com/feature/article/underground-matriarchy und https://ellenlupton.com/Underground-Matriarch (Abruf/accessed 11. Apr. 2022).

Ellen Lupton & Leslie Mia: There Is No Such Thing as Neutral Graphic Design, Design is Normative but It Can also Be Transformative, *Eye on Design*, 24. Mai/May 2021.

L. H. Makela & Ellen Lupton: Underground Matriarchy, *Eye Magazine* 4, Nr./no. 14 (Herbst/Autumn 1994): 42–47.

Claudia Mareis & Nina Paim (Hg./eds.): *Design Struggles. Intersecting Histories, Pedagogies, and Perspectives*, Amsterdam: Valiz, 2021.

Liz McQuiston, Guido Costa, Nan Goldin & Enrique Juncosa: *Suffragettes to She-Devils. The Developing Role of Graphics in the Struggle for Women's Liberation and Beyond*, London: Phaeton, 1997.

Reiner Meier: *Die Reklamekunst der Keksfabrik Bahlsen in Hannover 1885–1945*, Dissertation/dissertation, Münster, 1999.

MMS [Maryam Fanni, Matilda Flodmark & Sara Kaaman] (Hg./eds.): *The Natural Enemies of Books. A Messy History of Women in Printing and Typography*, London: Occasional Papers, 2020.

Linda Nochlin: *Why Have There Been No Great Women Artists?*, 1971, neu hg. / new ed. London: Thames & Hudson, 2021.

Katja Peglow & Jonas Engelmann (Hg./eds.): *Riot Grrrl Revisted. Geschichte und Gegenwart einer feministischen Bewegung*, Mainz: Ventil Verlag, 2011, 2. Aufl./ed. 2013.

Mary Pepchinski: *Feminist Space. Exhibitions and Discourses between Philadelphia and Berlin, 1865–1912*, Weimar: VDG, 2007.

Mary Pepchinski: Vom Women's Building zum Haus der Frau. Kulturtransport, Typologie und das Problem der Repräsentation, 1893–1914, in Anke Köth, Kai Krauskopf, Andreas Schwarting & Hans Lippert (Hg./eds.): *Building America. Eine große Erzählung*, Bd./vol. 2, Dresden: Thelem, 2008: 183–205.

Carl-Wolfgang Schümann: Das Haus der Frau, in *Der westdeutsche Impuls 1900–1914. Kunst und Umweltgestaltung im Industriegebiet. Die Deutsche Werkbund-Ausstellung Cöln 1914*, Katalog/catalog, Köln/Cologne, 1984: 233–241.

Martha Scotford: Messy History vs Neat History. Toward an Expanded View of Women in Graphic Design, *Visible Language* 28, Nr./no. 4 (Herbst/Autumn 1994), https://readings.design/PDF/messy-history-vs-neat-history-toward-an-expanded-view-of-women-in-graphic-design.pdf (Abruf/accessed 18. Nov. 2022).

Martha Scotford: Is There a Canon of Graphic Design History?, *AIGA Journal* 9, Nr./no. 2 (1991), Wiederabdruck in / repr. in Marie Finamore & Steven Heller (Hg./eds.): *Design Culture: An Anthology of Writing from the AIGA Journal of Graphic Design*, New York: Allworth Press, 1997.

Martha Scotford & Cipe Pineles: The Tenth Pioneer, *Eye Magazine* 5, Nr./no. 18 (Herbst/Autumn 1995), https://www.eyemagazine.com/feature/article/the-tenth-pioneer (Abruf/accessed 3. Aug. 2022).

Susan Sellers: How Long Has This Been Going On? Harper's Bazaar, Funny Face and the Construction of the Modernist Woman, *Visible Language* 29, Nr./no. 1 (1995): 13–35.

Catherine de Smet & Sara De Bondt (Hg./eds.): *Graphic Design. History in the Writing (1983–2011)*, Occasional Papers, 2012; zuerst veröffentlicht in / first printed in *Iconographie*, Nr./no. 6 (1973).

Prudence Stevenson, Susan Mackie, Anne Robinson & Jess Baines: *See Red Women's Workshop: Feminist Posters 1974–1990*, London: Four Corners Books, 2016.

Despina Stratigakos: Women and the Werkbund. Gender Politics and German Design Reform, 1907–14, *Journal of the Society of Architectural Historians* 62, Nr./no. 4 (2003): 490–511.

E. M. Thomson: Aims for Oblivion: The History of Women in Early American Graphic Design, *Design Issues* 10, Nr./no. 2 (1994): 27–48.

Christoph Thun-Hohenstein, Anne-Katrin Rossberg & Elisabeth Schmuttermeier (Hg./eds.): *Die Frauen der Wiener Werkstätte*, Katalog/catalog, MAK – Museum für angewandte Kunst Wien, Basel: Birkhäuser, 2020.

Aggie Toppins: Can We Teach Graphic Design History Without the Cult of Hero Worship?, *Eye on Design*, 29. Mai/May 2020, https://eyeondesign.aiga.org/can-we-teach-graphic-design-history-without-the-cult-of-hero-worship/ (Abruf/accessed 27. Jun. 2022).

Aggie Toppins: We Need Graphic Design Histories that Look beyond the Profession: Visual Communication Is Not Only a Professional Domain – It's an Active Cultural Practice Shared by All, *Eye on Design*, 10. Jun. 2021, https://eyeondesign.aiga.org/we-need-graphic-design-histories-that-look-beyond-the-profession/ (Abruf/accessed 27. Jun. 2022).

Teal Triggs: *Fanzines. The DIY Revolution*, San Francisco, CA: Chronicle Books, 2010.

S. Worden & J. Seddon (Hg./eds.): *Women Designing. Redefining Design Between the Wars*, University of Brighton, 1994.

KURZBIOGRAFIEN
SHORT BIOGRAPHIES

Danah Abdulla (geb. 1986)

Abdulla ist Designerin, Schriftstellerin und Verlegerin. Schwerpunkt ihrer Forschung ist die Kritik an den Erzählungen der Designgeschichte und -theorie. Sie entwickelte neue Narrative für die Designtheorie und -praxis, insbesondere unter dem Gesichtspunkt, arabische Kulturen, die von der westlichen Welt an den Rand gedrängt wurden, in die neuen Diskurse miteinzubeziehen. 2022 erschien ihr erstes Buch *Designerly Ways of Knowing. A Working Inventory of Things a Designer Should Know*. Die gebürtige Kuwaiterin lebt heute in London. Sie ist als Programmdirektorin für Grafikdesign am Camberwell und am Wimbledon College of Art, University of the Arts London (UAL), tätig und verantwortet hier die Durchführung verschiedener Examen im Grafikdesign. 2018 promovierte sie am Department of Design des Goldsmiths, University of London, mit der Arbeit *Design Otherwise. Towards a Locally-Centric Design Education Curricula in Jordan*. Sie ist zudem Gründungsmitglied der Plattform *Decolonising Design* und gründete das *Kalimat Magazine*, ein unabhängiges Non-Profit-Magazin über arabische Kultur.

Danah Abdulla (b. 1986)

Abdulla is a designer, writer, and publisher whose research focuses on critiquing the narratives of design history and theory. Her work has developed new narratives for design theory and practice, especially by integrating the perspectives of Arab cultures marginalized by the Western world into the new discourses she formulates. Her first book, *Designerly Ways of Knowing: A Working Inventory of Things a Designer Should Know*, appeared in 2022. Born in Kuwait, she now lives in London. She serves as program director for graphic design at Camberwell and Wimbledon Colleges of Art at the University of the Arts London (UAL), where she is responsible for administering various graphic design exams. In 2018, she received her PhD from the Department of Design at Goldsmiths, University of London, with the thesis *Design Otherwise: Towards a Locally-Centric Design Education Curricula in Jordan*. She is also a founding member of the platform *Decolonising Design* and founder of *Kalimat Magazine*, an independent nonprofit magazine about Arab culture.

Katharine Adams (1862–1952)

Adams, geboren in Bracknell, einer Stadt in Berkshire, England, wurde insbesondere bekannt für ihre Buchbindearbeiten aus feinem Leder. Ihre Kindheitsfreundinnen waren Jenny und May Morris, die Töchter von William Morris. Weitgehend autodidaktisch arbeitend, hat sie dennoch eine kurze Ausbildung bei Sarah Prideaux und T. J. Cobden-Sanderson in London genossen, gründete dann aber ihre eigene Werkstatt in Lechlade. 1898 gewann sie den ersten Preis auf der „Oxford Arts and Crafts Exhibition". 1901 gründete sie eine eigene Buchbinderei mit Namen Eadburgha Bindery in Gloucestershire, wo sie mit zwei Frauen zusammen arbeitete. Auftraggeber waren Emery Walker und Sydney Cockerell, das British Museum, die Doves Press, die Ashendene Press und die Kelmscott Press. Adams stellte ihre feinen Dekorationen, oft in Gold, auf der ganzen Welt aus. 1893 wurde sie zweite Vorsitzende der Women's Guild of Art und 1938 Fellow der Royal Society of Arts. Ihre Arbeiten, insgesamt etwa 300 Buchbindearbeiten, führte sie bis zu ihrem Tod im eigenen Haus, The Cherries, aus.

Katharine Adams (1862–1952)

Born in Bracknell, a town in Berkshire, England, Adams became known especially for her bookbinding work in fine leather. She counted Jenny and May Morris, daughters of William Morris, among her childhood friends. Largely self-taught, she nevertheless enjoyed a brief apprenticeship with Sarah Prideaux and T. J. Cobden-Sanderson in London, after which she set up her own workshop in Lechlade. In 1898, she won first prize at the Oxford Arts and Crafts Exhibition, and in 1901, she established her own bookbinding business, Eadburgha Bindery, in Gloucestershire, where she worked together with two women. Clients included Emery Walker and Sydney Cockerell, the British Museum, the Doves Press, the Ashendene Press, and the Kelmscott Press. Adams exhibited her fine decorations, often done in gold, around the world. In 1893, she became second president of the Women's Guild of Art, and in 1938 a fellow of the Royal Society of Arts. Until her death, she continued to produce work, ultimately totaling nearly 300 bookbindings, in her own home, which she called The Cherries.

Gail Anderson (geb. 1962)

Anderson ist eine der wenigen äußerst erfolgreichen Persons of Color in den USA in Graphic Design. Ihre Familie stammt aus Jamaika, sie selbst wurde in New York geboren. Dort besuchte sie einschlägige Designschulen wie die School of Visual Arts, an der die legendäre Grafikdesignerin Paula Scher lehrte. Anderson war von 1987 bis 2002 Art-Direktorin bei der designorientierten Musikzeitschrift *Rolling Stone*. Hier entwickelte sie ihre Begeisterung für Schrifttypen jeglicher Art, die sie unkonventionell miteinander kombinierte. Zusammen mit dem Grafikdesigner und Designkritiker Steven Heller stellte sie historische Schriften und neueste Fonts vor. Markant ist auch ihre Neigung zu starker Farbigkeit. Von 2002 bis 2010 war sie Creative Director of Design bei einer New Yorker Werbefirma, die für Broadway-Theater arbeitet. Darüber hinaus arbeitete sie als Designerin für *The Boston Globe Sunday Magazine* und Vintage Books.

Anderson wurde vielfach geehrt. 2008 empfing sie eine Medaille der AIGA (American Institute of Graphic Arts), der größten Vereinigung von professionellen Designer*innen in den USA. 2009 gewann sie den Richard Gangel Art Director Award. Es folgten Ehrungen für ihr Werk von renommierten Institutionen wie der Society of Publication Designers, des Type Directors Club, des Art Directors Club, Graphis, Communication Arts and Print. Als erste Woman of Color erhielt sie 2018 den Cooper Hewitt National Design Award für ihr Lebenswerk. Damit war sie die dritte Frau, die diesen Preis überhaupt empfing. Heute sind ihre Arbeiten Bestandteil der Sammlungen des Cooper Hewitt, Smithsonian Design Museum und der Library of Congress. Sie lehrt Grafikdesign an der School of Visual Arts, New York City.

Gail Anderson (b. 1962)

Anderson is one of the few highly successful persons of color in graphic design in the United States. Born in New York to a family from Jamaica, she attended design schools including the School of Visual Arts, where legendary graphic designer Paula Scher taught. From 1987 to 2002, Anderson was an art director at the design-conscious music magazine *Rolling Stone*. At Rolling Stone, she developed her enthusiasm for typefaces of all kinds, combining them in unconventional ways. Working with graphic designer and design critic Steven Heller, she often presented historical typefaces and the latest fonts. Another striking feature of her work is a tendency toward strong colors. From 2002 to 2010, she served as creative director of design at a New York advertising firm working for Broadway theaters. She has also worked as a designer for *The Boston Globe Sunday Magazine* and Vintage Books.

Anderson has been the recipient of many awards. In 2008, she received a medal from the AIGA (American Institute of Graphic Arts), the largest association of professional designers in the United States. In 2009, she also won the Richard Gangel Art Director Award. Honors for her work then followed from prestigious institutions, such as the Society of Publication Designers, the Type Directors Club, the Art Directors Club, Graphis, and Communication Arts and Print. In 2018, she became the first woman of color—and the third woman ever—to receive the Cooper Hewitt National Design Award for her life's work. Her work is held today by the collections of the Cooper Hewitt, Smithsonian Design Museum and the Library of Congress. She currently teaches graphic design at the School of Visual Arts in New York.

Ruth Ansel (geb. 1938)

Ansel schloss ihre Ausbildung zunächst als Künstlerin an der Alfred University in New York 1957 ab, anschließend arbeitete sie bei Columbia Records. Sie heiratete den Designer Bob Gill, der sie mit bekannten Designern New Yorks in Verbindung brachte. Das Paar trennte sich jedoch nach einigen Jahren. Als Grafikdesignerin ist Ansel vor allem bekannt für ihre Tätigkeit als – neben Bea Feitler – Co-Art-Direktorin von *Harper's Bazaar* in den 1960er Jahren. In den 1970er Jahren war sie Art-Direktorin des *New York Times Magazine* und in den 1980er Jahren von *House & Garden*, *Vanity Fair* und *Vogue*. Stets war sie, neben Bea Feitler, die einzige Frau in einer Männerwelt und in den 1960er Jahren die jüngste unter den Art-Direktor*innen. Aus der Zusammenarbeit mit Bea Feitler und dem Fotografen Richard Avedon resultierte im April 1965 das

Ruth Ansel (b. 1938)

Ansel first completed her training as an artist at Alfred University in New York in 1957, after which she worked at Columbia Records. She married designer Bob Gill, who connected her with well-known New York designers. However, the couple separated after a few years. As a graphic designer, Ansel is best known for her work as co–art director of *Harper's Bazaar* (alongside Bea Feitler) in the 1960s. In the 1970s, she worked as art director of the *New York Times Magazine* and in the 1980s of *House & Garden*, *Vanity Fair*, and *Vogue*. Together with Bea Feitler, she was a lone woman in a world of men, and in the 1960s she was the youngest of her art director peers. It was her collaboration with Bea Feitler and photographer Richard Avedon that led to the iconic cover image of model Jean Shrimpton in April 1965. In the 1970s, Ansel worked

ikonische Cover-Bild des Models Jean Shrimpton. In den 1970er Jahren arbeitete Ansel mit vielen Fotograf*innen und Künstler*innen zusammen, die berühmt wurden, neben Avedon mit Andy Warhol, Bruce Weber und Annie Leibovitz. Im Auftrag dieser Künstler*innen gestaltete sie später entsprechende Bücher, ebenso Titel wie *Alice in Wonderland*, das Fotografien von Richard Avedon enthält, sowie 1974 *The End of the Game* von Peter Beard. In den 1990er Jahren gründete sie ein eigenes Designstudio und gestaltete *Dark Odyssey* von Phillip Jones Griffiths, *The Sixties* von Richard Avedon, *Women and The White Oak Dance Project* von Annie Leibovitz und eine Monografie von Peter Beard beim Kölner Verlag Taschen. Ebenfalls in ihrem Studio entwarf sie Kampagnen für Versace, Club Monaco und Karl Lagerfeld. Ansel erhielt im Laufe ihrer Karriere die bedeutendsten Auszeichnungen, etwa 1970 die Gold Medal for Design des Art Directors Club, und wurde 1994 von der Society of Publication Design Award geehrt für Continuing Excellence in Publication Design. 2010 wurde sie mit einer eigenen Monografie in die Hall of Femmes aufgenommen, 2016 ernannte man sie zum Ehrenmitglied der AIGA (American Institute of Graphic Arts). Sie unterrichtete an der Cranbrook Academy in Michigan und an The School of Visual Arts in New York.

with many photographers and artists who became famous: Andy Warhol, Bruce Weber, and Annie Leibovitz, in addition to Avedon. She later designed books for these artists, as well as titles such as *Alice in Wonderland*, which includes photographs by Richard Avedon, and in 1974 *The End of the Game* by Peter Beard. In the 1990s, she established her own design studio and designed *Dark Odyssey* by Phillip Jones Griffiths, *The Sixties* by Richard Avedon, *Women and The White Oak Dance Project* by Annie Leibovitz, and a monograph by Peter Beard for the Cologne publisher Taschen. Other work she realized in her studio included campaigns for Versace, Club Monaco, and Karl Lagerfeld. Ansel has received the highest honors throughout her career, among them the Gold Medal for Design from Art Directors Club in 1970 and the Society of Publication Design Award in 1994 for Continuing Excellence in Publication Design. In 2010, she was inducted into the Hall of Femmes with her own monograph, and in 2016 she was named an honorary member of the AIGA (American Institute of Graphic Arts). She has taught at Cranbrook Academy in Michigan and at The School of Visual Arts in New York.

Vela Arbutina (geb. 1978)

Arbutina ist eine der Grafikdesignerinnen des Magazins *Girls Like Us*. Von 2001 bis 2003 absolvierte sie eine Ausbildung als Künstlerin und Grafikdesignerin am Central Saint Martins College of Art and Design in London, dann an der Gerrit Rietveld Academie in Amsterdam sowie von 2017 bis 2018 an der Zürcher Hochschule der Künste und anschließend für zwei Jahre an der Hochschule für Gestaltung und Kunst in Basel. Ihr Arbeitsfeld erstreckt sich von Editorial Design über Art-Direktion bis hin zur Kuratorentätigkeit.

Vela Arbutina (b. 1978)

Vela Arbutina is one of the graphic designers of the magazine *Girls Like Us*. From 2001 to 2003, she trained as an artist and graphic designer at Central Saint Martins College of Art and Design in London, then at the Gerrit Rietveld Academie in Amsterdam, and from 2017 to 2018 at the Zürcher Hochschule der Künste, followed by two years at the Hochschule für Gestaltung und Kunst in Basel. Her field of work ranges from editorial design to art direction and curatorial work.

Margaret Neilson Armstrong (1867–1944)

Armstrong lebte weitgehend in New York und wurde als Künstlerin, Grafikdesignerin und Illustratorin vor allem für ihre Bucheinbände berühmt. Zudem ist sie für Grafiken von Wildblumen bekannt, die sich bis heute großer Beliebtheit erfreuen. Ihr Vater war Diplomat und Glasmaler, sie hatte sechs Geschwister. Ihr Berufsweg als Grafikdesignerin begann in den 1880er Jahren. Sie arbeitete zunächst für den Verlag A. C. McClurg, später auch für Scribner's und andere Verlage. Um seltene Blumenarten zu erfassen, reiste Armstrong durch den US-amerikanischen Westen sowie durch Kanada und verfasste den ersten größeren Führer über diese Pflanzen. Sie schrieb auch Kriminal-

Margaret Neilson Armstrong (1867–1944)

Armstrong lived largely in New York and became famous as an artist, graphic designer, and illustrator, especially for her book covers. She is also known for her drawings of wildflowers, which are still very popular today. Her father was a diplomat and stained-glass artist; she had six siblings. Her career as a graphic designer began in the 1880s, with work for the publisher A. C. McClurg, and later for Scribner's and other publishing houses. Armstrong traveled throughout the western United States and Canada in order to document rare flower species, writing the first major guide to these plants. She also wrote crime novels and biographies. Her botanical interest motivated her to choose

Die Familie Armstrong, vordere Reihe v.l.n.r. / Armstrong family, front row, left to right: Maitland, Helen, Ham und Margaret Armstrong, um/around 1910

romane und Biografien. Aufgrund ihres botanischen Interesses wählte sie Pflanzenmotive für ihre Bucheinbände, wie sie auch der Jugendstil bevorzugte. Ihre vielen Einbände versah sie mit einem Monogramm, gebildet aus den sich leicht überlappenden Initialen ihres eigenen Namens.

plant motifs, also favored by art nouveau, for her book covers. She imprinted many of her bindings with a monogram formed from the slightly overlapping initials of her own name.

Jess Baines

Baines war von 1982 bis 1984 Mitglied des Frauenkollektivs See Red Women's Workshop in London. Nach 1984 studierte sie Keramik am Camberwell College of Art, später verlagerte sich ihr Schwerpunkt vom Design auf die theoretische Auseinandersetzung mit der Geschichte der radikalen Druckwerkstätten. Sie absolvierte einen Master in Kunstgeschichte und -theorie am Goldsmiths, University of London, und beschäftigte sich in ihrer Doktorarbeit an der London School of Economics (LSE) ebenfalls mit Design- und Drucker-Kooperativen. Heute ist sie Senior Lecturer for Contextual and Theoretical Studies an der Design School am London College of Communication und entwickelt dort Programme in grafischer Kommunikation.

Jess Baines

Jess Baines was a member of the See Red Women's Workshop collective in London from 1982 to 1984. After 1984, she studied ceramics at Camberwell College of Art, later shifting her focus from design to a theoretical exploration of the history of radical printmaking workshops. She completed a master's degree in art history and theory at Goldsmiths, University of London, and her doctoral research at the London School of Economics (LSE) focused on design and printer cooperatives. Today she is senior lecturer for contextual and theoretical studies in the Design School at the London College of Communication, where she develops programs in graphic communication.

Lillian Bassman (1917–2012)

Bassman hatte zwar eine Ausbildung als Grafikdesignerin an der Textile High School in Manhattan, New York, absolviert, arbeitete aber hauptsächlich in der Modefotografie. Als Tochter jüdischer Emigranten aus Russland konzentrierte sie sich zunächst auf fotografische Arbeiten zum Thema Krieg und Armut in Europa. Im Laufe der 1940er Jahre wandte sie sich vollständig der Fotografie zu und schuf ein großes Œuvre kommerzieller Modefotografien, vor allem für Magazine wie *Vogue* und *Harper's Bazaar*. Anfang der 1970er Jahre unterbrach sie diese Karriere für 15 Jahre und arbeitete im Bereich experimenteller Fotografie. Sie entwarf ihre eigene Modekollektion und unterrichtete Fotografie an der Parsons School of Design in New York. Mitte der 1990er begann sie erneut Mode zu fotografieren.

Lillian Bassman (1917–2012)

Bassman trained as a graphic designer at Textile High School in Manhattan but worked primarily in fashion photography. The daughter of Jewish emigrants from Russia, she initially concentrated on photographic works on the theme of war and poverty in Europe. During the 1940s, she turned her attention completely to photography and created a large oeuvre of commercial fashion photographs, mainly for magazines such as *Vogue* and *Harper's Bazaar*. In the early 1970s, she interrupted this career for fifteen years to work in the field of experimental photography. She designed her own fashion line and taught photography at Parsons School of Design in New York. In the mid-1990s, she once again began photographing fashion.

Edna Rudolph Beilenson (1909–1981)

Beilenson wurde am 16. Juni 1909 als Tochter der Künstler*innen John and Anna Rudolph in New York City geboren. Sie war eine amerikanische Typografin, Verlegerin von wertvollen Drucken, Buchdesignerin und Autorin. Zusammen mit ihrem Ehemann, Peter Beilenson, führte sie ab 1931 die Peter Pauper Press Nach dessen Tod 1962 blieb sie Eigentümerin der Druckerei. Beilenson stand einer Gruppe von Frauen vor, die in verschiedenen Bereichen des Buchgewerbes arbeiteten und sich gegen die männerdominierten Fachvereinigungen wehrten. Aus diesem Zusammenhang entstand 1937 das Buch *Bookmaking on the Distaff Side*. Bis auf zwei Männer waren

Edna Rudolph Beilenson (1909–1981)

Beilenson was born in New York City on 16 June 1909, the daughter of artists John and Anna Rudolph. She was an American typographer, publisher of valuable prints, book designer, and author. Together with her husband, Peter Beilenson, she ran the Peter Pauper Press from 1931 on. After his death in 1962, she remained the owner of the print shop. Beilenson presided over a group of women who worked in various areas of the book trade and resisted the male-dominated professional associations. This was the context from which the book *Bookmaking on the Distaff Side* originated in 1937. Except for two men, only women were involved. Under Beilenson's leadership,

daran nur Frauen beteiligt. Unter Beilensons Leitung formierten sich Mitglieder der Gruppe zur Distaff Press, die weitere Titel zur Geschichte von Frauen im Buchgewerbe herausgab. Beilenson bekleidete später zahlreiche ehrenvolle Ämter, 1958 beispielsweise wurde sie als erste Frau zur Präsidentin der AIGA (American Institute of Graphic Arts) gewählt. Sie zählte zu den ersten Frauen, die in den Roller Club gewählt wurden, wurde Ehrenmitglied der Royal Society of Arts und Präsidentin und Geschäftsführerin der Goudy Society. Für ihre Typografie erhielt sie zahlreiche Auszeichnungen.

members of the group formed Distaff Press, which published other titles on the history of women in the book trade. Beilenson later held numerous positions of leadership; in 1958, for example, she became the first woman to be elected president of the AIGA (American Institute of Graphic Arts). She was among the first women elected to the Roller Club, became an honorary member of the Royal Society of Arts, and was president and CEO of the Goudy Society. She received numerous awards for her typography.

Fritzi Berger (1894–1967)

Berger, die auch unter anderen Namen zeichnete (Friederike Berger, Friederike Hohenberg, Friederike Berger Hohenberg, Friedericke Berger Hohenberg), war eine der bekanntesten Mitarbeiterinnen der Wiener Werkstätte. In erster Linie war sie jedoch Modeentwerferin, machte eine Schneiderlehre und arbeitete für Modejournale. Ab 1912 war sie Mitglied der Wiener Werkstätte, für die sie zahlreiche Stoffmuster und einige Künstlerpostkarten entwarf. 1913 gewann sie einen Preis beim Wettbewerb des Jungwiener Modekomitees. 1916 gründete sie gemeinsam mit ihrer Schwester, der Schneiderin Hilde Berger, den Modesalon „Schwestern Berger". Er war in einem Otto-Wagner-Bau in Wien untergebracht und erfreute sich bald eines hohen Ansehens als elegantes und modernes Schneideratelier. Neben Mode schufen die Schwestern auch Bühnenkostüme. Im Jahr 1917 heiratete Berger den Ingenieur und Dichter Paul Hohenberg. 1927 wurde der Name des Modeateliers geändert zu „Friederike Hohenberg & Hilda Lampl, vormals Schwestern Berger". Wegen ihrer jüdischen Herkunft musste das Ehepaar mit den beiden Töchtern unmittelbar nach dem Einmarsch der Nationalsozialisten in Österreich 1939 in die USA emigrieren.

Fritzi Berger (1894–1967)

Berger, who also drew under other names (Friederike Berger, Friederike Hohenberg, Friederike Berger Hohenberg, Friedericke Berger Hohenberg), was one of the best-known collaborators of the Wiener Werkstätte. First and foremost, however, she was a fashion designer, completing an apprenticeship in dressmaking and working for fashion journals. From 1912, she was a member of the Wiener Werkstätte, for which she designed numerous fabric patterns and several artists' postcards. In 1913, she won a prize at the competition organized by the Jungwiener Modekomitee. In 1916, together with her sister, the dressmaker Hilde Berger, she founded the fashion salon Schwestern Berger. The salon was housed in an Otto Wagner building in Vienna and soon enjoyed a distinguished reputation as an elegant and modern dressmaking studio. Besides fashion, the sisters also created stage costumes. In 1917, Berger married the engineer and poet Paul Hohenberg. In 1927, the name of the fashion studio was changed to Friederike Hohenberg & Hilda Lampl, vormals Schwestern Berger. Because of their Jewish origins, the couple and their two daughters had to emigrate to the United States immediately after the Nazi invasion of Austria in 1939.

Helene Bernatzik (1888–1967)

Bernatzik arbeitete von 1914 bis 1922 für die Wiener Werkstätte, hier war sie ab 1916 Leiterin der neu gegründeten Künstlerwerkstätte in der Neustiftgasse. Sie stammte aus einer kulturell sehr interessierten Familie. Sie selbst machte von 1906 bis 1910 eine Ausbildung an der Kunstschule für Frauen und Mädchen und absolvierte anschließend von 1911 bis 1913 ein Studium an der Kunstgewerbeschule Wien in der Fachklasse Malerei bei Koloman Moser und in der Werkstätte für Textilarbeiten bei Rosalia Rothansl. 1920 heiratete sie den Sektionsrat im Handelsministerium Camillo Pfersmann.

Helene Bernatzik (1888–1967)

Bernatzik worked for the Wiener Werkstätte from 1914 to 1922, where she was head of the newly founded artists' workshop in Neustiftgasse from 1916. She came from a family with deep cultural interests. She herself trained at the Kunstschule für Frauen und Mädchen from 1906 to 1910 and then studied at the Kunstgewerbeschule Wien from 1911 to 1913 in the class devoted to painting with Koloman Moser, and in the textiles workshop with Rosalia Rothansl. In 1920 she married Camillo Pfersmann, a departmental official in the Ministry of Commerce.

Xenia Leonidowna Boguslawskaja
(1892–1973)

In Welik, Nowgorod, geboren, erhielt Boguslawskaja in einer St. Petersburger Kunstschule ersten Kunstunterricht. Ihre Mutter stammte aus Griechenland, ihr Vater war hoher Offizier der zaristischen Armee. Boguslawskaja war früh an sozialistischen Ideen interessiert. Sie musste deshalb unter falschem Namen aus der Heimat fliehen. Dank einer Amnestie konnte sie 1913 nach Sankt Petersburg zurückkehren. Später widmete sie sich mit ihrem Freund und späteren Ehemann Iwan Albertowitsch Puni der Organisation der russischen Avantgarde, insbesondere deren berühmten Ausstellungen „0,10", auf der sie gemeinsam mit Puni ein Manifest herausgab, und „Tramway V", beide 1915.

Ihren zukünftigen Mann Puni hatte sie mit 16 Jahren kennengelernt, nach ihrer Flucht begegnete sie ihm unter Exilrussen in Neapel wieder und sie zogen gemeinsam nach Paris. Hier besuchte Boguslawskaja eine russische Akademie und verdiente ihr Geld als Zeichnerin von Postkarten und Entwürfen von Stoffen. 1919 zogen sie und Puni kurzzeitig nach Witebsk, um auf Einladung des Direktors Marc Chagall an der dortigen Kunstschule zu lehren. Ende 1919 verließ das Paar Russland erneut und übersiedelte für fünf Jahre nach Berlin. Auf der „Großen Berliner Kunstausstellung" 1922 und 1923 waren beide mit einigen Werken zu sehen. Kurt Schwitters widmete Boguslawskaja sein Merzbild *Konstruktion für edle Frauen*. 1924 zogen die Eheleute für einen Neubeginn nach Paris. Boguslawskaja erwirtschaftete den gemeinsamen Lebensunterhalt als Kostümbildnerin und Stoffentwerferin. Nachdem Puni sich als Maler etabliert hatte, gab sie 1930 die eigene Arbeit auf und engagierte sich von nun an ausschließlich für Punis Werk. Sie organisierte für ihn Ausstellungen und veröffentlichte 1972 seinen Œuvrekatalog.

Kseniya Leonidovna Boguslavskaya
(1892–1973)

Born in Velik, Novgorod, Boguslavskaya received her first art lessons in a St. Petersburg art school. Her mother was from Greece, while her father was a high officer in the tsar's army. Interested in socialist ideas early in her life, Boguslavskaya had to flee her homeland under a false name. An amnesty allowed her to return to St. Petersburg in 1913. Later, together with her friend and later husband Ivan Albertovich Puni, she devoted herself to currents in the Russian avant-garde, organizing in particular its famous exhibitions *0.10*, the occasion for a manifesto she issued together with Puni, and *Tramway V* (both in 1915).

She first met her future husband Puni when she was sixteen, encountering him again among exiled Russians in Naples; after their marriage, the couple moved together to Paris. Here Boguslavskaya attended a Russian academy and earned her living drawing postcards and fabric designs. In 1919, she and Puni moved briefly to Vitebsk to teach at the art school there at the invitation of its director, Marc Chagall. At the end of 1919, the couple once again left Russia, moving to Berlin for five years. At the Great Berlin Art Exhibition in 1922 and 1923 both were represented by several works. Kurt Schwitters dedicated his Merzbild *Construction for Noble Women* to Boguslavskaya. In 1924, the couple moved to Paris for a fresh start. Boguslavskaya supported both of them with her work as a costume and fabric designer. After Puni had established himself as a painter, she gave up her own work in 1930 and from then on was exclusively committed to her husband's work. She organized exhibitions for him and published his oeuvre catalog in 1972.

Higgins Bond

Die US-amerikanische Grafikdesignerin Bond erlangte ein BFA Degree in Werbegrafik am Memphis College of Art. Ihre Arbeiten wurden 1974 am Metropolitan Museum of Art in New York ausgestellt und 1977 am DuSable Museum of African-American Art in Chicago. Sie ist Illustratorin der Black-Heritage-Briefmarken für den United States Postal Service und gestaltete vier Briefmarken für die United Nations Postal Administration. Sie war die erste afroamerikanische Frau überhaupt, die eine Briefmarke für die USA illustrierte. Bond arbeitet heute weitgehend als Buchdesignerin.

Higgins Bond

Bond, an American graphic designer, earned a BFA degree in advertising design from Memphis College of Art. Her work has been exhibited at the Metropolitan Museum of Art in New York (in 1974) and at the DuSable Museum of African-American Art in Chicago (in 1977). She is the illustrator of the U.S. Postal Service Black Heritage stamps and has designed four stamps for the United Nations Postal Administration. She was the first African-American woman to illustrate a postage stamp for the United States. Bond now works largely as a book designer.

Rosie Boycott (geb. 1951)

Rosel Marie „Rosie" Boycott, Baroness Boycott, war 1972 neben Marsha Rowe eine der Mitbegründerinnen der feministischen Zeitschrift *Spare Rib*. Privat ausgebildet im Cheltenham Ladies' College, Gloucestershire, arbeitete sie zunächst für etwa ein Jahr als Journalistin für das radikale Magazin *Frendz*. Später wurden Boycott und Rowe Leiterinnen des Verlagshauses Virago Press, das sich auf Frauenliteratur spezialisierte. Von 1992 bis 1996 war Boycott Herausgeberin der englischen Ausgabe von *Esquire*, danach bis 1998 von *The Independent* und *Independent on Sunday*, und schließlich vom *Daily Express* (bis 2001). Heute steht sie der Reiseredaktion des Magazins *The Oldie* vor und bekleidet zahlreiche weitere Positionen im Journalismus. Sie unterstützt die Women's Equality Party.

Rosie Boycott (b. 1951)

Rosel Marie "Rosie" Boycott, Baroness Boycott, was one of the cofounders in 1972 (with Marsha Rowe) of the feminist magazine *Spare Rib*. Privately educated at Cheltenham Ladies' College, Gloucestershire, she spent roughly the first year of her career working as a journalist for the radical magazine *Frendz*. Boycott and Rowe later became directors of Virago Press, a publishing house specializing in women's literature. From 1992 to 1996, Boycott was editor of the English edition of *Esquire*, then of *The Independent* and *Independent on Sunday* until 1998, and finally of the *Daily Express* until 2001. Today, she is the editor of the magazine *The Oldie* and holds numerous other journalistic positions. She supports the Women's Equality Party.

Bertha M. Boye (1883–1930)

Boye wurde in Oakland, Kalifornien, geboren. So berühmt ihr Wahlplakat „Votes for Women" (1911) ist, so wenig ist über ihr Leben bekannt. In erster Linie wird Boye als Malerin und Bildhauerin erwähnt. Sie studierte Kunst am Mark Hopkins Art Institute in San Francisco und lebte dort bis 1915. Dann zog sie um nach Ukiah, Kalifornien. Sie starb am 2. September 1930 bei einem Studienaufenthalt in Calais, Frankreich.

Bertha M. Boye (1883–1930)

Boye was born in Oakland, California. Though her campaign poster "Votes for Women" (1911) is widely famous, little is known about her life. She is mainly known as a painter and sculptor. She studied art at the Mark Hopkins Art Institute in San Francisco, where she lived until 1915 before moving to Ukiah, California. She died on 2 September 1930, during a study visit to Calais, France.

Daniela Burger (geb. 1969)

Burger ist selbständige Grafik-Designerin mit einem Studio in Berlin, seit 2010 Art-Direktorin von *Missy Magazine* und seit 2012 dessen Mitherausgeberin. Sie hat von 1996 bis 2001 Kommunikationsdesign an der FH Potsdam studiert und mit dem Diplom abgeschlossen, bevor sie beim Magazin *Spex* für die Gestaltung aller digitalen Formate zuständig war. Seither liegen ihre Schwerpunkte in der Umsetzung von Publikationen und visuellen Erscheinungsbildern. Außerdem ist sie als Dozentin an der Weißensee Kunsthochschule Berlin tätig.

Daniela Burger (b. 1969)

Burger is a freelance graphic designer with a studio in Berlin and has served as art director of *Missy Magazine* since 2010 and as its coeditor since 2012. After studying communication design at the University of Applied Sciences Potsdam from 1996 to 2001, graduating with a *Diplom*, she joined *Spex* magazine, where she was responsible for the design of all digital formats. Since then, her focus has been on realizing publications and visual design. She also teaches at the weissensee school of art and design Berlin.

Ece Canlı

Canlı versteht sich als Designforscherin, Performancekünstlerin und Sängerin. Sie wuchs auf in der Türkei und lebt heute in Porto, Portugal. In ihrer Dissertation an der Universität von Porto untersucht sie den Zusammenhang von Queer-Theorie und Design. Darüber hinaus absolvierte sie ein Master-Studium in Interdisziplinarität am Konstfack University College of Arts, Crafts and Design in Schweden. Sie ist Mitbegründerin der Plattform *Decolonising Design* und forscht seit einiger Zeit am CECS (The Communication and Research Centre) an der University of Minho in Braga, Portugal.

Ece Canlı

Canlı considers herself a design researcher, performance artist, and singer. She grew up in Turkey and now lives in Porto, Portugal. Her dissertation at the University of Porto explores the relationship between queer theory and design. She also completed a master's degree in interdisciplinary studies at Konstfack University College of Arts, Crafts and Design in Sweden. She is cofounder of the Decolonising Design platform and has conducted research at CECS (The Communication and Research Centre) at the University of Minho in Braga, Portugal.

Pamela Colman Smith, Foto aus / photo from The Craftsman (Okt./Oct. 1912)

Olga und Galina Chichagova
(1886–1958 und 1891–1966)

Die Schwestern Chichagova wurden durch ihre russischen Kinderbücher bekannt. Sie haben während ihrer gesamten Karriere zusammengearbeitet. Beide waren Töchter einer berühmten russischen Familiendynastie von Architekten, beide studierten von 1911 bis 1917 an der Stroganov-Akademie für Kunst und Industrie und setzten ihr Studium in den WCHUTEMAS fort. Ihre Kinderbücher zeigen eine starke Tendenz zur konstruktivistischen Ästhetik, die in den WCHUTEMAS gelehrt wurde. In der Bildgestaltung konzentrierten sich die Schwestern zudem auf Elemente der industriellen Produktion, weil sie Kinder auf die Zukunft der Sowjetunion als Industriestaat vorbereiten wollten. Ihr bekanntestes Buch ist *Charlies Reise*, 1923, mit einem Text von Nikolai Smirnov, dessen Werk sie häufig illustrierten.

Pamela Colman Smith (1878–1951)

Smith gilt als die Gestalterin der berühmtesten Tarot-Karten überhaupt. 1909 schuf sie ein Set von 78 einzelnen Karten mit jeweils unterschiedlichen Illustrationen. Sie wurde in London geboren, die Mutter war Jamaikanerin, der Vater weißer Amerikaner. Die Kindheit verbrachte sie in Manchester und Jamaika, ihre Ausbildung erhielt sie am Pratt Institute in New York City. Nach dem Tod der Mutter 1896 verließ Smith die Schule ohne Abschluss und führte ein nomadisches Leben mit einer Theatertruppe. Sie erwarb sich den Ruf als begabte Kostümbildnerin und Bühnenbildnerin. 1907 stellte sie in der Galerie des Fotografen Alfred Stieglitz in New York aus. Als talentierte Künstlerin geschätzt, entwickelte sie früh eine Vorliebe für Okkultes. Neben den Tarot-Karten illustrierte sie Bücher von Bram Stoker, William Butler Yeats und trug mit ihren Werken zur Suffrage-Bewegung bei. Obwohl ihre künstlerische Arbeit sehr populär war, erzielte sie keinen großen kommerziellen Erfolg. Auch erhielt sie keine Tantiemen für die Tarot-Karten. Smith verstarb verarmt und verschuldet in Cornwall.

Muriel Cooper (1925–1994)

Cooper zählt zu den Berühmtheiten der amerikanischen Grafikdesign-Szene. Sie war viele Jahre Direktorin der MIT Press und Mitbegründerin des MIT Media Lab. Nach einer einschlägigen künstlerischen und kunstpädagogischen Ausbildung – 1944 Bachelor of Arts in Ohio State, 1948 Bachelor of Fine Art in Design, 1951 Bachelor of Science in Education am Massachusetts College of Art – wurde sie 1952 Direktorin des neu gegründeten Office of Publications Institute des Massachusetts Institute of Technology (MIT). Im Anschluss an einen Aufenthalt in Mailand und die Gründung

Olga and Galina Chichagova
(1886–1958 and 1891–1966)

Working together throughout their careers, the Chichagova sisters became famous for their Russian children's books; both were daughters of a famous Russian architectural dynasty, both studied at the Moscow State Stroganov Academy of Industrial and Applied Arts from 1911 to 1917, and both continued their studies at VKHUTEMAS. Their children's books show a strong tendency towards the constructivist aesthetics taught at VKHUTEMAS. Their visual design focuses on elements of industrial production, with the aim of preparing children for the industrial future envisioned for the Soviet Union. Their best-known book is *Charlie's Journey*, published in 1923 with text by Nikolai Smirnov, whose work they often illustrated.

Pamela Colman Smith (1878–1951)

Smith is regarded as the designer of the most famous tarot cards ever. In 1909, she created a set of seventy-eight individual cards, each with a different illustration. Born in London to a Jamaican mother and a White American father, she spent her childhood in Manchester and Jamaica and received her education at the Pratt Institute in New York City. After her mother's death in 1896, Smith left school without a degree and led a nomadic life with a theater troupe. She earned a reputation as a talented costume and set designer, and in 1907 she exhibited her drawings and watercolors at the gallery of the photographer Alfred Stieglitz in New York. Well-regarded as a talented artist, she developed an early taste for the occult. In addition to Tarot cards, she illustrated books by Bram Stoker and William Butler Yeats and supported the suffrage movement with her work. Although her artistic work was very popular, she failed to achieve great commercial success. She also received no royalties for the tarot cards she designed, dying impoverished and in debt in Cornwall.

Muriel Cooper (1925–1994)

Cooper is one of the celebrities of the American graphic design scene. She was director of the MIT Press for many years and cofounder of the MIT Media Lab. After training in art and art education, with a bachelor of arts at Ohio State in 1944, a bachelor of fine art in design in 1948, and a bachelor of science in education at Massachusetts College of Art in 1951, she became director of the newly established Office of Publications Institute at the Massachusetts Institute of Technology (MIT) in 1952. After a stint in Milan and having founded her own graphic design studio in Boston, in 1967

eines eigenen Grafikstudios in Boston wurde sie 1967 die erste Art-Direktorin bei der MIT Press, deren Logo sie entwarf. Ihr Buchdesign, darunter ein bekannter Band über das Bauhaus in Deutschland, erhielt Auszeichnungen in zahlreichen Wettbewerben. Ab 1974 unterrichtete Cooper am MIT, 1977 wurde sie Assistenzprofessorin, 1981 Associate Professor und 1988 Professorin. Zudem war sie an anderen Universitäten in der Lehre tätig. Seit 1997 wird ihr zu Ehren der Muriel-Cooper-Preis für Design vergeben.

Hilda Dallas (1878–1958)

Dallas wurde in Japan geboren. Ihre Eltern waren britisch und kehrten später zurück nach England. 1901/02 besuchte sie die Slade School of Art in London. Ab 1909 kam sie, zusammen mit ihrer Schwester Irene, in Kontakt mit der Women's Social and Political Union (WSPU), wo sie weiter ausgebildet wurde. Zwischen 1910 und 1912 gestaltete sie Protestplakate für die Zeitschrift *Votes for Women*. Später arbeitete Dallas für *The Suffragette* und entwarf dort ein Plakat, auf dem Jeanne d'Arc als Heldenfigur zu sehen war. Während des Ersten Weltkriegs war sie als Pazifistin in karitativen Aktivitäten engagiert. Sie entwarf weiterhin Theaterkostüme.

Miki Denhof (1912–2000)

Denhof wurde in Triest, Italien, geboren, wuchs in Österreich auf und erhielt eine Ausbildung in Wien und Berlin. 1938 verließ sie Deutschland und emigrierte nach New York. In den USA wurde sie Assistentin des berühmten Designers Paul Rand und arbeitete für *Esquire* und *Apparel Arts Magazines*. Denhof gilt als eine der ersten Art-Direktorinnen. 1945 schloss sie sich dem einflussreichen Zeitschriftenmogul Condé Nast an und wurde wegen ihrer eleganten Typografie und der modernen Fotografie, die sie hinzuzog, schnell bekannt. Sie ging dann als Promotion Director zur *Vogue*. Später arbeitete sie in weiteren Magazinen wie *House & Garden* und *Glamour*. Sie war besonders darin begabt, junge Fotografinnen für die Magazine zu gewinnen. Später wurde sie auch Art-Direktorin von Condé Nast Books. 1977 verließ sie das Verlagshaus, wurde Ausstellungsdesignerin und gestaltete Kataloge für die Guild Hall in East Hampton. Dort wurde ihr auch eine Einzelausstellung gewidmet.

Julia de Wolf Addison (1866–1952)

Addison, geb. de Wolf Gibbs, wurde in Boston, Massachusetts, geboren und von einer Gouvernante in England erzogen und unterrichtet. 1878 kehrte sie nach Boston zurück und besuchte dort eine Privatschule. Anschließend unternahm sie Reisen nach England und Italien, um sich in Kunst ausbilden zu lassen. 1889 heiratete sie den Geistlichen Daniel Dulany Addison.

she became the first art director at MIT Press, whose logo she designed. Her book design, including a well-known volume on the Bauhaus in Germany, received awards in a number of competitions. Beginning in 1974, Cooper taught at MIT, becoming an assistant professor in 1977, associate professor in 1981, and full professor in 1988. She also held teaching positions at other universities. Since 1997, the Muriel Cooper Award for Design has been given in her honor.

Hilda Dallas (1878–1958)

Dallas was born in Japan to British parents, and she later returned to England. In 1901/02 she attended the Slade School of Art in London. Beginning in 1909, she, along with her sister Irene, came into contact with the Women's Social and Political Union (WSPU), where she received further training. Between 1910 and 1912, she designed protest posters for *Votes for Women* magazine. She later worked for *The Suffragette*, where she designed a poster featuring a heroic Joan of Arc. During World War I, she was involved in charitable activities as a pacifist. She continued to design theatrical costumes.

Miki Denhof (1912–2000)

Denhof was born in Trieste, Italy, grew up in Austria, and was educated in Vienna and Berlin. In 1938, she left Germany and emigrated to New York. In the United States, she became an assistant to the famous designer Paul Rand and worked for *Esquire* and *Apparel Arts Magazines*. Denhof is considered one of the first woman art directors. In 1945, she went to work for the influential magazine mogul Condé Nast and quickly became known for her elegant typography and the modern photography she employed. She then went to work as promotion director for *Vogue*, later working for other magazines such as *House & Garden* and *Glamour*. She was particularly gifted at attracting young woman photographers to the magazines. She eventually became art director of Condé Nast Books, though she left the publisher in 1977 and became an exhibition designer, creating catalogs for Guild Hall in East Hampton, which devoted a solo exhibition to her work.

Julia de Wolf Addison (1866–1952)

Addison, née de Wolf Gibbs, was born in Boston, Massachusetts, and was raised and educated by a governess in England. In 1878 she returned to Boston, where she attended a private school. She then traveled to England and Italy to be trained in art. In 1889, she married clergyman Daniel Dulany Addison. As a craftswoman, she became known for her work in

Sie wurde bekannt als Kunsthandwerkerin für Ornamentik, Mosaike, Metallarbeiten, Stickereien und war Illustratorin auf Pergamentpapier. Zugleich war sie Autorin zahlreicher Bücher, unter anderem von *Arts and Crafts in the Middle Ages. A Description of Mediaeval Workmanship in Several of the Departments of Applied Art, Together with Some Account of Special Artisans in the Early Renaissance*, Boston, L. C. Page & Co., 1908.

Sally Doust

Doust war, zusammen mit Kate Hepburn, eine der beiden Designerinnen des feministischen Alternativmagazins *Spare Rib*. Das erste Heft vom Juni 1971 zeigt beide als junge Frauen ungeschminkt (was für damalige Zeiten ungewöhnlich war) in einer fotografischen Großaufnahme auf dem Titelblatt. Sie dokumentieren mit diesem Bild eine Frauenfreundschaft: Sisterhood. Doust verließ die Schule 1960 mit 16 Jahren und absolvierte anschließend einen Grundkurs am Brighton College of Art. Während dieser Zeit heiratete sie ihren Studienkollegen Richard Doust, mit dem sie 1965 nach Australien ging. Sie wurde Art Editor von *Vogue Australia* und blieb fünf Jahre im Land. Zurück in England, schloss sich das Paar den Ko-Herausgeberinnen Rosie Boycott und Marsha Rowe von *Spare Rib* an. Mit Marsha Rowe hatte Doust schon bei *Vogue Australia* zusammengearbeitet. 2008 war sie Co-Kuratorin einer Ausstellung an der Royal Academy of Arts, London, und arbeitet seither als freiberufliche Grafikdesignerin.

Helen Dryden (1887–1981)

Dryden gilt als eine der bestbezahltesten Designerinnen ihrer Zeit. Sie wurde 1887 in Baltimore, Maryland, USA, geboren. Sie studierte mehrere Jahre bei dem Landschaftsmaler Hugh Breckenridge und absolvierte einen Sommerkurs an der Pennsylvania Academy of Fine Arts. 1909 zog sie nach New York City und vermarktete ihre Modezeichnungen bei den großen Frauenzeitschriften der damaligen Zeit, zunächst ohne nennenswerten Erfolg. Stilistisch ließ sie sich vom englischen Jugendstil anregen, zum Beispiel vom Karikaturisten Aubrey Beardsley, und nahm Anleihen beim japanischen Farbholzschnitt der Ukiyo-e-Drucke. Sie antizipierte zugleich den Mitte der 1920er einsetzenden, in den USA weit verbreiteten Stil des Art déco. Erst das Verlagshaus Condé Nast, das die *Vogue* und *Vanity Fair* herausgab, erkannte die Qualität ihrer Zeichnungen. Für die *Vogue* schuf Dryden etwa 100 verschiedene Titelblätter sowie eine große Anzahl von Illustrationen. Nach 13 Jahren bei Condé Nast arbeitete sie als Freiberuflerin für Titelblätter des *Delineator*-Magazins. Parallel dazu war sie Kostümbildnerin, unter anderem für Broadway-Theater, und befasste sich

ornamentation, mosaics, metalwork, and embroidery, and as an illustrator on parchment. She also authored numerous books, including *Arts and Crafts in the Middle Ages: A Description of Mediaeval Workmanship in Several of the Departments of Applied Art, Together with Some Account of Special Artisans in the Early Renaissance* (Boston: L. C. Page & Co, 1908).

Sally Doust

Along with Kate Hepburn, Doust was one of the two designers of the feminist alternative magazine *Spare Rib*. The first issue from June 1971 shows both of them as young women without makeup—unusual for the times—in a closeup photo on the cover. With this image, they were documenting a particular kind of friendship among women: sisterhood. Doust left school in 1960 at the age of sixteen and subsequently completed a foundation course at Brighton College of Art. During this time, she married fellow student Richard Doust, with whom she moved to Australia in 1965. She became art editor of *Vogue Australia*, remaining in the country for five years. After returning to England, the couple joined forces with coeditors Rosie Boycott and Marsha Rowe of *Spare Rib*; Doust had already worked together with Marsha Rowe at *Vogue Australia*. In 2008, she cocurated an exhibition at the Royal Academy of Arts, London, and has since worked as a freelance graphic designer.

Helen Dryden (1887–1981)

Dryden ranks among the highest paid designers of her time. Born in 1887 in Baltimore, Maryland, she studied for several years with landscape painter Hugh Breckenridge and took a summer course at the Pennsylvania Academy of Fine Arts. In 1909, she moved to New York City and pitched her fashion drawings to the major women's magazines of the day, initially without much success. Stylistically, she was inspired by English art nouveau, for example, by the caricaturist Aubrey Beardsley, and she borrowed from Japanese ukiyo-e color woodblock prints. At the same time, she anticipated the art deco style that became widespread in the United States in the mid-1920s. It was at Condé Nast, which published *Vogue* and *Vanity Fair*, where the quality of her drawings was first recognized. For *Vogue*, Dryden created some one hundred different covers, as well as a large number of illustrations. After thirteen years at Condé Nast, she worked as a freelance artist making covers for *Delineator* magazine. She also worked as a costume designer, with clients including Broadway theaters, and was involved in automotive design. Beginning in the

mit Automobildesign. Mit den 1930er Jahren kam ihr ästhetisch-modischer Stil aus der Mode. In Deutschland wurde besonders ihre Werbung für Lux-Seife bekannt, die in der Fachzeitschrift *Gebrauchsgraphik* 1928 veröffentlicht und farbig abgebildet wurde.

1930s, her highly fashionable, aestheticized style fell out of favor. In Germany, her advertising for Lux soap became particularly well known, as it was published in the trade journal *Gebrauchsgraphik* in 1928 with color illustrations.

Ellen M. Dunlap Hopkins (1854–1939)

Die Malerin und Philanthropin Dunlap Hopkins gründete 1892 die New York School of Applied Design for Women (NYSADW) – ein Jahr vor der für die amerikanische Kulturgeschichte so bedeutenden Weltausstellung in Chicago, auf der Frauen ein eigenes Gebäude für ihre kunsthandwerklichen und künstlerischen Arbeiten erhielten. Die NYSADW war eine einflussreiche Institution für die Ausbildung von Designerinnen und vertrat die amerikanische Arts-and-Crafts-Bewegung. Als erste Schule ihrer Art konzentrierte sie sich speziell auf die Berufsausbildung von Frauen, insbesondere von Frauen mit geringem Einkommen, um ihnen zu finanzieller Unabhängigkeit zu verhelfen. Ebenso wie Dunlap Hopkins für die Anerkennung der angewandten Künste kämpfte und deren Gleichstellung mit den bildenden Künsten anstrebte, rang sie um die Gleichberechtigung von Frauen. Die NYSADW war die einzige Ausbildungsstätte jener Zeit, die eigenes Land und ein eigenes Gebäude in der Lexington Avenue besaß. Dunlap Hopkins erhielt zahlreiche Preise, auch im europäischen Ausland. Die Royal School of Applied Arts for Women in London soll nach ihrem Vorbild eingerichtet worden sein. Nach ihrem Tod schloss sich die NYSADW mit einer anderen Kunstakademie zusammen, dem Phoenix Art Institute. Die nach kurzer Zeit umbenannte New York Phoenix School of Design war nun koedukativ ausgerichtet. 1974 verband sich die Schule mit dem Pratt Institute, um dann die Pratt-New York Phoenix School of Design zu werden.

Ellen M. Dunlap Hopkins (1854–1939)

Dunlap Hopkins, a painter and philanthropist, founded the New York School of Applied Design for Women (NYSADW) in 1892—one year before the Chicago World's Fair that would prove to be such a significant event in American cultural history, and which offered women a building of their own for their craft and artistic work. NYSDAW was an influential institution for the education of women designers and represented the American arts and crafts movement. The first school of its kind, it focused specifically on vocational training for women, and especially for low-income women, to help them achieve financial independence. Just as Dunlap Hopkins fought for recognition of the applied arts and endeavored for them to be treated as equals to the fine arts, she fought for equal rights for women. NYSDAW was the only educational institution of the time that owned its own land and building, located on Lexington Avenue. Dunlap Hopkins received numerous awards, in America and in Europe. The Royal School of Applied Arts for Women in London is said to have been established with her vision in mind. After her death, NYSDAW merged with another art academy, the Phoenix Art Institute. Soon renamed the New York Phoenix School of Design, it became a coeducational institution. In 1974, the school combined with the Pratt Institute to become the Pratt-New York Phoenix School of Design.

Sonja Eismann (geb. 1973)

Eismann war 2008 Mitbegründerin und Mitherausgeberin des *Missy Magazine*. 1973 in Heidelberg geboren, studierte sie in Wien, Mannheim, Dijon (Frankreich) und Santa Cruz (USA). Sie war 1999 Mitbegründerin der Zeitschrift *nylon. KunstStoff zu Feminismus und Populärkultur* und komoderierte eine zweiwöchentliche Musiksendung zu Pop und Feminismus beim Sender Orange 94.0, Wien. Daneben moderierte sie freiberuflich Jugendradiosendungen und war von 2002 bis 2007 Redakteurin beim Musikmagazin *Intro* in Köln. Sie arbeitete als freie Autorin für *Spex*, *taz*, *Jungle World*, *konkret*. Seit 2007 erhält sie Lehraufträge an Universitäten in Basel, Salzburg und Paderborn sowie an Kunstakademien in Wien, Linz und Zürich. Von 2007 bis 2008 war sie Mitarbeiterin beim Forschungsprojekt „Grrrl Zines" unter

Sonja Eismann (b. 1973)

In 2008, Eismann cofounded and coedited *Missy Magazine*. Born in Heidelberg in 1973, she studied in Vienna, Mannheim, Dijon (France), and Santa Cruz (USA). In 1999, she cofounded the magazine *nylon: KunstStoff zu Feminismus und Populärkultur* (Nylon: art[ificial] material on feminism and popular culture) and cohosted a biweekly music show on pop and feminism at the Vienna radio station orange 94.0. She also worked as a freelance moderator for youth radio programs and an editor at the music magazine *Intro* in Cologne. As a freelance writer, her clients have included the German magazines and newspapers *Spex*, *taz*, *Jungle World*, and *konkret*. Since 2007, she has taught at universities in Basel, Salzburg, and Paderborn and at art academies in Vienna, Linz, and Zurich. From 2007 to 2008, she was a collaborator in the

Leitung von Dr. Elke Zobl in Salzburg. 2007 erschien ihr Sammelband *Hot Topic. Popfeminismus heute*, 2011 war sie Mitherausgeberin von *Craftista. Handarbeit als Aktivismus* und, mit Chris Köver, *Mach's selbst. Do It Yourself für Mädchen*. 2012 stellte sie den Band *absolute fashion* für orange press zusammen.

research project "Grrrl Zines" under the direction of Elke Zobl in Salzburg. In 2007, she published an edited volume *Hot Topic: Popfeminismus heute* (Popfeminism today) and in 2011 she coedited *Craftista: Handarbeit als Aktivismus* (Handicrafts as activism) and, with Chris Köver, *Mach's selbst: Do It Yourself für Mädchen*. In 2012, she edited the volume *absolute fashion* for orange press.

Alexandra Exter (1882–1949)

Exter, geb. Grigorowitsch, war eine ukrainisch-französische Malerin, Designerin und Bühnenbildnerin. Nach dem Studium an der Kunstakademie von Kiew und der Heirat mit ihrem Cousin, einem wohlhabenden Rechtsanwalt, reiste sie bis zum Ausbruch des Ersten Weltkriegs nach Moskau, St. Petersburg, Kiew, Paris, Mailand und Rom und verkehrte in den wichtigen Kunstzirkeln dieser Zeit. Sie begegnete unter anderem Picasso, Léger, Apollinaire, teilte ein Atelier mit einem Künstler des italienischen Futurismus und nahm an allen großen Ausstellungen in Russland, Frankreich und Italien teil. Elemente von Kubismus, Futurismus, Suprematismus und Konstruktivismus flossen in ihre Gestaltung mit ein. Mit Ausbruch des Ersten Weltkriegs kehrte sie nach Russland zurück und schloss sich dem Kreis um Malewitsch an. Wie viele ihrer russischen Kolleginnen versuchte sie, Kunst für das nachrevolutionäre Russland fruchtbar zu machen. Sie unterrichtete Kinder in abstrakter Malerei mit geometrischen Formen und Rhythmus der Farben, arbeitete als Designerin und setzte sich für eine ganz neue Praktikabilität von Kleidung ein, wofür sie Mode- und Stoffdesigns entwarf. 1916 begann sie ihre fruchtbare Zusammenarbeit mit dem Leiter des Moskauer Kammertheaters, Alexander Tairow, im Rahmen derer sie eine neuartige Synthese von Bühnenbild, Kostümen und Schauspiel schuf. 1918 richtete sie sich ein Atelier in Kiew ein, in dem sie auch junge Künstler*innen unterrichtete. Zusammen mit ihren Schüler*innen stattete sie die großen Propagandaschiffe auf dem Dnjepr aus und bemalte einige der Propagandazüge, die durch das ganze Land fuhren. Nach der Gründung der Sowjetunion 1922 und Lenins Tod emigrierte Exter 1924 mit ihrem Mann nach Paris, entwarf Ballettkostüme und unterrichtete von 1926 bis 1930 an der Académie Moderne von Fernand Léger. Sie blieb bis zu ihrem Tod in Frankreich.

Aleksandra Ekster (1882–1949)

Ekster, née Grigorovich, was a Ukrainian-French painter, designer, and stage designer. After studying at the Kiev Art Academy and marrying her cousin, a wealthy lawyer, she traveled to Moscow, St. Petersburg, Kiev, Paris, Milan, and Rome until the outbreak of World War I. Frequenting the important art circles of the time, she met artists such as Picasso, Léger, and Apollinaire, shared a studio with an Italian futurist artist, and participated in all the major exhibitions in Russia, France, and Italy. Her design incorporated elements of cubism, futurism, suprematism, and constructivism. With the outbreak of World War I, she returned to Russia and joined the circle around Malevich. Like many of her Russian colleagues, she tried to make art a fertile contributor to postrevolutionary Russia. She employed abstract painting with geometric shapes and rhythmic color to teach children abstract painting, worked as a designer, and advocated for a totally new understanding of practical clothing, for which she created fashion and fabric designs. In 1916, she began her fruitful collaboration with the director of the Moscow Chamber Theater, Alexander Tairov, creating a novel synthesis of stage design, costumes, and acting. In 1918, she set up a studio in Kiev where she also taught young artists. Together with her students, she outfitted the large propaganda ships on the Dnieper and painted some of the propaganda trains that traveled throughout the country. After the founding of the Soviet Union in 1922 and Lenin's subsequent death, Ekster emigrated to Paris with her husband, designed ballet costumes, and taught at Fernand Léger's Académie Moderne from 1926 to 1930. She remained in France until her death.

Maryam Fanni

Die schwedische Grafikdesignerin Fanni lebt und arbeitet in Stockholm und Göteborg. Sie ist PhD-Studierende für Design an der HDK-Valand Academy of Art and Design, Universität Göteborg, sowie Mitbegründerin und Mitglied der Kollektive MMS, SIFAV und Mapping the Unjust City.

Bea (Beatriz) Feitler (1938–1982)

Feitler wurde in Rio de Janeiro, Brasilien, geboren, wohin ihre aus Deutschland stammenden jüdischen Eltern vor den Nationalsozialisten geflohen waren. Die meiste Zeit über lebte sie in den USA, wo sie die Parson's School of Design in New York City bis 1959 besuchte, die heute noch große Teile ihres Archivs verwaltet. Nach ihrem Examen in New York kehrte sie zurück nach Rio de Janeiro, um dort Kunst zu studieren. Gemeinsam mit zwei anderen Grafikdesigner*innen gründete sie das Estudio G, das sich auf Plakate, Plattencover und Buchdesign spezialisierte. Zusammen mit einer Werbeagentur arbeitete sie für das progressive Magazin *Senhor*. Bekannt wurde sie vor allem als Grafikdesignerin und Art-Direktorin von *Harper's Bazaar*, *Ms.*, *Rolling Stone* und *Vanity Fair*. Bei *Harper's Bazaar* arbeitete sie eng zusammen mit Ruth Ansel, beide reagierten visuell stark auf den politischen und kulturellen Wandel der 1960er Jahre. 1965 schuf sie mit Richard Avedon gemeinsam das ikonische Titelbild mit dem Model Jean Shrimpton. 1972 verließ Feitler *Harper's Bazaar*, um mit Gloria Steinem das feministische Magazin *Ms.* herauszugeben. Sie war dort Art-Direktorin und kreierte eine experimentelle Mischung aus Fotografie, Illustration und typografischen Elementen. Sie blieb bis 1974 bei *Ms.* und gestaltete einige Titelblätter. Zwischen 1974 und 1980 lehrte sie Design an der School of Visual Arts (SVA) und entwickelte zusammen mit Christian Dior, Diane von Fürstenberg, Bill Haire und Calvin Klein einige Plakate und Kostüme für die Alvin Alley Dance Company. Feitler entwarf zudem Plattenhüllen für die Rolling Stones und arbeitete sechs Jahre mit der Band zusammen. Als sie begann, für *Vanity Fair* zu entwerfen, war sie bereits mit einer seltenen Art von Krebs gezeichnet. Sie erlag der Krankheit im Alter von 44 Jahren.

Matilda Flodmark

Flodmark ist, zusammen mit Maryam Fanni und Sara Kaaman, Mitglied der schwedischen Gruppe MMS. Sie absolvierte einen Master of Arts an der Konstfack University of Craft and Design, 2011. Seitdem arbeitet sie als Art-Direktorin sowie Grafikdesignerin und künstlerisch mit handgemachtem Papier.

Maryam Fanni

A Swedish graphic designer, Fanni lives and works in Stockholm and Gothenburg. She is a PhD student in design at HDK-Valand Academy of Art and Design, University of Gothenburg, and a cofounder and member of the collectives MMS, SIFAV, and Mapping the Unjust City.

Bea (Beatriz) Feitler (1938–1982)

Feitler was born in Rio de Janeiro, Brazil, where her German-born Jewish parents had fled the Nazis. She lived for most of her life in the United States, where she attended Parson's School of Design in New York City until 1959, which still administers large portions of her archive. After graduating in New York, she returned to Rio de Janeiro to study art. Along with two other graphic designers she founded Estudio G, which specialized in posters, record covers, and book design, while also working for the progressive magazine *Senhor* in cooperation with an advertising agency. She became best known as a graphic designer and art director for *Harper's Bazaar*, *Ms.*, *Rolling Stone*, and *Vanity Fair*. At *Harper's Bazaar*, she worked closely with Ruth Ansel; through their visual designs, both women articulated potent responses to the political and cultural changes of the 1960s. In 1965, she collaborated with Richard Avedon to create their now iconic cover photo featuring model Jean Shrimpton. In 1972 Feitler left *Harper's Bazaar* to found, with Gloria Steinem, the feminist magazine *Ms.* At *Ms.*, she held the position of art director, which she used to create an experimental mix of photography, illustration, and typography. She remained with *Ms.* until 1974, designing a number of its covers. Between 1974 and 1980, she taught design at the School of Visual Arts (SVA) and developed several posters and costumes for the Alvin Alley Dance Company with Christian Dior, Diane von Fürstenberg, Bill Haire, and Calvin Klein. Feitler also designed record sleeves for the Rolling Stones, working with the band for six years. When she started working for *Vanity Fair*, she was already suffering from a rare type of cancer. She succumbed to the disease at the age of forty-four.

Matilda Flodmark

Together with Maryam Fanni and Sara Kaaman, Flodmark is a member of the Swedish group MMS. She graduated with a master of arts degree from Konstfack University of Craft and Design in 2011. Since then, she has been working as an art director and graphic designer and, in her art practice, with handmade paper.

Evelyn Gleeson (1855–1944)

Gleeson war eine englische Stickerei-, Teppich- und Wandteppichdesignerin. Sie war mit der Familie Yeats und anderen irischen Künstlerkreisen in London bekannt und ließ sich von der romantischen Vorstellung einer irischen Renaissance in Kunst und Literatur inspirieren. Sie engagierte sich in der Suffragettenbewegung und war Vorsitzende des Londoner Frauenclubs Pioneer Club. Zusammen mit Elizabeth und Lily Yeats gründete sie 1902 die Dun Emer Guild mit dem Ziel, junge Frauen in Buchbinderei und Druckerei sowie in Stickerei und Weberei auszubilden. Im Sommer 1902 fand Gleeson ein geeignetes Haus namens Runnymede in Dundrum, einem Vorort von Dublin. Lily Yeats leitete die Stickerei-Abteilung, denn sie hatte bei May Morris, der Tochter von William Morris, gelernt. Elizabeth Yeats leitete die Druckerei, wobei sie auf ihre Erfahrungen bei der Women's Printing Society in London zurückgreifen konnte. Sie war im übrigen Fröbel- und Kunstlehrerin. Gleeson war mit der Weberei und der Tapisserie betraut und verwaltete die Finanzen des Verlags. Die Werkstatt beschäftigte und bildete nur einheimische Mädchen aus. Der Schwerpunkt bei den Textilien lag auf der Verwendung hochwertiger irischer Materialien, um schöne, luxuriöse und dauerhafte gestaltete Objekte zu schaffen. Bis 1905 beschäftigte die Werkstatt 30 Frauen und Mädchen. Ein großer Teil der Aufträge kam von der katholischen Kirche. Weil die Zusammenarbeit nicht harmonisch verlief, wurde Dun Emer 1904 zwischen Gleeson und den Yeats-Schwestern aufgeteilt. Die Dun Emer Guild florierte weiter, wobei Gleeson mit ihrer Nichte Katherine MacCormack und Augustine Henrys Nichte May Kerley an Entwürfen arbeitete. 1910 wurde Gleeson eines der Gründungsmitglieder der Guild of Irish Art Workers und 1917 Meisterin. 1912 zogen die Werkstätten von Dundrum in die Hardwicke Street in Dublin um.

Natalja Gontscharowa (1881–1962)

Gontscharowa wurde als Tochter eines Architekten geboren und wuchs im Hause ihrer Großmutter auf. Ab 1898 studierte sie Bildhauerei an der Moskauer Hochschule für Malerei, Bildhauerei und Architektur. Dort begegnete sie dem Maler Michail Larionow, mit dem sie eine lebenslange Partnerschaft verband. 1906 zeigte sie ihre Arbeiten anlässlich des Pariser „Salon d'Automne" erstmals im westlichen Ausland. Zusammen mit Larionow nahm sie in den Jahren bis zum Ersten Weltkrieg an entscheidenden Ausstellungen der Avantgarde im Westen teil, unter anderem am „Blauen Reiter" 1912 in München und am „Ersten Deutschen Herbstsalon" 1913 in Berlin. 1910 war sie zusammen mit Larionow Gründerin der Künstlervereinigung

Evelyn Gleeson (1855–1944)

Gleeson was an English designer of embroidery, carpets, and tapestries. She was acquainted with the Yeats family and other Irish artistic circles in London and was inspired by the Romantic notion of an Irish Renaissance in art and literature. She was involved in the suffragette movement and was president of the Pioneer Club, a women's club in London. Together with Elizabeth and Lily Yeats, she founded the Dun Emer Guild in 1902, which sought to train young women in bookbinding and printing, in addition to embroidery and weaving. In the summer of 1902, Gleeson found a suitable location for the Guild, a house called Runnymede, in Dundrum, a suburb of Dublin. Lily Yeats headed its embroidery department, having learned from May Morris, daughter of William Morris. Elizabeth Yeats ran the print shop, drawing on her experience at the Women's Printing Society in London. She was also a children's teacher who followed the Froebel method and an art teacher. Gleeson was in charge of weaving and tapestry and managed the finances of the publishing house. The workshop employed and trained only local girls. For textiles, emphasis was placed on using high-quality Irish materials to create designed objects that were beautiful, luxurious, and durable. By 1905, the workshop employed thirty women and girls. A large fraction of the orders came from the Catholic Church. Because the collaboration was marked by tension, Dun Emer was divided between Gleeson and the Yeats sisters in 1904. The Dun Emer Guild continued to flourish, with Gleeson working on designs with her niece Katherine MacCormack and Augustine Henry's niece May Kerley. In 1910, Gleeson became one of the founding members of the Guild of Irish Art Workers, achieving the status of master in 1917. In 1912, the Dundrum workshops moved to Hardwicke Street in Dublin.

Natalia Goncharova (1881–1962)

Goncharova was born the daughter of an architect and grew up in her grandmother's house. Beginning in 1898, she studied sculpture at the Moscow College of Painting, Sculpture, and Architecture. It was at the college that she met the painter Mikhail Larionov, with whom she formed a lifelong partnership. In 1906 she showed her work for the first time in the West on the occasion of the Paris Salon d'Automne. Together with Larionov, she participated in important exhibitions showing work from the avant-garde in the West in the years leading up to World War I, including the *Blauer Reiter* in Munich in 1912 and the *Erster Deutscher Herbstsalon* in Berlin in 1913. In 1910, together with Larionov, she was the founder of the artists'

Karo-Bube, verließ diese aber bald wieder. 1912 gründeten die beiden die Gruppe Eselsschwanz. 1913 begann ihre produktivste Phase. Gleichzeitig erschien die erste Monografie über die Künstlerin. 1913 veranstaltete sie gemeinsam mit Larionow die Ausstellung „Zielscheibe" in der erstmals rayonistische Arbeiten gezeigt wurden. Im selben Jahr hatte sie als erste Frau in Russland eine Einzelausstellung, in dieser Retrospektive zeigte sie über 800 Arbeiten.

Gontscharowa war in erster Linie bildende Künstlerin, arbeitete aber auch in vielen Bereichen der angewandten Kunst, wie dem Bühnenbild und der Buchillustration. Bis zu ihrer Emigration aus Russland 1914 nach Frankreich trug sie maßgeblich zum künstlerischen Entwicklungsprozess der russischen Avantgarde bei. 1916 unternahm sie gemeinsam mit Sergej Diaghilev und Larionow eine Reise nach Spanien. Ab 1918 lebten Gontscharowa und Larionow kontinuierlich in Paris. In ihrem neuen Daueraufenthalt in Paris schuf sie 1929 im Todesjahr des Impresarios Sergei Pawlowitsch Diaghilev die Bühnenbilder der berühmten Ballets Russes. Anschließend wurde sie weltweit als Bühnenbildnerin engagiert, beispielsweise in USA, Litauen, Lateinamerika, England und Russland.

Gontscharowa war Kennerin der Ikonenmalerei und der russischen Volkskunst der sogenannten Lubki. Die Stile dieser Gattungen brachte sie nun in ihre Bilder ein und entwickelte den neoprimitivistischen Stil der russischen Avantgarde. Provokativ distanzierte sie sich von der westlichen Kunst. Sie illustrierte verschiedene Bücher russischer Futuristen.

Erst 1955 heiratete das Paar, dessen letzte Lebensjahre von Krankheit und Armut geprägt waren. 1962 verstarb Gontscharowa.

association Karo-Bube, though she soon left the group. In 1912, the two founded the group Eselsschwanz. The year 1913 marked the beginning of their most productive phase. At the same time, the first monograph about her was published. In 1913, together with Larionov, she organized the exhibition *Zielscheibe*, which showed rayonistic works for the first time. In the same year she became the first woman to have a solo exhibition in Russia; the retrospective showed over 800 works.

Goncharova was primarily a visual artist, but she also worked in many areas of applied art, such as stage design and book illustration. Until her emigration from Russia to France in 1914, she made major contributions to the artistic development of the Russian avant-garde. In 1916, she traveled to Spain together with Sergei Diaghilev and Larionov. Beginning in 1918, Goncharova and Larionov lived continuously in Paris. Now permanently settled in Paris, she created the stage designs for the famous Ballets Russes in 1929, the year in which the impresario Sergei Pavlovich Diaghilev died. She was subsequently engaged as a stage designer worldwide, in places including the United States, Lithuania, Latin America, England, and Russia.

Goncharova was an expert on icon painting and of the Russian folk art prints known as lubki. She integrated the styles of these genres into her paintings, developing the neoprimitivist style of the Russian avant-garde and provocatively distancing herself from Western art. She also illustrated various books by Russian futurists.

The couple, whose last years were marked by illness and poverty, did not marry until 1955. Goncharova died in 1962.

Bertha Matilda Sprinks Goudy (1869–1935)

Goudy war eine amerikanische Typografin und Mitinhaberin der Village Press in Oak Park, Illinois. Ab 1903 führte sie die Druckerei zusammen mit ihrem Mann, dem renommierten Typografen Frederic W. Goudy. Ein Jahr später zog das Ehepaar nach Hingham, Massachusetts, und 1906 nach New York City. Nach ihrem Tod 1935 forderten andere Frauen im Buchgewerbe Kollegen und Freunde von Bertha Goudy auf, an ihren Beitrag zur Typografie zu erinnern. Unter der Leitung von Edna Beilenson, Miteigentümerin der Peter Pauper Press, fand sich eine Gruppe zusammen, um 1937 das feministische Werk *Bookmaking on the Distaff Side* zu veröffentlichen. Zwei Jahre später veröffentlichte Frederic W. Goudy eine Hommage an seine Frau unter dem Titel *Bertha S. Goudy. Recollections by One Who Knew Her Best* (Marlboro, NY, The Village Press, 1939). Die Frauen der Distaff Press publizierten 1958 *Bertha S. Goudy. First Lady of Printing*. Die AIGA (American Institute of Graphic Arts) würdigte ihre Arbeit in einer

Bertha Matilda Sprinks Goudy (1869–1935)

Goudy was an American typographer and coowner of the Village Press in Oak Park, Illinois. Beginning in 1903, she ran the print shop together with her husband, the renowned typographer Frederic W. Goudy. A year later the couple moved to Hingham, Massachusetts, and in 1906 to New York City. After her death in 1935, other women in the book trade called on colleagues and friends of Bertha Goudy to commemorate her contribution to typography. Under the leadership of Edna Beilenson, coowner of the Peter Pauper Press, a group came together to publish the feminist work *Bookmaking on the Distaff Side* in 1937. Two years later, Frederic W. Goudy published a tribute to his wife under the title *Bertha M. Goudy: Recollections by One Who Knew Her Best* (Marlboro, NY: The Village Press, 1939), while the women of the Distaff Press published *Bertha S. Goudy: First Lady of Printing*, in 1958. The AIGA (American Institute of Graphic Arts) honored her work in an exhibit celebrating the thirtieth anni-

Natalja Gontscharowa, vor/before 1917

Ausstellung zum 30. Gründungsjubiläum der Village Press. Eines ihrer bekanntesten Werke war 1934 die Edition von Mary Shelleys *Frankenstein*. In Erinnerung an seine Frau Bertha M. Goudy gab Frederic Goudy seiner 100. Schrifttype den Namen Bertham.

versary of the Village Press. One of her most famous works was the 1934 edition of Mary Shelley's *Frankenstein*. In memory of his wife Bertha M. Goudy, Frederic Goudy named his one-hundredth typeface Bertham.

Kate Greenaway (1846–1901)

Greenaway war in erster Linie Illustratorin von Kinderbüchern. Wenngleich nicht im eigentlichen Sinne Grafikdesignerin, gestaltete sie auch die Einbände, Buchumschläge und Titel ihrer Bücher mit ihren Illustrationen. Sie entwickelte einen eigenen Stil, der viele Nachahmer*innen fand. Greenaway stammte aus Hoxton im Osten von London. Ihr Vater war Zeichner und Holzschnittkünstler, der für die *Illustrated London News* und *Punch* arbeitete, was ihre Begabung sicherlich förderte. Ihre Mutter war Näherin und Putzmacherin, sie unterhielt später ein Damenausstatter-Geschäft in Islington. Kates Begabung, Kinderkleider zu entwerfen, ging offensichtlich auf die Arbeit ihrer Mutter zurück. Die Liebe zur Natur hat sie durch lange Aufenthalte bei der Verwandtschaft auf dem Land erworben. Schon mit zwölf Jahren war sie Preisträgerin der South Kensington School of Art. Sie besuchte die Schule Heatherleys und die neu eröffnete Slade School of Fine Art. Greenaway war bereits in jungen Jahren erfolgreich, erwarb Preise, verfertigte Illustrationen für Zeitschriften wie *The Graphic* und *Illustrated London News*. Später erhielt sie einen mehrjährigen Vertrag mit dem renommierten Verlag Charles Scribner's Sons, der ihr ein stattliches Einkommen sicherte. Ihre Zusammenarbeit mit dem amerikanischen *The Ladies' Home Journal* war darüber hinaus hochprofitabel. Sie konnte es sich sogar leisten, den berühmten Architekten Richard Norman Shaw mit dem Bau eines Hauses zu beauftragen. Greenaways Kinderbücher wurden in zahlreiche Sprachen übersetzt; Museen und Galerien stellten ihre Arbeiten aus.

Kate Greenaway (1846–1901)

Greenaway was primarily an illustrator of children's books. Though not a graphic designer in the true sense, she also employed her own illustrations to design the covers, book jackets, and titles of her books. She developed her own style, which found many imitators. She hailed from Hoxton in east London. Her father was a draftsman and woodcut artist who worked for the *Illustrated London News* and *Punch*—a background that certainly encouraged her talent. Her mother was a seamstress and milliner, and she later ran a ladies' outfitter store in Islington; Kate's talent for designing children's clothes can clearly be traced back to her mother's work. She acquired her love of nature through long stays with relatives in the countryside. At the age of twelve she had already been recognized with a prize from the South Kensington School of Art. She attended Heatherley's School of Fine Art and the newly opened Slade School of Fine Art. Greenaway was successful at a young age, winning awards and producing illustrations for magazines such as *The Graphic* and *Illustrated London News*. Later she received a multiyear contract with the renowned publisher Charles Scribner's Sons, securing her a handsome income. Her collaboration with *The Ladies' Home Journal* in the United States was also highly lucrative. She even had the funds to hire the famous architect Richard Norman Shaw to build her residence. Greenaway's children's books have been translated into numerous languages, and many museums and galleries have exhibited her work.

April Greiman (geb. 1948)

Greiman ist eine der berühmten US-amerikanischen Grafikdesignerinnen und Typografinnen, die für ihre Arbeiten viele Auszeichnungen erhielt. Besonders einflussreich wurde sie durch den Einsatz digitaler Medien. In Long Island City geboren, studierte Greiman von 1966 bis 1970 Grafikdesign am Kansas City Art Institute und von 1970 bis 1971 in Basel an der Allgemeinen Kunstgewerbeschule, der heutigen Schule für Gestaltung. Dort war sie Schülerin von Armin Hofmann und Wolfgang Weingart. Danach arbeitete Greiman als Grafikdesignerin in New York und lehrte gleichzeitig am Philadelphia College of Art. 1976 zog sie nach Kalifornien und eröffnete in Los Angeles ihr Grafikbüro Made in Space, Inc. Zusammen mit dem Fotografen Jayme Odgers entwarf sie 1977

April Greiman (b. 1948)

Greiman is among the famous American graphic designers and typographers who have received many awards for their work. She became particularly influential through the use of digital media. Born in Long Island City, Greiman studied graphic design at the Kansas City Art Institute from 1966 to 1970 and in Basel at the Allgemeine Kunstgewerbeschule, now the Schule für Gestaltung, from 1970 to 1971. In Basel, she was a student of Armin Hofmann and Wolfgang Weingart. Greiman then worked as a graphic designer in New York while teaching at the Philadelphia College of Art. In 1976, she moved to California and opened her graphic design firm Made in Space, Inc. in Los Angeles. Together with photographer Jayme Odgers, she designed a poster for the California Institute

ein Plakat für das California Institute of Art, das in die Designgeschichte des New Wave eingegangen ist. Dem Rationalismus der Schweizer Schule weiterhin verpflichtet, verband sie ihren Grafikstil mit der amerikanischen Postmoderne. Ihre Grafiken sind oft collageartig zusammengefügt aus Schichten von Schrift und Bild. Man spricht ihr zu, den California-New-Wave-Stil mit seiner visuellen Transmedia-Sprache geprägt zu haben. In den 1980er Jahren wandte sie die Möglichkeiten der digitalen Medien an und entdeckte deren gestalterisches Potenzial. 1982 wurde sie Leiterin der Designabteilung des California Institute of the Arts. 1990 veröffentlichte sie das Buch *Hybrid Imagery. The Fusion of Technology and Graphic Design*. Sie arbeitet für zahlreiche berühmte Firmen der sogenannten Neuen Medien und für berühmte Architekturbüros.

of Art in 1977 that has gone down in new wave design history. Remaining committed to the rationalism of the Swiss school, she combined her graphic style with American postmodernism. Her graphics often resemble collages composed of layers of writing and images. She is credited with shaping the California new wave style with its visual, transmedial language. In the 1980s, she turned her attention to the possibilities of digital media to explore their creative potential. In 1982, she became head of the design department at the California Institute of the Arts. Her book *Hybrid Imagery: The Fusion of Technology and Graphic Design* was published in 1990. She works for a number of high-profile companies dealing with new media and for eminent architectural firms.

Kirsten Grimstad

Grimstad ist Literaturwissenschaftlerin. Sie gab 1973, zusammen mit Susan Rennie, den *The New Woman's Survival Catalog* heraus, ebenso die ersten zehn Hefte von *Chrysalis*. Geboren wurde sie in Wauwatosa, Wisconsin. Sie schloss ihr Studium mit einem Bachelor in Germanistik am Barnard College, einem Master in deutscher Sprache und Literatur an der Columbia University und einem PhD in Komparatistik am Union Institute & University ab. Ihr Interesse an deutscher Literatur und Geschichte geht auf einen Studienaufenthalt in Deutschland zurück. Nach 16 Jahren als Co-Direktorin des Master-Programms am Vermont College lehrt sie seit 2005 Literatur an der Antioch University, Los Angeles. Zurzeit ist sie Rätin des Getty Villa Council, einem von vier Councils des Getty Trusts, die kulturelle Programme unterstützen.

Kirsten Grimstad

Grimstad is a literary scholar. Working with Susan Rennin, in 1973 she published *The New Woman's Survival Catalog* as well as the first ten issues of *Chrysalis*. Born Wauwatosa, Wisconsin, she graduated with a BA in German studies from Barnard College, an MA in German language and literature from Columbia University, and a PhD in comparative literature from Union Institute & University. Her interest in German literature and history dates back to a visit she made to Germany as a student. After sixteen years as codirector of the master's program at Vermont College, she moved to Antioch University, Los Angeles, where she has taught literature since 2005. She is currently a member of the Getty Villa Council, one of four councils of the Getty Trust that support cultural programs.

Eva Grossberg (1924–2014)

Grossberg war die älteste Tochter des Industriemalers der Neuen Sachlichkeit, Carl Grossberg, ihre Mutter war die Musikerin Tilde, geb. Schwarz. Grossberg absolvierte 1943 ihr Abitur in Heidelberg und leistete danach (1943/44) ein Jahr Arbeitsdienst im Elsass. Von 1944 bis 1945 studierte sie an der Hochschule für Baukunst und Bildende Künste in Weimar Bühnenbild. Danach arbeitete sie als freie Malerin im Sommerhäuser Atelier ihres bereits 1940 verstorbenen Vaters. Grossberg war von 1947 bis 1989 Produkt- und Interiordesignerin bei der Firma Bahlsen. Sie gestaltete dort über 250 Luxus- und Geschenkdosen, die nach wie vor als Sammelobjekte gehandelt werden. Darüber hinaus entwarf sie Innengestaltungen für das Hannoveraner Stammhaus und prägte in der Zeit nach 1945 die Ausstattung der Firmengebäude. Von 1961 bis 1971 war sie außerdem verantwortlich für alle grafischen Arbeiten der Porzellanmanufaktur Fürstenberg.

Eva Grossberg (1924–2014)

Grossberg was the eldest daughter of Carl Grossberg, an industrial painter of new objectivity; her mother was the musician Tilde, née Schwarz. Grossberg graduated from high school in Heidelberg in 1943 and then in 1943/44 did a year of labor service in Alsace. From 1944 to 1945 she studied stage design at the Hochschule für Baukunst und Bildende Künste in Weimar. After that, she worked as a freelance painter in the Sommerhausen studio of her father, who had died in 1940. From 1947 to 1989, Grossberg was a product and interior designer at the company Bahlsen. At Bahlsen, she designed more than 250 luxury and gift boxes, which are still traded as collector's items. She also designed interiors for the company's Hannover headquarters and made her mark on the furnishings of the company's buildings in the period after 1945. From 1961 to 1971, she was also responsible for all graphic works at the Fürstenberg porcelain manufactory.

Guerrilla Girls

Die Guerrilla Girls sind eine bis heute anonym operierende Gruppe von Künstlerinnen in New York. Bekannt wurde die erste Gruppe 1985 mit einer spektakulären Aktion: Sie drang mit Gorillamasken bekleidet in das MoMA ein und machte, laut Plakat, darauf aufmerksam, dass in der Ausstellung „An International Survey of Recent Painting and Sculpture" zwar viele nackte Frauen zu sehen, neben 152 Künstlern jedoch nur 13 Künstlerinnen namentlich vertreten waren. Mit der Ausstellung war das neu renovierte und erweiterte Gebäude des MoMA 1984 eröffnet worden. Die Schau sollte einen Überblick über die bedeutendsten zeitgenössischen Künstler*innen vermitteln, die meisten von ihnen stammten aus Europa und den USA. Weitere Aktionen der Gruppe wiederholten sich in ähnlicher Form auch außerhalb der USA. Die Frauen arbeiteten mit schwarzen Blockbuchstaben auf weißem Papier, plakatierten anfangs nachts in SoHo oder East Village, verteilten später dann auch tagsüber Postkarten, Flyer und Plakate und forderten zur Mitarbeit auf. Die Guerrilla Girls arbeiten mit der Kulturtechnik des Culture Jamming, einer Guerillatechnik der Antiwerbung mit Störaktionen in Form von Postern, Publikationen, öffentlichen Auftritten und Aktionen. Sie kritisieren den Kunstbetrieb, insbesondere den vorherrschenden Sexismus und Rassismus. Gorillamasken tragen sie auch deshalb, um den Fokus auf Themen zu lenken und nicht auf die agierenden Künstlerinnen. Zur Anonymität tragen Pseudonyme bei, die meist auf verstorbene Künstlerinnen zurückgehen, wie Frida Kahlo, Käthe Kollwitz, Eva Hesse, Georgia O'Keefe und andere.

Jelena Guro (ca. 1877–1913)

Guro war eine russische Künstlerin, Buchillustratorin und Schriftstellerin und gilt bis heute als Multitalent. 1906 besuchte sie die private Kunstschule von Jelisaweta Swanzewa (1864–1921) in St. Petersburg, wo sie ihren Lebensgefährten und späteren Ehemann Michail Matjuschin kennenlernte. Mit ihm zusammen schloss sie sich zwischen 1909 und 1910 einer Impressionist*innengruppe an, mit der sie ihre Werke ausstellte. Sie hatte eine besondere Vorliebe für Landschaften, insbesondere für die Dünenlandschaft an der finnischen Küste nördlich von St. Petersburg, wo sie ein Sommerhaus besaß.

Guerrilla Girls

The Guerrilla Girls are a group of women artists in New York who have always operated anonymously. The group first became known in 1985 with a spectacular action: they barged into MoMA dressed in gorilla masks in order to draw attention to the fact, proclaimed on the posters they were carrying, that even though the exhibition *An International Survey of Recent Painting and Sculpture* featured many naked women, there were only 13 named women artists in the show compared to 152 men. The exhibition marked the opening of MoMA's newly renovated and expanded building in 1984. It was intended to provide an overview of the most significant contemporary artists, mostly figures from Europe and the United States. Further actions by the group were later repeated in similar form outside the United States. The women worked with black block letters on white paper, at first hanging their posters in SoHo or the East Village at night, later distributing postcards, flyers, and posters during the day as well, with a call for others to join them. The Guerrilla Girls work with the cultural strategy of culture jamming, a guerrilla technique of antipublicity that employs disruptive actions in the form of posters, publications, public appearances, and other activities. Their disruptions criticize the art business, especially its prevailing sexism and racism. The women also wear gorilla masks to direct attention to issues instead of the artists themselves. Their anonymity is further supported by pseudonyms based mostly on deceased female artists, such as Frida Kahlo, Käthe Kollwitz, Eva Hesse, Georgia O'Keefe, and others.

Jelena Guro (ca. 1877–1913)

Guro was a Russian artist, book illustrator, and writer but is known for being gifted in many areas. In 1906, she attended the private art school of Yelizaveta Zvantseva (1864–1921) in St. Petersburg, where she met her partner and later husband Mikhail Matyushin. Between 1909 and 1910, she joined a group of impressionists with whom she exhibited her works. She had a particular fondness for landscapes, especially the dune landscape on the Finnish coast north of St. Petersburg, where she owned a summer house.

Harmony Hammond (geb. 1944)

Die Künstlerin, Aktivistin und Schriftstellerin Hammond war eine bedeutende Vertreterin der feministischen Kunstbewegung der 1970er Jahre in New York und beteiligt an der Zeitschrift *Heresies*. Hammond wurde in Home-town, Illinois, geboren, zog nach Minneapolis und schloss dort 1967 ihr Studium an der University of Minnesota mit einem Bachelor in Malerei ab. Zusammen mit ihrem Ehemann zog sie 1969 nach New York, einige Monate nach den Stonewall Riots, den Protesten der Gay Community. Nach der Geburt ihrer Tochter trennte sie sich von ihrem Mann und begann ein lesbisches Leben. Hammond war 1972 Mitbegründerin der A.I.R. Gallery, einer von einem Frauenkollektiv geführten Kunstgalerie in New York, und 1976 von *Heresies. A Feminist Publication on Art and Politics*, deren Nummern 1, 3 und 9 sie bespielte. Insgesamt veröffentlichte sie Artikel in sieben Ausgaben der Zeitschrift. Sie war auch Lehrerin am New York Feminist Art Institute. Hammond kuratierte zahlreiche Ausstellungen lesbischer Kunst, beispielsweise „A Lesbian Show", 1978, und publizierte zu diesem Thema. 1984 zog sie nach New Mexico, wo sie bis heute lebt und arbeitet. Von 1988 bis 2005 lehrte sie an der University of Arizona in Tucson zu den Themen feministische, lesbische Kunst und Queer Art.

Harmony Hammond (b. 1944)

Hammond, an artist, activist, and writer, was a major figure in the feminist art movement of 1970s New York and involved in the magazine *Heresies*. Born in Hometown, Illinois, Hammond moved to Minneapolis and graduated from the University of Minnesota in 1967 with a bachelor's degree in painting. Together with her husband, she moved to New York in 1969, a few months after the Stonewall Riots launched by the queer community. After the birth of her daughter, she separated from her husband and began living as a lesbian. In 1972, Hammond cofounded the A.I.R. Gallery, an art gallery in New York run by a women's collective, and in 1976 she also cofounded *Heresies: A Feminist Publication on Art and Politics*, contributing to issues 1, 3, and 9. In total, she published articles in seven issues of the magazine. She also taught at the New York Feminist Art Institute. Hammond has curated numerous exhibitions of lesbian art, such as *A Lesbian Show* in 1978, in addition to publishing on the subject. In 1984, she moved to New Mexico, where she continues to live and work. From 1988 to 2005, she taught feminist, lesbian, and queer art at the University of Arizona in Tucson.

Sylvia Harris (1953–2011)

Die Schwarze US-amerikanische Grafikdesignerin und Dozentin wuchs in Richmond, Virginia, auf zu einer Zeit, in der die Bürgerrechtsbewegung auf dem Höhepunkt war. People of Color waren zu jener Zeit im Grafikdesign kaum vertreten. Harris hatte das Glück, sich auf unterstützende Mentoren wie Philip Meggs und Chris Pullman berufen zu können. Anfangs war sie in zwei der renommiertesten Architekturbüros Amerikas ausgebildet worden: unter Leitung von Walter Gropius in dessen amerikanischem Büro, The Architects Collaborative (TAC), und bei Skidmore, Owings und Merrill. Dann studierte sie Kommunikationsdesign an der Virginia Commonwealth University in Richmond und arbeitete anschließend beim öffentlich-rechtlichen Fernsehen der in Boston. Nach dem Bachelor-Abschluss 1975 erwarb sie 1980 den Master of Fine Arts an der Yale University. 1980 gründete Harris ihr eigenes Büro, Two Twelve Associates. Sie unterrichtete an der Purchase College State University in New York sowie im Grafikdesign-Programm von Yale und war Gastdozentin an verschiedenen Museen und Universitäten. 1994 gründete sie eine zweite Firma, Sylvia Harris, LLC, und spezialisierte sich auf die Gestaltung öffentlicher Informationssysteme. Ihr weiteres Büro Citizen Research & Design konzentrierte sich auf das Potenzial

Sylvia Harris (1953–2011)

A Black American graphic designer and lecturer, Harris grew up in Richmond, Virginia, at the height of the civil rights movement. People of color were scarcely represented in graphic design at the time. Harris was fortunate to be able to call on supportive mentors such as Philip Meggs and Chris Pullman. Initially, she had trained at two of America's most prestigious architectural firms: under the direction of Walter Gropius at his American office, The Architects Collaborative (TAC), and at Skidmore, Owings and Merrill. She then studied communication design at Virginia Commonwealth University in Richmond and went on to work at the public television station in Boston. After earning a bachelor's degree in 1975, she continued her studies, earning a master of fine arts degree from Yale University in 1980. In 1980, Harris founded her own firm, Two Twelve Associates. She taught at Purchase College State University in New York and in Yale's graphic design program and served as a guest lecturer at various museums and universities. In 1994, she founded a second firm, Sylvia Harris, LLC specializing in public information systems design. Her other practice, Citizen Research & Design, focused on the potential of graphic design in public spaces. Her work also includes the design of the Central Park Zoo, New York,

von Grafikdesign im öffentlichen Raum. Zu ihren Arbeiten zählen ferner die Gestaltung des Central Park Zoo, New York, das Design des United States Census Bureau, Census 2000, und ihre Briefmarkenentwürfe. Harris war Mitbegründerin der Public Policy LAB, ein Laboratorium, das mittels Design, multidisziplinärer Forschungen und entsprechender Strategien helfen soll, den öffentlichen Raum zu verbessern. Ihr zu Ehren wird der Sylvia Harris Citizen Design Award verliehen. 2014 erhielt sie die Ehrenmedaille der AIGA (American Institute of Graphic Arts).

a redesign of the census form for the U.S. Census Bureau in 2000, and stamps. Harris cofounded the Public Policy LAB, a laboratory designed to help improve public spaces through design, multidisciplinary research, and related strategies. The Sylvia Harris Citizen Design Award is presented in her honor. In 2014 she received the Medal of Honor of the AIGA (American Institute of Graphic Arts).

Deborah Hart

Hart war, zusammen mit Lilian Mohin und Sheila Shulman, Gründerin der Onlywomen Press, auch als The Women's Press bekannt. Die in London ansässige Druckerei war ein feministisches Unternehmen, hervorgegangen aus einer Gruppe lesbischer Schriftstellerinnen, die ihre Werke veröffentlichen wollten. Auf diese Weise erlangten sie die Kontrolle über ihr eigenes Werk. Darüber hinaus verlegten sie auch Arbeiten anderer Schriftstellerinnen. Der Druckbetrieb wurde 1974 aufgenommen und bis in die 1990er Jahre aufrechterhalten.

Deborah Hart

Hart, along with Lilian Mohin and Sheila Shulman, was founder of the Onlywomen Press, also known as The Women's Press. The London-based print shop was a feminist enterprise, born out of a group of lesbian writers who wanted to publish their work. This allowed them to gain control over their own work. They also published works by other women writers. Printing operations began in 1974 and were maintained until the 1990s.

Kate Hepburn

Hepburn entwarf zusammen mit Sally Doust das visuelle Konzept der feministischen Zeitschrift *Spare Rib*. Sie studierte an der Central School of Art and Design in London (heute University of the Arts) und anschließend am Royal College of Art. Sie lernte Sally Doust in den späten 1960er Jahren bei der Zeitschrift *Vogue Australia* kennen.

Kate Hepburn

Together with Sally Doust, Hepburn designed the visual concept of the feminist magazine *Spare Rib*. She studied at the Central School of Art and Design in London (now University of the Arts) and then at the Royal College of Art. She first met Sally Doust in the late 1960s at the magazine *Vogue Australia*.

Kathrin Hero

Hero gründete 2005 zusammen mit Jessica Gysel das Frauenmagazin *Girls Like Us*. Sie verantwortete anfangs das Editorial Design. Das Magazin wurde in Amsterdam konzipiert und international vertrieben. Heute gestaltet Hero Bücher und Magazine, ist spezialisiert auf Typografie und Ausstellungsdesign, auf visuelles Corporate Design und interaktive Projekte. Zunehmend interessiert sie sich für Medientheorie und Netzkritik und arbeitet mit vielen einschlägigen Institutionen zusammen, beispielsweise dem Mauritshuis und der Utrecht Graduate School of Visual Art and Design, daneben aber auch mit kleineren Unternehmen in der Kreativindustrie.

Kathrin Hero

Hero cofounded the woman's magazine *Girls Like Us* with Jessica Gysel in 2005. She was initially responsible for editorial design. The magazine was conceived in Amsterdam and distributed internationally. Today, Hero designs books and magazines and specializes in typography and exhibition design, visual corporate design, and interactive projects. She is increasingly interested in media theory and net criticism and works with many institutions, such as the Mauritshuis and the Utrecht Graduate School of Visual Art and Design, as well as with smaller companies in the creative industry.

Clemence Housman (1861–1955)

Housman, geboren in Bromsgrove, Worcestershire, war eine Schriftstellerin, Illustratorin und Aktivistin der Suffragettenbewegung. 1883 erlernte sie die kunsthandwerkliche Technik des Holzstichs und arbeitete für längere Zeit für die Zeitschrift *The Graphic*. 1908 wurde sie Mitglied der Women's Social and Political Union und ein Jahr später, zusammen mit ihrem Bruder, dem Schriftsteller und Illustrator Laurence Housman, Mitbegründerin des Suffrage-Ateliers. Vor allem entwarf sie Banner für die Frauenbewegung. 1910 wurde sie Mitglied der Women's Tax Resistance League. Sie kam 1911 ins Gefängnis, weil sie sich weigerte, Steuern zu bezahlen, wurde aber mit Unterstützung ihrer Anhänger nach einer Woche wieder entlassen. Zu ihren literarischen Werken zählte *The Were-Wolf*, 1896, *Unknown Sea*, 1898, und *The Life of Sir Aglovale de Galis*, 1905. Ihrem Bruder Laurence fühlte sie sich eng verbunden. Einige seiner Werke wie *The Blue Moon*, 1904, und *Moonshine & Clover*, 1922, illustrierte sie selbst.

Clemence Housman (1861–1955)

Housman, born in Bromsgrove, Worcestershire (UK), was a writer, illustrator, and activist in the suffragette movement. In 1883 she learned the artistic technique of wood engraving, working thereafter for a long time for the magazine *The Graphic*. In 1908, she became a member of the Women's Social and Political Union and a year later, along with her brother, writer, and illustrator Laurence Housman, cofounded the Suffrage Atelier. Above all, she designed banners for the women's movement. In 1910, she became a member of the Women's Tax Resistance League. She was jailed in 1911 for refusing to pay taxes, but was released after a week with the assistance of her supporters. Her literary works included *The Were-Wolf* (1896), *Unknown Sea* (1898), and *The Life of Sir Aglovale de Galis* (1905). She felt a close bond with her brother Laurence, illustrating several of his works such as *The Blue Moon* (1904) and *Moonshine & Clover* (1922).

Wera Michailowna Jermolajewa (1893–1937)

Jermolajewa war eine russischen Buchillustratorin und Malerin, die zur russischen Avantgarde gehörte. Sie war seit der Kindheit an den Beinen gelähmt. Ihre künstlerische Ausbildung erhielt sie von 1911 bis 1914 an einer privaten Kunstschule in St. Petersburg. 1918 gründete sie die Künstlergruppe Heute, die kunsthandwerkliche Bücher mit handkolorierten Linolschnitten im Stil der russischen Volkskunst Lubki herausgab. Danach lehrte sie an der 1918 von Marc Chagall gegründeten Kunstschule des Volkes von Witebsk, gemeinsam mit El Lissitzky und Kasimir Malewitsch. 1920 wurde sie Direktorin der Kunstschule und vertrat den Suprematismus in der angewandten Kunst. Sie war Mitglied der im selben Jahr in Wizebsk gegründeten Künstlergruppe UNOWIS. Auf der „Ersten Russischen Kunstausstellung" in Berlin 1922 wurden zwei Bühneninszenierungen von ihr zur russischen Oper *Sieg über die Sonne* gezeigt. 1922 kehrte sie gemeinsam mit Malewitsch, der an das Staatliche Institut für künstlerische Kultur (GIMChUK) berufen worden war, nach St. Petersburg zurück. Jermolajewa war dort bis 1926 Leiterin des Farblaboratoriums. Ab 1927 gestaltete sie vor allem Kinderbücher und Zeitschriften für Kinder, vorwiegend für den Staatsverlag Gosizdat. Wera Jermolajewa wurde im Zuge der stalinistischen „Säuberungen" 1934 verhaftet und zu fünf Jahren Lagerhaft verurteilt, während der sie verstarb.

Vera Mikhailovna Yermolayeva (1893–1937)

Yermolayeva was a Russian book illustrator and painter who belonged to the Russian avantgarde. Her legs were paralyzed since childhood. From 1911 to 1914, she received her artistic training at a private art school in St. Petersburg. In 1918, she founded the artists' group Today, which published craft books with hand-colored linocuts in the Russian folk-art style of lubki prints. Together with El Lissitzky and Kazimir Malevich, she then taught at the People's Art School of Vitebsk, founded by Marc Chagall in 1918. In 1920, she became the director of the art school and a proponent of suprematism in applied art. She was a member of the artist group UNOVIS, founded in the same year in Vizebsk. Two of her theatrical sets of the Russian opera *Victory over the Sun* were shown at the First Russian Art Exhibition in Berlin in 1922. In 1922, she returned to St. Petersburg together with Malevich, who had been appointed to the State Institute of Artistic Culture (INKhUK). Yermolayeva was head of the color laboratory at the institute until 1926. From 1927 onward, her design work was focused primarily on children's books and magazines for children, mainly for the state publishing house Gosizdat. Vera Yermolayeva was arrested in the course of the Stalinist purges in 1934 and sentenced to five years in the camps, during which she died.

Hilde (Hilda) Jesser (1894–1985)

Jesser war eine österreichische Malerin, Grafikdesignerin, Textilkünstlerin und Hochschullehrerin. Sie studierte von 1912 bis 1917 an der Kunstschule für Frauen und Mädchen und der Kunstgewerbeschule des K. K. Österreichischen Museums für Kunst und Industrie in Wien. Zu ihrem vielseitigen Werk zählen auch Entwürfe von Postkarten für die Wiener Werkstätte. 1922 übernahm sie eine Lehrtätigkeit an der Wiener Kunstgewerbeschule und wurde 1935 ordentliche Professorin. 1930 nahm sie in Wien an der Ausstellung „Wie sieht die Frau" teil. 1938 wurde sie von den Nationalsozialisten gezwungen, den Unterricht aufzugeben. 1945 nahm sie die Lehrtätigkeit an der Nachfolgeinstitution der Wiener Kunstgewerbeschule wieder auf und unterrichtete dort bis 1967. Jesser war Mitglied des Österreichischen Werkbundes und der Wiener Frauenkunst.

Sara Kaaman

Kaaman ist eine schwedische Grafikdesignerin, Pädagogin und Autorin. Sie studierte von 2006 bis 2008 Grafikdesign und Illustration am Konstfack University College of Arts & Crafts in Stockholm und von 2008 bis 2010 Grafikdesign an der Gerrit Rietveld Academie, Amsterdam. Sie erforscht Grafikdesign in verschiedenen Konstellationen. Seit 2012 ist sie die Grafikdesignerin (und gelegentlich Mitherausgeberin) des Frauenmagazins *Girls Like Us*. Mit Maryam Fanni und Matilda Flodmark bildet sie das Dreierkollektiv MMS, das sich unter anderem mit der Gegenwart und Geschichte von Frauen im Buchgewerbe auseinandersetzt. Beispielhaft hierfür ist das Buch *Natural Enemies of Books. A Messy History of Women in Printing and Typography*, 2020 bei Occasional Papers, London, erschienen, das sich mit einer ausschließlich von Frauen edierten Buchpublikation von 1937 auseinandersetzt. Seit 2016 ist Kaaman Senior Lecturer für Grafikdesign an der Konstfack University of Art, Crafts and Design in Stockholm und leitet seit 2020 das neue MA-Programm für Grafikdesign an der Estnischen Kunstakademie in Tallinn.

Anja Kaiser (geb. 1986)

Kaiser lebt und arbeitet vorwiegend in Leipzig, Deutschland. Sie studierte Grafikdesign an der Burg Giebichenstein Kunsthochschule Halle. Das Studium setzte sie 2012 in Amsterdam fort, wo sie am Design Department des Sandberg Instituut ihren Master-Abschluss mit der Arbeit „Sexed Realities. To Whom Do I Owe My Body?" machte und sich mit dem weiblichen Körper als Projektionsfläche verschiedenster Wünsche, auch technologischer Neuerungen, auseinandersetzte. Sie befasst sich mit der Aneignung von widerständigen Medien, undisziplinierten grafischen Methoden und übt

Hilde (Hilda) Jesser (1894–1985)

Jesser was an Austrian painter, graphic designer, textile artist, and university lecturer. She studied from 1912 to 1917 at the Kunstschule für Frauen und Mädchen and the Kunstgewerbeschule of the K. K. Österreichisches Museum für Kunst und Industrie in Vienna. Her diverse body of work also includes designs of postcards for the Wiener Werkstätte. In 1922, she took up a teaching position at the Vienna Kunstgewerbeschule, becoming a full professor in 1935. In 1930, she participated in the exhibition *Wie sieht die Frau* (How do women see it?) in Vienna. In 1938, she was forced by the Nazis to stop teaching. In 1945, she resumed teaching at the successor institution to the Vienna Kunstgewerbeschule, where she taught until 1967. Jesser was a member of the Österreichischer Werkbund and the Wiener Frauenkunst.

Sara Kaaman

Kaaman is a Swedish graphic designer, educator, and author. She studied graphic design and illustration from 2006 to 2008 at the Konstfack University College of Arts & Crafts in Stockholm and graphic design at the Gerrit Rietveld Academie in Amsterdam from 2008 to 2010. She explores graphic design in various constellations. Since 2012, she has been the graphic designer (and occasional coeditor) of the women's magazine *Girls Like Us*. With Maryam Fanni and Matilda Flodmark, she forms the three-person collective MMS, which explores topics including the present and history of women in the book trade. The group's aims are exemplified in the book *Natural Enemies of Books: A Messy History of Women in Printing and Typography* published in 2020 by Occasional Papers, London, which takes up a book from 1937 edited exclusively by women. Since 2016, Kamaan has been a senior lecturer in graphic design at Konstfack University of Art, Crafts and Design in Stockholm, and since 2020, she has led the new MA program in graphic design at the Estonian Academy of Arts in Tallinn.

Anja Kaiser (b. 1986)

Kaiser lives and works primarily in Leipzig, Germany. She studied graphic design at the Burg Giebichenstein Kunsthochschule Halle. She continued her studies in Amsterdam in 2012, where she completed her master's degree in the Design Department at the Sandberg Instituut with the work "Sexed Realities: To Whom Do I Owe My Body?," which explored the female body as a projection screen for a diverse array of desires, including some inspired by technological innovations. She is concerned with the appropriation of resistant media, undisciplined graphic methods, and critiques of conventional

Golnar Kat Rahmani © Golnar Kat Rahmani

Kritik an herkömmlichen Narrativen der Designgeschichte. Ein Fokus ihrer selbstbestimmten Arbeiten liegt auf feministischen Themen. Sie bewegt sich in einem aktivistischen Umfeld, in subkulturellen Szenen, die sie auch in ihre Arbeit integriert, und betrachtet Design als politisches Gestaltungsmittel. Seit dem Sommersemester 2021 vertritt Kaiser die Professur für Typografie an der Hochschule Burg Giebichenstein in Halle. Sie initiierte 2017 das Projekt „Whose.Agency" und präsentierte, zusammen mit Rebecca Stephany, ein *Unvollständiges Glossar des undisziplinierten Gestaltens von A bis Z*, um ihre Strategien und Werkzeuge im Grafikdesign zu diskutieren. Das Buch erschien 2021 bei Spector Books, Leipzig.

narratives in design history. One focus of the path she charts for her work is feminist themes. She works in an activist environment and in subcultural scenes that she also integrates into her design, and she considers design to be a political means of creating form. Since summer semester 2021, Kaiser has held the professorship for typography at Burg Giebichenstein Kunsthochschule Halle. In 2017, she initiated the project "Whose.Agency" and presented, together with Rebecca Stephany, an *Incomplete Glossary of Undisciplined Design from A to Z*, to discuss their strategies and tools in graphic design. The volume was published in 2021 by Spector Books in Leipzig.

Golnar Kat Rahmani (geb. 1983)

Rahmani, geboren in Gonbad-e-Kavoos, Iran, studierte Visuelle Kommunikation an der Universität Teheran und an der Kunstakademie Berlin-Weißensee. Heute lebt sie in Berlin und leitet das Studio Kat Rahmani. Sie spezialisiert sich auf Typografie, Editorial Design, Grafikdesign. Ihr Projekt *Type & Politics* versucht, die arabisch/persische Typografie durch spielerische Aktionen von ideologischen, insbesondere negativen Konnotationen zu befreien. Deshalb organisierte sie Typografie-Workshops an der UdK (Universität der Künste) in Berlin, der Kunstakademie in Berlin-Weißensee und der Hochschule Mainz. Sie nahm außerdem teil an verschiedenen Konferenzen wie Typo Berlin – International Design Conference, 2018, Letters and Typographics in New York, 2021.

Golnar Kat Rahmani (b. 1983)

Rahmani, born and raised in Iran, studied visual communication at the University of Tehran and at the Kunstakademie Berlin-Weißensee. Today she lives in Berlin and runs the Studio Kat Rahmani. She specializes in typography, editorial design, and graphic design. Her project *Type & Politics* attempts to liberate Arabic/Persian typography from ideological connotations and particularly those that are negative, through playful transformations. As part of the project, she organized typography workshops at the Universität der Künste in Berlin, the Kunstakademie in Berlin-Weißensee, and the Hochschule Mainz. She has also participated in various conferences such as Typo Berlin: International Design Conference (2018) and Letters and Typographics in New York (2021).

Jessie Marion King (1875–1949)

King war eine schottische Kinderbuchillustratorin und zählte zu den Glasgow Girls. Sie wurde in einem Pfarrhaus nahe Glasgow geboren, ihr Vater war Priester der Kirche von Schottland. Streng religiös erzogen, wurde ihr nicht gestattet, Künstlerin zu werden. Unterstützung bei der Verwirklichung ihres Berufswunsches erhielt sie von ihrer Gouvernante Mary McNab, die sie auch im späteren Leben begleitete. King wurde 1891 zur Kunstlehrerin am Outen Margaret College in Glasgow ausgebildet. Schon früh erwarb sie Auszeichnungen. Sie wurde 1899 Lehrerin für Buchdekoration und -design an der Glasgow School of Art, ein Beruf den sie auch nach der Heirat mit E. A. Taylor 1908 beibehielt. Auch ihren Mädchennamen führte sie weiter, was zu dieser Zeit ungewöhnlich war. King wurde vom Art nouveau beeinflusst, ähnlich wie die Glasgow Four. Sie gestaltete neben Büchern auch Schmuck, Textilien und bemalte Töpferware. Am bekanntesten wurde sie für ihre Buchtitel zwischen 1899 und 1902 für den Globus Verlag, Berlin. Der Verlag war dem Kaufhaus Wertheim zugeordnet, des-

Jessie Marion King (1875–1949)

King was a Scottish children's book illustrator and one of the Glasgow Girls. Born in a parsonage near Glasgow, with a father who was a priest in the Church of Scotland, she was raised following strict religious principles and was not allowed to become an artist. She received support in realizing her career aspirations from her governess, Mary McNab, who continued to be an important figure for King later in her life. King trained as an art teacher at Outen Margaret College in Glasgow in 1891 and was recognized with awards from an early age. She became a teacher of book decoration and design at the Glasgow School of Art in 1899, a profession she continued to practice after marrying E. A. Taylor in 1908. She also kept her maiden name, an unusual decision at the time. King was influenced by art nouveau, much like the Glasgow Four. In addition to books, she designed jewelry, textiles, and painted pottery. She became best known for the book covers she designed between 1899 and 1902 for Globus Verlag, Berlin. The publishing house was associated with the Wertheim department store, whose

sen Besitzer Georg Wertheim den „neuen schottischen Stil" propagierte. In den Jahren 1907 bis 1924 illustrierte King mehr als 20 Bücher für die Firma T. N. Folis aus Edinburgh. Insgesamt sind mehr als 100 Bücher von ihr bekannt, einige schrieb sie auch selbst.

1902 unternahm King eine Bildungsreise durch Deutschland und Italien, besonders beeinflussten sie die Gemälde von Sandro Botticelli. Auf der „Internationalen Ausstellung für moderne Dekoration" in Turin erhielt sie eine Goldmedaille für ihre Zeichnungen. King wurde führendes Mitglied der Glasgow Society of Artists (1903) und der Glasgow Society of Lady Artists (1905). 1908 zogen sie und ihr Ehemann nach Salford. Mary McNab versorgte den Haushalt, sodass King weiterhin künstlerisch arbeiten konnte. 1910 zog die Familie nach Paris, wo ihr Ehemann eine Professur an den Ernest Percyval Tudor-Hart's Studios erhielt. 1911 eröffneten beide die Sheiling Atelier School in Paris. Sie setzten Akzente im aufkommenden Art déco durch ihre Rezeption von Léon Bakst und der Ballets Russes von Diaghilev. King und Taylor zogen 1915 wieder zurück nach Schottland, wo sich King bis an ihr Lebensende weiterhin künstlerisch betätigte.

Mela Köhler (1885–1960)

Köhler, eigentl. Melanie Leopoldina Köhler-Broman, wurde in Wien geboren. Zwei Jahre lang besuchte sie die Malschule Hohenberger, danach von 1905 bis 1910 die Wiener Kunstgewerbeschule, wo unter anderem Koloman Moser ihr Lehrer war. Noch während dieser Zeit wurden ihre Arbeiten publiziert in *The Studio*, 1907, und *Jung Wien. Ergebnisse der Wiener Kunstgewerbeschule*, 1907. Neben der Malerei illustrierte sie Märchenbücher für den Verlag Konegen und war Mitarbeiterin der Zeitschrift *Wiener Mode*. Der Verlag Bedford beschäftigte sie als Buchkünstlerin. Daneben war sie für Unternehmen tätig, unter anderem für Bahlsen, Augarten (Keramik) sowie Munk und Kohn (Postkarten). Für die Wiener Werkstätte schuf sie Postkarten, Bilderbögen, Stoffe und Postkarten mit Stoffmustern. Hier signierte sie mit „Mela Koehler". Köhler war Mitglied des Österreichischen Werkbundes und der Wiener Frauenkunst. Sie emigrierte Anfang 1934 nach Schweden, schuf dort weiterhin Buchillustrationen, malte Figurenkompositionen in Aquarell und persönliche Porträts von Frauen und Kindern. Sie entwarf auch Kostüme für Theater und Ballett sowie Postkarten, unter anderem für den Verlag Sagokonst in Stockholm, 1940.

owner, Georg Wertheim, propagated the "new Scottish style." Between 1907 and 1924, King illustrated more than twenty books for the Edinburgh firm of T. N. Folis. In total, there are more than one hundred books of hers known today, some of which she not only illustrated but also wrote herself.

In 1902, King embarked upon an educational tour through Germany and Italy, particularly influenced by the paintings of Sandro Botticelli. At the International Exhibition of Modern Decoration in Turin she received a gold medal for her drawings. King became a leading member of the Glasgow Society of Artists (1903) and the Glasgow Society of Lady Artists (1905). In 1908, she and her husband moved to Salford. Mary McNab took care of the household so King could continue to work artistically. In 1910, the family moved to Paris, where her husband obtained a professorship at Ernest Percyval Tudor-Hart's Studios. In 1911, they together opened the Sheiling Atelier School in Paris. They had significant influence in the emerging movement of art deco through their reception of Léon Bakst and Diaghilev's Ballets Russes. King and Taylor moved back to Scotland in 1915, where King continued to be active artistically until the end of her life.

Mela Köhler (1885–1960)

Köhler, whose legal name was Melanie Leopoldina Köhler-Broman, was born in Vienna. For two years she attended the Malschule Hohenberger, then from 1905 to 1910 the Wiener Kunstgewerbeschule, where her teachers included Koloman Moser. Even during this time her work was published in *The Studio* (in 1907) and *Jung Wien: Ergebnisse der Wiener Kunstgewerbeschule* (in 1907). In addition to painting, she illustrated fairy tale books for the publishing house Konegen and was a contributor to the magazine *Wiener Mode*. The Bedford publishing house employed her as a book artist, and she worked for companies including Bahlsen, Augarten (ceramics), and Munk and Kohn (postcards). For the Wiener Werkstätte, she created postcards, picture posters, fabrics, and postcards with fabric patterns. She signed these designs with the name Mela Koehler. Köhler was a member of the Österreichischer Werkbund and the Wiener Frauenkunst. She emigrated to Sweden in early 1934, where she created book illustrations and painted figure compositions in watercolor and personal portraits of women and children. She also designed costumes for theater and ballet, as well as postcards, for clients including in 1940 for the publisher Sagokonst in Stockholm.

Mela Köhler © IMAGNO/Austrian Archives, Foto/photo: Trude Fleischmann

Änne Koken (1885–1919)

Koken hat, wie viele Künstlerinnen ihrer Zeit, neben der Malerei in vielen Bereichen des Kunstgewerbes und der Gebrauchsgrafik gearbeitet. Vor allem aber wurde sie mit ihrer Werbegrafik für die Firma Bahlsen bekannt. Als Tochter eines Kunstmalers zunächst von ihrem Vater ausgebildet, studierte sie drei Jahre Malerei in München und kehrte anschließend nach Hannover zurück. Dort eröffnete sie 1910 ein eigenes Atelier: Änne Koken, Werkstatt für angewandte Kunst. Von dort aus arbeitete sie für verschiedene namhafte Unternehmen, neben Bahlsen unter anderem für Appels Feinkost, die Lindener Samtfabrik, Günther Wagner (Pelikan) und die Hannoversche Waggonfabrik. Sie wurde zum Künstlerischen Beirat der Hannoverschen Cakes-Fabrik (Bahlsen) ernannt. Bei Bahlsen schuf Koken zwei Serien von Reklamemarken und Kekspackungen. Die Bandbreite ihrer Arbeiten umfasst aber auch Glasfenster, Schmuck, Kleidung – beispielsweise für die Reformzeitschrift *Neue Frauenkleidung und Frauenkultur* –, Hüte, Textilien, Plakate und Gebrauchsgrafik aller Art.

Leopoldine Kolbe (1870–1912)

Kolbe zählte zu den Frauen der Wiener Werkstätte. Sie wurde ausgebildet im Atelier des Wiener Frauen-Erwerbs-Vereins, der Frauen Bildungs- und Erwerbsmöglichkeiten bot. Dort erhielt sie Zeichenunterricht von Franz Čižek. Ab 1902 besuchte sie die Kunstgewerbeschule Wien und war in der Fachklasse von Koloman Moser, im Spezial-Atelier für Kunstweberei und Restaurierung von Leopoldine Guttmann und in der Fachklasse Schrift und Heraldik beim Kalligrafen Rudolf von Larisch. Kolbe erhielt 1903 ein Stipendium der Gesellschaft zur Förderung der Kunstgewerbeschule. Parallel erhielt sie eine Ausbildung als Lehrerin und erteilte in Fortbildungskursen des Vereins für erweiterte Frauenbildung Unterricht in den Fächern Freihandzeichnen und Darstellende Geometrie. In der Mal- und Zeichenschule von Franz Čižek war sie zwischen 1908 und 1912 provisorische Lehrerin. Für die Wiener Werkstätte gestaltete Kolbe Postkarten. Diese zeigen Blumen- und Pflanzenmotive in Körben und wurden als Werbematerial eingesetzt. Es heißt, die Körbchen der Blumenarrangements wären Inspiration für die Metallarbeiten der Wiener Werkstätte gewesen, besonders derjenigen von Koloman Moser.

Änne Koken (1885–1919)

Koken, like many women artists of her time, worked in myriad areas of decorative arts and commercial art in addition to painting. Above all, however, she became known for the advertising images she designed for the Bahlsen company. The daughter of a painter, she was initially trained by her father and studied painting in Munich for three years before returning to Hannover, where she opened her own studio in 1910: Änne Koken, Werkstatt für angewandte Kunst. She worked for a number of well-known companies, such as Appels Feinkost, the Lindener Samtfabrik, Günther Wagner (Pelican), and the Hannoversche Waggonfabrik, in addition to Bahlsen. At Bahlsen's Hannoversche Cakes-Fabrik, she was appointed to the Artistic Supervisory Board and created two series of advertising stamps as well as designs for cookie packaging. The range of her work, however, also encompasses stained glass windows, jewelry, clothing (for example, for the reform magazine *Neue Frauenkleidung und Frauenkultur*), hats, textiles, posters, and commercial images of all kinds.

Leopoldine Kolbe (1870–1912)

Kolbe was one of the women members of the Wiener Werkstätte. She was trained in the studio of the Wiener Frauen-Erwerbs-Verein, which provided educational and employment opportunities for women. There, she attended the drawing classes of Franz Čižek. From 1902 onward, she attended the Kunstgewerbeschule in Vienna in the class of Koloman Moser, in the studio for art weaving and restoration of Leopoldine Guttmann, and in the class for lettering and heraldry with the calligrapher Rudolf von Larisch. Kolbe received a scholarship from the Gesellschaft zur Förderung der Kunstgewerbeschule in 1903. At the same time, she received training as a teacher and gave lessons in freehand drawing and descriptive geometry in continuing education courses at the Verein für erweiterte Frauenbildung. She was a temporary teacher at Franz Čižek's painting and drawing school between 1908 and 1912. Kolbe designed postcards for the Wiener Werkstätte depicting flower and plant motifs in baskets, which were used as promotional material. It is said that the baskets of flower arrangements were the inspiration for the metalwork of the Wiener Werkstätte, especially that of Koloman Moser.

Käthe Kollwitz (1867–1945)

Kollwitz ist die berühmteste deutsche Grafikerin des 20. Jahrhunderts. Ihr Werk umfasst Radierungen, Lithografien, Holzschnitte und Zeichnungen sowie Plakate. Mit ihren Plakaten trat die Künstlerin mahnend und anklagenden für soziale Gerechtigkeit ein und reagierte auf aktuelle soziale Probleme. Das Schicksal von Frauen unterer Volksschichten in ihrer Zeit war eines ihrer größten Themen. In *Nieder mit dem Abtreibungsparagraphen!*, ein Plakat der Kommunistischen Partei Deutschlands (KPD) von 1924, spricht sie sich gegen die Not kinderreicher Familien aus, deren Armut sich mit jedem Neugeborenen nur noch vergrößere. In einer Abtreibung sahen viele Frauen damals den einzigen Ausweg. Auch das Plakat gegen Heimarbeit von Frauen anlässlich der „Deutschen Heimarbeit-Ausstellung", 1906, klagt die Lebens- und Arbeitsbedingungen armer Menschen an. Insgesamt hat Kollwitz nur 14 Plakate geschaffen, doch befinden sich darunter einige ihrer bekanntesten Werke, unter anderem die Lithografie *Nie wieder Krieg* – bis in die 1980er Jahre eine Ikone der Friedensbewegung.

Trotz ihrer frühen Bekanntheit wurde Kollwitz mit den Hürden konfrontiert, die Frauen bei der Ausbildung und der Ausübung ihres Berufes seinerzeit zu nehmen hatten. Sie musste Privatschulen besuchen, anschließend die sogenannte Damenakademie des Vereins der Berliner Künstlerinnen. Dort war sie dann von 1898 bis 1902/03 Lehrerin. 1933 wurde sie zum Austritt aus der Preußischen Akademie der Künste, deren Mitglied sie war, gezwungen und ihres Amtes als Leiterin der Meisterklasse für Grafik enthoben, da sie zu den Unterzeichnern des Dringenden Appells zum Aufbau einer einheitlichen Arbeiterfront gegen den Nationalsozialismus gehörte. 1937 wurden ihre Arbeiten in der zentralen Aktion „Entartete Kunst" aus vielen Museen entfernt. Kollwitz verstarb 1945, kurz vor Ende des Zweiten Weltkriegs.

Käthe Kollwitz (1867–1945)

Kollwitz is the most famous German graphic artist of the twentieth century. Her work includes etchings, lithographs, woodcuts, and drawings as well as posters. Kollwitz fought for social justice and responded to social problems of her day, admonishing viewers to not look away and to take action while calling out those who abused their power. The fate of lower-class women in her day was one of her greatest themes. In "Nieder mit dem Abtreibungsparagraphen!" (Down with the abortion law) a poster made for the Communist Party of Germany (KPD) in 1924, she speaks out against the plight of families with many children, whose poverty only grew with each new child. At the time, many women saw abortion as the only way to escape this fate. The poster against work done at home by women that she made for the *Deutsche Heimarbeit-Ausstellung* in 1906 similarly denounces the living and working conditions of poor people. Kollwitz created only fourteen posters in total, though some of these are her most famous works from any genre, including the lithograph "Nie wieder Krieg" (Never again war), an icon of the peace movement until the 1980s.

Despite her early prominence, Kollwitz was confronted with the hurdles women faced in training and in pursuing their professions at the time. She was forced to attend private schools, and then the *Damenakademien* (or ladies' academies), as they were called, of the Verein der Berliner Künstlerinnen, where she also later taught from 1898 to 1902/03. In 1933, she was forced to resign from the Prussian Akademie der Künste, where she was a member, and was relieved of her post as head of the master class for graphic arts because she had signed the Urgent Appeal to Build a Unified Workers' Front against National Socialism. In 1937, her works were removed from many museums during the Nazi-organized "Degenerate Art" campaign. Kollwitz died in 1945, shortly before the end of World War II.

Chris Köver (geb. 1979)

Köver ist eine deutsche Journalistin und Mitbegründerin sowie Mitherausgeberin der seit Oktober 2008 erscheinenden feministischen Zeitschrift *Missy Magazine*. Sie studierte ab 1999 in Lüneburg und Toronto Angewandte Kulturwissenschaften und absolvierte von 2006 bis 2008 ein Volontariat bei *Die Zeit*. Neben ihrer Arbeit als Redakteurin und Herausgeberin des *Missy Magazine* ist sie freie Journalistin und Autorin. In ihren Buchpublikationen befasst sie sich mit neuerem Feminismus in Popkultur, Film und Fernsehen sowie mit Netzkultur. So veröffentlichte sie beispielsweise 2012 zusammen mit

Chris Köver (b. 1979)

Köver is a German journalist and cofounder and coeditor of the feminist *Missy Magazine*, published since October 2008. Beginning in 1999, she studied applied cultural studies in Lüneburg and Toronto and completed an internship from 2006 to 2008 at the German news magazine *Die Zeit*. In addition to her work as editor and publisher of *Missy Magazine*, she is a freelance journalist and author. Her book publications focus on recent feminism in pop culture, film and television, and online culture, among them *Mach's selbst—Do It Yourself für Mädchen* (Do it yourself: do it yourself for girls)

Käthe Kollwitz, um/around 1906

Sonja Eismann *Mach's selbst – Do It Yourself für Mädchen* und 2015 mit Sonja Eismann und Daniela Burger *Hack's selbst! Digitales Do It Yourself für Mädchen*.

Dina Kuhn (1891–1963)

Kuhn, eigentlich Bernhardine Kuhn, war vor allem Keramikerin und arbeitete sowohl für die Wiener Werkstätte als auch für die Waechtersbacher Keramik in Deutschland. Nach Abschluss ihrer schulischen Ausbildung begann sie 1912 ein achtjähriges Studium an der Kunstgewerbeschule in Wien. Ihre Lehrer waren Josef Hoffmann, Franz Čižek, Koloman Moser, Oskar Strnad und Michael Powolny. In die Wiener Werkstätte trat sie 1917 ein, hatte aber schon vorher für die Künstler*innengemeinschaft gearbeitet. Bis 1922 schuf sie dort etwa 100 Entwürfe für Keramikfiguren, Tapeten und Stoffmuster. Für Oskar Strnads Edelraum der Österreichischen Werkstätten auf der „Deutschen Gewerbeschau" in München, 1922, fertigte sie zahlreiche keramische Wandreliefs an. Kuhn war Mitglied in der Vereinigung bildender Künstlerinnen Österreichs und in der Wiener Frauenkunst.

Valentina Kulagina (1902–1987)

Kulagina war neben ihrer Tätigkeit als Malerin auch Buchdesignerin, Plakatkünstlerin und Ausstellungsgestalterin. Sie war, wie auch ihr Ehemann Gustav Klucis, eine zentrale Figur der konstruktivistischen Avantgarde in Russland. Bekannt ist sie wegen ihrer sowjetischen Propaganda und der Verbundenheit mit dem Stalinismus. Kulagina studierte in den 1920er Jahren an den WCHUTEMAS bei ihrem Lehrer Klucis. 1921 heiratete das Paar. 1930 entwarf sie ein Plakat für den Internationalen Frauentag, wobei sie avantgardistische Techniken in der Typografie und der Fotomontage anwendete. Ihre Arbeit begann mit der Gestaltung des Russischen Pavillons auf der „Pressa" in Köln. Später arbeitete sie für die IZOGIZ (staatlicher Verlag für Kunstbücher), für VOKS (die sowjetische Gesellschaft für internationalen Austausch) und für VSKhV (die sowjetische Agentur für Landwirtschaft). Mitglieder ihrer Familie und ihr Ehemann wurden Opfer der stalinistischen „Säuberung".

Gabi Lagus-Möschl (1887–1961)

Lagus-Möschl war eine österreichische Malerin und Grafikerin. Sie besuchte von 1905 bis 1907 die Kunstschule für Frauen und Mädchen, anschließend bis 1911 die Wiener Kunstgewerbeschule, war Mitglied der Vereinigung bildender Künstlerinnen Österreichs (VBKÖ) und des Österreichischen Werkbunds. Vom VBKÖ spaltete sie sich mit anderen Künstlerinnen ab

with Sonja Eismann in 2012 and *Hack's selbst! Digitales Do It Yourself für Mädchen* (Hack it yourself: digital do it yourself for girls) with Sonja Eismann and Daniela Burger in 2015.

Dina Kuhn (1891–1963)

Kuhn, whose legal name was Bernhardine Kuhn, was primarily a ceramist and worked for both the Wiener Werkstätte and Waechtersbacher Keramik in Germany. After completing her school education, she began an eight-year course of study at the Kunstgewerbeschule in Vienna in 1912. Her teachers were Josef Hoffmann, Franz Čižek, Koloman Moser, Oskar Strnad, and Michael Powolny. She joined the Wiener Werkstätte in 1917, though she began working for the association before that. At the Werkstätte until 1922, she created nearly one hundred designs for ceramic figures, wallpaper, and fabric patterns. She created numerous ceramic wall reliefs for Oskar Strnad's Edelraum der Österreichischen Werkstätten (Nobleman's room of the Austrian workshops) at the Deutsche Gewerbeschau in Munich in 1922. Kuhn was a member of the Vereinigung bilden-der Künstlerinnen Österreichs and the Wiener Frauenkunst.

Valentina Kulagina (1902–1987)

In addition to being a painter, Kulagina was also a book designer, poster artist, and exhibition designer. Like her husband Gustav Klutsis, she was a central figure in the constructivist avant-garde in Russia, and today she is also known for her Soviet propaganda and ties to Stalinism. Kulagina studied at VKHUTEMAS in the 1920s under Klutsis, with the couple marrying in 1921. In 1930, she designed a poster for International Women's Day using avant-garde techniques in typography and photomontage. Her work began with the design of the Russian Pavilion at the Pressa in Cologne. Later she worked for IZOGIZ (the state publishing house for art books), for VOKS (the Soviet Society for International Exchange) and for VSKhV (the Soviet Agency for Agriculture). Members of her family, including her husband, became victims of the Stalinist purge.

Gabi Lagus-Möschl (1887–1961)

Lagus-Möschl was an Austrian painter and graphic artist. She attended the Kunstschule für Frauen und Mädchen from 1905 to 1907 and the Vienna Kunstgewerbeschule until 1911, and she was a member of the Vereinigung bilden-der Künstlerinnen Österreichs (VBKÖ) and the Austrian Werkbund. She split off from the VBKÖ with other women artists and officially founded

und gründete 1926 offiziell die Wiener Frauen-kunst, welche informell schon einige Jahre bestand. Hier wurde sie zur ersten Vizepräsidentin ernannt. In der Wiener Werkstätte arbeitete sie im Bereich der Stoffmalerei und Mode, schuf Einbände für Bücher und illustrierte Bände, unter anderem das Kinderbuch *Das seltsame Weihnachtserlebnis des kleinen Vigg*. Darüber hinaus entwickelte sie Grafiken für die Zeitschrift *Erdgeist*. Ab 1911 war sie auf den einschlägigen Ausstellungen in Europa vertreten sowie 1925 auf der „Exposition Internationale des Arts Décoratifs et Industriels Modernes" in Paris. 1938 wurde sie von den Nationalsozialisten mit einem Arbeitsverbot belegt. Daraufhin emigrierte sie mit ihrem Mann zunächst nach Rom, dann über Lissabon in die USA. Dort nannte sie sich Gabrielle Lagus. Zusammen mit ihrem Ehemann arbeitete sie in den USA hauptsächlich als Stoffdesignerin.

the Wiener Frauenkunst in 1926, after it had existed informally for several years. At the Wiener Frauenkunst, she was appointed first vice president. At the Wiener Werkstätte, she worked in the field of fabric painting and fashion and created bindings for books and illustrated volumes, including for the children's book *Das seltsame Weihnachtserlebnis des kleinen Vigg* (Little Vigg's curious Christmas tale). She also developed graphics for the magazine *Erdgeist* (Spirit of the earth). Beginning in 1911, she was present at all major exhibitions in Europe, and in 1925 at the Exposition Internationale des Arts Décoratifs et Industriels Modernes in Paris. In 1938, she was prohibited from working by the Nazis. She then emigrated with her husband, first to Rome, then via Lisbon to the United States, where she worked under the name of Gabrielle Lagus. Together with her husband she worked in the United States mainly as a fabric designer.

Lora Lamm (geb. 1928)

Die Schweizer Grafikdesignerin Lamm erhielt ihre Ausbildung als Grafikerin von 1946 bis 1952 an der Kunstgewerbeschule Zürich. Kurze Zeit war sie am Ort Werbegrafikerin, um dann 1953 in das wirtschaftlich prosperierende Mailand überzusiedeln. 1954 kam sie auf Empfehlung des Schweizer Grafikers Max Huber in die Werbeabteilung der eleganten Kaufhauskette La Rinascente und wurde dort Nachfolgerin von Huber als Art-Direktorin. Lamm beeinflusste durch ihr Design maßgeblich das Image des Kaufhauses. Sie arbeitete auch für das dazugehörige Billigkaufhaus Upim sowie für Pirelli, Elizabeth Arden, Niggi, Latte Milano. 1958 entschied sie sich, nur noch als freie Mitarbeiterin für La Rinascente zu entwerfen. 1963 kehrte sie mit ihrem Lebens- und Arbeitspartner Frank C. Thiessing wieder in ihre Heimat Zürich zurück, wo beide gemeinsam eine Agentur führten. Lamm erhielt viele Ehrungen. 2013 zeigte das m.a.x.museo in Chiasso ihre Arbeiten der italienischen Jahre, 2018 die Triennale in Mailand ihre Werbung für Pirelli.

Lora Lamm (b. 1928)

Lamm, a Swiss graphic designer, received her graphic design training from 1946 to 1952 at the Kunstgewerbeschule Zürich. For a short time, she worked as an advertising designer in the city, then in 1953 she moved to the economically flourishing city of Milan. In 1954, on the recommendation of Swiss graphic designer Max Huber, she joined the advertising department of the elegant department store chain La Rinascente, where she succeeded Huber as art director. Lamm significantly influenced the image of the department store through her design. She also worked for the associated budget department store Upim, as well as for Pirelli, Elizabeth Arden, Niggi, and Latte Milano. In 1958, she decided to continue her work with La Rinascente on an exclusively freelance basis. In 1963, she returned to her native Zurich with her life and work partner, Frank C. Thiessing, with whom she ran an agency. She has been the recipient of many honors: in 2013 the m.a.x.museo in Chiasso showed her works from her Italian years, and in 2018 the Triennale in Milan exhibited her advertising for Pirelli.

Eda Levenson

Levenson ist eine der beiden Gründerinnen von SOW, einer Organisation, die 2016 zur Unterstützung junger BIPoC-People gegründet wurde, die in den Bereichen Jugendkultur und Kunstpädagogik arbeiten. Zuvor war sie über zehn Jahre im Bereich Jugendarbeit tätig, arbeitete an öffentlichen Schulen, mit Non-Profit-Organisationen und Gesundheitseinrichtungen zusammen. Levenson absolvierte einen Master in Education an der Harvard Graduate School of Education und einen Bachelor of Arts in Community Studies an der University of California, Santa Cruz.

Eda Levenson

Levenson is one of the two founders of SOW, an organization established in 2016 to support young BIPOC people working in youth culture and arts education. Previously, she spent over ten years working with youth in public schools, with nonprofit organizations, and at health care facilities. Levenson earned a master's degree in education from the Harvard Graduate School of Education and a bachelor of arts degree in community studies from the University of California, Santa Cruz.

Sheila Levrant de Bretteville (geb. 1940)

Levrant de Bretteville gehört zur ersten Generation von Grafikdesignerinnen, deren Lehre und Designkritik sich mit feministischen Aspekten und der Beteiligung des Publikums auseinandersetzte. Sie war eine politische Aktivistin der 1960er und 1970er Jahre und in der Frauenbewegung dieser Zeit in den USA engagiert. 1971 etablierte sie das erste Programm für feministisches Design am California Institute of the Arts in Valencia im Los Angeles County. Zusammen mit Judy Chicago und Arlene Raven gründete sie das Woman's Building in Los Angeles, wo sie das Women's Graphic Center betrieb.

Levrant wurde 1940 in Brooklyn, New York City, als Kind einer polnischen Einwandererfamilie geboren. Sie studierte Kunstgeschichte am Barnard College für Frauen in New York City. 1964 schloss sie an der Yale University mit einem Master of Fine Arts in Grafikdesign ab. Mit ihrem Mann, dem Architekten Peter de Bretteville, zog sie nach Mailand und arbeitete dort unter anderem in einem Designstudio von Olivetti. Im Herbst 1969 kamen sie nach New York zurück, wo Levrant de Bretteville eine Stelle in einem Büro von Robert Mangurian und Craig Hodgetts annahm. Als stellvertretender Dekan der School of Design am California Institute of the Arts bat Hodgetts sie, das Branding der neu gegründeten Hochschule zu gestalten. 1970 übernahm sie auch das Design sowie die Redaktion einer Sonderausgabe von *Arts in Society*, die sich mit der Gründung des neuen California Institute of the Arts beschäftigte. Auf Anfrage des Dekans trat sie dem Fachbereich Design bei.

Levrant de Bretteville orientierte sich an der Pädagogik des Brasilianers Paulo Freire, der in den 1960er Jahren ein Alphabetisierungsprogramm für schnelles Lesen und Schreiben der armen brasilianischen Bevölkerung entwickelt hatte und es mit einer Methode der Bewusstseinsbildung verknüpfte.

Ein Jahr nach ihrer Anstellung erhielt sie die Genehmigung, zwei Unterrichtstage pro Woche dazu zu verwenden, Kurse nur für Frauen zu leiten. Auf diese Weise entstand der erste Studiengang für Frauendesign am California Institute of the Arts. Ihre Lehrtätigkeit war geprägt von einem egalitären und partizipatorischen Prozess. 1981 gründete sie den Fachbereich Kommunikationsdesign am Otis Art Institute of the Parsons School of Design in Los Angeles, dessen Vorsitzende sie bis 1990 war. 1990 wurde sie zur Direktorin des Studiengangs für Grafikdesign sowie zur ersten Frau mit Anstellung auf Lebenszeit an der Yale School of Art. Auch dort führte sie ihre schon in Los Angeles entwickelten neuen Lehrmethoden fort. Levrant de Bretteville wurde bereits mit mehreren Ehrendoktorwürden ausgezeichnet und ist heute eine Ikone feministischen Grafikdesigns.

Sheila Levrant de Bretteville (b. 1940)

Levrant de Bretteville is one of the first generation of women graphic designers whose teaching and design criticism addressed feminist issues and involvement of the public. She was a political activist during the 1960s and 1970s and involved in the women's movement of that time in the United States. In 1971, she established the first feminist design program ever, at the California Institute of the Arts in Valencia in Los Angeles County. Together with Judy Chicago and Arlene Raven, she founded the Woman's Building in Los Angeles, where she operated the Women's Graphic Center.

Sheila Levrant was born in Brooklyn, New York, in 1940 to a Polish immigrant family. She studied art history at Barnard College for Women in New York City. In 1964, she graduated from Yale University with a master of fine arts degree in graphic design. With her husband, the architect Peter de Bretteville, she moved to Milan where she worked at a number of places including an Olivetti studio. In the fall of 1969, they returned to New York, where Levrant de Bretteville took a job in an office run by Robert Mangurian and Craig Hodgetts. In the role of associate dean of the School of Design at California Institute of the Arts, Hodgetts asked her to design the branding for the newly established college. In 1970, she also took over the design and the editing of a special issue of *Arts in Society*, which focused on the founding of the new institution. She joined the design faculty at the request of the dean.

Levrant de Bretteville was inspired by the pedagogy of the Brazilian educator and philosopher Paulo Freire, who had developed a literacy program to teach rapid reading and writing among poor populations in Brazil in the 1960s that he regarded as a kind of consciousness raising.

A year after she was hired, she received permission to spend two of her teaching days a week leading classes just for women. This proved to be the beginning of the first women's design degree program, at the California Institute of the Arts. Her teaching was characterized by processes that were egalitarian and participatory. In 1981, de Bretteville founded the Department of Communication Design at the Otis Art Institute of Parsons School of Design in Los Angeles, serving as its chair until 1990. In 1990, she became the director of the graphic design program and the first woman tenured faculty member at the Yale School of Art. There, too, she continued the new teaching methods she had developed earlier in Los Angeles. Levrant de Bretteville has been awarded several honorary doctorates and is now an icon of feminist graphic design.

Maria Likarz (1893-1971)

Likarz besuchte von 1908 bis 1910 die Kunstschule für Frauen und Mädchen in Wien. Anschließend absolvierte sie von 1910 bis 1914 ein Studium an der Kunstgewerbeschule bei Josef Hoffmann, Rosalia Rothansl und Anton Kenner und war parallel und nach Abschluss des Studiums bis zur Auflösung der Wiener Werkstätte als Grafikerin dort tätig. Von 1916 bis 1920 arbeitete sie als Lehrerin in der Emaille-Werkstatt der Burg Giebichenstein Kunsthochschule Halle. Als Mitarbeiterin der Wiener Werkstätte war Likarz vor allem im werbegrafischen Bereich tätig. Sie entwarf Postkarten, Anzeigen, Plakate, Pack- und Marmorpapiere. Sie entwarf auch Dekorationen für Keramiken, Emaille und Textilien sowie für Mode und Bühnenbilder. Zusammen mit Vally Wieselthier gestaltete sie Reliefs in Oskar Strnads Edelraum der Österreichischen Werkstätten, der 1922 auf der „Deutschen Gewerbeschau" in München zu sehen war. Mit ihrem Ehemann, dem jüdischen Arzt Richard Strauss, emigrierte sie 1938 von Wien aus zunächst auf die kroatische Insel Korcula, anschließend nach Rom, wo sie hauptsächlich als Keramikerin arbeitete.

Stina Löfgren (geb. 1980)

Löfgren wurde in Wilhelmina, Lappland, geboren und lebt in Stockholm als Illustratorin, Designerin und Künstlerin. Ihren Master in Visueller Kommunikation absolvierte sie 2011 an der Kunsthochschule in Stockholm. Sie arbeitet als Illustratorin für Zeitschriften weltweit und ist, zusammen mit Sara Kaaman, Designerin für das Frauenmagazin *Girls Like Us*. Sie ist auch im Bereich Möbel- und Textildesign sowie Szenografie tätig.

Stefanie Lohaus (geb. 1978)

Lohaus wurde in Dinslaken geboren und studierte Angewandte Kulturwissenschaften in Lüneburg. 2008 gründete sie mit Chris Köver und Sonja Eismann das feministische *Missy Magazine*, dessen Mitherausgeberin sie seitdem ist. Sie ist außerdem Gründungsmitglied und Redakteurin des Blogs „10 nach 8" auf *Zeit Online* (bis 2015: „10 vor 8" auf faz.net). 2015 erschien ihr Buch *Papa kann auch stillen*, das sie gemeinsam mit ihrem Ehemann Tobias Scholz verfasst hat. Sie lebt als freie Journalistin in Berlin.

Friederike („Fritzi") Löw (1892-1975)

Löw, verheiratete Lazar, war eine Illustratorin und Grafikdesignerin der Wiener Werkstätte. Sie wurde in Wien geboren und besuchte von 1907 bis 1910 die Wiener Kunstschule für Frauen und Mädchen. Im Anschluss, von 1912 bis 1916, folgte ein künstlerisches Studium

Maria Likarz (1893-1971)

Likarz attended the Kunstschule für Frauen und Mädchen in Vienna from 1908 to 1910. She then studied at the Kunstgewerbeschule under Josef Hoffmann, Rosalia Rothansl, and Anton Kenner from 1910 to 1914, also working there as a graphic artist during and after completing her studies until the Wiener Werkstätte was dissolved. From 1916 to 1920, she worked as a teacher in the enamel workshop of the Burg Giebichenstein Kunsthochschule in Halle. As an employee of the Wiener Werkstätte, Likarz was primarily active in the field of advertising graphics. She designed postcards, advertisements, and posters as well as wrapping and marbled papers. She also designed decorations for ceramics, enamels, and textiles, as well as fashion and stage decoration. Together with Vally Wieselthier, she designed reliefs in Oskar Strnad's Edelraum der Österreichischen Werkstätten (Nobelman's room of the Austrian workshops), which was exhibited in 1922 at the Deutsche Gewerbeschau in Munich. She was forced to leave Vienna in 1938 with her husband Richard Strauss, a Jewish doctor, emigrating first to Croatia and then to Italy where she worked mainly as a ceramic artist.

Stina Löfgren (b. 1980)

Löfgren was born in Wilhelmina, Lapland, and lives in Stockholm as an illustrator, designer, and artist. She completed her master's degree in visual communication at the Stockholm School of Art in 2011. She works as an illustrator for magazines worldwide and, along with Sara Kaaman, is a designer for the women's magazine *Girls Like Us*. She is also active in the fields of furniture and textile design and scenography.

Stefanie Lohaus (b. 1978)

Lohaus was born in Dinslaken, Germany, and studied applied cultural sciences in Lüneburg. In 2008, together with Chris Köver and Sonja Eismann, she founded the feminist *Missy Magazine*, where she has been coeditor ever since. She is also a founding member and editor of the blog "10 nach 8" on *Zeit Online* (until 2015: "10 vor 8" on faz.net). In 2015 she published a book, *Papa kann auch stillen* (Papa can nurse the baby, too), coauthored with her husband Tobias Scholz. She lives as a freelance journalist in Berlin.

Friederike ("Fritzi") Löw (1892-1975)

Löw, who took the married name Lazar, was an illustrator and graphic designer for the Wiener Werkstätte. She was born in Vienna and attended the Kunstschule für Frauen und Mädchen in the city from 1907 to 1910. This was followed, from 1912 to 1916, by studies in art at

an der Wiener Kunstgewerbeschule bei Josef Hoffmann, Alfred Roller und Oskar Strnad. Von 1916 bis 1921 war sie Mitarbeiterin der Wiener Werkstätte. Sie illustrierte außerdem Erzählungen und Märchen von Eichendorff, Grillparzer, Keller, Mörike, Andersen, Brentano und Hauff mit Originallithografien, die als kleinformatige „Liebhaberausgaben" in den Jahren 1915 bis 1922 im Verlag Anton Schroll & Co. in Wien erschienen. Weitere künstlerische Arbeiten im Bereich der Buchgestaltung entwickelte sie für die Verlage Strache, Gerlach & Wiedling und die Gesellschaft für graphische Industrie. 1938 emigrierte Löw über Dänemark und England nach Brasilien. Dort war sie als Möbeldesignerin tätig. 1955 kehrte sie nach Wien zurück.

Luba Lukova

Lukova stammt aus Bulgarien und studierte an der National Academy of Fine Arts in Sofia. Sie reiste 1991 in die USA, nachdem ihre Arbeiten an der Colorado International Invitational Poster Exhibition gezeigt worden waren. Kurz darauf wurde sie von *New York Times Book Review* angestellt und sie gründete ein eigenes Studio in New York City. Sie arbeitet mit künstlerisch gestalteten Plakaten, die soziale Kritik ins Zentrum stellen. Ihre Auftraggeber sind international renommierte soziale wie humanitäre Einrichtungen, Universitäten, Broadway-Theater, Non-Profit-Organisationen. Sie entwarf auch Plakate für Shakespeare-Stücke, Choreografien und Arbeiten für die War Resisters League. Soziale Ungerechtigkeit, Zensur, Korruption, Prekariat, Umwelt-Bedingungen sind einige ihrer Themen. Zwar betrachtet sich Lukova nicht als Feministin, dennoch ist die Unterdrückung der Frauen ein Thema ihres Werkes. 2001 stellte sie unter dem Titel *The Printed Woman* eine Installation mit Drucken im Off-Off-Broadway-Theater LaMaMa aus. Lukovas Arbeiten sind weltweit geehrt, ihre Plakate werden von den renommiertesten Museen gesammelt. Sie trägt einen Ehrendoktortitel des Art Institute of Boston.

Ellen Lupton (geb. 1963)

Lupton ist eine US-amerikanische Grafikdesignerin, Autorin, Kuratorin und Lehrerin. Besonders bekannt ist sie für ihre zahlreichen Buchveröffentlichungen und Aufsätze. 1985 erwarb sie den Bachelor of Fine Arts an der The Cooper Union for the Advancement of Science and Art. 2008 promovierte sie in Kommunikationsdesign an der University of Baltimore. Als Lehrerin stellte sie 2003 das Graduiertenprogramm des Maryland Institute College of Art (MICA) in Baltimore auf. Zu ihren Publikationen zählen, zum Teil ausstellungsbegleitend, designtheoretische Werke und Monografien, etwa über Elaine Lustig

the Vienna Wiener Kunstgewerbeschule with Josef Hoffmann, Alfred Roller, and Oskar Strnad. From 1916 to 1921 she was an employee of the Wiener Werkstätte. She also illustrated stories and fairy tales by Eichendorff, Grillparzer, Keller, Mörike, Andersen, Brentano, and Hauff with original lithographs, which were published between 1915 and 1922 as small-format bibliophile editions by the Anton Schroll & Co. publishing house in Vienna. She additionally produced book designs for the publishing houses Strache, Gerlach & Wiedling, and the Gesellschaft für graphische Industrie. In 1938 she emigrated to Brazil, via Denmark and England, where she worked as a furniture designer. She returned to Vienna in 1955.

Luba Lukova

Born in Bulgaria, Lukova studied at the National Academy of Fine Arts in Sofia. She traveled to the United States in 1991 to see her work, which was being shown at the Colorado International Invitational Poster Exhibition. Shortly thereafter, she was hired by the *New York Times Book Review*, and she was able to establish her own studio in New York City. She works with artistically designed posters that focus on social criticism. Her clients are internationally renowned social and humanitarian institutions, universities, Broadway theaters, and nonprofit organizations. She has also designed posters for Shakespeare plays, choreography, and work for the War Resisters League. Social injustice, censorship, corruption, the precariat, and environmental conditions are some of her themes. While Lukova does not consider herself a feminist, the oppression of women is nevertheless one theme of her work. In 2001, under the title *The Printed Woman*, she exhibited an installation with prints at the off-off-Broadway theater LaMaMa. Lukova's works are honored worldwide, and her posters are held in the collections of the world's most prestigious museums. She holds an honorary doctorate from the Art Institute of Boston.

Ellen Lupton (b. 1963)

Lupton is a US graphic designer, author, curator, and teacher. She is particularly known for her numerous book publications and essays. In 1985 she earned a bachelor of fine arts degree from The Cooper Union for the Advancement of Science and Art, and in 2008 she received her doctorate in communication design from the University of Baltimore. As an instructor, she established the graduate program at the Maryland Institute College of Art (MICA) in Baltimore in 2003. Her publications include works and monographs on design theory, some of which were written to accompany exhibitions, among them books on Elaine Lustig Cohen (1995) and

Ellen Lupton, Foto/photo: Christina Chahyadi

Cohen, 1995, und Herbert Bayer, 2020. 2021 erschien *Extra Bold. A Feminist, Inclusive, Anti-racist, Nonbinary Field Guide for Graphic Designers*. Ein bekanntes frühes Werk von Lupton ist *Mechanical Brides. Women and Machines, from Home to Office* von 1993/94. Es handelt sich um den Katalog zu einer Ausstellung über gestaltete Objekte, die für Hausfrauen aus damaliger Sicht von Bedeutung waren wie Telefone, Schreibmaschinen, Waschmaschinen, Bügeleisen etc. Einige ihrer Bücher sind Anleitungen zum Selbermachen wie *D.I.Y.: Design It Yourself*, 2006, und *D.I.Y. Kids*, zusammen mit Julia Lupton, 2007. Neben vielen Aufsätzen ist das Interview mit Laurie Haycock Makela unter dem Titel „Neo-Ego. The Underground Matriarchy in Graphic Design" in *Eye*, 1994, besonders bekannt. Lupton ist Senior Curator am Cooper Hewitt, Smithsonian Design Museum in New York City, gleichzeitig auch unabhängige Kuratorin. Sie erhielt zahlreiche Auszeichnungen, zum Beispiel 2007 die Goldmedaille der AIGA (American Institute of Graphic Arts) für ihr Lebenswerk. 2019 wurde sie in die American Academy of Arts and Sciences gewählt.

Margaret MacDonald Mackintosh
(1864–1933)

Margaret MacDonald war die führende Künstlerin des schottischen Jugendstils und zählte mit ihren kunsthandwerklichen Arbeiten zu einer der einflussreichsten Gestalterinnen des Modern Style. Sie wurde als Tochter eines Bergbauingenieurs in der Nähe von Wolverhampton geboren. 1890 ließ sich die Familie in Glasgow nieder. Dort studierte sie mit ihrer Schwester Frances an der Glasgow School of Art. 1900 heiratete sie den Architekten und Designer Charles Rennie Mackintosh. Berühmt wurde sie mit ihrer Arbeit für die Wiener Sezession und mit ihren Wandbildern, zusammen mit ihrem Mann. MacDonald zählt mit ihrem Ehemann, ihrer Schwester Frances und deren Ehemann James Herbert McNair zur Glasgower Künstlergruppe The Four. Beide Schwestern bildeten zugleich das Zentrum der sogenannten Glasgow Girls, einer Gruppe von Künstlerinnen, die ihre Ausbildung an der Glasgow School of Art genossen hatten.

1915 ließ sie sich mit ihrem Ehemann in London nieder. Aufgrund ihres schlechten Gesundheitszustandes musste Margaret ab 1921 aber ihre künstlerische Tätigkeit beenden. 1923 reiste sie aus Gründen der niedrigeren Lebenshaltungskosten und des gesunden Klimas mit ihrem Ehemann nach Südfrankreich. 1927 kehrten beide nach London zurück und Margaret lebte nach Mackintoshs Tod bis 1933 zurückgezogen in Chelsea.

MacDonald war in verschiedenen kunsthandwerklichen Bereichen tätig, vor allem

Herbert Bayer (2020). In 2021, she published *Extra Bold: A Feminist, Inclusive, Anti-racist, Nonbinary Field Guide for Graphic Designers*. A well-known early work by Lupton is *Mechanical Brides: Women and Machines, from Home to Office* from 1993/94—the catalog of an exhibition of designed objects that were important for housewives of the time, such as telephones, typewriters, washing machines, irons, etc. Some of her books are do-it-yourself guides, such as *D.I.Y.: Design It Yourself* (2006) and *D.I.Y. Kids*, together with Julia Lupton (2007). In addition to many essays she has written, her interview with Laurie Haycock Makela titled "Neo-ego: The Underground Matriarchy in Graphic Design," published in 1994 in *Eye*, is particularly well known. Lupton is a senior curator at Cooper Hewitt, Smithsonian Design Museum in New York City and also works as an independent curator. She has received numerous awards, for example the Gold Medal of the AIGA (American Institute of Graphic Arts) in 2007 for her life's work. In 2019, she was elected to the American Academy of Arts and Sciences.

Margaret MacDonald Mackintosh
(1864–1933)

Margaret MacDonald was the leading woman artist of Scottish art nouveau, and her work in the field of arts and crafts established her reputation as one of the most influential designers of the modern style in Britain. She was born near Wolverhampton, UK, as the daughter of a mining engineer. In 1890, the family settled in Glasgow, where she later studied with her sister Frances at the Glasgow School of Art. In 1900 she married the architect and designer Charles Rennie Mackintosh. Together with her husband, she became famous with her work for the Vienna Secession and with her murals. MacDonald, her husband, her sister Frances, and her sister's husband James Herbert McNair comprise the Glasgow artist group The Four. Both sisters also formed the center of the Glasgow Girls, a group of women artists who were trained at the Glasgow School of Art.

In 1915, she settled in London with her husband. Poor health, however, forced Margaret to stop her artistic activity beginning in 1921. In 1923, she traveled to the south of France with her husband, taking advantage of the lower costs and healthy climate. In 1927, both returned to London and Margaret lived in seclusion in Chelsea after Mackintosh's death until 1933.

MacDonald was active in various arts and crafts, primarily as an interior decorator. Among her best-known works are the gesso panels *The Heart of The Rose* and *The White Rose and the Red Rose* (1901 and 1902, respec-

Margaret MacDonald Mackintosh, um/around 1901

als Ausstatterin von Innenräumen. Zu ihren bekanntesten Werken zählen die Gesso-Panels *The Heart of The Rose* und *The White Rose and the Red Rose*, 1901 bzw. 1902, und der sogenannte Wärndorfer-Fries *Die sieben Prinzessinnen* nach Motiven des belgischen Dichters Maurice Maeterlinck, 1902. Auch zahlreiche Plakate sind von ihr bekannt. 1901 entwarf das Ehepaar für den Wettbewerb „Haus eines Kunstfreundes" der deutschen Zeitschrift *Innendekoration* ein Wohnhaus mit Innenausstattung. Margaret entwickelte Zeichnungen für den Wettbewerbsentwurf. Das eigene Privathaus in Glasgow gestaltete das Ehepaar ganz im ästhetischen Sinne eines Gesamtkunstwerks.

tively) and the so-called Wärndorfer Frieze titled *The Seven Princesses*, based on motifs by the Belgian poet Maurice Maeterlinck (1902). She is also known for numerous posters. In 1901 the couple designed a residence in Darmstadt, Germany, including its interior spaces, for the competition "An Art Lover's Home," staged by the German magazine *Innendekoration*. Margaret developed drawings for the competition design. The couple designed their own private home in Glasgow as a Gesamtkunstwerk.

Frances MacDonald McNair (1873–1921)

Frances MacDonald ist, wie Margaret, eine der MacDonald-Schwestern. Zusammen mit Margaret MacDonald Mackintosh und ihrem Ehemann Charles Rennie Mackintosh bildeten sie und ihr Mann James Herbert McNair die bekannte Künstlergruppe The Four. Frances zählt auch zu den Glasgow Girls, einer Künstlerinnengruppe der Glasgow School of Art. Geboren wurde sie als zweite Tochter eines Bergbauingenieurs in der Nähe von Wolverhampton. 1890 ließ sich die Familie in Glasgow nieder, wo Frances und ihre Schwester Margaret an der Glasgow School of Art studierten. Dort lernte Frances ihren späteren Ehepartner kennen. Stilistisch verband sie der sogenannte Glasgow Style, eine Mischung von Elementen des englischen Art nouveau eines William Blake und Aubrey Beardsley, ferner nahmen sie Anleihen aus schottischer Kunsttradition auf, der englischen Arts-and Crafts-Bewegung und dem Symbolismus. Mitte der 1890er Jahre verließ Frances die Schule und richtete zusammen mit ihrer Schwester ein unabhängiges Studio im Zentrum der Stadt ein. Gemeinsam arbeiteten sie an Metall-, Grafik-, Textildesign und Buchillustrationen und konnten ihre Werke in London, Liverpool, Venedig und in der Wiener Sezession zeigen. Frances gestaltete das Titelbild von Anna Muthesius' *Das Eigenkleid der Frau*, 1903, das in Krefeld, Deutschland, herausgegeben wurde.

1899 heiratete Frances ihren langjährigen Freund James Herbert McNair und folgte ihm nach Liverpool, wo Frances an der School of Architecture and Applied Art unterrichtete. Das Paar entwarf die Innenräume seiner Wohnung in der Oxford Street 54 und stellte einen Lady's Writing Room auf der „Internationalen Ausstellung für moderne dekorative Kunst" in Turin aus. Ab 1907 unterrichtete Frances regelmäßig an der Glasgow School of Art. 1908 zogen sie und ihr Mann aufgrund finanzieller Schwierigkeiten zurück nach Glasgow. Frances, die Mutter eines Sohnes war, schuf eine Reihe von Aquarellen, die Ehe und Mutterschaft behandelten. Ihre

Frances MacDonald McNair (1873–1921)

Frances MacDonald was, like Margaret, one of the MacDonald sisters. Together with Margaret MacDonald Mackintosh and her husband Charles Rennie Mackintosh, Frances MacDonald and her husband James Herbert McNair comprised the well-known artist group The Four. Frances is also one of the Glasgow Girls, a group of artists from the Glasgow School of Art. She was born the second daughter of a mining engineer near Wolverhampton, UK. In 1890, the family settled in Glasgow, where Frances and her sister Margaret studied at the Glasgow School of Art, which is also where Frances met her future spouse. Stylistically, the couple were both proponents of the Glasgow style, a mixture of elements from the English art nouveau of William Blake and Aubrey Beardsley, while they also borrowed from the Scottish art tradition, the English arts and crafts movement, and symbolism. In the mid-1890s, Frances left school and set up an independent studio with her sister in the center of the city. Together they worked in metal, graphic, and textile design and created book illustrations, finding opportunities to show their work in London, Liverpool, and Venice and at the Vienna Secession. Frances designed the cover of Anna Muthesius's *Das Eigenkleid der Frau* (1903, Do-it-yourself women's dress), which was published in Krefeld, Germany.

In 1899, Frances married her longtime friend James Herbert McNair and followed him to Liverpool, where Frances taught at the School of Architecture and Applied Art. The couple designed the interiors of their apartment at 54 Oxford Street and exhibited a lady's writing room at the International Exhibition of Modern Decorative Art in Turin. From 1907, Frances taught regularly at the Glasgow School of Art. In 1908, financial difficulties prompted her and her husband to return to Glasgow. Herself a mother of a son, Frances created a series of watercolors dealing with marriage and motherhood. Her exhibitions were increasingly unsuccessful. In

Ausstellungen waren zunehmend erfolglos. 1913 reiste das Paar nach Kanada, kehrte aber 1914 vor Ausbruch des Ersten Weltkriegs wieder nach Schottland zurück.

Susan Mackie

Mackie war von 1974 bis 1982 Mitglied von See Red Women's Workshop und dort in Teilzeit Jugendarbeiterin im Kunsthandwerk. Anschließend studierte sie Sozialarbeit und engagierte sich danach acht Jahre lang im Lambeth Women and Children's Health Project, ein Gesundheitsprojekt auf der Basis von Selbsthilfe. Sie war Family Planning Association England Training Manager von 1998 bis 2005 und Training Manager bei Fostering Network England, einem Netzwerk von Pflegeeltern, von 2006 bis 2008. Im Anschluss arbeitete sie freiberuflich mit Pflegeeltern, Jugendarbeiter*innen und in Peer-Mentoring-Projekten mit jungen Menschen.

Shaz Madani

Madani ist eine Art-Direktorin in London. Neben vielen anderen Projekten gestaltete sie die Ausgaben 1 bis 12 des Magazins *Riposte*.

Ella Margold (1886–1961)

Von Margold, geb. Weltmann, sind vergleichsweise wenige Lebensdaten erhalten. Viele ihrer Arbeiten werden ihrem Ehemann, Emanuel Josef Margold, zugeschrieben, ihr Anteil an den gemeinsamen Ergebnissen ist kaum mehr identifizierbar. Zunächst arbeitete Ella Margold im Textildesign. Sie führte Entwürfe für Stickereien und Damenhüte ihres Mannes aus und war ab Oktober 1911 künstlerische und technische Mitarbeiterin in dessen Atelier auf der Mathildenhöhe in Darmstadt. Dort entwarf sie, wie auch ihr Mann, eine größere Anzahl von Blechdosen und Papierpackungen für die Firma Bahlsen in Hannover, eine Tätigkeit, die sich während der Abwesenheit ihres Mannes als Frontsoldat im Ersten Weltkrieg verstärkte und die sie bis etwa 1917 ausübte. In dieser Zeit lassen sich ihre Arbeiten eindeutig zuschreiben. Ähnlich wie ihr Mann, der 1909/10 Assistent seines Lehrers Josef Hoffmann an der Wiener Kunstgewerbeschule und Mitarbeiter der Wiener Werkstätte war, arbeitete Ella Margold mit Flächenmustern, wie sie von den Wienern Bertold Löffler und Carl Otto Czeschka bekannt waren, und entwickelte eine dem Art déco verwandte geometrische Ornamentik.

1913, the couple traveled to Canada, returning, however, to Scotland in 1914 before the outbreak of World War I.

Susan Mackie

Mackie was a member of the See Red Women's Workshop from 1974 to 1982, where she worked part-time supporting youth through instruction in arts and crafts. She went on to study social work and then spent eight years involved with the Lambeth Women and Children's Health Project, a self-help initiative. She worked as a training manager at the Family Planning Association England from 1998 to 2005 and then also at Fostering Network England, a network of foster caregivers, from 2006 to 2008. She went on to work freelance with foster parents, youth workers, and peer mentoring projects with young people.

Shaz Madani

Madani is an art director in London. Among many other projects, she designed issues 1 to 12 of *Riposte* magazine.

Ella Margold (1886–1961)

Not much is known about the life of Margold, née Weltmann. Many of her works are attributed to her husband, Emanuel Josef Margold, and it is hardly possible to identify the extent of her contributions to their joint projects. Initially, Ella Margold worked in textile design. She executed designs for her husband's embroidery and ladies' hats and from October 1911 was an artistic and technical assistant in his studio in the artists' colony Mathildenhöhe in Darmstadt. There, like her husband, she designed a large number of tin cans and paper packages for the Bahlsen company in Hannover, an activity that intensified during her husband's absence as a soldier on the front in World War I and which she continued until about 1917. During this period, her works can be clearly identified as her own. Similar to her husband, who was an assistant to his teacher Josef Hoffmann at the Vienna Kunstgewerbeschule and an employee of the Wiener Werkstätte in 1909/10, Ella Margold worked with decorative patterns for surfaces in the styles known from the Viennese artists Bertold Löffler and Carl Otto Czeschka, and she developed a geometric style of ornamentation akin to that of art deco.

Katherine McCoy (geb. 1945)

McCoy, geb. Katherine Jane Braden, lehrte an der Cranbrook Academy of Art in Bloomfield Hills, Michigan, am Illinois Institute of Technology's Institute of Design, am Royal College of Art in London und war Mitbegründerin von High Ground, einer Firma, die Designer*innen ausbildete. Geboren in Decatur, Illinois, studierte McCoy zunächst Interior Design an der Michigan State University, dann Industrial Design. Kurz nach ihrem Examen arbeitete sie für Unimark International, eine Designfirma, die bedeutende Vertreter der amerikanischen Moderne versammelte, unter anderem Massimo Vignelli und Herbert Bayer. Es folgten weitere Designfirmen. 1971 gründete sie das Büro McCoy & McCoy, Inc. zusammen mit ihrem Ehemann Michael McCoy. Gemeinsam mit ihm war sie Mitvorsitzende des „graduate design program" der Cranbrook Academy of Art, wo sie das Programm für Grafikdesign leitete und er das Industrial-Design-Programm. Die McCoys erwarteten von ihren Studierenden, dass sie sich intensiv mit der Geschichte und der Theorie von Design auseinandersetzten, außerdem sollten alle Studierenden ihren individuellen Zugang zu Design artikulieren. Studio-Experimente waren dabei mit Auftragsarbeiten vermischt. Katherine McCoy übernahm zahlreiche Buchgestaltungen. Eine ihrer bekanntesten war diejenige von Robert Venturis *Learning from Las Vegas*, 1972. Nach 24 Jahren kreativer Arbeit an den Schulen und für Firmen zogen die McCoys nach Buena Vista in Colorado, wo sie das Studio McCoy & McCoy Associates gründeten. Anschließend gaben sie bis 2004 jeden Herbst Unterricht am Illinois Institute of Technology's Institute of Design. Die Ehrungen für Katherine McCoy sind zahlreich und gehören zu den bekanntesten in den USA.

Blanche McManus Mansfield (1869–1935)

McManus, geboren auf der Talledega Plantation, East Feliciana Parish in Louisiana, war eine amerikanische Schriftstellerin und Buchillustratorin. Sie studierte Kunst in London und Paris, bevor sie 1893 ihr eigenes Studio in Chicago eröffnete. 1896 illustrierte sie viele Bücher für Stone & Kimball in Chicago sowie Dodd, Mead & Co in New York. Ihr erstes Kinderbuch *The True Mother Goose* wurde von Lamson, Wolffe & Co. herausgegeben. 1898 heiratete sie Milburg Franciso Mansfield, mit dem sie gemeinsam eine Reihe illustrierter Reiseliteratur verfasste. Sie reisten durch Europa und Nordafrika. Ihr Mann veröffentlichte unter dem Pseudonym Francis Milton. Er wurde Konsul der Vereinigten Staaten in Toulon, wo MacManus 1911 ihr illustriertes Buch *The American Woman Abroad* bei Dodd, Mead & Co publizierte. Insgesamt war sie eine äußerst produktive

Katherine McCoy (b. 1945)

McCoy, née Katherine Jane Braden, also has taught at the Cranbrook Academy of Art in Bloomfield Hills, Michigan, the Illinois Institute of Technology's Institute of Design, and the Royal College of Art in London and cofounded High Ground, a company that trained designers. Born in Decatur, Illinois, McCoy studied interior design, and then industrial design, at Michigan State University. Shortly after graduating, she worked for Unimark International, a design firm that brought together important figures from American modernism, including Massimo Vignelli and Herbert Bayer. Positions with other design firms followed. In 1971, she founded the firm McCoy & McCoy, Inc. with her husband, Michael McCoy, with whom she also was cochair of the graduate design program at the Cranbrook Academy of Art, where she headed the graphic design program and he the industrial design program. The McCoys expected their students to intensively engage with the history and theory of design; they also wanted each student to articulate their own individual approach to design. Studio experiments were mixed with commissioned works. Katherine McCoy also designed numerous books. One of her most famous was Robert Venturi's *Learning from Las Vegas* (1972). After twenty-four years of creative work at schools and for companies, the McCoys moved to Buena Vista, Colorado, where they founded the studio McCoy & McCoy Associates. They then taught classes at Illinois Institute of Technology's Institute of Design every fall until 2004. The honors awarded to Katherine McCoy are numerous and among the most illustrious in the United States.

Blanche McManus Mansfield (1869–1935)

McManus, born on Talledega Plantation, East Feliciana Parish in Louisiana, was an American writer and book illustrator. She studied art in London and Paris before opening her own studio in Chicago in 1893. In 1896, she illustrated a number of books for Stone & Kimball in Chicago and Dodd, Mead & Co in New York. Her first children's book, *The True Mother Goose*, was published by Lamson, Wolffe & Co. In 1898, she married Milburg Franciso Mansfield, with whom she coauthored a series of illustrated travel books. They traveled throughout Europe and North Africa. Publishing under the pseudonym Francis Milton, her husband became United States consul in Toulon, France, where MacManus published her 1911 illustrated book *The American Woman Abroad* with Dodd, Mead & Co. Overall, she was an extremely prolific illustrator. With her 1898 book *As Told by the*

Illustratorin. 1898 entwickelte sie mit *As Told by the Typewriter Girl* einen besonderen Stil. Der Buchtitel zeigt auf symmetrischem Doppelcover je eine Frau im roten Kleid, eingehüllt in ein Schreibmaschinenband. Die beiden spiegelbildlich angeordneten Motive treffen sich am Buchrücken, wo die Spule, von der sich das Band abwickelt, zur Basis eines Fächers wird. Dessen Gestaltung wiederum verweist auf die Anordnung der Typenhebel in der Schreibmaschine. McManus illustrierte unter anderem die Serie von *Alice's Adventures in Wonderland* von Lewis Carroll, 1899 und 1900. Auch *Our Little English Cousin* wurde 1905 von ihr verfasst und illustriert, desgleichen eine ganze Serie von Little Cousins aus vielen verschiedenen Ländern. In Woodville, Mississippi, erbte sie 1909 zusammen mit ihren beiden Schwestern ein historisches Herrenhaus, Hampton Hall, in dem sie die Wände der Salons bemalte. Über die Zeit nach 1912 existieren kaum noch Informationen über McManus. Ihre Buchillustrationen sind in amerikanischen Sammlungen sehr geschätzt.

Chia Moan

Moan zählt, neben Viv Mullett und Jenny Smith, zu den drei Gründerinnen des Lenthall Road Workshops im Londoner Stadtteil Hackney. 1975 übernahmen die Frauen eine bereits existierende Siebdruckwerkstatt und entwickelten daraus eine bis in die 1990er Jahre aktive kollektive Druckerei. Ihr Ethos war das der Selbstermächtigung von Frauen und die Adresse Lenthall Road 81 sollte das kreative Zentrum ihrer Aktivitäten sein. Die Adressatinnen waren Women of Color und Queer Communities. Moan produzierte zahlreiche Plakate.

Lilian Mohin (1938–2020)

Mohin war, zusammen mit Deborah Hart und Sheila Shulman, Gründerin der Onlywomen Press in London, auch als The Women's Press bekannt. Mohin wurde als Lilian Rodgers in Sevenoaks geboren. Ihre jüdischen Eltern stammten aus Wien und mussten wegen der Nationalsozialisten emigrieren, weshalb sie auch ihren Namen wechselten. Anfang der 1970er Jahre absolvierten Mohin, Sheila Shulman and Deborah Hart einen Zweijahreskurs am Camberwell College of Arts, um einen Verlag leiten zu können. Mohin studierte anschließend Buchbinderei und Papierproduktion am London College of Printing und arbeitete ein Jahr in einer kommerziellen Druckerei. 1974 starteten Mohin, Shulman, Hart und Jacky Bishop (die sich der Gruppe 1975 anschlossen) die feministisch-lesbische Onlywomen Press, deren Betrieb bis in die 1990er Jahre aufrechterhalten wurde. Treibende Kraft für die Gründung der Druckerei war einer Gruppe lesbischer Schriftstellerinnen, die ihre Werke veröffentlichen und zugleich

Typewriter Girl, she developed a special style: a symmetrical double cover shows two women, each in a red dress and wrapped in a typewriter ribbon. The two mirror-image motifs meet at the spine, where the coil from which the ribbon unwinds becomes the base of a fan. Its design, in turn, refers to the arrangement of the type levers on a typewriter. McManus's illustrated works include Lewis Carroll's series of *Alice's Adventures in Wonderland* (1899 and 1900). She also wrote and illustrated *Our Little English Cousin* in 1905, as well as an entire series of *Little Cousins* from many different countries. In 1909, she and her two sisters inherited a historic mansion in Woodville, Mississippi, known as Hampton Hall, where she painted the parlor walls. Little is known about McManus's life and work after 1912. Her book illustrations are highly prized in American collections.

Chia Moan

Along with Viv Mullett and Jenny Smith, Moan is one of the three founders of the Lenthall Road Workshop in the London borough of Hackney. In 1975, the women took over an existing silk-screen printing workshop, which they developed into a collective print shop that remained active until the 1990s. Their ethos was that of women's self-empowerment and the address 81 Lenthall Road was meant to be the creative center of their activities. The intended audience was women of color and queer communities. Moan produced numerous posters.

Lilian Mohin (1938–2020)

Along with Deborah Hart and Sheila Shulman, Mohin was founder of the Onlywomen Press in London, also known as The Womens's Press. Mohin was born Lilian Rodgers in Sevenoaks, UK. Her Jewish parents came from Vienna and were forced to emigrate, to Britain, because of the Nazis, where they also changed their name after arriving. In the early 1970s, Mohin, Sheila Shulman, and Deborah Hart took a two-year course at Camberwell College of Arts to learn how to run a publishing house. Mohin went on to study bookbinding and paper production at the London College of Printing and spent a year working in a commercial print shop. In 1974, Mohin, Shulman, Hart, and Jacky Bishop (who joined the group in 1975) launched the feminist-lesbian Onlywomen Press, which continued to operate into the 1990s. The driving force behind the founding of the print shop was a group of lesbian writers who wanted to publish and retain control over their own work, though Onlywomen also published works by

die Kontrolle über ihr eigenes Werk behalten wollten. Onlywomen Press verlegte aber auch Arbeiten anderer Schriftstellerinnen. 1977 organisierten Mohin und Hart die erste nationale Konferenz in England über Verlagswesen und Druckerei von Frauen.

Clara Lisette Möller-Coburg/Ehmcke
(1869–1918)

Möller-Coburg war eine der produktivsten Werbegrafikerinnen ihrer Zeit. Das Spektrum ihrer Arbeiten reichte von Exlibris, Werbeplakaten, Warenverpackungen, Visitenkarten, Vorsatzpapieren, Kinderkleidern, Web- und Stickarbeiten, Kinderspielzeug für die Deutschen Werkstätten, Verpackungen für die Parfümerie Hager, Stettin, bis hin zu Puppenkorbmöbel für die F. Baudler Rohrmöbelfabrik. Ihre künstlerische Ausbildung erhielt sie zunächst durch Privatunterricht bei ihrem Vater. In den späten 1890er Jahren ließ sie sich zuerst im privaten Atelier von Sophie Hormann in München in Malerei unterrichten, danach studierte sie an der sogenannten Damenakademie des Münchener Künstlerinnenvereins. 1900 und 1901 war sie Schülerin von Fritz Hegenbart und Maximilian Dasio und unternahm anschließend eine Reise nach Italien gemeinsam mit der Dichterin Margarete Susman, die damals Kunstgewerbe studierte, und zwei weiteren Künstlerinnen. Sie baute sich in München ein Netzwerk von gleichgesinnten Frauen auf, zu dem Gertrud Kleinhempel, Antonia Ritzerow, Viktoria Zimmermann, Edith von Herzer und Else Oppler zählten. Ihren Mädchennamen hatte sie um den Namen ihrer Geburtsstadt erweitert.

Möller-Coburg war anfangs am Jugendstil orientiert, stellte sich dann aber bei der renommierten Steglitzer Werkstatt in Berlin vor, die sich bewusst vom Jugendstil absetzte und eine größere Sachlichkeit entwickelte. Sie war von 1902 bis 1904 nicht nur Schülerin, sondern von Beginn an Mitarbeiterin der Werkstatt. Dort entwarf sie Werbegrafik für die Firma Syndetikon von Otto Ring, der die Werkstatt als Hauptauftraggeber weitgehend finanzierte, sowie Buchschmuck und Exlibris. Aus eigenen Mitteln etablierte sie eine Stickerei- und Modeabteilung, die Reformkleider produzierte und unterrichtete Maschinenstickerei. Nach ihrer Zeit in der Steglitzer Werkstatt konnte sie an der Handwerker- und Kunstgewerbeschule Magdeburg eine Stickerei-Abteilung aufbauen. Neben technischen Kenntnissen, die sie einbrachte, finanzierte sie auch die geeigneten Maschinen, sodass von April 1904 bis Februar 1905 eine Textilklasse entstehen konnte, in der sie als Lehrerin arbeitete. Die Leitung der Textilklasse wurde allerdings von Ferdinand Nigg übernommen. 1905 heiratete Möller-Coburg den renommierten Typografen und Buchgestalter Fritz Helmuth Ehmcke. Ihre Arbeiten kursieren bisweilen

other women writers. In 1977, Mohin and Hart organized the first national conference in the UK on women's publishing and printing.

Clara Lisette Möller-Coburg/Ehmcke
(1869–1918)

Möller-Coburg was one of the most prolific commercial artists of her time. The spectrum of her work included bookplates, advertising posters, merchandise packaging, business cards, endpapers, children's clothing, woven and embroidered works, children's toys for the Deutsche Werkstätten, packaging for Parfümerie Hager (in Stettin, today Szczecin in Poland), and rattan doll furniture for the F. Baudler Rohrmöbelfabrik. She initially received her artistic training through private lessons with her father. In the late 1890s, she first took painting lessons in Sophie Hormann's private studio in Munich, then studied at the so-called Damenakademie, or Ladies' Academy, of the Münchener Künstlerinnenverein. In 1900 and 1901, she was a student of Fritz Hegenbart and Maximilian Dasio, and then embarked on a voyage to Italy together with the poet Margarete Susman, who was studying arts and crafts at the time, and two other women artists. She built up a network of likeminded women in Munich, including Gertrud Kleinhempel, Antonia Ritzerow, Viktoria Zimmermann, Edith von Herzer, and Else Oppler. She created the extended form of her name by appending the name of the town where she was born.

Möller-Coburg initially began working in the style of art nouveau but was then hired by the renowned Steglitz workshop in Berlin, which deliberately set itself apart from art nouveau in its cultivation of greater objectivity. She was not only a student at the workshop from 1902 to 1904, but also an employee from the beginning. Working there she designed advertising graphics for Otto Ring's company Syndetikon; Ringer largely financed the workshop as its main client, in addition to commissioning book decorations and bookplates. Using her own funds, she established an embroidery and fashion department that produced clothing for the dress reform movement, while also teaching machine embroidery. After her time in the Steglitz workshop, she was able to set up an embroidery department at the Handwerker- und Kunstgewerbeschule Magdeburg. In addition to contributing technical knowledge, she also financed the machinery necessary to establish a textile workshop from April 1904 to February 1905, where she also worked as an instructor. The management of the textile class was, however, later taken over by Ferdinand Nigg. In 1905, Möller-Coburg married the renowned

deshalb auch unter dem Namen Clara Ehmcke. Aber auch in der Ehe behielt sie ihren Künstlernamen bei und war selbstständig tätig. Aus den drei Anfangsbuchstaben CMC, in einem Dreieck zusammengefasst, entwickelte sie ihr Signet als Künstlerin. Sie starb 1918 im Alter von 49 Jahren an den Folgen der Spanischen Grippe.

typographer and book designer Fritz Helmuth Ehmcke. Her works thus sometimes circulate under the name Clara Ehmcke. Even after she was married, however, she kept her artist's name and remained an independent artist. She developed her signet as an artist by combining the three initial letters of her name, CMC, in a triangle. She died in 1918 at the age of forty-nine as a victim of the Spanish flu.

May Morris (1862–1938)

Morris (geb. als Mary Morris) ist vor allem als Tochter ihres berühmten Vaters, William Morris, des Gründers der Arts-and-Crafts-Bewegung, und seiner Frau Jane Burden bekannt. Allenfalls fanden ihre Tätigkeiten in den Werkstätten ihres Vaters Erwähnung. In jüngerer Zeit widmeten sich Autorinnen ihrem eigenwilligen Leben und eigenständigen Werk in umfassenden Publikationen. May Morris' Schwerpunkt lag auf Glasmalerei und Textil, sie war aber auch Mitglied der Kelmscott Press und gestaltete Bücher, unter anderem mit kunstvoll gestickten Einbänden. Aufgewachsen im legendären Red House in Upton, Bexleyheath, zog die Familie nach London, als sie das Haus aufgeben musste. In London studierte sie von 1880 bis 1883 Textile Kunst an der South Kensington School of Design. Im Alter von 23 Jahren übernahm sie die Leitung der Stickerei-Abteilung der Firma Morris & Co. Für die damalige Zeit allgemein und auch für die Werkstatt ungewöhnlich, entwarf sie eigene Stickereien und führte alle neuen Entwürfe durch, gemeinsam mit Morris' Assistent John Henry Dearle. Von 1899 bis 1908 gab sie Unterricht in Sticken sowohl an der Central School of Arts & Crafts als auch der School of Art Needlework. Sie war eine bedeutende Schmuckdesignerin und stellte regelmäßig in der Arts and Crafts Society aus. Weil Frauen in der Art-Workers' Guild nicht zugelassen waren, gründete sie 1907 die Women's Guild of Arts und blieb deren Präsidentin bis 1935. Morris stellte ihre Arbeiten 1913 auf der Weltausstellung in Gent und 1914 auf der „Exposition d'Arts Décoratifs" in Paris aus. Nach dem Tod ihres Vaters 1896 veröffentlichte sie dessen Romane und Dichtungen in 24 Bänden.

Morris war, wie ihr Vater, der sozialistischen Bewegung ihres Landes verbunden. 1890 ging sie eine Ehe mit dem Sekretär der Sozialistischen Liga von Hammersmith, Henry Halliday Sparling, ein. Sparling, bäuerlicher Herkunft, wurde bei der Kelmscott Press angestellt. May nahm nach einiger Zeit ihre frühere Liebesbeziehung zu dem Schriftsteller George Bernard Shaw wieder auf und reiste mit ihm zum International Socialist Workers' Congress nach Zürich. Ihre Ehe wurde 1898 geschieden und May nahm wieder ihren Geburtsnamen an. Morris führte einen freien Lebensstil. Sie be-

May Morris (1862–1938)

Morris (born Mary Morris) is best known as the daughter of her famous father, William Morris, founder of the arts and crafts movement, and his wife Jane Burden. Until recently, her activities were mostly mentioned, if at all, in the context of her father's workshops. This has changed, however, as scholars have devoted extensive publications to her idiosyncratic life and independent work. May Morris's focus was on stained glass and textiles, but she was also a member of the Kelmscott Press and designed books, some of which possessed ornately embroidered covers. Raised in the legendary Red House in Upton, Bexleyheath, she moved to London with her family when they had to give up their manor. In London, she studied textile arts at the South Kensington School of Design from 1880 to 1883. At the age of twenty-three, she became head of the embroidery department of Morris & Co. Unusual for the time and for the workshop more specifically, she designed her own embroideries and executed all new designs together with Morris's assistant John Henry Dearle. From 1899 to 1908, she gave classes in embroidery at both the Central School of Arts & Crafts and the School of Art Needlework. She was also a prominent jewelry designer and exhibited regularly at the Arts and Crafts Society. Because women were not allowed in the Art-Workers' Guild, May Morris founded the Women's Guild of Arts in 1907; she remained its president until 1935. Morris exhibited her work at the 1913 World's Fair in Ghent and in 1914 at the Exposition d'Arts Décoratifs in Paris. After her father's death in 1896, she published his novels and poetry in twenty-four volumes.

Morris, like her father, was committed to her country's socialist movement. In 1890, she married Henry Halliday Sparling, secretary of the Hammersmith Socialist League. Sparling, originally from a peasant family, was employed by the Kelmscott printing company. Some time after marrying Sparling, however, May resumed her earlier love affair with the writer George Bernard Shaw, traveling with him to the International Socialist Workers' Congress in Zurich. She and Sparling divorced in 1898 and May reclaimed her birth name. Morris led a life marked by freedom. She befriended the erstwhile tractor operator and gardener of Kelm-

freundete sich mit der ehemaligen Traktoristin und Gärtnerin von Kelmscott Manor, Mary Lobb. 1910 reiste sie zusammen mit ihr in die USA und nach Kanada, wo sie auch Vorträge hielt. Dort verliebte sie sich in den amerikanischen Rechtsanwalt und Sammler von Manuskripten John Quinn, mit dem sie einen regen Briefwechsel führte, in dem sein Interesse an der Arbeit von May Morris deutlich wurde. Der Briefwechsel wurde sehr viel später in der John Quinn Memorial Collection der New York Public Library wiederentdeckt. Morris verfolgte über die Jahre die Idee eines Dorfgemeinschaftshauses für Kelmscott, das der mit ihr befreundete Architekt Ernest Gimson bereits plante. Er verstarb jedoch 1919.

Alice Cordelia Morse (1863–1961)

Morse gilt neben Margaret Neilson Armstrong und Sarah Wyman Whitman als eine der drei berühmtesten Buchgestalterinnen ihrer Zeit. Sie war, wie die meisten amerikanischen Grafikdesigner*innen, durch die Arts-and-Crafts-Bewegung beeinflusst. Morse wurde in Hammondsville, Ohio, geboren. Die Familie zog in ihrer frühen Kindheit um nach Williamsburg, Brooklyn. Sie besuchte von 1879 bis 1883 die Woman's School of Art der Cooper Union for the Advancement of Science and Art (Cooper Union), eine Privatschule in New York, wo sie einen Abschluss in Kunst und Design machte. Cooper Union öffnete sich früh dem Studium für Frauen, auch konnten Studierende unentgeltlich dort studieren. Danach absolvierte sie weitere Kunstschulen, unter anderem das Alfred State College in New York. Sie arbeitete zunächst als Künstlerin für Bleiverglasungen, zuerst bei John La Farge und dann bei Louis Comfort Tiffany. Nachdem sie mehrere Wettbewerbe in Buchgestaltung gewonnen hatte, konzentrierte sie sich auf dieses Handwerk. Hierfür begann sie 1889 noch einmal ein Studium an der Cooper Union bei Susan N. Carter. Von 1893 an war sie für zwei Jahre bei der New York Society of Decorative Art als Designerin angestellt. Zwischen 1887 und 1905 gestaltete sie über 80 Bucheinbände. Ihre Auftraggeber waren Houghton Mifflin, Charles Scribner's Sons, Harper & Brothers, G. P. Putnam's Sons, Dodd, Mead & Company. Plakate, Postkarten, dekorative Details von Büchern wie Vignetten, Titelblätter, Illustrationen zählten ebenfalls zu ihren Arbeiten. Zugleich interessierte sie sich für die romanische und renaissancistische Geschichte des Buchbindens, experimentierte mit keltischen, arabischen, gotischen und Rokoko-Formen und besonders mit der Art-nouveau-Stilistik.

Morse nahm an zahlreichen Ausstellungen teil, unter anderem 1893 an der Weltausstellung in Chicago, wo sie zum Planungskomitee des Woman's Building gehörte und Mitglied des

scott Manor, Mary Lobb, with whom she journeyed in 1910 through the United States and Canada, giving lectures. In Canada, she fell in love with John Quinn, an American lawyer and manuscript collector, with whom she maintained a lively correspondence that revealed his interest in May Morris's work. The correspondence was rediscovered much later in the John Quinn Memorial Collection of the New York Public Library. Morris pursued the idea of a village assembly hall for Kelmscott over the years, with early planning underway in collaboration with architect Ernest Gimson, a friend of hers; the plans, however, could not be completed because of his death in 1919.

Alice Cordelia Morse (1863–1961)

Morse is considered one of the three most famous women book designers of her time, along with Margaret Neilson Armstrong and Sarah Wyman Whitman. Like most American graphic designers, she was influenced by the arts and crafts movement. Morse was born in Hammondsville, Ohio. The family moved to Williamsburg, Brooklyn, in her early childhood. From 1879 to 1883 she attended the Woman's School of Art of the Cooper Union for the Advancement of Science and Art (Cooper Union), a private school in New York, where she earned a degree in art and design. Cooper Union accepted women early on and offered all students it accepted a free education. She went on to graduate from other art schools, including Alfred State College in New York. She began her career as a lead glazing artist, first for John La Farge and then for Louis Comfort Tiffany. After winning several competitions in book design, she refocused her work on this craft, returning to Cooper Union in 1889 to take an additional degree with Susan N. Carter. From 1893 to 1895, she worked as a designer for the New York Society of Decorative Art. Between 1887 and 1905, she designed over eighty book covers. Her clients included Houghton Mifflin, Charles Scribner's Sons, Harper & Brothers, G. P. Putnam's Sons, Dodd, and Mead & Company. Her work also encompassed posters, postcards, and decorative details of books such as vignettes, title pages, and illustrations. She was moreover interested in the Romanesque and Renaissance history of bookbinding, experimented with Celtic, Arabic, Gothic, and rococo forms and especially with the stylistic register of art nouveau.

Morse participated in numerous exhibitions, including the 1893 Chicago World's Fair, where she was part of the planning committee for the Woman's Building and a member of the Committee on Book Binding, Woodcuts, and Book Illustrations. Eleven of her own books were shown at the World's Fair, garnering her a number of honors. She also contributed a

Komitees für Bucheinbände, Holzschnitte und Buchillustrationen war. Elf ihrer eigenen Bücher wurden dort gezeigt, für die sie entsprechende Ehrungen erhielt. Zum Handbuch des Woman's Buildings trug sie ein Kapitel mit dem Titel „Women Illustrators" bei, in dem Abbildungen ihrer Bücher gezeigt wurden. Sie schuf auch die Einbände der berühmten *Distaff Series*, einer Serie von sechs Büchern, geschrieben, gestaltet und gesetzt von Frauen. Die Bücher wurden bei Harper & Brothers veröffentlich und im Woman's Building verkauft.

Künstlerisch gestaltete Bucheinbände verloren um 1900 an Attraktivität bei den Konsument*innen, weshalb Morse sich der Designlehre zuwandte. Sie begann 1896 eine Ausbildung am Pratt Institute in New York City, zog dann aber um in die damals reiche Stadt Scranton, Pennsylvania, wo sie eine Lehrposition an einer städtischen Schule übernahm. Sie stieg auf in die Scranton Central High School, die als eine der besten Schulen der Region galt. Ab 1917 war sie Direktorin aller Kunstprogramme der Schule in der Region. Sehr viele ihrer Bücher vermachte sie der Bibliothek des Metropolitan Museums in New York.

chapter titled "Women Illustrators" to the Woman's Building manual, featuring illustrations of her books, and she created the covers of the famous *Distaff Series*, a series of six books written, designed, and typeset by women. The books were published by Harper & Brothers and sold in the Woman's Building.

Artistically designed book covers lost their appeal among consumers around 1900, motivating Morse to turn to design pedagogy. She began training at Pratt Institute in New York City in 1896, later moving to the then-wealthy town of Scranton, Pennsylvania, where she took a teaching position in a city school. Moving up professionally, she obtained a teaching position at Scranton Central High School, which was considered one of the best schools in the region. From 1917 onward, she directed all school art programs in the region. She bequeathed a great many of her books to the library of the Metropolitan Museum in New York.

Viv Mullett

Mullett zählt neben Chia Moan and Jenny Smith zu den drei Gründerinnen des Lenthall Road Workshops im Londoner Stadtteil Hackney. 1975 übernahmen die Frauen eine bereits existierende Siebdruckwerkstatt und entwickelten daraus eine bis in die 1990er Jahre aktive kollektive Druckerei. Ihr Ethos war das der Selbstermächtigung von Frauen und die Adresse Lenthall Road 81 sollte das kreative Zentrum ihrer Aktivitäten sein. Die Adressatinnen waren Women of Color und Queer Communities.

Viv Mullett

Along with Chia Moan and Jenny Smith, Mullett is one of the three founders of the Lenthall Road Workshop in the London borough of Hackney. In 1975, the women took over an existing silk-screen printing workshop, which they developed into a collective print shop that remained active until the 1990s. Their ethos was that of women's self-empowerment and the address 81 Lenthall Road was meant to be the creative center of their activities. The intended audience was women of color and queer communities.

Anja Neidhardt

Neidhardt ist freiberufliche Designjournalistin und Kuratorin. 2016 schloss sie ihr Master-Studium im Fachbereich Design Curating and Writing an der Design Academy Eindhoven ab. Von 2012 bis 2014 gehörte sie zum Redaktionsteam des Magazins *Form*. Sie unterrichtet Designgeschichte und Designtheorie an der Frankfurter Akademie für visuelle Kommunikation und Design (Academy of Visual Arts). Gemeinsam mit der Designwissenschaftlerin Maya Ober leitet sie die Plattform *depatriarchise design*. 2021 schloss sich depatriarchise design mit dem nichtkommerziellen Studio für Designforschung common-interest zusammen, das sich 2018 gegründet hatte. 2019 schuf common-interest die website *Futuress*, die sich ein Jahr später als Online-Magazin und Plattform entwickelte. Neidhardt ist außerdem Redaktionsmitglied des Magazins *ROM*.

Anja Neidhardt

Neidhardt is a freelance design journalist and curator. In 2016, she completed her master's degree in design curating and writing at the Design Academy Eindhoven. From 2012 to 2014, she was part of the editorial team of the magazine *Form*. She teaches design history and design theory at the Frankfurt Academy of Visual Arts. Together with the design researcher Maya Ober, she spearheads the platform *depatriarchise design*. In 2021, depatriarchise design joined forces with the nonprofit design research studio common-interest, formed in 2018. In 2019, common-interest created the website *Futuress*, which developed a year later into an online magazine and platform. Neidhardt is also an editorial member of the magazine *ROM*.

Jessie Newbery (1864–1948)

Newbery war Mitglied der Glasgow Girls in Schottland. Sie spezialisierte sich auf Stickerei, wobei ihre Arbeiten auch bildhaften Charakter hatten. An der Glasgow School of Art gründete sie 1894 eine Abteilung Stickerei. Sie öffnete ihre Klassen für weibliche Studierende durch gelockerte Zulassungsformalia und ließ Frauen und Männer ungeachtet ihres sozialen Standes zu. Sie baute zudem eine Samstagsschule auf, damit werktätige Studierende am Unterricht teilnehmen konnten, und unterrichtete dort etwa 100 Frauen. 1889 heiratete sie den progressiven Direktor der Schule, Francis Newbery, der ein aktives Mitglied der Glasgow Society of Lady Artists war. Mit der Unterstützung von Freund*innen organisierte Jessie Newbery Ausstellungen und einen Raum für Künstlerinnen. Sie war aktives Mitglied der Women's Social und Political Union und fertigte Symbole für die Suffragetten, unter anderem eine Stickerei mit 80 Namen der zwangsernährten Suffragetten im Holloway-Gefängnis; die Arbeit wurde auf der Prozession Prison to Citizenship in London 1911 gezeigt. In späteren Jahren unterstützte Newbery die Planung einer Scottish Exhibition of National History, Art and Industry.

Maya Ober

Ober arbeitet als Designerin, Aktivistin und Lehrerin in Basel, Schweiz. Sie ist ausgebildet in Industrial Design. 2017 gründete sie die Non-Profit-Design-Plattform *depatriarchise design*.

Seit 2018 ist sie Forschungsassistentin am Industrial Design Institut und in der Lehre des Institute of Aesthetic Practice and Theory an der FHNW Academy of Art and Design in Basel, wo sie Programme zu Imagining Otherwise konzipiert. Sie ist Doktorandin im Fach Soziale Anthropologie an der Universität Bern und Stipendiatin der Swiss National Science Foundation. Ober setzt ihren Fokus auf eine feministische Designlehre und die Überschneidungen von aktivistischen Bewegungen.

Nina Paim (geb. 1986)

Paim ist eine in der Schweiz lebende brasilianische Grafikdesignerin und Kuratorin. Sie studierte zunächst Grafikdesign an der Escola Superior de Desenho Industrial (ESDI) in Rio de Janeiro, absolvierte dann ihren Bachelor in Grafikdesign an der holländischen Gerrit Rietveld Academie und ihren Master in Designforschung an der schweizerischen Hochschule der Künste, Bern. Sie hat in Aruba, Tschechien, Deutschland, Dänemark, Estland, Frankreich, Italien, Portugal, Großbritannien, den USA und der Schweiz unterrichtet und Vorträge gehalten. 2014 kuratierte sie im Rahmen der 26. Biennale für Grafikdesign in Brno die Ausstellung „Taking a Line for a Walk", für die sie 2015 mit dem

Jessie Newbery (1864–1948)

Newbery was a member of the Glasgow Girls in Scotland who specialized in embroidery, with works that often had a pictorial character. She founded an embroidery department at the Glasgow School of Art in 1894. It opened its classes to women students by relaxing its formal requirements for admission, accepting women and men regardless of social background. She also set up a Saturday school so that working students could attend classes, where she taught around one hundred women. In 1889 she married the school's progressive principal, Francis Newbery, who was an active member of the Glasgow Society of Lady Artists. Supported by friends, Jessie Newbery organized exhibitions and a space for women artists. She was an active member of the Women's Social and Political Union and made emblems for the suffragettes, including an embroidery of eighty names of the suffragettes subjected to forced feeding in Holloway Prison; the work was displayed at the Prison to Citizenship procession in London in 1911. In later years, Newbery supported the planning of a Scottish Exhibition of National History, Art, and Industry.

Maya Ober

Ober works as a designer, activist, and teacher in Basel, Switzerland. She is trained in industrial design. In 2017, she founded the non-profit design platform *depatriarchise design*.

Since 2018, she has been a research assistant at the Industrial Design Institute, while teaching at the Institute of Aesthetic Practice and Theory at the FHNW Academy of Art and Design in Basel, where she designs programs on Imagining Otherwise. She is a PhD candidate in social anthropology at the University of Bern and a Doc.CH grantee of the Swiss National Science Foundation. Her research focuses on feminist practices of design education and their intersections with activist movements.

Nina Paim (b. 1986)

Paim is a Brazilian graphic designer and curator living in Switzerland. She first studied graphic design at the Escola Superior de Desenho Industrial (ESDI) in Rio de Janeiro, then completed her bachelor's degree in graphic design at the Gerrit Rietveld Academie in Holland and her master's degree in design research at the Swiss University of the Arts, Bern. She has taught and lectured in Aruba, the Czech Republic, Germany, Denmark, Estonia, France, Italy, Portugal, the UK, the United States, and Switzerland. In 2014, she curated the exhibition *Taking a Line for a Walk* at the twenty-sixth Biennale of Graphic Design Brno, for which she was awarded the Swiss

Schweizer Designpreis ausgezeichnet wurde. Das begleitende Buch mit dem gleichen Titel hat sie mitkonzipiert und 2016 bei Spector Books, Leipzig, herausgegeben. Von 2017 bis 2018 war sie Programmkuratorin der Konferenz „Beyond Change. Questioning the role of design in times of global transformation" des Swiss Design Network, aus dem der Band *Design Struggles. Intersecting Histories, Pedagogies, and Perspectives* hervorging, den sie zusammen mit Claudia Mareis verantwortete. Paim ist Mitgründerin des nichtkommerziellen Studios für Designforschung common-interest. Als dessen Mitglied kuratierte sie 2018 im Rahmen der ersten Fikra Graphic Design Biennial in Sharjah (Vereinigte Arabische Emirate) die Ausstellung „Department of Non-Binaries". Sie ist außerdem Mitbegründerin und Co-Directorin des Online-Magazins und der Plattform *Futuress*, das die soziale und politische Praxis von Design in seinen Fokus stellt.

Marion Louise Peabody
(1869–vermutl. 1937)

Von der künstlerischen Buchbinderin Peabody sind nicht viele biografische Daten bekannt. Sie wurde in Boston, Massachusetts, geboren. Offensichtlich hat sie viele Reisen nach Italien unternommen. Einen Bucheinband gestaltete sie 1898 und 1899 für *The Fairy Spinning Wheel*.

Sarah Anne Worthington King Peter
(1800–1877)

Peter wurde 1800 in Chillicothe, Ohio, geboren und stammte aus einer angesehenen Familie. Ihr Vater war Gouverneur von Ohio und Mitglied des amerikanischen Senats. In erster Ehe war sie mit Edward King verbunden, in zweiter Ehe mit William Peter, einem britischen Konsul in Philadelphia. Nach seinem Tod zog sie nach Cambridge, Massachusetts. Während ihrer Zeit in Philadelphia gründete sie 1850 die Philadelphia School of Design for Women, heute Moore College of Art and Design. Nach dem Tod ihres Ehemannes widmete sich Peter kunstfördernden Maßnahmen sowie philanthropischen Initiativen. 1862 wurde sie Krankenschwester und verschrieb sich mit weiteren Schwestern karitativen Kriegsdiensten.

Design Prize in 2015. She was a coauthor of the accompanying book with the same title, published in 2016 by Spector Books in Leipzig. In 2017–18, she was program curator of the conference "Beyond Change: Questioning the Role of Design in Times of Global Transformation" organized by the Swiss Design Network, also the basis for the volume *Design Struggles: Intersecting Histories, Pedagogies, and Perspectives* that she edited with Claudia Mareis. Paim is cofounder of the nonprofit design research studio common-interest. As a member of common-interest, she curated the exhibition *Department of Non-Binaries* in 2018 as part of the first Fikra Graphic Design Biennial in Sharjah (United Arab Emirates). She is also the cofounder and codirector of *Futuress*, an online magazine and platform that focuses on the social and political practice of design.

Marion Louise Peabody
(1869–most likely 1937)

Not much is known about the life of Peabody, a bookbinder of art books. Born in Boston, Massachusetts, she also appears to have traveled many times to Italy. In 1898 and 1899, she designed a book cover for *The Fairy Spinning Wheel*.

Sarah Anne Worthington King Peter
(1800–1877)

Peter was born in Chillicothe, Ohio, in 1800, to a distinguished family. Her father was governor of Ohio and a member of the U.S. Senate. Her first husband was Edward King, and her second William Peter, a British consul in Philadelphia. After Peter's death, she moved to Cambridge, Massachusetts. During her time in Philadelphia, she founded the Philadelphia School of Design for Women, now the Moore College of Art and Design, in 1850. After the death of her husband, Peter devoted herself to fostering the work of artists and to philanthropy. In 1862, she became a nurse and joined other women nurses and in devoting her efforts to caring for soldiers during the American Civil War.

Cipe Pineles (1908–1991)

Pineles wurde 1908 in Österreich geboren und emigrierte 1915 mit ihrer Mutter und den Schwestern nach New York. 1926 schrieb sie sich ins Pratt Institute in Brooklyn ein, eine private Schule in New York, wo sie Kunst studierte. Karriere machte sie hingegen im Bereich von Gebrauchsgrafik und Printmedien. Sie wurde bei Condé Nast Art-Direktorin von Magazinen wie *Seventeen*, *Charm*, *Glamour*, *Vogue* und *Vanity Fair*. Sie war eine der Ersten, die in einer Männerwelt erfolgreich waren, und es gelang ihr, die Werke solch berühmter Künstler wie Andy Warhol, Ad Reinhardt und Ben Shahn in die von ihr betreuten Magazine zu integrieren. Neben ihrer Arbeit bei Condé Nast lehrte sie ab 1963 Publikationsdesign an der Parsons School of Design und war dort deren Leiterin. 1977 übernahm sie die Andrew-Mellon-Professur an der Cooper Union zur Förderung von Wissenschaft und Kunst, 1978 war sie im Gastkomitee der Harvard Graduate School of Design. 1943 wurde sie das erste weibliche Mitglied des Art Directors Clubs, in dessen Hall of Fame sie 1975 aufgenommen wurde. Pineles war zwanzig Jahre mit dem Designer William Golden verheiratet und nach dessen Tod mit dem Grafiker und Designer Will Burtin. In dieser Zeit gab sie viele Kochbücher heraus. Sie war Teil einer großen Gruppe von Designer*innen, Künstler*innen, Verlegern und Art-Direktor*innen in New York.

Cipe Pineles (1908–1991)

Pineles was born in Austria in 1908 and emigrated to New York with her mother and sisters in 1915. In 1926, she enrolled at the Pratt Institute in Brooklyn, a private school in New York, where she studied art, thereafter launching a successful career in the field of advertising graphics and print media. She went on to become art director at Condé Nast for magazines such as *Seventeen*, *Charm*, *Glamour*, *Vogue*, and *Vanity Fair*. One of the first woman designers to succeed in a man's world, she was able to including the work of such famous artists as Andy Warhol, Ad Reinhardt, and Ben Shahn in the magazines she directed. In addition to her work at Condé Nast, she taught publication design at the Parsons School of Design from 1963 onward, where she also served as director. In 1977, she accepted the Andrew Mellon Professorship at Cooper Union for the Advancement of Science and the Arts, and in 1978 she served on the visiting committee of the Harvard Graduate School of Design. In 1943, she became the first female member of the Art Directors Club and was inducted into its Hall of Fame in 1975. Pineles was married for twenty years to designer William Golden, and after his death, to graphic artist and designer Will Burtin. During this time, she published many cookbooks. She was part of a large group of designers, artists, publishers, and art directors in New York.

Esther Pissarro (1870–1951)

Pissarro wurde unter ihrem Mädchennamen Bensusan geboren. Sie studierte an der Crystal Palace School of Art der Crystal Palace Company in London. 1892 heiratete sie ihren Kollegen, den Künstler Lucien Pissarro, mit dem zusammen sie Inhaberin der Eragny Press war. Zu deren Gründung waren sie von William Morris' Kelmscott Press angeregt worden. Esther Pissarro illustrierte die Bücher der Eragny Press, wobei sie meist die Entwürfe ihres Mannes als Holzstiche umsetzte. Ihre Werke werden in der Tate Gallery und in der Royal Academy of Arts aufbewahrt.

Esther Pissarro (1870–1951)

Born under the maiden name of Bensusan, Pissarro studied at the Crystal Palace School of Art operated by the Crystal Palace Company in London. In 1892, she married a colleague, the artist Lucien Pissarro, with whom she then founded the Eragny Press, inspired by William Morris's Kelmscott Press. Esther Pissarro illustrated books for the Eragny Press, mostly executing her husband's designs as wood engravings. Her works are held in collections at the Tate Gallery and the Royal Academy of Arts.

Ljubow Sergejewna Popowa (1889–1924)

Für Popowa charakteristisch ist, dass sie sich in späteren Jahren von der Malerei, der „Staffelei"-Kunst, lossagte und sich der angewandten Kunst, der „Produktionskunst", zuwandte. Sie wurde auf einem Landgut in der Nähe von Moskau geboren. Im Zuge der Ausbildung zur Malerin besuchte sie die renommierten Privatateliers der Künstler Stanislaw Schukowski und Konstantin Juan in Moskau. Mehrere Studienreisen führten sie zwischen 1910 und 1914 nach Frankreich und Italien. Nach der Begegnung mit Wladimir Tatlin konnte sie in dessen legendären Moskauer Atelier Der Turm mitarbeiten und bildete zwischen 1913 und 1916 mit ihm zusammen eine Ateliergemeinschaft. Popowa nahm an den berühmtesten Ausstellungen der russischen Avantgarde jener Zeit teil: „Tramway V", „Magazin", „0.10" und 1921 an der Konstruktivistenausstellung „5 × 5 = 25". Auf ihrer Reise nach Samarkand in Usbekistan lernte sie die regionale Architektur und die Farben der alten Bauten kennen und integrierte sie in ihre „architektonische Malerei".

Ab 1918 arbeitete sie als Kunstprofessorin an den SWOMAS (Freie staatliche Ateliers) und WCHUTEMAS (Staatliche freie Kunstwerkstätten). Sie löste sich jedoch noch im selben Jahr von der freien Kunst und arbeitete in der angewandten Kunst, dem Buch-, Porzellan- und Textildesign. 1921 unterschrieben sie und viele ihrer Kolleg*innen ein Manifest, mit dem sie sich von der Staffelmalerei lossagten und der sogenannten Produktionskunst zuwandten. 1922 fertigte sie Szenen- und Kostümentwürfe für Wsewolod Emiljewitsch Meyerhold. Ihre Bühnenbilder wurden 1922 in Berlin auf der „Ersten Russischen Kunstausstellung" und in der Galerie Van Diemen ausgestellt. Von 1923 bis 1924 folgte die Arbeit an Kleidungs- und Textilentwürfen für die Erste Staatliche Textilfabrik in Moskau. Zusammen mit ihrer künstlerischen Weggefährtin Warwara Stepanowa arbeitete sie in ihren letzten Lebensjahren in einer Textilfabrik in Moskau und entwarf ein außergewöhnliches geometrisches Textildesign.

Lyubov Sergeyevna Popova (1889–1924)

Popova's work is characterized by her turning away, in her later years, from painting, or what she and others called "easel art," and toward applied art, or "production art". She was born on a country manor near Moscow. In the course of her training as a painter, she attended the renowned private studios of the artists Stanislav Zhukovsky and Konstantin Juan in Moscow. Several study trips took her to France and Italy between 1910 and 1914. After meeting Vladimir Tatlin, she was able to work in his legendary Moscow studio The Tower, forming a studio community with him from 1913 to 1916. Popova took part in the most famous exhibitions of the Russian avant-garde of the time, *Tramway V, Magazine, 0.10*, and the 1921 constructivist show *5 × 5 = 25*. On a journey to Samarkand in Uzbekistan, she became familiar with the regional architecture and the colors of the city's old buildings, integrating them into her "architectural painting."

From 1918 onward, she worked as an art professor at SVOMAS (the Free State Studios) and VKHUTEMAS (Free State Art Workshops). However, she broke away from fine arts that same year to work in applied arts and in book, porcelain, and textile design. In 1921, she and many of her colleagues signed a manifesto renouncing easel painting in favor of production art. In 1922, she designed scenery and costumes for Vsevolod Emilievich Meyerhold. Her stage designs were exhibited in Berlin in 1922 at the First Russian Art Exhibition and at the Van Diemen Gallery. From 1923 to 1924, she worked on clothing and textile designs for the First State Textile Factory in Moscow. Together with her artistic collaborator Varvara Stepanova, she worked in a textile factory in Moscow during the last years of her life, creating an extraordinary style of textile design based on geometric forms.

Helen Beatrix Potter (1866–1943)

Potter war eine der berühmtesten englischen Kinderbuchautorinnen und -illustratorinnen. Sie begann 1890 mit ihren Illustrationen, ihr bekanntestes Werk ist *Die Geschichte von Peter Hase*. Ihre Bücher werden bis heute verlegt. Potter stammte aus einer wohlhabenden Familie und wurde von Gouvernanten im Haus ihrer Eltern dem konventionellen Frauenbild entsprechend erzogen. Ihr Zeichentalent wurde von der Familie früh erkannt und Potter erhielt über viele Jahre privaten Zeichenunterricht.

Während der 1890er Jahre konzentrierte sich Potter zunächst auf naturkundliche Illustrationen; ihre ersten Kinderbücher wurden zwar erst zu Beginn des 20. Jahrhunderts publiziert, die Anfänge gehen aber auf die frühen 1890er Jahre zurück. Potter schrieb Bilderbriefe an Kinder ihrer Familie sowie an die Kinder ihrer ehemaligen Gouvernante. Daraus entstanden Kinderbücher, die der Verlag Frederick Warne & Company, zunächst ablehnend, dann aber doch mit Überzeugung edierte. Am 2. Oktober 1902 erschien dann *Die Geschichte von Peter Hase (The Story of Peter Rabbit)*.

Im Alter von 28 Jahren unternahm sie eine längere Reise. Mit 39 Jahren verlobte sie sich gegen den Widerstand ihrer Eltern mit dem Verleger Norman Warne, der ihr Talent außerordentlich schätzte. Warne starb jedoch kurz nach der Verlobung. Ihre Arbeiten wurden zunehmend nachgefragt und machten sie finanziell früh unabhängig. Sie konnte sich sogar ihren Wunsch erfüllen, Landbesitz im Lake District zu erwerben. Sehr naturverbunden, führte sie mit Leidenschaft ein Leben auf dem Land, dem nördlichen England, verbunden mit der Züchtung von Tieren und anderen landwirtschaftlichen Beschäftigungen.

Ihre Bücher waren kleinformatig (ca. 10 × 14 cm), damit sie von kleinen Kindern studiert werden konnten. Sie verkauften sich außergewöhnlich gut und wurden zunehmend auch im Ausland verbreitet. 23 Bände wurden veröffentlicht, alle im selben kleinen Format. Potter hat auch die Einbände mit ihren Illustrationen gestaltet.

Potter war zwar keine Anhängerin des Frauenwahlrechts, engagierte sich aber in anderen politischen Bereichen, zum Beispiel für Freihandelsabkommen, gegen eine unfaire Copyright-Gesetzgebung, für stärkere Schutz-Zölle.

Helen Beatrix Potter (1866–1943)

Potter was one of the most famous English children's book authors and illustrators, beginning her career in 1890 and most famously known for *The Story of Peter Rabbit*. Her books are still being published today. Potter came from a wealthy family and was raised by governesses in her parents' home following a conventional image of womanhood. Her talent for drawing was recognized early on by her family, and Potter received private drawing lessons for many years.

During the 1890s, Potter initially focused on natural history illustrations; although her first children's books were not published until the early twentieth century, their beginnings date back to the early 1890s. She wrote picture letters to the children in her family and to the children of her former governess. This led to her work on children's books, which the publisher Frederick Warne & Company first rejected but then enthusiastically published. This was followed on 2 October 1902 with *The Story of Peter Rabbit*.

At the age of twenty-eight, Potter embarked on a long journey, and at thirty-nine, against the wishes of her parents, she became engaged to the publisher Norman Warne, who held extraordinary regard for her talent. Warne died, however, shortly after the engagement. Potter's work was increasingly in demand, which made her financially independent at an early stage, allowing her even to fulfill her desire to purchase property in the Lake District. Feeling keenly close to nature, she embraced her life in the countryside of northern England with passion, passing her time with the breeding of animals and other agricultural pursuits.

Her books were small in size (about 10 × 14 cm) so that they could be enjoyed by young children. They sold exceptionally well and were increasingly distributed abroad. Eventually, twenty-three books of hers were published, all in the same small format. Potter also designed the covers, with illustrations of her own.

While she was not a supporter of women's suffrage, she was involved in other political issues, such as free trade agreements, unfair copyright legislation, and stronger protective tariffs.

Sarah Prideaux (1853–1933)

Prideaux, geboren in London, war eine angesehene englische Buchbinderin und -illustratorin. 1888, im Alter von 35 Jahren, begann sie mit dem Buchbinden in London unter Joseph Zaehndorf's Sohn Joseph W. und in Paris unter Antoine Joly. Im Laufe vieler Jahre des Experi-

Sarah Prideaux (1853–1933)

Born in London, Prideaux was a distinguished English bookbinder and illustrator. In 1888, at the age of thirty-five, she took up the craft of bookbinding in London under Joseph Zaehndorf's son Joseph W., and in Paris under Antoine Joly. Over the course of many years

Ethel Reed, um/around 1895, Foto/photo: Frances Benjamin Johnston

mentierens erschienen Hunderte Bücher mit ihrer Signatur. Sie war vor allem vom Art nouveau beeinflusst. Gleichzeitig entwickelte sich Prideaux zur Expertin auf dem Gebiet des Buchbindens und schrieb darüber Artikel in Magazinen. 1893 erschien ihr Buch *An Historical Sketch of Bookbinding*. Es folgte weitere Fachliteratur. Sie war Direktorin der Women's Printing Society. Die Vereinigung spielte eine wesentliche Rolle in der Frauenbewegung, sie unterstützte Literatur von Frauen und vermittelte einschlägige Berufsmöglichkeiten für Frauen in Bereichen, die weitgehend Männern vorbehalten waren.

Sybil Pye (1879–1958)

Wenngleich Autodidaktin im Kunsthandwerk der Buchbinderei, war Pye eine der bekanntesten Vertreterinnen des Art déco. Als Anna Sybella Pye in London geboren, war sie eines von sieben Kindern einer wohlhabenden und kulturell interessierten Familie. Ihre erste Anstellung hatte sie als Kindergärtnerin. Mit Thomas Sturge Moore verband sie seit 1899 eine enge lebenslange Freundschaft. Er machte sie mit Charles Rickett bekannt, einem Künstler und Buchdesigner, der Pyes Interesse an Buchbinderei weckte. Sie zog viele Kenntnisse aus dessen Buch *Bookbinding and the Care of Books*. 1906 eröffnete sie ihre erste Werkstatt im Haus ihres Vaters. Von 1910 bis 1946 wurden ihre Arbeiten regelmäßig in England und der ganzen Welt ausgestellt.

Ethel Reed (1874–1912)

Reed ist die bekannteste amerikanische Plakatdesignerin und Buchillustratorin des späten 19. Jahrhunderts und erlangte großes Renommee sowohl im eigenen Land als auch in Europa. Sie wurde in Newburyport, Massachusetts, geboren als Tochter eines Fotografen. Ihre Mutter war eine irische Immigrantin. Der Vater verstarb früh und Ethel wie ihre Mutter litten unter finanzieller Not. 1890 zogen sie nach Boston, wo Reed kurzzeitig an der Cowles Art School eine Ausbildung erhielt. Nach 1894 erfuhren ihre Illustrationen bereits öffentliche Anerkennung. Die Künstlerin Laura Hills wurde auf sie aufmerksam und unterstützte sie als ihre Mentorin. Etwa 20 Jahre lang erfuhren ihre Plakate und Buchillustrationen große Aufmerksamkeit. Wegen ihrer Schönheit war sie zugleich Model von bekannten Künstlern und Fotografen, insbesondere von Fred Holland. Als ihre Verlobung zerbrach, reiste sie mit ihrer Mutter nach Europa. Zusammen ließen sie sich 1897 in London nieder, wo Reed vor allem als Illustratorin der von Aubrey Beardsley mitbegründeten Vierteljahreszeitschrift *The Yellow Book* tätig war. Dennoch konnte sie in England nicht mehr an ihren alten Ruhm anknüpfen, sie verfiel der Drogensucht und starb im Alter von 38 Jahren.

of experimentation, hundreds of books with her signature mark appeared. Her main influence was art nouveau. At the same time, Prideaux became an expert in the field of bookbinding, writing articles about it in magazines. The year 1893 saw the publication of her book *An Historical Sketch of Bookbinding*. Additional studies by her on the craft followed. She was also the director of the Women's Printing Society, an association that played an essential role in the women's movement, supporting literature by women and providing career opportunities for women in fields largely reserved for men.

Sybil Pye (1879–1958)

Though self-taught in the craft of bookbinding, Pye became one of the best-known representatives of art deco. Born Anna Sybella Pye in London, she was one of seven children in a wealthy family with deep cultural interests. She first began working as a nursery school teacher. Beginning in 1899, she cultivated a close, lifelong friendship with Thomas Sturge Moore. It was Moore who introduced her to Charles Rickett, an artist and book designer who sparked Pye's interest in bookbinding. She learned a great deal from his book *Bookbinding and the Care of Books*. In 1906, she opened her first workshop in her father's house. From 1910 to 1946, her work was regularly exhibited in England and around the world.

Ethel Reed (1874–1912)

Reed is the most famous American poster designer and book illustrator of the late nineteenth century and achieved great renown both in the United States and in Europe. She was born in Newburyport, Massachusetts, to a father who was a photographer. Her mother was an Irish immigrant. Her father died early, causing Ethel and her mother to suffer financial hardship. In 1890, the two of them moved to Boston, where Reed briefly attended Cowles Art School. Soon thereafter, beginning in 1894, her illustrations began to receive public recognition, including the attention of artist Laura Hills, who supported Cowles in the role of mentor. Her posters and book illustrations continued to garner recognition for some twenty years. Her beauty also led to her serving as a model for famous artists and photographers, especially Fred Holland. Following the dissolution of an engagement for marriage, she traveled to Europe with her mother. Together they settled in London in 1897, where Reed was worked as the illustrator of the quarterly magazine cofounded by Aubrey Beardsley, *The Yellow Book*. Nevertheless, in England she failed to regain her former fame, fell into drug addiction, and died at the age of thirty-eight.

Susan Rennie

Rennie war zusammen mit Kirsten Grimstad Herausgeberin von *The New Woman's Survival Catalog*, 1973, und *The New Woman's Survival Sourcebook*, 1975. Beide gründeten zudem die Zeitschrift *A Magazine of Woman's Culture*, die von 1977 bis 1981 vom Woman's Building in Los Angeles herausgegeben wurde. Rennie absolvierte ihren Bachelor of Arts am Barnard College und promovierte in Politischer Philosophie an der Columbia University. Sie unterrichtete Sozialwissenschaft am Union Institute & University und arbeitete als Aktivistin in der Gesundheitspolitik.

Olga Rosanowa (1886–1918)

Rosanowa war eine russische Künstlerin, Buchillustratorin, Lyrikerin und Kunsttheoretikerin. Ab 1905 besuchte Rosanowa gemeinsam mit Nadeschda Udalzowa eine von Künstlern geleitete Privatschule in Moskau. Parallel dazu absolvierte sie ein Studium der angewandten Kunst an der Bolschakow- und der Stroganow-Schule in Moskau. 1910 zog sie nach St. Petersburg, wo sie ein Gründungsmitglied des Künstlerverbandes Union der Jugend wurde und zwischen 1912 und 1913 an der Swanzewa-Kunstschule studierte. Hier freundete sie sich mit Welimir Chlebnikow und Kasimir Malewitsch an. Zwischen 1911 und 1917 nahm Rosanowa unter anderem an solch berühmten Avantgarde-Ausstellungen wie „Tramway V", „0.10" und denjenigen der Künstlergruppe Karo-Bube teil. Anfang 1914 wurden fünf ihrer Werke auf der von Filippo Tommaso Marinetti in Rom veranstalteten Internationalen Futuristenausstellung gezeigt, so auch die Illustrationen zum Buch *Entennest* ihres späteren Mannes, des futuristischen Dichters Alexej Krutschonych, den sie 1916 heiratete. 1915 wandte sie sich der gegenstandslosen Kunstform zu und arbeitete 1916 an der ersten (unveröffentlichten) Nummer der suprematistischen Zeitschrift *Supremus* mit. 1918 wurde sie Mitglied in der Abteilung Industriekunst des ISO und arbeitete an der SWOMAS in verschiedenen Provinzstädten. In Bogorodsk entwarf sie zusammen mit Alexandra Exter Textildesign. Auch wirkte sie parallel bei verschiedenen Aktionen des Prolekults (Proletarischer Kulturbewegung) mit, die vor allem der Arbeiterbevölkerung zu einer authentischen Stimme verhelfen wollte. Die „Erste Russische Kunstausstellung" in Berlin 1922 zeigte einige ihrer Gemälde und Stickereientwürfe. In ihren letzten Jahren konzentrierte sie sich vor allem auf Design, Mode und Buchillustration.

Evelyn Rumsey Cary (1855–1924)

Rumsey wurde in Buffalo, New York, geboren und besuchte die Buffalo Seminary High School. 1879 heiratete sie Charles Cary.

Susan Rennie

Rennie was the coeditor, with Kirsten Grimstad, of *The New Woman's Survival Catalog* (1973) and *The New Woman's Survival Sourcebook* (1975). Both women also founded *A Magazine of Woman's Culture*, published by the Woman's Building in Los Angeles from 1977 to 1981. Rennie earned a bachelor of arts degree from Barnard College and her PhD in political philosophy from Columbia University. She taught social science at Union Institute & University in addition to work as a health policy activist.

Olga Rozanova (1886–1918)

Rozanova was a Russian artist, book illustrator, poet, and art theorist. Beginning in 1905, she attended a private school in Moscow run together with Nadezhda Udaltsova by a number of artists. She simultaneously studied applied arts at the Bolshakov and Stroganov schools in Moscow. In 1910, she moved to St. Petersburg, where she became a founding member of the Union Youth and studied at the Svantseva School of Art between 1912 and 1913. In St. Petersburg, she became friends with Velimir Khlebnikov and Kazimir Malevich. Between 1911 and 1917, Rosanova took part in famous avant-garde exhibitions such as *Tramway V*, *0.10*, and those staged by the artists' group Karo-Bube. In early 1914, five of her works were shown at the International Futurist Exhibition organized by Filippo Tommaso Marinetti in Rome, including the illustrations for the book *Duck's Nest* by the futurist poet Alexei Kruchonych, whom she married in 1916. In 1915 she turned to nonobjective art, and in 1916 she collaborated on the first (unpublished) issue of the suprematist journal *Supremus*. In 1918, she became a member of the Industrial Arts Division of the ISO and worked at SVOMAS in various provincial cities. In Bogorodsk she created textile design together with Aleksandra Exter. She also participated in various actions of the Prolekult (Proletarian Cultural Movement), which sought especially to give an authentic voice to the working-class population. The *Erste Russische Kunstausstellung* in Berlin in 1922 showed several of her paintings and embroidery designs. In her final years, she concentrated mainly on design, fashion, and book illustration.

Evelyn Rumsey Cary (1855–1924)

Rumsey was born in Buffalo, New York, and attended Buffalo Seminary High School. In 1879, she married Charles Cary. Early in her career,

Olga Rosanowa, Selbstporträt / self portrait, 1911

Schon früh stellte sie ihre Gemälde in der Jahres-schau der Buffalo Society of Artists aus. Rumsey war 1894 Gründungsmitglied des Twentieth Century Club. Der Club gilt als älteste private Vereinigung von Künstlerinnen in den USA, der von Frauen geleitet wurde und nur Frauen als Mitglieder führte. 1895 gestaltete sie das Titelblatt der Frauenausgabe des *Buffalo Courier*. Bekannt wurde sie in den USA für ihr Plakat für die „Pan American Exposition" 1901 in Buffalo. Es trägt den Titel *The Spirit of Niagara* und zeigt eine weibliche Figur vor den Niagarafällen. *Give Her Of the Fruit* von 1905 zeigt eine weibliche Figur, die wie ein Baum aus der Erde aufsteigt und ihre Hände wie die Zweige eines Baumes gegen den Himmel weitet; im Hintergrund ist das Weiße Haus zu sehen. Kommentiert ist es wie folgt: „Give her of the fruit of her hands and let her own works praise her in the gates". Das Plakat wurde sehr häufig von der Women's-Suffrage-Bewegung verwendet.

Betye Irene Saar (geb. 1926)

Saar wurde in Los Angeles geboren. In den 1970er Jahren wurde sie als Vertreterin der Black-Arts-Bewegung bekannt und hier insbesondere wegen ihrer künstlerischen Arbeit mit Assemblagen und Grafiken mit erzählerischem Charakter. Von Anfang an thematisierte sie die negativen Darstellungen von Afroamerikaner*innen sowie den Rassismus in den USA. Das Kunststudium begann sie am Pasadena City College, mit einem Stipendium wechselte sie dann auf die University of California, Los Angeles (UCLA). Darauf folgten 1947 ein Bachelor of Arts in Design und anschließend Kurse an verschiedenen Universitäten. Von 1952 bis 1970 war sie mit dem Keramikkünstler Richard Saar verheiratet. Betye Irene Saar begann Assemblagen mit gefundenen Objekten zu erstellen, die eine Verbindung zu den Kulturen ihrer Vorfahren hatten: zu Afroamerikaner*innen, Ir*innen und Native Americans. Motive von Black Power, Spiritualität, Mystizismus und Feminismus vereinen sich in ihrem Werk. Sie arbeitete teilweise zusammen mit Sheila Levrant de Bretteville. In den späten 1960er Jahren engagierte sich Saar in der Bürgerrechtsbewegung. 1970 traf sie andere afroamerikanische Künstlerinnen in der Gallery 32, die von der Künstlerin und Kunsthändlerin Suzanne Jackson geleitet wurde und ein Zentrum der African American Art Community im Los Angeles war. In den 1980er Jahren unterrichtet Saar an der University of California Los Angeles (UCLA) und dem Otis Art Institute of Art and Design. In dieser Zeit beschäftigte sie sich in ihren Werken mit Zusammenhängen zwischen zwei unterschiedlichen Wissenssystemen, von Technik und Voodoo.

she exhibited her paintings at the annual show of the Buffalo Society of Artists. Rumsey was a charter member of the Twentieth Century Club, founded in 1894. The club is considered to be the oldest private association of women artists in the United States that was led by women and admitted only women members. In 1895, she designed the cover of the women's edition of the *Buffalo Courier*. She became famous in the United States for her poster for the *Pan American Exposition* in Buffalo in 1901. Titled *The Spirit of Niagara*, it depicts a female figure in front of Niagara Falls. *Give Her of the Fruit* (1905) shows a female figure rising from the earth like a tree, stretching her hands towards the sky like its branches; in the background, the White House is visible. The text proclaims: "Give her of the fruit of her hands and let her own works praise her in the gates." The poster was used frequently by the Women's Suffrage Movement.

Betye Irene Saar (b. 1926)

Born in Los Angeles, Saar became known in the 1970s as a representative of the Black arts movement, especially for her artistic work with assemblages and narrative graphic works. From the outset, she addressed racism and negative portrayals of African Americans in the United States. She began studying art at Pasadena City College, continuing with a scholarship at the University of California, Los Angeles (UCLA). This was followed by a bachelor of arts in design in 1947 and then courses at various universities. From 1952 to 1970, she was married to the ceramic artist Richard Saar. Betye Irene Saar began creating assemblages with found objects that had a connection to the cultures of her ancestors: African American, Irish, and Native American. Her work combines motifs of Black power, spirituality, mysticism, and feminism. In some of her work, she collaborated with Sheila Levrant de Bretteville, and in the late 1960s, she became involved in the civil rights movement. In 1970, she came together with other African American women artists at Gallery 32, which was run by artist and art dealer Suzanne Jackson and served as a center for the African American art community in Los Angeles. In the 1980s, Saar taught at the University of California Los Angeles (UCLA) and the Otis Art Institute of Art and Design. Her work from this period deals with connections between two different systems of knowledge, namely technology and voodoo.

Amy Maria Sacker (1872–1965)

Amy Maria Sacker war eine US-amerikanische Buchdesignerin, Illustratorin, Malerin und Lehrerin. Sie wurde vor allem durch ihre Kinderbücher bekannt. Geboren in Boston, erhielt sie ihre Ausbildung zwischen 1889 und 1894 an der Schule des Museum of Fine Arts am Ort. Nach ihrem Schulabschluss lehrte sie Design an der Cowles Art School. 1901 gründete sie ihre eigene Schule unter dem Namen Sacker School of Design and Interior Decoration. Sie lehrte dort über 40 Jahre lang. Sacker entwarf Bucheinbände, Buchumschläge, Exlibris und Zeitschriftentitel für verschiedene Bostoner Verlage wie Joseph Knight, Estes & Lauriat, L.C. Page & Co, Houghton Mifflin und Little Brown. Ihr Design bestand weitgehend aus figurativen Kompositionen. Für ihre Arbeiten erhielt sie zahlreiche bedeutende Ehrungen. 1899 wurde Sacker zum Master Craftsman der Society of Arts and Crafts gewählt. Sie unterrichtete zusätzlich am Simmons College, unternahm Studienreisen nach Europa und beteiligte sich an mehreren Ausstellungen in den USA. Ein Jahrzehnt lang war sie Mitglied des Beratungsausschusses der Women's Educational and Industrial Union. Sacker beendete Mitte der 1940er Jahre ihre Arbeit an ihrer Schule, um sich auf Projekte für das Rote Kreuz zu konzentrieren.

Amy Maria Sacker (1872–1965)

Amy Maria Sacker was an American book designer, illustrator, painter, and teacher who became known primarily for her children's books. Born in Boston, she received her education between 1889 and 1894 at the school operated by the local Museum of Fine Arts. After graduating from high school, she taught design at Cowles Art School. In 1901, she founded her own school under the name Sacker School of Design and Interior Decoration, where she taught for over forty years. Sacker designed book covers, book jackets, bookplates, and journal covers for various Boston publishers including Joseph Knight, Estes & Lauriat, L. C. Page & Co, Houghton Mifflin, and Little Brown, with design that consisted largely of figurative compositions. She received numerous important awards for her work. In 1899, Sacker was elected as a master craftsman in the Society of Arts and Crafts. She additionally taught at Simmons College, traveled to Europe to enhance her education, and participated in several exhibitions in the United States. For a decade, she was a member of the Women's Educational and Industrial Union Advisory Committee. Sacker stopped working at her school in the mid-1940s to focus on projects for the Red Cross.

Paula Scher (geb. 1948)

Scher ist eine der renommiertesten Designer*innen der letzten vier Jahrzehnte. Sie hat neue Regeln im Grafikdesign aufgestellt und mit einigen der einflussreichsten Unternehmen zusammengearbeitet: Windows, Citibank, Bloomberg, Tiffany & Co., Walt Disney Company, Adobe und Coca-Cola. Sie entwickelte deren Branding. Bekannt wurde sie vor allem für ihre Arbeit in der Kulturbranche. Zu ihren Kund*innen zählen das Museum of Modern Art, das New York Ballet, die Metropolitan Opera und die New York Philharmonic. Mehr als 20 Jahre währte ihre Arbeit für The Public Theater in New York. Ab 1991 war sie Partnerin des New Yorker Büros von Pentagram. Scher ist bekannt für ihren illustrativen Gebrauch von Schriften. Sie erhielt zahlreiche Auszeichnungen in der Designbranche und unterrichtete an einigen der renommiertesten Designschulen der Welt. Ihr Werk wurde weltweit ausgestellt und befindet sich in den Sammlungen der renommiertesten Museen. Scher veröffentlichte eine Reihe von Büchern über Design wie *Make It Bigger*, 2002, *MAPS*, 2011, und *25 Years at the Public. A Love Story*, 2020.

Paula Scher (b. 1948)

Scher is one of the most renowned designers of the last four decades. She has established new standards in graphic design and collaborated with some of the most influential companies of the day, where she developed corporate branding; her clients have included Windows, Citibank, Bloomberg, Tiffany & Co, Walt Disney Company, Adobe, and Coca-Cola. She became known, however, primarily for her work in the cultural industry. Here, her clients have included the Museum of Modern Art, the New York Ballet, the Metropolitan Opera, and the New York Philharmonic. Her work for The Public Theater in New York lasted more than twenty years. In 1991, she became a partner in Pentagram's New York office, where she was also the first female director. Scher is known for her illustrative use of typefaces. She has received numerous awards in the design industry and has taught at some of the most prestigious design schools in the world. Her work has been exhibited worldwide and is in the collections of the most prestigious museums. She has also published a number of books on design such as *Make It Bigger* (2002), *MAPS* (2011), and *25 Years at the Public: A Love Story* (2020).

Martel Schwichtenberg, 1919, Foto/photo: Frieda Gertrud Riess, Courtesy of Das verborgene Museum, Berlin

Martel Schwichtenberg (1896–1945)

Schwichtenberg (eigentlich Justine Adele Martha Schwichtenberg), geboren in Hannover, ist in erster Linie als Malerin und Grafikerin bekannt, hinterließ jedoch ein umfassendes Werk als Grafikdesignerin. Besonders intensiv arbeitete sie für die ortsansässige Firma Bahlsen, für die sie unter anderem zahlreiche Verpackungen entwarf. Nach ihrem Studium an der Kunstakademie Düsseldorf wurde Schwichtenberg 1917 Mitarbeiterin des Architekten Bernhard Hoetger, mit dem sie die Entwürfe für die geplante TET-Stadt der Bahlsen-Werke in Hannover ausarbeitete. Wenngleich die Pläne nicht realisiert wurden, sind viele Werbeträger bis heute mit dem TET-Signet versehen. Schwichtenberg blieb auch in den Folgejahren für Bahlsen tätig, wodurch sie während ihrer Emigration nach Südafrika finanziell abgesichert war. Sie war Mitglied des Deutschen Werkbunds und der revolutionären Novembergruppe. 1929 nahm sie an der vom Verein Berliner Künstlerinnen organisierten Ausstellung „Die Frau von heute" teil, zeigte ihre Arbeiten in New York und in den Folgejahren in den großen Berliner Galerien, etwa bei Flechtheim. Anfang 1933 emigrierte sie nach Südafrika und arbeitete auch weiterhin auf Honorarbasis für die Bahlsenwerke. Von Schicksalsschlägen heimgesucht – 1938 wurden bei einem Brand ihr Haus und Hunderte ihrer Kunstwerke vernichtet –, erkrankte sie nach ihrer Rückkehr nach Deutschland an Depressionen und Alkoholsucht und starb im Alter von 49 Jahren. Sie hinterließ eine Autobiografie.

Martha Scotford

Martha Scotford war Buchdesignerin in Boston, bevor sie Lehrerin an Kunstakademien wurde. In ihrer Ausbildung erwarb sie eine Doppelqualifikation: Sie absolvierte einen Bachelor of Arts in Kunstgeschichte am Oberlin College und anschließend einen Master of Fine Arts in Grafikdesign an der Yale University. Heute ist sie in erster Linie bekannt für ihre designtheoretischen Essays, die sich auf das Thema Frauen im Design konzentrieren. Diese Ausrichtung klang schon in ihrem frühen Essay „Is there a Canon of Graphic Design?" im Herbst 1991 an, der in *The AIGA Journal* veröffentlicht wurde. Sie beschreibt hier die Unterrepräsentanz von Frauen im Design. Der bekannteste Essay aber ist „Messy History vs. Neat History. Toward an expanded view of women in graphic design", veröffentlicht in *Visible Language* im Herbst 1994. Hierin propagiert sie eine pluralistischere und individuellere Formensprache jenseits festgelegter Regeln, die eine Frauenperspektive zulässt. Neben vielen weiteren Artikeln in einschlägigen Designzeitschriften veröffentlichte sie 1999

Martel Schwichtenberg (1896–1945)

Hannover-born Schwichtenberg (whose legal name is Justine Adele Martha Schwichtenberg) is known primarily as a painter and graphic artist, but she left behind an extensive body of work as a graphic designer. In particular, she did a great deal of work for the Hannover company Bahlsen, producing a number of designs for packaging, among other things. After her studies at the Kunstakademie Düsseldorf, Schwichtenberg began working for the architect Bernhard Hoetger in 1917, with whom she developed the designs for the planned TET City for the Bahlsen factories in Hannover. Although the plans were not realized, the TET emblem can still be seen as part of many advertisements today. Schwichtenberg continued to work for Bahlsen in subsequent years, providing her with financial security during her emigration to South Africa. She was a member of the Deutscher Werkbund and the revolutionary Novembergruppe. In 1929, she took part in the exhibition organized by the Verein der Berliner Künstlerinnen (Berlin Association of Women Artists) called *Die Frau von heute* (The woman of today), and she showed her work in New York and in the following years in major Berlin galleries, such as Flechtheim. At the beginning of 1933, she emigrated to South Africa and continued her work for Bahlsen on a commission basis. After experiencing personal catastrophe (her home and hundreds of her artworks were destroyed in a fire in 1938), she fell ill with depression and alcoholism upon returning to Germany and died at the age of forty-nine. She left behind an autobiography.

Martha Scotford

Martha Scotford was a book designer in Boston before becoming an art school teacher. As part of her training, she acquired two degrees: she graduated with a bachelor of art in art history from Oberlin College, and then with a master of fine art in graphic design from Yale University. Today, she is primarily known for her essays in design theory focusing on women in design. This approach was echoed in her early essay "Is There a Canon of Graphic Design?," published in fall of 1991 in *The AIGA Journal*. In this essay, she describes the underrepresentation of women in design. Her most famous essay, however, is "Messy History vs. Neat History: Toward an Expanded View of Women in Graphic Design," published in *Visible Language* in the fall of 1994. In this essay, she argues for a more pluralistic and individual formal language beyond fixed rules that would allow for the perspective of women. In addition to many other articles in relevant design magazines, she published a book in 1999 titled *Cipe Pineles: A Life of Design*. This

ein Buch über *Cipe Pineles. A Life of Design*. Es folgte eine Untersuchung der Typografien von Mayakovsky und El Lissitzky 2000, des Weiteren kuratierte sie im Sommer 2013 eine Ausstellung über den Buchdesigner Ernst Reichl. 2001 verbrachte sie vier Monate an vier verschiedenen Institutionen als Fulbright Lecturer in Indien, eine Zeit, die sie in *Visible Language* und *Design Issues* beschrieb. Seit 2013 ist Martha Scotford emeritiert.

was followed by a study of the typographies of Mayakovsky and El Lissitzky (2000). She also curated an exhibition on the book designer Ernst Reichl in the summer of 2013. In 2001, she spent four months at four different institutions as a Fulbright lecturer in India, a time she described in *Visible Language* and *Design Issues*. Martha Scotford has been emeritus since 2013.

Mary Crease Sears (1880–1938)

Sears war eine der einflussreichsten Arts-and-Crafts-Buchbinderinnen in Boston. Sie besuchte die Schule des Museum of Fine Arts (MFA) am Ort und studierte nach ihrem Abschluss in Paris traditionelles Buchbindehandwerk. Dort lernte sie Agnes St. John kennen, die ihre langjährige Freundin und Mitarbeiterin wurde. Sears setzte ihre Ausbildung in London fort und kehrte dann nach Boston zurück, wo sie ein eigenes Studio eröffnete. Sie war mit dem gesamten Prozess der Buchherstellung vertraut. Ihre kunsthandwerkliche Neigung zeigte sich insbesondere in den aufwendig gestalteten Ledereinbänden; sie entwarf aber auch hand-gefertigte einfachere Ausgaben.

Mary Crease Sears (1880–1938)

One of the most influential arts and crafts bookbinders in Boston, Sears attended the School of the Museum of Fine Arts (MFA) in Boston and studied traditional bookbinding in Paris after her graduation. There she met Agnes St. John, who became her longtime friend and collaborator. Sears continued her training in London and then returned to Boston, where she opened her own studio. She was well-acquainted with the entire process of book production. Her penchant for arts and crafts was particularly evident in her elaborately designed leather bindings; however, she also designed handmade simpler editions.

Sheila Shulman

Shulman war, zusammen mit Deborah Hart und Lilian Mohin, Gründerin der Onlywomen Press in London, auch als The Women's Press bekannt. Die Druckerei war ein feministisch-lesbisches Unternehmen, das von 1974 an bis in die 1990er Jahre hinein produzierte. Sie ging hervor aus einer Gruppe lesbischer Schriftstellerinnen, die ihre Werke veröffentlichen wollten. Auf diese Weise erlangten sie die Kontrolle über ihr eigenes Werk. Weiterhin verlegte die Druckerei aber auch Arbeiten anderer Schriftstellerinnen.

Sheila Shulman

Along with Deborah Hart and Lilian Mohin, Shulman was founder of the Onlywomen Press in London, also known as The Womens's Press. The print shop was a feminist-lesbian enterprise that operated from 1974 until the 1990s. It emerged from a group of lesbian writers who wanted to publish, and thereby gain control over, their own work. Onlywomen continued to publish works by other women writers, however.

Jutta Sika (1877–1964)

Sika, geb. als Josepha Sika, war Keramikerin, Objekt- und Grafikdesignerin der Wiener Werkstätte und zugleich Gründungsmitglied des Österreichischen Werkbunds. Seit 1920 gehörte sie der Vereinigung bildender Künstlerinnen Österreichs an. Sie war auf fast allen bedeutenden internationalen Ausstellungen zum Kunstgewerbe vertreten. Nach Abschluss ihrer schulischen Ausbildung in Wien begann Sika 1895 ein zweijähriges Studium an der Graphischen Lehr- und Versuchsanstalt bei Joseph Eugen Hörwarter. Anschließend schrieb sie sich 1897 in die Fachklasse für Malerei an der Kunstgewerbeschule Wien ein. Ihre Lehrer waren unter anderem Koloman Moser und Alfred Roller. 1901 gründete sie gemeinsam mit anderen Mitgliedern der Kunstgewerbeschule die Vereinigung Wiener Kunst im Hause, einem Vorläufer der Wiener Werkstätte. Sika fokussier-

Jutta Sika (1877–1964)

Sika, born Josepha Sika, was a ceramist as well as object and graphic designer for the Wiener Werkstätte, in addition to being a founding member of the Österreichischer Werkbund. Beginning in 1920, she belonged to the Vereinigung bildender Künstlerinnen Österreichs, and she was represented at almost all major international exhibitions on decorative arts. After completing her school education in Vienna, Sika began a two-year course of study at the Graphische Lehr- und Versuchsanstalt under Joseph Eugen Hörwarter in 1895. She then enrolled in the painting class at the Vienna Kunstgewerbeschule in 1897. Her teachers included Koloman Moser and Alfred Roller. In 1901, together with other members of the Kunstgewerbeschule, she founded the association Wiener Kunst im Hause, a forerunner of the Wiener Werkstätte. Sika focused on porcelain

te sich auf Porzellan und Keramik und fertigte Modeentwürfe und Textilarbeiten an. Zudem widmete sie sich im Auftrag von Firmen dem Verpackungsdesign und entwarf Postkarten und Monogramme beispielsweise für die Wiener Werkstätte. Für die Firmen Kohansky, Löwit & Co. und W. Spitzer gestaltete sie Produktverpackungen, für die Firma Agentor wiederum Metallobjekte. Sika war auch als Lehrerin tätig und leitete von 1911 bis 1933 eine Zeichenklasse an der Gewerblichen Fortbildungsschule in Wien. 1913 ging sie erneut für zwei Jahre an die Kunstgewerbeschule, um bei Alfred Roller Aktmalerei und Kostümdesign zu studieren. Während des Zweiten Weltkriegs unterrichtete sie an Mädchenschulen.

Nina Simonovič-Efimova (1877–1948)

Simonovič-Efimova ist bekannt als Puppendesignerin, war aber auch als Gestalterin von Buchtiteln tätig. Zusammen mit ihrem Ehemann, Ivan Efimov, begründete sie die Tradition des Sowjetischen Puppentheaters. Sie wurde in St. Petersburg in eine deutsch-jüdische Familie geboren und war ein Kind von Sechslingen. Sie studierte Kunst in Russland und Paris. Ihre Mutter ließ sich in der Schweiz in der Fröbel'schen Erziehungsmethode ausbilden und eröffnete einen Kindergarten in St. Petersburg. Für ihre Puppen schuf Simonovič modernes Design und gab einschlägige Fachbücher heraus, in denen sie dieses beschrieb. Zudem fertigte sie zahlreiche Schattenfiguren. Nach der Oktoberrevolution passten sie und ihr Mann das Kindertheater den sozialistischen Richtlinien an. Sie veröffentlichten Bücher und Pamphlete, auch über die Geschichte des Puppentheaters. Sie wurden über die Grenzen Russlands hinaus bis in die USA bekannt.

Jenny Smith

Smith zählt, neben Viv Mullett und Chia Moan, zu den drei Gründerinnen des Lenthall Road Workshops im Londoner Stadtteil Hackney. 1975 übernahmen die Frauen eine bereits existierende Siebdruckwerkstatt und entwickelten daraus eine bis in die 1990er Jahre aktive kollektive Druckerei. Ihr Ethos war das der Selbstermächtigung von Frauen und die Adresse Lenthall Road 81 sollte das kreative Zentrum ihrer Aktivitäten sein. Die Adressatinnen waren Women of Color und Queer Communities.

Agnes Speyer (1875–1942)

Speyer studierte künstlerische Fächer wie Malerei und Bildhauerei, ihr Hauptwerk lag jedoch in der Gebrauchsgrafik. Sie gestaltete Plakate, Kalender, Postkarten, Bucheinbände und illustrierte Bücher und war weitgehend am Flächenstil der Wiener Secession um 1900 orientiert. Als Tochter eines jüdischen Laien-

and ceramics while also producing fashion designs and textile works. She also devoted herself to designing packaging for companies, in addition to designing postcards and monograms for clients including the Wiener Werkstätte. She designed product packaging for Kohansky, Löwit & Co., and W. Spitzer, and metal objects for Agentor. She also worked as a teacher and led a drawing class at the Gewerbliche Fortbildungsschule in Vienna from 1911 to 1933. In 1913, she returned to the Kunstgewerbeschule for two years to study nude painting and costume design with Alfred Roller. During World War II, she taught in schools for girls.

Nina Simonovič-Efimova (1877–1948)

Simonovič-Efimova is known as a doll designer, but she was also active as a designer of book covers. Together with her husband, Ivan Efimov, she founded the tradition of Soviet puppet theater. She was born in St. Petersburg into a German-Jewish family, as one of sextuplets. She studied art in Russia and Paris. Her mother was trained in the Froebel method of education in Switzerland and opened a nursery school in St. Petersburg. Simonovič created modern designs for her dolls, describing them in reference works. She also made numerous shadow puppets. After the October Revolution, she and her husband adapted the children's theater to conform with socialist ideals. They published books and pamphlets on topics including the history of puppet theater, becoming known widely outside of Russia, in countries as far away as the United States.

Jenny Smith

Along with Viv Mullett and Chia Moan, Smith is one of the three founders of the Lenthall Road Workshop in the London borough of Hackney. In 1975, the women took over an existing silkscreen printing workshop, which they developed into a collective print shop that remained active until the 1990s. Their ethos was that of women's self-empowerment and the address 81 Lenthall Road was meant to be the creative center of their activities. The intended audience was women of color and queer communities.

Agnes Speyer (1875–1942)

Speyer studied artistic disciplines such as painting and sculpture, but her main work was in advertising. She designed posters, calendars, postcards, book covers, and illustrated books and was largely influenced by the flat visual style of the Vienna Secession from around 1900. The daughter of a Jewish lay judge, she grew up in

richters wuchs sie in einem kulturell gut vernetzten Zuhause in Wien auf. Sie besuchte die Wiener Allgemeine Zeichenschule von Franz Pönninger am Kommunalpädagogicum und erhielt Malunterricht im Atelier von Imre Révész. Im Rahmen eines Aufenthaltes in Paris von 1901 bis 1903 studierte sie an der Académie Julian und der Académie Ranson. Sie ließ sich in den Ateliers der Bildhauer Aristide Maillol und Auguste Rodin ausbilden. In der Zeit von 1901 bis 1907 war sie an der Kunstgewerbeschule Wien eingeschrieben und studierte Bildhauerei bei Franz Metzner, Teppichrestaurierung bei Leopoldine Guttmann und Malerei bei Koloman Moser. Während ihrer Ausbildungszeit veröffentlichte Speyer Beiträge in der Kunstzeitschrift *Die Fläche* und illustrierte 1906 J. A. Lux' *3 Puppenspiele*. Ebenfalls 1906 entwarf sie einen Kalender und 1907 Postkarten für die Wiener Werkstätte. 1910 heiratete sie den Richter und späteren Oberlandesgerichtsrat Emil Ulmann, der in der Zeit des Nationalsozialismus zwangspensioniert wurde. Aus diesem Grund emigrierte die Familie 1939 in die USA.

a culturally well-connected home in Vienna. She attended the Vienna Allgemeine Zeichenschule of Franz Pönninger at the Kommunalpädagogicum and received painting lessons in the studio of Imre Révész. During a stay in Paris from 1901 to 1903, she studied at the Académie Julian and the Académie Ranson. She additionally trained in the studios of sculptors Aristide Maillol and Auguste Rodin. From 1901 to 1907, she was enrolled at the Vienna Kunstgewerbeschule, studying sculpture with Franz Metzner, tapestry restoration with Leopoldine Guttmann, and painting with Koloman Moser. While still completing her training, Speyer published articles in the art magazine *Die Fläche* and in 1906 illustrated J. A. Lux's *3 Puppenspiele*. Likewise in 1906, she designed a calendar, and in 1907 she created postcards for the Wiener Werkstätte. In 1910 she married Emil Ulmann, a judge and later member of the Superior Regional Court, who was forced into retirement under the Nazis. For this reason, the family emigrated to the United States in 1939.

Warwara Stepanowa (1894–1958)

Stepanowa stammte aus einer kleinbürgerlichen Familie, ihre Ausbildung erhielt sie von 1910 bis 1911 an der Kasaner Kunstschule. Dort lernte sie Alexander Rodtschenko kennen, mit dem sie später den Konstruktivismus vertrat. Er wurde ihr Arbeitskollege, Lebens- und späterer Ehepartner. 1912 zog sie nach Moskau. Von 1913 bis 1914 besuchte sie dort die Stroganoff-Kunstschule. Stepanowa schloss ihre Studien nicht ab, sondern arbeitete zunächst als Näherin und Buchhalterin und nahm Unterricht an Michail Leblans Schule. In den Jahren vor der Oktoberrevolution zählte sie zum Kreis der russischen Avantgarde. 1920 folgte sie Rodtschenko als Mitglied des INCHUK mit der Teilnahme an der Ausstellung „5×5 = 25". INCHUK war ein in Moskau gegründetes Institut innerhalb der Abteilung für Bildende Kunst des Volkskommissariats für Aufklärung, dessen Mitglieder die Zukunft Sowjetrusslands künstlerisch zu bestimmen suchten. Es war Zentrum der künstlerischen Avantgarde. Stepanowa nahm zudem mit mehreren Gemälden an der „Ersten Russischen Kunstausstellung" 1922 in Berlin teil. Ab den 1920er Jahren widmete sie sich stärker dem Design, sie entwarf Stoffe, Theaterkostüme und Bühneninszenierungen, unter anderem für ein Theaterstück von Meyerhold. Von 1923 bis 1924 arbeitete sie zusammen mit Ljubow Popowa für die Moskauer Erste Staatliche Textilfabrik. Gemeinsam mit Rodtschenko entwarf Stepanowa funktionale Arbeitskleidung, viele ihrer Modelle gingen in die Produktion. Stepanowa unterrichtete ab 1924 Textilgestaltung an der WCHUTEMAS

Varvara Stepanova (1894–1958)

Stepanova came from a petty-bourgeois family, and she received her education at the Kazan Art School from 1910 to 1911. It was there that she met Alexander Rodchenko, who would also become a proponent of constructivism. He became her colleague, life partner, and later spouse. In 1912, she moved to Moscow, where she attended the Stroganoff School of Art from 1913 to 1914. Stepanova did not complete her studies, working first as a seamstress and bookkeeper, while taking classes at Mikhail Leblan's school. In the years before the October Revolution she belonged to the circle of the Russian avant-garde. In 1920, she followed Rodchenko as a member of the INKhUK by participating in the exhibition *5 × 5 = 25*. INKhUK was an institute founded in Moscow within the Department of Fine Arts of the People's Commissariat for Enlightenment, whose members sought to artistically shape the future of Soviet Russia. It was the center of the artistic avant-garde. Stepanova also took part in the Erste Russische Kunstausstellung in 1922 in Berlin with several paintings. Beginning in the 1920s, she devoted herself more to design, creating fabrics, theater costumes, and stage designs, including one for a play by Meyerhold. From 1923 to 1924, she worked with Lyubov Popova for the Moscow First State Textile Factory. Together with Rodchenko, Stepanova designed functional work clothes; many of their designs were then mass produced. Stepanova taught textile design at the VCHUTEMAS (State Free Art Workshops) from 1924. From 1923 to 1925 she created illustrations for the magazines *LEF* and *Nowyi LEF*. From

(Staatliche freie Kunstwerkstätten). Von 1923 bis 1925 illustrierte sie für die Zeitschriften *LEF* und *Nowyi LEF*. Ab 1925 gestaltete sie mit Rodtschenko Plakate, Bücher, Zeitschriften und Literatur. Sie entwickelten einen besonderen Stil im Bereich der Fotomontage mit expressiven, politischen Botschaften. In den 1930er Jahren entwarf Stepanowa für die Zeitschrift *UdSSR im Aufbau*.

1925 onward, she designed posters, books, magazines, and literature together with Rodchenko. They developed a special photomontage style with expressive, political messages. In the 1930s, Stepanova designed for the magazine *USSR in Construction*.

Rebecca Stephany (geb. 1980)

Stephany ist eine deutsche Künstlerin und Designforscherin. Sie untersucht mit ihrer künstlerischen Praxis die Grenzen zwischen Kunst und Design, zwischen Autonomie und Dienstleistung. Sie studierte an der Gerrit Rietveld Academie und am Sandberg Instituut in Amsterdam. Von 2007 bis 2016 war sie Dozentin für Grafikdesign an der Gerrit Rietveld Academie. 2013 besuchte sie das Bard College in New York als Gastkünstlerin. Sie war bis 2022 als Professorin für Kommunikationsdesign an der Hochschule für Gestaltung Karlsruhe tätig und ist seitdem Professorin für Redaktionelles Gestalten an der Kunsthochschule Kassel. Stephanys Projekte und Kollaborationen reichen von Druckerzeugnissen, Installationen, Videoarbeiten, Performances bis hin zu kuratorischer Praxis und Schreiben. Einer breiteren Öffentlichkeit wurde sie bekannt durch das *Glossary of Undisciplined Design*, das sie zusammen mit Anja Kaiser herausgab. Es versammelt „ungehorsame Strategien", bestärkende Vorbilder und kritische Werkzeuge im Grafikdesign. Die Herausgeberinnen erhielten für das Projekt 2019 den INFORM Preis für konzeptionelles Design von der Galerie für Zeitgenössische Kunst in Leipzig. Jüngste Projekte sind „200 Sisters Souvenirs", eine Auseinandersetzung mit dem über 300 Publikationen umfassenden Katalogarchiv des Badischen Kunstvereins aus feministischer Perspektive. Stephany ging unter anderem den Spuren von *LAVA, Feministische Zeitung für Karlsruhe und überall*, nach, die von 1969 und 1994 mit 13 Ausgaben von einem Kollektiv herausgegeben wurde, und legte sie teils wieder neu auf. In einem Seminar an der Hochschule für Gestaltung Karlsruhe mit dem Titel „In Defense Of Style" untersuchte sie 2018/19 Kleidermode als soziokulturelles Phänomen und als Form nonverbaler Kommunikation mittels künstlerischer Inszenierungen. 13 Projekte in diesem Kurs widmeten sich dem gestalterischen Potenzial von Mode. Feministische Gesellschaftskritik ist ein wesentliches Element ihrer Projekte.

Rebecca Stephany (b. 1980)

Stephany is a German artist and design researcher. In her artistic practice, she explores the boundaries between art and design, and between autonomy and service. Stephany studied at the Gerrit Rietveld Academie and the Sandberg Instituut in Amsterdam. From 2007 to 2016 she was a lecturer in graphic design at the Gerrit Rietveld Academie. In 2013, she held a position at Bard College in New York as a visiting artist. Until 2022, she was a professor of communication design at the Hochschule für Gestaltung Karlsruhe, and has since been professor of editorial design at the Kunsthochschule Kassel. Stephany's projects and collaborations range from printmaking, installations, video works, and performances, to curatorial practice and writing. She became known to a wider public through the *Glossary of Undisciplined Design*, which she edited together with Anja Kaiser. This book compiles "disobedient strategies," empowering role models, and critical tools in graphic design. For the project, the editors received the 2019 INFORM Prize for Conceptual Design from the Galerie für Zeitgenössische Kunst in Leipzig. Recent projects include 200 SISTERS SOUVENIRS, a feminist "(mis)reading" of the Badischer Kunstverein's catalog archive of over 300 publications. Among other things, Stephany retraced the history of *LAVA, Feministische Zeitung für Karlsruhe und überall* (Feminist newspaper for Karlsruhe and everywhere), published by a collective from 1969 to 1994 with thirteen issues, some of which she reissued. In 2018/19, in a seminar at the University of Design Karlsruhe titled "In Defense of Style," she used artistic stagings to investigate clothing fashion as a sociocultural phenomenon and form of nonverbal communication. Thirteen projects from this course took up the design potential of fashion. Feminist social criticism is an essential element of her projects.

Prudence Stevenson

Stevenson war ab 1974 Mitglied des Frauenkollektivs von See Red Women's Workshop. Sie lehrte von 1983 bis 1985 Kunst in Her Majesty's Prison Holloway (HMP), einem Frauengefängnis in der Parkhurst Road im Londoner Stadtteil Holloway. Dort machte sie auf die inhumanen Zustände der psychiatrischen Abteilung aufmerksam, woraufhin sie Hausverbot bekam. Danach arbeitete sie von 1985 bis 1987 mit der Kampagne „Women in Prison" zusammen. Sie war Mitherausgebern von *Breaking the Silence*, einem Report über Frauengefängnisse in England und Wales, 1986, und *Insiders. Women's Experience of Prison*, 1988. Stevenson gründete 1987 die Gruppe WISH (Women in Secure Psychiatric Hospitals) und war deren Direktorin bis 1996. Sie erhielt bedeutende Auszeichnungen für ihre Arbeit. Sie betreute soziale Kampagnen in Jamaika, Nigeria und Ghana und gründete 2012 das Paddington Children's Holiday Scheme, das Kindern Ferien auf dem Land ermöglichte. Daneben betätigte sie sich weiterhin künstlerisch.

Prudence Stevenson

Stevenson was a member of the See Red Women's Workshop collective beginning in 1974. From 1983 to 1985, she taught art at Her Majesty's Prison Holloway (HMP), a women's prison on Parkhurst Road in the London Borough of Holloway. At the prison, she drew attention to the inhumane conditions of the psychiatric ward, prompting the administration to ban her from the building. She then worked with the Women in Prison campaign from 1985 to 1987. She was coeditor of *Breaking the Silence* (1986), a report on women's prisons in England and Wales, and *Insiders: Women's Experience of Prison* (1988). In 1997, Stevenson founded the group WISH (Women in Secure Psychiatric Hospitals), serving as its director until 1996. Her work has garnered significant awards. She has overseen social campaigns in Jamaica, Nigeria, and Ghana, and in 2012 she founded the Paddington Children's Holiday Scheme, which provided rural vacations for children. She has also continued her artistic work.

Synthia St. James (geb. 1949)

St. James ist eine afroamerikanische Grafikdesignerin. Sie wuchs in Los Angeles sowie in der Bronx, New York, auf. Neben Arbeiten im Buchdesign entwarf sie 1997 die erste Kwanzaa-Briefmarke für den United States Postal Service. 2016 gestaltete sie die Kwanzaa Forever Stamp. Kwanzaa stammt aus der Black-Power-Bewegung, das Wort ist aus dem Swahili abgeleitet. Es bezeichnet ein Fest, das in den USA von Afroamerikaner*innen zwischen dem 26. Dezember und dem 1. Januar gefeiert wird. Im Mai 2020 erhielt sie die Ehrendoktorwürde von der Saint Augustine's University, Raleigh, North Carolina. Sie ist Lehrerin an verschiedenen Akademien.

Synthia St. James (b. 1949)

St. James is an African American graphic designer who grew up in Los Angeles and in the Bronx, New York. In addition to work in book design, she designed the first Kwanzaa stamp for the United States Postal Service in 1997. In 2016, she designed the Kwanzaa Forever Stamp. Kwanzaa comes from the Black Power movement; its name taken from Swahili, the festival is celebrated in the United States by African Americans between 26 December and 1 January. In May 2020, St. James received an honorary doctorate from Saint Augustine's University, in Raleigh, North Carolina. She teaches at a number of art schools and universities.

Bertha Stuart (1869–1953)

Stuart war eine amerikanische Buchdesignerin, geboren in Clinton, Iowa. Die Familie zog später nach Chicago um. Dort studierte Stuart 1890 an der Schule des Art Institute of Chicago und gewann den 1. Preis für Decorative Designing. In den frühen 1890er Jahren zog die Familie nach Portland, Oregon, wo Stuart weiterhin zeichnete und illustrierte. Um 1900, nach ihrem Umzug nach New York, bewarb sie sich bei der Women's School at Cooper Union und besuchte zusätzlich Kurse bei der Art Student's League. 1902 gewann sie an der Cooper Union eine Bronzemedaille, später dann den Preis des besten Designs in Seide. Von 1904 bis 1914 arbeitete sie für Henry Holt's Publishing Company und gestaltete zahlreiche Buchtitel. Für A. Wessels Company, New York, illustrierte sie 1900 *Alice's Adventures in Wonderland & Through the Looking-Glass* von Lewis Carroll. Sie zog wieder zurück nach Portland und eröffnete dort ein eigenes Studio.

Bertha Stuart (1869–1953)

Stuart was an American book designer born in Clinton, Iowa. Her family eventually moved to Chicago, where she studied at the School of the Art Institute of Chicago in 1890 and won first prize of an award for decorative designing. In the early 1890s, her family moved to Portland, Oregon, where Stuart continued to draw and illustrate. Around 1900, after moving to New York, she applied to the Women's School at Cooper Union and attended additional classes at the Art Student's League. In 1902, she won a bronze medal at Cooper Union, and later a prize for the best design in silk. From 1904 to 1914, she worked for Henry Holt's Publishing Company, designing numerous book covers. In 1900 she illustrated *Alice's Adventures in Wonderland & Through the Looking-Glass* by Lewis Carroll for A. Wessels Company, New York. She then moved back to Portland and opened her own studio.

Emma Redington (Lee) Thayer (1874–1973)

Thayer, Pseudonym Lee Thayer, war eine amerikanische Künstlerin und Literatin. Sie studierte in New York an der Cooper Union for the Advancement of Science and Art und am Pratt Institute. Neben ihrer intensiven literarischen Tätigkeit gründete Thayer zusammen mit ihrem Ehemann Harry Thayer, der Künstler war, einen Kunstdienst für Verlage, die auf künstlerische Buchumschläge spezialisiert waren.

Marie Weißenberg (1900–?)

Weißenberg war Keramikerin und Gebrauchsgrafikerin um 1920 in der Wiener Werkstätte. Sie entwarf unter anderem Postkarten und Vorsatzpapiere. Von 1914 bis 1916 besuchte sie die Graphische Lehr- und Versuchsanstalt in Wien und studierte ab 1916 an der Kunstgewerbeschule am Ort bei Koloman Moser, Franz Čižek und Rudolf Larisch und anderen. Sie war Mitglied des Österreichischen Werkbundes. Ab 1938 wurde sie als Jüdin verfolgt. Ihr weiterer Lebensweg ist unbekannt.

Candace Wheeler (1827–1923)

Wheeler (geb. Thurber) war eine der bekanntesten amerikanischen Designerinnen, vorwiegend im Interior- und Textildesign. Sie war Feministin und verschaffte Frauen den Zugang zu Design und zu finanzieller Unabhängigkeit. Vor allem junge Frauen, die aufgrund des Bürgerkrieges die finanzielle Unterstützung ihrer Familie verloren hatten, profitierten von ihrer karitativen Arbeit. Sie gründete sowohl die Society of Decorative Art in New York City, 1877, als auch den New York Exchange for Women's Work, 1878. Selbst eine Frau der Mittelklasse, hatte sie weder den finanziellen noch den sozialen Hintergrund, um ihre Arbeit zu verwirklichen. Ein Netzwerk von Freunden, die Unterstützung ihres Ehemannes und ihrer wohlhabenden Brüder sowie großes Selbstbewusstsein und enorme Energie verhalfen ihr zum Erfolg. Wheeler war wesentlich beteiligt an der Vorbereitung des Woman's Building auf der Weltausstellung in Chicago 1893. Sie war eine der ersten Frauen ihrer Zeit, die darauf Wert legten, dass die Beschäftigung mit Design nicht nur Hobby war, sondern dem Lebensunterhalt von jungen Frauen diente. Sie unterstützte Frauen in ihrer Werkstatt Associated Artists, die nur von Frauen geführt wurde. Aufgrund ihres umfassenden Werks wurde sie zu Beginn des 20. Jahrhunderts zu einem Role Model für Frauen, die Gleichberechtigung im Berufsleben forderten. 1918 veröffentlichte Wheeler ihre Autobiografie *Yesterdays in a Busy Life*.

Emma Redington (Lee) Thayer (1874–1973)

Thayer, who went by the pseudonym Lee Thayer, was an American artist and author. She studied in New York at the Cooper Union for the Advancement of Science and Art and at the Pratt Institute. In addition to her significant literary activity, Thayer and her husband Harry Thayer, an artist, founded an art service for publishers specializing in artistic book covers.

Marie Weißenberg (1900–?)

Weißenberg was a ceramist and commercial artist in the Wiener Werkstätte around 1920. Among other things, she designed postcards and endpapers. From 1914 to 1916, she attended the Graphische Lehr- und Versuchsanstalt in Vienna, and from 1916 she studied at the local Kunstgewerbeschule under professors including Koloman Moser, Franz Čižek, and Rudolf Larisch. She was a member of the Austrian Werkbund. From 1938 onward, she was persecuted as a Jew; after that date, no more is known about her life.

Candace Wheeler (1827–1923)

Wheeler (née Thurber) was one of the best-known American designers, working primarily in interior and textile design. A feminist, she endeavored to provide women opportunities in design as well as financial independence. Young women who had lost the financial support of their families due to the American Civil War especially benefited from her charitable work. She founded both the Society of Decorative Art in New York City in 1877 and New York Exchange for Women's Work in 1878. A middle-class woman herself, she had neither the financial nor the social background to realize her work. Her success was enabled by a network of friends, the support of her husband and wealthy brothers, and her own tremendous self-confidence and enormous energy. Wheeler was instrumental in preparing the Woman's Building at the Chicago World's Fair in 1893. She was one of the first women of her time to emphasize that the pursuit of design was not just a hobby, but helped young women find a livelihood of their own. She supported women in her Associated Artists workshop, which was run only by women, and her extensive body of work had made her a role model for women demanding equal rights in the workplace in the early twentieth century. In 1918, Wheeler published her autobiography *Yesterdays in a Busy Life*.

Candace Wheeler, um/around 1870

Lorraine Wild (geb. 1953)

Die kanadische, in den USA lebende Grafikdesignerin Wild arbeitet zugleich als Designhistorikerin und Pädagogin. 1973 nahm sie ihr Studium an der Cranbrook Academy of Art in Bloomfield, Michigan, auf. Hier gehörte sie zur ersten Generation von Designer*innen, die unter der Anleitung von Katherine McCoy, der Leiterin des Grafikdesign-Programms, damit begannen, die klaren Raster und reduzierten Formen der Nachkriegsmoderne aufzulösen, um Collagen zu schaffen. Damit wollten sie der Brüchigkeit der sozialen Kommunikation ihrer Zeit besser entsprechen. 1975 schloss sie mit dem Bachelor of Fine Arts in Grafikdesign ab. Anschließend zog sie nach New York City, um für ein Jahr in der Designfirma Vignelli Associates zu arbeiten. Gleichzeitig beschäftigte sie sich mit Designgeschichte: Sie untersuchte das amerikanische Grafikdesign nach dem Zweiten Weltkrieg. Aufgrund ihres Interesses an Designgeschichte setzte sie ihr Studium an der Yale University fort und schloss 1982 mit der Arbeit *Trends in American Graphic Design. 1930–1955* den Master of Fine Arts ab. Während eines Großteils ihrer Karriere hat sich Wild auf Buchdesign spezialisiert, insbesondere auf eine visuell anspruchsvolle Zusammenarbeit mit Künstlern und Architekten, beispielsweise mit Daniel Libeskind, John Hejduk, Mike Kelley, Richard Tuttle, Bill Viola, Morphosis.

Als Lehrerin an der Architekturschule der Universität von Houston, Texas, schrieb sie den renommierten Essay „More Than A Few Questions about Graphic Design Education", der 1983 in *The Design Journal* veröffentlicht wurde. Daraufhin wurde sie Programmdirektorin des Grafikdesigns des California Institute of the Arts in Valencia, Kalifornien. Während ihrer Zeit als Direktorin konzipierte und implementierte sie ein neues Modell für Grafikdesign in die Ausbildung, das experimentelle, konzeptionelle Entwicklungen und individuell-emotionale Erfahrungen betonte. Anfang der 1990er Jahre war sie außerdem Gründungspartnerin der Designfirma ReVerb in Los Angeles. 1996 gründete sie ihr eigenes Studio, das heute unter dem Namen Green Dragon Office firmiert. Hier setzte sie ihre Zusammenarbeit mit Architekt*innen, Künstler*innen, Kurator*innen und Verleger*innen fort. Sie gestaltete weiterhin Kataloge für renommierte amerikanische Museen. 1998 erhielt sie im San Francisco Museum of Modern Art eine Einzelausstellung. Wild wurde vielfach geehrt, unter anderem 2006 mit der AIGA-Medaille (American Institute of Graphic Arts). Heute lebt und arbeitet sie hauptsächlich in Los Angeles.

Lorraine Wild (b. 1953)

Wild, a Canadian graphic designer living in the United States, also works as a design historian and educator. In 1973, she began her studies at Cranbrook Academy of Art in Bloomfield, Michigan. At Cranbook, she was part of a first generation of designers trained under Katherine McCoy, director of the graphic design program, who began to break down the clean grids and reduced forms of postwar modernism to create collages. Their aim was to better respond to the fragility of social communication of their time. In 1975, she graduated with a bachelor of fine arts in graphic design. She then moved to New York City to work for a year at the design firm Vignelli Associates. She has also done work in design history, examining American graphic design after World War II. Her interest in design history led her to continue her studies at Yale University, where she received a master of fine arts in 1982 with the thesis *Trends in American Graphic Design: 1930–1955*. For much of her career, Wild specialized in book design, particularly through visually sophisticated collaborations with artists and architects such as Daniel Libeskind, John Hejduk, Mike Kelley, Richard Tuttle, Bill Viola, and Morphosis.

As an instructor at the University of Houston School of Architecture in Houston, Texas, she wrote the renowned essay "More Than a Few Questions about Graphic Design Education," which was published in 1983 in *The Design Journal*. She then became program director of graphic design at the California Institute of the Arts in Valencia, California. As director, she conceived and implemented a new educational model for graphic design that emphasized experimental, conceptual development and individual-emotional experience. She was also a founding partner of the Los Angeles design firm ReVerb in the early 1990s. In 1996, she founded her own studio, which today operates under the name Green Dragon Office. At Green Dragon Office, she continued to collaborate with architects, artists, curators, and publishers. She also continued to design catalogs for prestigious American museums. In 1998, she was given a solo exhibition at the San Francisco Museum of Modern Art. Wild has been honored many times, including in 2006 with the AIGA Medal (American Institute of Graphic Arts). Today, she lives and works primarily in Los Angeles.

Julie Wolfthorn (1864–1944)

Wolfthorn war eine deutsche Malerin und Grafikdesignerin. Sie kam 1864 als fünftes Kind einer jüdischen Familie im westpreußischen Thorn zur Welt. Mit sechs Jahren wurde sie Vollwaise und wuchs bei den Großeltern auf. Mit 19 Jahren ging sie nach Berlin, wo Frauen das akademische Studium jedoch untersagt war. Aus diesem Grund besuchte sie die Privatakademie Colarossi in Paris und verbrachte mehrere Monate in der Normandie und in Grez-sur-Loing, einer Künstlerkolonie in Fontainebleau. Zurück in Berlin wurde sie Gründungsmitglied der Berliner Secession. Diese kämpfte für die Gleichberechtigung, vor allem forderten ihre Mitglieder die Zulassung von Frauen zum Kunststudium an der Königlich Preußischen Akademie. Julie Wolfthorn agitierte, zusammen mit Käthe Kollwitz, dagegen, doch vergebens.

Als aktives Mitglied des Deutschen Künstlerbunds, des Vereins Bildender Künstlerinnen zu Berlin, des Lyceum-Clubs war Wolfthorn in Berlin in den 1890er Jahren bestens vernetzt. Um 1902 schuf sie das Plakat *Vorwärts*, gedruckt bei der Kunstanstalt Hollerbaum & Schmidt, Berlin. Sie gehörte um die Jahrhundertwende zu den wenigen Frauen, die regelmäßig Aufträge erhielten, in ihrem Fall vom Magazin *Jugend*, für das sie Illustrationen und Titelblätter erstellte. Daneben setzte sie sich für Frauenrechte und das allgemeine Wahlrecht ein und engagierte sich für verbesserte Bedingungen für Künstlerinnen.

Jeden Sommer fuhr sie nach Hiddensee, eine deutsche Insel in der Ostsee, wo sich der Regisseur Billy Wilder, der Dichter Joachim Ringelnatz, die Schauspielerin Asta Nielsen, die Lyrikerin Masha Kaléko und viele andere Künstler*innen trafen. Hier gründeten Julie Wolfthorn, Clara Arnheim, Augusta von Zitzewitz und Henni Lehmann den Hiddenseer Künstlerinnenbund, eine Gruppe von zeitweise bis zu zwölf Frauen, die einmal im Jahr eine große Verkaufsschau veranstalteten. 1930 war sie in Berlin an der vom Deutschen Staatsbürgerinnenverband organisierten Ausstellung „Die gestaltende Frau" beteiligt. Als Jüdin wurde Wolfthorn Opfer der Shoa und 1942 in das Konzentrationslager Theresienstadt deportiert, wo sie zwei Jahre später starb.

Julie Wolfthorn (1864–1944)

Wolfthorn was a German painter and graphic designer. Born in 1864 as the fifth child of a Jewish family in Thorn, West Prussia, she became an orphan at the age of six and grew up with her grandparents. At the age of nineteen, she moved to Berlin. Yet since academic study was prohibited to women in Berlin, she attended the Colarossi Private Academy in Paris and spent several months in Normandy and Grez-sur-Loing, an artists' colony in Fontainebleau. After returning to Berlin, she became a founding member of the Berlin Secession. The group fought for equal rights; in particular, its members demanded that women be admitted to study art at the Royal Prussian Academy. Together with Käthe Kollwitz, Julie Wolfthorn fought to achieve these aims, without success.

As an active member of the Deutscher Künstlerbund, the Verein Bildender Künstlerinnen zu Berlin, and the Lyceum Club, Wolfthorn was extremely well connected in Berlin in the 1890s. Sometime around 1902, she created the poster *Vorwärts* (Forward), which was printed by the Kunstanstalt Hollerbaum & Schmidt, Berlin. She was one of the few women at the turn of the century who regularly received commissions, in her case from the magazine *Jugend* (Youth), for which she created illustrations and cover pages. She also campaigned for women's rights and universal suffrage and worked to improve conditions for women artists.

Every summer she spent time on Hiddensee, a German island in the Baltic Sea, where the director Billy Wilder, the poet Joachim Ringelnatz, the actress Asta Nielsen, the poet Masha Kaléko, and many other artists mingled. It was here that Julie Wolfthorn, Clara Arnheim, Augusta von Zitzewitz, and Henni Lehmann founded the Hiddenseer Künstlerinnenbund, a group of women, numbering at times as many as twelve, who organized a large sales show once a year. In 1930, she was involved in the exhibition *Die gestaltende Frau* (The designing woman) in Berlin, organized by the Deutscher Staatsbürgerinnenverband. As a Jew, Wolfthorn became a victim of the Shoa: she was deported in 1942 to the Theresienstadt concentration camp, where she perished in 1944.

Sarah Wyman Whitman (1842–1904)

Whitman, auch Sarah de St. Prix Wyman Whitman genannt, war eine US-amerikanische Künstlerin, die durch zahlreiche Bilder, die Erstellung von Kirchenfenstern und vor allem durch die Gestaltung von Buchtiteln berühmt wurde. Sie begann ihre künstlerische Karriere als Buchbinderin in den frühen 1880er Jahren. Als Reaktion auf das häufig prunkvolle und aufwendige Design von Buchtiteln vor 1880 entwickelte Whitman einen eigenen reduzierten Stil. Einfache und klare Formen und der Verzicht auf übermäßige Dekoration und auffällige Farben charakterisieren ihre Arbeiten. Da die Schlichtheit der Werke Whitmans auch den Vorteil hatte, in der Buchproduktion relativ kostengünstig zu sein, verbreiteten sich die Werke schnell an der gesamten Ostküste. Whitman machte sich nicht nur mit ihrem eigenen Werk, sondern auch mit der Förderung junger Talente einen Namen. So war sie Mitbegründerin der Boston Society of Arts and Crafts und Förderin des Radcliffe College der Howard University sowie des Tuskegee-Instituts. Ihr Engagement wurde ihr nicht zuletzt ermöglicht durch die Heirat mit dem reichen Bostoner Wollhändler Henry Whitman, der allerdings wenig Interesse für ihre künstlerischen Ambitionen zeigte.

Elizabeth Corbet Yeats (1868–1940)

Yeats war eine anglo-irische Kunstlehrerin und Verlegerin. Sie war Gründerin der Dun Emer Press; als Malerin arbeitete sie ausschließlich mit Handpressen. Sie wurde in London geboren, die Familie zog nach Irland. Zusammen mit ihrer Schwester schrieb sie sich 1883 in die Dublin Metropolitan School of Art ein und besuchte Kurse in der Royal Dublin Society. 1886 kehrte die Familie wieder zurück nach South Kensington, London. Yeats betätigte sich literarisch und veröffentlichte ein selbstfabriziertes Magazin, *The Pleiades*, zusammen mit Freund*innen. Sie besuchte zu dieser Zeit die Chiswick School of Art, gemeinsam mit ihrer Schwester Susan und ihrem Bruder Jack Butler Yeats. In den 1890er Jahren war sie Kindergärtnerin in London, die nach der Fröbel-Methode verfuhr, und wurde am Froebel College in Bedford, Bedfordshire, ausgebildet. Sie wurde dann Lehrerin an der Bedford Park High School und lehrte im Anschluss als Gastdozentin in der Froebel Society, Chiswick High School, und an der Central Foundation School. Sie gehörte dem Kreis um William Morris in London an. Auf Vorschlag von Emery Walker, der mit Morris zusammen an der Kelmscott Press arbeitete, ließ sie sich an der Women's Printing Society in London ausbilden.

In Dublin griff sie den Vorschlag von Evelyn Gleeson auf und gründete die Dun Emer Guild, die sie von 1902 an leitete. Sie befand sich im

Sarah Wyman Whitman (1842–1904)

Whitman, also known as Sarah de St. Prix Wyman Whitman, was an American artist who became famous for a large number of paintings and for creating stained glass windows and, most notably, book covers. She began her artistic career as a bookbinder in the early 1880s. Responding to the often ostentatious and elaborate design of book covers before 1880, Whitman developed her own pared-down style. Simple and clear forms and the eschewal of excessive decoration and flashy colors characterize her works. Since the simplicity of her designs had the additional advantage of being relatively inexpensive to produce for books, they quickly spread throughout the East Coast. Whitman furthermore made a name for herself not only with her own work, but also by encouraging young talent. She was a cofounder of the Boston Society of Arts and Crafts, for example, and a patron of Howard University's Radcliffe College and the Tuskegee Institute. Her engagement was made possible not least by her marriage to the wealthy Boston wool merchant Henry Whitman, even though he showed little interest in her artistic ambitions.

Elizabeth Corbet Yeats (1868–1940)

Yeats was an Anglo-Irish art teacher and publisher. Herself the founder of Dun Emer Press, as a painter she worked exclusively with hand presses. After her birth in London, her family moved to Ireland. Together with her sister, she enrolled in the Dublin Metropolitan School of Art in 1883 and attended classes at the Royal Dublin Society. In 1886, the family returned to South Kensington, London. Yeats was active as a writer and published a self-produced magazine, *The Pleiades*, together with friends. At the time, she attended the Chiswick School of Art, along with her sister Susan and brother Jack Butler Yeats. In the 1890s, she worked as a nursery school teacher in London, following the Froebel method, and was educated at Froebel College in Bedford, Bedfordshire. She then became a teacher at Bedford Park High School and subsequently taught as a guest lecturer at the Froebel Society, Chiswick High School, and Central Foundation School. She belonged to the circle around William Morris in London. At the suggestion of Emery Walker, who worked with Morris at the Kelmscott Press, she trained at the Women's Printing Society in London.

In Dublin, she took up the suggestion of Evelyn Gleeson and founded the Dun Emer Guild, which she headed from 1902. It was installed in the house of Evelyn Gleeson and sought to train young women in bookbinding and print-

Haus von Evelyn Gleeson und verfolgte das Ziel, junge Frauen in Buchbinderei und Druckerei sowie in Stickerei und Weberei auszubilden. Yeats' erstes Buch war *In the Seven Woods* von W. B. Yeats, 1903. Die Zusammenarbeit der Yeats-Geschwister und Evelyn Gleeson verlief auf Dauer nicht glücklich. 1908 gründeten Elizabeth und ihr Bruder eine eigene Druckerei, die Cuala Press. Sie veröffentlichen hier über 70 Bücher von vielen Autoren. Yeats arbeitete in der Druckerei bis kurz vor ihrem Tod.

ing as well as embroidery and weaving. Yeats' first book design was *In the Seven Woods* by W. B. Yeats, 1903. The collaboration between the Yeats siblings and Evelyn Gleeson was ultimately not a happy one. In 1908, Elizabeth and her brother founded their own printing company, the Cuala Press, where they published over seventy books by many authors. Yeats worked at the press until shortly before her death.

Bildnachweis
Picture Credits

10 Mela Köhler, © MAK Wien, Foto/photo: Kristina Wissik

11 Valentina Kulagina, © VG Bild-Kunst, Foto/photo: Museum für Gestaltung Zürich, Plakatsammlung

12 Lora Lamm, © Museum für Gestaltung Zürich, Plakatsammlung

13 Ljubow Popowa, Wikimedia Commons (gemeinfrei / public domain), https://commons.wikimedia.org/wiki/File:Muzykalnaya_Nov_no_11.jpg

14 Bea Feitler, © Bea Feitler papers, The New School Archives and Special Collections, The New School, New York

15 Margaret MacDonald Mackintosh, Wikimedia Commons, Scan von/from Nathaniel Harris: The Life and Works of Rennie Mackintosh, 1996, ISBN 075251448 (gemeinfrei / public domain), https://commons.wikimedia.org/wiki/File:Cranston%27s_exhibition_cafe.jpg

16 Lora Lamm, © Museum für Gestaltung Zürich, Plakatsammlung

17 Bea Feitler, © Bea Feitler papers, The New School Archives and Special Collections, The New School, New York

18 © Anja Kaiser

19 David Morales (Philipp und Keuntje), © Philipp und Keuntje, Berlin

20 © See Red Women's Workshop (Mo Cooling)

21 Wikimedia Commons, Foto/photo: Saelwill (CC BY-SA 4.0), https://commons.wikimedia.org/wiki/File:2015_Art_+_Feminism_Wikipedia_Edit-a-thon_at_LACMA_-_06.JPG

30 Ethel Reed, Wikimedia Commons, Foto/photo: Museu Nacional d'Art de Catalunya / Google Art Project (gemeinfrei / public domain), https://commons.wikimedia.org/wiki/File:Ethel_Reed_-_Miss_Tr%C3%A4umerei_-_Google_Art_Project.jpg

33 Candace Wheeler, © The Met Museum, Gift of Sunworthy Wallcoverings, a Borden Company, 1987

37 Margaret Neilson Armstrong, Gift of Friends of the Thomas J. Watson Library, The Metropolitan Museum (gemeinfrei / public domain), https://libmma.contentdm.oclc.org/digital/collection/p16028coll17/id/3260

38 Margaret Neilson Armstrong, Wikimedia Commons (gemeinfrei / public domain), https://de.wikipedia.org/wiki/Margaret_Neilson_Armstrong#/media/Datei:Armstrong_van-Dyke-1904.jpg

40 oben/top: Sarah Wyman Whitman, © Melinda Wallington; Museum of Rochester, New York; unten links / bottom left: Cordelia Alice Morse, Wikimedia Commons (gemeinfrei / public domain), https://commons.wikimedia.org/wiki/File:Dunbar-Poems_of_Cabin_and_Field.jpg; unten Mitte / bottom middle: Margaret Neilson Armstrong, Wikimedia Commons (gemeinfrei / public domain), https://commons.wikimedia.org/wiki/File:Armstrong_Dana-1902.jpg; unten rechts / bottom right: Sarah Wyman Whitman, © Museum of Rochester, New York, Foto/photo: Melinda Wallington

41 oben links / top left: Sarah Wyman Whitman, Boston Public Library, Special Collections (CC BY 2.0), https://www.flickr.com/photos/boston_public_library/2350744258; oben rechts / top right: Sarah Wyman Whitman, Boston Public Library (CC BY 2.0), https://www.flickr.com/photos/24029425@N06/2349920823; unten/bottom: Sarah Wyman Whitman, Boston Public Library, Special Collections, Rare Books (CC BY 2.0), https://www.flickr.com/photos/24029425@N06/2349956531

42 oben/top: Blanche McManus, The Met: Watson Library Digital Collections (gemeinfrei / public domain), https://libmma.contentdm.oclc.org/digital/collection/p16028coll17/id/2965/rec/2; unten/bottom: Blanche McManus, Wikimedia Commons (gemeinfrei / public domain), https://commons.wikimedia.org/wiki/File:Alice_by_Blanche_McManus.jpg

44 links/left: Ethel Reed, Boston Public Library, Print Department (CC BY 2.0), https://www.flickr.com/photos/24029425@N06/10713771163/; rechts/right: Ethel Reed, Library of Congress Prints and Photographs Division Washington, D.C. (gemeinfrei / public domain), https://www.loc.gov/pictures/item/2014645311/

45 Ethel Reed, © The Miriam and Ira D. Wallach Division of Art, Prints and Photographs: Art & Architecture Collection, The New York Library

49 Esther & Lucien Pissarro, Wikimedia Commons (gemeinfrei / public domain), https://upload.wikimedia.org/wikipedia/commons/e/e8/1903_Pissarro_Aucassin_et_Nicolette.jpg

50 Helen Scholfield, © The Victorian Web, Foto/photo: Edward Nudelman, https://victorianweb.org/victorian art/design/books/230.html

51 Kate Greenaway, Wikimedia Commons (gemeinfrei / public domain), https://commons.wikimedia.org/wiki/File:Kate_Greenaway_A_Apple_Pie_1886.jpg

53 links/left: Margaret McDonald Mackintosh, MCAD Library (CC BY 2.0), https://www.flickr.com/photos/69184488@N06/10276497515; rechts/right: Jessie M. King, Wikimedia Commons (gemeinfrei / public domain), https://commons.wikimedia.org/wiki/File:1907_Jessie_M._King_Bookplate.jpg

54 links/left: Margaret MacDonald Mackintosh, Wikimedia Commons (gemeinfrei / public domain), https://commons.wikimedia.org/wiki/File:Mackintosh_GlasgowHausEinesKunstfreundes_MIA_P98331151.jpg; rechts/right: Frances MacDonald McNair, Wikimedia Commons (gemeinfrei / public domain), https://commons.wikimedia.org/wiki/File:Frances_MacDonald_-_Glasgow_Institute_Of_The_Fine_Arts.jpg

55 Wikimedia Commons (gemeinfrei / public domain), https://commons.wikimedia.org/wiki/File:The_Immortals!.jpg

56 Frances MacDonald, Foto mit freundlicher Genehmigung der / photo courtesy of Kunstmuseen Krefeld

61 © MAK Wien, Foto/photo: Kristina Wissik

63 Felice Rex, © MAK Wien, Foto/photo: Kristina Wissik

65 Leopoldine Kolbe, Metropolitan Museum of Art (gemeinfrei / public domain), https://www.metmuseum.org/art/collection/search/388747

Bildnachweis

66–67 Mela Köhler, © MAK Wien, Foto/photo: Kristina Wissik

69–70 Maria Likarz, © MAK Wien, Foto/photo: Kristina Wissik

73 oben/top: Clara Möller-Coburg/Ehmcke, Foto mit freundlicher Genehmigung der / photo courtesy of Kunstmuseen Krefeld; unten/bottom: Clara Möller-Coburg/Ehmcke, Foto: privat / private photo

75–76 Änne Koken, Foto: privat / private photo

77 Mela Köhler, Foto: privat / private photo

78 links/left: Ella Margold, © Bahlsen-Archiv Hannover; rechts/right: Martel Schwichtenberg, © Bahlsen-Archiv Hannover

79 Martel Schwichtenberg, © Bahlsen-Archiv Hannover

81 F.H. Ehmcke, Clara Ehmcke, Düsseldorf, Flugschriften herausgegeben vom Deutschen Museum für Kunst in Handel und Gewerbe Hagen i. Westf., Nr./no. 1–2, Fr. Wilhelm Ruhfus, Dortmund, 1911, S./pp. 36–37.

82 Änne Koken, Foto: privat / private photo

87 © Museum of London

88 links/left: Clémentine Hélène Dufau, © Museum für Kunst und Gewerbe Hamburg; rechts/right: Anna Sóos Korány, © Museum für Kunst und Gewerbe Hamburg

89 links/left: Anna von Wahl, © Museum für Kunst und Gewerbe, Hamburg; rechts/right: Bertha Margaret Boye, © The Arthur and Elizabeth Schlesinger Library on the History of Women in America, Radcliffe Institute for Advanced Study, Harvard University

90 Unbekannt/unknown, © Museum für Gestaltung Zürich, Plakatsammlung

91 Käthe Kollwitz, © Museum für Gestaltung Zürich, Plakatsammlung

92 Käthe Kollwitz, Fotos: privat / private photos

93 oben/top: Käthe Kollwitz, © Deutsches Historisches Museum, Berlin; unten/bottom: Käthe Kollwitz: © Museum für Gestaltung Zürich, Plakatsammlung

95 Julie Wolfthorn, Wikimedia Commons (gemeinfrei / public domain), https://commons.wikimedia.org/wiki/File:Julie_Wolfthorn_-_VORWÄRTS._Mark_1,10_pro_Monat;_frei_ins_Haus.jpg

97–98 © Luba Lukova

103 Suffrage Atelier, Wikimedia Commons (gemeinfrei / public domain), https://en.wikipedia.org/wiki/Suffrage_Atelier#/media/File:Suffrage_Atelier_postcard,_c1909-1914_(38003316525).jpg

104 © Museum of London

105 oben/top: © Museum of London; unten/bottom: George Eastman Museum, Foto/photo: Charles Chusseau-Flaviens (gemeinfrei / public domain), https://www.flickr.com/photos/george_eastman_house/2678367136/in/set-72157606224254056/

106 links/left: Schlesinger Library, RIAS, Harvard University (gemeinfrei / public domain), https://www.flickr.com/photos/schlesinger_library/9555365303; rechts/right: Alfred Pearse (Pseudonym), Wikimedia Commons (gemeinfrei / public domain), https://commons.wikimedia.org/wiki/File:Force-feeding_poster_(suffragettes).jpg

107 Clemence Housman, © The Victorian Web, Foto/photo: George P. Landow, https://victorianweb.org/art/illustration/housman/8.html

108 links/left: Hilda Dallas, Schlesinger Library, RIAS, Harvard University (gemeinfrei / public domain), https://www.flickr.com/photos/schlesinger_library/17311553535/; rechts/right: Hilda Dallas, Wikimedia Commons (gemeinfrei / public domain), https://commons.wikimedia.org/wiki/File:Votes_For_Women.jpg; unten/bottom: Hilda Dallas, Schlesinger Library, RIAS, Harvard University (gemeinfrei / public domain), https://www.flickr.com/photos/schlesinger_library/9555468771/

110 Clemence & Laurence Housman, Foto/photo: Princeton University Library, Graphic Arts, Rare Books and Special Collections, http://libweb2.princeton.edu/rbsc2/ga/unseenhands/printers/Housman.html

111 Suffrage Atelier, © Schlesinger Library, RIAS, Harvard University

115 Alexandra Exter, Wikimedia Commons (gemeinfrei / public domain), https://commons.wikimedia.org/wiki/File:Alexandra_Exter,_1917,_Pikasso_I_Okrestnosti_(Picasso_and_Environs),_Moscow,_Tsentrifuga_(cover).jpg

116 Valentina Kulagina, © VG Bild-Kunst, Bonn, Foto/photo: © Museum für Gestaltung Zürich, Plakatsammlung

118 Vera Adamovna Gicevič, © VG Bild-Kunst Bonn, © Foto/photo: Museum für Gestaltung Zürich, Plakatsammlung

119 Valentina Kulagina, © VG Bild-Kunst, Foto/photo: © Museum für Gestaltung Zürich, Plakatsammlung

121 Ljubow Sergejewna Popowa, Wikimedia Commons (gemeinfrei / public domain), https://commons.wikimedia.org/wiki/File:Muzykalnaya_Nov_no_1.jpg

122 Ljubow Sergejewna Popowa, Foto/photo: Universität zu Köln, Bildarchiv Foto Marburg

123 oben links / top left: Ljubow Sergejewna Popowa, Wikimedia Commons (CC BY-SA 4.0), https://commons.wikimedia.org/wiki/File:Fabric_design_«_black-white-pink_stripes_»_by_Lyoubov_Popova_-_Rouge_Grand_Palais.jpg; oben rechts / top right: Ljubow Sergejewna Popowa, Wikimedia Commons (CC BY-SA 4.0), https://commons.wikimedia.org/wiki/File:Fabric_design_«_stars_in_circles_»_by_Lyoubov_Popova_-_Rouge_Grand_Palais.jpg; rechts/right: Ljubow Sergejewna Popowa, Wikimedia Commons (gemeinfrei / public domain), https://commons.wikimedia.org/wiki/File:Textile_design_-_Liubov_Popova_-_c.1924.jpg;

124 © Museum für Gestaltung Zürich, Plakatsammlung

125 Olga & Galina Chichagova, Russische Nationalbibliothek / Russian National Library (gemeinfrei / public domain), https://rusneb.ru/catalog/000200_000018_RU_NLR_A1SV_30989/

129–135 © See Red Women's Workshop

136 © Lenthall Road Workshop

141 Dun Emer Press, Foto/photo: Princeton University Library, Graphic Arts, Rare Books and Special Collections, http://infoshare1.princeton.edu/rbsc2/ga/unseenhands/printers/yeats.html

144 The Distaff Side, Foto/photo: Princeton University Library, Graphic Arts, Rare Books and Special Collections, http://libweb2.princeton.edu/rbsc2/ga/unseenhands/printers/GrabhornOne.html

145 The Distaff Side, Foto/photo: Princeton University Library, Graphic Arts, Rare Books and Special Collections, http://libweb2.princeton.edu/rbsc2/ga/unseenhands/printers/GrabhornOne.html

146 Fred & Bertha Goudy, Wikimedia Commons (gemeinfrei / public domain), https://commons.wikimedia.org/wiki/File:Good-king-wenceslas-illustrated-1904-p30.png

149 © Occasional Papers

152–157 The New Woman's Survival Catalog, mit freundlicher Genehmigung von / courtesy of Kirsten Grimstad, Susan Rennie & Primary Information, New York

160 © Chrysalis: A Magazine of Women's Culture, Foto: privat / private photo

163 oben/top: © British Library, https://www.bl.uk/collection-items/spare-rib-magazine-issue-122;
unten/bottom: Internet Archive (gemeinfrei / public domain), https://archive.org/details/Spare_Rib_Magazine_Issue_66

164 Foto/photo: https://douglasstewart.com.au/product/norman-lindsay-oz-magazine-london-issue-no-33-february-1971-3/

165 © Heresis Collective, New York City

166 © Mit freundlicher Genehmigung von / courtesy of Kristen Grimstad, Wikimedia Commons (fair use), https://en.wikipedia.org/wiki/File:Chrysalis1.jpg

167 © Roselia N. Meny Collection (MSS 303-1-4)

168 Brava-ngo.ch

170 © Das feministische Archiv, Courage, Fotoarchiv-Nr. / photo archive no. 1042

171 Courage, Foto: privat / private photo

172 © Emma Frauenverlag – www.emma.de

173 Die Schwarze Botin, Göttingen, Wallstein Verlag, 2020, Foto/photo: Vojin Saša Vukadinović

175 The Arab Institute for Women, Lebanese American University, https://aiw.lau.edu.lb/research/alraidajournal/

176 Wikimedia Commons (gemeinfrei / public domain), Karren Ablaze!, https://commons.wikimedia.org/wiki/File:Ablaze-issue-10-Huggy-Bear.jpg

178 Wikimedia Commons (CC BY-SA 3.0), Foto/photo: Denis Bochkarev, https://commons.wikimedia.org/wiki/File:Pussy_Riot_-_Denis_Bochkarev_5.jpg

181 © U.S. United States Postal Service or the predecessor postal agency of the U.S. government of the time, © 1970 United States Postal Service, Ward Brackett, Wikimedia Commons (gemeinfrei / public domain), https://upload.wikimedia.org/wikipedia/commons/5/5d/Stamp-US-1970-Woman-Suffrage.png

184 © Anja Kaiser, Rebecca Stephany, Glossary of Undisciplined Design, Leipzig, Spector Books, 2021

185 Sheila Levrant de Bretteville, Wikimedia Commons (CC BY-SA 2.5) https://de.wikipedia.org/wiki/Sheila_Levrant_de_Bretteville#/media/Datei:DebrettevillePink.jpg)

189 Anja Kaiser, Rebecca Stephany, Glossary of Undisciplined Design, Spector Books, Leipzig 2021: 94–95

193 Helen Dryden, Wikimedia Commons (gemeinfrei / public domain), https://commons.wikimedia.org/wiki/File:Vogue_cover._July_1st,_1919,_by_Helen_Dryden.jpg

195 Helen Dryden, Gebrauchsgraphik 5, Nr./no. 9 (1928): 20/29

197–199 Bea Feitler, © Bea Feitler papers, The New School Archives and Special Collections, The New School, New York

200 Bea Feitler, Ruth Ansel, The Richard Avedon Foundation Foto/photo: The New School Archives and Special Collection, The New School, New York, NY

206 oben/top: Rimini Berlin, © Museum für Kunst und Gewerbe Hamburg;
unten/bottom: © Mit freundlicher Genehmigung von / courtesy of Guerilla Girls, guerrillagirls.com

208 © Missy Magazine, Foto/photo: Nina Lüth

209 © Missy Magazine, Foto/photo: Jasmine Durhal

211 © Girls Like Us, Grafikdesign / graphic design: Vela Arbutina

213 © Riposte

217 © Gail Anderson, https://www.gailycurl.com/US-Postal-Service

218–219 Gail Anderson, © Thames & Hudson

220 Sylvia Harris, Wikimedia Commons, Creative Repute, LLC (CC BY-SA 4.0), https://commons.wikimedia.org/wiki/File:Sylvia_Harris_Creative_Repute_design_agency.jpg

221 links/left: Wikimedia Commons (gemeinfrei / public domain), https://commons.wikimedia.org/wiki/File:1990_Questionnaire_Sample.png
rechts/right: Sylvia Harris, Wikimedia Commons (gemeinfrei / public domain), https://commons.wikimedia.org/wiki/File:2000_long_form_sample.png

224 links/left: Foto/photo: Redbubble, https://www.redbubble.com/i/t-shirt/Audre-Lorde-Self-Care-by-Starbuck42/64256393.OS66D;
rechts/right:Foto/photo: Redbubble, https://www.redbubble.com/i/t-shirt/Audre-Lorde-by-TeeSwagDesings1/81566129.FB110

227–228 © Golnar Kat Rahmani

229 © Ganzeer, Foto/photo: Museum für Kunst und Gewerbe Hamburg

232–233 © Kalimat, https://kalimatmagazine.com/Issues

234–236 © Golnar Kat Rahmani

241 © Philipp und Keuntje

244 links/left: Cha Fun-Hye, © Friedrich Ebert Stiftung
rechts/right: Nahida Nisha, © Friedrich Ebert Stiftung

247 Foto/photo: MMS

248 © Futuress

251 © Anja Kaiser

252 Rebecca Stephany, Foto/photo: Felix Grünschloss

253 Lambsong, Wikimedia Commons (gemeinfrei / public domain), https://commons.wikimedia.org/wiki/File:UNLV_Art%2BFeminism_Wikipedia_Edit-a-thon.png

255 Pru.mitchell, Wikimedia Commons (CC BY-SA 4.0), https://commons.wikimedia.org/wiki/File:NGV_edit-a-thon.jpg

262 © Guerrilla Girls, mit freundlicher Genehmigung der Guerrilla Girls / courtesy of Guerrilla Girls, Foto/photo: Museum für Kunst und Gewerbe Hamburg

270 © Danah Abdulla

271 Creative Repute graphic design agency, Wikimedia Commons, nilelivingston (CC BY-SA 4.0), https://commons.wikimedia.org/wiki/File:Gail_Anderson_Creative_Repute_graphic_design_agency.jpg

272 © Vela Arbutina

273 Wikimedia Commons (gemeinfrei / public domain), https://commons.wikimedia.org/wiki/File:Armstrong_family_c._1910s.jpg

274 oben/top: © Jess Baines, University of the Arts London;
Unten/bottom: Anothermag, https://www.anothermag.com/art-photography/gallery/1734/in-memory-of-lillian-bassman/4

275 Österreichische Nationalbibliothek, Foto/photo: Grete Kolliner. Moderne Welt. Illustrierte Monatsschrift für Kunst, Literatur und Mode 2, Nr./no. 12 (1920/21): 39, https://anno.onb.ac.at/cgi-content/anno-plus?aid=dmw&datum=1921&page=151&size=33

276 oben/top: неизв, Wikimedia Commons (gemeinfrei / public domain), https://commons.wikimedia.org/wiki/File:О.IO_Розанова,_Богуславская,_Малевич.jpg;
unten/bottom: © Steven Harman, www.4050photo.com

277 oben/top: © Juliette Moarbes;
unten/bottom: © Ece Canlı

278 The Craftsman Magazine, Wikimedia Commons (gemeinfrei / public domain), https://commons.wikimedia.org/wiki/File:Pamela_Colman_Smith_circa_1912.jpg

281 American Club Woman Magazine, Wikimedia Commons (gemeinfrei / public domain), https://commons.wikimedia.org/wiki/File:HelenDryden1914.tif

282 oben/top: New York School of Applied Design for Women Collection, Pratt Institute Archives, https://libguides.pratt.edu/blog/New-York-School-of-Applied-Design-for-Women;
unten/bottom: Wikimedia Commons, Foto/photo: Jan Michalko/re:publica (CC BY-SA 2.0), https://commons.wikimedia.org/wiki/File:Sonja_Eismann_-_Re_publica_19_-_Day_1_(32846186967)_(cropped).jpg

283 Wikimedia Commons (CC BY-SA 4.0), https://commons.wikimedia.org/wiki/File:Oleksandra_Ekster_Photo.jpg

284 ADC, http://adcglobal.org/hall-of-fame/bea-feitler/

285 Wikimedia Commons (gemeinfrei / public domain), https://commons.wikimedia.org/wiki/File:Evelyn_Gleeson.jpg

286 University of Utah, J. Willard Marriott Library Blog, https://blog.lib.utah.edu/rare-books-digital-exhibition-the-pursuit-of-reading/

287 фотоархив. Wikimedia Commons (gemeinfrei / public domain), https://commons.wikimedia.org/wiki/File:Natalia_Goncharova_04.jpg

288 oben/top: Wikimedia Commons, M. H., Spielmann, / G. Layard: Kate Greenaway, London: Adam and Charles Black, 1905 (gemeinfrei / public domain), https://commons.wikimedia.org/wiki/File:Kate_Greenaway,_1880,_Elliott_%26_Fry.jpg;
unten/bottom: © April Greiman / Made in Space

289 © Kirsten Grimstad, https://www.antioch.edu/faculty/kirsten-grimstad/

290 oben/top: Foto/photo: Eric Huybrechts (CC BY-ND 2.0) https://www.flickr.com/photos/15979685@N08/15330478694/;
unten/bottom: Elena Guro, Wikimedia Commons (gemeinfrei / public domain), https://commons.wikimedia.org/wiki/File:Guro_selfport.jpg,

291 © No More Nice Girls Productions, http://heresiesfilmproject.org/women/harmony-hammond/

293 oben/top: Library of the London School of Economics and Political Science (Ausschnitt/crop) (gemeinfrei / public domain), https://www.flickr.com/photos/lselibrary/22967928012/
unten/bottom: Wikimedia Commons (gemeinfrei / public domain), https://commons.wikimedia.org/wiki/File: ера_Михайловна_Ермолаева.gif

294 Werner J. Schweiger, Wiener Werkstätte. Kunst und Handwerk 1903–1932, Wien, 1988

295 © Golnar Kat Rahmani

296 Wikimedia Commons (gemeinfrei / public domain), https://commons.wikimedia.org/wiki/File:Jessie_Marion_King.jpg

298 Mela Köhler, © IMAGNO/Austrian Archives, Foto/photo: Trude Fleischmann

300 Wikimedia Commons, Foto/photo: re:publica (CC BY-SA 2.0), https://commons.wikimedia.org/wiki/File:Ina_Freudenschuß,_Chris_Köver_auf_der_re_publica10_(4534331199)_(cropped).jpg

301 © Münchner Stadtmuseum, Foto/photo: Philipp Kester

302 oben/top: Projekt Waechtersbach, http://waechtersbach.org/fabrikgeschichte/pics/dinakuhn1a.jpg;
unten/bottom: Foto/photo: Gustav Klutsis, https://monoskop.org/Valentina_Kulagina

303 Foto/photo: Serge Liszewski

304 © Sheila Levrant de Bretteville Archives

305 oben/top: Foto/photo: MAK Wien
unten/bottom: © Stephanie Lohaus

306 © Luba Lukova

307 Foto/photo: Christina Chahyadi

309 Wikimedia Commons, James Craig Annan (gemeinfrei / public domain), https://commons.wikimedia.org/wiki/File:Margaret_MacDonald_Macintosh.jpg

310 Wikimedia Commons (gemeinfrei / public domain), https://commons.wikimedia.org/wiki/File:Frances_Macdonald.jpg

311 © Shaz Madani

313 oben/top: © Chia Moan;
unten/bottom: The Guardian, Foto/photo: Timothy Mohin

314 Kunstgewerbemuseum Dresden, Foto: privat / private photo https://kunstgewerbemuseum.skd.museum/ausstellungen/gegen-die-unsichtbarkeit/designerinnen/clara-moeller-coburg/

315 Georg Grantham Bain Collection at the Library of Congress (gemeinfrei / public domain), https://loc.gov/pictures/resource/ggbain.03901/

316 Wikimedia Commons (gemeinfrei / public domain), https://commons.wikimedia.org/wiki/File:Alice_Cordelia_Morse_ca_1893.jpg

317 Anja Neidhardt, https://designabilities.wordpress.com/tag/anja-neidhardt/

318 oben/top: Glasgow Museums and Art Gallery / Glasgow School of Art (gemeinfrei / public domain), https://upload.wikimedia.org/wikipedia/commons/b/b5/Jessie_Newbery.jpg; Mitte/middle: Foto/photo: depatriarchdesign.com;
unten/bottom: Foto/photo: Paco Zea Garcia

319 oben/top: American Trade Bindings, https://uncgbindingsandbeyond.blogspot.com/2015/11/marion-louise-peabody.html;
unten/below: Foto/photo: Matthieu Crozier

320 oben/top: Foto/photo: Trude Fleischmann;
unten/bottom: Historic Stage Services, Maler/painter: Jean Aubrey (gemeinfrei / public domain), http://drypigment.net/2018/10/05/tales-from-a-scenic-artist-and-scholar-part-526-raphael-strauss-of-noxon-strauss/

321 Wikimedia Commons (gemeinfrei / public domain), https:// commons.wikimedia.org/wiki/File:Lyubov_Popova.jpg

322 Wikimedia Commons, Foto/photo: Rupert Potter (gemeinfrei / public domain), (https://commons.wikimedia.org/wiki/File:B_Potter_and_her_husband_W_Heelis_1913.JPG

323 Ethel Reed, Foto/photo: Frances Benjamin Johnston

326 Ivanovo Regional Art Museum, Malerin: Olga Rosanova / painter: Olga Rozanowa, https://commons.wikimedia.org/wiki/File:Selfportrait_(Rozanova,_1912).jpg

328 oben/top: Amy Sacker, https://www.amysacker.net/documents/bookplategallery.html;
unten/bottom: Dale Simonson (Anschnitt/crop) (CC BY-SA 2.0) https://www.flickr.com/photos/45877650@N00/4643526082

329 Mit freundlicher Genehmigung von / courtesy of
Das Verborgene Museum, Berlin, Foto/photo: Gertrud Riess

330 © Martha Scotford

333 Wikimedia Commons (gemeinfrei / public domain), https://commons.wikimedia.org/wiki/File:Rodchenko-Stepanova.jpg

335 Synthia St. James, Foto/photo: Leroy Hamilton (CC BY-SA 3.0) https://commons.wikimedia.org/wiki/File:Synthia_SAINT_JAMES_-_photo_by_Leroy_Hamilton.jpg

337 The Met: Watson Library Digital Collections (gemeinfrei / public domain), https://libmma.contentdm.oclc.org/digital/collection/p15324coll10/id/48671/

338 Foto/photo: Design observer

339 Die weite Welt, 2/1902, Titelblatt / cover, in: Katja Behling, Anke Manigold: Die Malweiber. Unerschrockene Künstlerinnen um 1900, Insel Verlag, Berlin 2013, S./p. 66

340 Wikimedia Commons, Malerin/painter: Helen Bigelow Merriman (gemeinfrei / public domain), https://upload.wikimedia.org/wikipedia/commons/6/66/Sarah_Wyman_Whitman_by_Helen_Bigelow_Merriman_%28painting%29.jpg

Vorsatz-/Nachsatzpapier und Buchrücken: iStock.com/Jill_InspiredByDesign

Große Zitate / Large quotes

35 Candace Wheeler zit. n. / quoted from Coleman E. Bishop: American Decorative Art, Chautauquan 5 (Jul. 1885): 582–584, hier/on 583–584.

52 Feodora Gleichen zit. n. / quoted from Zoë Thomas: Women Art Workers and the Arts and Crafts Movement, Manchester: Manchester University Press 2020: 84.

57 Anna Muthesius zit. n. / quoted from Anna Muthesius: Das Eigenkleid der Frau, Krefeld: Kramer & Baum, 1903, 79.

143 Lilian Mohin zit. n. / quoted from Cath Jackson: A Press of One's Own, Trouble & Strife 26 (1993): 45–52, hier/on 47.

183 Sheila Levrant de Bretteville zit. n. / quoted from Ellen Lupton: Reputations: Sheila Levrant de Bretteville, Eye Magazine 2, Nr./no. 8 (1993), https://www.eyemagazine.com/feature/article/reputations-sheila-levrant-de-bretteville (Abruf/accessed 2. Jul. 2022).

194 Ruth Ansel zit. n. / quoted from Carol Kino: The Visionary, Bal Harbour Magazine 11.2010, https://static1.squarespace.com/static/561eaed4e4b09058780f2ad8/t/5629664ce4b0b0d8bdbd5518/1445553740889/Ruth+Ansel.pdf (Abruf/accessed 18. Jul. 2022).

205 Sara Kaaman, Jessica Gysel & Katja Mater zit. n. / quoted from Sara Kaaman, Jessica Gysel & Katja Mater: Anyone with a Link Can Edit, in Brad Haylock & Megan Patty (Hg./eds.): Art Writing in Crisis, Berlin: Sternberg Press, 2021: 179–190, hier/on 180.

240 Ilse Lenz zit. n. / quoted from Ilse Lenz: Von der Sorgearbeit bis #MeToo. Aktuelle feministische Themen und Debatten in Deutschland, APUZ. Aus Politik und Zeitgeschichte, 20. Apr. 2018, https://www.bpb.de/shop/zeitschriften/apuz/267940/von-der-sorgearbeit-bis-metoo/ (Abruf/accessed 23. Feb. 2023).

243 Philipp und Keuntje zit. n. / quoted from Philipp und Keuntje, Kampagne für Terre des femmes, https://puk.agency/gewalt-gegen-frauen-zur-sprache-gebracht/ (Abruf/accessed 18. Jul. 2022).

Gerda Breuer

Gerda Breuer ist pensionierte Professorin für Kunst- und Designgeschichte an der Universität Wuppertal. Sie war Leiterin des Industriemuseum Cromford und stellvertretende Leiterin der Rheinischen Industriemuseen sowie stellvertretende Leiterin des Instituts Mathildenhöhe in Darmstadt und Vorsitzende des wissenschaftlichen Beirates der Stiftung Bauhaus Dessau. Sie gab zusammen mit Julia Meer das Buch *Woman in Graphic Design 1890–2012. Frauen und Grafik-Design* (2012) heraus und zuletzt gemeinsam mit Petra Eisele den Band *Design. Texte zur Theorie und Geschichte* (2019).

Katja Lis

Katja Lis ist Kommunikationsdesignerin (HfG Offenbach am Main, University of the Arts London), Unternehmerin und Co-Gründern der Agentur dbf.design. Sie ist Rätin im Deutschen Designtag, Beirätin für Diversity im DDC Deutscher Design Club und Mitinitiatorin der *Women of DDC* – die Plattform zur Stärkung von Sichtbarkeit, Vernetzung und Unternehmerinnentum für Gestalterinnen. www.dbf.design

Gerda Breuer

Gerda Breuer is a retired professor of the history of art and design at the University of Wuppertal. She previously led the Cromford Industriemuseum in Ratingen as well as the Mathildenhöhe in Darmstadt, and was acting head of the Rheinische Industriemuseen in North Rhine-Westphalia. In addition to this, she chaired the scientific advisory board of the Stiftung Bauhaus Dessau. Together with Julia Meer she co-edited the book *Woman in Graphic Design 1890–2012. Frauen und Grafik-Design* (2012) and, more recently, she published the volume *Design. Texte zur Theorie und Geschichte* (2019) together with Petra Eisele.

Katja Lis

Katja Lis is a communication designer (HfG Offenbach am Main, University of the Arts London), an entrepreneur, and cofounder of the agency dbf.design. She is a committee member with the Deutscher Designtag, advisory board member for diversity in the DDC Deutscher Design Club, and coinitiator of the Women of DDC—its platform to strengthen visibility, networking, and entrepreneurship for female designers. www.dbf.design

Impressum
Imprint

© 2023 by jovis Verlag GmbH
Ein Unternehmen der Walter de Gruyter GmbH, Berlin/Boston
Part of Walter de Gruyter GmbH, Berlin/Boston
Das Copyright für die Texte liegt bei der Autorin. / Texts by kind permission of the author.
Das Copyright für die Abbildungen liegt bei den Fotograf*innen/Inhaber*innen der Bildrechte. / Pictures by kind permission of the photographers/ holders of the picture rights.

Alle Rechte vorbehalten. / All rights reserved.

Design und Satz / Design and setting:
Katja Lis, Anna Voß – dbf.design
Übersetzung / Translation:
Michael Thomas Taylor
Lektorat / Copyediting:
Maike Kleihauer (Deutsch/German),
Michael Thomas Taylor (Englisch/English)
Korrektorat / Proofreading:
Inka Humann (Deutsch/German),
Michael Thomas Taylor (Englisch/English)
Projektmanagement / Project management:
Theresa Hartherz
Herstellung / Production: Susanne Rösler
Lithografie / Lithography: Bild1Druck
Druck und Bindung / Printing and binding:
GRASPO CZ, a.s.
Papier / Paper: Munken Print White
Schriften / Typefaces:
Embury Text (Victoria Rushton);
Tablet Gothic Wide (José Scaglione, Veronika Burian)

Bibliografische Information der Deutschen Nationalbibliothek:
Die Deutsche Nationalbibliothek verzeichnet diese Publikation in der Deutschen Nationalbibliografie; detaillierte bibliografische Daten sind im Internet über http://dnb.d-nb.de abrufbar. / Bibliographic information published by the Deutsche Nationalbibliothek: The Deutsche Nationalbibliothek lists this publication in the Deutsche Nationalbibliografie; detailed bibliographic data are available on the Internet at http://dnb.d-nb.de.

jovis Verlag GmbH
Lützowstraße 33
10785 Berlin

www.jovis.de

jovis-Bücher sind weltweit im ausgewählten Buchhandel erhältlich. Informationen zu unserem internationalen Vertrieb erhalten Sie in Ihrer Buchhandlung oder unter www.jovis.de. / jovis books are available worldwide in select bookstores. Please contact your nearest bookseller or visit www.jovis.de for information concerning your local distribution.

ISBN 978-3-86859-773-8

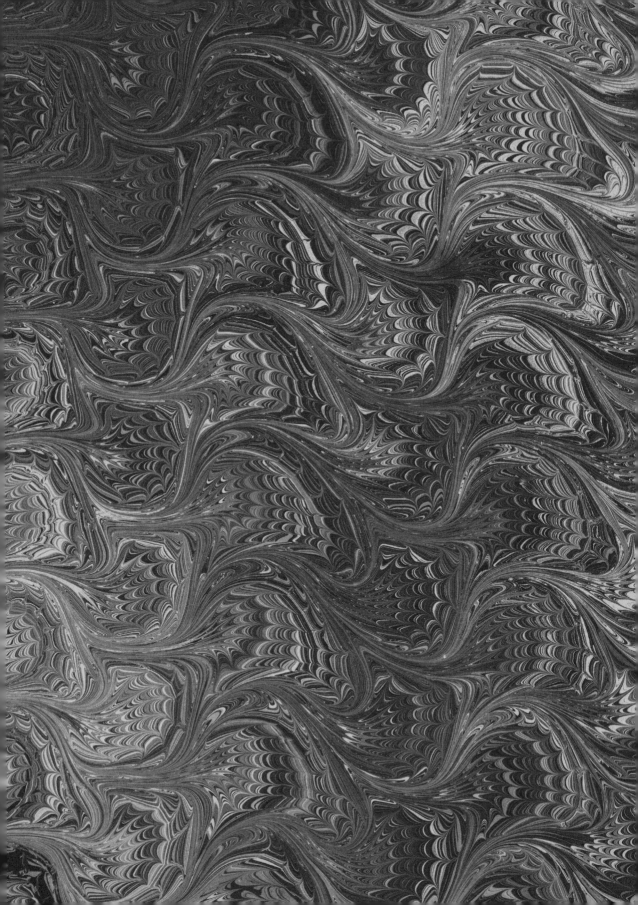